The Blackwell Companion to Jesus

The Wiley Blackwell Companions to Religion

The Wiley Blackwell Companions to Religion series presents a collection of the most recent scholarship and knowledge about world religions. Each volume draws together newly-commissioned essays by distinguished authors in the field, and is presented in a style which is accessible to undergraduate students, as well as scholars and the interested general reader. These volumes approach the subject in a creative and forward-thinking style, providing a forum in which leading scholars in the field can make their views and research available to a wider audience.

Recently Published

The Blackwell Companion to Contemporary Islamic Thought
Edited by Ibrahim M. Abu-Rabi'

The Blackwell Companion to the Bible and Culture
Edited by John F. A. Sawyer

The Blackwell Companion to Catholicism
Edited by James J. Buckley, Frederick Christian Bauerschmidt, and Trent Pomplun

The Blackwell Companion to Eastern Christianity
Edited by Ken Parry

The Blackwell Companion to the Theologians
Edited by Ian S. Markham

The Blackwell Companion to the Bible in English Literature
Edited by Rebecca Lemon, Emma Mason, John Roberts, and Christopher Rowland

The Blackwell Companion to the New Testament
Edited by David E. Aune

The Blackwell Companion to Nineteenth Century Theology
Edited by David Fergusson

The Blackwell Companion to Religion in America
Edited by Philip Goff

The Blackwell Companion to Jesus
Edited by Delbert Burkett

The Blackwell Companion to Paul
Edited by Stephen Westerholm

The Blackwell Companion to Religion and Violence
Edited by Andrew R. Murphy

The Blackwell Companion to Christian Ethics, Second Edition
Edited by Stanley Hauerwas and Samuel Wells

The Wiley Blackwell Companion Practical Theology
Edited by Bonnie J. Miller-McLemore

The Wiley Blackwell Companion to Religion and Social Justice
Edited by Michael D. Palmer and Stanley M. Burgess

The Wiley Blackwell Companion to Chinese Religions
Edited by Randall L. Nadeau

The Wiley Blackwell Companion to African Religions
Edited by Elias Kifon Bongmba

The Wiley Blackwell Companion to Christian Mysticism
Edited by Julia A. Lamm

The Wiley Blackwell Companion to the Anglican Communion
Edited by Ian S. Markham, J. Barney Hawkins IV, Justyn Terry, and Leslie Nuñez Steffensen

The Wiley Blackwell Companion to Inter-Religious Dialogue
Edited by Catherine Cornille

The Blackwell Companion to Jesus

Edited by

Delbert Burkett

WILEY Blackwell

Registered Office
John Wiley & Sons Ltd, The Atrium, Southern Gate, Chichester, West Sussex, PO19 8SQ, UK

Editorial Offices
350 Main Street, Malden, MA 02148-5020, USA
9600 Garsington Road, Oxford, OX4 2DQ, UK
The Atrium, Southern Gate, Chichester, West Sussex, PO19 8SQ, UK

For details of our global editorial offices, for customer services, and for information about how to apply
for permission to reuse the copyright material in this book please see our website at www.wiley.com/
wiley-blackwell.

Library of Congress Cataloging-in-Publication Data

The Blackwell companion to Jesus / edited by Delbert Burkett.
        p. cm. – (Wiley Blackwell companions to religion)
    Includes bibliographical references and index.
    ISBN 978-1-4051-9362-7 (cloth) – ISBN 978-1-118-72410-1 (pbk.)
1. Jesus Christ–History of doctrines.   I. Burkett, Delbert Royce.   II. Title: Companion to Jesus.
    BT198.B543 2011
    232'.809–dc22

                            2010016187

A catalogue record for this book is available from the British Library.

Cover image: Byzantine mosaic of Chris from Sant'Apollinare Nuovo, Ravenna, Italy, 6th century. Photo
The Bridgeman Art Library.
Cover design by Nicki Averill Design & Illustration

Set in 10/13 pt Photina by Toppan Best-set Premedia Limited

1 2014

Contents

List of Figures   viii
Notes on Contributors   ix
Acknowledgments   xv

Images of Jesus: An Overview   1
Delbert Burkett

Part I   Jesus in the New Testament   11

1   Mark's Portrait of Jesus   13
    William R. Telford

2   Who Do You Say That I Am? A Matthean Response   30
    Elaine M. Wainwright

3   Jesus in Luke-Acts   47
    Delbert Burkett

4   John's Portrait of Jesus   64
    Mary L. Coloe

5   Jesus in Q   81
    Christopher Tuckett

6   Paul, Jesus, and Christ   94
    Edward Adams

7   Jesus in the General Epistles   111
    Harold W. Attridge

8 Jesus in the Apocalypse   119
   Ian Boxall

9 Constructing Images of Jesus from the Hebrew Bible   127
   Warren Carter

Part II Jesus Beyond the New Testament   143

10 Ancient Apocryphal Portraits of Jesus   145
    J. K. Elliott

11 Gnostic Portraits of Jesus   160
    Majella Franzmann

12 The Christ of the Creeds   176
    Khaled Anatolios

13 Jesus in Atonement Theories   193
    Stephen Finlan

Part III Jesus in World Religions   213

14 Jewish Perspectives on Jesus   215
    Michael J. Cook

15 Islamic Perspectives on Jesus   232
    Reem A. Meshal and M. Reza Pirbhai

16 Hindu Perspectives on Jesus   250
    Sandy Bharat

17 Buddhist Perspectives on Jesus   267
    Peggy Morgan

Part IV Philosophical and Historical Perspectives on Jesus   283

18 Skeptical Perspectives on Jesus' Resurrection   285
    Michael Martin

19 The Quest for the Historical Jesus: An Overview   301
    David B. Gowler

20 The "Jesus" of the Jesus Seminar   319
    Robert J. Miller

21 The Quest for the Historical Jesus: An Appraisal   337
    Helen K. Bond

Part V   Modern Manifestations of Jesus   355

22   Modern Western Christology   357
     John P. Galvin

23   Christology in Africa, Asia, and Latin America   375
     Veli-Matti Kärkkäinen

24   Jesus in American Culture   394
     Paul Harvey

25   The Black Christ   410
     Kelly Brown Douglas with Delbert Burkett

26   Feminist Christologies   427
     Lisa Isherwood

27   The "Gay" Jesus   443
     Theodore W. Jennings Jr.

28   Modern Mystifications of Jesus   458
     Per Beskow

Part VI   Jesus in Art, Fiction, and Film   475

29   Jesus in Christian Art   477
     Robin M. Jensen

30   Jesus Novels: Solving Problems with Fiction   504
     Zeba A. Crook

31   Jesus in Film   519
     Adele Reinhartz

Index   532

Figures

1   Jesus as the Good Shepherd. Catacomb of Peter and Marcellinus.   480

2   "Christ Healing the Sick," Rembrandt Harmensz van Rijn, ca. 1647.
British Museum, London.   482

3   Jesus as healer and wonder-worker. Sarcophagus of Marcia Romania
Celsa, Musée départemental Arles antique.   483

4   Madonna and Child, mid sixth century. From the Basilica of Sant'
Apollinare Nuovo, Ravenna.   485

5   Baptism of Christ, late fifth or early sixth century. From the Arian
Baptistery, Ravenna.   487

6   Transfiguration. Portable mosaic from Constantinople, ca. 1200 CE.
Louvre Museum, Paris.   488

7   Jesus' entry into Jerusalem, last quarter of the fourth century.
Sarcophagus from the Vatican Museo Pio Cristiano.   489

8   Last Supper, early sixth century. From the Basilica of Sant' Apollinare
Nuovo, Ravenna.   490

9   Arrest and trial of Jesus, ca. 350. Sarcophagus from the Vatican
Museo Pio Cristiano.   491

10   Jesus crucified, ca. 432. Panel from the wooden doors of Santa
Sabina, Rome.   492

11   Christ resurrected, Fra Angelico, 1438. Museo di San Marco, Florence.   494

12   Trinity creating Adam and Eve, mid-fourth century. Sarcophagus
from the Vatican Museo Pio Cristiano.   496

13   Christ giving the new law to Peter and Paul, ca. 350. Mosaic from an
apse of Santa Constanza (Mausoleum of Constantina), Rome.   498

14   Last Judgment, ca. 1230. Tympanum of west portal, Notre Dame
Cathedral, Paris.   499

15   Portrait of Christ, mid-sixth century. From the Basilica of
San Vitale, Ravenna.   501

Notes on Contributors

Edward Adams is Senior Lecturer in New Testament Studies in the Department of Theology and Religious Studies, King's College London. He is the author of *Constructing the World: A Study in Paul's Cosmological Language* (T&T Clark 2000) and *The Stars Will Fall from Heaven: Cosmic Catastrophe in the New Testament and its World* (T&T Clark 2007).

Khaled Anatolios is Associate Professor of Historical Theology at the Boston College School of Theology and Ministry. He is the author of *Athanasius: The Coherence of his Thought* (Routledge 1998, 2004) and the *Athanasius* volume of the Routledge Early Church Fathers series, as well as many articles on topics in early Christian, systematic, and Eastern Christian theology.

Harold W. Attridge, Dean and Professor of New Testament at Yale Divinity School, has made scholarly contributions to New Testament exegesis, the study of Hellenistic Judaism, and the history of early Christianity. His publications include *Hebrews: A Commentary on the Epistle to the Hebrews* (Fortress 1989), and *Nag Hammadi Codex I: The Jung Codex* (Brill 1985), as well as numerous book chapters and scholarly articles.

Per Beskow is Assistant Professor of Religious Studies at the University of Lund, Sweden. His main field is patristic studies. His works include *Rex Gloriae: The Kingship of Christ in the Early Church* (Almquist & Wiksell 1962). *Strange Tales about Jesus* (Fortress 1982/1983) is an example of his interest in literary forgeries.

Sandy Bharat is former director, now trustee, of the International Interfaith Centre at Oxford. Her publications include *Christ Across the Ganges: Hindu Responses to Jesus* (O-Books 2007). She has an honours degree in theology from the University of

Exeter, has edited for the *Encyclopaedia of Hinduism* project (India Heritage Research Foundation and University of South Carolina), and manages two websites, Interfaith Information Online (www.interfaithinfo.net) and Spirituality for Daily Life (www.spiritualityfordailylife.com).

Helen K. Bond is Senior Lecturer in New Testament at the University of Edinburgh. Interested in the historical, political, and social background to the gospels and in the life (and execution) of Jesus, she has published *Pontius Pilate in History and Interpretation* (Cambridge 1998) and *Caiaphas: Friend of Rome and Judge of Jesus?* (Westminster John Knox 2004). She is currently writing a book on the historical Jesus for Continuum's *Guide for the Perplexed* series.

Ian Boxall is Senior Tutor and Tutorial Fellow in New Testament at St Stephen's House, University of Oxford. He is the author of *Revelation: Vision and Insight* (SPCK 2002) and *The Revelation of St John* in the Black's New Testament Commentary series (Hendrickson, Continuum 2006).

Delbert Burkett, Professor of Religious Studies at Louisiana State University, has written on the gospels and teaches a course on images of Jesus in history and tradition. Two volumes of his series *Rethinking the Gospel Sources* have appeared: *From Proto-Mark to Mark* (T&T Clark 2004) and *The Unity and Plurality of Q* (Society of Biblical Literature 2009). Other books include *An Introduction to the New Testament and the Origins of Christianity* (Cambridge 2002), and *The Son of Man Debate* (Cambridge 1999).

Warren Carter is Professor of New Testament at Brite Divinity School, Texas Christian University. His scholarship has focused on the gospels and on the diverse ways in which early Jesus-believers negotiated the Roman imperial world. He has written numerous articles and books, including *John and Empire: Initial Explorations* (T&T Clark/Continuum 2008); *John: Storyteller, Interpreter, Evangelist* (Hendrickson 2006); and *Matthew: Storyteller, Interpreter, Evangelist* (rev. edn, Hendrickson 2004).

Mary L. Coloe PBVM is Associate Professor of the School of Theology at Australian Catholic University in Melbourne, Australia. She is the author of numerous articles and several books, including *Dwelling in the Household of God: Johannine Ecclesiology and Spirituality* (Liturgical 2007) and *God Dwells with Us: Temple Symbolism in the Fourth Gospel* (Liturgical 2001).

Michael J. Cook is Sol and Arlene Bronstein Professor of Judeo-Christian Studies at Hebrew Union College–Jewish Institute of Religion, Cincinnati campus. He is the only rabbi in America with a Full Professorial Chair in New Testament, and more than one thousand rabbis have been graduated from his New Testament courses. His numerous publications include *Modern Jews Engage the New Testament: Enhancing Jewish Well-Being in a Christian Environment* (Jewish Lights 2008).

Zeba A. Crook is Associate Professor of Religion at Carleton University in Ottawa, Canada. He is the author and editor of several books and is currently writing a book on representations of Jesus in modern fiction. On this topic, he has made several public lectures and published one article: "Fictionalising Jesus: Story and History in Two Recent Jesus Novels," *Journal for the Study of the Historical Jesus* 5 (2007): 33–55.

Kelly Brown Douglas is the Chair of Philosophy and Religion at Goucher College, where she holds the Elizabeth Conolly Todd Distinguished Professorship. She was the first black woman to be ordained as an Episcopal priest in the Southern Ohio Diocese. A leading voice in the development of a womanist theology, she has published numerous essays and articles and several books, including *The Black Christ* (Orbis 1994).

J. K. Elliott is Professor (Emeritus) of New Testament Textual Criticism at the University of Leeds, England. He is the editor of *The Apocryphal New Testament* (Clarendon 1993) and *The Apocryphal Jesus* (Oxford 1996). He has also written many books and articles on Greek New Testament manuscripts and on textual criticism. He is secretary of the International Greek New Testament Project, having previously been the executive editor of the Project's two-volume critical apparatus to Luke's Gospel.

Stephen Finlan is adjunct faculty at Salve Regina University in Newport, Rhode Island, and has taught at the University of Durham, where he obtained his PhD. He is the author of *The Background and Content of Paul's Cultic Atonement Metaphors* (SBL/Brill 2004); *Problems with Atonement: The Origins of, and Controversy about, the Atonement Doctrine* (Liturgical 2005); *Options on Atonement in Christian Thought* (Liturgical 2007); and *The Apostle Paul and the Pauline Tradition* (Liturgical 2008).

Majella Franzmann is Pro-Vice-Chancellor for Humanities and Professor of Religion at the University of Otago, New Zealand. She has published *Jesus in the Nag Hammadi Writings* (T&T Clark 1996), *Jesus in the Manichaean Writings* (T&T Clark 2003), and translations and analysis of the fourth-century Manichaean Syriac remains from ancient Roman Kellis in Egypt. More recently she has been working on the fourteenth-century Christian Syro-Turkic tombstones in Quanzhou, China.

John P. Galvin, Professor of Systematic Theology at The Catholic University of America, Washington, DC, received his doctorate in theology from the University of Innsbruck, Austria, in 1970. He is the co-editor, with Francis Schüssler Fiorenza, of *Systematic Theology: Roman Catholic Perspectives* (2 vols., Fortress 1991), to which he also contributed the chapter on Jesus Christ.

David B. Gowler is the Dr Lovick Pierce and Bishop George F. Pierce Professor of Religion at Oxford College of Emory University. He is also affiliated with the Center for Ethics at Emory. His books include *What Are They Saying About the Historical Jesus?* (Paulist 2007). He has published dozens of articles, book chapters, and book reviews and has edited several other books. His current project is *James Through the Centuries* (Blackwell, forthcoming).

Paul Harvey is Professor of History and Presidential Teaching Scholar at the University of Colorado. He is the author of *Freedom's Coming: Religious Cultures and the Shaping of the South, from the Civil War through the Civil Rights Era* (2005) and the co-editor of the *Columbia Guide to Religion in American History*.

Lisa Isherwood is Professor of Feminist Liberation Theologies and Director of Theological Partnerships at the University of Winchester. She is executive editor of the international journal *Feminist Theology* and editor of five international book series. She has published seventeen books in the area of feminist theologies, gender, and sexuality. She is Director of the Britain and Ireland School of Feminist Theology and has served as Vice-President for the European Society of Women in Theological Research.

Theodore W. Jennings Jr. is Professor of Biblical and Constructive Theology at Chicago Theological Seminary. In 1991 he initiated the program in Gay Studies there, which is now the Center for LGBTQ Religious Studies. In addition to lecturing at many universities in Latin America, Africa, and Asia, he has written scores of essays and more than fifteen books, including *The Man Jesus Loved: Homoerotic Narrative in the New Testament* (Pilgrim 2003).

Robin M. Jensen is the Luce Chancellor's Professor of the History of Christian Art and Worship at Vanderbilt University, where she holds a joint appointment in the Divinity School and the Department of the History of Art. Her books include *Understanding Early Christian Art* (Routledge 2000); *Face to Face: Portraits of the Divine in Early Christianity* (Fortress 2005); and *The Substance of Things Seen: Art, Faith and the Christian Community* (Eerdmans 2004).

Veli-Matti Kärkkäinen is Professor of Systematic Theology at Fuller Theological Seminary and Docent of Ecumenics at the University of Helsinki. He has authored eleven scholarly books, including *The Trinity: Global Perspectives* (Westminster John Knox 2007) and *Christology: A Global Introduction* (Baker Academic 2003), as well as more than one hundred articles that have appeared in several languages. Dr Kärkkäinen is also co-editor of the *Global Dictionary of Theology* (with William Dyrness; InterVarsity 2008).

Michael Martin has a PhD in Philosophy from Harvard University and is Professor Emeritus at Boston University. He is the author of many articles and reviews as well as several books, including *Atheism: A Philosophical Justification* (Temple University

1990) and *The Case Against Christianity* (Temple University 1991). He is the editor of *The Cambridge Companion to Atheism* (2007) and co-editor with Ricki Monnier of *The Improbability of God* (Prometheus 2006) and *The Impossibility of God* (Prometheus 2003).

Reem A. Meshal holds a PhD in Islamic Studies from McGill University. She is currently Assistant Professor of Religious Studies at Louisiana State University. Her specialization is Islamic Law and Society in the Ottoman Era. She has published articles in two edited volumes and has one forthcoming in the *Journal of Islamic Studies*. She is currently working on a book on the Shari'a courts of Ottoman Cairo.

Robert J. Miller is Rosenberger Professor of Christian Thought and Religious Studies at Juniata College in Pennsylvania. Miller has been an active member of the Jesus Seminar since 1986 and has served on the steering committee for the Society of Biblical Literature Historical Jesus Section since 2004. His publications include *The Jesus Seminar and its Critics* (Polebridge 1999) and *Born Divine: The Births of Jesus and Other Sons of God* (Polebridge 2003).

Peggy Morgan tutors courses in the study of religions for the Faculty of Theology at Oxford. Her published work includes the section on Buddhism in *Ethical Issues in Six Religious Traditions*, which she also edited (with Clive Lawton; 2nd edn, Edinburgh University Press 2007), *Get Set for Religious Studies* (with Dominic Corrywright; Edinburgh University Press 2006), and "Buddhism" in *Jesus in History, Thought and Culture* (ed. Leslie Houlden; ABC/Clio 2003).

M. Reza Pirbhai received a PhD in history from the University of Toronto (2004) and is currently Assistant Professor of History at Louisiana State University. His specialization is Islamic thought and institutions in Modern South Asia. He has published articles in *Modern Intellectual History* and *Journal of Asian History*. He is also author of the book *Reconsidering Islam in a South Asian Context* (Brill 2004).

Adele Reinhartz is Professor in the Department of Classics and Religious Studies at the University of Ottawa in Canada. Her main areas of research are the Gospel of John, early Jewish–Christian relations, feminist criticism, and, most recently, the Bible and Film. Her most recent book is a study of the Jesus movies, entitled *Jesus of Hollywood* (Oxford 2007). She is the author of numerous articles and several other books, including *Scripture on the Silver Screen* (Westminster John Knox 2003).

William R. Telford is Senior Lecturer in Christian Origins and the New Testament at Durham University. His research interests include the historical Jesus, the Gospel of Mark, methods of biblical interpretation, and the Bible in literature and film. His books on Mark include *Writing on the Gospel of Mark* (DEO 2009), *Mark* (T&T Clark

2003), *The Theology of the Gospel of Mark* (Cambridge 1999), and *The Barren Temple and the Withered Tree* (JSOT 1980).

Christopher Tuckett is Professor of New Testament Studies in the University of Oxford, having also worked in the University of Manchester. He has published widely on matters concerning the Synoptic Problem and Q, New Testament christology, non-canonical gospels, and other New Testament topics. His books include *Q and the History of Early Christianity* (T&T Clark 1996), *Christology and the New Testament* (Westminster John Knox 2001), and *The Gospel of Mary* (Oxford 2007).

Elaine M. Wainwright is Professor of Theology and Head of the School of Theology at the University of Auckland, New Zealand. She specializes in New Testament Studies, in particular, the Gospel of Matthew. She has published widely including *Toward a Feminist Critical Reading of the Gospel according to Matthew* (De Gruyter 1991), *Shall We Look for Another? A Feminist Rereading of the Matthean Jesus* (Orbis 1998) and *Women Healing/Healing Women: The Genderization of Healing in Early Christianity* (Equinox 2006).

Acknowledgments

Figure 1   The International Catacomb Society. Photo: Estelle Brettman.
Figure 2   Photo credit: © The Trustees of the British Museum/Art Resource, NY.
Figure 3   Photo: author, with permission of Musée départemental Arles antique.
Figure 4   Photo: author.
Figure 5   Photo: author.
Figure 6   Photo credit: Réunion des Musées Nationaux/Art Resource, NY.
Figure 7   Photo: author, with permission of the Vatican Museo Pio Cristiano.
Figure 8   Photo credit: Sacred Destinations Images.
Figure 9   Photo: author, with permission of the Vatican Museo Pio Cristiano.
Figure 10   Photo credit: Lee Jefferson.
Figure 11   Photo credit: Erich Lessing/Art Resource, NY.
Figure 12   Photo: author, with permission of the Vatican Museo Pio Cristiano.
Figure 13   Photo: author.
Figure 14   Photo credit: Sacred Destinations Images.
Figure 15   Photo: author.

Images of Jesus: An Overview

Delbert Burkett

Jesus of Nazareth is arguably the most influential person in human history. As the founding figure of Christianity, the largest of the world religions, his influence has extended to the billions of people who have professed this religion, as well as to the billions of others who have been affected by it. Christians past and present have worshiped Jesus as a god, prayed to him for assistance, looked to him for salvation, and professed to emulate his life and teachings. They have traversed the globe to bring the knowledge of his name to the entire world.

Jesus' influence on the world has been complex and varied. In his name, his adherents have practiced pacifism or launched crusading armies, initiated missions of mercy and assistance or participated in pogroms and inquisitions, withdrawn from the world or established social and political movements. No single conception or image of Jesus could have spawned such diversity. From the beginning of Christianity, the image of Jesus has been protean, adaptable to the different perspectives and needs of different communities and individuals.

The *Blackwell Companion to Jesus* explores these diverse conceptions and images of Jesus that have arisen over the past 2,000 years, from the beginning of Christianity to the present. While no single volume can claim to cover all of these, the present volume does examine the most significant ways in which Jesus has been imagined or portrayed.

Jesus in the New Testament

Diverse conceptions of Jesus appear already in the earliest accounts of his life that have been preserved: the four gospels of the New Testament. The Gospel of Mark (see

The Blackwell Companion to Jesus, First Edition. Edited by Delbert Burkett. ©2014 John Wiley & Sons, Ltd. Published 2014 by John Wiley & Sons, Ltd.

chapter 1) never suggests that Jesus is anything more than human. Though he is adopted as God's "son" and appointed as the "Christ," his special character comes not from his genes, but from the Spirit that God has given him, thus enabling him to perform miraculous deeds. In contrast, the Gospel of Matthew (see chapter 2) elevates Jesus to the rank of a demigod, the literal offspring of a divine father and a human mother. Additionally, it presents Jesus as a Jewish rabbi, an interpreter of the Jewish Law. But while some passages present Jesus as a lenient rabbi, others make him very strict. The Gospel of Luke (see chapter 3) retains the portrayal of Jesus as a demigod but lacks the image of Jesus as a strict rabbi. For Luke, Jesus is primarily a friend of the poor and oppressed, the outcast and the sinner, women and non-Jews. Only in the Gospel of John (see chapter 4) does Jesus exist in some form prior to his birth on earth, and only this gospel calls him "God." For John, Jesus is a pre-existent divine being who comes from heaven to become incarnate as a human being, to accomplish God's will, and to ascend back to the heavenly realm.

These gospels probably used earlier sources and traditions that have not been preserved, such as the one that New Testament scholars call "Q," a source common to the Gospels of Matthew and Luke (see chapter 5). These earlier sources and traditions did not necessarily present the same perspective on Jesus. Consequently, as the authors of the gospels combined them in their own works, the gospel portraits of Jesus that emerged were not necessarily consistent internally or with each other.

Other writings in the New Testament contribute other significant images of Jesus. The letters written by or attributed to the apostle Paul (see chapter 6) focus on the crucified and resurrected Christ as the means of salvation for those who confess that he is Christ, Son of God, or Lord. Jesus is also the "last Adam," whose obedience to God reversed the consequences of Adam's disobedience. The "cosmic Christ" of Colossians reconciles the entire world to God. Among the general or non-Pauline epistles (see chapter 7), the letter to the Hebrews is unique in presenting Christ as a heavenly high priest, comparable to, but superior to, those high priests that served in the Jewish tabernacle. The book of Revelation (see chapter 8) symbolically portrays Jesus not only as a lamb that had been slain, but also as a victorious rider on a white horse, leading the armies of heaven into war.

These images, for the most part, were not based on personal knowledge of Jesus. Paul did not know Jesus personally, though he knew people who did. Nor did the authors of the gospels know Jesus, according to New Testament scholars, but wrote forty to seventy years after his death. Nevertheless, new images of Jesus continued to emerge after Jesus' death, from people who never met him. In some cases, they could attribute their conceptions of Jesus to the "Spirit" of God, who inspired them and taught them new things about Jesus (John 14:25–26; 15:26; 16:12–15). In other cases, they developed their images of Jesus from passages in the Hebrew Bible or "Old Testament" (see chapter 9). Since they believed that these scriptures spoke about Jesus, they used them to construct their conceptions of him.

Jesus Beyond the New Testament

Other conceptions of Jesus appear in the early centuries of the Christian era in the "apocryphal" writings (see chapter 10). These circulated alongside those writings that eventually became the canon of the New Testament. Some of these sought to fill in the gaps in the life of Jesus that were left by the canonical gospels. For example, the Infancy Gospel of Thomas relates stories about Jesus' childhood. The young Jesus portrayed in this gospel is occasionally volatile, as when he curses another child who offends him and the child drops dead. Other apocryphal writings used Jesus to promote certain religious beliefs or practices. For example, the Acts of John promotes a "docetic" perspective by portraying Jesus as a purely spiritual being who only appeared to be human. In the Acts of Thomas, Jesus, in the form of his identical twin and apostle Thomas, functions as a mouthpiece to promote the "encratite" practices of abstinence from marriage, wine, and certain foods.

Diverse images of Jesus continued to emerge as various Christian groups competed for supremacy. Judaic Christian groups generally regarded Jesus as a human being. Since these groups continued to view the Jewish Law as the way to God, they placed little emphasis on the death of Jesus, typically regarding it as the death of a rejected prophet. Jesus' primary importance lay in his role as the future Messiah, who would return to liberate the Jewish people from Roman domination. For Proto-Orthodox groups, the precursors of what would later become "mainstream" or orthodox Christianity, Jesus was both human and divine. His primary importance lay in his death, seen as a sacrifice for others. The shedding of his blood atoned for sins. For Gnostic Christian groups (see chapter 11), who combined Christian ideas with Hellenistic philosophy, the problem for human beings was not sin, but ignorance of their true selves. Human souls were sparks of divine light that had fallen from the heavenly realm to become ensnared in material bodies. Jesus' primary importance lay in his role as a revealer, who descended from the heavenly world to bring self-knowledge to ensnared souls so that they might ascend back to the heavenly realm. Many Gnostics regarded the Christ who performed this task as a purely spiritual being who never became ensnared in a material body.

In the early centuries of Christianity, the question of Jesus' "nature," whether human or divine, became a topic of considerable debate. On one end of the spectrum, adoptionists regarded Jesus as a purely human being. On the other end, docetists and many Gnostics saw him as a purely divine being. While some theologians wished to make him partly human and partly divine, others wanted him fully human and fully divine. These debates continued unabated through the eighth century and resulted in the formulation of the major creeds of Christendom (see chapter 12). The creed adopted at the Council of Nicea in 325 described Jesus as "of the same substance (homoousios) as the Father." Theologians from Cappadocia explicated this to mean that Jesus was one of three "persons" of the Trinity, who shared a single divine "nature." The creed adopted at the Council of Chalcedon in 451 insisted that Jesus had two natures, divine and human, which in some inexplicable way were neither mixed nor separated. Through these creeds and writings, emperors and bishops sought to establish one official interpretation of Jesus as the "orthodox" view, thus rendering all other views "heretical." This attempt only partially succeeded, since a number of Christian groups never accepted the official interpretations of Jesus' nature.

Interpretations of Jesus' death have been similarly diverse, though never reduced to an official creedal statement. Some early passages in the gospels present Jesus' death as that of a prophet. God sent Jesus to Israel not in order to die, but to deliver his message. Jesus' death came from those who rejected that message. Alongside this conception developed another, in which Jesus' death did not contravene God's will, but fulfilled it. God sent Jesus to die, and in some way he died on behalf of others as an "atonement" for sins (see chapter 13). While this conception prevailed to become the dominant view of Christianity, theologians and critics have continued to debate why Jesus needed to die and how his death could be for others.

During the Middle Ages, Christian theologians understood the nature of Jesus within the parameters set earlier by the creeds, though new theories of the atonement were developed by Anselm and Abelard. Thomas Aquinas justified the real presence of Christ in the Mass by the theory of "transubstantiation." Mystics sought mystical union with Jesus, while monks and nuns emulated his life of celibacy and poverty. Images of Jesus for the masses portrayed him primarily as hanging on the cross or presiding at the last judgment.

In the sixteenth century, the Protestant Reformation splintered Europe into warring factions. Reformers generally continued to restate earlier doctrines about Jesus. Building on earlier theories of atonement, Martin Luther and John Calvin developed the "penal substitutionary theory." A controversy over the Lord's Supper arose as Luther continued to accept the bodily presence of Jesus in the elements, while Calvin did not. Anabaptists who died for their faith looked to the suffering of Jesus as their model.

Jesus in World Religions

Alongside these developments, Jesus became a figure in religious traditions other than Christianity. Christianity has traditionally presented Jesus as the only way to the divine. As adherents of other religious traditions have encountered this claim, they have often found themselves compelled to respond. As part of their response, they have produced alternative visions of Jesus that are compatible with their own religious traditions.

Since Jesus was a Jew, as were his earliest followers, Judaism had the first encounter with Jesus (see chapter 14). As Jewish Christians preached that Jesus was the Christ, this message found little acceptance among Jews but had greater success among non-Jews. Christianity thus became a religion primarily of Gentiles, who increasingly developed hostility toward the Jews who rejected their view of Jesus.

After Christianity became the official religion of the Roman Empire in the fourth century, it had the power to put this animosity into effect. Jews throughout Europe became a persecuted minority in a hostile Christian environment. Not surprisingly therefore, Jews developed a less than positive attitude toward the Jesus in whose name they suffered. Ancient and medieval Jewish sources portray Jesus as an illegitimate child, an apostate from Judaism, a sorcerer who led Israel astray into idolatry, who was rightly condemned for blasphemy. Not until the nineteenth century, when Jews became more fully integrated into European culture, did Jewish scholars develop a more positive conception of Jesus as a Jewish prophet or sage, whose teachings have a place alongside those of other Jewish sages.

When Muhammad founded the religion of Islam in the seventh century, Christianity was a dominant power that required a response. The Qur'an provides a response by presenting an image of Jesus acceptable to the monotheistic faith of Islam (see chapter 15). This portrait adopts many aspects of the Christian Jesus: Jesus is born of a virgin, he is the Messiah, he performs miracles, and he is taken up to God. However, unlike the Jesus of Christianity, this Jesus is neither God nor the son of God nor a member of a divine Trinity. In the Qur'an, Jesus himself repudiates such claims. He is the greatest prophet other than Muhammad, but he is not divine. Nor did he die as an atonement for sins. In fact, he did not die at all, but was raised up to God alive. Later Islamic literature develops the portrait of Jesus in line with this basic image.

As Hindus have encountered the Jesus preached by Christian missionaries, they have developed images of Jesus that understand him within the context of Hinduism (see chapter 16). Hindus have no trouble accepting Jesus as an incarnation of God in human form, since the Hindu tradition itself includes the concept of an "avatar," a divine being who descends to the world to bring revelation of the truth. Some Hindus therefore regard Jesus as an avatar. However, they part company with the Christian view when it claims that Jesus was the only incarnation of God. For Hindus, Jesus was one avatar among others, such as Rama and Krishna. Other Hindus regard Jesus not as an avatar, but as a teacher of morality and ethics.

Similarly, Buddhists understand Jesus within the context of Buddhism (see chapter 17). In the most common appropriation of Jesus in Buddhism, he is a bodhisattva, a being who postpones entrance into nirvana in order to help other sentient beings toward enlightenment. Since there are many bodhisattvas, this perspective too rejects the Christian claim that Jesus is the only way to ultimate reality. Buddhists also regard Jesus as a spiritual teacher. They especially appreciate Christian teachings about love, which correspond to the Buddhist emphasis on the virtue of compassion.

Philosophical and Historical Perspectives on Jesus

With the Enlightenment of the seventeenth and eighteenth centuries, a new era dawned in perceptions of Jesus. Ideas about Jesus based on tradition or revelation or theological speculation came under suspicion. Since that time, rational philosophical enquiry, applied to the traditional image of Jesus, has raised doubts about the supernatural aspects of it. Jesus' birth from a virgin, his divinity, his miracles, his resurrection from the dead, the whole concept of the Trinity, have all come under scrutiny (see chapter 18 on the resurrection). Many critics have regarded these claims about Jesus as impossible, improbable, or incredible.

A similar result has issued from secular historical methods applied to the story of Jesus. The historical-critical method understands the past as analogous to the present. If the events that occur in the present have a natural explanation, then the same must be true for events that occurred in the past. Consequently a historical reconstruction gives natural explanations for the events of Jesus' life, just as it would for the life of Alexander the Great or any other figure of history. A reconstruction of Jesus as a historical figure presents Jesus in purely human terms.

The application of this method to the gospel accounts of Jesus' life has led to an ongoing quest for the historical Jesus (see chapters 19, 20, and 21). New Testament scholars engaged in this quest seek to place Jesus firmly within the historical context of first-century Judaism in the Roman Empire. But since the sources about Jesus are few and subject to interpretation, this quest has produced not one, but many different images of the historical Jesus. Scholars have portrayed Jesus as a revolutionary seeking to overthrow Roman domination, as an eschatological prophet announcing that God was about to establish his kingdom on earth, as a social reformer trying to improve the society in which he lived, as a Jewish rabbi concerned about the correct interpretation of the Jewish Law, as a magician, a sage, and even a feminist.

Modern Manifestations of Jesus

Alongside these various forms of the historical Jesus, other images of Jesus have also emerged in the modern era. Christian theologians, primarily in Europe and North America, have grappled with the problem that modernity poses for traditional conceptions of Jesus (see chapter 22). Some have embraced the Enlightenment goal of "religion within the limits of reason alone," seeking an understanding of Jesus that is credible within those limits but still relevant for Christian faith. Others have rejected those limits and developed more traditional christologies based on revelation and faith.

Theologians in Africa, Asia, and Latin America have also produced christologies that have relevance for their particular cultures (see chapter 23). South American theologians find most meaningful an understanding of Jesus as a liberator of the poor and oppressed. Theologians in Asia use various cultural analogies to make Christ relevant for that context, including the Hindu concept of the avatar to understand the incarnation of Jesus, the Chinese concept of yin and yang to understand the divine and human in Jesus, and the analogy of the guru to understand Jesus as a spiritual teacher. Similarly theologians in Africa portray Jesus in terms from their own culture, as an ancestor, a chief, or a medicine man (healer).

If Jesus has thus been adaptable to different cultures, that has been true nowhere more than in the United States, where Jesus has been a ubiquitous cultural icon (see chapter 24). In America, Jesus has ousted God the Father as the central figure of Christian devotion. Freed from creeds and tradition, he has become an intensely personal Savior. Members of the Ku Klux Klan take him as their role model, football players give thanks to him when they score, and presidents look to him for guidance in their foreign policy.

Since Jesus is typically portrayed as a white male, many black people have found it ironic to worship a Christ who resembles the white people responsible for their oppression. The struggle of blacks in the United States for liberation thus gave rise to an image of Christ as black (see chapter 25). In one sense, to call Christ black means that he supports blacks in their struggle for freedom; in another sense, it means that Jesus was ethnically black with dark skin. Proponents of the Black Christ have adopted one sense or the other or both, producing an image of Christ with which black people can identify.

While the whiteness of the traditional Christ has alienated many blacks, his maleness has posed a problem for many women. The depiction of God and Christ as male has traditionally justified the subjugation of women. Consequently the relevance of Jesus for women has come under scrutiny by the feminist movement that arose in the 1970s. While some feminists regard Jesus and his religion as incompatible with their goal of liberation, many Christian feminists have sought to retain Jesus by developing feminist christologies (see chapter 26). These have sought to develop an understanding of Christ that supports the goals and aspirations of women. "Womanist" christologies have developed such an understanding specifically for black women (see chapter 25). From these efforts, new images of Jesus have emerged, such as the Jesus who is a prophet of Sophia, a feminine personification of God's wisdom in the Jewish tradition. This is a Jesus who opposes patriarchal structures.

While the maleness of Jesus raises one issue for women, it raises another for gay men (see chapter 27). Can Jesus be relevant for gays? Could Jesus himself have been gay? Some interpreters have in fact found evidence that Jesus engaged in a homoerotic relationship with another man, pointing to his relationship with "the disciple whom Jesus loved" in the Gospel of John (John 13:21–26; 19:26–27, 34–35; 20:1–10; 21:1–8, 18–24). Depictions of Jesus as homoerotic also occur in art, literature, and theater. Some theologians argue that a "gay" Jesus is not incompatible with Christian theology.

Outside of official Christianity or the academic study of religion, more popular images of Jesus have abounded (see chapter 28). Modern apocrypha, forged texts that claim to be ancient documents, present a variety of perspectives about Jesus. For example, the *Life of Issa* fills in the "lost years" of Jesus between the ages of twelve and thirty, by relating how he traveled to India and studied with Hindu and Buddhist teachers. The *Essene Letter* describes how Jesus survived the crucifixion. Without using a forged text, modern "mystifications" – unverified speculations about Jesus – continue this tradition. Among these new mythologies is that disseminated most successfully in *The Da Vinci Code* by Dan Brown. This claims that Jesus and Mary Magdalene had children whose descendants are still among us. While Brown's book is fiction, it relies on works that actually make this claim.

Jesus in Art, Fiction, and Film

It is not surprising that a figure as popular as Jesus has frequently been depicted in art, fiction, and film. The history of Christian art testifies to various conceptions of Jesus (see chapter 29). Artists have depicted him as the good shepherd, the teacher of true philosophy, a healer and wonder-worker, a member of the Trinity, the creator, the giver of the new covenant, and the judge at the final judgment. Icons of Jesus have invited the veneration of the faithful.

Literature too has produced its own portrayals of Jesus. Since 1770, around 300 novels about Jesus have appeared in English, no two of which are exactly alike (see chapter 30). Most of these attempt to harmonize the differences between the four stories of Jesus in the gospels, in order to produce a single unified account. By rewriting the story, novelists are able to provide what they consider satisfactory solutions to problems in the gospel narratives. They answer such problematic questions as how Jesus' virgin birth occurred, how he regarded himself, what he thought he was doing, how he could perform miracles, who was responsible for his death, and what happened to his body. The novel allows the author to present his or her own perspective on Jesus, which may be characterized by devotion, cynicism, or humor.

Similarly, since the invention of motion pictures in the late nineteenth century, hundreds of movies about Jesus have appeared (see chapter 31). Like Jesus novels, most of these attempt to harmonize the four gospels. Yet no two portray exactly the same Jesus. While *King of Kings* presents a clear-headed and self-confident messiah of peace, *The Last Temptation of Christ* portrays a man beset by doubts and struggling with his own desires. While *The Greatest Story Ever Told* depicts a pious Christ, whose every word drips with solemnity, *Jesus Christ Superstar* gives us a hippy Jesus who sings his dialogue to the accompaniment of rock music.

Reflections on Jesus

Jesus of Nazareth would probably have a hard time recognizing himself in the plethora of different images that have borne his name over the past 2,000 years. How should we explain this diversity? No doubt a variety of factors were involved, but here I will focus on only one: the Christian claim that Jesus is "the truth." This claim emerged as early as the Gospel of John, in which Jesus proclaims, "I am the way, the truth, and the life. No one comes to the Father except through me" (John 14:6).

But if a particular understanding of Jesus represents ultimate truth, then all those who do not accept it are aligned with falsehood to a correspondingly ultimate degree. Christianity has frequently promoted precisely this perspective: it has claimed the status of ultimate truth for its own understanding of Jesus and thus condemned all those who reject it. To such a potent claim, spread by Christian missionizing, some communities and individuals have responded by putting forward a counter-image, an alternative image of Jesus as the truth. Such responses have produced numerous images of Jesus, because every community and individual has a different conception of the truth.

Some communities have rejected Jesus as a symbol for the truth, yet even such rejection may produce an image of Jesus. For example, the Jews of antiquity and the Middle Ages rejected the Jesus of their oppressors. In the process, they created a counter-image of Jesus as the opposite of the truth, as a deceiver who led Israel astray.

More frequently, communities have accepted Jesus as a symbol for the truth but have assimilated his image to their own particular truths. This process is attested already in the earliest writings about Jesus. A Jewish community that strictly followed the Law portrayed Jesus as a strict rabbi. One that had a more lenient attitude toward the Law depicted him as a lenient rabbi. Communities immersed in Hellenistic culture portrayed him as a demigod or incarnation. Another steeped in the tradition of sacrifice regarded him as a sacrifice for sins. Each of these communities produced a Jesus who reflected and supported its own particular truth.

This process continued as various world religions encountered the Jesus of Christianity. Islam adopted a Muslim Jesus who supported the truth of Islam. Hindus and Buddhists likewise assimilated Jesus to the truths of their own traditions, imagining him as an avatar or bodhisattva. This process has continued down to the present, as images of Jesus have emerged that support the particular truths of black people, feminists, and gay men.

Ultimately humans have created Jesus in their own image, and since humans are infinitely diverse, this diversity has extended to their images of Jesus. These images may not tell us a great deal about Jesus of Nazareth, but they do tell us about the people who conceived or imagined them. The continuing influence of Jesus in the future will depend on his ability to maintain this protean character, his ability to be all things to all people.

PART I
Jesus in the New Testament

1   Mark's Portrait of Jesus   13
     William R. Telford

2   Who Do You Say That I Am? A Matthean Response   30
     Elaine M. Wainwright

3   Jesus in Luke-Acts   47
     Delbert Burkett

4   John's Portrait of Jesus   64
     Mary L. Coloe

5   Jesus in Q   81
     Christopher Tuckett

6   Paul, Jesus, and Christ   94
     Edward Adams

7   Jesus in the General Epistles   111
     Harold W. Attridge

8   Jesus in the Apocalypse   119
     Ian Boxall

9   Constructing Images of Jesus from the Hebrew Bible   127
     Warren Carter

CHAPTER 1
Mark's Portrait of Jesus

William R. Telford

It is fitting that this volume, the *Blackwell Companion to Jesus*, which is dedicated to exploring the diverse ways in which Jesus has been considered significant in human culture over the past 2,000 years, should begin with Mark's portrait of Jesus. The Gospel of Mark is considered by many to be the primary compendium of Jesus traditions, and the first connected narrative account of the life of Jesus resulting therefrom. The status of the gospel in this regard cannot, therefore, be overestimated. While there are still those who would assign it a secondary role in the development of the Jesus tradition, for example, by casting doubt on its position as the first gospel to be written, and claiming that honor for the Gospel of Matthew (e.g., Peabody et al. 2002), most scholars nowadays would accept the case for Markan priority, and hence a scholarly consensus resulting from over two centuries of debate on the interrelationship of the gospels (e.g., Head 1997; for a full summary of scholarship over the last quarter century on the issue of Markan priority and posteriority, see Telford 2009, 4–5). The apostle Paul, of course, was the first to establish a Christian literary tradition through his epistolary activity, but his letters offer us little in the way of a description of Jesus. The compilers of Q (the other putative source used by Matthew and Luke in addition to Mark) may have been the first to compile a collection of Jesus' sayings, but nothing that resembles a picture of Jesus emerges from them. The Markan evangelist, on the other hand, was the first to bring together into a coherent form the various traditions that had grown up over a generation regarding Jesus' teaching and activity, and by placing not only his sayings but also his deeds within the framework of a story recounting his life and death, he it is who provides us with our first real portrait of Christianity's founder.

Being *first* at anything in human life and experience brings with it its own kudos, but in the case of Mark, the *first* evangelist, and the Gospel of Mark, the *first* gospel, we can recognize an achievement that, in historical, literary and theological terms, was to have profound significance for the emergence, development, and influence

The Blackwell Companion to Jesus, First Edition. Edited by Delbert Burkett. ©2014 John Wiley & Sons, Ltd. Published 2014 by John Wiley & Sons, Ltd.

of early Christianity, as well as for the subsequent history of western civilization itself. The Jesus portrayed by Mark, the Markan Jesus, was a major influence on the Matthean Jesus, the Lukan Jesus, and the Johannine Jesus, the later canonical writers using Mark's gospel directly (in the case of Matthew and Luke) and (arguably) indirectly (in the case of John) as one of their sources. The Markan Jesus was the progenitor of and inspiration for countless other representations of Jesus, and elements of Mark's portrait of Jesus can be discerned elsewhere in the New Testament; in ancient apocryphal, orthodox, and Gnostic portraits of Jesus; in the history of art, literature, and film; in modern historical reconstructions of Jesus; or in contemporary ideological constructions influenced by feminism, for example, or liberation theology; in short, in many of the Jesuses that this volume will be treating.

The significance of Mark's portrait as the first real portrait of Christianity's founder does not lie, however, in the assumption that it is, of necessity, a historically reliable portrait, for what the evangelist offers, if you like, is a literary "construct," or "fixation," of the developing tradition surrounding Jesus some forty years after his death. Although Mark's gospel may be reckoned the earliest of such accounts, primitiveness should not be confused with historicity. The significance of Mark's gospel does not lie, furthermore, in the claim that it is a literary masterpiece, for while the gospel's effectiveness as a literary vehicle for the "good news" of (or about) Jesus has stood the test of time, other more striking or compelling portraits have emerged in the ensuing development of the Jesus tradition, as this volume will demonstrate. Neither does Mark's significance lie in the sophistication or profundity of its theology, although, as we shall see, the evangelist can be claimed to have made an important contribution to the theological history of early Christianity, and his role as a theologian, therefore, notwithstanding the simplicity of his literary style, should not be dismissed. Where the significance of the Gospel of Mark does lie is in the fact that the primary images of Jesus that it presents, in scenes that have etched their way into the religious consciousness and literary imagination of believer and non-believer alike, have provided the basis for an array of Jesus constructions over the past 2,000 years.

Mark, then, has played a seminal role in the shaping of the traditions about Jesus, and it will be one of the aims of this chapter to explore this aspect of his achievement in relation to the portrait of Jesus that it has produced. As we shall see, Mark's portrait of Jesus, in this respect, is not an altogether uniform one, for the Jesus portrayed is a product or even, to some extent, an amalgam of the various prior traditions that the evangelist has attempted to incorporate and reconcile. Before the Markan Jesus, there was the Jesus of the pre-Markan tradition (or, to complicate things in the interests of greater accuracy, the Jesuses of the pre-Markan traditions).

In recognizing this, one must also acknowledge the decisive role that Mark has likewise played in the formation of the Jesus story, and it will be another of the aims of this chapter to examine this further facet of his achievement. While the Markan gospel gives evidence of its composite nature, the reader of the Markan text nevertheless gains the impression that a story, with its own plot, characters, and settings is gradually being unfolded. The Jesuses of these pre-Markan traditions, in other words, appear to have been replaced by a narrative Jesus who acts with seeming consistency within the story-world that the evangelist has attempted to construct.

Although he has made a significant contribution to the characterization of the central figure of his gospel, Mark was concerned not with the character of Jesus as such, but with his status, with what his words and his deeds reveal about who he is. Theology (a form of ideology) underpins his traditio-historical and literary enterprise, and the ideology that underlies his representation of Jesus has in turn been influential in the subsequent development of christology. When all of this is taken into consideration, therefore, it becomes obvious that Mark's portrait of Jesus is capable of being understood from different perspectives, in particular, the historical, the literary, and the theological; and it is the examination of these three distinct aspects of his achievement that will constitute the specific objectives of this chapter.

Some Preliminary Questions and Answers

Any consideration of "Mark's portrait of Jesus," then, must take account of the complexities that face us in examining this gospel text. At this point, it would be useful to highlight and explore some of these and to offer some observations and reflections on them. The very title, "Mark's Portrait of Jesus," raises a number of preliminary questions.

First, who is the "Mark" of the title? Is it the "Mark" referred to by Papias[1] as the interpreter of Peter, the John Mark of the New Testament,[2] or an anonymous figure whose identity in fact remains hidden from us? I would continue to uphold the position argued in my previously published work (Telford 1995b, 15–20 = Riches et al. 2001, 133–137; Telford 1999, 9–12), and maintained by most Markan scholars in the last quarter century, that the internal evidence of the Markan text hardly suggests, far less supports, Papias' testimony and that we should opt for an anonymous author, a profile of whose cultural background, socio-political situation and religious concerns can, nevertheless, to some extent be constructed.

Second, what is implied by the word "portrait"? The term conjures up the image of an artist with his subject in person before him, who attempts to capture on canvas the special features and enduring characteristics of the sitter. But few scholars would accept nowadays that the anonymous writer of this text had any personal knowledge of Jesus, and hence that his "portrait" was painted with the benefit of such individual experience. As a second-generation Christian, Mark, as we have said, had the role of shaping the traditions about Jesus.

But how should we envisage the "role" of this "Mark" in the shaping of such traditions? In light of advances in our knowledge of the literary and theological aspects of Mark's achievement, can the judgment, voiced by Dibelius (1934, 3) so long ago, that the evangelist, in common with the other synoptic writers, should be considered principally as a collector, a compiler, a vehicle of tradition, a mere editor and only to the smallest extent an author, still be maintained? In brief, I would consider him, if not an "author" in the literary sense, then a "highly creative redactor" of the traditions at his disposal, and one who, at times, gives evidence not only of an "authorial" voice in his shaping of the traditions about Jesus but also of theological creativity in his treatment of them. Redaction criticism[3] has taught me to respect this first gospel for what it was, a synthetic and constructive exercise in narrativizing the disparate Jesus traditions, to appreciate the evangelist's role in the selection, arrangement, modification, alteration, and even creation of these traditions, and to recognize the influence of the evangelist's theology in the construction of his portrait of Jesus. Over the years, moreover, I have owed an increasing debt to literary criticism, and in particular narrative criticism, which has in turn has made me conscious of the evangelist's literary ability, has enabled me to recognize the signs of literary artifice in the shaping of the traditions about Jesus, and to value Mark's considerable skill as a storyteller.

How, then, did the evangelist "shape" the traditions at his disposal, what was his contribution to the developing Jesus story, and to what extent was he a master of his material? There is no doubt, as the early form critics recognized, that he supplied notes of place, time, and audience where these were missing, seams uniting the individual units of tradition or pericopae, and summary and transitional passages linking series of pericopae. Redaction critics have gone further, however, and demonstrated more extensive redactional activity on his part. Composition critics have, likewise, pointed to chiastic structure and topical arrangement in the gospel; rhetorical critics have illuminated the numerous literary techniques and rhetorical devices at work in the shaping of the traditions; and narrative critics have exposed the various themes, motifs, and concerns that give the text its literary coherence, as well as offering evidence of the use of plot, characterization, and settings to provide unity and narrative progression.

The reasonably high degree of internal coherence which Mark has thereby imposed on his materials means that we must now treat him as more than a mere collector or editor of traditions, as formerly conceived; but – and here we should acknowledge the contribution of those early form and source critics – the countervailing evidence of disjunction in the narrative, of inconsistencies, aporias, and discrepancies should lead us to be cautious, in my view, in attributing too much authorial creativity to him. Due weight needs to be given, then, to both the textually-integrative and the textually-disintegrative factors in Mark's narrative, due attention to both his story-world and the real or historical world that impinges upon it, due regard for both his literary activity and for the pre-Markan traditions about Jesus that he has pressed into service, the incorporation of which has left a number of incongruities in the narrative (for a list and discussion of these, see Telford 1999, 18–19).

Mark was a highly creative redactor of the traditions about Jesus, traditions that he shaped both in a literary and in a theological way. But what were these traditions, and what form did they take? The case for written sources in Mark has still, in my view, to be proved, and so I am inclined to agree with most scholars that his sources were oral, and, in line with the classic form critics, that they consisted of sayings and stories about Jesus that had been circulating for a generation in various Jewish- or Gentile-Christian communities before they came to literary expression and theo- logical (re)interpretation at his hands. Their specific content and form and his treatment of them will occupy us later.

And, finally, who is the "Jesus" that we are talking about when we speak of Mark's portrait of Jesus? From one point of view, this Jesus is, of course, the *historical* Jesus, reconstructed by the modern historian and approached through critical anal- ysis and evaluation of the available sources. From another point of view, it is the Jesus of *culture*, constructed by the literary or religious imagination and propagated in the interests of the believing community or society. As has already been empha- sized, however, the Jesus that confronts us in the Markan text is first and foremost a *narrative* Jesus who has been given a story, and has been shaped by the evangelist out of the prior Jesus, or better, Jesuses, of the pre-Markan tradition. Any attempt to engage ultimately with the historical Jesus must begin first of all, in my view, with the *Markan Jesus*, and then proceed backwards, as the evidence allows, to the pre- Markan Jesus or Jesuses on which it is based. Any endeavor to come to grips with the *cultural* Jesus, and hence to understand the diverse ways in which Jesus has been considered significant in human culture over the last 2000 years, must also start with *Mark's portrait of Jesus*, but, conversely, move forwards in order to recognize what human artifice, need, and circumstance have added to that picture. Mark's portrait of Jesus is a focal point, therefore, for a whole spectrum of Jesus studies, and that portrait, as I have indicated, can be examined from different points of view, and in particular from a historical, literary, or theological perspective. It is these three particular dimensions of Mark's portrait that we shall now consider.

Historical Perspective: Forms, Sources, and Redaction

The evangelist's debt to the pre–Markan tradition

The first of these perspectives on Mark's portrait of Jesus requires us to ask what might have been the historical basis for the evangelist's depiction of Jesus, and what sources, oral or written, might have been at his disposal for such a portrait. Classic form criticism, with its emphasis on the oral tradition, has established the principal forms of the sayings and narrative tradition on which Mark drew for his portrait of Jesus: apophthegms, paradigms or pronouncement stories, prophetic or apocalyptic sayings, legal sayings, community rules, christological sayings, para- bles, miracle stories, historical stories and legends, and a passion narrative.

It is clear, too, that this material has been placed in certain main groupings, thereby illustrating the key features of Jesus' teaching and activity:[4]

- miracle stories (1; 4:35–5:43; 6:35–52; 7:25–8:9, 22–26);
- controversy stories (2:1–3:6; 3:20–35; 7:1–23; 11:27–12:40);
- parables (4:1–33);
- teaching about discipleship (8:27–10:45);
- apocalyptic discourse (13);
- passion narrative (14–16).

It is also obvious that this material has been placed in a loose, overall geographical framework by the evangelist, thereby indicating the main contours of Jesus' career:

- Jesus in Galilee (1:14–5:43);
- Jesus in Galilee and the surrounding Gentile area (the northern journey) (6:1–9:50);
- Jesus' journey to Judea and Jerusalem (10:1–52);
- Jesus in Jerusalem (11–16).

As indicated earlier, the work of source critics on the gospel has highlighted the fact that there is insufficient evidence that Mark used extensive written sources in creating his gospel. Some collections of material (e.g., miracle stories in 1, 4:35–8:26; controversy stories in 2:1–3:6, 11–12; parables in 4; apocalyptic material in 13; passion narrative in 14–16) might be pre-Markan, but the overall arrangement is more likely to be the product of his own redactional (or editorial) activity. Werner Kümmel once summarized scholarly consensus on the Markan sources in the classic judgment, "We cannot go beyond declaring that Mk is probably based on no extensive written sources, but that more likely the evangelist has woven together small collections of individual traditions and detailed bits of tradition into a more or less coherent presentation" (Kümmel 1975, 85). This verdict, I think, can still stand, although nowadays, as I have suggested, there would be more respect on the part of scholars for the coherence of the resulting Markan presentation and for Markan creativity in the shaping of these Jesus traditions than was previously entertained.

Where the redaction critics and their understanding of the editorial process is concerned, judgments would vary as to the precise purpose of Mark's redactional activity (although most scholars would agree, I think, that the overall purpose was theological, or more specifically, christological). Nevertheless, as indicated in several of my publications on Mark (Telford 1995b, 77–78 = Riches et al. 2001, 184; Telford 1999, 28), a gathering scholarly consensus would now probably identify the following features of the gospel as of prime importance in determining Mark's theological purpose insofar as it can be garnered from his redactional activity:

- the secrecy motif and the writer's interest in the true but hidden identity of Jesus;
- an interest in the passion of Jesus (his suffering, death, and resurrection) and its significance for christology;

- an interest in the nature and coming of the kingdom of God and in the question of Jesus' return as Son of Man;
- an interest in Galilee;
- his use of the term "gospel" (*euangelion*);
- an interest in Gentiles and the Gentile mission;
- an interest in persecution, suffering, and martyrdom and the true nature of discipleship;
- his harsh treatment of the Jewish leadership groups, Jesus' family, and especially his original disciples.

The pre-Markan Jesus(es)

Armed with knowledge of the components of the inherited pre-Markan tradition, with appreciation of the evangelist's redactional methods and interests, and with respect for his literary achievement in welding these materials together, contemporary Markan scholars are in some ways better equipped than an earlier generation, despite the complexities involved, to make the move I earlier referred to from the Markan Jesus, or the narrative Jesus, to the pre-Markan Jesus (or Jesuses) and thence to the historical Jesus.

My own position on this has been made clear in my published work (Telford 1995b, 126–127 = Riches et al. 2001, 225–227; Telford 1999, 33–35, 88–103). In keeping with a normal tradition-critical approach to the gospel, I have asserted that Mark has taken over traditional material already stamped with particular estimates of Jesus' significance. Three pre-Markan traditions in particular can be isolated: Jesus as *teacher*, Jesus as *prophet* and Jesus as *miracle-worker*. These three traditions are likely to be pre-Markan, since they form the core of the sayings and narrative traditions isolated by the form critics, and they are multiply attested in our early sources (for example, in Q). They also have a claim to go back to the historical Jesus.

One of the earliest impulses in the Jesus movement was the collection of Jesus' sayings, as the "sayings" tradition underlying the gospels indicates. In Q, indeed, as we previously noted, attention focuses mainly on Jesus' sayings and there is little interest otherwise in his life, death, or resurrection. In this early source, which is independent of Mark, Jesus is principally portrayed as a teacher, preacher, or prophet of the coming kingdom of God.

This tradition of Jesus as a prophet is also deeply embedded in primitive Christianity as well as in Mark. Jesus is believed to have had close connections with John the Baptist, whose disciple he may have been. Jesus' own consciousness appears to have been a prophetic one (cf. e.g., Mark 6:4; Luke 13:31–35), and it is certain that he was regarded as such (cf. e.g., Mark 6:14–16; 8:27–28). A substantial number of the sayings attributed to him are prophetic or apocalyptic ones, with many regarded by form critics as authentic. Certain activities associated with him, it has been suggested, may originally have been examples of dramatic prophetic action (e.g., the feeding in the wilderness, the triumphal entry, the cleansing of the temple, the cursing of the fig tree, the last supper). Traditions furthermore concerning his possession by the Spirit (e.g., Mark 1:9–11), ecstatic experience (e.g., Luke 10:21–22/Matt 11:25–27), clairvoyance (e.g., Mark 2:8), and even celibacy would also fit the prophetic mould.

The Jesus of the pre-Markan tradition was also deemed a miracle-worker, most notably a healer and an exorcist. The proclamation of Jesus' "mighty deeds" was another of the early impulses in the Jesus movement, as the "miracles" tradition also underlying the gospels indicates. Mark, of course, offers us the most notable evidence of this (with subsequent developments and embellishments provided by Matthew and Luke), for Q presents few, if any, actual miracle stories, and John, although he offers his readers a series of Jesus' "signs" (e.g., John 2:1–11; 4:46–54; 5:2–9; 6:1–15, 16–21; 9:1–7; 11:1–44), presents no exorcisms. Q, however, reveals knowledge of such a tradition by preserving a saying ("But if it is by the Spirit of God that I cast out demons, then the kingdom of God has come upon you"), which indicates that the significance of Jesus' miracle-working was eschatological; i.e., it vindicated his claim to be an eschatological prophet and provided evidence that the kingdom of God was imminent, as he proclaimed (Matt 12:28/Luke 11:20; cf. Matt 11:2–6/Luke 7:18–23). This saying not only has a high claim to authenticity, but it also links together all the essentials of this threefold pre-Markan tradition, namely Jesus' exorcisms, his teaching, and his prophetic proclamation, thereby lending support for the historicity of at least the core elements in Mark's parallel traditions.

Historical criticism and the Jesus of history

Even the most stringent historical criticism, therefore, cannot sever the link between the Markan Jesus, the pre-Markan Jesus (or Jesuses), and the Jesus of history, however one may wish to understand that "link." Though a literary composition, Mark's gospel shows evidence of being connected with a real or historical world. That world is the political world of the Roman Empire, and the cultural and religious worlds of Hellenism and Judaism. In constructing his portrait of Jesus, the evangelist refers to historical characters and groups (John the Baptist, Jesus' disciples, Pharisees, Sadducees, Herod, Pontius Pilate, etc.). In sketching the career of Jesus, he refers to historical regions (Galilee, the Decapolis, Judea, etc.), places (Capernaum, Tyre, Sidon, Caesarea Philippi, Jericho, Jerusalem, etc.), and even localities (Mount of Olives, Gethsemane, etc.).

Mark also has historical roots in the sectarian community out of which his gospel springs. That community has preserved the popular tradition of Jesus as a Jewish teacher, prophet, and healer-exorcist but is also in debt to Jewish Christian estimates of him as a Messianic figure. As I shall assert later, he may even be in tension with such traditions, for the evangelist clearly also has a debt to the Hellenistic Christianity that was to exalt him even further and to see in him a divine figure with salvific significance for the wider Greco-Roman world.

Mark's portrait of Jesus is more complex, then, than it first seems. From a historical perspective, it is manifestly not a complete or even adequate portrait, for it contains important lacunae (e.g., details of Jesus' birth and education, material relating to the first thirty or so years of his life, etc.). Nevertheless, by virtue of its debt to a pre-Markan tradition, the gospel does present data that has a claim to authenticity: Jesus' baptism by John the Baptist, his eschatological teaching and preaching, his gathering of disciples, his healings and exorcisms, his conflict with Jewish leadership groups, his death at the hands of the Romans. It is worth keeping these historical data in mind when one comes to consider the second dimension of his portrait, namely, the literary aspect.

Literary Perspective: Plot, Settings, and Characterization

Mark as story

Emphasis on the literary features of the Gospel of Mark has been a significant facet of Markan studies in the last quarter century, and the notion of Mark as *literature* has rivaled, although not eclipsed, the gospel's treatment as *history*. Literary studies have explored the question of the gospel's genre, its language and style, its composition and structure, its literary techniques and rhetorical devices. Approaching the gospel as a story, and providing analyses of the narrator, the characters, the plot and settings, a number of scholars have drawn attention to the insights that are to be gained by reading Mark through the lens of the storyteller (e.g., Minor 2001), or sought to demonstrate that Markan theology, which we shall consider shortly, can be appreciated by paying attention to the storyline (e.g., Humphrey 1992).

This storyline, or plot (which one would not expect, one notes, in a text that was *merely* a collection of traditions), leads to a recognizable climax, namely, the death and resurrection of Jesus, and has two major strands. The first is the conflict between Jesus and his opponents, the Jewish leadership groups, which is built up section by section (2:1–3:6; 3:22–30; 7:1–23; 10:2–9; 11–12; 14–15) and culminates in Jesus' visit to Jerusalem, his besting of his opponents in argument, his arrest, trial, and crucifixion. The second plot theme is the conflict between Jesus and his disciples, who, despite his repeated instructions to them, fail to understand who he is (4:41; 6:52; 8:21) – indeed, in the second half of the gospel (from 8:30 on), positively misunderstand the true nature of his divine status and mission as well as the Christian discipleship springing from it – and are left in the dark at the end after the announcement by the young man of his resurrection (16:1–8).

Apart from Jesus, whom we shall consider presently, and these major supporting characters (Jewish leaders and disciples), a host of minor ones, many of them, like the young man, unnamed (e.g., Jairus' daughter, the woman with the hemorrhage, the Syro-Phoenician woman, the rich young ruler, the poor widow, etc.), excite the reader's interest. The evangelist, too (or, in some cases, the tradition before him) has supplied the individual scenes with a variety of interesting settings (wilderness, sea, house, synagogue, boat, hills/mountain, way/road, temple, tomb), and these give the story a further literary (and, arguably, theological) texture.

An informed reader of the Gospel of Mark cannot also fail to recognize the very rich tapestry of quotations of or allusions to the Old Testament (or Hebrew Bible) that offer an implicit invitation to interpret the story of Jesus in light of them. A number of scholars, indeed, have called special attention to such intertextuality and have argued for the generative power of the Old Testament in forming Mark's story of Jesus.[5]

Literary techniques and rhetorical devices

But it is not only plot, characters, settings, and intertextuality that have contributed from a literary perspective to Mark's portrait of Jesus. The evangelist has employed a number of literary techniques and rhetorical devices to construct a unified narrative out of his inherited traditions.

Prominent, for example, among these has been the use of *intercalation* (Telford 1980, 39–68), what, in cinematic circles, would be called *intercutting*, one scene being spliced with another for effect, or *montage*, the juxtaposition of parallel scenes so that the interpreter is led to view the one scene in light of the other (e.g., 3:21, *22–30*, 31–35; 4:1–9, *10–12*, 13–20; 5:21–24, *25–34*, 35–43; 6:7–13, *14–29*, 30; 11:12–14, *15–19*, 20–25; 14:1–2, *3–9*, 10–11; 14:17–21, *22–26*, 27–31; 14:53, 54, *55–65*, 66–72; 15:40–41, *42–46*, 15:47–16:8).

Along with chiasmus and inclusio, this is one of the many ways that Mark shapes the traditions about Jesus, and we owe a considerable debt to composition critics for highlighting these techniques as instances of the wider phenomenon of sandwich patterning, concentric arrangement, or ring composition in antiquity that was employed and recognized both in oral teaching and in written discourse as a structuring mechanism.

A text that is a mere collection of traditions, and not a story, will not necessarily speak with a uniform voice, and another device that helps Mark achieve literary coherence for his story of Jesus is that of the "omniscient, intrusive, third-person narrator" (Petersen 1978). The narrator of Mark's gospel (in this case, the implied author) appears to control the narrative. As we read the text, we are conscious that he is present in every scene, unbound by time and space, and that he exercises a sovereign freedom in communicating to us what his characters think and feel ("inside views"), so establishing them in our minds as "reliable" or "unreliable" characters.

The narrator, in other words, evinces a definite and consistent "point of view," one that he identifies with that of his central character, Jesus. Moreover, by divulging or withholding information, or by arranging the order of events – for example, by *prospective devices*, that is, by foreshadowing what is to come (3:6) or *retrospective devices*, for example, by flashbacks (6:17–29) – he guides the reader throughout and suborns him or her into accepting his own ideological stance.

Narrative criticism and the narrative Jesus

Though connected with a real or historical world, the world that first confronts us, then, in Mark's gospel is a narrative world, a story-world, a world in which Jesus traditions have been selected, arranged, interpreted, and retold (or re-presented) in line with the evangelist's ideology, and in which characters, plot, and settings are constructed in such a way as to enlist the reader's sympathetic support for (indeed, allegiance to) the central character, and to engender antipathy for his detractors.

Moreover, just as the evangelist has historical roots in a first-century Mediterranean community that has clearly preserved both Jewish Christian and Hellenistic Christian traditions and estimates of Jesus, so, too, his gospel has literary antecedents that may have influenced the form of his presentation. Although some would maintain that Mark's so-called "gospel" is a unique literary genre – his own invention, if you like – others have pointed out the resemblances between this work and Greco-Roman biography, Greek tragedy, Hellenistic romance, or Jewish novelistic literature (Telford 1995b, 94–100 = Riches et al. 2001, 199–204; Telford 2009, 9; Burridge 1992; Inch 1997; Tolbert 1989; Vines 2002).

Whatever literary antecedents (or genres) might have provided a model for Mark's presentation of Jesus, the characterization of Jesus in his "gospel" is his major achievement. In contradistinction to flat characters like the disciples, or stock characters like the Jewish leaders, the Markan Jesus is what narrative critics call a round character (Rhoads, Dewey, and Michie 1999, 104), one distinguished, that is, by his many and varied traits, and one toward whom the narrator, as we have seen, maintains a consistently favorable point of view. Though the Markan Jesus' "human" traits are often emphasized (note his anger, 3:5; harshness, 8:33; impatience, 9:19; even vindictiveness, 11:13–14!), the evangelist's real concern is to highlight his "divine" characteristics. The Markan Jesus is a figure endowed with power (*dunamis*; e.g., 5:30) and authority (*exousia*; e.g., 1:22, 27). He wields this power over nature (e.g., 4:35–51), he works miracles (e.g., 4:35–5:43), he possesses supernatural knowledge (e.g., 2:8) and he can be dramatically "metamorphosed" before his disciples (9:2–8).

Theological Perspective: Christology and Soteriology

Narrative theology and the theological Jesus

These "divine," and hence theological, elements, clearly in evidence in the literary portrait of Jesus just adumbrated, make us realize that in the Gospel of Mark we are dealing with more than a historical document, with its deposit of traditions, and indeed more than a literary composition, with its storybook world. Mark's gospel is finally a vehicle for religious ideas, and an exercise, if you like, in narrative theology. A key consequence of this, of course, is that the deductive move from the Markan Jesus to the Jesus (or Jesuses) of the pre-Markan tradition and thence to the historical Jesus is made all the more problematic for the scholar, for he or she must come to grips with the *theological world* that confronts us in the gospel and the *theological Jesus*, who addresses us from its pages.

The reader who enters Mark's world enters a religious world in which angels, demons, and other supernatural agencies are at work, a world in which storms can be stilled by a word of command, in which seas can be traversed with no visible means of support, and in which unfruitful trees can be withered with a curse. This world is a world in which theological concepts (kingdom of God, the Holy Spirit, the preaching of "good news," faith, unbelief, blasphemy, signs from heaven, etc.) or religious practice (baptism, the confession and forgiveness of sins, prayer and fasting, the keeping of the Law, the observance of the Sabbath, attendance at the synagogue or Temple, etc.) inform the narrative but make their own demands on the reader. This world is also familiar to us from the Old Testament, whose influence on Mark we have already commented upon. To understand Mark's portrait of Jesus, therefore, one must not only have an appreciation of the gospel's historical context, or its literary environment, but also its theological background.

Further theological, or in this case christological, elements are also very much in evidence when one considers the narrative images by which Mark's central figure is characterized. As we have seen, he appears as an authoritative teacher (e.g., 1:21–22), a charismatic prophet (8:27–28), and a popular healer and exorcist (e.g., 1:32–34). He is described as the "Nazarene" (e.g., 10:47) and addressed as "Teacher" (e.g., 4:38), "Rabbi" (e.g., 9:5), or "Lord" (7:28). He is acclaimed, moreover, as the "Holy One of God" (1:24), greeted as the "Son of David" (10:47), and confessed as "Christ" (8:29) or "Son of God" (15:39). He speaks of himself, however, as the "Son of Man" and defines his role as that of a servant (e.g., 10:45). Given this multifaceted presentation, the move that can be made (backwards) from Markan christology to the christology or christologies of the pre-Markan tradition and thence to the historical Jesus is a further challenge to the student of early Jesus traditions, who wishes to understand the process that led to Mark's portrait of Jesus.

The developing pre-Markan christological tradition

The first move is made when we recognize, as we have indicated, that the theological world of the Gospel of Mark is the religio-cultural world of both Judaism and Hellenism, and in the case of the evangelist, more specifically, that of first-century Jewish and Hellenistic Christianity. A second move is when we acknowledge that a number of the estimates of Jesus within this pre-Markan tradition have Jewish

Christian roots, while others convey a much wider Hellenistic perspective. Allowing for overlap or ambiguity, some differentiation between them, therefore, can be attempted. Impulses within the tradition to view Jesus in *eschatological* terms, to see him, in other words, as the proclaimer of the coming kingdom of God, or as God's "strong man" in the defeat of Satan and his legion of demons, or to describe him in *Messianic* terms, as God's agent in the inauguration of the new age, are clearly of Jewish Christian provenance. Tendencies within the tradition to see Jesus in *epiphanic* terms, that is, to see him as divine (or semi-divine), a supernatural being from another world, or a manifestation of God himself, clearly act in the face of Jewish monotheism, and are more likely to represent a Hellenistic Christian orientation. The final move has already been made in the recognition that we reach historical bedrock in the (sociological) categorization of Jesus as a Jewish teacher, prophet, and exorcist.

Depictions of Jesus in the gospel as Messiah or Christ (1:1; 8:29; 9:41; 12:35–37; 13:21, 22; 14:61; 15:32), apocalyptic Son of Man (2:10, 28; [3:28]; 8:31, 38; 9:9, 12, 31; 10:33, 45; 13:26; 14:21, 41, 62), royal Son of David (10:47–48; 11:10; 12:35–37), or suffering Servant (e.g., 10:45) clearly have Jewish roots, and, while much ink has been spilt by scholars explaining the meaning and precise use of these terms, their background in the Old Testament and intertestamental, particularly apocalyptic, Judaism is not really in doubt. The term "Son of Man" has occasioned particular difficulty, but I myself would share the view of those scholars who claim that it was applied to Jesus in accordance with the belief entertained in apocalyptic Judaism in an exalted, transcendent, heavenly figure (styled variously as "one like a son of man," "that Son of Man," or "the Man") who would appear at the end-time to judge the world, punish the wicked, and vindicate the righteous (Dan 7:1–14; 1 Enoch 48; 69:26–29; 71:14–17; 4 Ezra 13:1–13).

While Jewish usage can be cited, appellations such as Lord (e.g., 1:3; 2:28; 5:19; 7:28; 11:3; 12:35–37) or Son of God (1:1, 11; 3:11; 5:7; 9:7; 13:32; 14:61; 15:39) are more at home in the wider Hellenistic world, and in Hellenistic Christianity, as is the notion of a Jesus who can still storms (4:35–41), walk on water (6:45–52), and appear before his disciples in resplendent glory (9:2–8). These *epiphanic* elements suggest that a process of divinization has been at work on the pre-Markan Jesus, one that is clearly more credible in a Hellenistic Christian than a Jewish Christian religious environment, and one that has come to find its literary and theological expression in Mark's portrait of Jesus.

Markan christology and soteriology

In addition to popular estimates of Jesus, then, Mark appears to have also inherited a more developed christological tradition in which Jesus had come to be regarded in Jewish Christian circles not only as a teacher, prophet, and exorcist, but also as a victorious Messianic figure, the earthly Son of David or the heavenly Son of Man.

He was also heir, it seems, to a Hellenistic Christian tradition influenced, one might suggest, by Paul, "the apostle to the Gentiles," who, likewise, saw in Jesus the divine "Son of God" (Gal 4:4; Rom 1:3–4; 8:3), who had died for the sins of the world (Rom 3:23–25; 5:8–9, 18–19), and who was now to be addressed as the believing community's exalted "Lord" (1 Cor 12:3). How, then, has the evangelist, in his role of interpreter as well as transmitter of traditions, shaped these various prior estimates about Jesus theologically? Here we touch on what has undoubtedly been one of the major preoccupations of Markan scholars in the last quarter century, namely, the question of Mark's own christology (see Telford 2009, 17–19, where I have tried to chart the ongoing debate on this subject).

The first clue lies in one very important, indeed distinctive, aspect of his literary portrait of Jesus, namely, the secrecy motif, mentioned earlier as one of the eight features of the gospel, treated by William Wrede in his ground-breaking book, *Das Messiasgeheimnis in den Evangelien* [The Messianic Secret in the Gospels] (1901), but hitherto only touched upon. Whoever reads the gospel is instantly struck by the aura of secrecy that surrounds the person and activity of the Markan Jesus: e.g., his puzzling commands to silence (1:25, 34, 44; 3:11–12; 5:43; 7:36; 8:26; 8:30; 9:9); the private instruction he gives to his disciples (4:11–12, 33–34; 4:41; 6:52; 7:17–23; 8:14–21, 31–33; 9:2–13, 28–41; 10:1–14, 32–45); his parabolic teaching to the crowd (4:11–12), which conceals the "mystery" or "secret" of the kingdom of God; his curious self-concealment (1:35–37, 45; 3:7; 4:35; 6:31, 45–47; 7:24; 9:30); and his refusal to give a sign (8:11–13).

Though opinions vary as to its nature and function in the gospel, the secrecy motif is arguably Mark's supreme literary and theological device. It illumines (but also characteristically obfuscates) the evangelist's theological shaping of the traditions about Jesus. By means of this motif, the reader is made a party to the secret of Jesus' true identity, as Mark perceives it. With the exception of the supernatural world (the demons, 1:24, 34; 3:11–12) and one Gentile centurion (15:39), none of the characters in Mark's story are a party to this secret. By means of the secrecy motif, the Markan scholar, too, can gain some understanding of Mark's christology, and hence some appreciation of how he shaped the Jesus traditions theologically.

How, then, to repeat our question, has the evangelist, in his role of interpreter as well as transmitter of traditions, shaped these various prior estimates about Jesus theologically? In common with a number of Markan scholars, I myself would maintain that Mark did not impose a christology upon pre-Markan traditions that had *no* christological stamp, as Wrede thought, but rather that he sought to *develop* or *counter*, by means of his own, the christology (or christologies) already *implicit* in the various traditions that we have outlined. My own view is that by both employing and correcting the emphases of these separate traditions, by a discriminating use of christological titles, and, above all, by means of the secrecy motif, Mark has presented these traditions in such a way as to leave his readers in no doubt as to the significance that ought to be attached to the pre-Markan Jesus, namely, that he is the *supernatural* "Son of God" as well as the *suffering* "Son of Man."

Mark in part rejects, in part modifies, these earlier common traditions of Jesus as teacher, prophet, and miracle-worker and those more developed particularist Jewish Christian estimates, I believe, in two ways, namely, christologically and soteriologically. Christologically, he presents Jesus essentially as he was seen by Gentile Christians, viz., as the divine Son of God, and not as the Jewish Messiah, the Son of David. By means of the secrecy motif, the Jesus of Jewish Christian tradition is presented to the reader as the bearer in his earthly life of the more exalted (but concealed) status of the (divine) Son of God. This is presented as a "revelation" to the reader, if not to the characters in the Markan story who remain "blind" (Jewish leaders and disciples), but in reality it reflects the evangelist's own christology, or that of the Hellenistic Christianity by which he has been influenced, and it marks thereby a significant advance on the Jewish Christian estimates of Jesus that antedate it.

Soteriologically, by including the "passion" elements in his story of Jesus, he presents Jesus' suffering and death not only as predestined but also as salvific, as fundamental to salvation (e.g., 10:45). Mark retains the Jewish Christian tradition of Jesus as the triumphant apocalyptic Son of Man (perhaps because it accorded more transcendence to Jesus than did the notion of a purely human, Davidic Messiah), but by means of the passion predictions (8:31; 9:31; 10:33–34), the other suffering "Son of Man" sayings (9:9, 12; 10:45; 14:21 [twice], 41) and the passion narrative, the *suffering, death, and resurrection* of the returning (apocalyptic) Son of Man is presented as a pre-ordained part of the divine plan for redemption carried out by the Son of God.

And so, with these emphases, therefore, Mark reflects a shift away, I believe, from a historical tradition of Jesus as teacher, prophet, and healer-exorcist, as well as from an earlier Jewish Christian tradition of Jesus as Messianic Son of David or apocalyptic Son of Man toward one reflecting the influence of a Hellenistic Christian theology of the cross, particularly that of Paul, for whom, likewise, the proclaimer of the coming kingdom of God of the Jewish Christian tradition had become the one whose saving death, as well as resurrection, is the content of the message of salvation, the "gospel" proclaimed among the Gentiles, the "mystery" or "secret" now being made manifest to them (see Telford 1999, esp. 155–156, where this conclusion is more fully worked out).

Conclusion

What, to conclude, was Mark's role in the shaping of traditions about Jesus and his contribution to our first portrait of Jesus? A very considerable one, I think, and one characterized by significant contributions at the historical, literary, and theological levels. From a historical point of view, Mark has provided us with a document that offers the historian core traditions relating to the main features of Jesus' life: his baptism by John the Baptist; his Galilean ministry; his calling of disciples; his activity as a teacher, prophet, healer, and exorcist; his conflict with the authorities; his death at the hands of the Romans.

From a literary perspective, he has given us our first connected narrative account of the life of Jesus, and, with literary skill and artifice, has shaped these traditions into a story that was to have a powerful effect on church and society for generations to come.

From a theological viewpoint, he has combined disparate Jesus traditions under the influence of a christology and a soteriology closer to Paul, I believe, than to Jesus' original disciples, and he has done this in the service of a Gentile Christian community struggling to make sense of its Jewish Christian heritage within a Hellenistic world that is henceforth to be its mission field.

And finally, from the standpoint of posterity, he has produced a Markan Jesus who has in turn influenced the Matthean Jesus, the Lukan Jesus, (directly or indirectly) the Johannine Jesus, and, to some extent, the apocryphal Jesuses that followed in other centuries. Mark's gospel, too, is the text out of which novelists and filmmakers, from the very conception of the cinema, have created their literary and cinematic lives of Christ, and from whose pages they have manufactured their literary and filmic versions of scenes in Jesus' life made famous by Mark himself.

Notes

1   As cited by Eusebius, *Ecclesiastical History* III.39, who quotes its ascription by Papias, bishop of Hieropolis, ca. 140 CE, to a contemporary, "the Elder."
2   Cf. Acts 12:12, 25; 13:13; 15:37–39; Col 4:10; Philemon 24; 2 Tim 4:11; 1 Pet 5:13.
3   For a description of the hermeneutical methods mentioned in this chapter, see, for example, Telford 1995b, 46–56 (source criticism and Mark's sources), 56–69 (form criticism and the forms in Mark), 69–82 (redaction criticism and the editorial process in Mark), 86–94 (literary approaches to Mark) = Riches et al. 2001, 158–167, 167–177, 177–188, 192–199, resp.; for the history of scholarship in connection with them, see Telford 1995a; for a comprehensive account and analysis of the use and results of these methods in Markan scholarship up until the present, see Telford 2009.
4   Note, however, the exceptions to this otherwise schematic arrangement: the single miracle pericopae in 9:14–27 and 11:12–14, 20–25, the single controversy story in 10:2–9, the single parable in 12:1–11.
5   For example, Schneck 1994, who detects the influence of Isaiah on Mark 1–8, or Roth 1988, the influence of the Elijah–Elisha narrative in 1 Kings 17–2 Kings 13.

References

Burridge, Richard A. (1992). *What Are the Gospels? A Comparison with Graeco-Roman Biography.* Cambridge: Cambridge University Press.
Dibelius, Martin (1934). *From Tradition to Gospel.* London: Ivor Nicholson & Watson.

Head, Peter M. (1997). *Christology and the Synoptic Problem: An Argument for Markan Priority.* Cambridge: Cambridge University Press.

Humphrey, Hugh M. (1992). *"He is Risen!" A New Reading of Mark's Gospel.* New York: Paulist.

Inch, Morris A. (1997). *Exhortations of Jesus According to Matthew and Up From the Depths: Mark As Tragedy.* Lanham, MD: University Press of America.

Kümmel, Werner G. (1975). *Introduction to the New Testament.* London: SCM.

Minor, Mitzi L. (2001). *The Power of Mark's Story.* St. Louis, MO: Chalice.

Peabody, David B., Lamar Cope, and Allan J. McNicol, eds. (2002). *One Gospel from Two: Mark's Use of Matthew and Luke. A Demonstration by the Research Team of the International Institute for Renewal of Gospel Studies.* Harrisburg, PA: Trinity.

Petersen, Norman R. (1978). " 'Point of View' in Mark's Narrative." *Semeia* 12:97–121.

Rhoads, David, Joanna Dewey, and Donald Michie (1999). *Mark as Story: An Introduction to the Narrative of a Gospel.* Minneapolis: Fortress.

Riches, John, William R. Telford, Christopher M. Tuckett, and Scot McKnight (2001). *The Synoptic Gospels.* Sheffield: Sheffield Academic Press.

Roth, Wolfgang (1988). *Hebrew Gospel: Cracking the Code of Mark.* Oak Park, IL: Meyer-Stone.

Schneck, Richard (1994). *Isaiah in the Gospel of Mark, I–VIII.* Vallejo, CA: BIBAL.

Telford, William R. (1980). *The Barren Temple and the Withered Tree: A Redaction-Critical Analysis of the Cursing of the Fig-tree Pericope in Mark's Gospel and its Relation to the Cleansing of the Temple Tradition.* Sheffield: JSOT.

Telford, William R. (1995a). "The Interpretation of Mark: a History of Developments and Issues." In William R. Telford (ed.), *The Interpretation of Mark* (pp. 1–61). Edinburgh: T&T Clark.

Telford, William R. (1995b). *Mark.* Sheffield: Sheffield Academic Press.

Telford, William R. (1999). *The Theology of the Gospel of Mark.* Cambridge: Cambridge University Press.

Telford, William R. (2009). *Writing on the Gospel of Mark.* Leiderdorp: DEO; London: SCM-Canterbury.

Tolbert, Mary Ann (1989). *Sowing the Gospel: Mark's World in Literary-Historical Perspective.* Minneapolis: Fortress.

Vines, Michael E. (2002). *The Problem of Markan Genre: The Gospel of Mark and the Jewish Novel.* Atlanta: Society of Biblical Literature.

CHAPTER 2

Who Do You Say That I Am? A Matthean Response

Elaine M. Wainwright

The central gospel question – "Who do you say that I am" (Matt 16:15) – is one that has engaged Christians since it was first asked in the gospel narratives (see also Mark 8:29; Luke 9:20). While for some it might seem that there is a clear and unambiguous answer – "You are the Messiah, the Son of the living God" (Matt 16:16) – an exploration of both the Gospel of Matthew and recent scholarship on this gospel would suggest that its answer is neither clear nor unambiguous but rather opens up multiple dimensions of meaning.

Gospel portraits of Jesus are complex. They are *formed* and shaped as a reader encounters the web of plot, character interaction, images and metaphors (including titles), and a range of other rhetorical devices. They are *informed* by the theological or interpretive perspectives that scholars bring to their readings of the narrative. Also, the use of a range of biblical methodologies or interpretive strategies leads to variations in interpretations. Matthean scholarship, with the portraits of Jesus proposed therein during the second half of the twentieth century into the first decade of the new millennium, has been no stranger to this complexity.

Given the wealth of this scholarship, it would be impossible to summarize it in this chapter. What I propose to do, therefore, is to draw attention to the major emphases in the Matthean portrait of Jesus. At the same time, I will note some of the shifts in biblical methodologies that have impacted scholars' constructions of this portrait across the proposed timeframe and some of the hermeneutical perspectives they have brought to their interpretation. Detailed discussion and extensive critical engagement will not be possible. It is my hope, however, that this chapter will invite readers into the complex map of responses in the Matthean gospel to the Jesus question – "Who do you say I am?" – while at the same time providing a compass that can guide the traversing of this map.

The Blackwell Companion to Jesus, First Edition. Edited by Delbert Burkett. ©2014 John Wiley & Sons, Ltd. Published 2014 by John Wiley & Sons, Ltd.

Titles Given to Jesus

One characteristic of historical critical scholarship on Matthew's gospel has been and is its concern with the titles given to Jesus: whether "Son of Man," "Son of God," "Messiah," "Lord," "Son of David," or others were dominant in the Matthean gospel. This approach has been exemplified in the work of Jack Dean Kingsbury ([1975] 1989; 1984) and others.

Foundational to Kingsbury's historical critical approach to Matthean christology was his proposed structuring of the gospel. He divided the gospel into three sections (1:1–4:16; 4:17–16:20; and 16:21–28:20) on the basis of the marker "[f]rom that time on Jesus began to ..." in 4:17 and 16:21 (1989, 1–39). Kingsbury drew attention to one set of markers in the Matthean narrative, but it was one among many. The traditional division of the gospel into five major discourses with the key marker "when Jesus had finished ... ," the phrase that concludes each of the five major discourses (7:28; 11:1; 13:53; 19:1; 26:1), was one other (Meier 1979, 45–46), and it focused attention on Jesus as teacher/preacher. On the basis of his emphasis on the formula in 4:17 and 16:21, Kingsbury, however, argued that the Matthean gospel is the unfolding story of Jesus as Messiah (1989, 7–25), a title which occurs sixteen times in the gospel (1:1, 16, 17, 18; 2:4; 11:2; 16:16, 20; 22:42; 23:10; 24:5, 23; 26:63, 68; 27:17, 22). Within his proposed structure of the unfolding story of Jesus Messiah, he claims that "Son of Man" is the way that Jesus designates himself or interacts with the world (Kingsbury 1975; Matt 8:20; 9:6; 10:23; 11:19; 12:8, 32, 40; 13:37, 41; 16:13, 27, 28; 17:9, 12, 22; 19:28; 20:18, 28; 24:27, 30, 37, 39, 44; 25:31; 26:2, 24, 45, 64) but that "Son of God" is a confessional title and hence is central even though it occurs as an explicit title fewer times in the narrative (4:3, 6; 8:29; 14:33; 16:16; 26:63; 27:40, 43). He privileges confession over narrative and a single title over a multiplicity of titles.

Kingsbury does not articulate a particular hermeneutic shaping his interpretation, but it is worth noting that, with the emergence of a narrative approach to the gospels in the mid-1980s, he participated in this shift (1988). While his methodological approach purportedly shifted, his christological focus was still on titles, with the accompanying claim that the title Son of God dominated. In a frequently cited response to Kingsbury, David Hill raises the question as to whether for him the christological probe "was already settled and delivered and would accord with what Kingsbury has strongly argued for elsewhere and by other means" (1984).

John Meier, on the other hand, highlighted the significance of the Son of Man title. He, however, did not claim the dominance of any one title but emphasized that titles function together within the context of the gospel and should not be pitted over against one another (1979). More recently, Dennis Duling (1992) has drawn attention to the contribution that the title Son of David (Matt 1:20; 9:27; 12:23; 15:22; 20:30, 31; 21:9, 15; 22:42) makes to the Matthean portrait of Jesus, using three social scientific models to demonstrate the multivalence or plurisignificance of this term in the gospel. The most recent comprehensive exploration of a Matthean title is that of Joel Willitts, in which he explores the motif of Shepherd-King through the lens of what he calls "concrete-political Davidic Messianism" (2007, 4).

It is evident from the above that these and other titles given to Jesus in the Matthean gospel are multiple and function across the text to develop an understanding of Jesus. However, together with the metaphoric designation of God as Father, especially in relation to Jesus as Son, that occurs extensively across the Matthean gospel, these titles construct an androcentric symbolic universe within the gospel, while titles such as "Lord" and "King" construct an imperial one. Such aspects need to be engaged critically so as not to underpin contemporary justification for ongoing patriarchy, androcentrism, imperialism, or colonialism.

Attention to titles, does not, however, exhaust the gospel portrait. Closely related to the function of titles in shaping the characterization of Jesus are certain motifs that are developed in the unfolding of the gospel story. One such motif is that of Wisdom. Celia Deutsch, for instance (1996; cf. Suggs 1970; Burnett 1981), examines the metaphor of Lady Wisdom in the sapiential literature. She points to the tensive nature of metaphor that enables it to evoke ever new meanings in new situations. She then goes on to examine ways in which the Matthean gospel, especially in 11:2–13:58 and 19:1–25:46, "presents Jesus as Wisdom by ascribing to Jesus qualities and roles attributed to Lady Wisdom in other Jewish sources ... Jesus is hidden and revealed, accepted and rejected. He is teacher and prophet" (1996, 42). In a later article, she brings an explicitly feminist hermeneutic to bear on the Matthean portrayal of Jesus as Wisdom (2001). While the Wisdom motif may not necessarily speak from women's experience in the Matthean communities, it can provide contemporary interpreters with a female metaphor that may begin to subvert the androcentrism noted above.

While Deutsch traced the use of the metaphor of Wisdom to characterize Jesus in the Matthean narrative, Dale C. Allison examined how a Moses-typology that had been developing in the Hebrew Bible and other religious literature available to the Matthean author functioned to inform the gospel's portrait of Jesus (Allison 1993). For him, this was not a motif visible only in certain sections of the gospel, such as Matthew 2 (the bringing of Jesus out of Egypt) or Matthew 5–7 (in which Jesus is presented as a new lawgiver). Rather, for Allison, it characterized the entire narrative.

All the above studies could be designated as literary-critical in their approach within the context of the broader methodological approach of historical criticism – the scholars who examined titles, motifs, metaphors, and typologies characterizing the Matthean Jesus were seeking the intention of the Matthean author/s in relation to the portrait of Jesus. They explored how these titles and motifs were informed by the variety of meanings emerging from both the Hebrew Bible and other Jewish texts circulating in the late Hellenistic and early Roman empires, an aspect that I have not been able to develop in this brief article. What is becoming clear, however, is that the Matthean portrait of Jesus is multidimensional, informed by a web of such typologies and titles, motifs and metaphors. What tended to be missing from these studies, however, was the integrating aspect of the gospel story. In the early 1980s, narrative criticism emerged as a way of addressing such a lacuna, and it is to this that I now turn.

Narrative Portrayals of Jesus

It seems almost a truism to state that Jesus is a character, albeit the major character, in the Matthean narrative, but Mark Allan Powell (1991, 48) makes it very explicit when he says, "[t]he plot of Matthew's gospel is basically the story of its central character, Jesus." Turning attention to plot and characterization as narrative techniques has further informed an understanding of the Matthean Jesus. In 1987, Frank Matera, using Chatman's literary critical theory of "kernels" and "satellites" as constitutive of plot, shifted attention from historical criticism's identification of markers in the text indicating structure to key events and what emerges from them in the shaping of a story. He summarized his determination of plot in this way. By birth Jesus was the Davidic Messiah. After John was imprisoned, he began to preach, heal, and teach, exclusively among the people of Israel. Though most segments of Israel rejected him, his disciples acknowledged him as the Messiah. After explaining to them that he would suffer, die, and be resurrected, he went to Jerusalem, where his cleansing of the temple brought about his death. His death meant that Israel had rejected its Messiah, and consequently, the gospel was transferred to the Gentiles (Matera 1987, 245–246).

Powell (1991, 48–51) advanced the narrative study of Jesus further, demonstrating the intimate link between plot and characterization. He drew attention to conflict as constitutive of the Matthean narrative (1992a; 1992b), examining how other characters interact around Jesus the main character in the conflict-laden story. In the opening scenes, many bear witness to Jesus: the narrator, the *magoi* from the East, John the Baptist, and the heavenly voice. This cumulative witness authorizes Jesus for preaching, teaching, and healing roles that draw opposition. The culmination of this opposition occurs in the condemning of Jesus to death and his vindication in being raised up by God. Powell's final sentence in the section on the character of Jesus seems to suggest, however, that the narrative portrayal falls short of Matthean theology, concluding in relation to 28:20 that "Matthew indicates that Jesus cannot ultimately be understood as a character but must be seen as a living presence in the midst of his church" (1992c, 361). It could be argued, however, that the final aspect of the narrative portrayal of the character Jesus is that he, as risen one, will be with the addressees of the narrative, until the end of time. Matthean theology is conveyed through narrative characterization.

I have dealt further with this issue of the theological function of narrative in constructing the gospel portrait of Jesus (Wainwright 1998), arguing that narrative functions by being heard/read, that narrative makes meaning, including theological meaning, in and among readers/hearers, and that this was as true for the first century as for the twentieth and the twenty-first. The gospel story of Jesus would have been heard *differently* within the *different* households constituting the Matthean community or communities of the first century, whether they were located in Antioch (Carter 2000) or in northern Galilee – either Tiberias or Sepphoris (Overman 1990, 158–161; Gale 2005) – or whether they functioned as "a rather loosely confederated group of congregations, united by missionaries" across "an arc of settlement that included both the Galilee ... and Pella ... arched into Syria through Antioch and Edessa," with Galilee and Antioch being two fixed points (Segal 1991, 26–27).[1] Wherever the community or however constituted, although I am inclined toward Segal's position, its various households would have made theological meaning from the narrative. So too will this gospel story of Jesus be heard/read/received differently, so too will it make theological meaning of Jesus with different emphases in different communities today, be they scholarly or faith communities (Davies 1993, 11–17).

This aspect of difference came to my attention as a result of my feminist hermeneutic. This criticizes the androcentric language and worldview and the patriarchal structures encoded in the biblical text and revisions the gospel storytelling to include the meaning-making of both women and men of the Matthean communities and of today's interpretive communities. Bringing such a perspective to the task of reading the Matthean Jesus also made me attentive to the ways in which centuries of reflection on christology have influenced interpreters (1) to separate the maleness of Jesus from his many other characteristics, giving it undue emphasis; (2) to fix attention on the titles of Jesus without recognition of how they reflect the dominant androcentric worldview, resulting in many other aspects of the narrative such as the Wisdom motif noted above being obscured; and (3) to read with an isolated focus on Jesus rather than on his functioning as one character among many within the unfolding narrative (Wainwright 1998, 9–18).

I undertook a critical reading of selected texts from the Matthean narrative, attentive to the possibility of different aspects of the Matthean portrait of Jesus being emphasized in different types of households of interpretation. This enabled me to demonstrate, by way of example, that Jesus could have been understood within some Matthean households as coming from the lineage of Tamar, Rahab, Ruth, Bathsheba, Rachel, and many other mothers omitted from the Matthean genealogy, as well as from the lineage of David and Abraham and the thirty-seven other patriarchs (Matt 1:1–17). He may have been seen as an endangered child of an endangered mother (1:18–25), who needed to be liberated by God before he could take up his role of liberator/savior (Matt 2). Some households may have emphasized his characterization as a doer of deeds rather than a bearer of titles (11:1–6) or as Wisdom justified by her deeds (11:19). I suggested further that metaphors may have emerged from the characterization of Jesus in relationship with others in the text, such as that of the boundary walker of Matthew 15:21–28. On the border with Tyre and Sidon, Jesus encountered a Canaanite woman whose engagement with him brought him to a new understanding of his mission, namely that the bread of the children belonged to all who would demonstrate the "great faith" that she did (15:28). Jesus' preaching, teaching, and healing among the "lost sheep of the house of Israel" (10:5–6; 15:24) had been extended through this encounter beyond boundaries of gender, ethnicity, and religion. Amy-Jill Levine (1988) and Anthony Saldarini (1994) both, however, emphasize that such an extension to include Gentiles within the ministry of Jesus does not constitute a rejection of Israel, an important recognition that can counter some of the anti-Jewish characterizations of Jesus and the Jewish leaders that have constituted Matthean scholarship (Levine 2006, 87–117).

As a result of such a reading of the Matthean Jesus, I concluded that "[d]iverse voices of interpretation need to be heard so that the reading of Jesus is not controlled or confined in the hands of a few ... but is available to many ... in communities of Christian faith and praxis" (1998, 119–120). Matthean scholarship in the latter decades of the twentieth century into the twenty-first has contributed to this diversity of interpretation, and I turn now to aspects of the Matthean portrait of Jesus that have not yet been highlighted in this chapter.

Expanding the Portrait

Since the emergence of narrative criticism, at least two approaches have contributed to the expansion of the Matthean portrait of Jesus: namely, social scientific criticism (Neyrey 1998; Love 2009) as well as a renewed focus on the context of the Roman Empire (Carter 2001; Riches and Sim 2005). Diverse hermeneutical perspectives have also shaped an understanding of the Matthean Jesus, among them postcolonialism and an awareness of the explicitly Jewish context and character of the Matthean gospel and the tendency of Christian interpreters to read this through a supersessionist lens (Saldarini 1994; Overman 1990; Gale 2005; Levine 2006). Given the limitations of an article such as this, I will not be able to explore fully this hermeneutical and methodological potential for new understandings of the Jesus of Matthew. Rather, I will highlight aspects of the unfolding story of Jesus in dialogue with such perspectives and methodologies.

The opening verse/s of a narrative are particularly important in engaging the reader, and the opening phrase of Matthew's story of Jesus, the "book of the genealogy of Jesus Christ," is no exception. This phrase, "book of the genealogy" (Revised Standard Version), may seem rather mundane until it is recognized that this phrase could have evoked and can evoke for its hearers/readers Genesis 2:4 – the *genealogy* of the heavens or sky and the earth and all they contained, including the birds of the air, the fish of the sea, and all living creatures, including male and female of the human species (Gen 2:4) – and then explicitly the *genealogy* of the human community in Genesis 5:1–2, male and female. In my current research, I am seeking to develop an ecological hermeneutic for reading Matthew's portrait of Jesus, and from such a perspective, the evocation in the opening phrase of the gospel extends the genealogy of Jesus far beyond the first named ancestor, Abraham, and even beyond the emergence of the human community that is male and female, to the emergence of the heavens and earth, with all the complexity of this unfolding that we now know through cosmology (Wainwright 2009). The end of the gospel (28:18) also situates the authorizing power of Jesus within the context of the heavens and the earth, thus providing a cosmic frame around the narrative for the reader attentive to this evocation in 1:1. Within such a frame, Jesus is designated as Emmanuel ("God with us"), the one in whom God is with God's people (1:23; 28:20), inviting ever new reflection on who this God is and how this God is known in the Matthean portrait of Jesus.

Particularity emerges in the second part of the opening verse. The genealogy is of the one designated *Jesus Christos*. Later in 1:21, an angelic voice announces to Joseph that Mary will bear a son who is to be named "Jesus" (derived from Hebrew "he saves") because he will save or liberate, as the name indicates. The term "Christos" evokes the multiple expectations and hopes that were circulating around that name in first-century Judean/Galilean/Syrian Jewish communities (Neusner, Green, and Frerichs 1987). For some *Christos* pointed to an authoritative royal figure who would reconstitute Israel (hence the link to "Son of David"; see Willitts 2007); for others, it may have evoked the popular messianic figures leading liberation movements (Horsley and Hanson 1985, 89–96). Warren Carter demonstrates that the situation of the Matthean households within the context of the Roman Empire, with its religio-political and socio-economic symbol systems, would have also shaped the understanding of Jesus called forth by the opening verse of the narrative (Carter 2005, 147–148). He summarizes the outcome of his detailed investigation in this way:

> In the gospel's opening verse, the aspirations associated with David, the Christ, Jesus/ Joshua, and (new) creation evoked in relation to Jesus collide with and contest Roman imperial claims. The verse functions to dispute the truthfulness of the imperial claims, suggesting Rome's demise, offering some present relief and proclaiming an alternative and just social vision under way now but yet to be fully realized in the future new creation (2005, 165).

I turn next to Jesus' emergence in the narrative as an adult, who is paralleled with John the Baptist in two carefully structured scenes – in the wilderness and by the Jordan (3:1–4:11). Both John and Jesus are liminal characters, associated with the wilderness (3:1; 4:1), that space which is outside temple, palace, city, or village (Levine 1988, 7–8). John, in particular, is characterized as a prophet (Matt 3:4; cf. 2 Kings 1:8), and McVann argues, using the social-scientific understanding of ritual process and the liminality associated with it, that John leads Jesus through a rite of passage, making him "one of the prophets" (1993).

John and Jesus, the wilderness prophets, are both designated as proclaiming a call to hearers/readers to repent, to change their perspective, their way of seeing the world, because the *basileia* (kingdom) of the heavens is near at hand (3:2; 4:17). For

John, this preaching culminates in the "fulfilling of all righteousness" when he takes Jesus through the authorizing ritual of baptism in accordance with Jesus' desire (3:15). For Jesus, the *basileia* of the heavens, the *basileia* of God, becomes the core of his proclamation (the gospel of the *basileia* – see 4:23 and 9:35).

In Matthew, the account of Jesus' baptism is passed over very cursorily. It is, however, followed by two statements to which the reader's attention is drawn by the phrase *kai idou* (and behold) in 3:16 and 17. The one whose birth is from the spirit named as holy has a spirit that is "of God" come upon him as he is being authorized for prophetic ministry, and a heavenly voice, presumably of God, proclaims him as son/beloved in whom God is well pleased. For many Matthean hearers/readers, the narration of the spirit coming upon Jesus may have been understood intertextually with Isaiah 61:1 (Jesus is the anointed one of God) or with Psalm 2 (he is the anointed one who is called "son"). The language and imagery of divine sonship in Matthew 3 and 4 (baptism and temptations) is polyvalent. In the Greco-Roman world, such language or imagery was associated with the birth, the crowning, or the apotheosis of a new emperor (Ovid, *Metamorphoses* 14.804–851; 15.843–848; see Cotter 2001). In the Jewish world, it designated Israel as God's beloved (Exod 4:22–23; Jer 31:9, 20; Hos 11:1) or the righteous one (Wis 2:18; Sir 4:10).

One of the first actions of the newly designated prophet and holy one, Jesus, is to gather around him a new fictive kinship, symbolized by the four fishermen: Peter, Andrew, James, and John (4:18–22). Only then, surrounded by this group, does Jesus begin to go "throughout Galilee, teaching in their synagogues and proclaiming the *good news of the kingdom* and curing every disease and every sickness among the people" (4:23; cf. 9:35). There is ambivalence in the narrative at this point. Those whom Jesus gathers are not his own family or kin (see 12:46–50). Rather he invites followers to make a radical break with their families and with all the resources associated with kinship relationships, in order to form a new kinship group around the proclamation of this new *basileia* vision (4:17). Indeed Jerome Neyrey claims from a sociological perspective, using the cultural code of honor and shame, that it is the members of this new kinship who are proclaimed blessed or honored by Jesus in the beatitudes (1998, 164–189).[2]

The new kinship group formed by Jesus is all male at this point. I have argued, however, that in Matthew's gospel the structure of the "healing" of Peter's mother-in-law is parallel to that of the calling of male disciples in Matthew 4:18–22 and 9:9, except for the phrase "and the fever left her." Where they follow, she serves, both words indicating discipleship in the gospel.[3] This parallel suggests that at least some Matthean households contested the view that disciples of Jesus could only be male (Wainwright 1991, 180–182). This theme of the significant inclusion of women in the unfolding story of Jesus runs like a thread through the Gospel of Matthew, forming a subverted and a subversive narrative, as I have demonstrated elsewhere (Wainwright 1991).[4] This theme, together with the general theme of discipleship, helps to characterize Jesus.[5]

The summary passage of Matthew 4:23–25 forms a narrative transition into Jesus' preaching of what we call the Sermon on the Mount (Matt 5–7). The Matthean imagery of the mountain and Jesus' teaching from a seated position confirm his authority to teach, an authority conferred in and through his baptism. The Matthean community characterizes Jesus as a lawgiver like Moses (5:1–2, 17–19, 21–48; Allison 1993), thus providing authorization for itself as standing within the tradition of Judaism, albeit in a sectarian struggle according to the studies of Overman (1990, 86–94), Saldarini (1994, 84–167), and Gale (2005).[6] He is also presented as a sage or wise one, a wisdom teacher, seated and interpreting the tradition in macarisms or beatitudes (blessings; 5:1–12) or as the two paths of the wise and foolish (7:24–27; Crosby 1988, 147–195).

The beatitudes that open this first major discourse capture intertextually the characteristics of the righteous ones of God in the tradition of Israel's scriptures.[7] They are poor in spirit (Isa 61:1–10), meek (Ps 37:11), merciful (Ps 85:10), and makers of peace (Ps 37). The poetry of the gospel storyteller is revealed in the structuring of these beatitudes, that are framed by the phrase "the *basileia* (or kingdom) of the heavens" (5:3, 10). Interpolated into this frame in vv. 6 and 10 is the notion of righteousness/justice or the right ordering that God desires (Green 2001). Jesus is preacher of a *basileia* characterized by this right ordering or justice (5:20; 6:10, 33; 7:21; Crosby 1988; see Hannan 2006 for a comprehensive treatment of this motif of the *basileia* across the gospel).

Jesus, teacher of the *basileia*, presents scriptural injunctions concerning murder, adultery, divorce, swearing falsely, retaliation, and love of enemies (5:21–48), issues which had an explicit first-century context. The teaching on divorce, for instance (5:31–32; 19:3–12), is addressed to the man only and gives him power over a woman in marriage (Carter 2000, 147–149); it forbids divorce and remarriage after divorce and promotes celibacy for those who do divorce on the grounds of *porneia*, the exception clause in this ruling, whose meaning still puzzles scholars. Jesus, the teacher, and his teachings may not have been liberating and especially not for women. Levine (2006) warns against interpreting such texts to portray Jesus as "liberating women from an oppressive, misogynistic Judaism" (143) in an attempt to present a monolithic image of Jesus. Rather, today's communities of interpretation will need to engage with such teachings in the light of contemporary insights and ethics, exploring both the biblical text and today's multiple and varied contexts.

The frame of 4:23 and 9:35 includes the healings in Matthew 8–9 within Jesus' *basileia* ministry. Jesus is cast in the role of an itinerant folk healer (8:1–15; 8:23–9:8; 9:18–34), whose healings are interspersed with other forms of ministry (8:16–22; 9:9–17). He carries on the healing role that is ascribed to God in the Hebrew Bible or is one like the Roman healing deity, Asclepius, about whom narratives of healing, sharing some similarities with the gospel stories, were inscribed on the walls of the Asclepium (LiDonnici 1995; Wainwright 2006, 85–87). In recent years, John Pilch (2000) has brought a medical-anthropological perspective to gospel healings, situating them within a broader regional healthcare system that included varied practices and beliefs. This approach underscores Jesus' role as a folk healer, whose healings raised questions about whether his power was from Beelzebul or the spirit of God (12:27–28; 13:53–58). On the other hand, Lidija Novakovic argues that Jesus' healings demonstrate his messiahship and that they constitute an explicit fulfillment of the scriptures, as Matthew 8:16–17 attests (Novakovic 2003). The healing work of Jesus is not confined to two chapters of the gospel (8–9) but continues up to his healing of the blind and lame in the temple (12:9–14, 22–23; 15:21–28; 17:14–18; 20:29–34; 21:14). It is also reiterated in summary passages (11:1–6; 12:15–21; 14:14, 34–36; 15:29–32; 19:2).

Having provided a developing portrait of Jesus as preacher, teacher, healer within the context of a *basileia* ministry, the gospel has Jesus passing on this ministry to his disciples, commissioning them to preach in the mission discourse (10:7), although the gospel does not recount any such mission being undertaken. Like John and Jesus, they are to proclaim that the *basileia* of the heavens, or God's *basileia*, is near at hand (3:2; 4:17; 10:7), and they are to continue the healing ministry that Jesus began (10:1–8). One contentious issue in relation to Jesus' proclamation of the *basileia* and its continuation by the disciples is that it seems to be limited within the ministry of Jesus to "the lost sheep of the house of Israel" (Matt 10:5; 15:24), while at the same time Jesus heals a Roman centurion's servant (8:5–13) and the daughter of a Canaanite woman (15:21–28) as well as commissioning the disciples to make disciples of "all nations" (28:19). Amy-Jill Levine has undertaken a comprehensive exploration of this issue (1988), suggesting that there is a temporal axis along which the mission to Israel and then to the nations can be placed. There is also a social axis, along which those with little social status respond to Jesus, while those with power and prestige, like Herod and Pilate, do not. The Canaanite woman of 15:21–28 is one of those low on the social axis who shift the focus of Jesus' *basileia* mission to include whoever is in need.[8]

Matthew 1–10 presents Jesus as a teacher/preacher and healer, interweaving this portrait with titles and motifs within the context of the unfolding narrative, as discussed above. Although there are hints of human opposition and questioning (2:1–12; 9:3, 11, 14, 34), these do not emerge strongly until Matthew 11 and beyond. Indeed, Matthew 11 opens with John questioning whether Jesus is, indeed, the *Christos* or coming one (11:2–3). The reply given by Jesus confirms his characterization in the narrative to this point. He will be known by what one has seen him doing and heard him saying (11:5). It is not titles (*Christos* or "coming one") that best characterize Jesus, but his preaching of the *basileia* in word and in deed.

Later in the gospel, titles will be used by Peter and the other disciples in response to Jesus' questions about his identity (16:13, 15), and it is the reply of Peter, "you are the *Christos*, the son of the living God," which Jesus affirms (16:16, 17). Jesus will be questioned and mocked under this title later in the narrative (26:63; 27:40, 43). It is important, however, that such titles are not considered apart from the narrative. Rather Jesus' characterization by a title (16:13–21) functions in tension with his characterization by word and deed (11:2–6) in a narrative context, demonstrating that the characterization of Jesus must take account of the variety of perspectives that the gospel presents.

As is clear from this pericope (16:13–21) and elsewhere in the narrative, interaction between Jesus and others is one of the key narrative techniques for portraying a character. There are four groups whose responses shape the Matthean portrayal of Jesus. They are the disciples, the crowds, the Jewish leaders (variously named as scribes, Pharisees, Sadducees, elders, and chief priests), and the Roman procurator, Pilate, and his soldiers. There have been book-length studies on each of the first three groups (Brown 2002 and Wilkins 1988; Cousland 2001; van Tilborg 1972). I cannot take up this aspect of the characterization of Jesus, except to draw attention to Matthew 23, which pits Jesus over against the scribes and the Pharisees in a series of woes.

This is one of the most difficult chapters in the gospel, in that it presents Jesus proclaiming prophetic condemnation or woes upon the designated teachers/leaders of the Jewish people as a culmination of growing contention and opposition to his preaching and ministry (5:20; 7:29; 9:11, 34; 12:14, 24; 16:21; 20:18; 22:34). If the Matthean community considers itself still within Judaism (see Carter 2000; Sim 1998; and Carter 2007 for a discussion of the problematic terminology "Jewish Christianity" and "Christian Judaism" currently being used by scholars), then this diatribe represents the bitterness of its struggle against Judaism and carries connotations of the woes proclaimed over Israel by the prophets (Isa 3:8–12; Jer 13:27; Hos 7:11–16). If the community has already broken with the synagogue, as Stanton (1992) and Levine (2006, 110–111) suggest, then the words of the Jesus portrayed in the Matthean gospel are not only anti-Jewish but have tragically acted as a foundation for centuries of Christian anti-Judaism.

Carter (2000, 449–450) offers three possible explanations for the invective, thus "limiting its applicability." First, as noted above, it has a place in the plot of the gospel, which depicts, as he says, a "life-and-death conflict between Jesus and the religious elite as characters in this story," and, I would add, must be engaged critically. His second point is that its historical context is the post-70 debates within Judaism over the destruction of Jerusalem and its temple and the Matthean community's claim for the legitimacy of its interpreters of Jesus and the scriptures. Finally, Carter places the invective within "the polemical and stereotypical nature of language" in the Jewish and Greco-Roman world of the first century (note also the violent language attributed to God and directed toward those designated as the "evil" and "unrighteous" who do not respond adequately – 5:45; 13:40–42, 49–50; 18:34–35; 21:41; 22:13–14; 24:51; 25:45–46; see Reid 2004). Critical engagement with this chapter will prevent its being used to fuel anti-Jewish sentiment and will encourage contemporary Christian communities to reflect on how they should respond to these prophetic woes that Jesus preaches to hearers of the gospel.

The narrative of Jesus' death and resurrection continues and concludes the gospel's characterization of its central character. Matthew 26–28 is framed by instructions to the disciples (26:1–2; 28:16–20); by the gathering and consulting together of the chief priests and elders (26:3–5; 28:11–15); and by the response of a woman and women to Jesus (26:6–13; 28:1–10). Despite the impending betrayal by members of his chosen group of disciples (26:14–16, 31–35, 47–56, 69–75) and the fact that all of them will flee (26:56), Jesus eats with them a final symbolic meal, in which he offers his body that has been prepared for burial by the unnamed woman who anointed him with healing ointment (26:17–30; 26:6–13). He prays with them in the agony of facing death (26:36–46), and he commissions the women disciples who stay with him during the crucifixion (27:55–56; 28:10) to send the male disciples to Galilee so that they can be reconciled to Jesus and so that he can pass on the task of continuing to make disciples for the *basileia* of God (28:9–10; 16–20). Just as Jesus remained faithful to his *basileia* ministry, teaching and preaching, faithful unto death when opposition rendered this inevitable, so too must disciples remain faithful.

Titles that previously had been used to proclaim Jesus become contentious in the conflict of the final chapters. Before Caiaphas, the high priest, Jesus is charged as Messiah, Son of God (26:63), and Son of Man (26:64); and in the trial before Pilate, as King of the Jews (27:11) and Messiah (27:17, 22). Also, he is mocked and dishonored as King of the Jews (27:29), Son of God (27:40), King of Israel (27:42), and God's Son (27:43). Finally, a Roman centurion, seeing the extraordinary phenomena surrounding Jesus' final breath, calls him "a son of God," as Roman emperors were named when such phenomena accompanied their deaths. The one, however, who is buried and raised is named simply as Jesus (27:58; 28:5–7, 9–10, 16, 18). For the Matthean community, finally, it is Jesus, the crucified and raised one who has, through the theologizing process of the gospel, been restored to honor and who now commissions disciples, both male and female, to continue the work of the *basileia*.

Donald Senior (1985, 163–171), who has studied Matthew's passion extensively, notes four aspects of the theology of Jesus' death and resurrection: namely, that Jesus' death fulfils the scriptures and through it he is faithful to God's will; that it frees God's people from sin and death; that it is the pathway to life; and that it is an exemplar of authentic faith. More recently, scholars have questioned the ransom theology of the gospel (20:28; 26:28). Such theology has often been used to maintain the subservience of women, of colonized peoples, of the weakest and most vulnerable. If today's readers are attentive to such a critique of this view of Jesus' death, then they can read the passion narrative as providing a model for a life lived for the sake of justice and in fidelity to God, lived in a way that could lead to a martyr's death, especially in unjust imperial situations like that of first-century Palestine.

Jerome Neyrey (1998, 139–162) provides another lens for reading the death of Jesus in a way that seeks to deal with the shame associated with Roman crucifixion. He reads the narrative as an encomium that reverses the shame by way of praise of the person's death as noble, making use of phenomena such as an earthquake and an opening of a tomb. I do not have the space to engage further with this approach, but it leads us to the close of the gospel. Jesus is raised up by the power of

God symbolized in that very earthquake and the opening of the tomb, and he authorizes a continuation of his *basileia* ministry by instructing the reconciled disciples to
go out into the whole world inviting all nations into a new fictive kinship as Jesus
did and teaching all that Jesus taught. The final characterization of the Matthean
Jesus, crucified and raised, is that he will indeed be a presence with this expanding
group of disciples until the end of the age (28:20).

Conclusion

The gospel question "Who do you say that I am?" has indeed received many nuanced
answers in the Matthean gospel, answers reflecting the theologizing processes going
on not just in one community but in the different households constituting communities across an arc linking northern Galilee with Syrian Antioch. Struggles over both
names and authority, mission and identity, have given rise to the different perspectives that move in and out of focus in the gospel narrative, much more indeed than
it has been possible to highlight in this chapter. Contemporary appropriation of this
same gospel must deal also with not only difference and conflict over issues that have
emerged from centuries of reading the gospel in very diverse contexts but contentious issues in the portrait itself. And so just as story, titles/metaphors, character
interaction, plot and other features combined in the context of diverse communities
of the first century, so too they continue to combine creatively and critically in
today's myriad contexts of interpretation to provide the rich depiction of Jesus that
is the Matthean gospel's portrait and which answers the gospel's question: "Who do
you say that I am?"

Notes

I wish to acknowledge here the service of my colleague Professor Amy-Jill Levine,
who read an early draft of this chapter. Her critique enabled me to reshape it quite
significantly, but the final version gives witness to my own insights, and any potential errors are likewise mine.

1   The complex nature of these contexts and of Jewish communities within them
    during the latter half of the first century add further weight to my claim that the
    gospel shows evidence of different perspectives on Jesus both in its shaping and its
    reception, which are interactive in the meaning-making process of narrative. For
    instance, Jesus Messiah could have been understood by some as messianic liberator of
    an oppressed people, by others as one with royal power. Such different interpretations
    would have been particularly operative in settings in which orality was the dominant
    mode for the majority of the community. Some of the different types of households
    could have included those with scribal leadership engaged in the Jewish sectarian

conflict/s of the first century (Overman 1990; Gale 2005); the more "egalitarian" households in which women functioned in leadership and contributed to the storytelling (see Beavis 2007 for a discussion of the term "egalitarian" in relation to the first century); and the poorer households suffering under Roman occupation (Wainwright 1998, 35–49).

2   The social-scientific approach used by Neyrey and others draws attention to the function of social codes and the ways in which these are embedded within narrative, honor and shame being one such code. There is a tendency within this approach, however, to study these codes as fixed rather than being constantly negotiated and as overriding other aspects of the biblical text.

3   Matt 8:15; cf. 20:28, in which serving characterizes Jesus, and 27:55, where it describes a group of women faithful to the foot of the cross.

4   I argue that the references to women or stories in which women function as key characters can be read as a sub-narrative, as there is significant narrative development from the role of women in the birth narrative (1:3, 5, 6, 16, 18–25; 2:11, 13, 14, 20, 21) through accounts of women relating to Jesus (8:14–15; 9:18–26; 15:21–28; 20:20–28; 27:55–56, 61) to 28:1–10, when the women who encounter the risen Jesus are commissioned to go and tell the good news that Jesus has been raised and to instruct the male disciples who fled from Jesus' crucifixion and burial to go to Galilee where they will see Jesus. This sub-narrative is not itself monolithic but is subverted by the story of Herodias (Matt 14:1–12).

5   Stuart Love's title, *Jesus and Marginal Women* (2009), suggests that his study of some of the female characters in the Matthean gospel using social-scientific categories contributes to that gospel's portrait of Jesus. While this study will make an important contribution to Matthean studies, the models used tend to obscure the gospel text as well as most of the earlier work of women scholars on these same texts.

6   Amy-Jill Levine (2006, 112–114) warns that such an approach may obscure the fact that the gospel concludes with a mission to the Gentiles and includes a final Matthean polemic against "the Jews" in 28:11–15. She thus questions whether the community is not more Gentile than Jewish. See also Stanton (1992), who argues that the gospel writer is a "Gentile Christian for whom the relationship of church and synagogue was not a primary concern."

7   Use of the term "righteous" to describe those who belong to God occurs extensively across the Psalms, the wisdom literature, and the prophets.

8   For another perspective on this issue, see David Sim (1998, 215–256).

References

Allison, Dale C. (1993). *The New Moses: A Matthean Typology*. Minneapolis: Fortress.

Beavis, Mary Ann (2007). "Christian Origins, Egalitarianism, and Utopia." *Journal of Feminist Studies in Religion* 23 (2): 27–49.

Brown, Jeannine K. (2002). *The Disciples in Narrative Perspective: The Portrayal and Function of the Matthean Disciples*. Leiden: Brill.

Burnett, Fred W. (1981). *The Testament of Jesus-Sophia: A Redaction-Critical Study of the Eschatological Discourse in Matthew*. Washington: University Press of America.

Carter, Warren (2000). *Matthew and the Margins: A Socio-Political and Religious Reading.* Sheffield: Sheffield Academic Press.

Carter, Warren (2001). *Matthew and Empire: Initial Explorations.* New York: Continuum.

Carter, Warren (2005). "Matthean Christology in Roman Imperial Key: Matthew 1.1." In John Riches and David C. Sim (eds.), *The Gospel of Matthew in Its Roman Imperial Context* (pp. 143–165). London: T&T Clark.

Carter, Warren (2007). "Matthew's Gospel: Jewish Christianity, Christian Judaism, or Neither?" In Matt Jackson-McCabe (ed.), *Jewish Christianity Reconsidered: Rethinking Ancient Groups and Texts* (pp. 155–179). Minneapolis: Fortress.

Cousland, J. R. C. (2001). *The Crowds in the Gospel of Matthew.* Leiden: Brill.

Crosby, Michael H. (1988). *House of Disciples: Church, Economics, and Justice in Matthew.* Maryknoll, NY: Orbis.

Cotter, Wendy (2001). "Greco-Roman Apotheosis Traditions and the Resurrection Appearances in Matthew." In David E. Aune (ed.), *The Gospel of Matthew in Current Study* (pp. 127–153). Grand Rapids: Eerdmans.

Davies, Margaret (1993). *Matthew.* Sheffield: JSOT.

Deutsch, Celia M. (1996). *Lady Wisdom, Jesus and the Sages: Metaphor and Social Context in Matthew's Gospel.* Valley Forge, PA: Trinity.

Deutsch, Celia M. (2001). "Jesus as Wisdom: A Feminist Reading of Matthew's Wisdom Christology." In Amy-Jill Levine (ed.), *A Feminist Companion to Matthew* (pp. 88–113). Sheffield: Sheffield Academic Press.

Duling, Dennis C. (1992). "Matthew's Plurisignificant 'Son of David' in Social Science Perspective: Kinship, Kingship, Magic, and Miracle." *Biblical Theology Bulletin* 22: 99–116.

Gale, Aaron M. (2005). *Redefining Ancient Borders: The Jewish Scribal Framework of Matthew's Gospel.* London: T&T Clark.

Green, H. Benedict (2001). *Matthew, Poet of the Beatitudes.* Sheffield: Sheffield Academic Press.

Hannan, Margaret (2006). *The Nature and Demands of the Sovereign Rule of God in the Gospel of Matthew.* London: T&T Clark.

Hill, David (1984). "The Figure of Jesus in Matthew's Story: A Response to Professor Kingsbury's Literary-Critical Probe." *Journal for the Study of the New Testament* 21: 37–52.

Horsley, Richard A., and John S. Hanson (1985). *Bandits, Prophets, and Messiahs: Popular Movements at the Time of Jesus.* San Francisco: Harper.

Kingsbury, Jack Dean (1975). "The Title 'Son of Man' in Matthew's Gospel." *Catholic Biblical Quarterly* 37: 193–202.

Kingsbury, Jack Dean (1984). "The Figure of Jesus in Matthew's Story: A Literary-Critical Probe." *Journal for the Study of the New Testament* 21: 3–36.

Kingsbury, Jack Dean (1988). *Matthew as Story.* 2nd edn. Philadelphia: Fortress.

Kingsbury, Jack Dean ([1975] 1989). *Matthew: Structure, Christology, Kingdom.* Minneapolis: Fortress.

Levine, Amy-Jill (1988). *The Social and Ethnic Dimensions of Matthean Salvation History: "Go Nowhere among the Gentiles ... ." (Matt. 10:5b).* Lewiston: Edwin Mellen.

Levine, Amy-Jill (2006). *The Misunderstood Jew: The Church and the Scandal of the Jewish Jesus.* New York: HarperOne.

LiDonnici, Lynn R. (1995). *The Epidaurian Miracle Inscriptions: Text, Translation and Commentary.* Atlanta, GA: Scholars.

Love, Stuart L. (2009). *Jesus and Marginal Women: The Gospel of Matthew in Social-Scientific Perspective*. Eugene: Cascade Books.

Matera, Frank J. (1987). "The Plot of Matthew's Gospel." *Catholic Biblical Quarterly* 49 (2): 233–253.

McVann, Mark (1993). "One of the Prophets: Matthew's Testing Narrative as Rite of Passage." *Biblical Theology Bulletin* 23: 14–20.

Meier, John P. (1979). *The Vision of Matthew: Christ, Church and Morality in the First Gospel*. New York: Crossroad.

Neusner, Jacob, William Scott Green, and Ernest S. Frerichs, eds. (1987). *Judaisms and Their Messiahs at the Turn of the Christian Era*. Cambridge: Cambridge University Press.

Neyrey, Jerome H. (1998). *Honor and Shame in the Gospel of Matthew*. Louisville, KY: Westminster John Knox.

Novakovic, Lidija (2003). *Messiah, the Healer of the Sick: A Study of Jesus as the Son of David in the Gospel of Matthew*. Tübingen: Mohr Siebeck.

Overman, J. Andrew (1990). *Matthew's Gospel and Formative Judaism: The Social World of the Matthean Community*. Minneapolis: Fortress.

Pilch, John J. (2000). *Healing in the New Testament: Insights from Medical and Mediterranean Anthropology*. Minneapolis: Fortress.

Powell, Mark Allan (1991). *What is Narrative Criticism?* Minneapolis: Fortress.

Powell, Mark Allan (1992a). "The Plot and Subplots of Matthew's Gospel." *New Testament Studies* 38: 187–204.

Powell, Mark Allan (1992b). "The Plot of Matthew's Story." *Interpretation* 46 (4): 347–356.

Powell, Mark Allan (1992c). "The Major Characters of Matthew's Story." *Interpretation* 46 (4): 357–367.

Reid, Barbara E. (2004). "Violent Endings in Matthew's Parables and Christian Nonviolence." *Catholic Biblical Quarterly* 66 (2): 237–255.

Riches, John, and David C. Sim, eds. (2005). *The Gospel of Matthew in Its Roman Imperial Context*. London: T&T Clark.

Saldarini, Anthony J. (1994). *Matthew's Christian-Jewish Community*. Chicago: Chicago University Press.

Segal, Alan F. (1991). "Matthew's Jewish Voice." In David L. Balch (ed.), *Social History of the Matthean Community* (pp. 3–37). Minneapolis: Fortress.

Senior, Donald (1985). *The Passion of Jesus in the Gospel of Matthew*. Collegeville, MN: Liturgical.

Sim, David C. (1998). *The Gospel of Matthew and Christian Judaism: The History and Social Setting of the Matthean Community*. Edinburgh: T&T Clark.

Stanton, Graham N. (1992). *A Gospel for a New People: Studies in Matthew*. Louisville, KY: Westminster John Knox.

Suggs, M. Jack (1970). *Wisdom, Christology, and Law in Matthew's Gospel*. Cambridge: Harvard University Press.

van Tilborg, Sjef (1972). *The Jewish Leaders in Matthew*. Leiden: Brill.

Wainwright, Elaine M. (1991). *Toward a Feminist Critical Reading of the Gospel according to Matthew*. Berlin: De Gruyter.

Wainwright, Elaine M. (1998). *Shall We Look for Another? A Feminist Rereading of the Matthean Jesus*. Maryknoll, NY: Orbis.

Wainwright, Elaine M. (2006). *Women Healing/Healing Women: The Genderization of Healing in Early Christianity*. London: Equinox.

Wainwright, Elaine M. (2009). "The Book of the Genealogy ... How Shall We Read It?" In Felix Wilfred, Luis Carlos Susin, and Elaine M. Wainwright (eds.), *Ecotheology: New Questions and Debates*. London: SCM, forthcoming.

Wilkins, Michael J. (1988). *The Concept of Disciple in Matthew's Gospel as Reflected in the Use of the Term Μαθητης*. Leiden: Brill.

Willitts, Joel (2007). *Matthew's Messianic Shepherd-King: In Search of "The Lost Sheep of the House of Israel."* Berlin: De Gruyter.

CHAPTER 3

Jesus in Luke-Acts

Delbert Burkett

In the Gospel of Luke, the inner self of Jesus occasionally emerges. He feels compassion at the death of a widow's son (Luke 7:13); he exults at the success of his emissaries (10:21); and he gets frustrated at his disciples' lack of faith (9:41). In other instances, we can infer his feelings from the words that he speaks. If he ever became impassioned, it was probably when he heaped woes on the rich (6:24–26) or uttered scathing denunciations of the Pharisees and lawyers (11:39–52). It is hard to imagine that anyone could mount such verbal attacks calmly and without rancor. For the most part, however, the Gospel of Luke gives us little indication of Jesus' inner life or personality. We are left therefore with other aspects of Luke's portrayal, such as the designations that Jesus receives and the activities in which he engages.

The same person who wrote the Gospel of Luke also wrote the Acts of the Apostles, as the relation between their prefaces shows (Luke 1:1–4; Acts 1:1–2). We do not know for sure who wrote these texts, but ancient tradition attributes them to "Luke." That name will do as well as any for our purpose. Luke describes his first volume as a narrative about what Jesus "began" to do and teach (Acts 1:1), implying that his story of Jesus continued in the second volume. To get Luke's full story of Jesus, therefore, we must consider both volumes. In composing these texts, Luke probably drew on a number of different sources that had different ideas about Jesus. We may find therefore that not all of what Luke says about Jesus is completely consistent.

Studies of Jesus in Luke-Acts usually focus on its "christology," that is, its teaching about the nature or identity of Jesus, especially as this affects his relation to God and his role in salvation.[1] Our own study will examine not only the identity of Jesus, but also Luke's story of his life and activities. This story encompasses five stages of Jesus' life and career: his birth and childhood; his public ministry; his passion, resurrection, and ascension; his reign in heaven; and his anticipated reign on earth. We will examine Luke's portrait of Jesus in each of these stages.

Jesus' Birth and Childhood

Luke begins his story with the births of John the Baptist and Jesus (1:5–2:40). This starting point distinguishes Luke's story from the Fourth Gospel, which portrays Jesus as a divine being who existed with God "in the beginning" (John 1:1). Unlike the Fourth Gospel, Luke never suggests that Jesus existed before his birth, as a divine being or otherwise.[2]

One function of Luke's birth narrative is presumably to provide background information about Jesus. Like Matthew, Luke names Jesus' parents as Joseph and Mary, his birthplace as Bethlehem, and his home town as Nazareth. Unlike any other source, Luke portrays Jesus and John the Baptist as related through their mothers. He names John's parents as Zechariah and Elizabeth. The primary function of Luke's birth narrative, however, is not historical but christological: to reveal what Luke considers significant aspects of Jesus' identity and his role in the purpose of God. In particular, Luke portrays the infant Jesus as the Davidic Messiah and as the son of God.

Jesus as Davidic Messiah

Luke's birth narrative has a primary emphasis on identifying Jesus as the Davidic Messiah or Christ (Strauss 1995, 76–125). Twice it refers to Jesus as "Christ": once in the expression "Christ the Lord" (Luke 2:11) and again in the expression "the Christ of the Lord" (2:26). The Greek term *christos*, meaning "anointed," translates the Hebrew *messiah*. In ancient Israel, consecrated individuals, such as priests, prophets, and kings, were anointed with oil. This act involved pouring oil over the person's head, which apparently symbolized God pouring out his Spirit on the anointed one. Certain passages of the Hebrew scriptures refer to Israel's king in particular as "the anointed of the Lord" (e.g., 1 Sam 24:6, 10; 26:9, 11, 16, 23). In the southern kingdom of Judea, this king always came from the line of David, and, according to tradition, God promised that David's line would never end (2 Sam 7:12–16). When the dynasty of Davidic kings did come to an end, at the Babylonian conquest of Judea in 587 BCE, Jewish prophets reinterpreted this promise to mean that God would raise up a new king from the line of David. As the "Messiah," this king would be anointed with the Spirit of God, would defeat Israel's oppressors, and would reestablish an independent kingdom for the Jewish people (Isa 11). In the time of Jesus, the Jewish people had various ideas about a messiah or messiahs, but many continued to hope that the Davidic Messiah would arise to deliver them from the Romans, who ruled over them at that time (e.g., Psalm of Solomon 17).

In referring to Jesus as the Christ, Luke's birth narrative clearly means the Davidic Messiah. The angel Gabriel says of Jesus that "the Lord God will give to him the throne of David his father, and he will reign over the house of Jacob forever, and of his kingdom there will be no end" (1:32–33). Zechariah says of him that God "has raised a horn of salvation for us in the house of David his child" (1:69). The genealogy has the purpose of confirming that Jesus descended from David (3:23, 31), as does the story of Jesus' birth in Bethlehem, the city of David (2:4, 11).

The role of the Davidic Messiah in Luke's birth narrative remains what it was in traditional Jewish thought. As the Messiah, Jesus would sit on the throne of David and reign over Israel (1:32–33). He would bring "redemption" (1:68; 2:38) and "salvation" (1:69, 71; 2:30; cf. 2:11) to Israel and Jerusalem. Only Luke among the evangelists refers to Jesus as a "savior" and to his work as "salvation." However, in the birth narrative this salvation is political. As the Davidic Messiah, Jesus' salvation would be directed toward the Jewish people. And he would save them not from sin or hell, but from their oppressors (1:71, 74). The birth narrative does not mention the Romans by name but does refer to "our enemies" and "those who hate us" (1:71, 73). Mary's song anticipates their defeat by God: "He brought down the mighty from their thrones and exalted the humble" (1:52). Obviously the baby Jesus did not yet reign as the Messiah. In designating him as the Christ, the birth narrative indicates that he had been born to become the Messiah.

In Luke's birth narrative, Jesus' identity as the Messiah is no secret but is revealed to numerous individuals. The angel Gabriel reveals it to Mary (1:32–33; cf. 1:46–55), and both Elizabeth (1:43) and Zechariah (1:69) know it without being told. An angel reveals it to some shepherds (2:11). The old man Simeon realizes it when he sees Jesus (2:26, 30–32) as does the prophetess Anna, who "spoke about him to all those awaiting the redemption of Jerusalem" (2:38). This open announcement of Jesus' identity as the Christ stands in sharp contrast to the "messianic secret" that appears later in Luke's narrative.

Jesus as son of God

The second main emphasis of the birth narrative is to present Jesus as the son of God. This identification is related to Jesus' role as the Davidic Messiah. In the same tradition that promised an unending dynasty to David, God proclaimed that David's offspring would be God's own son (2 Sam 7:14; Ps 2:7). Originally this sonship was metaphorical or adoptive. Though David's child came from David's own body (2 Sam 7:12), God recognized or adopted him as his own son. Possibly the original version of Luke's birth narrative presented Jesus as God's son in this adoptive sense, which would not conflict with the view that Jesus descended from David through Joseph. In its present form, however, the narrative presents Jesus as the son of God in a more literal sense. Though Mary has never had intercourse with a man, she conceives when God's Spirit comes upon her (1:34–35). This depiction does conflict with the view that Jesus descended from David through Joseph.

Nowhere in previous Jewish tradition does God have children through mortal women, though there is a story in which angels did (e.g., Gen 6:1–4). In Greek thought, however, gods or goddesses frequently mated with mortals to produce sons or, less frequently, daughters (Burkett 2002, 79–80, 529–535). Such sons of the gods, or "demigods," included not only mythical or legendary characters, such as Heracles and Achilles, but also historical figures, such as Plato, Alexander the Great, and Augustus Caesar. This tradition of sons born from one divine and one human parent seems to have influenced the way Luke thought of Jesus as the literal son of God. Luke's account does differ in one respect from these Greek stories. In these, the gods appeared in human or animal form to physically mate with mortal women. The Jewish Law, however, forbade anyone to represent God in any such visible form (Exod 20:4–6). Luke respects these Jewish sensibilities in having the invisible Spirit of God come over Mary and overshadow her in the act of conceiving Jesus.

Jesus' Public Ministry

Luke's narrative skips from the twelfth year of Jesus to the thirtieth, from his boyhood to the second stage of his life, his public ministry (Luke 3:1–21:38). After Jesus is baptized, apparently by John the Baptist, and undergoes a period of testing, he becomes an itinerant preacher in Galilee. He goes through the cities and villages of Galilee, preaching and teaching in the synagogues, healing the sick, and casting out demons.

Luke's Jesus breaks his ties with any form of settled existence. He has no home (9:57–58) and no job, relying on others to support him (8:1–3). He renounces his ties with his family (8:19–21) and makes no attempt to settle down and get married. He apparently lives this uprooted lifestyle for the sake of his ministry, not out of an impulse toward asceticism, i.e., renunciation of bodily appetites. While John fasted, Jesus eats food and drinks wine, to such a degree that his critics label him "a glutton and a drunkard" (7:33–34; cf. 5:33–34).

Along the way, Jesus attracts followers. Following Luke's Jesus is no easy matter. He requires his disciples to adopt his own lifestyle. They must abandon home, family, and possessions to follow him (9:57–58; 14:25–33). He especially emphasizes the need to put following him ahead of family ties and obligations (8:19–21; 11:27–28; 12:51–53). He does not permit his followers time to bury their parents or to say goodbye to their families (9:59–62). They must hate their father, mother, wife, children, brothers, and sisters, and even their own lives (14:26).

Jesus has more to do with women in Luke than in any other gospel. They appear as his followers, as recipients of his healing, and as characters in the stories about him. Yet Jesus' attitude remains patriarchal. When he chooses twelve apostles to exercise positions of authority, they are all men (6:12–16).

To get a better sense of Jesus' public ministry, we will examine his message, his mighty deeds, and his identity.

Jesus' message

Luke's Jesus spends a good deal of time preaching and teaching. He proclaims "the kingdom of God," which is "good news" (4:43; 8:1) and sends out emissaries to make the same announcement (9:2, 6; 10:1, 9, 11). The good news is that God's reign over the earth has arrived or almost arrived. Such a kingdom would replace the empire of the Romans, whom the early Christians viewed as agents of Satan. In one instance, Luke's Jesus portrays the kingdom as already invisibly present (17:20–21). In other instances, Jesus refers to the kingdom as coming visibly in the near future, when Jesus would return from heaven (9:27; 21:31–32). In yet other instances, Luke's Jesus speaks as though his return, and thus the coming of the kingdom, would be delayed longer than expected (12:45; 18:1–8).

Luke's Jesus announces the kingdom as good news specifically for the poor (4:18; 7:22). He is concerned about the inequities of society, about the disparity between rich and poor. He teaches that the coming kingdom will bring a reversal of status in society: the first will be last and the last first (13:30; cf. 1:51–53). The kingdom of God belongs to the poor (6:20). God will bless the poor, the hungry, and those that weep, but bring woe on the rich, the full, and those that laugh (6:20–21, 24–25; cf. 14:15–24; 16:19–31).

While Luke's Jesus anticipates this reversal of society, he is not content to wait for it, but advocates a program of economic distribution. Even now, those who host a banquet should invite "the poor, the maimed, the lame, and the blind" (Luke 14:12–14). Creditors should reduce the debts of those who owe them (16:1–9). The rich should sell their possessions and give to the poor (12:33–34; 18:22–23; 19:8–9).

Since the kingdom would bring God's judgment on sin, Luke's Jesus preaches that his hearers should repent in order to receive forgiveness of sins. He states specifically that he came "to call sinners to repentance" (5:32). He warns his hearers that unless they repent, they will all perish (13:1–5). Apparently Jesus' message goes unheeded for the most part, since he frequently castigates the unrepentant (10:12–15; 11:32; 13:6–9; 14:34–35).

In order to bring his message of repentance to those who need it most, Jesus eats and drinks with "sinners." Chief among sinners in the gospels are the tax collectors, either because of their dishonesty or because they worked for the Romans. Jesus' association with such people draws criticism from his critics on three separate occasions (5:27–32; 7:34; 15:1–2), moving Jesus to justify his actions (5:31–32; 15:3–7, 8–10, 11–32). Jesus not only preaches repentance to sinners, but also forgives their sins, another practice that draws criticism from the Pharisees (5:17–26; 7:36–38, 48–50).

As a Jewish teacher, Luke's Jesus maintains that the Jewish Law remains valid (16:17). Twice he teaches that one inherits eternal life by keeping the command-ments of the Law (10:25–28; 18:18–20). While he upholds the Law, his inter-pretations of Jewish Law and custom do not always agree with those of other Jewish teachers, the scribes and Pharisees. Jesus' interpretations often offend the Pharisees (e.g., 5:17–6:11), but theirs seem to offend him even more. He attacks the Pharisees, lawyers, and scribes with scathing denunciations of their practices and motivations (11:39–54; 12:1; 20:45–47).

Luke's Jesus teaches on a variety of other topics as well. He instructs his disciples how to pray (11:1–4) and teaches that God answers prayer (11:5–13; 18:1–8). In this respect, he practices what he preaches, since he prays more often in Luke than in any other gospel (3:21; 5:16; 6:12; 9:13; 9:28–29; 22:39–46). He also teaches frequently about the need for humility (9:46–48; 14:7–11; 16:14–15; 18:9–14; 22:24–27).

Jesus' mighty deeds

The Holy Spirit that fills Jesus at his baptism provides the "power" (*dynamis*) that enables him to perform miracles (4:14; 5:17; 6:19; 8:46). He heals people, he casts out unclean spirits "with authority (*exousia*) and power (*dynamis*)" (4:36), and he exercises power over nature (e.g., 8:22–25).

In one passage, Jesus addresses the significance of his healings. When John sends to ask Jesus if he is "the one coming," Jesus instructs John's messengers to tell John what they have seen and heard: "the blind recover sight, the lame walk, people with skin disease are cleansed and the deaf hear, the dead are raised, good news is announced to the poor" (7:18–23). Some of these events are mentioned in Isaiah 35:4–6 and 61:1, descriptions of the time when God comes to save his people. Jesus' answer, though indirect, indicates that his ministry of healing is a sign that the time of God's deliverance has come and that Jesus is the one through whom it has come. This explanation does not satisfy his critics, who charge that Jesus' power over demons comes not from God, but from "Beelzebul, the ruler of the demons" (11:14–15).

Jesus' identity

Luke gives Jesus certain designations that reveal his identity. These include "son of God," "Christ," "son of man," "son of David," "Lord," and "prophet."

Son of God   Luke's Jesus is related to God as his son, but Luke explains this relation in two different ways. In the birth narrative, Jesus' relation to God differs in kind from that of other people: the Holy Spirit "overshadows" Mary, making Jesus the literal son of God. One would thus expect Jesus to manifest the powers of God or the Spirit innately as a semi-divine being. This concept of Jesus as innately powerful does in fact appear in the non-canonical Infancy Gospel of Thomas, in which Jesus performs miraculous deeds as a child.

Luke, however, presents a different concept in his account of Jesus' public ministry: Jesus receives the Spirit of God and its powers only at his baptism, at which time he is acknowledged as the son of God (3:21–22). In this account, Jesus' relation to God differs not in kind, but only in degree, from that of other servants of God. Just as Jesus is filled with the Spirit, so were the prophets of ancient Israel. So are John, Elizabeth, Zechariah, and Simeon in Luke's birth narrative (1:15, 41, 67; 2:25–27).

In fact, God, as a good father, gives the Holy Spirit to all of his children who ask for it (11:13).

Jesus' reception of the Spirit is unique in one respect. When the Spirit comes upon Jesus, the perceptive reader will recognize that Jesus has been anointed with the Spirit, that he has become the anointed one, the Messiah, the Christ. And when the voice says to him, "You are my son," the reader will recognize that God has adopted the Messiah, just as he promised to adopt the son of David whose kingdom would last forever (2 Sam 7:12–16). Thus in the account of Jesus' public ministry, the designation "son of God" forms part of Luke's portrayal of Jesus as the Christ.

Christ   John A. T. Robinson (1956) argued that Luke has included three inconsistent ideas about Jesus as the Christ: (1) that Jesus was the Christ already in his lifetime and therefore suffered as the Christ (Luke 24:26, 46; Acts 3:18; 17:3; 26:23); (2) that Jesus became the Christ only at his exaltation to heaven (Acts 2:33–36); and (3) that Jesus would become the Christ only when he came from heaven to rule on earth (Acts 3:19–21). These ideas are probably not three inconsistent conceptions, but three stages in a single conception of the Christ. This multi-stage understanding arose as early Christians adapted traditional Jewish ideas to the actual circumstances of Jesus' life and death. *First stage*: the Christ or "anointed one" would be the one anointed with the Spirit of God. Jesus was anointed with the Spirit at his baptism, and in that sense became the "Christ" even during his public ministry. *Third stage*: but the Christ was also the one who would drive out the Romans and rule over Israel, an authority that Jesus did not exercise during his lifetime. In the early Christian conception, therefore, Jesus would rule on earth as the Christ at his return. *Second stage*: but since Jesus had not yet returned, there must be an intermediate stage as well, in which he reigned in heaven.

During Jesus' public ministry, therefore, he is already the Christ in the sense of being anointed with the Spirit. However, he keeps this identity a secret, presumably so that no one will expect him to establish the messianic kingdom at this stage of his career. The Gospels of Matthew, Mark, and Luke all portray Jesus as keeping this "messianic secret." In Luke's story, Jesus never makes any public claim to be the Christ or the son of God, and the people never catch on to his identity. They regard him variously as John the Baptist raised from the dead, as Elijah returned, or as one of the prophets of old (9:7–8, 18–19). They do not suspect him of being the Messiah, probably because he does nothing that the Messiah was supposed to do, such as driving out the Romans and restoring independence to Israel.

While Jesus' identity remains a secret to the people, it cannot be hidden from the Devil and his minions. The Devil knows that Jesus is the son of God (4:3, 9). The demons also know that Jesus is "the holy one of God," "the son of God," and the "Christ," but Jesus prohibits them from revealing this knowledge to the people (4:34–35; 4:41; 8:28).

At first, Jesus' disciples know as little as the people (8:25). Eventually, however, Peter recognizes Jesus as "the Christ of God" (9:20). After this, Jesus speaks more openly to his disciples. On one occasion, he speaks of his relation to God in terms that would be at home in the Gospel of John (10:22). While Jesus does reveal himself to his disciples, he forbids them to reveal him to others (9:21, 36).

Son of man   While Jesus avoids the designations "Christ" and "son of God," he openly refers to himself as the "son of man." This expression, a Hebrew or Aramaic idiom meaning "human being," probably alludes to Daniel 7:13–14, where "one like a son of man" comes to God "with the clouds of the sky" and receives an everlasting kingdom. Early Christians identified this figure as Jesus and created a conception of the Messiah that served as an alternative to the traditional concept of the Davidic Messiah. In this conception, Jesus was the son of man who ascended to God in heaven in order to receive from him an everlasting kingdom (Luke 22:29; Acts 7:56). This conception explained why Jesus did not drive out the Romans and establish God's kingdom as expected: he first had to ascend to heaven to receive it (Luke 19:11, 12, 15). It also explained why Jesus was not around at present (17:22). Once he received the kingdom of God in heaven, he would return to establish it on earth (12:40; 17:24, 26, 30; 18:8; 21:27) and to function as a judge (21:36).

In this conception, in order for the son of man to ascend to heaven, he first had to be on earth. Therefore, Jesus could be called the son of man during his lifetime, even before he ascended to heaven. Luke's Jesus thus calls himself the son of man as he conducts his ministry (e.g., 5:24; 6:5; 7:34) and when he speaks about his suffering, death, and resurrection (e.g., 9:22, 44).

Son of David   The birth narratives present Jesus as the Davidic Messiah, traditionally known as the son (i.e., descendant) of David. Likewise in Jesus' public ministry, a blind man calls Jesus the son of David (18:38, 39). Jesus, himself, however, argues that the Christ is not the son of David, but one who is exalted to heaven as Lord (20:41–44). These two alternative conceptions stand side by side in Luke without harmonization.

Lord   Luke's Jesus is thus also "Lord" (*kyrios*). In numerous instances in Luke-Acts, this term clearly refers to God; in numerous others, it clearly refers to Jesus; and in still others, it is unclear whether it refers to God or to Jesus.[3]

The term "Lord" occurs in the New Testament in two different senses: an exalted sense and a normal sense. In the exalted sense, this title functioned as the name of God. Since the Jewish people felt that it was irreverent to pronounce the personal name of God ("Yahweh"), some of them substituted the title "Lord" (Fitzmyer 1979). In Luke-Acts, Jesus becomes "Lord" at his ascension, when he is exalted to the right hand of God (Luke 20:41–44; Acts 2:34–36). In this context, the term "Lord" probably has the exalted sense as the term that substitutes for the personal name of God (cf. Phil 2:9–11). This use of the term "Lord" for both God and Jesus enabled early Christians to transfer the functions of God to Jesus. Thus the celestial signs that originally accompanied the coming of God on "the day of the Lord" (e.g., Isa 13:6–13) were transferred to the coming of Jesus (Luke 21:25–28).

In other contexts, the term "Lord" has its normal sense: it is simply the equivalent of "master" (or "owner") and may refer to any individual who has subordinates, such as slaves, servants, disciples, or petitioners. Luke frequently uses it to refer to other "masters" besides Jesus (e.g., Luke 19:33; Acts 10:4; 16:16, 19, 30; 25:26).

The term probably has its normal sense when characters in the story refer to Jesus as "lord" or "master" during his public ministry. Thus Jesus' disciples address him as "Lord" (e.g., 9:54, 61; 10:17, 40) or refer to him as "the Lord" (19:31, 34; 24:34). Likewise others in the story who come to Jesus as subordinates address him in the same way (5:12; 7:6; 18:41; 19:8). From the perspective of these characters, Jesus has not yet ascended to receive the name of "Lord" in the exalted sense, but already they acknowledge him as their master in the normal sense.

The meaning of the term is more ambiguous when Luke himself uses it as the narrator (e.g., 7:13; 10:1, 39, 41). From Luke's perspective, Jesus had already ascended to heaven to receive the exalted name of "Lord." Therefore when Luke uses the term in his narration, he may well give it the more exalted sense rather than the normal sense that it would have for the characters in his story.

Prophet   Luke also designates Jesus as a "prophet."[4] In his sermon at Nazareth, Jesus identifies himself as a prophet, complaining that "no prophet is acceptable in his homeland" (4:24). He implies that, like the prophets Elijah and Elisha, he will be accepted only by those outside Israel (4:25–27). Yet Jewish people in the story do accept him as a prophet. When he raises a widow's son (7:11–17), as did the prophet Elijah (1 Kings 17:8–24), it is Jewish people who conclude that "A great prophet has been raised up among us" (Luke 11:16). In fact, the people generally do regard Jesus as a prophet, either as the prophet John restored to life, as the prophet Elijah returned, or as one of the prophets of old (9:7–8, 18–19; cf. 7:39). It is only his disciples who finally recognize that he is the Christ (9:20). Despite the fact that the people accept his prophetic role, Jesus considers it the normal fate of a prophet to be rejected and killed, specifically in Jerusalem (11:47–51; 13:31–35). After his death, at least two of his followers continue to regard him as "a man who was a prophet" (24:19).

The tensions within these passages suggest that Luke has incorporated two different perspectives on the designation of Jesus as a prophet. One perspective regarded the term as an appropriate designation for Jesus, especially as one who was rejected and killed (4:24–27; 7:16; 11:47–51; 13:31–35). The other perspective saw the designation as inappropriate, because it was inadequate: it represented a misconception on the part of the people, who did not grasp that Jesus was the Christ (9:7–8, 18–20).

Jesus' Passion, Resurrection, and Ascension

At the conclusion of his public ministry, Jesus enters the third stage of his career, in which he experiences his passion (suffering), resurrection, and ascension. This part of the story occurs primarily in Luke 22–24, but a number of earlier passages help to prepare for it.

Jesus' passion

In Luke, Jesus' identity as the Messiah is openly known in the birth narrative, a well kept secret during Jesus' public ministry, but once again openly known in the passion narrative. Luke has done nothing to harmonize or explain this inconsistency.

Though Jesus never reveals his identity, both the people and the authorities know it in the passion narrative. Up to this point, the people have been clueless about Jesus' messianic identity, generally regarding him as a prophet. However, as Jesus nears Jerusalem, a blind man addresses him as "the son of David" (18:38, 39), and the crowd that accompanies him into Jerusalem calls him a "king" (19:38). At Jesus' trial before the Sanhedrin, the authorities know to demand, "If you are the Christ, tell us," and to ask, "So you are the son of God?" (22:67, 70), even though Jesus has kept these designations secret throughout his public ministry. When these authorities take Jesus to Pilate, they accuse him of "saying that he is Christ, a king" (23:2), though Jesus has never publicly made such a claim. Pilate then says to Jesus, "You are the king of the Jews?" (23:3). When Jesus is crucified, the rulers and the soldiers challenge him to save himself if he is "the Christ of God," i.e., "the king of the Jews" (23:35–36), and the superscription over the cross reads, "This is the king of the Jews" (23:38). One of the criminals crucified with him demands, "Aren't you the Christ?" while the other requests, "Jesus, remember me when you come into your kingdom" (23:39, 42).

The entire passion narrative thus proceeds as though Jesus had claimed to be the Christ. His own statements, however, are less direct. When the Sanhedrin asks if he is the Christ and the son of God, he does not give an unqualified "I am" as in Mark, but replies ambiguously, "You say that I am," and identifies himself instead as the son of man who will sit at God's right hand (22:67–70). When Pilate asks if he is the king of the Jews, he gives a similarly ambiguous reply (23:3). Thus in the passion narrative, Jesus resists being identified with traditional conceptions of the Messiah and presents himself as Messiah in the new Christian sense, in which he first had to ascend to heaven to receive the kingdom before he could return to establish it on earth.

As in all the gospels, Jesus has complete foreknowledge concerning his fate. At his transfiguration, Moses and Elijah speak to him about his "departure" (*exodus*) to heaven, which will occur in Jerusalem (9:30). Three times in his public ministry he predicts his death and resurrection (Luke 9:22; 9:44; 18:31–33). He knows who will betray him (22:21–23) and who will deny him (22:31–34). In short, he goes not as a victim, but as one who willingly drinks the cup that God has given him (22:41).

Like the Jesus of Mark and Matthew, Luke's Jesus presents his passion as a necessity for the son of man: he affirms that the son of man "must" suffer and be raised

(9:22; 17:25; cf. 9:44; 18:31–33). This necessity is grounded in the scriptures: "all that is written through the prophets about the son of man" must be completed (18:31). Only Luke's Jesus presents the passion as a similar necessity for "the Christ." The Christ too "must" suffer and be resurrected in order to fulfill the scriptures (Luke 24:25–27; 24:44–47; cf. Acts 3:18; 17:2–3). It is not clear to what scriptures Jesus is referring, since no passage in the Hebrew Bible explicitly states that either the Messiah or the son of man would suffer and be raised from the dead.

Luke's Jesus gives two different interpretations of the significance of his death. In traditional Christian theology, God sent Jesus to die to atone for the sins of others. This idea occurs only once in the Gospel of Luke. When Jesus institutes the Lord's Supper, he speaks of the bread as his body "that is given for you," and of the wine as his blood "that is shed for you" (22:19–20). Elsewhere in Luke, Jesus dies because he is a prophet, because it is supposedly the normal fate of a prophet to be rejected and killed in Jerusalem (13:33–34; cf. 11:47–51). Jesus expresses this idea in the parable of the wicked tenants (20:9–19). This symbolically portrays the idea that God sent Jesus not to die, but for the same reason that he sent all the other prophets: to deliver a message. Jesus also died for the same reason as all the other prophets: those to whom he was sent rejected his message.

Jesus' resurrection

Jesus differs from other prophets, however, in that he does not stay dead. On the first day of the week a group of women find his tomb empty (Luke 24:1–12). While in the other gospels the resurrected Jesus appears first to Mary Magdalene or a group of women, Luke's Jesus appears first to Peter and to two disciples on the road to Emmaus (Luke 24:13–35; cf. 1 Cor 15:5). He then appears to the eleven and others with them (Luke 24:36–49). This appearance occurs in Jerusalem, whereas in Matthew it occurs in Galilee (Matt 28:16–20). Though the risen Jesus in Luke assures his disciples that his body consists of "flesh and bones" (Luke 24:39), he changes his appearance and appears and disappears at will, demonstrating powers beyond the normal abilities of flesh and bone.

Jesus' ascension

After his resurrection, Luke's Jesus ascends to heaven. Luke gives two different accounts of this ascension. At the end of Luke, after Jesus appears to his disciples, he leads them out to Bethany and, as he blesses them, is parted from them and borne up into the sky (Luke 24:50–51). At the beginning of Acts, Jesus stays with the disciples for forty days, talking about the kingdom of God, before a cloud takes him into the sky (Acts 1:1–11).

In a popular Christian conception of today, souls of good people "go to heaven" when they die. That conception had not yet become dominant at the time that Luke wrote. In his day, most people, whether good or bad, expected that at death their souls would enter an underground domain, known to the Jews as "Sheol" and to the Greeks as "Hades" (cf. Luke 16:22–23). Only a few elite individuals ascended to heaven. In Jewish tradition, these included Elijah (2 Kings 2:1–12) and Enoch (1 Enoch 71). In Greco-Roman tradition, they included Romulus, Heracles, and many of the Roman emperors. At least in the Greco-Roman tradition, such special individuals ascended not only to dwell with the gods, but also to become gods themselves, thus undergoing *apotheosis* or deification (Burkett 2002, 80–81, 536–538).[5] Though Luke does not refer to Jesus' ascension as an apotheosis, it results in something similar to a deification of Jesus: he is enthroned at the right hand of God and becomes "Lord" (Acts 2:33–36). That is, he now has the same name as God and the authority to act in that name.

Jesus' Reign in Heaven

Luke's Gospel ends with Jesus' ascension to heaven, but Acts carries the story forward into the time of Jesus' sojourn in the heavenly realm. This fourth stage of Jesus' story represents an interim period between Jesus' ascension and his expected return. Luke marks off these two limits in the introduction to Acts. Here Jesus ascends to heaven in the clouds, and, as the disciples watch, two men tell them that Jesus will return from heaven in the same way (Acts 1:9–11). The rest of Acts is Luke's story of what transpires in between. During this period, the exalted Jesus appears occasionally in person, but is more often proclaimed in the preaching and actions of his followers.

Jesus at the right hand of God

Luke provides no narrative description of what happened when Jesus arrived in heaven. He does, however, reveal this through the preaching of Peter, who interprets Jesus' ascension to heaven in light of Psalm 110:1: "The Lord said to my Lord, 'Sit at my right hand, until I make your enemies a stool for your feet'" (Acts 2:34–35). Originally this passage relayed a message from God to the Davidic king at his enthronement in Jerusalem. Early Christian interpreters, however, took it as a message from the Lord God to the Lord Jesus, a reference to the enthronement of Jesus in heaven. Thus when Jesus arrives in heaven, he sits at God's right hand.

In Luke's account, Peter presents this enthronement as a change in Jesus' status: "God has made him both Lord and Christ" (2:36).[6] As "Lord," Jesus receives the same name as God, an indication that he acts in the name of God. The functions of God have been transferred to him (Tuckett 1996, 77; Dunn 1998, 252). As "Christ" or Messiah, he receives authority as king of the kingdom of God in heaven.

However, his authority as Christ would not be fully manifested until he returned to rule on earth.

Testimony to Jesus

Once Jesus ascends to the right hand of God, he pours out the Spirit on his disciples at the festival of Pentecost (Luke 24:49; Acts 1:4–5; 2:1–5, 33). Once he empowers them with the Spirit, they have the task of being his "witnesses" (Acts 1:7–8).

In their preaching, the disciples occasionally refer to Jesus' public ministry (2:22; 10:36–38) or to the ministry of John (13:24–25; 19:4). Far more often they preach about Jesus' death and resurrection (e.g., 2:23–32; 10:39–41; 13:27–37) and sometimes mention his exaltation (2:33–35; 3:13; 5:31; 7:55–56).

They also testify to the identity of Jesus: he is Lord (2:36; 7:59–60; 11:20–21; 20:21; 28:31), Christ (e.g., 2:36; 3:20; 4:26–27; 5:42), the servant or child (*pais*) of God (3:13, 26; 4:27, 30), the holy and righteous one (3:14; 7:52; 22:14), the author of life (3:15), the promised prophet like Moses (3:22–23; cf. 7:37), the one to whom the prophets bear witness (3:24; 10:43; 13:27; 26:22; 28:23), the cornerstone rejected by the builders (4:11), leader (5:31), savior (5:31; 13:23), the son of man (7:56), a sheep led to the slaughter (8:32–35), the son of God (9:20; 13:33), judge of the living and the dead (10:42; 17:31), and David's posterity (13:33).

The disciples also testify to the role of Jesus in salvation: in his name one receives forgiveness of sins, the gift of the Holy Spirit, and salvation on the day of the Lord (e.g., 2:20–21, 38–40). Yet Luke does not clarify in what way Jesus is actually necessary for any of these benefits (Tuckett 1996, 91–92), which in Jewish thought God himself could provide without any help.

As witnesses of Jesus, the disciples not only testify about Jesus, they act in his name. Though Jesus himself is absent, the disciples carry on his ministry in his name. In his name, they speak his message (4:17–20; 5:27–29, 40; 9:27, 29), baptize (2:38; 8:12, 16; 10:48; 19:5), heal the sick and infirm (3:6, 16; 4:7–10; 9:34), cast out demons (16:18), perform other signs and wonders (4:30), and suffer imprisonment and dishonor (5:41; 9:16, 21; 21:13).

Jesus and Gentiles

Luke's Jesus is concerned about Gentiles as well as Jews. In the birth narrative, Simeon predicts that Jesus will be "a light for revelation of Gentiles" (Luke 2:32; cf. Isa 42:6; 49:6). This does not happen during Jesus' ministry, though he does praise a Gentile centurion's faith (7:9) and hint that others besides the invited Jews would enter God's kingdom (13:28–29; 14:23–24).

After his resurrection, Jesus commissions his disciples to preach to "all the nations," i.e., Gentiles (Luke 24:7), but in Acts the disciples act as though they had never heard such a thing. It takes a special vision from God to Peter to get them to realize that he wants them to preach to Gentiles (Acts 10:1–11:18). However, it is not until Paul comes along that the Gentile mission gets into full swing, and in this the exalted Jesus plays a major role, as we shall see next.

Appearances of Jesus

While Jesus' disciples represent him on earth, Jesus himself also puts in a personal appearance from time to time, once to Stephen and several times to Paul. For the martyr Stephen, the heavens open, enabling him to see Jesus as the son of man standing at the right hand of God (7:55–56). Jesus seems to take a special interest in Paul. While God, the Holy Spirit, and angels communicate with various individuals, the exalted Jesus speaks only to Paul or someone that he sends to Paul.

His first appearance to Paul is on the road to Damascus. Paul is blinded by a light and hears the voice of a speaker, who identifies himself as Jesus (9:3–9; 9:27; 22:6–11; 26:12–18). On the same occasion, Jesus appears in a vision to a disciple named Ananias in Damascus, sending him to restore Paul's sight (9:10–19; cf. 22:12–16). Jesus confides to Ananias his interest in Paul: "He is a vessel of my choosing to carry my name before Gentiles and kings and sons of Israel" (9:15). Subsequently, when the Jews in Jerusalem do not accept Paul's message, Paul falls into a trance as he is praying and sees Jesus (22:17–21). Jesus warns him to leave the city, saying, "Go, because I will send you far away to Gentiles" (22:21). Jesus appears several more times to Paul, each time giving encouragement or instruction concerning his mission (16:7; 18:9–10; 23:11). Jesus thus intervenes directly in the story to ensure that his name is carried to the Gentiles through Paul.

Jesus' Reign on Earth

From Luke's perspective, the future would bring the fifth and final stage in the story of Jesus: his reign in the kingdom of God on earth. Chronologically, Luke would have placed this part of the story after the story of Acts, but since it had not occurred, he devotes no separate narrative to it. We must therefore construct a description of this stage from predictions about it in the previous stages of the story.

This stage would begin with the return of Jesus. Certain eschatological events would lead up to that return (Luke 21:5–24). Then Jesus, who had gone away to receive a kingdom, would return to exercise its authority (Luke 19:12). He would return accompanied by the celestial signs traditionally associated with the day of the Lord (Luke 21:25–26; cf. Isa 13:9–10, 13). He would return in a cloud as the son of man, the one to whom God had given great power and glory (Luke 9:26; 21:27; Acts 1:9–11). His coming would be unexpected, like the coming of a thief (Luke 12:39–

40) or a flash of lightning (Luke 17:22–24) or the springing of a trap (Luke 21:34–36). It would bring sudden destruction on those unprepared (Luke 17:26–30).

The coming of Jesus would mark the beginning of "the age to come" (Luke 18:30; 20:35), which would bring a resurrection of the dead (Luke 20:27–40). At that time Jesus would conduct a judgment of the living and the dead (Acts 10:42; 17:31), separating the righteous from the wicked like wheat from chaff (Luke 3:17). He would condemn the unrepentant (Luke 10:12–15; 11:31–32) and slay those who did not want him to reign (Luke 19:14, 27).

At that time, Jesus would restore an independent kingdom to Israel, over which he would reign (Acts 1:6–7).[7] As the Davidic Messiah, he would rule over the Israelites in a kingdom that would have no end (Luke 1:32–33). He would regather the twelve tribes of Israel and place his twelve apostles on twelve thrones governing them (Luke 22:28–30). Jesus' other followers would also share in his reign (Luke 12:32). He would put some of his faithful servants in charge of five cities and others in charge of ten (Luke 19:15–19; cf. 12:42–44). While this kingdom would be a restoration of the fallen kingdom of David over Israel, it would include Gentiles as well, all those called by the name of the Lord (Acts 15:14–17).

If this stage of the story had occurred, Luke's story of Jesus would have come full circle back to the beginning. All of the hopes and expectations placed on the newborn Jesus in the birth narrative would have been fulfilled. Jesus would have sat on the throne of David reigning over Israel. He would have become a "horn of salvation," bringing the Jewish people deliverance from the Romans. He would have brought down the mighty from their thrones and exalted the humble. Unfortunately for Luke, he never saw these hopes fulfilled. Consequently, Luke's story of Jesus remains incomplete, ending in Acts with Jesus' disciples still awaiting his return.

Notes

1   Buckwalter (1996, 6–24) surveys a number of previous attempts to describe what is central in the christology of Luke-Acts.

2   Buckwalter (1996, 192) thinks that Luke and his readers "firmly believed that Jesus was by nature as much God as God the Father was." Luke fails to mention this belief because "such knowledge was already common to his readers." However, Luke explicitly states that he wrote in order to confirm what his readers had already been taught (Luke 1:4). If they had been taught that Jesus was a pre-existent divine being like God, this would seem an important teaching for Luke to confirm.

3   Dunn (1998, 245–251) seeks to determine when "Lord" refers to God and when to Jesus in Acts. Rowe (2006, 27) thinks that Luke uses the term "Lord" in such a way that God and Jesus are inseparable in the narrative: the narrative establishes for them a shared identity.

4   Johnson, among others, has argued that "Luke's Jesus is fundamentally a prophetic figure," specifically the prophet like Moses promised in Deuteronomy 18:15–19

(Johnson 1999, 63). This assertion probably overstates the case (Tuckett 1996, 84–85; 1999, 145–148).

5   Zwiep (1997, 194–196) thinks that the Jewish stories provide a more adequate context for understanding Luke's ascension story than the Greco-Roman stories, because of Luke's Jewish monotheism. However, Luke's monotheism did not prevent him from using a Greco-Roman model in portraying Jesus as a demigod in his birth narrative.

6   Zwiep (1997, 145–166, 196–197), among others, thinks that Luke's Jesus is enthroned at the right hand of God on Easter Sunday before the resurrection appearances, so that in these appearances Jesus had already been exalted to heaven. But Luke mentions only one ascension of Jesus to heaven, and he places this after the resurrection appearances in Luke 24:50–51, in Acts 1:1–11, and in Acts 2:32–36. It is more likely then that Luke's Jesus is not enthroned at the right hand of God until his ascension (Franklin 1975, 29–41).

7   According to Tuckett, when Jesus' disciples ask him when he will restore the kingdom to Israel (Acts 1:6–7), he brushes the question aside as irrelevant and unimportant (Tuckett 2001, 143), because he does not intend to restore a this-worldly kingdom to Israel (Tuckett 1999, 162–164; 2001, 142–143). However, in the context, Jesus has been teaching his disciples about the kingdom for forty days (Acts 1:3). Presumably therefore their question develops out of Jesus' teaching and does not represent a misapprehension on their part. Jesus does not tell them that they have the wrong idea; he only tells them not to worry about the timing (Franklin 1975, 40).

References

Buckwalter, H. Douglas (1996). *The Character and Purpose of Luke's Christology*. Cambridge: Cambridge University Press.

Burkett, Delbert (2002). *An Introduction to the New Testament and the Origins of Christianity*. Cambridge: Cambridge University Press.

Dunn, James D. G. (1998). "ΚΥΡΙΟΣ in Acts." In James D. G. Dunn, *The Christ and the Spirit: Collected Essays of James D. G. Dunn*. Vol. 1: *Christology* (pp. 241–253). Grand Rapids: Eerdmans.

Fitzmyer, Joseph A. (1979). "The Semitic Background of the New Testament *Kyrios*-Title." In Joseph A. Fitzmyer, *A Wandering Aramean: Collected Aramaic Essays* (pp. 115–142). Chico, CA: Scholars.

Franklin, Eric (1975). *Christ the Lord: A Study in the Purpose and Theology of Luke-Acts*. Philadelphia: Westminster.

Johnson, Luke Timothy (1999). "The Christology of Luke-Acts." In Mark Allan Powell and David R. Bauer (eds.), *Who Do You Say That I Am? Essays in Christology* (pp. 49–65). Louisville, KY: Westminster John Knox.

Robinson, John A. T. (1956). "The Most Primitive Christology of All?" In *Twelve New Testament Studies* (pp. 139–153). London: SCM.

Rowe, C. Kavin (2006). *Early Narrative Christology: The Lord in the Gospel of Luke*. Berlin: De Gruyter.

Strauss, Mark L. (1995). *The Davidic Messiah in Luke-Acts: The Promise and Its Fulfillment in Lukan Christology*. Sheffield: Sheffield Academic Press.

Tuckett, Christopher M. (1996). "The Person and Work of Jesus." In *Luke* (pp. 72–93). Sheffield: Sheffield Academic Press. Reprinted London, New York: T&T Clark, 2004.

Tuckett, Christopher M. (1999). "The Christology of Luke-Acts." In Joseph Verheyden (ed.), *The Unity of Luke-Acts* (pp. 133–164). Leuven: Leuven University Press & Peeters.

Tuckett, Christopher M. (2001). "Luke-Acts." In *Christology and the New Testament: Jesus and His Earliest Followers* (pp. 133–147). Louisville, KY: Westminster John Knox.

Zwiep, A. W. (1997). *The Ascension of the Messiah in Lukan Christology*. Leiden: Brill.

CHAPTER 4

John's Portrait of Jesus

Mary L. Coloe

In John we have a visionary – a theologian and poet, a mystic and a realist. Whatever we may discover about the identity of "John," he writes from his experience of the Jesus-event. Only one who knows experientially could make the claims that he does: "we have beheld his glory" (1:14), "from his fullness we have all received" (1:16), "he who saw it has borne witness" (19:35). Writing from within the experience of Jesus, after decades of community living, oral storytelling, proclamation, and reflection, the author of John's gospel offers a distinctive portrait of Jesus. Where Mark's narrative begins with Jesus' adult baptism as the moment of his divine acknowledgment, "You are my beloved Son," (Mark 1:11), and Matthew and Luke take that moment back to his conception (Matt 1:18; Luke 1:32), John places Jesus' divine origins, "in the beginning ..." (John 1:1). Jesus, according to John, can only be fully understood from the perspective of God's own timelessness.

The Prologue (John 1:1–18) is the first place to begin looking for clues to John's christology. According to Carson (1991, 249–277), these verses function as a foyer in a building, "simultaneously drawing the reader in and introducing the major themes." The reader thus knows, before the narrative begins, essential information about Jesus' identity and mission, and this knowledge guides the reading process and adds to its drama. The reader shares a certain omniscience that the characters in the narrative do not have. As readers, we watch the development of the traditional Jesus story and observe the characters in the story as they struggle to understand who Jesus is and what he is doing. Our knowing what the characters do not know adds an ironical edge to the reading process.

There are many varied approaches to John's portrait of Jesus. The three major clues in the Prologue that I wish to focus on are presented with disarming simplicity: Word (1:1), Tabernacle (1:14), and Son (1:14, 18). I have chosen these three images because they are introduced in the Prologue, giving them a particular hermeneutical significance; they then continue to operate across the entire narrative, and, as I will show, they interact with each other, especially in "the hour" of Jesus' passion, thus providing narrative and theological coherence to the gospel. This chapter will

The Blackwell Companion to Jesus, First Edition. Edited by Delbert Burkett. ©2014 John Wiley & Sons, Ltd. Published 2014 by John Wiley & Sons, Ltd.

show that these three terms are fundamental to John's portrait of Jesus both in his identity and in his mission.

Jesus the Word / Wisdom of God

"In the beginning was the word/*logos*" (1:1)

A first-century audience, familiar with the Jewish scriptures, on hearing the opening lines of the gospel would immediately recall the first chapter of Genesis and its narrative of creation. In Genesis, God's word is the agent of creation, drawing light from darkness, separating the waters, populating the land. The Prologue then continues by stating the theological and christological mystery at the heart of this gospel: "the word was with God and the Word was God" (1:1). "Was with" expresses a duality: the "word" and "God." "Was" expresses a singularity: "Word/God." What sense could a first-century audience make of this startling claim that appears to refute the heart of Israel's faith acclamation: "Hear, O Israel, the Lord our God, the Lord is One"?

For some centuries, Israel's theologians had been struggling to name their experience of God as both Other, the utterly transcendent One, and immanent, as a creative and salvific presence known in their history and in creation. In the post-exilic writings, these two experiences of God were expressed in two different types of literature, known as "Apocalyptic" and "Wisdom." Where Apocalyptic writing stressed God's transcendence, the Wisdom writings affirmed an experience of God's immanence. The prophets had spoken of the Word going forth from the mouth of God to accomplish God's purpose in the world (Isa 55:10–11), of the Spirit being set within Israel (Ezek 22:26; 37:14). The sages in the post-exilic community chose the term "Wisdom" (*hokmah/sophia*) to describe God's self-being in the world.

At first, God's Wisdom, like God's power, God's majesty, God's compassion, was simply an attribute – a way of saying "God is wise," just as "God is powerful," "God is compassionate." In time, with the freedom of poetic imagination, Wisdom developed into a figure of speech, a personification of God's self. And Wisdom, like the Johannine Word, is described as being with God at the dawn of creation.

> The Lord created me, the beginning of his ways for his works. Before eternity he established me, in the beginning before he made the earth ... When he prepared the heavens, *I was with him, ... I was beside him, his "darling child" ('āmôn) rejoicing before him always.*[1] He rejoiced when he finished the world [lit. dwelling place], and rejoiced in the midst of humanity. (Prov 8:22–31, Septuagint)

Word and Wisdom

Israel's prophets frequently spoke of the power and effectiveness of God's word, but this word never took on the personification we find with Wisdom. The only text where God's word takes on a quasi-personal reality is in the book of Wisdom, and its use here can be instructive for understanding John's use of the term *Logos*:

> For while gentle silence enveloped all things, and night in its swift course was now half gone, your all-powerful word (*logos*) leaped from heaven, from the royal throne, into the midst of the land that was doomed, a stern warrior carrying the sharp sword of your authentic command, and stood and filled all things with death, and touched heaven while standing on the earth. (Wis 18:14–16)

Beginning in chapter 10, the Book of Wisdom recounts Israel's history, and Sophia/Wisdom is named as the one who delivered Israel from Egypt, guiding them by day and night, leading them through deep waters and drowning their enemies (e.g., Wis 10:15–19; cf. Sir 24:1–34). The change in chapter 18 from "Wisdom," which is given feminine gender in both Hebrew and Greek, to "Word," which is given masculine gender, may have been needed because in the passage quoted above, the savior figure is imaged in masculine terms as a "stern warrior."[2]

There have been a number of studies on the influence of the Wisdom Literature on the Fourth Gospel. Some of these deal with specific themes or sections of the gospel (Ashton 1986; Cory 1997; Ringe 1999), while others present a systematic study of Wisdom across the entire gospel (Willett 1992; Scott 1992; Witherington 1995; Ringe 1999). Here, I will briefly outline some major points of similarity between Wisdom and the Johannine Word and then examine in greater detail one characteristic of Wisdom as it operates in the narrative.

In considering the possible background to the Prologue, Schnackenburg states, "The closest parallels in thought are to be found in Jewish Wisdom speculation" (1968–1982, 1:481; cf. Dodd 1953, 274–275; Brown 2003, 259–265). The Johannine Word, like Wisdom, pre-exists with God (Sir 1:1; Prov 8:23; John 1:1), is an active agent in creation (Prov 8:27–31; John 1:3), and has come to dwell in Israel (Sir 24:8–12; Bar 3:36–4:1; John 1:11a). The Word and Wisdom are both described as "one of a kind" (*monogenes*; Wis 7:22; John 1:14, 18; 3:16, 18; Willett 1992, 41 n. 123), and both are described as having a parent–child relationship with God (Prov 8:30; John 1:18). Like Wisdom, the Word has received various responses, both rejection and acceptance (1 Enoch 42:1–2; John 1:11b). The gospel narrative continues to present similarities between the Word and Wisdom, who gathers disciples, inviting them to dwell with her (Sir 51:23; John 1:35–51; Feuillet 1965, 89–91), offering them nourishment (Sir 24:19–22; Prov 9:1–6; John 6) and salvation (Wis 9:18; John 3:16; Sinnott 2004). The disciples of Wisdom are called children/sons (Prov 2:1; Sir 2:1; 4:10–11; Wis 2:13; John 13:13) and friends (Wis 7:27; John 15:15). Wisdom lives with God and is loved by God (Prov 8:30–31; Wis 8:3; John 5:20; 10:17); she is an initiate in the knowledge of God and an associate in God's works (Prov 8:30; Wis 8:4; John 8:29, 38, 42, 55). In the words of Michael Willett: "Wisdom strides through the Gospel in the person of Jesus of Nazareth. He is Wisdom incarnate, God reaching out to humanity to the fullest extent, as a human being" (1992, 127).

Wisdom / Creation christology

A striking feature of Wisdom in the Old Testament is her involvement in creation. It is this aspect of Wisdom that is given great emphasis in the Fourth Gospel. Not only does this gospel begin with the first words of the Genesis creation narrative, but the Prologue appears to follow the structure of this narrative. The Prologue has an introduction (vv. 1–2) and a conclusion (v. 18) that recapitulates and develops the opening verses – the process of this development is shown in the intervening verses (3–17). The central section can be set out in a parallel array that traces the historical development of the Word's presence in the world (vv. 3–5, 14), the prior witness of John the Baptist (vv. 6–8, 15), then the arrival and responses to the Word (vv. 9–13, 16–17). At first the story of the Word in the world is reported in the third person (vv. 3–13), but at verse 14 the report changes to personal testimony, using first person verb forms and pronouns – "us," (14b), "we" (14c, 16b), "I" (15c), and "me" (15c, d, e).

This structure can be shown schematically:

Introduction (1–2): Logos/Theos in eternity

The story of the Word/reported		The story of the Word/Testimony
A (3–5)	have seen	A' (14)
B (6–8)	have heard	B' (15)
C (9–13)	have experienced	C' (16–17)

Conclusion (18): Son/Father in history

The introduction (vv. 1–2) establishes the relationship between the Word and God before moving to the relationship between the Word and the created world. These opening verses echo the description of Wisdom, with God from the beginning (Prov 8:22–26), the first of God's creative acts (Prov 8:22), and beside God in the process of creation (Prov 8:30). The Word is within the world of history from v. 3, from the very moment when all things came into being through him. The presence of the Word in creation and human history draws on traditions of both Wisdom and Word, whereby the world is the locus of divine revelation (von Rad 1972, 62; Brown 2003, 25).

The motif of Divine Wisdom continues in verses 9–13, where there are echoes of two contradictory Wisdom myths. In one myth, Wisdom finds a dwelling within Israel and is identified with the Torah:

> Among all these I sought a resting place; I sought in whose territory I might lodge. Then the Creator of all things gave me a commandment, and the one who created me assigned a place for my tent, and said, "Make your dwelling in Jacob, and in Israel receive your inheritance." From eternity, in the beginning, he created me, and for eternity I shall not cease to exist. In the holy tabernacle I ministered before him, and so I was established in Zion. (Sir 24:7–10)

> All this is the book of the covenant of the Most High God, the law which Moses com-
> manded us as an inheritance for the congregations of Jacob. (Sir 24:23; cf. Bar 4:1)

The book of Enoch presents a contradictory myth where Wisdom finds no home in
the world and so returns to the heavens:

> Wisdom found no place where she might dwell; then a dwelling-place was assigned her
> in the heavens. Wisdom went forth to make her dwelling among the children of men,
> and found no dwelling-place: Wisdom returned to her place, and took her seat among
> the angels. (1 Enoch 42:1–2; in Charles 2004, 2:213)

According to the Prologue, the Lord's heritage (*ta idia*) who have embraced
Wisdom now reject the *logos*. But there are some who do receive him, who believe
in his name, and these are gifted with the power to become children of God (John
1:12).

The bipartite structure of the Prologue outlined above, framed by an introduction
and conclusion, is found in the first creation account in Genesis 1:1–2:4a.

Johannine Prologue		Genesis	
Introduction (1–2)		Introduction (1–2)	
A (3–5) have seen	A' (14)	A (3–5) light <=> darkness	A' (14–19)
B (6–8) have heard	B' (15)	B (6–8) heaven <=> earth	B' (20–23)
C (9–13) have experienced	C' (16–17)	C (9–13) land <=> waters	C' (24–31)
		Climax: The Sabbath (2:1–3)	
Conclusion (18)		Conclusion (2:4a)	

Genesis has one significant difference, in that the six days of creation in this
narrative from the Priestly tradition lead to the establishment of the Sabbath on
the seventh day: "Thus the heavens and earth were finished and all their multitude.
And on the seventh day God finished (LXX *suneteleō*) the work that he had done ..."
(Gen 2:1–2a).

The Prologue has no equivalent to the "seventh day" in its structure, which suggests that in the Johannine perspective, the creative work of God had not been
completed "*in the beginning.*" The gospel narrative then presents Jesus/Sophia as
one continuing the creative work of God. Jesus says to his disciples, "my food is
to do the will of the One who sent me and to finish (*teleiōsō*) the work" (4:34). In
John 5, "the Jews" "persecute" Jesus for working on the Sabbath, and Jesus states,
"My Father is working still and I am working" (5:17). As Divine Wisdom incarnate,
Jesus continues God's creative work and for this is he rejected. The ultimate rejection
of Jesus/Sophia is presented in the "hour" of the passion, which this gospel presents
as the completion of Wisdom's creative work.

The "hour" continues to draw upon the Genesis creation narrative (Manns 1991,
401–429; Barker 1991, 57–95). Only in this gospel is Jesus arrested and buried in
a garden (18:1; 19:41). As Frédéric Manns notes, "The symbol of the garden frames

this section" (Manns 1991, 409). At the center of the garden, as in Genesis, is a tree of life (Gen 2:9; John 19:18). Standing at the foot of this "tree" is a man, and a woman who is called "mother" (*mētēr*, 19:25), echoing the name Adam gave the woman in Genesis because "she is the mother (*mētēr*) of all the living" (Gen 3:20). This garden will be the crux of a new creation in John's resurrection narrative, where the first scenes with the women and the disciples take place at the garden tomb (20:1–18). The first day of a new creation dawns with the resurrection, and the second gathering of disciples, including Thomas, occurs "eight days later," again making this the Sunday evening, since the beginning and end day of a period of time are both counted (Schnackenburg 1968–1982, 3:331). In early Christian symbolism, the eighth day signaled the dawn of the new eschatological age, and this terminology first appears in Christian literature in the Epistle of Barnabas (ca. 95–135).

> He further says to them, *Your new moons and Sabbaths I disdain.* Consider what he means: Not the Sabbaths of the present era are acceptable to me, but that which I have appointed to mark the end of the world and to usher in the eighth day, that is, the dawn of another world. This, by the way, is the reason why we joyfully celebrate the eighth day – the same day on which Jesus rose from the dead; after which He manifested himself and went up to heaven. (Barn 15:8–9)

In the gospel, the disciples gather "on the first day" and then again, "eight days later." The theme of the eschatological new creation is suggested by these two details of time, particularly given the placement of the crucifixion, burial, and resurrection in a garden (18:1; 19:41).

Wisdom's work of creation is only completed in the life and death of Jesus. His dying word, "It is finished" (*tetelestai*), echoes the use of the same verb (*teleō*) used in the Greek version of Genesis to announce the finish of God's initial work of creation (Gen 2:1). In the death of Jesus, the scriptures that opened with the words "In the beginning ..." (Gen 1:1; John 1:1) have been brought to fulfillment. "The work is now finished, and the Sabbath that begins after Jesus' death (xix 31) is the Sabbath of eternal rest" (Brown 2003, 2:908, cf. 1:217).

Toward the end of the first century, after the destruction of the Temple by Rome, two groups with origins in Second Temple Judaism were struggling to express their identity in this new situation. Both groups looked to their traditions, seeking continuity with the God who had acted in their past, in order to articulate faith in the ongoing activity of God in the present. One group looked to the Law as the embodiment of Wisdom, while the Johannine community saw Wisdom incarnate in Jesus. The rabbinic leadership at Jamnia and the local synagogue found God's Wisdom in the Torah that God revealed to Moses; John's community, however, found it in Jesus (Carter 1990, 47).

The six-strophe structure of the Prologue, like the six days of creation in Genesis 1, requires one final act to bring it to completion. For the gospel, this act begins in 1:19 with the narrative of God's final work, to be accomplished in the life and death of Jesus. Until this story has been told, there can be no "seventh day." Wisdom's creative activity is still unfolding, and the final creative word has not yet been spoken. Israel's past history and traditions are part of this unfolding activity, which is now being brought to fulfillment when Wisdom/Word is spoken in a new way within human history: "the Word became flesh ..."

Jesus the Tabernacle / Temple

"The Word became flesh and tabernacled among us" (1:14)

The Gospels of Matthew and Luke speak of God's coming into human history as a birth; John's gospel draws on Israel's long history of God's presence in its midst and speaks of the Word/Wisdom's tabernacling (*eskēnōsen*) among us. The verb *skēnoō* means to pitch a tent, and the noun form *skēnē* is used in the Greek Old Testament to speak of the tabernacle. Again this verse develops the Word/Wisdom imagery, for in the book of Sirach Wisdom says,

> Then the Creator of all things gave me a commandment,
> and the one who created me assigned a place for my tent (*skēnēn*)
> And he said, "Make your dwelling (*kataskēnōson*) in Jacob" ...
> In the holy tabernacle (*en skēnē hagia*) I ministered before him
> and so I was established in Zion. (Sir 24:8, 10)

This passage from Sirach draws on Israel's experience of God's presence in the wilderness of Sinai. Following the Exodus and the revelations at Sinai, Moses was commanded to "make an ark of acacia wood" (Deut 10:3). In the Deuteronomic tradition, the ark was a box containing the stone tables of the law, and the people carried this with them on their journey. This box becomes the symbol of God's presence guiding and protecting Israel (Num 10:35–36). After David's capture of Jerusalem, Solomon built a temple, and the ark was brought into the Holy of Holies at the heart of the temple (1 Kings 8:6). The memory of the Exodus ark and Tent of Meeting (Exod 33:7–11) was developed further in the later Priestly tradition of the tabernacle (Exod 35–40). So when the sage writes of Wisdom coming to dwell in Zion within the holy tabernacle (Sir 24:10), he summarizes Israel's long history of God's immanence, which came to be symbolized in the temple.

The temple was the great symbol and physical reality that proclaimed to the people of Israel that "God dwells in our midst." When the Solomonic temple was destroyed by the Babylonians in 587 BCE, the prophets of Israel's exile kept alive a future hope of restoration when once more God would establish God's dwelling in the midst of a renewed people (Ezek 37:26–28). A new Israel would then settle in a cleansed and revitalized land with the temple as its center. When the temple was rebuilt by the returning exiles (ca. 516 BCE), it failed to usher in the longed-for restoration, so Israel's hopes were projected to a future end-time when God would intervene and raise up the eschatological temple in a new and glorified Jerusalem (Zech 12–14).

An aspect of the temple's significance lies in its mythological meaning (Barker 1991; Rubenstein 1995). As the earth's navel, it is the very center point of God's life-giving contact with the earth (Terrien 1983, 192; Levenson 1984, 284). This mythic understanding of the temple transcends the history of a particular building in Solomon's Jerusalem. It perceives the temple in cosmic terms as the link between heaven and earth, as the place in this world that corresponds to the heavenly throne of God and where the life-giving waters of God's throne make first contact with earth. The temple, as a cosmic symbol of God's presence, reaches back in time to the first acts of creation, when God's Spirit hovered over the waters of the deep (Gen 1:2) and God caused water to rise and form the four rivers bringing life to Eden (Gen 2:6, 10–14).

The Johannine temple

The historical and mythic significance of the temple, described above, lies behind its use in the Fourth Gospel (Coloe 2001; Kerr 2002; Fuglseth 2005; Hoskins 2006). As a time-transcending symbol, it reaches back to the protological beginnings of creation and forward to its eschatological fulfillment. In John, the temple scene is placed as Jesus' first public act in Jerusalem, and in this scene Jesus renames Israel's "house of God" as the "house of my Father" (2:16). The renaming of the temple is the first of a number of changes made across the Johannine narrative, through which the meaning of the temple, as the place of God's dwelling, is transferred to the person of Jesus and then to the community of disciples.

The first movement in this transfer of meaning is in John 2, when Jesus enters the temple, dispels the sacrificial animals, and overturns the tables of the money changers (2:13–17). At Passover time, the money changers enabled pilgrims to change their Roman coinage, inscribed with the head of Caesar, to non-idolatrous Tyrian coinage, with which they paid their annual temple tax to support the temple's ongoing sacrificial system. The tables for the money changers were set up in the outer precincts of the temple in the weeks leading up to Passover. Similarly, having sacrificial animals in these outer precincts aided the many pilgrims coming to the feast. The money changers and animals do not therefore represent a corruption of Israel's worship: "their presence made possible the cultic participation of every Israelite, and it was not only not a blemish on the cult but part of its perfection" (Neusner 1989, 289). Because the money changers and animals are essential for Israel's cultic system, it is incorrect to call this scene a temple "cleansing." Jesus is enacting a prophetic critique of the temple and announcing that Israel's sacrificial system and cultic way of coming to God is over (Neusner 1989, 290). This is stated quite explicitly in the dialogue following the temple action, when Jesus announces that the temple will be destroyed but he will raise it in three days. The narrator then adds, "He spoke of the temple of his body" (2:21). From chapter 2, the temple provides a major symbol of Jesus' identity and also a major focus for the ongoing plot of this gospel. In telling the traditional story of Jesus, the fourth evangelist is going to depict it from a new perspective, for alongside the narrative of a death and resurrection, this gospel will narrate the destruction and raising of a temple. Utilizing the temple as a major christological image is an aspect of John's unique portrait of Jesus.

In the festival of Tabernacles, Jesus appropriates the key symbols of the feast. He is a source of water for the thirsty (7:37) and light for the world (8:12), and it is during this feast that the temple symbolism begins a second transference of meaning from being the "temple of his body" to being a future temple of believers. Just as the temple is imbued with a mythological meaning as the source of creation's life-giving waters, Jesus speaks of himself as a source of water for those who thirst: "Let anyone who is thirsty come to me" (7:37a). His next words speak of a future time when the Spirit will be given, and at that time believers will also become sources of water.

> "As the scripture has said, 'Out of his [the believer's] heart shall flow rivers of living water.'" Now he said this about the Spirit, which believers in him were to receive; for as yet there was no Spirit, because Jesus was not yet glorified. (7:37b–39)[3]

The third and final transference of meaning occurs within Jesus' farewell meal with his disciples (John 13–17): "In my father's house are many dwellings; if it were not so, would I have told you that I go to prepare a place for you?" (John 14:1–2). In chapter 14, the phrase "in my father's house" needs to be interpreted in the light of the similar expression in chapter 2, where "my father's house" referred to the Jerusalem temple, the building (2:16). The scene in chapter 2 begins in the physical temple building, but by the end of the chapter the temple has been reinterpreted as a person: "he spoke of the temple of his body" (2:21). In chapter 2, the meaning of "my father's house" is thus transferred from a building (the temple) to a person (Jesus). In the Hebrew scriptures, the phrase "my father's house" always has a personal sense, in that this phrase refers to the group of people who make up the household, such as the parents, children, servants, and even the future descendants. The following example illustrates this usage:

> Now then, swear to me by the LORD that as I have dealt kindly with you, you also will deal kindly with my father's house, and give me a sure sign, and save alive my father and mother, my brothers and sisters, and all who belong to them, and deliver our lives from death. (Josh 2:12–13)

In speaking of the temple with this phrase in chapter 2, the evangelist began to move away from temple-as-building to something personal and relational – the temple of his body (2:21). In chapter 14, this movement continues and extends beyond one person, Jesus, to a group of people in a household or in familial relationship. Chapter 14 develops this personal and relational understanding even further with the shift from the word "house" (*oikos*), the term used in chapter 2, to "household" (*oikia*), used in chapter 14.

The shift from a building to personal relationships suggested by the phrase "in my father's household" requires a similar shift in understanding what the evangelist means by "many dwellings." What are these many dwellings? The chapter itself provides the best interpretive clue to the particular Johannine meaning of this phrase.

Chapter 14 uses derivatives of "dwell" (*menō*) and "dwelling" (*monē*) to describe a variety of interpersonal relationships between the Father, Jesus, the Paraclete, and believers. The relationships are usually described with the translation "abiding" or "dwelling." These series of relationships are introduced by the phrase "many dwellings": "In my father's house are many dwellings ..." (14:2) – namely,

- the Father is "dwelling" (*menōn*) in Jesus (v. 10);
- the Paraclete "dwells" (*menei*) with believers and in the future will be in them (v. 17);
- the Father and Jesus will make their "dwelling" (*monēn*) with the believer (v. 23);
- and Jesus is "dwelling" (*menōn*) with the disciples (v. 25).[4]

Many commentators would see the metaphor as a reference to God's heavenly dwelling, where the believers will abide at some future time. But the subject of the verb "dwell" throughout chapter 14 is not *the believer* but *God*. The action therefore is not the believers coming to dwell in God's heavenly abode, but the Father, the Paraclete, and Jesus coming to dwell with the believers. Given that the emphasis in chapter 14 is on the Divine dwelling with the believers, it is appropriate that this theology is introduced with an image that draws on Israel's symbol of the divine presence dwelling in its midst – the temple, Israel's "house of God," which had been renamed by Jesus in chapter 2 as "my father's house" (2:16).

From the above analysis, the statement "in my father's house are many dwellings" is best understood, within the context of this gospel, to refer to a series of interpersonal relationships made possible because of the indwellings of the Father, Jesus, and the Paraclete with the believer. These divine indwellings in the midst of a believing community make it appropriate to speak of the community as "the father's house," a living temple, where God can now be found. The community is the "house (household) of God." In the words of David Aune, the term "house/household," as it is used here and in 8:35, "reflects the self-designation of the Johannine community" (1972, 130).

Faced with the impending death and loss of Jesus, the disciples are offered words of consolation that the experience of Jesus' departure will at the same time usher in a new experience of God's presence. They will not be left orphans (14:18). The divine presence, who tabernacled in the flesh of Jesus, will continue to dwell with them. The indwelling relationship between Father, Son, and Spirit will become their relationship, building them into a temple/household of God.

Why use the temple as the great symbol of God's presence, not only in the life of Jesus, but in the ongoing life of the Christian community? To understand this, we need to realize that this gospel was written at a time when the magnificent temple of Jerusalem no longer existed, just as the historical Jesus was no longer present with disciples.[5] At the same time as the fourth evangelist was offering consolation to his community, the Jewish rabbis were trying to understand how they could maintain contact with their God in the absence of the temple, its priesthood, and its system of sacrifices. Both communities faced the stark loss of their point of contact with God. For both groups, the temple represented most dramatically a past presence of God and evoked the current painful possibility that God had abandoned the world.

The rabbis turned to the Torah, seeing in Torah the promise of God's abiding presence. Once again the Wisdom traditions provide the interpretive means of associating temple and Torah.

> Afterward she [Wisdom] appeared upon earth and lived among men. She is the book of the commandments of God, and the law that endures for ever. All who hold her fast will live, and those who forsake her will die. (Bar 3:36–4:1; see also Sir 24:7–12, 23, quoted above)

The rabbis sought a theological meaning for the temple's destruction and alternative ways of living lives acceptable to God. The Torah provided this alternative, as is illustrated in this later rabbinic tale: Once as Rabbi Yohanan ben Zakkai and Rabbi Joshua observed the temple in ruins, Rabbi Joshua lamented that the place of atonement for the iniquities of Israel had been destroyed.

> "My son," Rabban Yohanan said to him, "be not grieved. We have another atonement as effective as this. And what is it? It is acts of loving kindness, as it is said, *For I desire mercy and not sacrifice.*" (Hos 6:6) (Avot de Rabbi Natan, ch. 6; quoted in Neusner 1972, 324)

Following the destruction of Jerusalem, the evangelist is engaged in the same task as the Jewish rabbis. The rabbis sought to ensure the survival of Judaism and the means of redemption without the Temple cult, and their answer was Torah. The Johannine community focused on the person of Jesus. Both groups turned to their common tabernacle/temple traditions and the Wisdom myth to find the means of expressing their claims to cultic continuity. For the Johannine community, holy Sophia/Logos, present with God in the beginning, had tabernacled in the midst of Israel in the flesh of Jesus, the one and only Son.

Jesus the Son

> "No one has ever seen God; the only begotten Son, who is in the bosom of the Father, has made him known" (1:18)

In examining the two terms given in the Prologue so far, Word/Wisdom and Tabernacle, we have seen that there is a strong resonance between them, as Wisdom took up her dwelling in the tabernacle. This overlap of terms continues when we consider the third image offered in the Prologue, Jesus as the one and only Son.[6] The Fourth Gospel gives a unique emphasis to Jesus' sonship, whether it be as Son of God, Son of Man, or simply Son (Moloney 1978; Kim 1983; Burkett 1991; 1999; Pazdan 1991). The title "Son" draws together and gives added meaning to the two themes discussed above: Jesus as the creative Word/Wisdom of God and Jesus as the tabernacle/temple of God's presence.

As mentioned above, the evangelist makes use of two different Wisdom myths to describe the coming of the Word into the world: one where Wisdom is accepted and dwells in Zion, and another where Wisdom finds no place and returns to the heavens. In the Prologue, these two myths are expressed in the form of two responses to the Logos: "He came to his own (*eis ta idia*), and his own did not receive him, but those who did receive him, he gave them the power to become the children (*tekna*) of God" (1:11–12). Once again the Prologue hints at what the gospel narrative will reveal. As Son, Jesus is the one and only revealer of the Father, and nowhere is his sonship more critical than in the hour of his passion.

The royal temple–builder

Two of the unique elements in the Johannine passion are the title placed above Jesus' head (19:19) and the scene with the mother of Jesus and the Beloved Disciple (19:25–30). These elements will draw together the two images from the Prologue presented so far, Divine Wisdom/Logos, who participates in God's ongoing creative activity, and the temple as God's dwelling place in the world.

Pilate insists on the title "Jesus the Nazarene, the King of the Jews" (19:19). In fact, two titles are used synonymously, "the Nazarene" and "the King of the Jews," and only the Fourth Gospel calls these words a "title" (*titlon*).[7] Because the Fourth Gospel does not emphasize Jesus' upbringing or ministry in Nazareth, the evangelist is able to use "Nazarene" as a unique and emphatic title for Jesus in his hour (18:5, 7; 19:19).

The words "Nazareth" and "Nazarene" have their root meaning in the Hebrew word *netzer*, describing the future royal branch from the house of David: "There shall come forth a shoot from the stump of Jesse, and a branch (*netzer*) shall grow out of his roots" (Isa 11:1).[8] As well as referring to royal line of David, the term "branch" is also the symbolic name of the one who will build the future temple:

> Take from them silver and gold, and make a crown, and set it upon the head of Joshua, the son of Jehozadak, the high priest; and say to him, Thus says the LORD of hosts, "Behold, the man whose name is the Branch (*tzamah*): for he shall grow up in his place, and he shall build the temple of the LORD. It is he who shall build the temple of the LORD, and shall bear royal honor, and shall sit and rule upon his throne." (Zech 6:11–13)

Although the Hebrew words for "branch" are different in Isaiah (*netzer*) and Zechariah (*tzamah*), by the first century the words are used as equivalent terms, as evidenced in the Dead Sea Scrolls. The community of Qumran looks to a future son of David and applies to him the term "branch": "There shall come forth a shoot from the stump of Jesse, and a branch (*netzer*) shall grow out of his roots" (Isa 11:1). The quotation from Isaiah follows the Hebrew text and uses *netzer* (branch), but, in the commentary immediately following, the term *netzer* is rendered "the shoot (*tzamah*) of David," using the term for "branch" from Zechariah 6:12 (4Q161 [4QpIsa[a] line 11] in García Martínez and Tigchelaar 1997, 1:316).[9] These texts show that, by the time of the Qumran writings, the two terms *tzamah* and *netzer* are synonymous and the roles of both have become fused. The man named "Branch" who will build the temple of the Lord, according to Zechariah 6, has been identified as the Messianic shoot of David, the *netzer*.

Jesus is identified as the Nazarene only in his "hour" (18:5, 7; 19:19). When the soldiers come to the garden, they ask twice for Jesus "the Nazarene" – *ton Nazōraion* (18:5, 7), then Jesus is lifted up on the cross bearing Pilate's title, "the Nazarene" (19:19). This is the formal charge and final title applied to him in the pre-Easter narrative. Given this particular narrative usage, its historical background in contemporary Jewish literature, as well as the overall emphasis on the temple across the entire gospel, this title "Nazarene/Branch" is a reference to Jesus' messianic role as the builder of the eschatological temple (Zech 6:12). Jesus is condemned and dies as the Nazarene temple-builder. As his body is lifted up on the cross, his prophetic words in chapter 2 are fulfilled, the temple of his body is destroyed, but as "the Nazarene," the "Branch" of Zechariah, he is simultaneously raising a new temple.

The new temple/household of God

At the foot of the cross stand the mother of Jesus and the Beloved Disciple (19:25–26). The form of the words Jesus speaks to each of them – "Woman behold your son … behold your mother" (vv. 26–27) – is very similar to the formula of adoption. The double use of the term "behold" (*ide*) informs the reader that Jesus' words are a prophetic revelation (de Goedt 1961–1962; Barrett 1978, 552). These two phrases, "behold your son" and "behold your mother," create a new relationship between the disciple and the mother of Jesus (mother/son), and in so doing they establish a new relationship between the disciple and Jesus as brothers (de Goedt 1961–1962, 145).

If the woman always called "the mother of Jesus" is presented also as the mother of the Beloved Disciple, then Jesus' sonship is now extended to embrace others. This scene depicts the fulfillment of the promise of divine filiation given in the Prologue: "to all who received him, who believe in his name, he gave power to become the children of God" (1:12). Here, at the cross, is the moment when believers, represented by the Beloved Disciple, are incorporated, through the Spirit, into the sonship of Jesus. The expression "to his own" (*eis ta idia*), describing the Beloved Disciple's action at the foot of the cross (19:27), forms an *inclusio* with the same expression used in the Prologue, "he came *eis ta idia*" (1:11), indicating that the action of Jesus coming to his own is now brought to completion. Verses 26 and 27 are the climax of the narrative, and the narrator confirms this in v. 28 when he relates that "After this, Jesus knew that all was now finished." The personalizing of the temple, begun in the transfer of temple imagery to Jesus, then continued with the promise of the divine indwellings in the community of believers constituting them as "my Father's house/hold" (14:2), is completed in this scene when the disciples become "son/daughter" and "sister/brother." This divine filiation is the ultimate revelation of the "hour" and brings Jesus' mission to its completion. Those who believe, who receive the incarnate *logos*, are drawn into the intimate relationship between Father and Son as the Prologue had promised (1:12; cf. 17:24, 26). The new identity of believers is confirmed in the next chapter, when Jesus says to Mary Magdelene, "Go to my brothers and sisters (*tous adelphous mou*) and say to them, I am ascending to my Father and your father, to my God and your God" (20:17).[10] The gift of divine filiation is only possible because of Jesus' unique sonship. In drawing believers into his own sonship, a new humanity comes into being at the cross. As Jesus bows his head and hands down the promised gift of the Spirit (v. 30), a new household of God is created (Barrett 1978, 554; Brown 2003, 2:931). This is the "work" of creation that Jesus, holy Wisdom, has been engaged in across the gospel, and this is why Jesus can now say, "It is finished" (19:30).

Conclusion

The above approach to John's portrait of Jesus has taken its starting point from three images presented in the Prologue: Word/Wisdom (1:1), tabernacle/temple (1:14), and Son (1:18). While there are other approaches to examining the portrait of Jesus in John (Brown 2003, 249–277), the Prologue provides the "key to the understanding of this gospel" (Lightfoot 1956, 78). These three images provide the reader with the necessary interpretive lenses with which to read the following narrative. These images then function across the narrative, serving to reveal Jesus' identity and express his mission. The knowing readers then observe how individuals respond to him with either acceptance or rejection of his claims. In the hour, these images coalesce, as the cross is the moment of a new creative act when believers become children of God, participating in Jesus' sonship[11] and in him becoming members of his Father's house/hold and a temple of God's dwelling in the world.

Notes

1   I am following Willett's translation of the word '*āmôn*, which could mean "craftsman," "nursling," "counselor" (1992, 12).

2   In much the same way, the maleness of Jesus may have necessitated using the masculine gendered "Logos/Word," rather than the feminine "Sophia/Wisdom" in the Prologue.

3   John 7:37 is a notoriously difficult verse to understand (see Coloe 2001, 125–134).

4   The imagery of "many dwellings" continues into chapter 15 where the verb "dwell" is again used to describe the believers dwelling in Jesus. The shift to the community of believers is reflected by a shift in the metaphor from "house" to "vine," since the vine was a common image for the community of Israel.

5   The Gospel of John is dated toward the end of the first century, around 95 CE. Jerusalem and its temple had been destroyed by the Roman army in the year 70 CE.

6   On four occasions, Jesus is called the "one-and-only Son" (1:14, 18; 3:16, 18). On nine occasions, he is called "Son of God" (1:49; 5:25; 10:36; 11:4; 11:27; 19:7; 20:31). On thirteen occasions, he is called "Son of Man" (1:51; 3:13, 14; 5:27; 6:27, 53, 62; 8:28; 9:35; 12:23, 34, 34; 13:31). On sixteen occasions, he is called simply "Son" (3:17; 3:35, 36, 36; 5:20, 21, 22, 23, 23, 26; 6:40; 8:36; 14:13), and in his prayer in chapter 17, "your Son" (17:1).

7   In Mark and Luke, they are termed an inscription (*epigraphē*, Mark 15:25; Luke 23:38), while in Matthew the words are called the "charge" (*aitia*, Matt 27:37).

8   From the Greek, it was not clear if "Nazareth" would be spelt in Hebrew with a *tz* or the simpler *z*. Excavations at Caesarea in 1962 found a clear Hebrew inscription referring to a family from Nazareth using the letter *tz*, thus clarifying that Nazareth is derived from *ntzr* (Strange 1992, 1050–1051).

9   For a similar interchange of these words see 4QFlor col 1,11 and 4QpGen col 5,3–4.

10 I read *tous adelphous mou* as an inclusive expression, since Mary Magdalene is surely included in "your Father."

11 The righteous one who possesses Wisdom can be called a "child" of God (Wis 2: 13), can call God "his father" (Wis 2:16), and is counted among "the sons of God" (Wis 5:5).

References

Ashton, John (1986). "The Transformation of Wisdom: A Study of the Prologue of John's Gospel." *New Testament Studies* 32: 161–186.

Aune, David E. (1972). *The Cultic Setting of Realized Eschatology in Early Christianity*. Leiden: Brill.

Barker, Margaret (1991). *The Gate of Heaven: The History and Symbolism of the Temple in Jerusalem*. London: SPCK.

Barrett, C. K. (1978). *The Gospel According to St. John*. 2nd edn. London: SPCK.

Brown, Raymond E. (2003). *An Introduction to the Gospel of John*. Edited by Francis J. Moloney. 2 vols. Anchor Bible Reference Library. New York: Doubleday.

Burkett, Delbert (1991). *The Son of the Man in the Gospel of John*. Sheffield: Sheffield Academic Press.

Burkett, Delbert (1999). *The Son of Man Debate: A History and Evaluation*. Cambridge: Cambridge University Press.

Carson, Donald A. (1991). *The Gospel According to John*. Grand Rapids: Eerdmans.

Carter, Warren (1990). "The Prologue and John's Gospel: Function, Symbol and the Definitive Word." *Journal for the Study of the New Testament* 39: 35–58.

Charles, Robert Henry, ed. (2004). *Pseudepigrapha of the Old Testament*. Bellingham, WA: Logos Research Systems.

Coloe, Mary L. (2001). *God Dwells with Us: Temple Symbolism in the Fourth Gospel*. Collegeville, MN: Liturgical.

Cory, Catherine (1997). "Wisdom's Rescue: A New Reading of the Tabernacles Discourse (John 7:1–8:59)." *Journal of Biblical Literature* 116: 95–116.

de Goedt, Michel (1961–1962). "Un Schème de Révélation dans la Quatrième Évangile." *New Testament Studies* 8: 142–150.

Dodd, C. H. (1953). *The Interpretation of the Fourth Gospel*. Cambridge: Cambridge University Press.

Feuillet, André (1965). *Johannine Studies*. Staten Island: Alba House.

Fuglseth, Kare Sigvald (2005). *Johannine Sectarianism in Perspective: A Sociological, Historical, and Comparative Analysis of the Temple and Social Relationships in the Gospel of John, Philo, and Qumran*. Leiden: Brill.

García Martínez, Florentino, and Eibert J. C. Tigchelaar (1997). *The Dead Sea Scrolls Study Edition, 1qq–4q273*. 2 vols. New York: Brill.

Hoskins, Paul M. (2006). *Jesus as the Fulfillment of the Temple in the Gospel of John*. Milton Keynes, UK: Paternoster.

Kerr, Alan R. (2002). *The Temple of Jesus' Body: The Temple Theme in the Gospel of John*. Sheffield: Sheffield Academic Press.

Kim, Seyoon (1983). *The "Son of Man" as the Son of God*. Tübingen: Mohr Siebeck.

Levenson, Jon D. (1984). "The Temple and the World." *Journal of Religion* 64: 275–298.

Lightfoot, R. H. (1956). *St. John's Gospel: A Commentary*. London: Oxford University Press.

Manns, Frédéric (1991). *L'Évangile de Jean à la lumière du Judaïsme*. Jerusalem: Franciscan Printing Press.

Moloney, Francis J. (1978). *The Johannine Son of Man*. 2nd rev. edn. Biblioteca Di Scienze Religiose 14. Rome: LAS.

Neusner, Jacob (1972). "Judaism in a Time of Crisis: Four Responses to the Destruction of the Second Temple." *Judaism* 21: 313–327.

Neusner, Jacob (1989). "Money-Changers in the Temple: The Mishnah's Explanation." *New Testament Studies* 35: 287–290.

Pazdan, Mary Margaret (1991). *The Son of Man: A Metaphor for Jesus in the Fourth Gospel*. Collegeville, MN: Liturgical.

Ringe, Sharon H. (1999). *Wisdom's Friends: Community and Christology in the Fourth Gospel*. Louisville, KY: Westminster John Knox.

Rubenstein, Jeffrey (1995). *The History of Sukkot in the Second Temple and Rabbinic Periods*. Brown Judaic Studies. Atlanta, GA: Scholars.

Schnackenburg, Rudolf (1968–1982). *The Gospel According to St. John*. Trans. K. Smyth et al. 3 vols. London: Burns & Oates.

Scott, Martin (1992). *Sophia and the Johannine Jesus*. Sheffield: JSOT.

Sinnott, Alice (2004). "Wisdom as Saviour." *Australian Biblical Review* 52: 19–31.

Strange, James (1992). "Nazareth." In David Noel Freedman (ed.), *Anchor Bible Dictionary* (vol. IV, pp. 1050–1051). New York: Doubleday.

Terrien, Samuel (1983). *The Elusive Presence: Toward a New Biblical Theology*. New York: Harper & Row.

von Rad, Gerhard (1972). *Wisdom in Israel*. London: SCM.

Willett, Michael E. (1992). *Wisdom Christology in the Fourth Gospel*. San Francisco: Mellen Research University Press.

Witherington, Ben, III (1995). *John's Wisdom: A Commentary on the Fourth Gospel*. Louisville, KY: Westminster John Knox.

CHAPTER 5

Jesus in Q

Christopher Tuckett

The title of this chapter, when placed alongside the titles of other chapters in this section of the volume, i.e., "Jesus in the New Testament," which includes essays on Jesus in texts such as the Gospels of Matthew, Mark, Luke, and John, demands at least some brief explanation before we attempt to tackle the issue of the chapter's contents. Unlike the four gospels, Q is not a document that we have extant in any form as such; least of all is it a document in the collection we call the "New Testament." In some ways, Q is a scholarly construct.

The theory of the existence of an entity called Q arises from the problem of seeking to explain the agreements between the three synoptic gospels. As is well known, there is extensive agreement, both in wording and in order, between all three synoptic gospels taken together; and this is frequently explained by the theory of "Markan priority," i.e., the theory that Mark's gospel was written first and was then used by Matthew and Luke independently. This theory, however, only explains the agreements between Matthew and Luke where there is a Markan parallel. It is well known that the Matthew–Luke agreements are considerably more extensive than those which can be explained by dependence on Mark. Thus at times, Matthew and Luke agree almost verbatim in their Greek texts: cf., for example, the accounts of Matthew 3:7–10//Luke 3:7–9 (the words of John the Baptist's preaching) or Matthew 7:7–8//Luke 11:9–10 (Jesus' teaching about asking and receiving). In these instances, the Matthew–Luke agreements cannot be explained by dependence on Mark since there is no Markan parallel. For a variety of reasons, many scholars have argued that the agreements here are best explained by the theory that, rather than one gospel being directly dependent on the other, both depend on a common source, or tradition, and that source is usually known as Q.

There is no space here to discuss this theory in any detail. Full treatments of the issues concerned can be found elsewhere (see Catchpole 1993, 1–59; Tuckett 1996, 1–39; Kloppenborg 2000, 11–54, and 2008, 1–40). Also it needs to be acknowledged fully that the theory of the existence of such a Q source is by no means universally accepted by scholars today. Some would argue that the Matthew–Luke agreements are better explained by a theory of direct dependence (usually in the form of Luke being directly dependent on Matthew: see Goulder 1989, 3–71; Goodacre 2002). Others would argue that such a neat theory of synoptic origins is too simplistic and there may have been a much more complex set of relations between the gospels. Nevertheless, some form of Q hypothesis is widely held today. Further, many would argue that Q is not merely a body of amorphous tradition shared by Matthew and Luke; rather, it may have been a more unified body of material, perhaps a single unified source that may have been available to Matthew and Luke in *written* form, probably in Greek (to explain the verbatim agreements in Greek, which are such a striking feature of the agreements generally). The reasons for these judgments can again be found elsewhere (e.g., Kloppenborg 2000, 56–80), and there is no time to go into the arguments in detail in this context.

I shall therefore assume that Q was a written document, probably written in Greek, which served as a source for Matthew and Luke when they came to write their gospels. It has certainly been a feature of much recent study of Q that the material contained in Q might have a distinctive theological profile, i.e., that there might be something we could reasonable identify as a "theology of Q." Indeed, it might be the case (in part) that, *if* such a distinctive profile could be found, this in turn might help to strengthen the case that Q did indeed exist as a document in its own right at some stage in the development of early Christianity, and that it might make more sense to think of Q as a unified whole, rather than just as an amorphous mass of unrelated traditions that only came together for the first time when they were used by Matthew and Luke (see Catchpole 1993, 5; Tuckett 1996, 37–38). And in this search for a possible "Q theology," the issue of "christology" generally, i.e., the ideas implied concerning the identity of Jesus, has always played an important role.

One other issue should be mentioned briefly. In any reconstruction of the contents of Q, most scholars have restricted themselves to the traditions where Matthew and Luke are closely parallel and where their agreements with each other cannot be explained by dependence on Mark. However, it is a well-known feature of the Markan material in the gospels that, although most of it is contained in Matthew and Luke, some is contained in only one of the other gospels (and a little is contained in neither): at times Matthew and Luke must have omitted material from Mark. *A priori* there is no reason why the same might not have happened with Q materials: hence it might be that some material in Matthew and/or Luke alone might be Q material that the other evangelist has omitted (see Tuckett 1996, 93–96). In turn, the inclusion of such material in the body of what is taken to be Q could have a significant effect on one's assessment of Q's theology and/or christology (cf. below). On the other hand, such theories are inherently somewhat speculative, and arguments about whether a particular passage unique to Matthew or Luke belonged to Q or not might become rather circular in the present context. For the most part, I will therefore avoid including such material in any assessment of Q's christology and confine attention to those materials which are "unquestionably" Q (at least for those who accept some form of Q theory), i.e., materials that are parallel in Matthew and Luke and cannot be explained by common dependence on Mark. What then can we say about Q's christology? Are there distinctive and/or characteristic features of the portrayal of the figure of "Jesus in Q"?

Implicit Christology in Q

That Jesus is in some way "special" for Q is perhaps trite, but important. (In one way, of course, such a claim applies to all parts of any group claiming to view the figure of Jesus positively, i.e., to be regarded as "Christian" in some sense, however one defines that term.) In terms of content, a large proportion of the Q tradition comprises teaching by Jesus. The very fact that this is the teaching *of Jesus* is then significant simply for this fact. Moreover, there is in some sense a striking *silence* in Q about any justification being claimed by the Jesus of Q for having the right, or authority, to teach in the way he does. It is simply assumed that the teaching of Jesus has an almost innate claim to be taken with the utmost seriousness without any need to provide warrant or supporting authority for it. As we shall see shortly, one possible "category" in which the Jesus of Q might be placed is that of a "prophetic" figure; but it is very striking that nowhere does the Jesus of Q introduce any of his teaching with the typically prophetic introduction, "Thus says the Lord ... ," with its implicit claim to be speaking with divine authority. The Jesus of Q is assumed to be his own authority with no need for any external support or validation.

Further, it is noteworthy that at many points in Q sayings, it is assumed that the time of Jesus constitutes a time of eschatological fulfillment, at least in some sense. For example, in Q 7:22 (= Luke 7:22 and the Matthean parallel; it has become conventional to refer to Q verses by their chapter and verse numbering Luke), Jesus replies to the messengers of John the Baptist by referring to his activity in his own ministry ("the blind receive their sight, the lame walk, the lepers are cleansed, the dead are raised, and the poor have the good news preached to them"); but it is also significant that this is stated in terms that clearly recall a number of prophecies from Isaiah, probably about a future eschatological age (Isa 29:18–19; 35:5; 61:1). The implication is clear: the time of Jesus is the time of the fulfillment of these eschatological hopes, and hence Jesus' actions in his ministry (of curing various sick people and "preaching the good news" to the "poor") constitute the fulfillment of important aspects of hopes by (some) Jews for the new age. Q 10:23–24 is similar (though set in slightly more general terms): the future longed for by prophets and others in the past, the things that many people in the past desired to see and encounter, is now being experienced by the disciples of Jesus ("you") in the present.

Perhaps the clearest example of this comes in Q 11:20: "If I by the Spirit/ finger of God cast out devils, then the Kingdom of God has come upon you." The activity of Jesus in exorcising is claimed here to be equivalent to the arrival and

presence of the kingdom itself. (It is universally agreed that the Greek verb translated "has come" here implies the arrival and presence of the kingdom, not merely
as something that is imminent but not quite present yet.)

Similarly, in Q 11:31–32 (the threats of coming judgment against "this generation" and the comparisons made between this generation and the Ninevites who
encountered Jonah and the "Queen of the South") culminate in the claim that
"something greater than" both Jonah and Solomon is "here" now. Nothing is said
that is explicitly christological as such (it is "some*thing* greater," not some*one*). But
the implication is not far away: the "something" is, in context, clearly tied up, and
intimately connected, with the work and ministry of Jesus himself. Hence the time
of Jesus is claimed to be a time of eschatological fulfillment. (For similar ideas, cf. too
Q 12:51–53; 13:18–21; 16:16. For more details, see Tuckett 1996, 209–212.)

Thus deeply embedded in the Q tradition is what one might call an "implicit
christology," an assumption that in and through the life and ministry of Jesus,
something of profound significance is happening, especially when viewed through
a lens of Jewish eschatological hopes for the future. By implication Jesus is thus
considered to be "special" in a very real way. What is not stated explicitly here is
just how "special" he is. How, if at all, can one be more precise?

Christological Categories in Q

The question of how one can/should introduce more precision into a discussion of
New Testament christology has been debated many times. In particular, there has
been debate about the merits (or otherwise) of focusing on christological "titles" to
gain greater precision in any understanding of New Testament christology. An
(almost exclusive) focus on such "titles" was a feature of a number of older treatments of New Testament christology (e.g., Cullmann 1959; Fuller 1965). Such an
approach has been radically questioned in more recent study (see especially Keck
1986), partly because such an approach may work with too rigid an idea of what
any supposed "title" may have meant at the time, and also because it may miss other
vitally important pieces of evidence that contribute to the overall picture of how
Jesus is presented and/or what Jesus is claimed to be. These factors may be particularly relevant for study of Q, since there is something of a dearth of christological
"titles" in Q! Q expresses the significance of the person of Jesus very often in other
ways than using grand titles or explicit descriptions.

There is too the problem, particularly acute in study of a "text" such as Q, of
knowing how to interpret what appear to be "gaps" in the tradition as we have it.
Does the Q that we can access (in any case only indirectly, via Matthew's and Luke's
use of Q) give us anything approaching a full and complete set of evidence for the
picture of Jesus that those who preserved and compiled the Q collection may have
held? This is a particularly acute problem in relation to the slightly broader theological question of the significance attached by Q to the death of Jesus. As far as our
evidence will allow us to determine, it seems that Q did not contain a passion nar-

rative. Did this mean that the person or persons responsible for collecting and preserving the Q material had no ("theological") interest in the death of Jesus? Very
different answers have been given to this question! Some have argued that Q indeed
does represent a distinctive stream within primitive Christianity that, unlike say
Paul, saw little if any positive significance in the death of Jesus (e.g., Mack 1993).
Others have argued equally strongly that an argument from silence is particularly
dangerous here: we do not have anything approaching a full, comprehensive statement of the beliefs and practices of whoever it was that assembled the Q materials
into a single text, and hence we cannot deduce anything from an (apparent) absence
of a passion narrative in Q in relation to theories about broader claims relating to
the significance (or otherwise) of the death of Jesus for "Q Christians" (see, e.g.,
Hengel 1983, 37; cf. too Manson 1949, 16).

Nevertheless, despite these caveats, a focus on "titles" may be at least partly relevant in determining the christology of a writer or group (though bearing in mind
the danger of arguing from silence in relation to any absence of titles). I start with
two "titles" that may be all but absent in Q.

Christ

The term "Christ" (Greek *christos*, corresponding to the Hebrew *mashiah* = "Messiah")
is, as far as one can tell, completely absent from Q. There is no Q text where one can
say with any certainty that the term "Christ" is mentioned in Q. Matthew 11:2 mentions John the Baptist in prison hearing about "the works of the Messiah," but this
is widely regarded as Matthew's redaction of a vaguer Q wording, perhaps more
accurately reflected in Luke's parallel, which speaks only of John hearing about "all
these things" (Luke 7:18).

The evidence of 1 Corinthians 15:3, "Christ died for our sins" (almost certainly a
pre-Pauline formulation cited here by Paul, hence pre-dating Paul by some time),
suggests that the term "Christ" was applied very early to Jesus, and indeed by this
very early date had already been attached so firmly to Jesus that it lost its definite
article ("*the* Christ") and hence perhaps its original significance (where "Christ/
Messiah" is a description of a role) and became virtually just another proper name,
which here has even displaced the name "Jesus." Further, the category of messiahship is one that is at home, and only at home, within a Jewish context. Given that
Q appears to have been a very "Jewish" kind of text, and indeed arguably stemming
from Galilee (so Kloppenborg 2000 and 2008), it is quite surprising that Q gives no
instance of Jesus being referred to, either by himself or by others, as "Christ/Messiah."

Lord

The other christological "title" that is frequently used in other parts of primitive
Christianity is the term "Lord" (Greek *kyrios*). For example, Paul in 1 Corinthians
12:3 appears to assume that it is the *sine qua non* of any Christian confession: anyone

who calls Jesus "Lord" possesses the Spirit of God; and conversely, no one can say the polar opposite ("Jesus is cursed") through the Sprit. Again perhaps surprisingly, Q rarely seems to imply that Jesus is thought of as "Lord." The evidence is not entirely clear.

In Q 7:6, the centurion addresses Jesus as "Lord" with the vocative case (*kyrie*). However, the vocative of *kyrios* is notoriously ambiguous and can be used as simply a polite form of address (as "Sir!" can be used in slightly older-style English, without implying that the person addressed has received a knighthood!). At the end of the Great Sermon in Q, Jesus bemoans those who call him "Lord, Lord," but do not put his teaching into practice in their ethical conduct (Q 6:46: the rest of the saying is very different in wording in Matthew and Luke, but there is enough agreement in the meaning, as well as the opening reference to such people calling Jesus "Lord, Lord," to be fairly sure that this is indeed part of Q.) It would seem then that invoking Jesus as "Lord" is clearly regarded as in some sense a "standard" activity by Jesus' followers; but the thrust of the saying is to call into question radically the sufficiency of such an invocation (and hence Q 6:46 is the diametrical opposite of 1 Corinthians 12:3 in this respect!). What is far more important than any "title" being ascribed to Jesus is that his teaching be taken seriously and be obeyed.

Prophet

It is clear from other parts of Q that Jesus' teaching is not considered in isolation from the rest of his ministry; and in part, this broader picture of Jesus' activity may implicitly place him in a slightly more precise category, viz., that of a "prophetic" figure.

In the section Q 7:18–23, the question of Jesus' identity is raised by the question posed by John the Baptist in prison: is Jesus the "coming one" or should one be looking for another figure? The reply that the Jesus of Q gives comes in Q 7:22–23. As noted above, this reply alludes to the language used in a number of passages from Isaiah (Isa 29, 35, 61), but its prime reference is to the activity of Jesus himself in various acts of healing the blind, the lame, lepers, and so on. Thus the claim is being made that, in Jesus' miracle-working activity of healing, the longed-for new age is present.

The climax of the reply comes in the last clause: "the poor are evangelized." This is universally accepted as an allusion to the language of the prophecy of Isaiah 61:1, "The Spirit of the Lord is upon me, because he has anointed me, he has sent me to bring good news to the poor" (Greek lit. "evangelize the poor"). The implicit claim being made by the Jesus of Q 7:22 is thus that his own preaching (as well as his healing activity) constitutes the fulfillment of this Isaianic expectation. Moreover, in Isaiah it is almost certainly the case that the figure described there is thought of as having a *prophetic* role. Q 7:22 thus implicitly claims that a vitally important aspect of Jesus' activity is to fulfill this prophetic role in his preaching and teaching. Jesus is thus the prophet of Isaiah 61.

The same may well also be implied by the beatitudes, which appear at the start of the Great Sermon in Q 6:20–21. Matthew and Luke differ in wording here, so one cannot be certain of the Q wording in detail. Nevertheless, a strong case can be made for claiming that the beatitudes in Q pronounced a blessing on the "poor" (Luke 6:20: Matthew's "poor in spirit" [Matt 5:3] may be Matthew's change to Q), and promised "comfort" to those who "mourn" (Matt 5:4: Luke's slightly different wording may be secondary. For details, see Tuckett 1996, 223–225.) This is then very close indeed to the language of Isaiah 61:1–2, which claims that the task of the prophetic figure is to preach the good news to the "poor" (v. 1) and to "comfort all who mourn" (v. 2). Thus right at the start of Jesus' preaching in Q, Jesus is made to claim implicitly that the program set out in Isaiah 61:1–2 is being put into practice in his own preaching and ministry.

We may also note that some of the activities mentioned in Q 7:22 are hard to explain wholly from the Isaianic texts. In particular, the reference to healing lepers is not mentioned in Isaiah. So too the motif of raising the dead is not so easy to parallel (though cf. Isa 26:19). However, in the Old Testament the two figures most distinctively associated with these activities are Elisha (healing Naaman the leper in 2 Kings 5) and Elijah (bringing the widow of Zarephath's son back to life in 1 Kings 17). Jesus is thus being presented in Q as acting in very similar ways to these "classic" prophets of the Jewish tradition. (There is also a striking parallel between the language of Q 7:22 and one of the Qumran scrolls, viz., 4Q521, which may well be referring to the work of an Elijah-type figure: see Collins 1995, 117–122.)

This general idea (of Jesus as an eschatological prophetic figure) would be strongly confirmed if it could be shown that Luke 4:16–30, the account of Jesus' rejection in Nazareth, where he is portrayed as explicitly citing the text from Isaiah 61:1–2 and claiming that it is being fulfilled in his own present, were also part of Q. Claiming that a passage in Matthew or Luke alone might have been part of Q is always an uncertain process (see above). A case can be made in this instance for taking the citation of Isaiah 61 as part of Q (see further Tuckett 1996, 226–236). For example, it is striking that both Matthew and Luke give the name of the village in the form "Nazara" (Matt 4:13; Luke 4:16), perhaps then reflecting the existence of a tradition common to Matthew and Luke here, i.e., Q. Further, while it is widely argued that the citation of Isaiah 61 in Luke 4 acts as a programmatic summary for the Lukan story to come (and hence many argue its presence here is due entirely to Lukan redaction), there are some features that make it hard to see as a redactional creation *in toto*. For example, the unusual form of the citation combines a phrase from Isaiah 58:6 in the middle of the lines from Isaiah 61:1. These passages are linked via common use of the Greek word *aphesis*, which here must be taken in a non-Lukan sense as meaning something like "release" (from bondage or illness). Elsewhere in Luke-Acts, the word is used frequently, but with the meaning "forgiveness" (of sins). It may be then that the text form, and the presence of the text itself at this point, comes to Luke from an earlier tradition and, given the agreement with Matthew in the form of the name Nazara, that source may be Q. If so, then the explicit application of the citation from Isaiah 61 to Jesus confirms the importance of the category of (eschatological) prophet for the Jesus of Q. (It is also noteworthy that in Luke 4:25–27, reference is made to the figures of Elijah and Elisha as implicitly prefiguring the fate of Jesus: this would then link with the parallels noted earlier between what is said in Q 7:22 and the Elijah–Elisha stories.)

Wisdom and the prophets

This same theme is reinforced by a related complex of ideas that appears to be highly distinctive within the Q tradition. This concerns the theme of the figure of (personified) Wisdom sending prophets who regularly then experience rejection and suffer violence. The theme of personified Wisdom is one that appears in a number of Old Testament passages (cf. Prov 1, 8, etc.). So too, there is a well attested theme in a number of Old Testament (and later) texts of (all) the prophets being sent to recalcitrant Israel but all being rejected and suffering violence (see Neh 9:26; cf. also 1 Kings 18:4, 13; 19:10, 14; 2 Chron 36:14–16). There is of course a strong element within the Wisdom tradition whereby Wisdom herself is a figure who is rejected and finds no welcome (cf. 1 Enoch 42). But what is distinctive in the Q tradition is that these two themes coalesce (apparently for the first time) so that Wisdom becomes the agent who sends out the prophets, all of whom then suffer violence and rejection. This is clearest perhaps in the doom oracle of Q 11:49, where Luke is widely regarded as preserving the Q wording most accurately: here Jesus says that "the Wisdom of God said 'I will send them prophets ... some of whom they will persecute and kill.' " (Matthew characteristically equates Jesus himself with the figure of Wisdom and has the saying in the first person: Jesus himself says "I will send you prophets ... .") A similar network of ideas occurs in the lament over Jerusalem in Q 13:34–35: "O Jerusalem, Jerusalem, the city that kills the prophets and stones those who were sent to you ... ." Taken on its own, the Wisdom reference is not explicit, though the saying is redolent of wisdom motifs. In any case, the two sayings are contiguous in Matthew (Matt 23:34–36 + 37–39), so that *if* Matthew's ordering of the Q material is original here (which is at least possible), it may be that for Q the two sayings were assumed to be by the same speaker, viz., Wisdom.

Elsewhere in the Q tradition, similar ideas emerge. The saying in Q 9:58 ("the Son of Man has nowhere to lay his head") is strongly reminiscent of the passage in 1 Enoch 42, which talks of Wisdom seeking a home but finding none. And in Q 7:35 ("Wisdom is justified by her children") the figure of Wisdom is associated with figures who suffer hostility and rejection (cf. the criticisms of Jesus and John the Baptist reflected in Q 7:33–34).

In part, many of these sayings relate to Jesus' followers: they will experience rejection and suffering akin to the prophets (explicitly in the final beatitude in Q 6:22–23; also Q 11:49). But equally, by implication, it seems that this rejection and hostility is also experienced by Jesus himself (cf. Q 9:58, where the "Son of Man" for Q almost certainly means Jesus and Jesus alone; also Q 7:34 before Q 7:35: the reference to

Wisdom is preceded by a note recalling how Jesus receives no welcome but is rejected as a "glutton and a wine-bibber, a friend of tax-collectors and sinners"). It would seem then that in one way a relatively "low" christological outlook is being expressed here, in that Jesus is not necessarily being distinguished from his followers. He, and they, will experience the same fate as the prophets. The pattern of rejection of God's prophetic messengers is reaching its climax in the events surrounding Jesus and his followers.

Yet Jesus is being given (as are his followers) a significant status in the overall dispensation envisaged here: they *are* akin to prophets. Thus Jesus is implicitly being given a prophetic role here. It is also noteworthy that, via this scheme, Q does appear to give some measure of "interpretation" to the hostility experienced by Jesus and hence, perhaps by implication, to his passion and death. Q may very well not have a passion *narrative* as such (see above). But that does not necessarily mean that Q ignores the suffering of Jesus completely and gives no evaluation of it: rather, Q may well envisage the death of Jesus within this broad schema of the violence suffered by the prophets. This may be very different from other New Testament passages that develop ideas about Jesus' suffering being "vicarious" ("for us") in some sense (cf. the creedal summary cited by Paul in 1 Corinthians 15:3; the general theme is very prominent elsewhere in Paul's writings). Q may not have any idea (at least explicitly) of Jesus' death as atoning. Indeed it is not entirely clear that Q thinks of the suffering of Jesus as "unique" in being qualitatively different from the suffering endured by others: the model assumed here seems to presuppose that the suffering of Jesus is in a line of direct continuity with the suffering of others, past and present. Nevertheless, Q does have a scheme, or a model, in which the death of Jesus is interpreted and given some positive significance.

Son of Man

It is striking that in many of the Q passages considered above linking ideas of Wisdom and her (suffering) prophetic messengers, there is as often as not a reference to Jesus as "Son of Man." Thus in Q 9:58, Jesus says that "the Son of Man" has nowhere to lay his head. The Wisdom saying in Q 7:35 is preceded by the saying in Q 7:34, which talks about "the Son of Man" coming, eating and drinking, and experiencing hostility and rejection. In the beatitude of Q 6:22–23, the followers of Jesus are said to be suffering "for the sake of the Son of Man." (Matthew's first person "for *my* sake" is probably due to Matthew himself, and Luke most likely preserves the Q wording here: see Tuckett 1996, 180 with further references.)

The problems surrounding the use of the term "Son of Man" in the gospels are enormous, and it is probably fair to say that "the Son of Man problem" is one of the most intractable in all aspects of gospel studies today. Nevertheless, it is probably fair to say that much of "the problem" about the use of the term "Son of Man" in the gospels has focused on the issue of what Jesus himself may have meant if/when he used the phrase, probably in Aramaic. Various theories have been proposed that at an earlier stage in the tradition, perhaps at the level of the historical Jesus, the "Son of Man" figure was thought of as a figure other than Jesus (see, e.g., Bultmann 1951, 28–31; survey in Burkett 1999, 37–39). Alternatively it has been argued that in the Aramaic that underlies our Greek gospel tradition, the equivalent phrase, *bar nash* or *bar nasha*, may have meant simply "a man," or "someone," or had some such quasi-"generic" meaning (see, e.g., Casey 1979; Lindars 1983; survey in Burkett 1999, ch. 8). However, by the time one gets to the stage of the gospel writers writing in Greek, and even perhaps also Q (if Q was in Greek), the situation may be clearer. As far as the evangelists are concerned, it seems that they are convinced that the "Son of Man" figure is none other than Jesus and Jesus alone.

Further, in the gospels, it is clear that the reference to the figure of the "Son of Man" is directly related to the language and imagery of Daniel 7:13 and the vision that "Daniel" has of a figure who has the appearance of "one like a son of man." We know that that vision, and the figure of the "one like a son of man," caught the imagination of a number of writers, Christian and non-Christian, in the period, and various literary developments of the tradition are now clearly evidenced (in texts such as 1 Enoch, 4 Ezra, as well as the New Testament gospels: cf. Collins 1995, ch. 8). Whether Q represents the same development is not absolutely certain but seems very likely. (There are no absolutely clear echoes of Danielic language in the Q sayings, unlike, e.g., Mark 13:26; 14:62, where the reference to the Son of Man figure "coming on the clouds" is widely taken as a verbal allusion to the vision of Daniel 7.)

The interpretation of the figure of the vision of Daniel 7 is disputed: whether he is an angelic figure, a human figure, or whatever is debated. Further, there is no unanimity about whether one should regard the figure as a *suffering* figure or not. The vision comes from a time when loyal Jews are suffering intense persecution during the time of Anitochus Epiphanes (just before the Maccabean revolt) for their commitment to their true religion and their refusal to compromise their religious beliefs and practices in any way. The vision then provides them with encouragement, in that the "Son of Man" figure of the vision receives vindication and reward at the heavenly throne: he "represents" them in some way so that the vision serves to provide reassurance and encouragement to the loyal suffering Jews that they too will be rewarded. In the vision itself, the Son of Man figure is (simply) a glorious figure who receives the favorable judgment in the heavenly court and is as a result given a highly privileged position himself. But in the context of Daniel 7, it may be implied that the figure who is glorified in this way is precisely one who has experienced prior suffering. Otherwise, the vision fails to communicate hope and encouragement to its readers. Thus inherent in the vision of Daniel 7 may be the twin themes of suffering and subsequent vindication. Such twin themes clearly fit well with the body of Son of Man sayings in the Gospel of Mark, where Jesus *qua* Son of Man is one who must suffer (cf. all the passion predictions in Mark 8:31; 9:31; 10:33–34, which are all couched in terms of Jesus as Son of Man) but who will come on the clouds of heaven at the end of time (Mark 13:26; 14:62).

What is striking is that the same pattern seems to be present in the Q Son of Man sayings as well. Jesus *qua* Son of Man in Q is one who experiences hostility and rejection, and hence by implication suffering (see Q 7:34; 9:58, though there is no explicit reference in these sayings to the suffering or death of Jesus). But equally there is another side to the coin. And just as in Mark, so too in Q, Jesus will exercise a significant eschatological role. He will act as witness in the final judgment, speaking on behalf of ("confessing") those who have been true to him ("confessed him") on earth (Q 12:8). He will come like a "thief in the night" (Q 12:42) on his "day," which will arrive with terrifying suddenness and which will mean disaster for those who are unprepared (Q 17:22–37). In this then, unlike some of the other evidence considered so far, Jesus seems to be ascribed a role that is somewhat "higher" than that for other human beings. He and he alone will confess those who have confessed him, and indeed he is the one who is in a position to be "confessed" (Q 12:8); and the language of the "day of the Son of Man" (Q 17) seems to be a deliberate allusion, and parallel, to language in the Jewish Bible about the "Day of the Lord." Thus many would see this as a distinctive feature of a "Q christology" here, so that it is appropriate to say that Q has a "Son of Man christology" (cf. Tödt 1965, and many others since).

Yet it is also worth noting that even this exalted language about Jesus in Q serves as much to unite Jesus with his followers as it does to exalt him over and above them. As noted above, the verbal picture of Jesus as the rejected Son of Man serves in a significant way to act as a paradigm or example for his followers, who are told to expect the same rejection and hostility. For example, the saying in Q 9:58 ("The Son of Man has nowhere to lay his head") acts in Q as a quasi-"heading" for the mission charge that probably follows in Q (Q 10:1–16), where Jesus warns his followers that they too may experience hostility and rejection.

But equally the more exalted language associated with the eschatological activity of Jesus *qua* Son of Man does not serve necessarily to distinguish Jesus from his followers. For in what is probably the final (and hence probable climactic) saying of Q, Jesus tells the disciples that they themselves will "sit on the thrones judging the twelve tribes of Israel" (Q 22:30). Thus even in the most exalted role of exercising final judgment itself, the role of Jesus is one that, according to the Q tradition, he shares with his disciples. Any "christology" here then is one that serves to unite Jesus with his followers, rather than to distinguish him from them.

Son of God

The same may also apply in the case of the other christological "title" that occurs occasionally in Q, viz., "Son of God." The phrase occurs in two Q passages, viz., the temptation narrative of Q 4:1–13 and the so-called "Johannine thunderbolt" of Q 10:21–22. Both passages have been seen as slightly unusual within the rest of Q, in part precisely because of their references to Jesus as Son of God: and as such, they have sometimes been regarded as later additions to Q (cf. Kloppenborg 1987 and others). However, it may be that these passages fit well with the general pattern emerging from the rest of Q, where Jesus is seen as united with his followers, rather than distinct from them.

In the temptation narrative, the force of the story may be in part to set up the figure of Jesus as a model figure who is obedient to God's word and who refuses to rely on anyone other than God (Tuckett 1992). Thus, precisely as Son of God, Jesus is portrayed as obedient to God: when confronted by the Devil and addressed there with "If you are the Son of God ...," Jesus stands firm, citing scripture back at the Devil and refusing to put God to the test or to worship anyone or anything other than God himself. This pattern of divine sonship as implying obedience serves to align the Q temptation narrative with other parts of Q where Jesus' followers are also sons or daughters of God too. They are to be "merciful," just as their heavenly "Father" is merciful (Q 6:36); they are to address God as their "Father" in prayer (Q 11:2); and they can rely on God as their Father who knows all their needs to care for them (Q 12:30). The fact then that Jesus is the "son" of God, or correlatively that God is the "Father" of Jesus, is something that serves to unite Jesus with his followers quite as much as to distinguish him.

The "Johannine thunderbolt" (Q 10:21–22) is an extremely complex passage. Its popular description as a "thunderbolt" reflects the view of many that the saying is somewhat out of line with much of the rest of the synoptic tradition (not only Q), and more "Johannine" in its ideas (including the category of divine sonship and the apparently extremely "high" christology implied here). Many have argued that Wisdom ideas are here very prominent, though with Jesus implicitly being presented not just as the envoy of Wisdom but as Wisdom herself. Thus the exclusive mutual knowledge of the Father and the Son ("no one knows the Father except the Son, and no one knows the Son except the Father") can be paralleled in sayings from the Wisdom tradition about God knowing Wisdom (Job 28; Sir 1:6, 8) and Wisdom knowing God (Prov 8:12; Wis 7:25ff.), as well as Wisdom revealing God to others (e.g., Wis 7:21; Sir 4:18).

The first phrase in Q 10:22, "all things have been delivered to me by my Father," is however more reminiscent of "apocalyptic" language, especially language associated with the figure of the Son of Man (cf. Dan 7:14: "to him was given dominion and glory and kingship"). Further, the "title" used of Jesus here is not "wisdom" but "son." In fact the language of the saying may have closer links with some of the sonship language used in Wis 2–5 (which in any case may be related to the Son of Man tradition), where it is the righteous sufferer, and perhaps the follower of Wisdom, who is the "son" of God (Wis 2:16) and who may also be thought to have (or to claim to have) "knowledge of God" (cf. the taunt by opponents in Wis 2:13: "he claims to have knowledge of God"). It may therefore be wrong to try to press the saying here into a single christological mould or category. In any case, the saying may be closer to some of the other Q traditions than some have allowed in the past (it may be less of a "thunderbolt" than some have suggested!) and may be presenting Jesus in ways similar to other parts of Q, viz., as one who is obedient to God and who shares his status of sonship, and his position of possessing close knowledge of God, with others.

References

Bultmann, Rudolf (1951). *Theology of the New Testament*. Vol. 1. London: SCM. (German original 1948.)

Burkett, Delbert (1999). *The Son of Man Debate*. Cambridge: Cambridge University Press.

Casey, P. Maurice (1979). *Son of Man: The Interpretation and Influence of Daniel 7*. London: SPCK.

Catchpole, David R. (1993). *The Quest for Q*. Edinburgh: T&T Clark.

Collins, John J. (1995). *The Scepter and the Star: The Messiahs of the Dead Sea Scrolls and Other Ancient Literature*. New York: Doubleday.

Cullmann, Oscar (1959). *The Christology of the New Testament*. London: SCM.

Fuller, Reginald H. (1965). *The Formation of New Testament Christology*. London: Lutterworth.

Goodacre, Mark S. (2002). *The Case against Q: Studies in Markan Priority and the Synoptic Problem*. Harrisburg, PA: Trinity.

Goulder, Michael D. (1989). *Luke: A New Paradigm*. Sheffield: JSOT.

Hengel, Martin (1983). "Christology and New Testament Chronology." In *Between Jesus and Paul*. London: SCM.

Keck, Leander E. (1986). "Toward the Renewal of New Testament Christology." *New Testament Studies* 32: 362–377.

Kloppenborg, John S. (1987). *The Formation of Q*. Philadelphia: Fortress.

Kloppenborg, John S. (2000). *Excavating Q: The History and Setting of the Sayings Gospel*. Minneapolis: Fortress.

Kloppenborg, John S. (2008). *Q, The Earliest Gospel: An Introduction to the Original Stories and Sayings of Jesus*. Louisville, KY and London: Westminster John Knox.

Lindars, Barnabas (1983). *Jesus Son of Man*. London: SPCK.

Mack, Burton L. (1993). *The Lost Gospel: The Book of Q and Christian Origins*. San Francisco: HarperSanFrancisco.

Manson, T. W. (1949). *The Sayings of Jesus*. London: SCM.

Tödt, H. E. (1965). *The Son of Man in the Synoptic Tradition*. London: SCM.

Tuckett, Christopher M. (1992). "The Temptation Narrative in Q." In F. Van Segbroek et al. (eds.), *The Four Gospels 1992. Festschrift Frans Neirynck* (pp. 479–507). Leuven: Leuven University Press & Peeters.

Tuckett, Christopher M. (1996). *Q and the History of Early Christianity*. Edinburgh: T&T Clark.

Further Reading

Jacobson, Arland D. (1992). *The First Gospel: An Introduction to Q*. Sonoma, CA: Polebridge.

Tuckett, Christopher M. (1993). "The Son of Man in Q." In M. C. de Boer (ed.), *From Jesus to John. Essays on Jesus and New Testament Christology in Honour of Marinus de Jonge* (pp. 196–215). Sheffield: Sheffield Academic Press.

Tuckett, Christopher M. (2001). "The Son of Man and Daniel 7: Q and Jesus." In A. Lindemann (ed.), *The Sayings Source Q and the Historical Jesus* (pp. 317–394). Leuven: Leuven University Press & Peeters.

CHAPTER 6

Paul, Jesus, and Christ

Edward Adams

Paul is the earliest Christian author to whose views about Jesus we have first-hand access. His letters, or at least those letters that scholars accept as genuinely written by him, are (very probably) the earliest writings in the New Testament, dating broadly from 50 to 60 CE, about twenty to thirty years or so after the death of Jesus. Paul was a highly influential figure in the early church, and he is sometimes, at a popular level, credited with almost single-handedly turning the man Jesus into a divine being. However, Paul was much more influential after his lifetime than during it, and his role in the development of christology in his own day was a lot less significant than is popularly thought. In many respects, his christology reflects ideas about Jesus that were current in the early church at the time of writing. I will return to this point at the end.

This chapter gives an overview of Paul's christology, discussing his attitude toward the earthly Jesus, the main titles he accords to Jesus, his "Adam christology," and the question of whether Paul attributes pre-existence and "deity" to Jesus. It is conventional within Pauline scholarship to distinguish between the undisputed and disputed Pauline letters. Seven letters are generally accepted as authentic: Romans, 1 and 2 Corinthians, Galatians, Philippians, 1 Thessalonians, and Philemon. In examining Paul's views of Jesus, I will restrict my database to these epistles. The christological teaching of the disputed letters will be treated separately, and inevitably, more briefly.

Paul and the Earthly Jesus

In Martin Scorsese's film, *The Last Temptation of Christ*, Jesus is shown a future in which he survives the cross and goes on to live a normal family life. In a memorable scene, he encounters Paul fervently proclaiming the good news of Jesus Christ, the

The Blackwell Companion to Jesus, First Edition. Edited by Delbert Burkett. ©2014 John Wiley & Sons, Ltd. Published 2014 by John Wiley & Sons, Ltd.

Son of God, who was crucified, resurrected, and taken into heaven. Jesus angrily disputes these claims, insisting that he is just a man. He orders Paul to stop telling such lies about him. Paul eventually accepts that the figure remonstrating with him is indeed Jesus of Nazareth, but he vows to carry on preaching his gospel regardless, since what is important to him, and what people need, is the crucified, risen, and exalted Christ, not the man Jesus.

This filmic exchange presents in an extreme form (with Paul being depicted as a fraudster) an opinion that has often been expressed in popular contexts in scholarship: that the historical Jesus was of no real interest to Paul.[1] The most notable scholarly proponent of this view was Rudolf Bultmann (1966, 220–246). According to Bultmann, Paul's letters barely show traces of Jesus' life-history and preaching: "All that is important to him in the story of Jesus is the fact that Jesus was born a Jew and lived under the Law (Gal 4:4) and that he had been crucified" (1952, 188). For Paul what mattered was the Christ of Christian preaching (the *kerygma*) not the earthly Jesus. Bultmann found support for this view in 2 Corinthians 5:16: "From now on, therefore, we regard no one from a human point of view; even though we once knew Christ from a human point of view, we know him no longer in that way."[2] He interpreted this text to mean that Paul eschewed knowledge of the activities and personality of the historical Jesus (1966, 239).

Certainly, in Paul's letters there is a remarkable dearth of explicit reference to Jesus' teaching or details of his ministry. Twice, Paul cites a "command" of Jesus: in 1 Corinthians 7:10–11, referring to Jesus' prohibition of divorce (cf. Mark 10:9–12 and parallel; Matt 5:32 and parallel); and in 1 Corinthians 9:14, alluding to the missionary charge/s of Matthew 10:9–10 and Luke 10:4, 7. In 1 Corinthians 11:23–25, he quotes Jesus' words of institution at the Last Supper (Mark 14:22–25 and parallels). These are the only explicit appeals to Jesus' speech in Paul's letters (the "word of the Lord" in 1 Thessalonians 4:15–17 may be another, but this is much less certain). Apart from Jesus' crucifixion and resurrection, to which he constantly refers, the only facts about Jesus' life that Paul directly mentions are that he was born of a woman (Gal 4:4); that he lived as a Jew under the Law (Gal 4:4); that he was a descendent of David (Rom 1:3); that he had brothers (1 Cor 9:5), one of whom was James (Gal 1:19); and that on the night of his betrayal, he spoke certain words over the bread and cup (1 Cor 11:23–25). Paul says nothing about Jesus' baptism, his call of disciples, his ministry in Galilee, his healings and exorcisms, his parables, his conflicts with the Pharisees, his transfiguration, his triumphal entry into Jerusalem, or his arrest and trial/s.

Yet, we should not make light of the few sayings of Jesus that Paul does quote and the few facts about Jesus that he does reveal. In themselves, they are sufficient to show that Jesus Christ, for Paul, is no docetic figure (a purely spiritual being with no human reality), but a real man who lived, taught, and died (Bruce 1966, 24).

There is evidence to suggest, though, that Paul knows rather more about the earthly Jesus than he openly indicates. Apart from the more or less direct citations of Jesus' words, we can detect in Paul's letters echoes of sayings of Jesus known from

the canonical gospels. The exhortation of Romans 12:14 ("Bless those who persecute you; bless and do not curse them") is "a virtually certain echo" of Matthew
5:44, paralleled in Luke 6:27–28 (Thompson 1991, 105). Paul's claim that "the
whole law is summed up in a single commandment, 'You shall love your neighbor
as yourself'" (Gal 5:14; cf. Rom 13:8–10), seems to reflect the teaching of Jesus in
Mark 12:28–34 and parallel. Romans 14:14 calls to mind Mark 7:15, 1 Corinthians
13:2 appears to echo Matthew 17:20 (and its parallel Luke 17:6), and so on. There
is intense debate about the number of such echoes[3] and also their significance,[4] but
many now would agree that Paul's knowledge of Jesus' teaching extends, at least
somewhat, beyond the few explicit citations. There are also hints that Paul knows
more of the narrative tradition about Jesus. He knows of Jesus' life of poverty (2 Cor
8:9). He seems to know the tradition of the sending out of the apostles (1 Cor 9:14;
Horrell 2005, 214–222). Arguably, he knows of Jesus' practice of addressing God
as "Abba" (Rom 8:15; Gal 4:6). He has some sense of the circumstances leading up
to Jesus' death (1 Cor 11:23), and he is aware that Jesus was crucified as a messianic
pretender (1 Cor 1:23).

Paul tells us that several years after his conversion, he went to Jerusalem to visit
Peter, staying with him for fifteen days (Gal 1:18). It seems highly likely that he
would have spent some of this time acquiring information about Jesus. It is not
Paul's concern in 2 Corinthians 5:16 to repudiate such information. The contrast
Paul is drawing in this verse is one between his former, i.e., "pre-conversion," attitude to Jesus – and to everyone in general – and his current, i.e., "post-conversion,"
view of Jesus. Whereas he had previously regarded Jesus as a false prophet who died
a hateful and accursed form of death, he now views him as Messiah, Son of God and
Lord. He is not contrasting historical knowledge of Jesus with the preaching of Christ
in the gospel.

Yet, however much Paul did know about Jesus, the fact remains that he does not
say much about the deeds and teaching of the earthly Jesus in his extant writings,
and this calls for explanation (see the survey of proposed reasons in Thompson
1991, 70–76). An important consideration is the fact that Paul wrote *letters*, and
the epistle was not the natural literary genre for providing detailed biographical
information (though it did not necessarily preclude the provision of biographical
data). In their lack of allusion to events in Jesus' life, Paul's letters are generally no
different than the other New Testament epistles. It was precisely to meet the need
for extensive written narratives of Jesus' ministry, death, and resurrection that the
gospels – a subset of ancient biography (Burridge 2004) – were eventually produced.
What Paul wrote about in his letters was to a large extent determined by the needs
and questions of his addressees, and there is little indication in the surviving letters
that his readers sought from him fuller information about the earthly Jesus. This
may suggest that they already had a certain level of knowledge about Jesus' historical life and ministry, acquired from the oral circulation of Jesus traditions, and
perhaps even from their initial evangelization. It seems likely that Paul's own missionary proclamation of Christ's death and resurrection included at least a sketch of

the life of Jesus. As Graham Stanton has argued, the apostle's preaching of "Christ crucified" (1 Cor 1:23) would have made little sense without it, especially in a Gentile context (2004, 53).[5] Another reason for the paucity of references to Jesus' earthly activities in Paul's writings may simply be that this apostle, unlike others, was not a witness of Jesus' ministry (Bruce 1966, 25). He was not a follower of Jesus, and he had probably never met or even seen the earthly Jesus. Thus, he prefers to speak more about his own experience of the living Jesus, stemming from the calling he received on the road to Damascus. Perhaps the most significant reason for Paul's apparent inattention to the earthly life of Jesus is the massive theological weight he attaches to the cross and resurrection. Christ's passion and resurrection are the basis of salvation; they are also "apocalyptic" occurrences, overturning the old age and inaugurating the new (2 Cor 5:15–17; Gal 6:14–15). As such, these events overtake and eclipse Jesus' preceding ministry. As Michael Thompson puts it, "Everything Jesus said and did before his death and vindication paled in significance by comparison to the Christ-Event" (1991, 73). It is not, then, that Paul is uninterested in or dismissive of the deeds and teaching of Jesus; rather, he is overwhelmingly more interested in Christ's cross and resurrection, events that have completely reconfigured his worldview and self-identity (Gal 2:20).

Recent studies by David Horrell (2005, 204–45) and Richard Burridge (2007, 81–154) have emphasized the importance of Jesus as moral exemplar in Paul's ethics.[6] Paul exhorts readers to imitate Jesus and/or to copy himself as he seeks to emulate Christ (1 Cor 10:33–11:1; 1 Thess 1:6; cf. 1 Cor 4:1; Phil 3:17; 4:9). He appeals to the example of Christ (Rom 15:1–3, 2 Cor 8:9; Phil 2:5–11). He refers to Christ's moral virtues (2 Cor 10:1) and his ministry of service (Rom 15:8). In certain instances, the paradigm of Christ's self-sacrifice and self-renunciation seems to underlie his ethical instruction, even if the moral example of Jesus is not explicitly cited (e.g., 1 Cor 8:7–13; 10:23–24; Gal 6:2). It is little wonder that Horrell can claim that "the normative pattern of Christ's self-giving is woven into the fabric of Paul's ethics" (2005, 242). To be sure, it is often Christ's self-giving on the cross that is in mind. But in 2 Corinthians 10:1, "meekness and gentleness" are general character traits of Jesus and not just dispositions manifested on the cross. And in 2 Corinthians 8:9 and Philippians 2:5–9, the whole scheme of Christ's earthly career, from incarnation to exaltation, is in view. These texts show that the earthly life of Jesus is sometimes ethically significant for Paul. There is also evidence that the pre-crucifixion life of Jesus is *salvifically* significant for him. In Romans 5:19, Paul speaks of the many being made righteous by Christ's obedience. Whether the reference is to Christ's life or his death is keenly debated. The immediate context seems to indicate that Christ's obedience on the cross is uppermost in Paul's thought (see further below). Yet, Christ's submission to God's will in going to the cross is surely understood here as the outgrowth and climax of a faithful and obedient life (cf. Phil 2:8).[7] In 2 Corinthians 5:21, Paul seems to suggest that Christ's sinless life was a precondition of his being "made sin" on the cross (cf. Gal 3:13). Such references intimate a link between the life Jesus lived and his redemptive death.[8]

It would thus be incorrect to maintain that the pre-crucifixion life of Jesus was of no theological consequence to Paul. *How* Jesus lived, at least in general terms, was important to the apostle, certainly for ethics and arguably for salvation. Furthermore, it matters to Paul that the crucified, risen, and living Lord is continuous and consistent with the pre-crucified Jesus. The idea that the apostle could happily go on preaching his gospel fully knowing that the historical reality of Jesus completely undermined his christological claims, we can safely say, is pure fiction.

Paul's Main Christological Titles

While the christological thinking of a New Testament writer cannot be wholly subsumed under the titles he uses for Jesus, the titles and their usage nonetheless constitute important christological data. We focus here on the three christological designations that Paul uses most frequently: "Christ," "Son of God," and "Lord."[9]

Christ

Christos (the Greek word translated "Christ") is the title Paul applies most often to Jesus. It occurs around 270 times in the undisputed letters, more than half the 531 instances in the New Testament (Hurtado 2003, 98–99). Paul uses "Christ," almost, simply to fill out the name of Jesus: "Jesus Christ" (Rom 1:1, 6, 8, etc.) or "Christ Jesus" (Rom 3:24; 6:3, 11, etc.). We commonly find the combination "Lord Jesus Christ" (Rom 1:7; 5:1, 11, etc.). And very frequently, Paul uses "Christ" on its own to identify Jesus (Rom 5:6, 8; 6:4, etc.), a usage already established in the tradition: "Christ" is used to signify Jesus in the pre-Pauline formula of 1 Corinthians 15:3.

Paul's habitual and automatic use of "Christ" for Jesus has often been taken as indicating that the term no longer carries messianic significance for him; it simply functions as a name for Jesus. But what it rather shows is how "firm and routinized" the identification of Jesus as Messiah has become (Hurtado 2003, 99).[10] Paul's application of *Christos* to Jesus always encodes a messianic claim.[11] Paul never makes any attempt in his letters to prove that Jesus is the Messiah. The messianic identity of Jesus is simply taken for granted.

Yet, it is clear that traditional Jewish notions of messiahship have undergone radical transformation in the application of this title to Jesus. This comes out above all in Paul's talk of "Christ crucified" (1 Cor 1:23; 2:2; Gal 3:1) and of the "cross of Christ" (1 Cor 1:17; Gal 6:12, 14; Phil 3:8). There is still no conclusive evidence that first-century Jews expected a crucified Messiah. By preaching "Christ crucified," Paul was making an "absurd paradox" the center of his message (Tuckett 2001, 47).

One of Paul's most characteristic uses of the term "Christ" is in the formula "in Christ" (sometimes "in the Lord": Rom 14:14; 16:2, etc.), rarely found outside of Paul's writings (cf. 1 Pet 3:16; 5:10, 14). The phrase varies in meaning and nuance, but in a significant number of instances, Paul employs it to convey the idea that believers are somehow "included" in Christ (e.g., 1 Cor 15:22; 2 Cor 5:17; Phil 4:21), a key concept in his theology.

Son of God

The designation "Son of God" is much less prominent in Paul than "Christ" and "Lord." It occurs fifteen times (in the undisputed letters); the exact expression "Son of God" is found only three times (Rom 1:4; 2 Cor 1:19; Gal 2:20; cf. Eph 4:13). Nevertheless, it is generally accepted that this christological classification is an important one for Paul. It occurs most often in Romans (1:3, 4, 9; 5:10; 8:3, 29, 32; elsewhere, 1 Cor 1:9; 15:28; 2 Cor 1:19; Gal 1:16; 4:4, 6; 1 Thess 1:10).

One of the applications of the phrase in Judaism was to the Messiah (e.g., 4Q246). But although Paul refers in Romans 1:3 to the Davidic ancestry of God's Son, the designation "Son of God" does not serve as a messianic title in Paul. The expression, in Paul's usage, conveys Jesus' essential relationship to God (especially in talk of Jesus as God's "own" son: Rom 8:3, 32).

References to Jesus as God's Son occur in connection with his death (Rom 5:10; 8:32; Gal 2:20), resurrection (Rom 1:4), return (1 Thess 1:10), and ultimate subjection to the Father (1 Cor 15:28). In Romans 8:3 and Galatians 4:4, Paul speaks of the sending or sending forth of the Son. The verbs "send" (Rom 8:3) and "send forth" (Gal 4:4) need not imply the Son's pre-existence. In the Old Testament, prophets are frequently said to be have been "sent" by God (e.g., Jer 25:4); such "sending" does not presuppose their prior existence. Yet, the thought of the Son appearing in human form, found in both Romans 8:3 and Galatians 4:4, strongly suggests that a schema of pre-existence and incarnation is in play. In Romans 1:3–4, in what is widely accepted as a pre-Pauline formula, we read that Christ "was declared (or appointed) to be Son of God with power ... by resurrection from the dead." The wording seems to aver that Jesus' divine sonship dates from his being raised from the dead. However, the creedal affirmations of vv. 3–4 are governed by Paul's introductory words, "concerning his Son" (1:3), implying that Jesus was God's Son during his "fleshly" earthly existence (and probably before). It may be, as some have argued, that the creedal formulation originally expressed a more adoptionist christology, and that by introducing it in the way he does, and by (allegedly) inserting the words "with power" in v. 4, Paul tries to soften the adoptionist inferences that might be drawn from it (see Jewett 2007, 107). At any rate, the passage as it stands is best interpreted as teaching not that Christ *became* the Son of God at the resurrection (which would be at odds with other statements in Paul about Jesus as God's Son), but rather that at the resurrection Jesus was powerfully shown to be who he was.

Although Paul clearly views Jesus as God's Son in an exclusive sense, he also teaches that believers are drawn into a filial relationship with God modeled on the Son's relationship with the Father. Thus those who have received the Spirit of

God's Son may emulate Jesus in calling God "Abba, Father" (Gal 4:4–7; cf. Rom 8:14–17).

Lord

The title "Lord," *kyrios* in Greek, is used about 180 times of Jesus in the undisputed letters (Hurtado 1993a, 563; 2003, 108). It appears in different formulations: "the Lord Jesus" (Rom 14:14; 1 Cor 5:4; etc.), "the Lord Jesus Christ" (Rom 13:14; 1 Cor 6:11; etc.), "our Lord Jesus Christ" (Rom 5:1, 11; etc.), and "Jesus Christ our Lord" (Rom 1:4; 5:21; etc.). Most often (around 100 times), it is used on its own (with the definite article), designating Jesus as "the Lord" (Rom 14:6, 8; 16:2, 8, 11, 12, 13, 22; etc.).

It is generally accepted that "Jesus is Lord" (Rom 10:9; 1 Cor 12:3) was an early confessional formula. The pre-Pauline application of the appellation "Lord" to Jesus is reflected in the Aramaic expression *Maranatha*, cited by Paul in 1 Corinthians 16:22, which invokes Jesus as Lord (*marêh*) to come (cf. Rev 22:20).

The word *kyrios* was used as a title of respect in the world of the New Testament and often meant "master." The term was also applied to cult deities (e.g., Lord Sarapis). More significantly, it is virtually certain that *kyrios* was employed by Greek-speaking Jews for God's name, YHWH in Hebrew (Tuckett 2001, 20; Hurtado 2003, 109).

A striking feature of Paul's use of the title is his application to Jesus, through citation and allusion, of Old Testament passages referring to God as "the Lord," YHWH (see Capes 1992). Thus in Romans 10:13 he cites Joel 2:32, "everyone who calls on the name of the Lord shall be saved," implicitly identifying Jesus as the Lord (see also 1 Cor 1:31; 2 Cor 10:17; etc.). Philippians 2:9–11 alludes to the words of Isaiah 45:23 ("unto me every knee shall bow, every tongue shall swear") and applies them to Jesus, as the one who has been given "the name that is above every name," i.e., the name "Lord." Isaiah 45:22–23 is one of the strongest monotheistic affirmations in the Old Testament, so its transference to Jesus is a startling move. No less striking is Paul's "christologizing" of the Old Testament eschatological motifs of "day of the Lord" and the coming of the Lord (cf. Zech 14:5). The former becomes the "day of Christ" (Phil 1:10; 2:16), or "the day of the/our Lord Jesus Christ" (1 Cor 1:8; 2 Cor 1:14; see Kreitzer 1987, 112–128), while the latter becomes the coming/*parousia* of the Lord Jesus (1 Thess 3:13; 4:16–17; see Adams 2006).

It would be easy to conclude from this evidence that Paul is equating God with Christ, but this would be too simplistic (a simple equation of Christ and God would make Paul a Christomonist). There are a significant number of Old Testament citations and allusions in which Paul retains the original reference to God (Rom 4:17; 9:9, 13, etc.). Moreover, in numerous passages, Paul distinguishes the Lord Jesus from God or the Father (Rom 1:7; 5:1; 15:6; 1 Cor 3:1; etc.). Even in Philippians 2:9–11, with its exalted claims about Christ, a hierarchical distinction is drawn between Jesus Christ the Lord and God the Father.

An important indication of how Paul understood the Lordship of Jesus Christ in relation to God is found in 1 Corinthians 8:5–6, another text which many scholars take to be a pre-Pauline formulation (with Pauline insertions). The wording of 8:6 is unmistakably influenced by Deuteronomy 6:4, part of the *Shema*, the traditional Jewish confession of God's oneness. The Greek (Septuagintal) version of Deuteronomy 6:4 reads, "Hear Israel: The Lord our God, the Lord is one." 1 Corinthians 8:6 affirms that "there is one God, the Father ... and one Lord, Jesus Christ ... ." The Jewish confession of God's uniqueness is thus split between God and Christ. In this "dramatically redrawn monotheism" (Hurtado 1993a, 565), Christ is included in the "divine identity"[12] as "Lord," while distinguished from "God, the Father." Such a conceptual distinction seems generally to underlie Paul's application of "Lord," in its divine sense, to Jesus.

On numerous occasions, Paul uses the term "Lord" of Jesus not, or at least not principally, as a divine title, but with the primary meaning "master." Thus, for example, in 1 Corinthians 7:32, to "please the Lord" means to please Jesus as the one to whom allegiance is owed (see also 1 Cor 6:13, 17; 7:22, 34, 35, 39; etc.). In his careful analysis of the relevant data in Paul, Larry Hurtado has noted that Jesus is referred to as "Lord" in three main contexts (1993a, 566–569): hortatory (relating to Christian conduct), eschatological (with reference to the *parousia*, coming judgment, etc.), and liturgical (in passages having to do with or reflect the church's worship). In hortatory contexts, Hurtado argues, *kyrios* primarily means "master"; in eschatological texts, Christ is accorded the end-time role of God; and in liturgical contexts, *kyrios* designates Jesus as the transcendent one who has been incorporated into the church's devotional life.

We may, therefore, distinguish varying nuances and connotations of the title *kyrios* as it is given to Jesus. It is clear, though, that in a good number of instances, the application of it to Jesus reflects and expresses an extremely high christology, associating Jesus with God the Father in the closest possible way and including Jesus in the divine identity.

Paul's Adam Christology

Another title used of Jesus by Paul is "the last Adam" (1 Cor 15:45), identifying Jesus as a new and final Adam. Paul's Adam christology is arguably his most distinctive christological contribution (see Barrett 1962; Dunn 1980, 108–113; 1998, 199–204). The notion of Jesus as a new Adam may be detected elsewhere in the New Testament, outside Paul (in the story of Jesus' temptation and in Hebrews 2:5–9), but it is Paul who develops the Adam–Christ parallel most explicitly and extensively. In Romans, the Adamic role of Jesus is central to the soteriology developed therein (Adams 2002, 26–39).

There are two places where Paul explicitly draws a comparison between Adam and Christ: Romans 5:12–21 and 1 Corinthians 15. Although the latter was written first, it makes sense to take Romans 5:12–21 first, since it focuses on the Christ's death, while 1 Corinthians 15 dwells on his resurrection.

In Romans 5:12–21, Adam and Christ are presented as determinative figures: persons whose actions affect the destiny of others. A basic similarity between the two individuals is assumed (v. 14). Yet, it is the contrast between the two that receives the greater attention. Whereas Adam was disobedient, Christ was obedient and faithful. Adam's disobedience resulted in sin, death, and condemnation for all; Christ's obedience brings righteousness, life, and acquittal. Paul understands Adam's transgression (in the Garden of Eden) as the means of entry into the world of sin and death as tyrannical powers. A causal connection between Adam's sin and subsequent human sinfulness is assumed. The precise nature of that connection, however, is not made clear. As noted earlier, the "obedience" of Christ in this passage is specifically his death on the cross (though as the culmination of an obedient life). The word "obedience" in v. 19 is rhetorically equivalent to "act of righteousness" (*dikaiōma*) in the previous verse, which points to a singular deed. The contrast with Adam's transgression also looks for a definitive expression of obedience. What Christ has achieved by means of his obedient death more than compensates for Adam's trespass ("much more," 5:15, 17; "abounded," 5:15; "abundance of grace," 5.17; "abounded all the more," 5:20), and its positive results more than outweigh the negative outcome of Adam's misdeed. In rectifying the plight initiated by Adam, Christ makes available again the "eternal life" (5:21) that the first man forfeited (cf. Gen 2:9; 3:22).

In 1 Corinthians 15, the Adam–Christ parallel forms part of Paul's defense of and rationale for bodily resurrection. In vv. 21–22, having identified the risen Christ as "the first fruits" of the resurrection of the dead (v. 20), he draws a contrast between Adam, as the means through which death entered the world (cf. Rom 5:12), and Christ, as the source of resurrection life. In vv. 45–49, he draws a further contrast between Adam and Christ in the course of explaining the difference between the present body and the resurrection body. Adam is presented as the archetype of the "physical body," *sōma psychikon*, and Christ, the archetype of the "spiritual body," *sōma pneumatikon*. Adam, the first human, formed from the dust, was made a living *psyche* (Gen 2:7). Christ, the final Adam, became – through his resurrection – a life-giving *pneuma* (Spirit). All human beings bear the image of Adam and possess a mortal and corruptible body like his. But at the coming resurrection, those who are Christ's will bear his image and will be given a glorious, imperishable body. Christ is thus portrayed here as the progenitor and prototype of a new humanity.

In 1 Corinthians 15:48–49, Christ is called "the man of heaven" in contrast to Adam as "the man of dust" (vv. 48–49). The designation is intriguing. Paul could be referring to Jesus' heavenly status as risen and ascended Lord. However, the formulation more readily points to Christ's heavenly origin, and so seems to indicate his pre-existence.

Paul's Adam christology is not confined to these texts. It is implicit in the application of Psalm 8:6 to Christ in 1 Corinthians 15:27 and Philippians 3:21, and in his talk of Christ as the image of God who transforms people into that image (2 Cor 3:18;

4:4; cf. Rom 8:29). A contrast with Adam may also be at work in Philippians 2:5–11 (see below).

Pre-existence and Divinity

Whether Paul ascribes pre-existence to Jesus and whether he regards him as a divine being are key issues in the scholarly discussion of Paul's christology. We have already touched on these issues, but we must now address them more directly.

The debate about pre-existence is fairly recent. James D. G. Dunn, in a study first published in 1980 (Dunn 1980; see also 1998, 266–293), challenged the consensus by arguing that there is no clear belief in Christ's personal pre-existence and incarnation in the Pauline epistles: such a belief only comes to expression in the late first century (John 1:1–18). The debate has been a lively one, but the majority of scholars still agree that there are some passages in Paul that do reflect the idea of Christ's previous existence. We noted above several texts that seem to involve the notion (Rom 8:3; Gal 4:4; 1 Cor 15:47–49). To this list may be added 1 Corinthians 8.6, discussed above in another connection. Here Christ, as Lord, is said to be the one "through whom are all things." This statement accords him the role of God's agent in creation. Dunn (1998, 274) argues that Christ is seen here as the human embodiment of God's attribute of wisdom, which is sometimes depicted in personified terms (Prov 8:22–31; Wis 7:22–8:21). Thus, what is being affirmed is the pre-existence of divine wisdom, not the personal pre-existence of Christ. The problem with this reading, as Hurtado points out, is that it is not what the text actually says. Even if wisdom is being drawn upon and adapted here, this text does "attribute to Jesus personally a pre-existence and a central role in creation" (Hurtado 2003, 126). Another passage that seems to convey the thought of Christ's pre-existence is 2 Corinthians 8:9, which states "that though he was rich, yet for your sakes he became poor." That "he was rich" suggests a former state of existence.

For most scholars, the clearest expression of Christ's actual pre-existence in Paul is Philippians 2:5–11, widely regarded as a hymn used in early Christian worship that Paul is citing. Consequently this passage has been the most intensely debated. Verses 6 to 8 contain the key statements:

> 6. who, though he was in the form of God,
> did not regard equality with God
> as something to be exploited,
> 7. but emptied himself,
> taking the form of a slave,
> being born in human likeness.
> And being found in human form,
> 8. he humbled himself
> and became obedient to the point of death –
> even death on a cross. (New Revised Standard Version)

Traditionally, these verses have been interpreted as describing Christ's pre-human status and incarnation. Dunn argues that the text refers to the earthly Jesus, with no real thought of his previous existence (1998, 283–288). According to Dunn, Jesus is being contrasted with Adam, who was in the "form of God," which Dunn takes to be synonymous with being made in God's "image" (Gen 1:26–27), and who succumbed to the temptation to be "like God" (Gen 3:5). Unlike Adam, Jesus resisted grasping at equality with God and instead humbled himself and took the path that led to the cross.

However, there is little evidence that the phrase "form of God," *morphē theou*, was used as equivalent to "image of God," *eikōn theou* (Hurtado 2003, 122). When Jewish writers want to allude to the Genesis 1 notion of being created in God's image, the word *eikōn* is regularly used (Wis 2:23; Sir 17:3). Paul himself, when evoking this theme, consistently uses *eikōn* (Rom 8:29; 1 Cor 11:7; 15:49; 2 Cor 3:18; 4:4; cf. Col 3:10). Also, "equality with God" is most likely to be understood as a status *already held* by Christ, one which he refused to take advantage of for selfish gain.[13] Moreover, talk of Christ *actively existing* (this is the sense of the verb employed) in the form of God and then *taking* the form of a servant strongly suggests a prior and subsequent state, with the lines of v. 7b indicating that the change of state involved becoming human ("being born" is literally "having become").

One can still recognize a comparison with Adam, but with Christ's decision to empty himself understood as taking place in a heavenly setting. We have seen from 1 Corinthians 15:47–49 that Paul can hold together an Adamic view of Christ and a notion of Christ's heavenly origin. As Hurtado observes, a heavenly figure exercising humility and descending into a human life of service, and a human being vainly attempting to rise above his creaturely status make for a rather powerful contrast (1993b, 745).[14]

As to the question of Christ's divinity,[15] we have noted that the attribution to Jesus of a divine status is involved in the designation "Son of God" (at least in some instances) and, at least in certain passages, in the application to him of the title "Lord." In two places, Paul seems to refer to Christ as God: Romans 9:5 and Philippians 2:6. The interpretation of Romans 9:5 partly involves a decision about how it ought to be punctuated (the earliest Greek manuscripts are unpunctuated). The disputed line can be read either as "from them [the patriarchs] comes the Christ, who is God over all, blessed forever" or as "from them comes the Christ. God, who is over all, [be] blessed forever." The word order definitely favors the first reading, i.e., the identification of Christ as God (Jewett 2007, 567–568). On the other hand, Paul is talking in this context about "the Christ," i.e., the Messiah as a figure of Jewish expectation, and not specifically about Jesus, and there is little evidence that first-century Jews thought of the Messiah as God. This would favor the second reading, which sees a separate blessing directed to God. The verse is at best ambiguous and so should probably not be used as a proof-text for Paul's belief in the deity of Jesus.

Philippians 2:6, as we have seen, is also debated. However, as I have pointed out, it is unlikely that the text is merely saying that Christ, like Adam, was a human being made in God's image. The Greek word *morphē*, as commentators have stressed (e.g.,

Fee 1995, 204; O'Brien 1991, 210), signifies a form that genuinely expresses the underlying reality. Thus, the claim that Jesus was in the "form of God" means that he possessed a divine status. Alongside the attribution of "equality with God" (understood as something Christ possessed but did not exploit), it makes Christ, in some sense, a divine being.

It must be emphasized again, though, that Paul does not straightforwardly equate Christ and God. Christ as Lord or Son is consistently distinguished from God the Father, and at key points *subordinated* to him (1 Cor 15:27–28; Phil 2:9–11).

The Christological Teaching of the Disputed Letters

We turn our attention now, and more briefly, to the disputed Pauline letters.

2 Thessalonians

2 Thessalonians exhibits a strong eschatological interest, but in terms of christology, worthy of note is the extent to which "the Lord Jesus" takes on the traditional role of God in his eschatological coming. At a number of points, the author alludes to Old Testament "coming of God" texts and applies them to Jesus as returning Lord: 2 Thessalonians 1:7 (Zech 14:5); 1:8 (Isa 66:15); 2:1 (Isa 66:18); and 2:8 (Isa 30:27–28).

Colossians and Ephesians

Colossians and Ephesians, sometimes called the "Deutero-Pauline Letters" are usually discussed in tandem, with Colossians taken first, and the Pastoral Epistles treated as a distinct set. The christological titles "Christ" and "Lord" are frequent in both Colossians and Ephesians. "In Christ" language is especially prominent in Ephesians (1:1, 3, 4, 9, etc.). The designation "Son (of God)" occurs just once in each letter (Col 1:13; Eph 4:13).

Colossians is rich in christological content. The most important christological passage is Colossians 1:15–20. Most scholars agree that this portion of text represents a pre-formed unit, possibly a hymn like that of Philippians 2:5–11. Although details of the hymnic structure are debated, a two-part division, with each "stanza" beginning with "He is ... ," is widely recognized. The first stanza celebrates Christ's role in creation (Col 1:15–17), while the second focuses on his redemptive role (1:18–20).

Christ is said to be "the image of the invisible God" and "the firstborn of all creation" (v. 15). The latter phrase appears to suggest that Christ belongs to the order of creation. However, the immediate context rules this out: the verses that follow make clear that he is prior to creation, distinct from it, and above it. The underlying Greek is thus better translated, "firstborn *over* all creation." The three phrases "in him," "through him" and "for him" have connotations derived from ancient philosophy (Sterling 1997). They identify Christ as the agent and goal of creation.

Agency in creation was assigned to Christ in 1 Corinthians 8:6, but the thought that all things were made for *his* benefit (rather than God's) is new. Not only is he the purpose of creation, he is also its principle of coherence: "in him all things hold together" (Col 1:17). Again, the statement has philosophical evocations, suggesting a force that binds everything together, imposing and maintaining the stability that makes the world a cosmos (ordered system).

There are clearly parallels between how Christ is described in this half of this hymn and what is said of divine wisdom (cf. Dunn 1998, 269–270): "an image of his goodness" (Wis 7:26), "the fashioner of all things" (Wis 7:22), something that "pervades and penetrates all things" (Wis 7:24).[16] However, it would be missing the point to deduce that these verses are honoring an attribute of God that subsequently came to be embodied in the man Jesus. The repetition of "He is" in 1:18 makes clear that the subject of the first stanza is also the subject of the second, and there is no doubt that the latter is the person of Jesus Christ. Moreover, in the literary context, the "He is" of 1:15 refers back to the "beloved Son" of v. 13.

From Christ's role in creation, the thought moves to his redemptive significance. The claim that he is "the head of the body, the church" (v. 18) emphasizes his sovereignty over the redeemed people. He is said to be "the beginning," which probably means "the beginning *of the new creation*," matching the epithet, "firstborn from the dead." The latter is equivalent to the phrase "first fruits of those who have died" in 1 Corinthians 15.20. We are told that all the divine "fullness" was pleased to dwell in him and to reconcile "all things" to him. The reference to "all things" underscores the cosmic compass of Christ's redemptive work, the reconciling effects of the cross extending to the whole created order.

Striking christological claims are also found in the rest of the letter, some of which reinforce and extend statements in the hymn: that "in him the whole fullness of deity dwells bodily" (2:10); that "he is the head of every ruler and authority" (2:10); and that "Christ is all and in all" (3:11).

The cosmic significance of Christ is also underlined in Ephesians. Ephesians 1:10 speaks of God's intention to "gather up all things in him, things in heaven and things on earth." In 1:20–23, the climax of the opening prayer, we read that Christ has been exalted to God's right hand, "far above all rule and authority and power and dominion." The statement that follows, that God has "put all things under his feet" (alluding to Psalm 8:6) and has made him "head over all things," further emphasizes Christ's cosmic sovereignty. It is noteworthy that Christ is said to have been made cosmic head for the sake of "the church" (v. 22), defined as "his body." This is indicative of the close relation between christology and ecclesiology in the letter. The final clause of v. 23 makes the church the "fullness" of Christ, as he progressively fills the whole universe (cf. 4:10). The theme of Christ as head of the church is reiterated in 4:15 and 5:23. In 5:23, 31–32, Christ's relation to the church is represented as that of husband to wife.

One of the most puzzling christological remarks in the letter is the mention in 4:9–10 of Christ's descent into "the lower parts of the earth" (explicating Psalm

68:18). This appears to be an early reference to Christ's descent into Hades after the crucifixion and before the ascension, though some see a reference to the incarnation. Much less likely is an allusion to Christ's descent into the church, through the Spirit, at Pentecost, though this interpretation is preferred by Lincoln (1990, 244–247).

The Pastoral Epistles

The christological titles "Christ" and "Lord" are well represented in the Pastoral Epistles. The title "Son," though, does not appear. A title that does crop up quite often is "savior" (given to Christ in Phil 3:20 and Eph 5:23). On six occasions it is used of God (1 Tim 1:1; 2:3; 4:10; Titus 1:3; 2:10; 3:4) and four times, it is applied to Jesus (2 Tim 1:10; Titus 1:4; 2:13; 3:6). The sharing out of this title between God and Christ, according to Hurtado, points to "a deliberate effort to link them" (Hurtado 2003, 516).

In 1 Timothy, there are three key christological confessions. The first, in 1:15, states that "Christ Jesus came into the world to save sinners." The words "came into the world" may simply indicate that Christ was born, like every human being, but they could also imply his pre-existence (cf. John 3:17; 6:14; 10:36; 11:27; 16:28; Heb 10:5). The second, in 2:5–6, lauds Christ Jesus as "the one mediator between God and humankind." The third, in 3:16, summarizes the career of Christ:

> He was revealed in flesh, vindicated in spirit,
> seen by angels, proclaimed among Gentiles,
> believed in throughout the world, taken up in glory.

This formulation consists of three pairs of contrasting statements. "Revealed in flesh" encompasses the earthly life of Christ; "vindicated in spirit" seems to refer to his resurrection (cf. Rom 1:4). "Seen by angels" alludes to his post-resurrection appearance in heaven, which is counterbalanced by the proclamation of his exaltation "among Gentiles" (or "among the nations"). The third line contrasts his acceptance on earth by those who have believed the gospel with his glorious reception in heaven at the ascension. Whether the initial phrase "revealed in flesh" implies Christ's pre-existence is debated.

1 Timothy 6:13 refers to Christ's trial before Pilate as an illustration of faithful testimony. This is a rare instance in the Pauline epistles of an appeal to Jesus' example with reference to a specific incident his life.

Titus 2:13 *may* refer to Jesus as God. The text speaks of a glorious divine manifestation, which is either that of Jesus *and* God or that of Jesus alone, who is identified as "our great God and savior." It is difficult to know which of these two meanings is intended. But even if "our great God" and Jesus Christ are distinguished here, they are nevertheless so closely associated as to be joint subjects of a singular eschatological manifestation.

Conclusion

For Paul, Jesus is Christ, Son of God, Lord, and the last Adam. As Christ, he fulfills and transforms messianic expectation. As Son of God, he holds a unique status and enjoys a unique relationship with God (though he confers some of the benefits of his sonship upon others). As Lord, he is the supreme master, acts in the divine capacity (in some contexts), and receives the divine name (again in some contexts). As last Adam, he triumphs where the first Adam failed, replacing condemnation with justification; he is the founder of a new humanity, and the one who brings to fulfillment God's original purposes in creating human beings. Jesus can be spoken of as preexistent and as divine, and placed alongside God the Father.

It is quite astonishing that a writer can accord such titles, roles, and attributes to Jesus within twenty to thirty years (or thereabouts) of his execution. Yet Paul was no christological innovator, foisting upon the early church an understanding of Jesus alien to existing thinking. The main titles Paul ascribes to Jesus (Christ, Son of God, Lord) were already part of pre-Pauline tradition, and Christ's pre-existence and "divinity" were, so it seems, already being celebrated in the churches through creedal formulation and hymn. Thus while it is staggering that Paul can say the things he does about Jesus so quickly after Jesus' death, even more remarkable is the christological development that had already taken place by the time Paul wrote (Hurtado 2003, 153; Tuckett 2001, 66).

Notes

1   For an overview of the scholarly debate on the relation between Jesus and Paul, see Barclay 1993.
2   All quotations of the Bible in this chapter are taken from the New Revised Standard Version.
3   One may contrast the minimalist position of Walter (1989), who recognizes only the explicit citations, with the maximalist approach of Wenham (1995), who finds very many echoes of Jesus' teaching in Paul.
4   Why are these echoes mixed in with other maxims and not specifically flagged as sayings of Jesus?
5   Admittedly, there is no evidence of such a sketch in the brief glimpses Paul gives us of the content of his missionary preaching (1 Thess 1:9–10; 1 Cor 2:2); cf. Barclay 1993, 499.
6   Bultmann (1966, 239) insisted that *Christ is not an exemplar* for Paul.
7   Whether or not Paul's teaching on justification *requires* some notion of Christ's "active" obedience (i.e., perfect obedience to God's will manifested throughout the course of his life) is quite another matter.
8   In Romans 5:10, Paul speaks of being "saved" by Christ's life, but here Christ's risen life seems to be in view (cf. Rom 6:10).

9   Other designations include "wisdom of God" (1 Cor 1:24, 30), "power of God" (1 Cor 1:24), "our paschal lamb" (1 Cor 5:7), "image of God" (2 Cor 4:4), "savior" (Phil 3:20), and "servant" (Rom 15:8).

10   Paul refers to "the Christ" as a figure of Jewish messianic expectation in Romans 9:5.

11   Wright (1991, 41) contends that the term *Christos* in Paul should regularly be read as "Messiah."

12   The term "divine identity" comes from Bauckham (1998), who argues that New Testament christology is "a Christology of divine identity" (p. viii).

13   This seems to be the sense of the key phrase *ouch harpagmon hēgēsato*: see Hoover 1971; Wright 1991, 62–90.

14   On the compatibility of Adam christology and the idea of incarnation, see Wright 1991, 90–97.

15   In discussing this question, one must be careful not to project back onto Paul the categories of later christological debates and confessions.

16   Yet what is said of Christ in these verses is not fully understandable against the background of wisdom. For the influence of contemporary Greco-Roman cosmological thought, see Van Kooten 2003, 121–129.

References

Adams, Edward (2002). "Paul's Story of God and Creation." In Bruce W. Longenecker (ed.), *Narrative Dynamics in Paul: A Critical Assessment* (pp. 19–43). Louisville, KY: Westminster John Knox.

Adams, Edward (2006). "The Coming of God Tradition and its Influence on New Testament Parousia Texts." In Charlotte Hempel and Judith M. Lieu (eds.), *Biblical Traditions in Transmission: Essays in Honour of Michael A. Knibb* (pp. 1–19). Leiden: Brill.

Barclay, J. M. G. (1993). "Jesus and Paul." In Gerald F. Hawthorne, Ralph P. Martin, and Daniel G. Reid (eds.), *Dictionary of Paul and His Letters* (pp. 492–503). Downers Grove, IL, and Leicester: InterVarsity.

Barrett, C. K. (1962). *From First Adam to Last: A Study in Pauline Theology*. London: Black.

Bauckham, Richard J. (1998). *God Crucified: Monotheism and Christology in the New Testament*. Carlisle: Paternoster.

Bultmann, Rudolf (1952). *Theology of the New Testament*. Vol. 1. London: SCM.

Bultmann, Rudolf (1966). *Faith and Understanding*. Vol. I. New York: Harper & Row.

Bruce, F. F. (1966). "Jesus and Paul." *Theological Students Fellowship Bulletin* 46: 21–26.

Burridge, Richard A. (2004). *What are the Gospels? A Comparison with Graeco-Roman Biography*. 2nd edn. Grand Rapids: Eerdmans.

Burridge, Richard A. (2007). *Imitating Jesus: An Inclusive Approach to New Testament Ethics*. Grand Rapids: Eerdmans.

Capes, David B. (1992). *Old Testament Yahweh Texts in Paul's Christology*. Tübingen: Mohr Siebeck.

Dunn, James D. G. (1980). *Christology in the Making*. London: SCM.

Dunn, James D. G. (1998). *The Theology of Paul the Apostle*. Grand Rapids: Eerdmans.

Fee, Gordon D. (1995). *Paul's Letter to the Philippians*. Grand Rapids: Eerdmans.

Hoover, Roy W. (1971). "The Harpagmos Enigma: A Philological Solution." *Harvard Theological Review* 64: 95–119.

Horrell, David G. (2005). *Solidarity and Difference: A Contemporary Reading of Paul's Ethics*. London, New York: T&T Clark.

Hurtado, Larry W. (1993a). "Lord." In Gerald F. Hawthorne, Ralph P. Martin, and Daniel G. Reid (eds.), *Dictionary of Paul and His Letters* (pp. 560–569). Downers Grove, IL, and Leicester: InterVarsity.

Hurtado, Larry W. (1993b). "Pre-existence." In Gerald F. Hawthorne, Ralph P. Martin, and Daniel G. Reid (eds.), *Dictionary of Paul and His Letters* (pp. 743–746). Downers Grove, IL, and Leicester: InterVarsity.

Hurtado, Larry W. (2003). *Lord Jesus Christ: Devotion to Jesus in Earliest Christianity*, Grand Rapids and Cambridge: Eerdmans.

Jewett, Robert (2007). *Romans: A Commentary*. Minneapolis: Fortress.

Kreitzer, Larry J. (1987). *Jesus and God in Paul's Eschatology*. Sheffield: JSOT.

Lincoln, Andrew T. (1990). *Ephesians*. Dallas: Word.

O'Brien, Peter T. (1991). *The Epistle to the Philippians: A Commentary on the Greek Text*. Grand Rapids: Eerdmans.

Stanton, Graham N. (2004). *Jesus and Gospel*. Cambridge: Cambridge University Press.

Sterling, Gregory E. (1997). "Prepositional Metaphysics in Jewish Wisdom Speculation and Early Christian Liturgical Texts." In David T. Runia and Gregory E. Sterling (eds.), *Wisdom and Logos: Studies in Jewish Thought* (pp. 219–238). Atlanta, GA: Scholars.

Thompson, Michael B. (1991). *Clothed with Christ: The Example and Teaching of Jesus in Romans 12.1–15.13*. Sheffield: JSOT.

Tuckett, Christopher M. (2001). *Christology and the New Testament*. Edinburgh: Edinburgh University Press.

Van Kooten, Geurt Hendrik (2003). *Cosmic Christology in Paul and the Pauline School: Colossians and Ephesians in the Context of Graeco-Roman Cosmology, with a New Synopsis of the Greek Texts*. Tübingen: Mohr Siebeck.

Walter, Nikolaus (1989). "Paul and the Early Christian Jesus-Tradition." In A. J. M. Wedderburn (ed.), *Paul and Jesus: Collected Essays*. Sheffield: JSOT.

Wenham, David (1995). *Paul: Follower of Jesus or Founder of Christianity?* Grand Rapids: Eerdmans.

Wright, N. T. (1991). *The Climax of the Covenant*. Edinburgh: T&T Clark.

CHAPTER 7

Jesus in the General Epistles

Harold W. Attridge

The general or "catholic" epistles (Hebrews; James; 1, 2, and 3 John; 1 and 2 Peter; and Jude) include all the letters in the New Testament other than those attributed to Paul. They represent several strands of Christian tradition of the late first and early second century CE. All affirm the significance of Jesus as the ground of Christian life. They do so with few references to his deeds or explicit teaching, but with considerable attention to his death, exaltation, and return in judgment. Discussions of Jesus in these letters can be found elsewhere in surveys of New Testament christology (e.g., Powell and Bauer 1999; Tuckett 2001) and in more narrowly focused monographs (e.g., Bechtler 1998; Mason 2008; McCruden 2008).

The Epistle of James

The opening salutation of the Epistle of James signals the significance of Jesus. The letter comes from "James, a servant of God and of the Lord Jesus Christ" to "the twelve tribes in the Dispersion" (James 1:1). The author invokes faith in the glorified Jesus as the shared presupposition of his addressees, particularly as he begins his discourse on impartiality: "My brothers and sisters do you with your acts of favoritism really believe in our glorious Lord Jesus Christ?" (2:1). The second coming of Jesus frames the eschatological horizon within which the community lives: "Be patient, therefore, beloved, until the coming of the Lord" (5:7).

Despite these prominent references to Jesus, James provides no other explicit data about his life, deeds, teaching, death, or resurrection. Hence the appeal to Jesus seems to be rather formal, and the letter says nothing to justify the significance of the present or future Lordship of Jesus.

The epistle's exhortations do, however, occasionally echo the teachings of Jesus. That one should be doer and not just a hearer of the word (1:22) recalls Jesus'

The Blackwell Companion to Jesus, First Edition. Edited by Delbert Burkett. ©2014 John Wiley & Sons, Ltd. Published 2014 by John Wiley & Sons, Ltd.

admonition not just to listen but to act (Matt 7:26). The emphasis in the same context on doing the "perfect Law of freedom" (James 1:25) recalls the version of Jesus' teaching found in the Sermon on the Mount in Matthew, where he solemnly proclaimed that "not one letter, not one stroke of a letter" from the Law would be abrogated, "until all is accomplished" (Matt 5:8). Matthew and James thus share an approach to Christian life that, at least in theory, is Torah-observant and critical of those who rely solely on faith (James 2:14–26), perhaps a critique of Pauline circles. While James stands with Matthew, the epistle does not explicitly cite Jesus in favor of its position.

Neither does the epistle mention Jesus when it names the core principle of the "royal Law according to the Scripture, 'You shall love your neighbor as yourself'" (James 2:8, citing Lev 19:18). Jesus cited the same verse in the synoptic accounts of the love command (Matt 19:19; 22:39; Mark 12:31; Luke 10:27), as did Paul in his letters (Rom 13:9; Gal 5:14).

For the Epistle of James, therefore, Jesus is the past and future Lord of those whose morals the author wants to shape, with teachings that at least recall those attributed to Jesus.

The Johannine Epistles

The Johannine epistles afford a window into the community connected with the Gospel of John and probably reflect controversies within the Johannine community over the interpretation of the gospel and the kind of belief and practice that it requires.

The opening paragraph of 1 John, replete with allusions to the gospel, heralds its focus on Jesus by proclaiming that "truly our fellowship is with the Father and with his Son Jesus Christ" (1 John 1:3). It is not the Jesus of sacred memory that is important, but the Jesus who is present to the community of his disciples, through whom they now enjoy fellowship with God, like the branches on the true vine (John 15:1–17).

Having fellowship with God through Jesus involves professing certain fundamental truths about him (1 John 2:24). Many of these claims focus on the salvific work that Jesus accomplished: his blood cleanses us from all sin (1 John 1:7; 2:2); he appeared to destroy the works of the devil (1 John 3:8); the Father sent him "to be the atoning sacrifice (*hilasmos*) for our sins" (1 John 4:10) and "the savior of the world" (1 John 4:14). Other affirmations involve his continuing role as mediator, or advocate (*paraklētos*) for his community before the Father (1 John 2:1; cf. John 14:26; 16:13). Proper recognition of Jesus is essential for the relationship: "God abides in those who confess that Jesus is the Son of God, and they abide in God" (1 John 4:15; cf. 5:1, 5).

The necessity for a proper christological confession can also be expressed negatively. The "liar" who "denies that Jesus is the Christ" is an "antichrist" (1 John 2:22). The position being castigated may either be that of those who oppose any form of adherence to Jesus or to those who have a defective form of Christian faith.

The latter is certainly the situation in the contrast between what true believers profess and what "false prophets" and the "antichrist" teach: "Every spirit that confesses that Jesus Christ has come in the flesh is from God and every spirit that does not confess Jesus is not from God" (1 John 4:2–3). At issue here is some form of "docetism," either a denial of the full humanity of Jesus or a denial that his human nature was significant for his followers. The epistles of Ignatius of Antioch provide roughly contemporary evidence for the presence of such claims among early second-century Christians.

Other important truths about Jesus that one must affirm to have a proper relationship to him are that the community lives in the last hour (1 John 2:18) and awaits his return (1 John 2:28). Symbolic actions also mediate the presence of Jesus, who comes "by water and blood" (1 John 5:6). This phrase may allude to aspects of the story of Jesus' earthly life, which began in his encounter with John the Baptist (although the Fourth Gospel does not record Jesus' baptism) and ends with the shedding of his blood on the cross. The phrase may also refer to the mixture of water and blood that flows from Jesus' side in the Johannine account of the crucifixion (John 19:34). Whatever elements of the story of Jesus are evoked by the phrase, it introduces a reflection on the unity of "the Spirit, the water, and the Blood," which hints at the rites of baptism and eucharist through which the Spirit is present to the disciples. (The passage on the unified triad of Spirit, blood, and water in 5:7–8 attracted a Trinitarian interpolation found primarily in the Latin tradition, the so-called *Comma Johanneum*.)

Subscribing to certain dogmatic claims about Jesus is of fundamental importance but is not enough. Keeping his commandments is the way in which the law of love is perfected (1 John 2:4–5; cf. John 13:34–35; 15:10). The commandments to be kept are not specified. The central moral imperative, as in the gospel, is to love (1 John 2:7; 4:7), a love grounded in the love that God showed to the world by sending his Son (1 John 4:8–12). To live by that command is to walk in the light (1:5; cf. John 8:12; 12:35). To claim to be in the light but to hate one's brother or sister is in fact to be in darkness (1 John 2:9). To hate one's brother or sister is equivalent to murder (1 John 3:15; cf. Matt 5:22). Similarly, "desire of the flesh, the desire of the eyes, the pride in riches" (1 John 2:16) are all aspects of loving the world that are incompatible with the commandment to love.

The overall message of 1 John can be summarized in its version of the great commandment: "And this is his commandment, that we should believe in the name of his Son Jesus Christ and love one another, just as he has commanded us" (1 John 3:23).

1 Peter

The first epistle of Peter, purportedly "an apostle of Jesus Christ," offers a message of encouragement to the "elect sojourners of the Diaspora, in Pontus, Galatia, Cappadocia, (the province of) Asia and Bithynia" (1 Pet 1:1). The author, claiming to write from "Babylon" (i.e., Rome) with Mark, "his son," with him (5:13), makes several oblique references to the challenges that these followers of Jesus were facing (1:6; 3:14; 4:12–19). They may have been socially marginalized, true "aliens and sojourners" (2:11), or it may be that their adherence to Christ had brought them persecution and opprobrium. The author in fact refers to the persecution of these disciples "as Christians" (3:16), and expresses concern with how they might give an "apology" for themselves (3:15).

The letter's overarching strategy is to reinforce for these Christians a vision of their identity as God's special people, "an elect race, a royal priesthood, a holy nation, a people set apart" (2:9), called upon to distinguish themselves by their behavior. The author points to Jesus as the essential element of the identity that he wants to support and as an example of the behavior that he wants to encourage. Through his death and resurrection, appropriated through baptism (3:21–22), God has provided a new possibility of life for the addressees, which they are called upon to understand and to live (5:10).

The conceptual structure of this hortatory epistle is clear from the first chapter. The author reminds his addressees of the effect of Christ's resurrection on their lives, as the source of a "new birth into a living hope and into an inheritance that is imperishable, undefiled, and unfading" (1:3–4). That hope has an eschatological focus in the second coming of Christ, when those who believe in him will receive "praise and glory and honor" (1:7). The author also recalls the effect of Christ's death, in which believers were "ransomed" by the "precious blood of Christ" (1:18–19). Those who have been ransomed share in the Spirit of Christ (1:7), which now should guide their behavior, leading them to holiness (1:16), focused on love (1:22).

The rest of the epistle reflects further on the Christ event and offers exhortations to live up to the possibilities that it created. The author continues by evoking the image of the community as a living temple (2:1–10), a "holy priesthood" (2:5) founded on the cornerstone that is Christ. To develop that image, the author calls upon scriptural texts (2:6–8): Isaiah 28:16 for the "stone in Zion," and Psalm 118:22 for the rejected stone that has become the cornerstone, a stone that also causes some to stumble (Isa 8:14). Psalm 118:22 at least is known from other early Christian traditions (Matt 21:42; Acts 4:11), and all of the "stone" texts in this section may have circulated as a catena applied to Christ, the foundation on which the community is built and also a cause of scandal to those without.

As part of his call to holiness, the author urges both symbolic marginalization, as "aliens and exiles from the desires of the flesh" (2:11), and actual submission to structures of social and political authority. All "servants of God," who "live as free people" (2:16) must obey governing authorities (2:13). The author then exhorts people in various stations in life to accept the specific form of authority appropriate to them (2:13–3:7). In commenting on the duties of slaves to obey their masters, he explicitly cites the model of Christ, who "suffered for you, leaving you an example" (2:21). Once again a scriptural passage, from one of Isaiah's servant songs, "He committed no sin and no deceit was found in his mouth" (Isa 53:9), drives home the point.

The evocation of Christ's suffering, initially used to ground a call to obedience by slaves, then serves a more general hortatory purpose to inspire the audience to endure persecution and pursue a moral life. The addressees are called to "sanctify Christ as Lord," by being ready to give "an account of the hope that is in you" (3:15). Even if one is maligned in the process or suffering results from such a confession, it should be accepted, following the example of Christ who suffered for all, righteous and unrighteous (3:18).

Christ's passion also should inspire the addressees to be guided not by human desires, but by the will of God (4:1–2). The author spells out some of what that means, highlighting above all the requirement to love one another, "for love covers a multitude of sins" (4:8). As in several of the other general epistles, the love command thus appears in a central place in the structure of the Christian life, although, once again, there is no explicit reference to the teaching of Jesus on the subject. It is Christ's example that counts. That appears to be the import of the claim that by living in accordance with the principle of love and providing hospitable service, God is "glorified in all things through Jesus Christ" (4:11).

For 1 Peter then, Jesus Christ is the ground and model for the life of his followers, a life that willingly accepts suffering of various sorts, knowing that, as in the case of Jesus, suffering leads to heavenly glory (5:10).

2 Peter and Jude

The related texts of Jude and 2 Peter say little about Jesus. Jude, a brief but testy condemnation of those who "pervert the grace of God and deny our only Master and Lord, Jesus Christ" (Jude 4), calls upon his addressees to keep themselves in the love of God, looking forward "to the mercy of our Lord Jesus Christ that leads to eternal life" (Jude 21), though whom the community gives honor and glory to God (Jude 25).

Belief about Jesus focuses on his coming again in judgment, a belief grounded in a citation from a book of Enoch (Jude 14–15). The author also attributes to the "apostles of Jesus Christ" insight into a future marked by "scoffers" (Jude 17–18), a claim that may evoke the predictions of the synoptic apocalypse (Mark 13:5–6 and parallels). A reverently defensive hope in Christ's return is at the heart of this text's piety.

2 Peter is an even more bitter tirade directed at "scoffers" (2 Pet 3:3), who mock belief in the second coming of Christ (3:3–7), as well as at other unspecified teachers reviled as "false prophets" and "waterless springs and mists driven by a storm" (2:17). The author, writing probably in the second century, when Pauline epistles are being debated (3:15–16), adopts the persona of Peter, who has written previously (3:1). More importantly, Peter was a witness of the ministry of Jesus. His experience of the transfiguration, when a voice from heaven declared Jesus to be "My Son, my Beloved" (2 Pet 1:16–18; cf. Mark 9:2–7 and parallels) constitutes the one clear reference in the general epistles to an episode of the life of Jesus reported in the synoptic gospels.

Like the other general epistles, 2 Peter grounds Christian life in Christ, using the formula of the "knowledge of our Lord Jesus Christ" (1:2, 8). That knowledge leads to a moral life, characterized by self-control, godliness, mutual affection, and love, through which believers become "participants in the divine nature" (1:4) and gain entry to the "eternal kingdom of our Lord and Savior Jesus Christ" (1:11).

The Epistle to the Hebrews

The Epistle to the Hebrews, actually a homily with an epistolary conclusion, was addressed to a group of Christians not unlike the recipients of 1 Peter. Like them, these Christians had experienced persecution in days gone by (Heb 10:32–34) and perhaps had begun to wane in their commitment to their faith (10:25). The anonymous homilist addresses them with a "word of exhortation" (13:22), offering a vision of the significance of the death of Jesus that grounds an appeal to renewed fidelity modeled on his faithful obedience.

Hebrews devotes little attention to the details of the life of Jesus, citing no dominical sayings nor mentioning any of the deeds of Jesus during his public ministry. The homily focuses on Christ's passion, death, and exaltation, and the significance of those events for the life of the faithful. While it does cite two "sayings" of Jesus, both are quotations taken from scripture and contribute to the interpretation of Christ's death and exaltation.

The epistle's preface celebrates the Son, through whom God speaks at the end of days, who is the "reflection of God's glory" and the "imprint of his very being." (1:3). These terms, and the following affirmation of the Son as the instrument of creation and sustaining force of all that is, echo the hymn to Wisdom in the Wisdom of Solomon 7:25–28. Like other early Christian texts (John 1:1–14; Col 1:15–20; 1 Cor 8:6) that rely on sapiential traditions (Prov 8; Sir 24), Hebrews highlights the cosmic significance of Christ. The "incarnational" perspective, insisting on the heavenly origin of the Son, will surface again in Hebrews (1:6; 10:5), but this perspective does not form the cornerstone of the epistle's christology. Instead, the homily focuses on Christ's exaltation, announced in the next verses of the prefatory paragraph, which celebrates the fact that Christ "sat down at the right hand of the majesty on high" (1:3).

This phrase evokes the key text, Psalm 110:1, a passage that originally depicted the enthronement of a Davidic king but was widely used by early Christians to celebrate Christ's exaltation (cf. 1 Pet 3:22; Eph 1:20–21; Acts 2:34). That psalm also provided the verse (Ps 110:4: "Thou art a priest forever according to the order of Melchizedek") that grounds the homily's claims that Christ was a special high priest (Heb 7).

Following the preface, a catena of scriptural texts tells of the divine address to the Son (Heb 1:5: Ps 2:7), his introduction into the world (Heb 1:6: Deut 32–43 LXX and Ps 97:7), and his final enthronement (Heb 1:7–12: Ps 45:6–7; 102:25–27; 110:1). However the rest of the catena is to be read – and some interpreters find not an incarnational moment in 1:6, but another reference to exaltation – the climactic point is clear. The Son is exalted above all heavenly powers at the right hand of God, a position that assures the future of his followers.

The exalted Christ, however, is only one of the two christological foci of the homily. The second is his death, understood as an act of radical obedience to the divine will. Attention to the death of Jesus, interpreted through the Psalms, appears in chapter 2. The homilist interprets Psalm 8, which celebrates the high status of humankind in creation, as a description of Christ's death and exaltation. The rereading is effected by eliminating the parallel between the two affirmations "made a little (or for a little while) lower than the angels" and "crowned with honor and glory." For the author, the two phrases refer not to the same universal human status in different terms, but to two points in the history of the Son. The exegesis of the Psalm in Hebrews 2:8–9 makes this christological reading clear and focuses its application: the suffering and exalted Son "tasted death" for all, a phrase that emphasizes his humanity. The homilist then turns to the benefits of that death.

Plays on words often mark the homily's most profound points, and so it is in the next move, to explain how the Son's actions have an impact. Jesus is the *archēgos*, the one who leads the way for many sons and daughters to heavenly glory (2:10). This epithet, which will appear again with slightly different connotations at 12:2, suggests both the Son's importance as the "pioneer" or "pathfinder," who opens the way for his followers, and his role as "model" whose action exemplifies what the followers are supposed to do, a combination that also appeared prominently in 1 Peter. The balance between these two dimensions of the Son's role characterizes the rest of the homily.

The depiction of the *archēgos* continues in chapter 2, where the voice of Jesus is heard for the first time. What it says consists of texts from scripture (Heb 2:12–13), which declare the purposes of Jesus: to proclaim God's name among his brethren, to sing a hymn to God in the assembly (*ekklēsia*) (Ps 22:23), and to trust in God (Isa 8:17) along with the children God has given him (Isa 8:18). These texts thus establish the solidarity between Christ and other members of his community in their shared relationship of fidelity to God. On the basis of that relationship, Jesus frees the "seed of Abraham," who share in flesh and blood with him, from their fear of death (Heb 2:15). In offering that salvation, Jesus shows himself to be a faithful and merciful high priest (2:17–18), tested by experience.

Themes of fidelity and mercy continue in the following chapters, focusing first on Jesus as an example of filial fidelity greater than that of Moses (3:1–6) or that of Joshua (4:8) in leading his people to their promised rest. Like other priests, he serves as an intermediary with God (5:1–4), but again, his mediation is based on his experience of solidarity with suffering humankind. A vivid passage about the prayers of Jesus, uttered with "cries and tears" (5:7), drives home the point, echoing a well-known Greek proverb, that Jesus learned obedience through what he suffered (5:8). The passage recalls the scene of the tormented Jesus in the Garden of Gethsemane (Mark 14:32–42 and parallels), although the note that he was "heard because of his reverent submission" (Heb 5:7) suggests either a different tradition or a different understanding of the scene.

Although the homily treats Jesus as a high priest in these passages, the case that he merits the title still needs demonstration. Chapter 7 offers such a demonstration, through a bold interpretation of the two Old Testament texts that mention Melchizedek: Psalm 110:4, assumed to be addressed by God to his Son, and Genesis 14:17–20. Recognizing that by traditional standards, Jesus, as a member of the tribe of Judah, could not be priest (7:13), the homilist argues that he is a priest of a different, eternal order, symbolized by Melchizedek, who in scripture is "fatherless, motherless, and without genealogy" (7:3), but who is said to "live" (7:8).

This chapter paves the way for the central argument of Hebrews, made in chapters 8–10. Here the homilist argues that the "new covenant" promised by Jeremiah (Jer 31:31–34), a covenant written on hearts and minds, was established by the high-priestly act of Christ, who, in his exaltation, entered the "true" heavenly tabernacle to produce real atonement for sins, not the superficial cleansing effected by the blood of animals. The homily's characterization of Christ's priestly act is encapsulated in the claim that his sacrificial bloodshed was consummated "through the eternal spirit" (9:14). Citation of another scriptural text, set on the lips of Jesus, grounds that claim (10:5–7). Psalm 40:7–9, in its Greek form, declares the intention of Jesus as he "enters the world" (10:5). That intention is to submit to God's will, and by that willing submission his followers are sanctified (10:10).

The faithful obedience of Jesus, by inaugurating a new covenant, has created a "new and living way" for his followers to have access to God (10:20). The remainder of the homily limns the characteristics of that way, citing numerous scriptural examples of fidelity (Heb 11), all of whom culminate in Jesus, "the pioneer (archēgos) and perfecter of faith" (12:3). The homily concludes with a call to its addressees to follow him "outside the camp, bearing his shame" (13:13), like him reciting a psalm of trust in God (Ps 118:6; Heb 13:6).

For Hebrews, then, as for other general epistles, the divine vindication of Jesus who gave his life for his brothers and sisters establishes a new possibility of relationship with God, based on an imitation of the faithfulness that Jesus exemplified.

References

Bechtler, Richard Steven (1998). *Following in His Steps: Suffering, Community, and Christology in 1 Peter*. Atlanta, GA: Scholars.

Mason, Eric F. (2008). *You Are a Priest Forever: Second Temple Jewish Messianism and the Priestly Christology of the Epistle to the Hebrews*. Leiden: Brill.

McCruden, Kevin B. (2008). *Beneficent Christology in the Epistle to the Hebrews*. Berlin: De Gruyter.

Powell, Mark Allan, and David R. Bauer, eds. (1999). *Who Do You Say That I Am? Essays in Christology*. Louisville, KY: Westminster John Knox.

Tuckett, Christopher M. (2001). *Christology and the New Testament: Jesus and His Earliest Followers*. Louisville, KY: Westminster John Knox.

CHAPTER 8

Jesus in the Apocalypse

Ian Boxall

Visitors to medieval cathedrals such as Chartres or Angers in France are confronted with an awesome vision in the tympanum above the central entrance. Sculpted in stone, Christ sits enthroned as judge, the Lamb's book of life in his hand, attended by the four living creatures, which in Christian tradition have become symbols for the four evangelists. This sculpted scene is but one example of the profound influence of the book of Revelation on the Christian perception of Jesus.

Revelation (or the Apocalypse of John, following its Greek title) claims to be a report of visions received by John while on the island of Patmos in the eastern Aegean. Like other Jewish and Christian apocalypses, it describes the revelation of heavenly mysteries, received by the visionary through a combination of ascent to heaven and angelic mediation. Although popular interpretation of the Apocalypse tends to treat it as a vision of the End, scholars have emphasized that it unveils the true reality of the original author's own world. Through its terrifying visions of monsters and a harlot-city, a holy war and a butchered Lamb, Revelation unmasks the beastly character of first-century Rome and its emperors. Most scholars follow the second-century Christian author Irenaeus in dating the book to ca. 90-96, though a good case can be made for an earlier date in the late 60s, either during or more likely just after the reign of Nero (Boxall 2006, 7–10).

Revelation's visionary character, its use of apocalyptic symbolism, and its reworking of Old Testament prophecy (most notably Ezekiel and Daniel), have left their mark on the book's idiosyncratic portrayal of Jesus. Unlike the gospels, the Apocalypse has little interest in the earthly life and ministry of Jesus of Nazareth. Instead it offers dramatic visions of the heavenly Christ in a number of guises, presenting a kaleidoscope of words and images that engage the imagination of the hearer. This preference for images poses particular challenges for an interpreter wishing to engage with Revelation's christology. It means that attention to the titles used for

The Blackwell Companion to Jesus, First Edition. Edited by Delbert Burkett. ©2014 John Wiley & Sons, Ltd. Published 2014 by John Wiley & Sons, Ltd.

Jesus (a so-called "titular christology"), illuminating though that is, will only provide part of the picture.

Many of these titles betray the Jewish Christian character of Revelation. Jesus is described in royal messianic terms as the Lion of the tribe of Judah (Rev 5:5; cf. Gen 49:9), the Root of David (Rev 5:5; 22:16; cf. Isa 11:10), and the bright morning star (Rev 22:16; cf. Num 24:17), who holds the key of David (Rev 3:7). Elsewhere, titles hitherto belonging to Israel's God are now shared with Jesus Christ. He is "Lord of lords and king of kings" (Rev 17:14; 19:16; cf. Deut 10:17; Ps 136:3; Dan 4:37 LXX). He is the "first and the last" (Rev 1:17; 22:13; cf. Isa 44:6; 48:12), the "Alpha and the Omega" (Rev 22:13; cf. 1:8), designations that give him a role in protology as well as eschatology.

To understand Revelation's view of Jesus, however, depends as much upon how Jesus is characterized within the unfolding visionary narrative, as on what titles he receives. As the architects of the medieval cathedrals, or artists in every generation, have recognized, the impression of Jesus' divinity that a portrayal of Jesus produces depends upon its overall impact, its power to move, to inspire awe and mystery. Hence many have recognized that Revelation contains one of the "highest" christologies in the New Testament. It is a highly distinctive example of how early Christians found purely human categories (e.g., prophet, messiah, teacher) inadequate to express their experience of Jesus Christ.

The Son of Man

The first appearance of Christ in the Apocalypse occurs in John's inaugural vision on Patmos "on the Lord's Day" (1:9–20). That this is a vision of Jesus is confirmed by his self-designation as the "first and the last" (used by Christ elsewhere at 22:13) and as the living one who died (1:18). However, John describes not the earthly Jesus, but the exalted Jesus, "one like a son of man" (see also 14:14). The probable meaning of this latter phrase is that, like angels in the Old Testament and Jewish apocalypses (e.g., Gen 18:2; Josh 5:13; Zech 1:8; 1 Enoch 87:2; 90:14), Christ is a heavenly being appearing in human form. His celestial origin is conveyed by his glorious appearance: his fiery eyes, his feet like polished bronze, his face shining like the blazing sun. John's reaction – to fall down at his feet "as if dead" (1:17) – is an appropriate human response to a supernatural being. Scholars often use the designation *angelomorphic* of the son of man figure, to convey that Christ here appears in angelic form but is no mere angel. He certainly fulfills a similar role to the angelic interpreter of other apocalypses, guiding the seer and revealing heavenly mysteries (e.g., Rev 1:20; 4:1). His angelomorphic presence here also stresses the closeness of this heavenly being to his Church (Carrell 1997, 119–128).

John's description echoes two visions in the book of Daniel. The first is Daniel 7:13, where "one like a son of man" (possibly the archangel Michael) is the heavenly representative of God's people who are vindicated through suffering and persecution. Second, John's description also has strong parallels with Daniel's vision of the "man clothed in linen" (Dan 10:5–6; cf. *Apocalypse of Abraham* 11; *Joseph and Aseneth* 14), notably the gold belt, fiery eyes, and legs of burnished bronze. Daniel's figure is thought by some to be the archangel Gabriel (cf. Dan 9:21) but is more likely a manifestation of the "glory of the Lord," separated from the divine throne (Ezek 1:26–28; Rowland 1980).

The exalted status of John's Christ is confirmed by the description of his hair as white "like wool which is white as snow," echoing the hair and clothing of the Ancient of Days at Daniel 7:9. For some scholars, this is evidence that the figure John describes participates in divinity rather than belonging to the created angelic order. They point to the likely influence of Daniel 7:13 in the Septuagint (LXX), where one like a son of man comes not "to" but "as" or "like [*hōs*] the Ancient of Days" (Rowland 1985, 106). Others point to the similar description of figures from the created realm, such as the principal angel Iaoel at *Apocalypse of Abraham* 11:2, and the angel-like Noah at 1 Enoch 106:2. As we shall see, however, Jesus is described elsewhere in the Apocalypse in ways that suggest participation in divinity rather than membership in the angelic ranks.

Revelation's heavenly Son of Man is also the high priest, a role ascribed to Jesus in the letter to the Hebrews as well. He wears the foot-length robe typical of the Jewish high priest (*podērē*: cf. Exod 28:4, 31; 29:5 LXX; Josephus, *Antiquities* 3.153–155, 159) and has a golden belt around his breast. He is depicted standing in the heavenly sanctuary "in the midst of the seven lampstands" (symbols of the seven churches, 1:20). Early Christian congregations would draw strength from the proximity of their high priest, a reminder that their small earthly assemblies were participations in the great heavenly liturgy.

However, the heavenly high priest does not merely comfort his people. John's inaugural vision prefaces a series of prophetic oracles or messages (often misnamed "seven letters," Rev 2–3), one to each of the angels of the seven named churches of Asia. They contain words of challenge as well as consolation from the "one like a Son of Man." With his sword of judgment emerging from his mouth (cf. Isa 11:4), he judges the early Christian congregations and finds some of them wanting (only Smyrna and Philadelphia receive undiluted praise).

The Lamb

Perhaps the most pervasive portrayal of Christ in the Apocalypse is as the Lamb (Greek *arnion*). This character is first introduced in the throne-room vision of Revelation 4–5 and is a key player throughout the remainder of this book. The image of the Lamb presents in symbolic form the achievements of the human Jesus. It replicates a regular feature of Jewish and Christian apocalypses, the depiction of human figures in animal guise. The four terrifying beasts of Daniel 7 symbolize four kings (Dan 7:17). In the *Animal Apocalypse* (1 Enoch 85–90), various nations and individuals in the history of salvation are represented as a variety of animals, including bulls and sheep. Similarly Revelation's Messiah – announced as the "Lion of the tribe of Judah" (Gen 49:9–10; 4 Ezra 11:37; 12:31–32) – manifests himself as the Lamb.

Scholars disagree as to the primary background of the Lamb imagery. Some think that the symbol stresses the weakness of a lamb as a slaughtered sacrificial animal (e.g., Guthrie 1994, 400–402). Others, given the paradox that the slain lamb "stands," and John's preference for the Greek word *arnion* rather than *amnos*, see it as a powerful, warrior lamb, like the victorious ram of 1 Enoch 90:9–13 (thought to represent Judas Maccabeus) or the destroying lamb in the *Testament of Joseph* 19:8–9. The seven horns signify its omnipotence, and the seven eyes its omniscience.

The wider narrative of Revelation may provide the hermeneutical key, suggesting that the dual aspects of weakness and power should be held in creative tension. According to the preferred reading of Revelation 1:5, Christ has "set us free us from our sins by his blood," an idea that puts Jesus in the role of a sacrificial lamb. Afterwards, the story of Israel's exodus from Egypt is in John's sights. The woman clothed with the sun relives Israel's exodus experience by flying into the wilderness with "the two wings of the great eagle" (12:14; cf. Exod 19:4). Later, the Lamb's followers stand beside a sea of glass, singing "the song of Moses and the song of the Lamb" (15:2–3). This vision ushers in a new sequence of seven bowl plagues, reminiscent of the plagues of Egypt (Exod 7–12). In light of these references to the exodus, memorialized among Jews at Passover by the slaughter of a lamb, the Lamb of Revelation is probably the unblemished Passover Lamb.

This interpretation explains the victory theme at the heart of this Lamb christology. Salvation has been achieved by the shedding of Christ's blood on the cross (e.g., 1:5; 12:11). This claim is full of apocalyptic paradox, for Christ's enemies are defeated through the death of the liberator himself. Hence in Revelation the sacrificial victim-lamb now appears as the exalted victor. He stands on Mount Zion, surrounded by his army of 144,000 (14:1–5), "who have not been defiled with women." The probable meaning is that they are in a state of priestly purity, appropriate to those ready to fight in the eschatological war (cf. 1QM 7:3–6). They are most likely the army of martyrs, male and female, Jewish and Gentile, "from every nation and tribe, from every people and language" (Rev 7:9). They are unafraid to bear faithful witness even in the face of death, thus conquering the dragon by the blood of the Lamb and their word of witness (Rev 12:11).

Paradoxically, the Lamb in Revelation is also a shepherd (7:17), fulfilling a role played elsewhere by God himself (e.g., Ps 23:1; Ezek 34:15). Although common authorship of the Apocalypse and the Fourth Gospel is unlikely, the two books share this Johannine motif. In the Fourth Gospel, the Good Shepherd offers life to his sheep through laying down his own life (John 10:1–18). In Revelation, the slaughtered and risen Lamb "shepherds" (*poimanei*) his flock, leading them to "springs of the water of life." His flock consists of "those who pass safely through the great tribulation" (7:14), who find protection, from the one who has also suffered, and refreshment after their tribulation. The scene reflects Isaiah's vision of Yahweh leading the Babylonian exiles by springs of water (Isa 49:10).

The Woman's Male Child

Revelation 12 describes a heavenly vision of a pregnant woman, clothed with the sun and wearing a crown of twelve stars. She is pursued by a great red dragon, identified as the devil. In this vision, Jesus is portrayed as the woman's male child, who is caught up to God's throne after birth. Although the woman has often been identified as Mary, the oldest exegetical tradition prefers a more corporate interpretation. She is the Church, or Israel, or the people of God of both covenants (Boxall 1999). In contrast with the opening vision of "one like a son of man," this vision highlights Christ's humanity and his ethnic origin as a member of the Jewish people. He is born out of and as a member of a specific community, which has undergone struggle and even persecution throughout the centuries (for the image of the "birth pangs" referring to community tribulation, see 1QH 3; Mark 13:8; John 16:20–22).

The human child has specifically royal messianic credentials. Running like a thread throughout the vision is Psalm 2, probably a coronation psalm, which describes the coronation of the Davidic king as the "begetting" of God's son on Mount Zion in Jerusalem. The king in the psalm smashes the nations whose own kings have plotted against him (Ps 2:2, 9). Revelation exploits the ambiguity of the Septuagint's *poimanein* (a verb already used of the Lamb at Rev. 7:17) and *rhabdos sidēra*. The son will "rule" or "shepherd" all the nations with a "rod of iron" or "iron staff" (Rev 12:5). What from the enemy's perspective may be a harsh rule, however, is felt by his followers as the shepherding of the Lamb, wielding his pastoral staff (cf. Rev 7:17).

Adela Yarbro Collins has shown how Revelation 12 reworks ancient forms of the so-called "Combat Myth," in which order is re-established through the subjugation of a chaos monster (Yarbro Collins 1976). The closest pagan form of the myth to John's description relates the birth of Apollo to Leto, despite the threats to his pregnant mother from the dragon Python. This would have been a familiar story to the first recipients of the Apocalypse, living in cities in western Asia Minor, not far from Apollo's shrine at Didyma. Patmos in John's day was also steeped in the cult and mythology of Apollo and his sister Artemis. In Revelation's radical retelling of the ancient myth, informed by Old Testament antecedents, peace and order are brought about not by Apollo but by Jesus Christ.

First-century Christian readers would have further detected political implications in Revelation 12, since the Apollo–Leto myth was used by the imperial propaganda machine. Nero, for one, presented himself as an Apollo figure and was likened by his troops to Pythian Apollo (van Henten 1994, 506). According to such propaganda, the emperor would be the woman's male child, the Savior who establishes peace through slaying the chaos monster. The Apocalypse radically subverts this mythology by identifying the male child as Christ and placing the emperor on the wrong side of the order/chaos divide, associating him with the Satanic dragon (13:3; 17:9–11). It exploits the irony that a victim of Rome's tyranny, the crucified Jesus of Nazareth, is the true victor over the powers of evil and injustice.

The Divine Warrior

The motif of holy war links the portrayals of Christ as the Lamb and as the woman's male child. The Lamb has an army and conquers its enemies (e.g., 17:12–14). The male child conquers the dragon in order to rule the nations (e.g., 12:5, 10–12). This divine warrior theme finds its most explicit expression in the vision of Christ as a terrifying rider on a white horse (19:11–16). Once again, the Christ portrayed here shares in God's mission. In the background is Isaiah's vision of the Lord returning from battle against the Edomites (Isa 61:1–3), together with Wisdom's angelomorphic description of the Word of God, leaping down from his royal throne to destroy the firstborn of Egypt (Wis 18:14–16). Indeed, Christ is explicitly called the Word of God here (Rev 19:13). A terrifying vision such as this, combined with descriptions of the Lamb witnessing the torments of the beast's worshipers (14:10) or of humans recoiling in horror from the "wrath of the Lamb" (6:16), has left Revelation open to the charge of replacing one tyranny – that of the beast – with another of equal cruelty (e.g., Moyise 2001).

But there is another side to the rider's ferocity. It is possible that the blood spattered on his garment is his own blood, since battle has not yet been engaged (Reddish 1988, 89–90). The armies following him may be not angelic hosts, but the white-robed martyrs, whose testimony required the shedding of their blood. This passage would thus be a visionary reminder of the effects of Christ's cross and resurrection, and the paradigm it provides for his followers. The nonviolent warrior and his troops have conquered by dying at the violent hands of the enemy (Bredin 2003).

Moreover, the weapon wielded by this warrior (19:15; cf. 1:16; Isa 11:4) is consonant with his role as the divine Word. The sharp sword is a biblical symbol of God's word spoken through the prophets (e.g., Isa 49:2; Heb 4:12). In this vision, the emphasis is upon the role of God's Word in revelation and judgment. The sword-like word is certainly a powerful weapon, capable of destruction. But the destruction, though real, is mythical rather than literal. No weapons are wielded by hand. The divine warrior proclaims the word of truth, which unmasks the powers and their imperial manifestations, defeating them and robbing them of their power to enslave.

Jesus and God

What is Revelation's understanding of the relationship between Jesus and God? Given the book's apocalyptic visionary character, scholars have recognized that this is a difficult assessment to make. Although Jesus is seen as an exalted heavenly being in Revelation 1 and 19, his angelomorphic appearance echoes figures such as Iaoel, who, however exalted in the celestial realm, are clearly part of the created order. He performs functions properly belonging to God, such as judgment (e.g., 19:11), yet such activity befits his role as the Lord's vice-regent, the royal Messiah (e.g., 5:5; 11:15; 12:5; 22:16). As heavenly warrior, divine attributes such as the Word or *Logos* (e.g., 19:13) are ascribed to him.

Nevertheless, other evidence suggests that the author believes Jesus participates in divinity rather than merely sharing in its functions. From the start of the book, Christ shares divine titles. He declares himself to be the Alpha and the Omega, and the beginning and the end (22:13), both self-designations used by the Lord God (1:8; 21:6). He shares with the one on the throne the title *kurios*, Lord (e.g., 1:10; 11:8; 14:13; 17:14; 22:20), almost certainly a substitute for the divine name Yahweh (e.g., 1:8; 4:8, 11; 6:10; 15:3).

Particularly dramatic is the claim that the Lamb shares God's throne. The first possible reference to this (5:6) is admittedly ambiguous in the Greek. It could be taken to mean that the Lamb occupies the space between the throne and the four living creatures, as in the New Revised Standard Version, although the New International Version prefers the bolder interpretation according to which the Lamb stands in the center of the throne itself. In support of the latter reading is the joint ascription of "praise and honor, glory and strength" to the one on the throne and the Lamb in 5:13.

There is little ambiguity, however, by chapter 7, where the great multitude stand before the throne and before the Lamb, who is explicitly located "in the middle of the throne" (7:17; cf. 22:1, 3; at 3:21 the son of man speaks of sharing his Father's throne). God and the Lamb are jointly acclaimed in a context of worship in 7:10. In other words, by this stage in the action, the reader has witnessed the enthronement of the Lamb on God's throne-chariot or *Merkavah*. This is very different from the tradition of enthronement at God's right hand (Knight 2001, 46–48). This tradition, rooted in an exegesis of Psalm 110:1, is used elsewhere in the New Testament to describe Jesus' ascension. By contrast, the Apocalypse's assertion that the Lamb shares God's own throne lacks the subordination implicit in such "right-hand" passages. It portrays two beings with one shared authority (compare 1 Enoch 61:8; 69:29). This impression is supported by other passages that closely associate the one on the throne and the Lamb, often using a singular verb or pronoun for the two (Rev 6:16–17; 11:15; 21:22; 22:1–4).

Most compelling for the divine character of Jesus in the Apocalypse is the fact that he is the object of worship. Richard Bauckham has highlighted the theological significance of worship in Revelation as making a clear distinction between creator and creature (Bauckham 1993b, 31–35). Fundamental to Revelation's political critique of Rome is its contrast between authentic and false worship, and its exposure of seductive idolatry, which includes participation in Roman political and commercial life. This warning against idolatry extends even to the worship of angels. On two occasions, John is firmly rebuked for attempting to worship his angelic interpreter (cf. *Ascension of Isaiah* 7:21; Tobit 12:16–22; *Apocalypse of Zephaniah* 6:15). The only worship permitted in the Apocalypse is to "worship God" (19:10; 22:8–9). By contrast, there are no strictures against the adoration of the Lamb who shares the divine throne (e.g., 5:12, 14; 7:9–12). This adoration is more than the *proskunēsis* (bowing down) that could be directed toward humans without compromising divine worship (Bauckham 1993a, 133–140). In short, the Apocalypse's vision of the enthroned Lamb confronts the reader with the extraordinary claim that one of the human race, the crucified and risen Jesus, is worthy of the worship due to Israel's God alone.

References

Bauckham, Richard (1993a). "The Worship of Jesus." In *The Climax of Prophecy: Studies on the Book of Revelation* (pp. 118–149). Edinburgh: T&T Clark.

Bauckham, Richard (1993b). *The Theology of the Book of Revelation.* Cambridge: Cambridge University Press.

Boxall, Ian (1999). "Who is the Woman Clothed with the Sun?" In M. Warner (ed.), *Say Yes to God: Mary and the Revealing of the Word Made Flesh* (pp. 142–158). London: Tufton Books.

Boxall, Ian (2006). *The Revelation of Saint John.* Black's New Testament Commentaries. Peabody, MA: Hendrickson; London: Continuum.

Bredin, Mark (2003). *Jesus, Revolutionary of Peace: A Nonviolent Christology in the Book of Revelation.* Carlisle: Paternoster.

Carrell, Peter R. (1997). *Jesus and the Angels: Angelology and the Christology of the Apocalypse of John.* Cambridge: Cambridge University Press.

Guthrie, Donald (1994). "The Christology of Revelation." In Joel B. Green and M. Turner (eds.), *Jesus of Nazareth: Lord and Christ. Essays on the Historical Jesus and New Testament Christology* (pp. 397–409). Eerdmans: Grand Rapids; Carlisle: Paternoster.

Knight, J. (2001). "The Enthroned Christ of Revelation 5:6 and the Development of Christian Theology." In Steven Moyise (ed.), *Studies in the Book of Revelation* (pp. 43–50). Edinburgh and New York: T&T Clark.

Moyise, Steven (2001). "Does the Lion Lie Down with the Lamb?" In Steven Moyise (ed.) *Studies in the Book of Revelation* (pp. 181–194). Edinburgh and New York: T&T Clark.

Reddish, Mitchell G. (1988). "Martyr Christology in the Apocalypse." *Journal for the Study of the New Testament* 33: 85–95.

Rowland, Christopher (1980). "The Vision of the Risen Christ in Rev. i.13ff.: The Debt of an Early Christology to an Aspect of Jewish Angelology." *Journal of Theological Studies* 31: 1–11.

Rowland, Christopher (1985). "A Man Clothed in Linen: Daniel 10.6ff. and Jewish Angelology." *Journal for the Study of the New Testament* 24: 99–110.

van Henten, Jan Willem (1994). "Dragon Myth and Imperial Ideology in Revelation 12–13." In Eugene H. Lovering Jr. (ed.), *Society of Biblical Literature 1994 Seminar Papers* (pp. 496–515). Atlanta, GA: Scholars.

Yarbro Collins, Adela (1976). *The Combat Myth in the Book of Revelation.* Missoula, MT: Scholars.

Further Reading

Rowland, Christopher (1982). *The Open Heaven: A Study of Apocalyptic in Judaism and Early Christianity.* London: SPCK.

Stuckenbruck, Loren T. (1995). *Angel Veneration and Christology: A Study in Early Judaism and in the Christology of the Apocalypse.* Tübingen: Mohr Siebeck.

CHAPTER 9

Constructing Images of Jesus from the Hebrew Bible

Warren Carter

Stumbling block, suffering servant, son of David and king, eschatological (end-time) judge, high priest, son of Abraham, Wisdom – these images used of Jesus in New Testament writings differ considerably, but they have at least one thing in common. They all draw on passages found in the Hebrew Bible.

New Testament writers frequently evoke the Hebrew Bible in their constructions of the significance of Jesus. Citations of, allusions to, and language from the Hebrew Bible pervade the New Testament writings. The presence of these links to the Hebrew Bible raises a number of questions: did the Hebrew Bible always speak about Jesus? If so, why did many people – other than followers of Jesus – not understand it to be doing so? How did followers of Jesus use citations of, allusions to, and themes from the Hebrew Bible in their writings, and what images of Jesus did they construct? We will consider these sorts of questions in this chapter.

The authors of the New Testament writings used the language and ideas of the Hebrew scriptures to construct a variety of images of Jesus. Centuries after these writings had addressed their own time and situation, the New Testament writers, as committed followers of Jesus, read the Hebrew scriptures wearing their "Jesus glasses." They read their scriptures expecting them to provide insight into Jesus' identity and roles in relation to God's workings. Not surprisingly, that is what they found. They used understandings and language about God's activity and about faithful life in relationship to God to construct images of Jesus in their own writings.

Introduction

In constructing images of Jesus, the opening sections of several New Testament writings readily indicate their indebtedness to the language and contents of the Hebrew

The Blackwell Companion to Jesus, First Edition. Edited by Delbert Burkett. ©2014 John Wiley & Sons, Ltd. Published 2014 by John Wiley & Sons, Ltd.

scriptures. Matthew's gospel, for instance, begins by locating Jesus in relation to a seventeen-verse genealogy that highlights Abraham, David, and exile in Babylon (Matt 1:1–17). The association with Abraham portrays Jesus as a means of God's blessing for all people (Gen 12). The association with David presents Jesus as a king who represents God's rule (cf. Ps 72). Then throughout chapters 1–2, Matthew employs citations from the Hebrew Bible to portray Jesus as the one who manifests God's presence (Emmanuel, Matt 1:22–23), and as God's son (2:15) opposed by King Herod (2:18). Moreover, several events such as his conflict with Herod and flight into Egypt echo the life of (the unnamed) Moses.

Paul begins his letter to the Romans by locating Jesus in relation to the unnamed Isaiah (by using the term "gospel"), then in relation to unspecified "prophets and the holy scriptures," and to David (1:1–3). Hebrews begins with a string of seven verses from the Hebrew Bible to present Jesus as greater than the angels (Heb 1:5–14). The prologue of John's gospel locates Jesus "in the beginning" with God, from whence he comes to earth to reveal God's life, is rejected by many but received by some, and returns to be with God (John 1:1–18). Without explicitly saying so, this passage presents Jesus as the revealer of God by evoking traditions from the Hebrew Bible about the revealer figure, Lady Wisdom, who is with God in the beginning but comes among humans to reveal God's life (Prov 8; Sir 24; Wis 7:22–8:1; Ringe 1999). The book of Revelation begins by imaging Jesus as the firstborn, the faithful witness, and ruler of the kings of the earth, by alluding to Psalm 89:28, 38 (Rev 1:5). Several verses later, in 1:17, the image changes with an allusion to Isaiah 44:6. Jesus is "the first and the last," the beginning (source) and end (goal) of all things, the Alpha and Omega. In Isaiah the phrase refers to God (as it does in Rev 1:8; 22:13), while its use for Jesus in Revelation 1:17 portrays him as the one who is sovereign over creation and history.

These instances indicate some of the diverse uses of the Hebrew Bible in the New Testament and some of the diverse portraits of Jesus that result.

Citations

One use (common in Matthew 1–4 and Hebrews) involves *citations*, often introduced by a formula such as "so it has been written by the prophet." This formula, for example, introduces a citation in Matthew 2:5 from Micah 5:2 and 2 Samuel 5:2 to portray Jesus as a ruler in the line of David. Similar introductions appear in John 12:38 (Isaiah) and Acts 2:16 (Joel). Paul uses a shorter formula, "for it is written," to introduce a citation from Isaiah 54:1 into his allegorical interpretation of the story of Hagar and Sarah (Gal 4:27; cf. Eph 4:8; James 4:6). But in Matthew 22:37–39, Jesus responds directly to an inquiry about the greatest commandment by directly quoting Deuteronomy 6:5 (love God) and Leviticus 19:18 (love neighbor) without any introductory formula (Carter 2008b). By one count, there are some 195 such citations in the New Testament. Their distribution is quite uneven, with most appearing in the gospels, Acts, Romans, and Hebrews. None appears, for example, in Colossians or Revelation. Arguably the most extensively used Hebrew Bible book, Psalms (along with Isaiah and Deuteronomy), is not explicitly cited in Philippians, 1 or 2 Thessalonians, 1 or 2 Timothy, Titus, Philemon, James, 2 Peter, the Johannine epistles, or Jude (Moyise and Menken 2004).

Allusions

Another use of material from the Hebrew Bible involves *allusions*, where material is not quoted in a separate, clearly introduced statement, as the citations are, but is incorporated into the account without any identifying markers. The book of Revelation includes no explicit citations of the Hebrew Bible but continually alludes to the scriptural tradition and expects its readers to understand this language (Moyise 2004). Without explicit markers, allusions can be difficult to identify. How many words might be needed for an allusion? Hebrews 1:2, for example, describes Jesus as "the heir of all things." Some have seen an allusion here to the royal psalm, Psalm 2:8, where the same term, "heir/inheritance," is used to describe the nations that are given to the king to rule over "as your inheritance." While the translation differs a little in English, it is the same term in Greek. Are a couple of words enough to claim an allusion? The answer probably depends on the circumstances or context of each use. In this instance, a reader's attention is directed to Psalm 2 by the term "son" in Hebrews 1:2 (used in Ps 2:7) and again in Hebrews 1:5, which directly quotes Psalm 2:7. These contextual clues suggest that the allusion, albeit a very brief one, is likely thereby presenting Jesus as a ruler over the nations and God's agent or son. Mark 13:26, on the other hand, is much more clearly an allusion. Jesus says, "and then you will see 'the Son of Man coming in clouds' with great power and glory." Incorporated into the verse smoothly – and identified here (but not in the Greek text) with quotation marks – are words from Daniel 7:13–14. There is no introductory formula ("as Daniel says") and no textual clue that a quotation is being made. We as readers are expected to recognize the quote from Daniel 7, which constructs an image of Jesus as the coming one who will establish God's rule over all empires. Because of the difficulty in recognizing allusions, Hays has suggested seven criteria by which to recognize their presence: availability, volume (use of shared words), recurrence (same passage used elsewhere), thematic coherence, historical plausibility, history of interpretation (recognition by other readers), and satisfaction (does the reading make good sense?) (Hays 1989, 29–32).

Word associations

A third use of Hebrew Bible texts consists of *word associations*. This usage is perhaps a subset of allusion, involving a person, place, event, tradition, or idea. Matthew's opening seventeen-verse genealogy, for example, leaves the reader to elaborate from the Hebrew Bible the stories associated with each person's name. Similarly, Romans 1:3 associates Jesus and David but requires the reader to understand that the link establishes Jesus as king. Beyond names, Paul's double use of the term "gospel" in Romans 1:1, 3 requires readers to know passages from Isaiah (40:9; 52:7; 61:1) concerning God's victory over the Babylonian empire. The kinship term "Son" (Rom 1:3) evokes various usages of the term in the Hebrew Bible, which refer to figures in intimate relationship with God who are agents of God's purposes, such as kings (Ps 2:7) and Israel (Hos 11:1). Associated with Jesus, the term designates his role as agent of God's rule. Interestingly, both terms set up a further "intertextual" relationship with contemporary cultural claims about Roman imperial power in order to present Jesus as a superior rival to the Roman emperor, who was also commonly known as son of God and whose reign was sometimes described as "gospel" (i.e., "good news").

Intertextual echoes

A fourth use involves *intertextual echoes* (Hays 1989). Unlike "word associations," intertextual echoes are not made explicit by the authors but are discernible for those who know Israel's scriptures. In Matthew 2, for example, the story of infant Jesus delivered in Egypt from a violent king echoes the story of the infant Moses rescued from Pharaoh, even though Moses is not mentioned. The echo supplies a subtext that presents Jesus as one who, like Moses, comes into conflict with ruling power, is protected by God, and carries out his God-given commission to deliver God's people. Similarly, the wisdom traditions evoked by John 1:1–18, but not explicitly mentioned, present Jesus as revealer of God's life and purposes.

Christological and ecclesiological uses of scripture

Citations, allusions, word associations, and echoes, then, indicate something of the pervasive significance and diverse uses of the Hebrew scriptures on images of Jesus in the New Testament writings. The New Testament writers evidence at least two assumptions as they read texts of the Hebrew Bible. We have noted the first, namely that they read with "Jesus glasses," whereby they read the texts in relation to Jesus. In addition to this *christological* approach, they also read with the assumption that the final age, in which God is completing God's purposes, is underway in Jesus. This *eschatological* approach spanned both the present and the future, with some writers oriented more to the present (John's gospel; Ephesians) and others oriented more to the future (Paul; Matthew). God's final purposes had, in the person of Jesus, broken into the present, with their final goal yet to be completed.

While texts of the Hebrew Bible are cited or used in presenting Jesus, it should also be noted that they are also frequently used to construct images of the church or followers of Jesus. Paul collects a "chain" (or "catena") of verses in Romans 3:10–18 to establish the sinfulness of all people. In 2 Corinthians 4:6, he presents his new-covenant ministry as the revelation of truth, by applying Genesis 1:3–5 (creation) and Isaiah 9:1 (liberation from Assyria) to preaching the gospel, something he continues to do in adversity as a faithful person (2 Cor 4:13, citing Ps 116:10). Hebrews 3:7–4:13 reads Psalm 95:7–11 ecclesiologically, whereby the exodus experience is evoked in order to warn the church against hardening their hearts against God. Hebrews 12:5–6 quotes Proverbs 3:11–12 to underscore the importance of God's discipline for believers. 1 Peter 2:9–10 employs a series of covenant metaphors taken from Exodus 19:6 and Isaiah 43:20–21 to construct an image of the church as a "chosen race, a royal priesthood, a holy nation, God's own people." In this chapter, we will focus on the christological-eschatological, rather than ecclesiological, uses of the Hebrew scriptures in the New Testament writings.

Reading the Hebrew Bible through Jesus Glasses

In this section, we consider five issues related to how the New Testament writers construct images of Jesus by reading the Hebrew Bible through Jesus glasses.

The practice of quotations and allusions

The New Testament practice of borrowing passages and language from another writing (in this case the Hebrew Bible) is not unique to the New Testament writers. Classical writings employed the practice (Stanley 1990) as did the Hebrew Bible, where later writings borrowed material from earlier writings for new and different contexts. The prophet known as Deutero-Isaiah (responsible for Isa 40–55), for example, borrows the image of the exodus from Egypt to depict God liberating the people from exile in Babylon (Exod 15; Isa 40:18–20; 41:17–20; 43:1–7, 16–17).

Writings from Early Judaism also utilized this technique. The first-century CE Jewish writing 4 Maccabees, written to persuade its Hellenistic-Jewish readers that faithfulness to the Law was the highest display of devout reason, depicts the death of martyrs as "an atoning sacrifice" (4 Macc 17:22). The writer borrows an image from the Day of Atonement ceremony (Lev 16), just as Paul does in Romans 3:25 to interpret Jesus' death as an atoning sacrifice. Practices of citation and allusion are extensive in the Dead Sea Scrolls found at Qumran (Brooke 2004). The writers, for instance, read the prophet Habakkuk, not in relation to the sixth-century BCE world and events from which it originated, but in relation to their own experiences some four or five centuries later (1QpHab). No one else interpreted Habakkuk in this way (cf. Paul's interpretation of Hab 2:4 in Rom 1:17); without wearing "Qumran glasses" it is impossible to do so.

In evoking the Hebrew scriptures, whether by citation, allusion, word association, or intertextual echoes, the New Testament writers adopted a literary practice that was common in the ancient world. The distinctive dimension of the New Testament usage is that the scriptures are read with a christological-eschatological perspective in order to construct images of Jesus.

The roles of authors and audience in making meaning

The practice of quoting from or alluding to the Hebrew Bible in order to construct images of Jesus raises important literary and theological questions (Snodgrass 2001; Moyise 2008). In the interpretation of Habakkuk from Qumran, or in the New Testament documents, do the writers faithfully reproduce the intent and meaning of the original authors, discover new meaning, or create entirely new meanings?

Some approaches privilege the intentions of the authors of the Hebrew Bible. Proponents of one such approach reject the notion that in using texts from the Hebrew Bible, New Testament authors misinterpreted them by giving them new meanings. Rather, they argue, New Testament authors were faithful to the intentions of the authors of the Hebrew Bible. So some readers have claimed that writers of the Hebrew Bible, under the influence of God's spirit, wrote about Jesus centuries before his time. In this way of reading, no one recognized the reference to Jesus until Jesus and the New Testament writers centuries later. While such a claim of authorial intent makes sense from a particular theological perspective, it is difficult to sustain on literary and historical grounds. It fails to give adequate regard to historical factors such as the context that the text originally addressed, the human finitude of authors restricted to their own circumstances, and the difficulty of establishing authorial intent several thousand years later when we are not able to quiz long-dead authors.

A variation on this approach argues that texts have a "communicative intent" that includes but surpasses the context of origin (Beale 1994; 1999; Vanhoozer 1998). The text has a "fuller" meaning beyond its original application that allows it to address future situations that might be analogous and even unforeseen by the author or speaker. This "communicative intent" is open-ended, and a text of the Hebrew Bible can be "extended" to address new situations, such as presenting images of Jesus. Advocates of this approach often see a close link between this "communicative intent" of a text and the intent of an author. So in citing or alluding to the Hebrew Bible in relation to Jesus, the New Testament writers, so it is claimed, are actualizing this communicative intent, or at least its spirit. Beale comments, "someone like Isaiah, if he were living in the first century, might well think the extended application of his prophecies to Jesus would fall within the parameters of his understanding of what he wrote" (Beale 1999, 157).

This claim to know what the eighth-century BCE prophet Isaiah would be thinking some 700 years, and then 2,800 years, after he lived highlights one of the difficulties with this approach. Discerning the "intent" or motivations of someone who wrote several millennia ago is very difficult. Moreover, there were, according to numerous scholars, three "Isaiahs" (so to speak), linked to different parts of the Isaiah collection, whose followers continued to develop the tradition (Isa 1–39; 40–55; 56–66). The notion of "authorial" and "communicative intent" is complicated by these complex circumstances of origin and by multiple participants in a traditioning process. The presence of such development alerts us to a further issue that we experience in daily communication. The originator of a verbal or written statement cannot control its reception. Indeed "authorial intent" is not the final word in any communication, and in some communication is of no consequence at all.

Those who seek to privilege authorial and communicative intent in explaining the use of the Hebrew Bible by New Testament writers also often employ a theological justification. This theological conviction concerns the existence of a divinely inspired canon whose unity of content is guaranteed by God: "... [O]ne divine mind stands behind it all" (Beale 1994, 401). Apparently this divine mind, at least in Beale's reconstruction, prefers unity and coherency in images of Jesus, rather than diversity, and ensures the "truth" of the (Christian) canonical material so that New Testament writers interpret texts of the Hebrew Bible in ways consistent with their authors' intent. But it is not clear why this "divine mind" secures the authority of the Christian scriptures and their re-reading of the Hebrew Bible but does not care very much, for example, for Qumran's re-reading of Habakkuk.

Not surprisingly, then, many interpreters have preferred to pay less attention to the elusive, and ultimately irretrievable "intentions" of the authors of the Hebrew Bible, and much more attention to understanding the New Testament writers as interpreters of the texts of the Hebrew Bible (Moyise 2008). In other words, more important than what a speaker or author intends is what audiences or readers "make" of the texts in various contexts. They may at times actualize the communicative intent, but equally they may reject it, ignore it, or be unaware of it and, in being unconstrained by it, create a different meaning.

In comparison with the original authors of the Hebrew Bible, New Testament writers interpret these texts in a different context, namely their commitment to Jesus, and with a different purpose, namely to express understanding about him through various images. At times, they see analogies between particular texts of the Hebrew Bible and circumstances involving Jesus. Hence Matthew uses Hosea 11:1 to link Jesus' escape to safety into Egypt with God's rescue of the people in Egypt in the exodus (Matt 2:15). This link presents Jesus as protected by God, and his mission as delivering or saving people (1:21), just as Moses did. The writer of John's gospel portrays Jesus' life-giving crucifixion, resurrection, and exaltation with an analogy of the serpent lifted up on a pole by Moses for the people in the wilderness ("just as ... so must ... " [Num 21:8–9; John 3:14–15]).

At other times, New Testament writers seem to be quite creative in applying texts of the Hebrew Bible to Jesus. Mark, for instance, begins his gospel by claiming to quote "the prophet Isaiah" (1:2). But while Mark 1:3 cites Isaiah 40:3, Mark 1:2b ("I am sending my messenger ahead of you") does not. Who does Mark quote in 1:2b? Perhaps it is Malachi 3:1 (referring to one who will purify priests in the temple) or Exodus 23:20 (referring to an angel who will guide the people into the promised land). Whichever one it is, Mark mistakenly attributes the verse to Isaiah. And whatever the verse's original meaning, Mark now creatively applies it to Jesus – or so it seems at first glance. Mark mentions Jesus in verse 1, so the "messenger [whom] I send ahead of you" could refer to Jesus as the messenger sent ahead to prepare for the coming of God. But another reading is possible. Perhaps Mark applies it to John the Baptist as the messenger who is sent ahead of Jesus! After quoting Isaiah 40:3 in the next verse (referring to whom?), Mark then narrates the activity of John the Baptist (Mark 1:4–8). So perhaps he applies the citations from the Hebrew Bible in both verse 2b and verse 3 to John rather than Jesus. Whichever it is, the link is creative, and the original context or "communicative intent" of the texts from the Hebrew Bible does not control either Mark's or our interpretive activity.

Likewise, when Jesus enters Jerusalem, Mark's crowd shouts "Hosanna! Blessed is the one who comes in the name of the Lord!" (Mark 11:9). These words cite Psalm 118:26. Psalm 118 was originally a psalm recited by pilgrims, especially the king and the people, as they approached the temple, giving thanks to God for deliverance. Mark uses it to portray Jesus as a victorious king in whom God's final (or eschatological) salvation is being encountered. The psalm did not originally refer to Jesus. Nor, as a liturgical psalm recited perhaps annually at the festival of Tabernacles, did it refer to eschatological or final salvation. Mark's creative interpretive work shows Jesus implementing this completion.

The christological and eschatological presuppositions of the New Testament writers (their Jesus glasses) and their purposes in addressing communities of Jesus' followers shape the new meanings that are formulated.

Continuity, discontinuity, creativity in interpretive process

The recognition of a reader's role in making meaning from a text is clarified in the work of an influential literary theorist, Wolfgang Iser (1974; 1978). Iser argues that texts have "gaps" that readers must fill, in order to complete the text. This process happens as readers engage a text in their particular contexts. Hence New Testament writers read the texts of the Hebrew Bible in relation to Jesus or the church, while those at Qumran read them in relation to their own circumstances and produce quite different interpretations. This does not mean that readers can make a text mean anything, but it does recognize that texts are somewhat open-ended and that readers play an active and creative part in making meaning.

These observations suggest that both continuity and discontinuity mark the ways in which New Testament writers use the Hebrew Bible to construct images of Jesus. Continuity is often found in the understanding that texts of the Hebrew Bible speak of God's ways, purposes, and agents, as well as of human life in relation to God. These are foundational perspectives for New Testament understandings of Jesus. As God's agent, Jesus enacts God's purposes, and lives in faithful relation to God. Discontinuity, however, is found in the way that the New Testament writers put these texts to use in relation to Jesus. Prior to his life and activity, these texts did not speak of him. Followers of Jesus made this connection and creatively interpreted texts of the Hebrew Bible in relation to him. So Acts 3:22–23 takes God's promise of a prophet like Moses (Deut 18:15) and reinterprets it christologically and eschatologically to portray Jesus as this prophet. There is continuity in that God works through a chosen agent. There is discontinuity (and creativity) in the declaration that the crucified and risen Jesus is this one of whom Deuteronomy speaks.

To what purpose: apologetic or understanding?

In employing texts of the Hebrew Bible to portray Jesus, who were New Testament writers addressing? Some scholars have argued that they were primarily addressing non-believers. Texts of the Hebrew Bible were used, so it was argued, on behalf of the gospel in order to convince non-believers of the significance of Jesus (Dodd 1936; 1952; Lindars 1961). Dodd focused on the citations in the speeches or sermons in Acts (Acts 2:16; 3:18; 13:23–33; 17:2–3), partly because he saw these sermons as incorporating material that came from earliest Christian proclamation in Jerusalem. Moreover Dodd reached his conclusion that their purpose was apologetic because these sermons had narrative settings involving "public" groups before whom the gospel was defended or advocated (Acts 2:14–39; 3:13–26; 4:10–12; 5:30–32). Dodd thereby concluded, it seems, that the citations performed an apologetic role, defending and advocating the faith to outsiders.

Neither of Dodd's contentions, however, has proved durable. In concluding that the citations have a primarily apologetic purpose, Dodd's confidence in the historical value of Acts and its speeches has generally been judged to be misplaced (Dibelius 1956). More seriously, Dodd confuses the narrative setting and audience of the citations for the actual setting and audience of Jesus-believers addressed by Acts. His assumption that New Testament writings were being read by outsiders has not proved persuasive.

These factors suggest, then, that in using texts of the Hebrew Bible to construct images of Jesus, New Testament writers were not defending or advocating the faith to outsiders (apologetic or polemical purposes) but were providing understanding for Jesus-believers (Juel 1988). That is, the texts of the Hebrew Bible were read by those already committed to Jesus in order to gain further insight about him. The scriptures provided ways of understanding the significance of his life and implications for the way believers live.

Which texts of the Hebrew Bible are chosen? What images of Jesus result?

The New Testament writers draw more from Isaiah and from Psalms than any other writings of the Hebrew Bible.

Isaiah   By one count, there are in the New Testament writings around fifty citations of Isaiah and even more allusions (Moyise and Menken 2005). Paul's use of Isaiah is quite extensive in Romans (some sixteen citations; Wagner 2005) but less so in the Corinthian correspondence, with only four explicit citations and about ten or eleven allusions. Interestingly, most of the citations in Romans appear in chapters 9–11, a section rich in citations of Isaiah: Rom 9:27–28 (Isa 10:22–23; 28:22), Rom 9:29 (Isa 1:9), Rom 9:33 (Isa 8:14), Rom 9:33/10:11 (Isa 28:16); Rom 10:15 (Isa 52:7); Rom 10:16 (Isa 53:1); Rom 10:20–21 (Isa 65:1–2), Rom 11:8 (Isa 29:10), Rom 11:26–27 (Isa 27:9; 59:20–21). In Romans 9–11, Paul discusses how God works through human history to accomplish God's saving purposes that embrace both Jews and Gentiles. The texts cited from Isaiah especially underline God's active faithfulness to God's purposes despite the failure of many in Israel and among the Gentiles to embrace those purposes (Rom 9:27–29, 33; 10:16, 20–21; 11:8), which are encountered in Jesus Christ (Rom 9:33; 10:11). These latter verses portray Jesus as a stumbling block, citing Isaiah 8:14 and 28:16. Yet while these texts underline rejection, Isaiah is also employed to declare the final and sure accomplishment of God's redemptive purposes. After "the full number of the Gentiles has come in" (Rom 11:25), "all Israel will be saved" when a "Deliverer from Zion" banishes Israel's ungodliness and takes away sin (Isa 59:20–21 in Rom 11:26–27). Jesus is portrayed first as a stumbling block that trips up some people, and then as the deliverer who faithfully completes God's life-giving purposes. Paul does not make clear here *how* Jesus will deliver. By comparison, Revelation also uses Isaiah to form a distinctive image of Jesus as a deliverer. Revelation 19:11 alludes to Isaiah 11:4 to present Jesus as a messianic warrior who judges righteously and makes war on God's opponents.

1 Peter also portrays Jesus as a stone, using the same texts from Isaiah that Paul uses. First, Jesus is a precious cornerstone for believers (1 Pet 2:6–7, citing Isa 28:16) and then a stumbling block for unbelievers (1 Pet 2:8, citing Isa 8:14 and Ps 118:22). The image emphasizes the preciousness of Jesus as well as the division between believers who are honored and unbelievers who stumble or are dishonored. An ecclesiological emphasis is apparent in at least four other citations of Isaiah in 1 Peter (1:24–25, citing Isa 40:6–8; 2:9, citing Isa 43:20b–21; 3:14–15, citing Isa 8:12–13; 4:14, citing Isa 11:1).

In its remaining citation, in 2:22–25, 1 Peter portrays Jesus as a suffering servant, with a mixture of citation and allusion drawn from Isaiah 53:4–12. This portrayal makes three assertions, the first two of which are explicitly christological. Using Isaiah 53:7, 9, the passage in 1 Peter 2:22–23 asserts Jesus' innocence and non-retaliation in the face of abuse. 1 Peter 2:24b asserts that Jesus bears "our sin," drawing on Isaiah 53:4–5, 6b, 12b. But the third assertion is ecclesiological, with the impact of Jesus' actions on the letter's readers and their way of living elaborated in 2:24b ("so that free from sins we might live for righteousness"). The christological assertions shape the way of life of the community of Jesus-believers.

The gospels use Isaiah extensively for constructing images of Jesus. Matthew has at least nine explicit citations, Mark six (with at least eighteen allusions), Luke four (and a further five citations in Acts), and John four. Matthew's citations from Isaiah affirm that various aspects of Jesus' life interpret or actualize ("fulfill") Isaiah's words, beginning with Jesus' conception and commission to manifest God's presence (Isa 7:14 in Matt 1:23) and continuing with John's role in preparing for Jesus' coming (Isa 40:3 in Matt 3:3). Various other dimensions of Jesus' activity fulfill or actualize

Isaiah's words: his ministry beginning in Capernaum in Galilee under Gentile/Roman rule (Isa 8:23b–9:1 in Matt 4:15–16; Carter 2001), his healings (Isa 53:4 in Matt 8:17), his sonship empowered by the Spirit and expressed in justice among the nations (Isa 42:1–4 in Matt 12:17–21), responses of rejection and hostility (Isa 6:9–10 in Matt 13:13–15), his condemnation of the Pharisees (Isa 29:13 in Matt 15:8–9), his attack on the temple and vision of it as a house of prayer (Isa 56:7 in Matt 21:13), and his eschatological condemnation of the world under Roman power (Isa 13:10, 34 in Matt 24:29). Matthew seems to have taken over five of these citations from Mark (the role of John the Baptist, responses of rejection and hostility, condemnation of the Pharisees, temple attack, eschatological judgment) and uses them to portray Jesus carrying out God's saving purposes.

Luke uses two of Mark's citations (concerning John the Baptist and the temple) and adds two more. One citation introduces Jesus' public ministry, as Jesus in the Nazareth synagogue reads from Isaiah 58:6 and 61:1–2 (Luke 4:18–19). These passages from Isaiah belong to a tradition that anticipated a time of restoration in the Jubilee year involving the cancellation of debt, restoration of land, and release from slavery, along with the creation of physical wholeness (Ringe 1985). By citing Isaiah, Luke introduces Jesus' ministry as an act of radical transformative justice.

Luke's other use of Isaiah appears in Luke 22:37, "and he was counted among the lawless," which cites Isaiah 53:12. While the context involves mission instructions for disciples, this statement involving the citation of Isaiah refers to Jesus. But there is considerable debate as to what image of Jesus it creates. One view sees it referring to Jesus' association with sinners and marginal people, an association that attracts a hostile response (Luke 7:34, 39; 15:1–2; Green 1997, 775–776). Another view sees the comment anticipating Jesus' imminent fate in Jerusalem, where he will be crucified with two "lawless" criminals (Luke 23:32–33, 39). On this latter reading, the citation presents Jesus' death as accomplishing God's purposes, interprets Jesus' death as vicarious suffering whereby he, though innocent, suffers on behalf of and for the benefit of the lawless and sinners, and depicts his being "counted" as lawless by outsiders as being according to the scriptures (Johnson 1991, 347).

If we choose the second reading, this reference is the only citation in the gospels that possibly links Isaiah's figure of the suffering servant with Jesus' death (along with perhaps Mark 10:45; Hooker 1959). It has often been claimed that Isaiah's figure of the servant of the Lord (Isa 42:1–4; 49:1–6; 50:4–9; 52:13–53:12) provides the image for all of Jesus' ministry and death (Dodd 1936; 1952). Isaiah's suffering servant provides a paradigm or "spirituality" of life lived in relationship to God whereby the righteous one, faithful to God, experiences opposition from unidentified enemies of both the righteous person and God. The righteous person suffers on behalf of or in the place of others, feels abandoned by God, and complains or laments to God. God finally vindicates the righteous person over the enemies. This paradigm, so it is argued, supplies something of a unifying "plot" for understanding Jesus' life. The scattered references to these passages of Isaiah assume this larger paradigm. Thus, by using citations from Isaiah, Jesus' healings (Isa 53:4 in Matt 8:17), ministry of justice (Isa 42:1–4 in Matt 12:17–21), and conflict and suffering (Isa 6:9–10 in

Matt 13:13–15) are linked together to portray Jesus as a suffering servant. Yet, perhaps surprisingly, only Luke 22:37 (and perhaps Mark 10:45) apply citations from Isaiah's servant songs to Jesus' death.

Short text–segments or longer traditions? This discussion of how the larger tradition of the suffering servant might function to create this image of Jesus raises an important issue. In citing and alluding to texts of the Hebrew Bible, New Testament writers typically quote short text-segments comprising only a verse or two. Are interpreters of the New Testament texts to focus only on the quoted segment itself (Gundry 1967), or are we to understand the text-segment as prompting us to elaborate the much larger text and/or tradition from which the text-segment has been drawn (Dodd 1936; 1952; Juel 1988)? Focusing on the short verse often means the verse is understood as a "proof-text" that functions to express or confirm an insight about Jesus. Focusing on a much larger text or tradition often evokes an image of Jesus that is based on a larger paradigm or narrative about God's ways of working.

For example, twice in the opening four chapters, Matthew cites verses from Isaiah 7–9. The first appears in 1:23 (Isa 7:14, "the virgin shall conceive ...") and the second, in relation to the location of Jesus' ministry, in 4:15–16 (Isa 8:23b–9:1, concerning Galilee). What is the significance of evoking Isaiah 7–9 twice in chapters 1–4? John Foley, a scholar of oral cultures and narratives, argues that oral-derived narratives typically employ the technique of metonymic intertextuality, whereby a brief citation represents and evokes a much larger tradition or narrative known to the audience (Foley 1991). The audience is expected to elaborate this larger cultural tradition or narrative. Applying this understanding to Matthew's two citations of Isaiah 7–9 in the first four chapters, I have argued that the citations function not as brief proof-texts to confirm a claim about Jesus, but as a means of evoking the larger account of king Ahaz of Judah in Isaiah 7–9 (Carter 2001). Ahaz is threatened by imperial forces, Syria and Israel to the north as well as the powerful Assyrian empire. Isaiah 7–9 provides three perspectives on imperial power: God opposes it, God uses it, and God delivers from it. I suggest that this double evoking of Isaiah 7–9 provides important images of Jesus' mission. Matthew's community faces a situation analogous to the situation of those whom Isaiah addresses, namely the challenge of negotiating imperial power, but now in the form of the Roman empire that had crucified Jesus and had within the last decade or so destroyed Jerusalem and the temple. Evoking Isaiah offers insights into and encouragement for Matthew's community by presenting an image of Jesus. While God opposes Rome, and uses it in the destruction of Jerusalem (cf. Matt 22:7), God will in the return of Jesus deliver from it (24:27–31; Carter 2003).

Psalms Other than Isaiah, the book of Psalms is the most frequently cited book of the Hebrew Bible. We will briefly consider the use of just two types of psalms. Royal psalms (Pss 2; 110) are used to portray Jesus as a king and high priest, while lament psalms (Pss 22; 69) depict him as one who suffers in being faithful to God but is vindicated by God. Regrettably there is not space to consider other prominent psalms used in the gospels nor the key role of various psalms in Romans (e.g., Ps 143; Stanley 1992; Hays 1989; Keesmaat 2004; Moyise 2004).

Royal psalms such as Psalms 2 and 110 (and other passages such as 2 Samuel 7) celebrate the enthronement and rule of the king in the line of David as representative of God's rule. As God's "son," the king in Psalm 2 enjoys intimate relationship with God and victory over his enemies (the nations). The citation of Psalm 2:7 ("you are my son"), first at Jesus' baptism and then at his transfiguration, identifies Jesus as a chosen Son and king who is in intimate relationship with God, represents God's rule, and will be victorious over his enemies (Mark 1:11; 9:7; Matt 3:17; 17:5; Luke 3:22; 9:35; also quoted in Acts 4:25–26; 13:33; Heb 1:5). Spoken by God, the citation provides divine sanction for Jesus' identity and mission as the kingly representative of God's purposes. Revelation employs Psalm 2 to portray the victory of Jesus as Messiah (Rev 2:26–27; 11:15, 18; 12:5; 19:15). And texts such as 2 Samuel 7:10–14, with its promise to David of a descendent whose throne will be established forever, are also significant for portraying Jesus as king in the line of David (quoted or alluded to in Heb 1:5, Luke 1:32–33, Acts 13:23, John 7:42).

The widely quoted Psalm 110 (see Mark 12:37; 14:62; Matt 22:44; 26:64; Luke 20:42–43; Acts 2:34–35; Heb 1:13; 5:6; 7:17, 21) provides similar sanction for an image of Jesus as God's exalted son and king. Jesus is currently exalted in the place of honor at the right hand of God and shares in divine rule (Eph 1:20–23 with Ps 8:7). Paul uses it in 1 Corinthians 15:25 (along with Psalm 8:7 in 1 Corinthians 15:27) to emphasize the future, final, eschatological destruction of every ruler, power, and authority placed under Christ's feet and subjected to God in the yet-future subjection of all creation to God's rule.

Lament psalms of the righteous sufferer, especially Psalms 22 and 69, like the passages about Isaiah's suffering servant, narrate the experience of a righteous person who suffers at the hands of enemies and the powerful, but is vindicated by a faithful and powerful God. This paradigm, or way of understanding God's workings, is especially used to understand Jesus' conflict with the Roman-allied, Jerusalem-based authorities, his crucifixion, and his resurrection. So citations from or allusions to Psalm 22 appear in the passion narratives in relation to the presence of Jesus' enemies (Mark 15:1, 2–15; Matt 27:1–2, 11–26), division of Jesus' garments (Ps 22:19; Mark 15:24; Matt 27:35; Luke 23:34; also John 19:24), Jesus' cry of Godforsakenness (Ps 22:2; Mark 15:34; Matt 27:46), and the mockery of the crowd (Ps 22:9; Mark 15:29; Matt 27:43).

John uses another lament psalm, citing Psalm 69 twice. The first citation, Psalm 69:10 in John 2:17 ("Zeal for your house will consume me"), explains the central role that Jesus' conflict with the temple powers has in his death. And in the crucifixion account, the image of Jesus as the righteous sufferer is emphasized by the citation of Psalm 69:22 in the detail of Jesus being thirsty on the cross (John 19:28).

Hebrews draws extensively on the Hebrew Bible for citations and allusions in portraying Jesus, and the Psalms play a significant role (Attridge 2004). The opening sequence of psalms in Hebrews 1:5–14 includes Psalms 2:7 and 110:1 to portray Jesus as greater than the angels and exalted by God to share in God's reign. The royal psalm, Psalm 110:4, is crucial for presenting Jesus not just as a ruler but more especially as an eternal, heavenly high priest in the order of the mysterious figure Melchizedek. This verse is explicitly cited in Hebrews 5:6, 7:17, and 10:12 as part of several discussions of Jesus as the great high priest (Heb 4:14–5:10; 7:1–17). The citing of another psalm (Ps 40:6–8) in Hebrews 10:5–7 shifts the image from Jesus as the high priest to Jesus as the sacrifice for sin, presenting the ideas that God does not want animal sacrifices and that Jesus does God's will in his death. These images of Jesus as high priest and sacrifice are elaborated by other Hebrew scriptures. So Hebrews 7 uses Genesis 14 to develop the reference to Melchizedek, as well as referring to the priesthood from the line of Aaron (the focus of Leviticus) to assert Jesus' superiority as high priest. Exodus and Leviticus provide the source for references to previous (inferior) and displaced sacrifices (Lev 16; Heb 9:6–7, 13–14, 19) and the wilderness tent-sanctuary (Exod 25–26; Heb 9:1–10). Likewise, Jeremiah 31:31–34 is quoted at length in Hebrews 8:8–12 and 10:15–18 to establish the superiority of the new covenant, which through Jesus' superior sacrifice accomplishes the forgiveness of sins. Hebrews regrettably employs an explicitly supersessionist approach in its christological and eschatological reading of the Hebrew Bible, whereby Jesus' roles as high priest and sacrifice are presented as replacing Israel's cultic traditions.

Daniel 7 and the Son of Man; Zechariah 9–14   Apocalyptic texts such as Daniel 7:13–14 and Zechariah 9–14 provide imagery for Jesus' eschatological roles. The use of Daniel 7 presents Jesus as a returning judge and agent of God's rule. Daniel 7 envisions a future judgment scene involving a heavenly figure who is identified as "one like a son of man." God gives this figure "an everlasting dominion" and kingship over "all peoples, nations, and languages" (Dan 7:14). The subsequent explanation indicates that this granting of everlasting dominion ends the rule of the empires of the world (Dan 7:15–28). The gospels draw on this scene to present Jesus' *parousia* or coming as the Son of Man soon to return to earth (Juel 1988, 158–170; Carter 2000). As Son of Man, Jesus will come (Matt 24:27; Luke 17:24) suddenly and surprisingly (Matt 24:37–44; Luke 17:26–35; 12:39–40), with power (Mark 13:26 and parallels), as God's agent, who will overpower the current Rome-allied leaders (Mark 14:62 and parallels), exercise judgment (Mark 8:38 and parallels; John 5:27), and establish God's rule as the enthroned king judging all the nations of the earth (Matt 25:31–46). Similar emphases on Jesus' roles in representing God's reign (enthronement) and enacting judgment are evoked in Revelation (Rev 1:7; 14:14). Citing or alluding to this scene from Daniel 7 thereby depicts Jesus as a future figure who will end all empires (notably Rome's), exercise judgment on God's behalf, and establish God's reign and purposes.

Zechariah 9–14, with its vision of the reassertion of God's reign over oppressive rulers, also provides a source for these eschatological descriptions, though it is used less often. Jesus' entry to Jerusalem from the Mount of Olives evokes the vision of Zechariah 14:4, which describes a time when God will stand on that mount to exercise judgment and salvation (Mark 11:1; Matt 21:1; Luke 19:29). Further, both Matthew 21:5 and John 12:15 cite Zechariah 9:9 to portray Jesus' entry into Jerusalem as that of Israel's king coming to establish God's reign. John has Jesus condemn the temple as a marketplace (John 2:16), echoing the declaration in Zechariah 14:21 that when God's reign is established there will be no traders in God's house (Carter 2008a, 256–288). And Matthew evokes Zechariah 12:10–14 in 24:30 in presenting Jesus' *parousia* as Son of Man as the establishment of this reign. Significantly, Matthew 24:3 (cf. Mark 13:3) makes the Mount of Olives the setting for Jesus' eschatological discourse, thereby employing the vision of divine judgment and salvation from Zechariah 14:4 to frame Jesus' words about his return (Ham 2008).

Conclusion

While various factors were at work in producing the New Testament's diverse images of Jesus, the Hebrew Bible played a significant role as New Testament writers used it in citations, allusions, word associations, and intertextual echoes. Reading the Hebrew Bible through their "Jesus glasses," these writers found rich resources that they employed to present a wide range of insights into Jesus' significance.

References

Attridge, Harold W. (2004). "The Psalms in Hebrews." In S. Moyise and M. J. J. Maartens (eds.), *The Psalms in the New Testament* (pp. 197–212). London: T&T Clark.

Beale, G. K. (1994). *The Right Doctrine from the Wrong Texts? Essays on the Use of the Old Testament in the New*. Grand Rapids: Baker.

Beale, G. K. (1999). "Questions of Authorial Intent, Epistemology, and Presuppositions and Their Bearing on the Study of the Old Testament in the New: A Rejoinder to Steve Moyise." *Irish Biblical Studies* 21: 151–180.

Brooke, George J. (2004). "The Psalms in Early Jewish Literature in the Light of the Dead Sea Scrolls." In S. Moyise and M. J. J. Maartens (eds.), *The Psalms in the New Testament* (pp. 5–24). London: T&T Clark.

Carter, Warren (2000). *Matthew and the Margins: A Sociopolitical and Religious Reading*. Maryknoll, NY: Orbis.

Carter, Warren (2001). "Evoking Isaiah: Why Summon Isaiah in Matthew 1:23 and 4:15–16." In *Matthew and Empire: Initial Explorations* (pp. 93–107). Harrisburg, PA: Trinity.

Carter, Warren (2003). "Are There Imperial Texts in the Class? Intertextual Eagles and Matthean Eschatology as 'Lights Out' Time for Imperial Rome (Matthew 24:27–31)." *Journal of Biblical Literature* 122: 467–487.

Carter, Warren (2008a). *John and Empire: Initial Explorations*. New York: T&T Clark.

Carter, Warren (2008b). "Love as Societal Vision and Counter-Imperial Practice in Matthew 22:34–40." In Thomas R. Hatina (ed.), *Biblical Interpretation in Early Christian Gospels*. Vol. 2: *The Gospel of Matthew* (pp. 30–44). London: T&T Clark.

Dibelius, Martin (1956). *Studies in the Acts of the Apostles*. New York: Scribner.

Dodd, Charles H. (1936). *The Apostolic Preaching and Its Developments*. New York and London: Harper.

Dodd, Charles H. (1952). *According to the Scriptures*. London: Nisbet.

Foley, John M. (1991). *Immanent Art: From Structure to Meaning in Traditional Oral Epic*. Bloomington: Indiana University Press.

Green, Joel B. (1997). *The Gospel of Luke*. Grand Rapids: Eerdmans.

Gundry, Robert H. (1967). *The Use of the Old Testament in St. Matthew's Gospel. With Special Reference to the Messianic Hope*. Leiden: Brill.

Ham, Clay A. (2008). "Reading Zechariah and Matthew's Olivet Discourse." In Thomas R. Hatina (ed.), *Biblical Interpretation in Early Christian Gospels. Vol. 2: The Gospel of Matthew* (pp. 85–97). London: T&T Clark.

Hays, Richard (1989). *Echoes of Scripture in the Letters of Paul*. New Haven: Yale University Press.

Hooker, Morna (1959). *Jesus and the Servant*. London: SPCK.

Iser, Wolfgang (1974). *The Implied Reader: Patterns of Communication in Prose Fiction from Bunyan to Beckett*. Baltimore: Johns Hopkins University Press.

Iser, Wolfgang (1978). *The Act of Reading*. Baltimore: Johns Hopkins University Press.

Johnson, Luke T. (1991). *The Gospel of Luke*. Collegeville, MN: Liturgical.

Juel, Donald (1988). *Messianic Exegesis: Christological Interpretation of the Old Testament in Early Christianity*. Philadelphia: Fortress.

Lindars, Barnabas (1961). *New Testament Apologetics*. London: SCM.

Keesmaat, Sylvia C. (2004). "The Psalms in Romans and Galatians." In S. Moyise and M. J. J. Maartens (eds.), *The Psalms in the New Testament* (pp. 139–161). London: T&T Clark.

Moyise, Steve (2004). "The Psalms in the Book of Revelation." In S. Moyise and M. J. J. Maartens (eds.), *The Psalms in the New Testament* (pp. 231–246). London: T&T Clark.

Moyise, Steve (2008). *Evoking Scripture: Seeing the Old Testament in the New*. London: T&T Clark.

Moyise, Steve, and Maarten J. J. Menken, eds. (2004). *The Psalms in the New Testament*. London: T&T Clark.

Moyise, Steve, and Maarten J. J. Menken, eds. (2005). *Isaiah in the New Testament*. London: T&T Clark.

Ringe, Sharon (1985). *Jesus, Liberation, and the Biblical Jubilee: Images for Ethics and Christology*. Philadelphia: Fortress.

Ringe, Sharon (1999). *Wisdom's Friends: Community and Christology in the Fourth Gospel*. Louisville, KY: Westminster John Knox.

Snodgrass, Klyne (2001). "The Use of the Old Testament in the New." In David Alan Black and David S. Dockery (eds.), *Interpreting the New Testament: Essays on Methods and Issues* (pp. 209–229). Nashville: Broadman & Holman.

Stanley, Christopher D. (1990). "Paul and Homer: Greco-Roman Citation Practice in the First Century CE." *Novum Testamentum* 32: 48–78.

Stanley, Christopher D. (1992). *Paul and the Language of Scripture: Citation Technique in the Pauline Epistles and Contemporary Literature*. SNTSMS 74. Cambridge: Cambridge University Press.

Vanhoozer, Kevin (1998). *Is There a Meaning in This Text? The Bible, the Reader, and the Morality of Literary Knowledge*. Grand Rapids: Zondervan.

Wagner, Ross (2005). "Isaiah in Romans and Galatians." In S. Moyise and M. J. J. Menken (eds.), *Isaiah in the New Testament* (pp. 117–132). London: T&T Clark.

PART II

Jesus Beyond the New Testament

10   Ancient Apocryphal Portraits of Jesus   145
     J. K. Elliott

11   Gnostic Portraits of Jesus   160
     Majella Franzmann

12   The Christ of the Creeds   176
     Khaled Anatolios

13   Jesus in Atonement Theories   193
     Stephen Finlan

CHAPTER 10

Ancient Apocryphal Portraits of Jesus

J. K. Elliott

From a period soon after the completion of the writing of the last book in what became (by the fourth century) the recognized New Testament canon of twenty-seven scriptures, other Christian writings were being written, books such as the Apostolic Fathers[1] together with a vast number of other texts now often labeled the New Testament Apocrypha. This umbrella title is the (less than ideal) name for an amorphous body of literature, most commonly written in imitation of the genres of writing found in the New Testament proper, i.e., gospels, letters, acts, and apocalypses. These texts generally deal with the teachings, exploits, and often the deaths of characters who figure to a larger or (often) lesser degree in the New Testament itself. Such writings emerged in the second century (some would say even the first) and proliferated up to the Middle Ages. The most influential and usually the oldest such writings may be accessed in various modern scholarly collections,[2] although inevitably, given the sheer numbers of such apocrypha, these modern editions seldom agree in their contents.

Not surprisingly, no single picture of Jesus emerges from such a diffuse collection of apocrypha, written over many centuries in different parts of Christendom. Just as one cannot write one biography or one theological assessment of Jesus from the New Testament gospels *en bloc* (although one may attempt to portray the Jesus of Matthew or the Jesus of Luke), so too one can only look to the theology or christology of each apocryphon in turn. However, the theological content of these apocryphal texts is less profound than that of the canonical writings. One does not find another Gospel of John with its elevated poetry and multifaceted layering of meanings. The apocrypha are more ephemeral, popular, and belong to pious fiction and sheer entertainment rather than to elevated intellectual enquiry. Most are quite orthodox. Generally they were based on or were influenced by the writings that were the earliest and most widespread in use, and of course it was those that became the New Testament. Scholars who brand these writings "apocryphal" are possibly correct to use such a

The Blackwell Companion to Jesus, First Edition. Edited by Delbert Burkett. ©2014 John Wiley & Sons, Ltd. Published 2014 by John Wiley & Sons, Ltd.

term to describe these texts as secondary (i.e., when compared to the New Testament) and derivative. Whether or not their theological content is due to their being a debased form of writing, an inevitable state of affairs once the first Christian flush of spiritual enthusiasm and inspirational writing that accompanied the sub-apostolic age had evaporated, is debatable.

Nonetheless, these texts, and especially those from the second to fourth century or so, are historically important, revealing the impact of Christianity (now increasingly accepted as a state religion) on the ordinary worshiper. These writings are unlikely to contain much about the historical origins of the first-century faith. Few of these texts aspire to great theological teaching, but they serve as a corrective to the impressions that we receive from the contemporary intellectual writings of the famous church fathers and ecclesiastical councils, as they, at the same period, were hammering out dogmas, doctrines, and creeds. The apocryphal texts reflect simpler faith but were nonetheless influential. They reflect a contemporary teaching but also fueled a wider interest in the beliefs and practices of such teaching.

Birth and Infancy Narratives

Those who have only a scant acquaintance with the New Testament apocryphal texts may nonetheless be aware of some of the bizarre tales about Jesus as a child found in the Infancy Gospel of Thomas (hereafter, InfGTh).[3] This is the document that has the tale of Jesus making birds out of clay:

> When this boy Jesus was five years old he was playing at the crossing of a stream, and he gathered together into pools the running water, and instantly made it clean, and gave his command with a single word. Having made soft clay he moulded from it twelve sparrows. And it was the Sabbath when he did these things. And there were also many other children playing with him. When a certain Jew saw what Jesus was doing while playing on the Sabbath, he at once went and told his father Joseph, "See, your child is at the stream, and he took clay and moulded twelve birds and has profaned the Sabbath." And when Joseph came to the place and looked, he cried out to him, saying, "Why do you do on the Sabbath things which it is not lawful to do?" But Jesus clapped his hands and cried out to the sparrows and said to them, "Be gone!" And the sparrows took flight and went away chirping. The Jews were amazed when they saw this, and went away and told their leaders what they had seen Jesus do. (InfGTh 2)

It is a tale that is known even in Islam: "I create for you something resembling the form of birds, and I blow into it and it becomes birds by God's leave" (Sura 3:49; cf. Sura 5:110).[4] And it is a tale that appears in a twelfth-century carved wooden ceiling of the remote church St Martin in Zillis in Canton Graubünden in Switzerland, where it is the only non-canonical depiction of Jesus amid some ninety-eight comparable painted carvings of biblical scenes.

It is of course a charming tale that serves simply to show Jesus' uniqueness. The assumptions and teachings here, namely that Jesus is the Lord of the Sabbath, whose word alone is efficacious in initiating action and who is a giver of life and a creator, are orthodox, and the tale is an effective vehicle for what is in essence a high christology. On this higher theological level, the story may be interpreted as proof of Jesus' divinity: Jesus, like God in Genesis 1:20, breathes life into birds. The picture of Jesus as the pre-existent *logos* and a partner in creation (John 1:1–5) may well lie behind the thinking of the Infancy Gospel of Thomas, where it emerges as a simple folk tale.

Some of the other stories of the child Jesus in Infancy Thomas have caused consternation among the faithful – stories such as the sequel to the bird-making scene:

> Now the son of Annas the scribe was standing there with Joseph; and he took a branch of a willow and with it dispersed the water which Jesus had collected. When Jesus saw what he had done he was angry and said to him, "You insolent, godless ignoramus, what harm did the pools and the water do to you? Behold, now you also shall wither like a tree and shall bear neither leaves nor root nor fruit." And immediately that child withered up completely; and Jesus departed and went into Joseph's house. But the parents of the boy who was withered carried him away, bemoaning his lost youth, and brought him to Joseph and reproached him, asking, "What kind of child do you have, who does such things?" (InfGTh 3)

A comparable story relates the following: "a child ran and knocked against his shoulder. Jesus was angered and said to him, 'You shall not go further on your way', and immediately he fell down and died" (InfGTh 4).

What picture of Jesus emerges or is intended by the author? Clearly his miraculous powers and his divine status are highlighted. But many readers coming across such stories may well find that this is not the Christian Jesus they expect and that such a depiction in InfGTh is responsible for the (to them correct) judgment of this novella as "apocryphal" (in its popular definition as "spurious," even "unorthodox"). However, the participants' reactions to the events in the stories are deliberately significant and challenging. But the stories above, where Jesus on the face of it looks like an *enfant terrible* (rather than like the pacific Christ, beloved of later interpreters), are compatible with the "angry" Jesus of the leper story in the authentic reading at Mark 1:41 and with the vengeful Jesus of Mark's story of the blasting of the fig tree (Mark 11:12–14).

The stories in InfGTh reveal Jesus' power over life and death. There are of course other stories there where the child Jesus is a *Wunderkind*. In those, he is a force for good, showing the beneficent side of his abilities, as when he raises a dead child or heals an injured foot. In the latter case, the people who observe the healing worship Jesus and say, "Truly the spirit of God dwells in this child" (InfGTh 10).

In another story, Jesus is depicted as superior to his teachers and surpasses their knowledge even of the secret meanings of the alphabet. That story appears with variations three times in this short gospel, showing its obvious popularity in the second century. It is probably based on the canonical story of Jesus in the Temple at age twelve (Luke 2:41–52). After admitting defeat to his pupil, one teacher, Zacchaeus, exclaims, "Whatever great thing he is, a god or an angel, what should I say?" (InfGTh 7). Again, as in the extract from InfGTh 10, the climax of the story is a high christological declaration.

We have concentrated on the InfGTh, because it was a popular book. Many manuscripts of this text survive, and its stories were repeated in other later apocrypha such as the Gospel of Pseudo-Matthew (= Ps-Mt). Ps-Mt probably dates from the eighth century but utilized and repeated stories from earlier gospels, especially the Protevangelium of James (= Protev) as well as the InfGTh. One new story in it continues that same tradition:

> After these things Joseph departed with Mary and [the child] Jesus to go into Capernaum by the sea-shore, on account of the malice of his adversaries. And when Jesus was living in Capernaum, there was in the city a man named Joseph, exceedingly rich. But he had wasted away under his infirmity and died, and was lying dead in his couch. And when Jesus heard people in the city mourning and weeping and lamenting over the dead man, he said to Joseph, "Why do you not grant the benefit of your favour to this man, seeing that he is called by your name?" And Joseph answered him, "How have I any power or ability to grant him a benefit?" And Jesus said to him, "Take the kerchief which is upon your head, go and put it on the face of the dead man and say to him, 'Christ save you,' and immediately the dead man will be healed and will rise from his couch." And when Joseph heard this, he went away at the command of Jesus and ran and entered the house of the dead man, and put the kerchief, which he was wearing on his head, upon the face of him who was lying in the couch and said, "Jesus save you." And forthwith the dead man rose from his bed and asked who Jesus was. (Ps-Mt 40)

Again it is the final question that is important, in which the readers are addressed – the theological message of Ps-Mt is in the expected answer to the question. Here Jesus is used as an intercessor, and his powers are with him *ab initio* – in itself, a powerful theological statement. Wordsworth's line states, "the Child is the father of the Man"; in Jesus' case that is expressly fulfilled as he performs his divine mission from the beginning of his life (and in some theological teachings from the start of time itself). The familiar story in Protev 20 (itself another popular nativity gospel, going back to the second century) has the hand of the incredulous midwife, Salome, consumed with fire because of her disbelief that Jesus' mother is still a virgin, and she is healed by Jesus, the neonate.

In the following tale, which also comes from Ps-Mt, Jesus is portrayed as master over the created world:

> And having come to a certain cave, and wishing to rest in it, Mary dismounted from her beast, and sat down with the child Jesus in her lap. And on the journey there were with Joseph three boys, and with Mary a girl. And behold, suddenly there came out of the cave many dragons; and when the boys saw them they cried out in great terror. Then Jesus got down from his mother's lap and stood on his feet before the dragons; and they worshipped Jesus and then departed. Then was fulfilled that which was said by David the prophet, "Praise the Lord from the earth, dragons, and all you ocean depths." ... Likewise, lions and panthers adored him and accompanied them in the desert. Wherever

Joseph and Mary went, they went before them showing them the way and bowing their heads; they showed their submission by wagging their tails, they worshipped him with great reverence. ... And the lions kept walking with them, and with the oxen and the asses and the beasts of burden, which carried what they needed, and did not hurt a single one of them, though they remained with them; they were tame among the sheep and the rams which they had brought with them from Judaea and which they had with them. They walked among wolves and feared nothing; and not one of them was hurt by another. Then was fulfilled that which was spoken by the prophet, "Wolves shall feed with lambs; lion and ox shall eat straw together." (Ps-Mt 18–19)

In this selection, Jesus demonstrates his control over all animals. In other apocrypha, especially in the apocryphal Acts, where the apostles act as Jesus' emissaries and invoke Jesus' name, snakes, dogs, asses, a tuna fish, and even bedbugs are among the menagerie of creatures who serve Christ's message (see Spittler 2008).

The following selection, also from Ps-Mt, portrays Jesus as the destroyer of paganism. Here the unassailability of his message is evident:

And it came to pass that, when Mary went into the temple with the child, all the idols prostrated themselves on the ground, so that all of them were lying on their faces shattered and broken to pieces; and thus they plainly showed that they were nothing. Then was fulfilled that which was said by the prophet Isaiah, "Behold, the Lord will come upon a swift cloud and will enter Egypt, and all the handiwork of the Egyptians shall be moved before his face." (Ps-Mt 23)

Above, we have concentrated on the Protev, InfGTh, and Ps-Mt, all of which are nativity or infancy gospels. Two other such accounts are the Armenian Infancy Gospel (= ArmInfG) and the Arabic Infancy Gospel (= ArabInfG). These read like the *Thousand and One Nights* – long picaresque novels dealing predominantly with Jesus and the Holy Family in Egypt. In a moralistic tale from ArmInfG 30 (Terian 2008), Jesus reconciles a couple about to seek a divorce. The characters acknowledge Jesus' status by bowing and recognize his divine status: "You are God who came to give us life." The story may well be an adaptation of Matthew 19:1–12, with an allusion to Deuteronomy 24:1–4, but it is all the more effective being dramatized in a simple tale.

The flavor of these texts can also be seen in the following selection from the Arabic Infancy Gospel:

On another day the Lord Jesus went out into the road, and seeing some boys who had met to play, he followed them; but the boys hid themselves from him. The Lord Jesus, therefore, having come to the door of a certain house, and seen some women standing there, asked them where the boys had gone; and when they answered that there was no one there, he said again, "Who are these whom you see in the furnace?" They replied that they were young goats of three years old. And the Lord Jesus cried out and said, "Come out, O goats, to your Shepherd." Then the boys, in the form of goats, came out, and began to skip round him; and the women, seeing this, were very much astonished, and were seized with trembling, and speedily supplicated the Lord Jesus, saying, "O our Lord Jesus, son of Mary, you are truly that good Shepherd of Israel; have mercy on your handmaidens who stand before you, and who have never doubted: for you have come, O our Lord, to heal, and not to destroy." And when the Lord Jesus answered that the sons of Israel were like the Ethiopians among the nations, the women said, "You, O Lord, know all things, nor is anything hid from you; now, indeed, we beseech you, and ask you of your mercy to restore these boys, your servants, to their former condition." The Lord Jesus therefore said, "Come boys, let us go and play." And immediately, while the women were standing by, the kids were changed into boys. (ArabInfG 40)

The picture of Jesus that emerges from these two stories is orthodox (as understood and later defined). The illustrations may be simple, unsophisticated sermons, but in the Armenian story, the announcement is that Jesus' divinity is central: he is addressed as God, and his role as having come "to give us life" is consistent with John 10:10 and other comparable statements in the canonical gospels. In ArabInfG, the child Jesus, as in InfGTh, is master of life and death and is shown as such in his miraculous powers, as well as in his titles, "Lord," "Shepherd," and "Son of Mary."

Although he is regularly identified as "God" or Godlike, he nevertheless is fully human – and that significant element distinguishes the proto-orthodox and ultimately canonical writings, and indeed the bulk of the New Testament apocrypha, from the teachings of Gnostics and docetists (on which more below). In all the infancy gospels, Jesus is fully incarnate. In the Infancy Gospel of Thomas, Jesus is seen as a "normal" child working in his father's carpentry shop and running errands for his mother.

But in one infancy story, known as Arundel 404 (*Liber de Infantia Salvatoris*), a docetic view is possibly present. Jesus is born as an intense bright light, which "gradually shrank, imitated the shape of an infant, then immediately became outwardly an infant like a child born normally" (Arundel 72–74). But is this docetic? May it not be merely poetic, a dramatizing of Jesus as the Word-became-flesh and, more particularly here, as the Light of the World?

One significant element in this apocryphon is the silencing of nature, which occurs immediately before the child is born:

In that hour, a great silence descended with fear. For even the winds stopped, they made no breeze; there was no movement of the leaves on the trees, nor sound of water heard; the streams did not flow; there was no motion of the sea. All things born in the sea were silent; no human voice sounded and there was a great silence. For the pole itself ceased its rapid course from that hour. The measure of time almost stopped. Everyone was overwhelmed with great fear and kept silent; we were expecting the advent of the most high God, the end of the world.

Such a description occurs also in the Protevangelium of James 17, when Joseph, at the moment of Jesus' birth, describes the cessation of time and the catalepsy of nature. That monologue is a passage of purple prose in the apocrypha, a body of literature not generally distinguished by great writing. In it, the created world acknowledges the cosmic significance of Jesus' incarnation. It develops the phenomena already present in the birth stories of Matthew and Luke, such as the star that heralds Jesus' coming, and may be compared to the passages in the canonical gospels that associate Jesus' death with such otherworldly events as the solar eclipse during the crucifixion, the earthquakes, the rending of the temple's veil, and the opening of graves. The suspension of time parallels Revelation 8:1, with the "half hour silence in the heavens." The uniqueness and cosmic significance of Jesus' birth is hereby enhanced in the apocrypha by the story in the Arundel manuscript, and in Joseph's monologue in the Protevangelium.

Jesus' Public Ministry

Gospels like Ps-Mt, InfGTh, and the Protev are nativity-childhood gospels, not gospels of the ministry like the canonical gospels of Matthew, Mark, Luke, or John. Possibly they were originally composed to fill in gaps in the biography of Jesus and are part of a process that began soon after Jesus' own day. Paul in his letters pays little attention to Jesus' earthly ministry or sayings and concentrates on the effect of his death and resurrection, because he wishes to concentrate only on the changed relationship between man and God that resulted from Jesus' redeeming death, and/ or because he was ignorant of details about the ministry of Jesus, not having had first-hand experience of that career.

Once the canonical gospels were being composed, the need had already been felt, and was consequently then being met, to explain to outsiders how and why Jesus met his death. It is a cliché in biblical studies that Mark can largely be seen as a passion gospel with an introduction, one third of that short gospel being taken up with only one week in Jesus' ministry; the remaining two thirds being largely concerned with passion plots, controversies, and warnings about Jesus' fate. Later accounts, i.e., Matthew and Luke, in writing Jesus' story, as it were, from his death backwards, give flesh to his teaching and ministry, increasing the number of incidents in the pre-Jerusalem phase of Jesus' life, and prefacing the accounts with two separate ways of describing Jesus' birth. The process of filling in gaps had already started. It was to continue in the second century.

Nevertheless, the writings from the second to third centuries onwards did not significantly fill in the events of Jesus' public ministry. A few fragments survive in isolated papyri, such as Egerton 2 and Oxyrhynchus Papyrus 840, that tell stories of a synoptic-gospel type, but it is not known if these remains came from a full-fledged gospel comparable in scale to, say, Matthew or Luke. Little is of significance in those fragments to supplement our portrait of Jesus. Part 1 of the Gospel of Nicodemus, also known as the Acts of Pilate (= APil), is a rewriting of the trial narratives. The Gospel of Peter (GPet) survives only as a passion story, and we cannot know how much material prior to that story was originally contained in this writing. It seems as if writers of this time wanted to concentrate mainly on the very beginnings of Jesus' career and, as we shall see in a moment, on the period immediately consequent upon his death.

An exception may be the apocryphal sayings of Jesus; it may be argued that some of these at least could go back to the earthly Jesus. The Gospel of Thomas (= GTh) contains some 114 logia, mostly sayings attributed to Jesus. Although the contexts are not given, it is likely that they were intended to be read as the *ipsissima verba* of the incarnate Jesus of the ministry period, not the *dicta* of the risen redeemer. The purpose was (as also in, say, the Sermon in Matthew 5–7 or the hypothetical sayings document Q, which many think lay behind Matthew and Luke) to record pronouncements allegedly from Jesus' own lips. Such teachings would be worthy of attention and would have been promoted as uniquely authoritative, because they were spoken by the one whom Christians believed had been sent by God and who was soon to be resurrected.

Some sayings in GTh are close to those known elsewhere in the New Testament, e.g., logion 9, which is a version of the parable of the sower, or logion 73: "Jesus said, 'The harvest is great but the laborers are few, so pray to the Lord to send laborers to the harvest'" (= Matt 9:37–38; Luke 10:2). Others are quite different from New Testament sayings – e.g., logion 18:

> The disciples said to Jesus, "Tell us in which way our end will occur." Jesus said, "Have you indeed discovered the beginning, that you search for the end? In the place where the beginning is, there the end will be. Blessed is he who will stand at the beginning: he will know the end and he will not taste death."

Logion 23 is another saying of this type: "Jesus said, 'I shall choose you, one from a thousand, and two from ten thousand, and they shall stand as a single one.'"

Some of the logia have been branded as docetist or Gnostic, but, as we have seen throughout this examination, those judgments may not be clear-cut, and logion 28, in which Jesus states that he "stood in the midst of the world and appeared to them in the flesh," is conspicuously anti-docetic. The problem with trying to assess the overall picture of the theology of the Jesus of these and other *agrapha* is that no one picture emerges, just as no one portrait of Jesus is apparent in the collected canonical sayings. One of the main reasons why GTh has lent itself to the charge of being Gnostic is that the full, Coptic version of this apocryphon was found at Nag Hammadi among tractates that are Gnostic. GTh has been tarred with the same brush and is thus guilty by association. It is certainly conceivable that GTh would have proved congenial reading matter to those who also knew and used other Nag Hammadi texts; but we need to remember that second-century Christianity was open to syncretism, and it would be surprising if innovative new texts were not tainted from time to time with alternative, even opposing, variants of Christianity. GTh is the end-product of a growing and heterogeneous collection. As a consequence, no one theology of it can be written. Richard Valantasis (1997) notes that, although GTh lacks anything on Jesus' passion, death, and resurrection, his ministry sayings reveal him to be a living voice rather than only a historic person set in a particular time: he is nonetheless the revealer of mysteries, but is one who has a mission and disciples.

Jesus' Descent into Hades

The other large perceived gap in Jesus' career, to which we previously alluded, was that mysterious time between Jesus' death and the discovery of his empty tomb. 1 Peter 3:19 may have been responsible for many of the questionings that later piety tried to satisfy. Reconstructions of that period immediately after Jesus' death (and the dramatization of the creedal statement "He descended into Hell") occur in such apocryphal tales as the *Descensus*, part 2 of the Gospel of Nicodemus or Acts of Pilate (cf. GPet 10.41–42). It is there where Jesus breaks into the Underworld, hitherto controlled by Satan (and Hades personified), and where the following scene occurs:

> While Satan and Hades were speaking to one another, a loud voice like thunder sounded, "Lift up your gates, O rulers, and be lifted up, O everlasting doors, and the King of Glory shall come in." When Hades heard this, he said to Satan, "Go out, if you can, and withstand him." So Satan went out. Then Hades said to his demons, "Secure strongly and firmly the gates of brass and the bars of iron, and hold my bolts, and stand upright and keep watch on everything. For if he comes in, woe will seize us." When the forefathers heard that, they all began to mock him, saying, "O all-devouring and insatiable one, open, that the King of Glory may come in." The prophet David said, "Do you not know, blind one, that when I lived in the world, I prophesied that word: 'Lift up your gates, O rulers'?" Isaiah said, "I foresaw this by the Holy Spirit and wrote, 'The dead shall arise, and those who are in the tombs shall be raised up, and those who are under the earth shall rejoice. O death, where is your sting? O Hades, where is your victory?'" Again the voice sounded, "Lift up the gates." When Hades heard the voice the second time, he answered as if he did not know it and said, "Who is this King of Glory?" The angels of the Lord said, "The Lord strong and mighty, the Lord mighty in battle." And immediately at this answer the gates of brass were broken in pieces and the bars of iron were crushed and all the dead who were bound were loosed from their chains, and we with them. And the King of Glory entered as a man, and all the dark places of Hades were illuminated. Hades at once cried out, "We are defeated, woe to us. But who are you, who have such authority and power? And who are you, who without sin have come here, you who appear small and can do great things, who are humble and exalted, slave and master, soldier and king, and have authority over both the dead and the living? You were nailed to the cross, and laid in the sepulchre, and now you have become free and have destroyed all our power. Are you Jesus, of whom the chief ruler Satan said to us that through the cross and death you would inherit the whole world?" Then the King of Glory seized the chief ruler Satan by the head and handed him over to the angels, saying, "Bind with irons his hands and his feet and his neck and his mouth." Then he gave him to Hades and said, "Take him and hold him fast until my second coming." (APil 5 [21])

Jesus subsequently raises the faithful dead, a scene known to the medieval mystery plays as the Harrowing of Hell.

The Apocryphal Acts

The bulk of the New Testament apocrypha is concerned not directly with Jesus himself nor with perceived gaps in his biography, but with the lives and especially the deaths of his faithful followers, the apostles. Apocryphal acts were produced in abundance and seem to have been the Christian equivalents of the erotic novel, beloved of a leisured, literate, and moneyed upper class. The big five apocryphal Acts are those of Andrew (= AA), of Paul (= APaul), of Peter (= APet), of John (= AJ), and of Thomas (= ATh). But successors were prolific, e.g., the Acts of Philip, the Acts of Andrew and Matthias (= AAM), the Acts of Andrew and Paul, the Acts of Barnabas, and others.

In these verbose tales, the picture of Jesus that emerges is striking. He is prayed to, often as "savior" (APet 10, 32 [3]; ATh 25, 47). He is the center of much of the apostolic preaching that makes up a high proportion of these books. The following comment by Marcellus, a character in the Acts of Peter, is typical: in APet 10 he declares that the apostle's preaching is "the true faith of Christ." Jesus is invoked during the sacraments, as in ATh 26, 27, 49–50 (during the eucharist), and in the story of Thecla's auto-baptism "into Christ's name" (APaul 34), and in that distinctive sacrament of "sealing" (ATh 49). In all of these ceremonies, Christ is established as central to Christian initiation, life, and teaching.

But occasionally these apocryphal Acts betray ambiguities, especially regarding the nature of Jesus' resurrected body. Those queries reflect early Christianity's difficulties in describing and understanding resurrection, a problem already detected in the earliest Easter stories and in 1 Corinthians 15.

In Acts of John 87–106, a section of the second-century Acts, which many think was influenced by Gnostic or docetic ideas, questions are raised about the nature of Jesus' body before the resurrection. In recalling his earlier career with the earthly Jesus, "John" says,

> And my brother said, "John, this child on the sea shore who called to us, what does he want?" And I said, "What child?" He replied, "The one who is beckoning to us." And I answered, "Because of our long watch that we kept at sea you are not seeing straight, brother James: but do you not see the man who stands there, fair and comely and of a cheerful countenance?" But he said to me, "Him I do not see, brother; but let us go and we shall see what it means." And so when we had landed the ship, we saw him helping us to beach the ship.
>
> And when we left the place, wishing to follow him again, he again appeared to me, bald-headed but with a thick and flowing beard; but to James he appeared as a youth whose beard was just starting. We were perplexed, both of us, as to the meaning of what we had seen. But when we followed him, we both became gradually more perplexed as we thought on the matter. Yet to me there appeared a still more wonderful sight; for I tried to see him as he was, and I never at any time saw his eyes closing but only open. And sometimes he appeared to me as a small man and unattractive, and

then again as one reaching to heaven. Also there was in him another marvel; when I sat at table he would take me upon his breast and I held him; and sometimes his breast felt to me to be smooth and tender, and sometimes hard, like stone, so that I was perplexed in myself and said, "What does this mean?" (AJ 88–89)

At AJ 91 we read that "[Jesus'] unity has *many* faces" – that teaching is taken quite literally in many apocryphal Acts, as are so many other such images by the second-century Christians.

In some other stories, Jesus is similarly changeable and amorphous. At APet 17, the reappearing Jesus is described as a naked boy; at APet 21, he is variously described as an old man and a young boy; in Acts of Paul and Andrew 3, he is seen as a twelve-year-old boy. During the sacrament of chrism in ATh 27, a young man (presumably the risen Jesus) is seen with a symbolically brilliant blazing lamp. In AJ 73, he is a beautiful smiling youth; in AAM 5, he is camouflaged as a ship's captain; in AAM 18 and 33, he is a "beautiful small child." One may find such metamorphoses in the New Testament, as in the transfiguration account (Matt 17:1–8 and parallels), and when Jesus is not readily recognized as such by the travelers to Emmaus (Luke 24:13–35), nor by Mary in the garden (John 20:14), as well as in those stories when the risen Christ can pass out of his sealed tomb (Matt 27:66; 28:6) or through the locked doors of the upper room (John 20:19, 26). In one of the apocryphal writings about the assumption, the Virgin Mary sees a thirty-year-old youth, and he is identified as the risen Christ (*Discourse of Theodosius II*). In the Epistle of the Apostles (= EpAp), on which more below, Jesus is said to have been metamorphosed *before* the incarnation. In the story in EpAp 14, Jesus is Gabriel announcing his own role in Mary's conception (recalling "I, the Lord, went into her and became flesh") and thus was responsible for his own incarnation.[5] These multifaceted portrayals of Jesus and his polymorphism are part of a wider phenomenon (Foster 2007) and help to show that each individual with the eye of faith who accepts the ongoing guiding example set by Christ receives him as active in the present; there is indeed no one uniform vision.

A prophecy by Jesus, predicting that his disciples will heal the sick or raise the dead after his death and that they will then suffer (Matt 10:8, 18), is already seen to have been fulfilled within the canonical Acts of the Apostles, where Peter, Paul, and the other apostles are indeed arraigned before kings and governors and show that the apostles replace the absent Christ. They follow in his footsteps and are his *alter ego*. Not surprisingly, that connection of Jesus with each apostle results in a typically literal depiction in the apocryphal Acts. Thus in AA 47 (15), Jesus appears disguised as Andrew. And in the following selection from ATh, Jesus, replacing Thomas, becomes the preacher:

The king requested the groomsmen to leave the bridal chamber. When all had left, and the doors were shut, the bridegroom raised the curtain of the bridal chamber, that he might bring the bride to himself. And he saw the Lord Jesus talking with the bride. He had the appearance of Judas Thomas, the apostle, who shortly before had blessed them and departed; and he said to him, "Did you not go out before them all? And how is it that you are here now?" And the Lord said to him, "I am not Judas Thomas, I am his brother." (ATh 12)

Compare also ATh 34, which says that the apostle was known to exist in two forms: i.e., as himself and as Jesus. Clearly these writings were susceptible to docetic interpretation. A Jesus who can transform himself at will in post-Easter visions could be said by some to have had a similar ability during the ministry, if indeed he were not fully human. For the proto-orthodox writers of the apocryphal Acts, this motif had a different purpose; it was merely to show the experiences of those who claim to have seen the risen Lord, or to depict in a symbolic and dramatic way how the eponymous hero as the *alter ego* of Christ was indistinguishable from his risen master, in whose footsteps he was following.

Dialogues with the Risen Christ

To have the risen Jesus reappear and impart teachings is a major development, and it is a theme that becomes a major literary device in New Testament apocryphal apocalypses and also especially in the Gnostic literature. Visions cut across orthodox definitions of authority, which were based on a privileged hierarchy and on aboriginal texts, although a claim for the authority of visions had a precedent in the period of earliest Christianity itself with Paul (that quintessential anti-authoritarian and *soi-disant* apostle), who claimed a personal commission from his visionary experience of the risen Lord during his Damascus Road conversion. But such personalized revelatory experiences were looked on with suspicion, not least once Montanism had emerged in the second half of the second century. In that movement, spiritual outpourings on its own prophets and prophetesses are dominant.

In the apocryphon the Epistle of the Apostles, we have a typical example of a dialogue with the Redeemer. The risen Jesus answers his questioners:

> And we said to him, "O Lord, how many years yet [until Christ's second coming]?" And he said to us, "When the hundred and fiftieth year is completed, between Pentecost and Passover will the coming of my Father take place." And we said to him, "O Lord, now you said to us, 'I will come,' and then you said, 'he who sent me will come.'" And he said to us, "I am wholly in the Father and the Father in me." Then we said to him, "Will you really leave us until your coming? Where will we find a teacher?" And he answered and said to us, "Do you not know that until now I am both here and there with him who sent me?" And we said to him, "O Lord, is it possible that you should be both here and there?" And he said to us, "I am wholly in the Father and the Father in me after his image and after his likeness and after his power and after his perfection and after his light, and I am his perfect word." (EpAp 17)

And so the questions and answers continue. See EpAp 20–30, where the questions center on the nature of Jesus' resurrected body, giving another clear instance of that major concern that Christian believers had expressed ever since the issues were voiced in 1 Corinthians 15.

Similar questioning is evident in other apocryphal apocalypses, especially in the Apocalypse of Peter, where the risen Lord himself gives Peter a guided tour of the Other World, during which Peter incessantly bombards Jesus with inquiries:

> And he showed me in his right hand the souls of all men. And on the palm of his right hand the image of that which shall be accomplished at the last day; and how the righteous and the sinners shall be separated, and how those who are upright in heart will fare, and how the evil-doers shall be rooted out to all eternity. We beheld how the sinners wept in great affliction and sorrow, until all who saw it with their eyes wept, whether righteous or angels, and he himself also.
>
> And I asked him and said to him, "Lord, allow me to speak your word concerning the sinners, 'it were better for them if they had not been created.'" And the Saviour answered and said to me, "Peter, why do you say that not to have been created were better for them? You resist God. You would not have more compassion than he for his image: for he has created them and brought them forth out of not-being. Now because you have seen the lamentation which shall come upon the sinners in the last days, therefore your heart is troubled; but I will show you their works, whereby they have sinned against the Most High." (Apoc Peter 3)

The apocryphal writing the Questions of Bartholomew (= QBarth) is another good example of the genre:

> Bartholomew said to him, "Declare to us, Lord, what sin is more grievous than all sins?" Jesus said to him, "Truly I say to you that hypocrisy and backbiting are more grievous than all sins: for because of them the prophet said in the psalm that 'the ungodly shall not rise in judgement, neither sinners in the council of the righteous,' neither the ungodly in the judgement of my Father. Truly, truly, I say to you, that every sin shall be forgiven to every man, but the sin against the Holy Ghost shall not be forgiven." And Bartholomew said to him, "What is the sin against the Holy Ghost?" Jesus said to him, "Whosoever shall decree against any man who has served my holy Father has blasphemed against the Holy Ghost. Every man who serves God with reverence is worthy of the Holy Ghost, and he who speaks anything evil against him shall not be forgiven." (QBarth V, 1)

The picture of Jesus that emerges throughout this and the other apocrypha is of the living Jesus, almighty and obviously still highly efficacious as the divine teacher inspiring his followers. To present such a picture is the purpose and message of such writings. Their authors may well sometimes be filling in gaps in Jesus' biography or be telling tales of his apostles' careers as they traveled to spread the good news of his teachings and mission, but, in so doing, they reveal historical information not about the first-century characters or events, but about the world at the time of their composition. In so doing, they provide an invaluable insight for modern readers into a period that all too often is a dark age or a time when only the prevailing orthodoxy is being promulgated by Christian councils and intellectual patristic giants amid simmering conflicts. The apocrypha allow us tantalizing, incomplete, but often revealing insights into the multilayered interests and theological concerns of their authors and the early Christian communities.

Appendix

In the Middle Ages, the Letter of Lentulus, written in the thirteenth century, purports to show what Jesus looked like. This then is literally a portrait:

> In these days there appeared, and there still is, a man of great power named Jesus Christ, who is called by the Gentiles the prophet of truth, whom his disciples call the Son of God, raising the dead and healing diseases – a man in stature middling tall, and comely, having a reverend countenance, which those who look upon may love and fear; having hair of the hue of an unripe hazel-nut and smooth almost down to his ears, but from the ears in curling locks somewhat darker and more shining, flowing over his shoulders; having a parting at the middle of the head according to the fashion of the Nazareans; a brow smooth and very calm, with a face without wrinkle or any blemish, which a moderate red colour makes beautiful; with the nose and mouth no fault at all can be found; having a full beard of the colour of his hair, not long, but a little forked at the chin; having an expression simple and mature, the eyes grey, flashing, and clear; in rebuke terrible, in admonition kind and lovable, cheerful yet keeping gravity; sometimes he has wept, but never laughed; in stature of body tall and straight, with hands and arms fair to look upon; in talk grave, reserved and modest, fairer than the children of men.

Many apocryphal stories influenced later artists,[6] although one must also be alert to the opposite influence, that is, an iconic representation described by later writers. The Letter of Lentulus seems to be an example of the latter, namely a writing that is describing an actual painting before the author's very eyes. In written form, it helped perpetuate a conventional portraiture of what Jesus looked like. Many likenesses of the type written up by "Lentulus" were created, and even today these features of Jesus are the usual ones commonly recognizable.

Notes

1   A relatively modern term for a number of essentially Christian guides (e.g., the Didache, the Epistle of Barnabas, the Shepherd of Hermas, 1 and 2 Clement) concerning matters such as church order, Sabbath observance, and the correct interpretation of circumcision.

2   All the translated texts that appear in this chapter are taken from Elliott 1993 and are reproduced by permission of Oxford University Press. Other published compendia of apocryphal texts include Bernhard 2006; Elliott 1996; Klauck 2002, 2005, 2008b;

Schneemelcher 1990, 1997; and Terian 2008. For introductions and essays, see Foster 2008 and Lapham 2003.

3   For a study into the milieu in which this apocryphon developed and a discussion of it as a typical childhood biography of a great man, see Chartrand-Burke 2008.

4   The *Tafsīr* of Abū Ja'far al-Tabarī, the oldest commentary on the Koran extant, quotes from another form of this story. See Robinson 1989.

5   See Cartlidge and Elliott 2001, 84–85, figures 4.6 and 4.7. There artists interpret "the Word became flesh" literally as a fetus, traveling along a tube from God's mouth to (typically) the virgin's ear.

6   Cartlidge and Elliott (2001) set out the many links between apocryphal stories and artists' depictions of those characters and scenes.

References

Bernhard, Andrew E., ed. (2006). *Other Early Christian Gospels: A Critical Edition of the Surviving Greek Manuscripts*. London, New York: T&T Clark.

Cartlidge, David R., and J. Keith Elliott (2001). *Art and the Christian Apocrypha*. London and New York: Routledge.

Chartrand-Burke, Tony (2008). "The Infancy Gospel of Thomas." In Paul Foster (ed.), *The Non-Canonical Gospels* (pp. 126–138). London: T&T Clark.

Elliott, J. K., ed. (1993). *The Apocryphal New Testament*. Oxford: Clarendon.

Elliott, J. K., ed. (1996). *The Apocryphal Jesus: Legends of the Early Church*. Oxford: Oxford University Press.

Foster, Paul (2007). "Polymorphic Christology: Its Origins and Development in Early Christianity." *Journal of Theological Studies* n.s. 58: 66–99.

Foster, Paul, ed. (2008). *The Non-Canonical Gospels*. London: T&T Clark.

Klauck, Hans-Josef (2002). *Apokryphe Evangelien*. Stuttgart: Katholisches Bibelwerk. English translation: Klauck, Hans-Josef (2003). *Apocryphal Gospels: An Introduction*. London, New York: T&T Clark.

Klauck, Hans-Josef (2005). *Apokryphe Apostelakten*. Stuttgart: Katholisches Bibelwerk. English translation: Klauck, Hans-Josef (2008a). *The Apocryphal Acts of the Apostles*. Waco: Baylor.

Klauck, Hans-Josef (2008b). *Die Apokryphe Bibel*. Tübingen: Mohr Siebeck.

Lapham, Fred (2003). *An Introduction to the New Testament Apocrypha*. London, New York: T&T Clark.

Robinson, Neal (1989). "Creating Birds from Clay: A Miracle in the Qur'an and in Classical Muslim Exegesis." *Muslim World* 79: 1–13.

Schneemelcher, Wilhelm (1990, 1997). *Neutestamentliche Apokryphen*. 2 vols. 6th edn. Tübingen: Mohr Siebeck. English translation: R. McL. Wilson, ed. (1991, 1992). *New Testament Apocrypha*. 2 vols. Cambridge: Clarke; Louisville, KY: Westminster John Knox.

Spittler, Janet E. (2008). *Animals in the Apocryphal Acts of the Apostles*. Tübingen: Mohr Siebeck.

Terian, Abraham (2008). *The Armenian Gospel of the Infancy*. Oxford: Oxford University Press.

Valantasis, Richard (1997). *The Gospel of Thomas*. London, New York: Routledge.

CHAPTER 11

Gnostic Portraits of Jesus

Majella Franzmann

Gnostic groups who believed in Jesus as their savior and revealer represent one of the major movements within the history of early Christianity. The categorization of these particular Christian groups as "Gnostics" (from the Greek word *gnōsis* = insight, knowledge) emphasizes one major aspect of their belief system: namely, that salvation is primarily, though not exclusively, the result of waking up to the insight that one is a child of the Father, or highest God. Not all Gnostic groups are classified as Christian, but those that are so classified were involved in negotiating a place for themselves in the religious and socio-political worlds of early Christianity along with other groups, some of which developed into the Christian group that was eventually regarded as the mainstream.

Early modern scholars' knowledge of the Gnostics owed much to what could be gleaned from the writings of mainstream Christian groups who held different ideas or theologies about Jesus, principally from apologists or heresiologists like Justin Martyr, Irenaeus, Hippolytus, Tertullian, Clement of Alexandria, Origen, Eusebius of Caesarea, and Epiphanius of Salamis. Pearson (2007, 25–60) and Rudolph (1987, 10–25) provide excellent overviews of these writers and of the various groups and individuals that came under their attack. Mainstream Christians and Christian Gnostics appear generally to be seeking the same goal in developing their theologies: namely, to understand Jesus and find words to adequately describe him and his relationship to them. For the most part, apologists and heresiologists of mainstream groups attack the perceived heretical nature of Gnostic beliefs, especially about Jesus, but also about the God who creates the world and other entities. Some of these writers provided snippets from writings of the Gnostics themselves; others described their beliefs and behavior, sometimes from information derived first-hand, but more frequently from what had been passed on to them by others.

There is a distinct disadvantage in having to rely on the apologists for information, since their writings are explicitly polemical, so the discovery of primary texts

The Blackwell Companion to Jesus, First Edition. Edited by Delbert Burkett. ©2014 John Wiley & Sons, Ltd. Published 2014 by John Wiley & Sons, Ltd.

from Christian Gnostics themselves has been a boon to scholarship. A jar full of ancient manuscripts was discovered at Nag Hammadi in Egypt in 1945, and a number of these writings can be categorized as Christian Gnostic (Robinson 1988; Layton 1987). More recently, Codex Tchachos, which contains the Gnostic Gospel of Judas, has been made available for scholarly study (Kasser and Wurst 2006).

In addition to these writings, there is a great body of texts from the Manichaeans, a very highly developed Gnostic group founded by the Persian Mani. Many Manichaean texts were discovered in Egypt and also by expeditions along the Silk Road in Central Asia in the nineteenth and twentieth centuries. While Manichaeism is a religion in its own right, nevertheless the central focus on Jesus by Mani and those who followed him make these writings a rich source for Gnostic views of the figure of Jesus. These Manichaean texts include the following.

Cologne Mani Codex (Cameron and Dewey 1979)
Chinese Hymn Roll (in Schmidt-Glintzer 1987)
Homilies (Polotsky 1934)
Kephalaia (Gardner 1995)
Psalm Book (Allberry 1938)
Šābuhragān (MacKenzie 1979)
Tractate Pelliot (in Schmidt-Glintzer 1987)

Gnostic writings reveal a diverse range of mythologies and theologies. However, some degree of commonality can be identified within that diversity. Humans inhabit a dualistic universe, divided between a realm of light, goodness, and spirit, and a realm of darkness, evil, and matter. The realm above is a world of light where the ineffable God or Father of Light exists. From this supreme God, various spiritual beings called "aeons" emanate. The realm below is the place of matter, the world, and human flesh. These are evil or at best fatally flawed, the work of a Demiurge, the evil and ignorant creator, who together with dark cosmic powers under his command, the archons, creates an evil or flawed world and the first human beings (Letter of Peter to Philip 135.8–136.5; Second Apocalypse of James 58.2–6; Gospel of Philip 75.2–11). Gnostics emanated from the light as spirits or souls in the realm of light but became embodied in the world below at birth. They consider themselves essentially strangers or "passers-by" (Gospel of Thomas 42) in the world, trapped here in the flesh ("nets of flesh"; Interpretation of Knowledge 6.28–29) and in the world that is the prison of the spirit. By *gnōsis*, Gnostics become aware of their spiritual origin from the world of light, where the ineffable God or Father of Light exists, and of their destiny to return to that world of light.

Gnōsis, the insight or knowledge that saves, may encompass knowledge of God, knowledge of heavenly mysteries, or knowledge of oneself, but most frequently it comprises a combination of all three. The Teachings of Silvanus affirm that when believers truly know themselves – their birth, their original substance, race, and species, their original divine nature (90.29–31; 92.10–15) – they are able to know

God, Christ, the Spirit and the heavenly powers (117.3–5). The believer may acquire knowledge that ranges from simple basic truths, to the knowledge required to pass after death through the levels of the heavens to the Father. The latter information is provided, for example, in the First Apocalypse of James, where James must know how to answer the questions posed by the heavenly toll-collectors who would hinder his passage after death. Jesus reveals to James the correct answers to their questions:

> When you come into their power, one of them who is their guard will say to you, "Who are you or where are you from?" You are to say to him, "I am a son, and I am from the Father." He will say to you, "What sort of son are you, and to what father do you belong?" You are to say to him, "I am from the Pre-existent Father, and a son in the Pre-existent One." (33.11–24)

Herrick (2003, 178) sums up the "Gnostic impulse" succinctly as manifested "in the veneration of secret spiritual knowledge, the elevation of spiritual elites in possession of such knowledge, a denigration of time and history, a tendency to view the physical realm as evil and a corresponding tendency to view human embodiment with suspicion."

Plotting the emergence of the various early Christian groups with any degree of certainty is not an easy task. Christian Gnostic thinking reveals major influences from Greek philosophy, dualistic systems of thought, and movements within Judaism that focused on apocalyptic themes and the revelation from heavenly figures often found in apocalypses. Scholars can identify no clear beginning point of Gnosticism, no Gnostic group in a particular geographical or cultural context from which scholars may draw lines of development into more complex groups and systems, toward what has been termed "classical" or Sethian Gnosticism (e.g., Pearson 2007, 10).

Williams (1996, 51–53) suggests that the categorization of these groups as "gnostic" owes more to scholars than to the groups themselves. Others propose that the term "gnostic" should not be used since it is a term that has been used pejoratively by writers like Irenaeus (*Against Heresies* 1.11.1; 1.25.6). Pearson (2005; 2007, 9–12) continues to defend the use of the term. In the end, Karen King's suggestion may be the most helpful: "It is important not so much to eliminate the term *per se*, but to recognize and correct the ways in which reinscribing the discourse of orthodoxy and heresy distort our reading and reconstruction of ancient religion" (2003, 218). Antti Marjanen (2005, 1–53) provides a very helpful overview of the use of the term and of the scholarly debate over its continuing use.

Gnostic Portraits of Jesus

Portraits of Jesus emerge in Gnostic groups, as they do in other Christian groups, from individual and communal experiences of Jesus and reflection on those experiences. Sources for Gnostic concepts about Jesus are varied: personal experience, community reflection, the writings of other Gnostic groups, and scriptures common to both Gnostics and mainstream Christian groups. Gnostic groups frequently used the canonical gospels to support their theological positions. The use of the Gospel of Matthew, for example, is well documented in major texts like the Manichaean Psalm Book (see the index in Allberry 1938). General references to the commandments of Jesus and gospel sayings are sprinkled liberally through Manichaean texts, often introduced by "the Savior says" or something similar (e.g., Cologne Mani Codex 84.20–85.4; Psalm Book 16.4; 51.20–21; 177.2–6; Kephalaia 201.29–31; 210.31–32; 223.3–5; 229.10–15; 264.3–12; etc.; Persian texts M 399 and M 1738 [Sundermann 1968, 403–404; Klimkeit 1991, 153–155]). Canonical Christian scriptures are also well attested in the Nag Hammadi texts (Evans et al. 1993).

The collection of works from Nag Hammadi and the writings of the Manichaeans will be the major sources for the outline of Gnostic portraits of Jesus below. These represent a range of views, from what we might call the first flowering of Gnosticism to its last and greatest flowering in Manichaeism, and from geographical areas as far distant as Egypt and China. Clearly when we put together all the concepts about Jesus found in these numerous writings from a wide variety of groups and geographical areas, no single unified portrait of Jesus emerges. These texts contain different emphases for different circumstances and times. Some texts may have been written when times were good and there was ample opportunity for listening to teachings and having key points explained; such texts might place more emphasis on the revealing and teaching aspects of a savior. Other texts may have been written in times of persecution, when solidarity in suffering with a suffering savior might be a much more meaningful focus for reflection. Thus the colors and structures of Jesus' portraits may change with time and with the varying circumstances of individuals and the community. In what follows, we will present examples of the variety of views of Jesus as we follow the major episodes of his story – who he is; where he comes from and what he does there; how he enters the world; what he does and what is done to him in the world; how he leaves the world but continues to be present to believers; and what happens at the end of his dealings with the world.

Who is Jesus?

Some of these texts contain detail about Jesus as he existed before he came into the world. Descriptions of the heavenly region from which he came may be quite complicated and his place and his relationships within that region also complicated. Some texts refer to multiple heavenly characters, of which one is Jesus; others refer to multiple manifestations of one character, who is Jesus; still others refer to multiple manifestations of one character, and one of these manifestations may be Jesus. An example of this kind of complexity is found in the Tripartite Tractate, which appears to present three distinct Son-Savior figures: the Son of the Father in the highest level of heaven, the Savior of the Logos below the second limit, and the earthly Savior. However, these three Son-Savior figures are manifestations of the same character, the first-born and only Son of the Father (57.18–19), before whom there was no other (57.15) and after whom no other Son exists (57.16–17).

Perhaps the most complicated presentation of Jesus, in both heavenly and earthly contexts, is found in the Manichaean writings, which refer to six Jesus figures – Jesus the Splendor, Jesus the Apostle, Jesus the Judge, Jesus Patibilis, Jesus the Youth, and Jesus the Moon. However, as the present author has shown (Franzmann 2003), only one Jesus is intended within the Manichaean system. The clearest attestation that this is so is to be found in the Šābuhragān, a text which may date back even to Mani himself, and where at least the four major manifestations of Jesus – Splendor, Apostle, Judge, and Patibilis – are conflated.

Where does he come from and what does he do there?

Nag Hammadi texts speak in general of Jesus originating in the heavenly region or coming from the highest God or Father, who is variously named as Father, Light, the Great Power, and so on. It is this highest God who sends him into the world (e.g., Apocryphon of John 1.22–24; 4.17–18; Acts of Peter and the Twelve Apostles 6.18–19; Letter of Peter to Philip 137.28–30). Manichaean texts like the Psalm Book describe Jesus as the son of God (121.11 and 15), the son of the kingdom (121.13), and the son of the Father (121.17). According to Kephalaia, Jesus the Splendor is the son of, or emanation of, "the greatness" or the Father of Greatness (e.g., 28.26–28; 37.27–28; 72.28–73.3).

The heavenly Jesus figure has a part to play in a number of creative activities prior to entering the world, most often as the agent of the Father. In the Second Treatise of the Great Seth, he is said to have brought forth a word and an imperishable thought to the glory of the Father (49.20–25). In the Teachings of Silvanus, as the Word who is the hand of the Father, he has created everything; he is the mother of all, from whom the all has come into being (115.3–9, 16–19), and he gives life and nourishes all things, ruling over all and giving life (113.15–20). The Interpretation of Knowledge describes his part in continuing the creative work of the Father. The Father does not keep the Sabbath but actuates the Son, and, through the Son, continues to provide himself with the Aeons (11.33–35).

The Manichaean Jesus descends into the world a number of times, as we shall see below. Prior to the first descent, Jesus the Splendor is described as a creative, life-giving being. The closing hymn of Tractate Pelliot (T.85c26–86a4 /P.586), calls him the ocean of immortality for all living things (v. 8) and the one who gives eternal life to the dead (v. 13). In Kephalaia 35.13–14, he is the one through whom eternal life shall be given. In the heading of the Persian hymn M 28 II, he is the "life-giver" (Andreas and Henning 1933, 312), and in Psalm Book 116.7 and the Chinese Hymn Roll (7–8, 12, 72) he is the Tree of Life itself.

How does he enter the world?

In ideas prevalent at the time, the heavenly world had a complex structure, comprising multiple layers. One would therefore expect Gnostic versions of how Jesus enters the world below to be similarly complex. His coming into the world usually includes a number of stages. Where the "mechanics" of his descent are given in detail, he requires various garments, forms, or vehicles. These may actually enable him to move through certain "places"; they may assist him in communicating with the beings who are in those places; or perhaps by using them, he can remain unnoticed while in those dangerous in-between spaces, until at last he takes on a human shape, or appearance, or flesh, and reaches the level of the world that humans inhabit.

The Manichaean Jesus is said to descend three times to the world: as the revealer, Jesus the Splendor, who brings *gnōsis* to Adam; as Jesus the Apostle, who comes to Palestine as revealer and savior; and at the end of the world as Jesus the King and Judge. In Kephalaia 61.17–28, Jesus the Splendor descends to the world by first taking on the form of angels, and then he takes on the form of flesh. The descent of Jesus the Apostle is described in similar fashion in Psalm Book 193.13–197.8, where he takes on the form of those beings who inhabit and control the in-between spaces: "He passed the powers by taking their likeness. He mocked the principalities by likening himself to them" (193.27–28).

Christian Gnostic ideas about the nature of Jesus and how he enters the human world differ markedly from mainstream Christian ideas. Gnostic understandings of the world and human beings provide a different context for thinking about how a savior can enter and act in that world and affect the lives of human beings. For the various Christian Gnostic groups, the heavenly revealer and savior must not be caught and imprisoned in the world of darkness and flesh, unless he intentionally puts himself in that position of risk. The more human-like the form that Jesus chooses, the more he immerses himself in the world of the flesh, the more he will be in danger from the dark powers that rule there. One finds a wide range of reflection on this issue in the Gnostic texts, from portraits of a Jesus who is a purely spiritual being so that the world is of no danger to him, to a Jesus who comprises two distinct and discrete natures, taking on real flesh or a human nature when entering the world, but without compromising his spiritual nature in any way. Thus the Tripartite Tractate 116.26–28 presents a Jesus who has spiritual "flesh," so that there is no division between his heavenly and spiritual "earthly" self. On the other hand, the Treatise on Resurrection 44.14–19; 21–33 describes an earthly setting for a Jesus who has real flesh, necessitating a clear and discrete division of his person into Son of God and Son of Man.

Though the Gnostic texts themselves are in no way in complete agreement as to how the nature of Jesus should be understood, we can say generally that they are not receptive to the idea of the savior Jesus having a real human birth in real human flesh and later a real death. The Gospel of Philip manages to avoid any difficulty for the heavenly Jesus in the human world, by proposing that Jesus has two sets of parents, the earthly parents Mary and Joseph, and the heavenly parents, the Father of All and the Holy Spirit: "If Jesus had not had two fathers, an earthly and a heavenly, he would not have said, 'My Father who is in heaven,' indicating the heavenly one, but simply 'My Father.' Thus, his earthly father is Joseph, whose offspring or 'seed' he is" (73.9–15). Of course, such a concept of double parentage can serve as a basis for belief in his two discrete natures.

Other texts describe what appears to be a human birth for Jesus, at least with the involvement of one human parent. The Testimony of Truth, for example, states clearly that Christ is born of a virgin and takes flesh (39.29–31). He is first begotten by the Word through the Virgin Mary (45.9–11). Thereafter he passes through her womb (45.14–16). When she has finished giving birth, she is found to be a virgin again (45.16–18). Thus his conception and birth appear to have no lasting effect upon her physical state, and one could argue by corollary that he also is unaffected by the physicality of the organ that opens to receive him and then closes again to its original state. Interestingly, this same passage contrasts Jesus with John the Baptist, who is also begotten by the Word through the woman Elizabeth, who is clearly not a virgin and whose womb is "worn with age" (45.6–8, 12–14). The virginity of Mary is clearly essential to the kind of "human" Jesus becomes.

What does he do in the world and what is done to him?

Christian Gnostic portraits of Jesus focus overwhelmingly on his role as savior and revealer. In some cases, the differences in approach to this role by the Gnostics and by mainstream Christian groups do not appear to be very great. The Gospel of Truth, for example, describes Jesus as the hidden mystery or Word of the Father of truth who enlightens believers, teaches them a way of truth, and shows them a way out of the darkness (16.31–38; 18.11–21). This wording has clear parallels with the canonical Gospel of John (e.g., 1:5; 14:6).

The most important role for the Gnostic Jesus is as savior. In general, while the mainstream Jesus saves from God's judgment, which is directed against sin, the Gnostic Jesus saves the soul from imprisonment in the material world, imprisonment that is caused by ignorance, the lack of *gnōsis*. The Gospel of Philip provides a summary of his work: he came as a savior to ransom those who were strangers, making them his own (52.35–53.1, 3–4); to save others (53.1–2), specifically the soul (53.10–13); and to redeem the good and the evil (53.2–3, 13–14; see also 60.26–28). Salvation, liberation, and revelation may be combined in his activity, as in the Sophia of Jesus Christ, where the Savior struggles to destroy the work of the archons, who oppose his revelatory activity, and breaks the bonds in which they have imprisoned Immortal Man (107.15–16; Codex Berolinensis 8502 121.15–122.3).

Jesus' liberating work in the earthly realm also affects elements of the heavenly region, both by dividing or opening them up and by reuniting them. In the Dialogue of the Savior 120.20–26, he opens up a way for believers out of the earthly region into the heavens. In the Gospel of Truth, as he opens a way, he also reunites the elect with the Father by bringing them out of ignorance into knowledge of him (18.9–11; 24.30–32). In the Gospel of Philip, he reconciles what has been divided – the above and below, the outside and the inside (67.30–34) – and thus ensures access to the heavenly region (68.17–22). He also repairs the separation (i.e., death) begun with Adam and Eve, so as to give life to those who died as a result of the separation and to unite them (70.12–17).

The second most important role for the Gnostic Jesus is as revealer. In general, the revelation offered by Jesus is concerned with the revealer himself and secret knowledge from him (e.g., Trimorphic Protennoia 37.8–20; 47.13–15), and/or it is revelation from the highest God or Father through the revealer (Apocalypse of Peter 70.23–25; 71.9–13; First Apocalypse of James 26.6–8; On the Anointing 40.19–20; Tripartite Tractate 114.22–30; Sophia of Jesus Christ 94.5–13). This revelation may be straightforward information, as for example in the First Apocalypse of James, which describes features of the twelve hebdomads or archons and the seventy-two heavens (26.2–30), or in the Letter of Peter to Philip, which is concerned with the aeons and archons, and what role the apostles play within the scheme of things (134.18–135.2). A much more detailed exposition is provided by the Apocryphon of John, which describes the nature of the Father, the evolution of the powers in the heavenly region, the development of the human race, and the salvation of souls; and by the Sophia of Jesus Christ, which describes various figures of the heavenly realm and relates how cosmogonic events have occurred. These are truths upon which ordinary human beings cannot even begin to speculate (92.6–93.8).

In the Dialogue of the Savior, Jesus reveals more about the end of things than about the beginning. His revelation includes instructions on how one should act in relation to the world now and information about the time of dissolution (the time for the journey of the soul to heaven), the heavenly garment, and the path to be followed on that journey. Such detail brings together the themes of revelation and liberation of the soul. The Gospel of Truth too contains a clear statement about Jesus' liberating activity, accomplished through revelation that brings enlightenment. The major work of the "earthly" Jesus in this gospel is enlightenment, and even his death is an allegory for this work: "He was nailed to a tree; he became a fruit of the knowledge of the Father ..." (18.24–26); "He put on that book; he was nailed to a tree; he published the edict of the Father on the cross" (20.24–27).

In the Apocryphon of James, much more conventional teaching is to be found about salvation (11.1–2), the kingdom of God/heaven (6.2–8; 7.22–35; 12.22–27; 13.17–19), and the cross and death of Jesus (5.6–6.18). It includes exhortation to remember the cross and death of Jesus, which will bring life (5.33–35), to hearken to the word (9.18), to understand knowledge (9.19), to love life (9.19–20), to pray to the Father/God (10.32–34), and to repent (10.11–12). Common canonical forms of teaching and associated activity are found in the Manichaean texts, where Jesus teaches in parables (see esp. the parable of the good and bad tree in Kephalaia 17.2–9; 19.21–25; 21.23–26) and performs signs and wonders (Kephalaia 7.18–27).

A number of texts focus on the secret or special nature of Jesus' teaching. In its prologue, the Gospel of Thomas characterizes its sayings as secret sayings given to

Thomas by Jesus. In saying 13, Jesus takes Thomas aside and tells him three things that he must not tell the other disciples, because it would pose a risk to them. While saying 62 refers to the mysteries that Jesus tells, the secret teaching is never explicitly revealed, although the rest of the text could perhaps be regarded as secret teaching in its own right. The Book of Thomas the Contender claims to give the secret words (138.1–2) or talk about the secret things (138.24–25) of Jesus. The Apocryphon of John refers to secret teaching presented in a mystery (32.2; see also 31.31). And in the Gospel of Judas, Jesus orders Judas to step aside from the other disciples so he can tell him "the mysteries of the kingdom" (35.21–25).

Generally, Jesus gives revelation to believers or to those who oppose the world and its evils. Surprisingly then, in the Interpretation of Knowledge, Christ is said not only to destroy the Demiurge (the arrogant teacher; 9.19–20), but also to teach him (10.13–18), who was himself teaching the church to die (9.20–21, 26–27).

Some descriptions of Jesus' activity use imagery that is reminiscent of sacramental practice. In clear reference to the Christian eucharist, the Gospel of Philip relates that Christ came as nourisher or life-enhancer, as the Perfect Man who brought bread from heaven to nourish humankind (55.12–14), and the food of the truth by which one has life and does not die (73.23–27). Similarly a reference to baptism can be found in Psalm Book 59.8–9, 25–27, which says that Manichaean believers who are defiled by the world and the guile of the archons are washed clean in the "holy waters," cleansed by the Savior's members and made spotless.

The savior Jesus is clearly a powerful liberator and revealer, with insight and secret knowledge to impart, but he is not otherwise easily described, and the texts differ quite markedly in how they present him. The Gospel of Judas, for example, offers a portrait of a rather cold and distant figure, who often ridicules the disciples for their lack of understanding. Even Judas, whom he singles out for special revelation (35.24–25), fares no better. In the Apocryphon of James, Jesus frequently speaks against the disciples, calling them "wretches," "unfortunates," "pretenders to the truth," "falsifiers of knowledge," and "sinners against the Spirit' (9.24–28), but at the same time he suggests that they ignore his apparent rejection of them and rejoice in the promise of life and the kingdom of heaven (14.10–14). On the other hand, in the First Apocalypse of James, the relationship between James and Jesus is warm and affectionate. When Jesus appears to James after his passion, James embraces him and kisses him (31.3–5), and Jesus sits beside James on a rock to comfort him when James is afraid and distressed at the thought of his own impending passion (32.13–22).

How does he leave the world but continue to be present to believers?

The process by which Jesus leaves the world parallels that by which he enters the world. He needs to change garments, find another vehicle, or take off the flesh in some way, in order to move upwards through the levels of the heavens. In the

Apocryphon of James, Jesus describes his second departure from the earth, which involves using a chariot of the spirit to ascend (14.33–34). While doing so, he strips himself in order to clothe himself (14.35–36), clearly meaning that he strips away the garment of the flesh in order to put on a spiritual garment and re-enter the heavenly region.

In most texts, Jesus engages in some kind of struggle, either on his own behalf or for others, as he frees himself (and others) from the rulers of the world. But as he struggles to leave the world, he generally does so as a powerful figure. To win against death is to conquer it.

Only rarely does one find in the texts the paradox that Jesus dies a humiliating death as the means of conquering the archons. The Teachings of Silvanus, for example, emphasize the humiliating death of Jesus. They describe him as the Wisdom of God who became a type of fool for the believer, so that he might take the believer up and make him a wise man (107.9–13). He is also the Life who died for the believer when he was powerless, so that through his death he might give life to him who had died (107.13–17).

Some texts appear to attest to a real death for Jesus. The Tripartite Tractate says that the Savior suffers (113.33–34; 114.34–35), having taken upon himself the death (i.e., ignorance) of humankind (115.3–6), since he is a compassionate Savior (114.31–32). It also refers to his burial in a tomb as a dead man (133.30–134.1). That the suffering is more than an experience of ignorance may be supposed from the description of his persecution by the powers of the left (both men and angels [121.19]), who deny him and plot evil against him (122.5–6) and do wicked things to him including causing his death (121.10–14), thinking to rule the universe by slaying the one proclaimed as king of the universe (121.14–18).

Kephalaia 267.24–27 makes it clear that the suffering and crucifixion of Jesus the Apostle forms a part of his revelation in the world: "He has been reve[ale]d therein! He suffered tribulation and persecution. They hung h[im] on the cross, and his enemies perpetrated against him the tor[ment] and shame of their evil-doing." Several rather detailed summaries of the events within the passion-resurrection story of Jesus the Apostle appear in eastern and western Manichaean texts. Psalm Book 195.23–196.8 gives considerable detail, though not in the same order as the canonical accounts: the scribes oppose Jesus; Judas takes a bribe and apparently accuses him; the scribes condemn Jesus and deliver him to "the judge" (presumably here Pilate because of what follows); he is crucified at the sixth hour; he is crowned as king with a garland; he is clothed in a robe of purple, with a reed put in his hand; he drinks vinegar and myrrh; he is pierced with a spear; and the sun goes dark.

However, even where texts appear to suggest that Jesus dies a real physical death, one needs to take care to examine that idea within the writings as a whole. For example, the Manichaean Psalm Book seems to imply that Jesus the Apostle enters the world taking on real flesh. He descends through the powers and finally to earth, at which point he, a God, becomes man (Psalm Book 194.2), taking on the likeness of the flesh (194.1), the likeness of a man, which for him is a garment of slavery

(194.3). Such a situation would provide the necessary physical context in which Jesus could then experience real death, yet only a little before this passage in the same work, one finds a description of the passion that puts this idea into question. In the so-called "Amen" hymn of Psalm Book 190.21–191.14, Jesus reveals his "wonders" to the apostles on the Mount of Olives in a series of seemingly paradoxical statements about his suffering (191.4–8):

> Amen, I was seized; Amen again, I was not seized.
> Amen, I was judged; Amen again, I was not judged.
> Amen, I was crucified; Amen again, I was not crucified.
> Amen, I was pierced; Amen again, I was not pierced.
> Amen, I suffered; Amen again, I did not suffer.

The two verses that follow these five antitheses give the clue to their meaning:

> Amen, I am in my Father; Amen again, my Father is in me.
> But thou desirest the fulfilment of Amen:
> I mocked the world, they could not mock me.

It appears that Jesus is able to overcome the torture of his crucifixion because he is in the Father and the Father in him. Each part of the statement is correct: "I am in my Father ... my Father is in me." Likewise in the preceding apparent antithetical statements, each part is true: he was seized and not seized, judged but not judged, and so on. Both parts can be true about Jesus because he has both a human *schēma* or outward form, discerned by others through their physical senses, and an inner divine reality. Under the outward form he appears to suffer, but in effect he does not suffer, because in reality he is an untouchable god. This aspect of Jesus is most clearly described in the events following his death. In Psalm Book 196.20–26, in the context of Jesus' descent into Hades, Death seeks Jesus, but does not find what it expects among those of the dead – Jesus has no flesh, no blood, no bones, no sinews, no likeness of Death, which is fire and lust. All Death finds is a figure, a *schēma*, like a mask (196.26), and the illusion clearly enables Jesus to escape from Death and to bring others with him out of Death's clutches.

In many cases, the plot by the archons or rulers of the world to kill Jesus fails, and his enemies become figures of ridicule. Four sections of the Treatise of the Great Seth deal with the events of the passion or crucifixion of Jesus in summary form (54.23–56.17; 56.20–57.18; 58.13–59.11; 59.15–26), describing his bonds, the crown of thorns, the cross, the drink of gall and vinegar, and his being nailed to the tree. In the end, however, the archons themselves are overpowered: darkness overtakes them (58.20–22), and they condemn themselves by their own action (56.2–4). Jesus is not afflicted, even though he is punished, and he does not really die as people think, but only appears to (55.10–19, 26–28, 30–34; see also 53.24–25). As in the Psalm Book, his persecutors do not see him through their blindness. They only think they see him and punish him (55.36–56.1, 4–6). Instead, they punish their own man, their father, Simon (55.34–35; 56.6–11). This passage is similar to one in the

Apocalypse of Peter, where the Savior's enemies mistakenly crucify "the son of their glory" instead of the servant of the Savior, Jesus (82.1–3), who is glad and laughing on the tree/cross (81.10–11), laughing at the blindness of those who thought to persecute him, as they are divided among themselves (82.26–83.4). In the Second Treatise of the Great Seth likewise, Christ's reaction to the persecution is to laugh at the ignorance of his opponents while he rejoices in the height (56.13–17).

A number of texts that refer to the death of Jesus attest also to the fact of his resurrection from the dead (e.g., the Sophia of Jesus Christ 90.15–16; Letter of Peter to Philip 139.20–21), although providing little detail of the event. Melchizedek 5.1–11 includes rising from the dead in the list of what has really happened to Jesus, contrary to the incorrect teaching of some people.

For the Treatise on Resurrection, the Son of Man who was known to believers is he who rose from among the dead, being the destruction of death (46.14–19). This Lord and Savior, Jesus Christ, is the one through whom the resurrection has come into being (48.16–19). However, this text uses the term "resurrection" in a metaphorical sense. It means not that the body is brought back to life, but that the inward living self leaves behind the body that is subject to death (47.30–48.3).

Both Kephalaia 13.5–6 and 264.13–14 report briefly that Jesus was in the tomb three days, suggesting that he was "among the dead." These passages seem to imply that he appeared dead so as to be placed in a tomb, and being among the dead means, at least in some way, that he went into the abode of the dead. The Parthian hymn M 18 also gives a brief summary in Jesus' words from Luke 24:6–7: "They will hand me over and crucify me, on the third day I will rise from among the dead" (Müller 1904, 35).

Psalm Book 196.15–31 goes much further than these brief accounts, providing detail about what happens in the abode of the dead, how Jesus destroys its fortifications and means of keeping the dead imprisoned – he opens the closed doors (15), breaks the doors and bars (16), shines his Light into the darkness (17–18), and breaks the sepulchers and tombs (29). Thus not only can he escape the abode of the dead (20), but he can also revive the righteous (30) and bring these prisoners of death with him as he escapes (21).

The time after the resurrection is important for the Gnostic texts. Much of the revelation from Jesus in the Nag Hammadi texts comprises post-resurrection teaching. Similarly the setting of Psalm Book 190.30–31 is the Mount of Olives, where Jesus reveals the glory and wonders of his passion. Kephalaia 13.10 too, clearly places his ascent to the heights after his post-resurrection appearances to the disciples, even though resurrection and ascension, as found in canonical Christian sources, are not always clearly delineated in the Manichaean texts.

There are a number of ways of describing the final ascension of Jesus that decisively ends his connection with the earthly context. He may ascend directly from the experience of passion or the cross, as in Trimorphic Protennoia 50.12–15 or in the Concept of our Great Power 42.18–19, or he may rise from the tomb, as outlined above. In the Manichaean texts, each time Jesus ascends after working in the earthly context, we learn little more than that he ascends back to his light ship (Kephalaia

59.28) or to the heights (Kephalaia 56.26). Kephalaia 61.17–28 states simply that, at the end of his activity, Jesus ascends to rest in the light. The Apocryphon of James provides a narrative closest to what one finds in the synoptic accounts of an ascension. Jesus' farewell speech from 10.22 onwards is introduced by, "Behold, I shall depart from you and go away ..." (10.22–23). The disciples are exhorted to remember him after his departure (12.34) and to follow him quickly (10.26–27).

There is little in these texts that specifically deals with Jesus' continuing presence with believers after his final ascent to the heavens. The Acts of Peter and the Twelve Apostles relates that, while he is no longer with his disciples, he has power to affect what happens to them: he provides the opportune moment for their going down to the sea (1.14–16), and the kindness of the sailors is also ordained by him (1.20–23). Peter expects him to give the apostles power to walk the road to the city of Lithargoel (6.11–12), and the apostles ask him in prayer to give them the power to do what he wishes at all times (9.26–29). Similarly Manichaean sources know the power of prayer to Jesus. A Sogdian text contains the story of Mani's healing of Nafsha, the sister of Queen Tadi, after she has prayed to Jesus for help (So. 18.222 = TM 389c; Sundermann 1981).

What role does he play at the end of the world?

The Greek loan word *parousia* ("coming," i.e., second coming of Jesus) occurs only five times in the entire Nag Hammadi collection (Siegert 1982, 284). Some few texts include the expectation of a final return of Jesus, in some cases linked with a final judgment. Often Jesus returns after the community of believers has endured a period of struggle (e.g., Apocalypse of Peter 78.6). The Book of Thomas the Contender warns that the end, or the day of judgment (143.8), will not be long in coming (141.14). Those who love the fire (141.29–31), and those who turn away from or sneer at the word of Thomas as he preaches the words of Jesus, will be thrown into Hades and imprisoned there and undergo torment (141.32–41; 142.2; 142.26–143.5). On the other hand, the elect will receive rest and will reign and be joined with the good one/the king (145.12–16). A similar judgment scene occurs in Šābuhragān and Homilies 35–39, in which Jesus the Judge comes to make a judgment between the righteous and sinners at the end of the world. The Manichaeans believed in a return of Jesus at the end of time, on the "day of Jesus." There would be a *parousia* in the conventional Christian understanding, which would occur after a period of peace and power for the Manichaean community following the Great War (Homilies 27.2–4; 28.14–16; 29.12–15).

The Use of Portraits

The Gnostic portraits sketched out above seem fairly straightforward in intention, albeit sometimes obscure in their delivery. They are painted to give us information, or a clue, or a brief glimpse of who Jesus is, what he did, and how he was important within the various Gnostic theologies. While portraits may be intended to give an idea about a person, they may also be used for other purposes. Gnostic portraits or ideas about Jesus could be used for argument or ridicule as much as for presenting the subject of the portrait. The Gospel of Philip, for example, uses teaching about the birth of Jesus to ridicule mainstream Christian teaching that the Virgin Mary conceived Jesus by the power of the Holy Spirit (55.23–27), by stating that no woman can impregnate another, a statement clearly influenced by the feminine gender of the original Aramaic word for "Spirit" (*rûah*).

This article has been concerned with texts and the word pictures they paint of Jesus, but did Gnostic groups actually have pictures of Jesus? Irenaeus of Lyons, (*Against Heresies* 1.25.6) wrote of the Carpocratians that they had portraits of Christ, and the philosophers Pythagoras, Plato, and Aristotle, and others (Coxe 1885). However, there are no extant physical portraits of Jesus from Gnostic groups, apart from Manichaean paintings. There are small etchings of figures with a cock's head or a lion's head, some with a serpent's tail or feet, with names like Sabaoth or Ialdabath, names also found in Gnostic texts. These do not include portraits of Jesus (see Rudolph 1987, 23; Pearson 2007, 48), although the representation of the serpent with Adam and Eve on one gem (Pearson 2007, 49) may symbolically represent him. Recently identified Chinese Manichaean paintings in a private collection in Osaka depict Jesus (Furukawa and Yoshida 2010), and Gulácsi (2008, 11–12; 2009) has argued for the identification of Jesus in other Manichaean paintings, found in Central Asia and in Japan. In general, however, apart from the didactic paintings used in Manichaean communities and mission, Gnostic groups were not interested in such portraiture for the purpose of recording physical features for Jesus, since in their thinking such features would be simply a sham or mask hiding the true spiritual features of the savior.

Conclusion

In putting together snippets of texts from Christian Gnostic writings above, we have identified important aspects of the Jesus figure in whom they believed – a savior and revealer who descends from the realm of light into the world of darkness, takes on a garment of flesh, imparts insight through his revelation of the mysteries to believers trapped in the flesh, overcomes the powers of darkness and Death, and opens a way of truth to ensure that believers can return to their real home with the Father of Light. There is much in these aspects that are both similar to, and different from, the beliefs about Jesus expressed by mainstream Christian groups. Both Christian Gnostic and mainstream Christian groups developed their portraits of Jesus out of reflection on traditions and key scriptures handed down to them; each group relied on their ongoing experience of Jesus to guide what they were saying and writing about him. The Christian Gnostic portraits of Jesus provide a rich source for building up a more complete picture of the reflections about Jesus by a wide variety of groups during the early centuries of the Christian tradition.

References

Allberry, C. R. C. (1938). *A Manichaean Psalm-Book, Part II*. Manichaean Manuscripts in the Chester Beatty Collection. Vol. 2. Stuttgart: Kohlhammer.

Andreas, Friedrich Carl, and W. B. Henning, eds. (1933). "Mitteliranische Manichaica aus Chinesisch-Turkestan, II." In *Sitzungsberichte der Preußischen Akademie der Wissenschaften 1933.7* (pp. 292–363). Berlin: Akademie der Wissenschaften.

Cameron, Ron, and Arthur J. Dewey, eds. (1979). *The Cologne Mani Codex: "Concerning the Origin of his Body."* Missoula, MT: Scholars.

Coxe, A. Cleveland (1885). *Ante-Nicene Fathers*. Vol. 1: *The Apostolic Fathers, Justin Martyr, Irenaeus*. Edinburgh: T&T Clark; Grand Rapids: Eerdmans.

Evans, Craig A., Robert L. Webb, and Richard A. Wiebe, eds. (1993). *Nag Hammadi Texts and the Bible: A Synopsis and Index*. Leiden: Brill.

Franzmann, Majella (2003). *Jesus in the Manichaean Writings*. London: T&T Clark.

Furukawa, Shoichi, and Yutaka Yoshida (2010). "Cosmogony and Church History Depicted in the Newly Discovered Chinese Manichaean Paintings." *Yamato Bunka* 121: 3–34.

Gardner, Iain M. F., ed. (1995). *The Kephalaia of the Teacher: The Edited Coptic Manichaean Texts in Translation with Commentary*. Nag Hammadi and Manichaean Studies 37. Leiden: Brill.

Gulácsi, Zsuzsanna (2008). "A Visual Sermon on Mani's Teaching of Salvation: A Contextualized Reading of a Chinese Manichaean Silk Painting in the Collection of the Yamato Bunkakan in Nara, Japan." *Studies on the Inner Asian Languages* 23: 1–15.

Gulácsi, Zsuzsanna (2009). "A Manichaean *Portrait of the Buddha Jesus (Yishu Fo Zheng)*: Identifying a 12th/13th-Century Chinese Painting from the Collection of Seiun-ji Zen Temple, Near Kofu, Japan." *Artibus Asiae* 69: 1–38.

Herrick, James A. (2003). *The Making of the New Spirituality: The Eclipse of the Western Religious Tradition*. Downers Grove, IL: InterVarsity.

Kasser, Rodolphe, and Gregor Wurst, eds. (2006). *The Gospel of Judas: Critical Edition*. Includes the Gospel of Judas, the Letter of Peter to Philip, the Book of James, and the Book of Allogenes from Codex Tchacos. Washington, DC: National Geographic Society.

King, Karen (2003). *What Is Gnosticism?* Cambridge, MA: The Belknap Press of Harvard University Press.

Klimkeit, Hans-Joachim (1991). "Die Kenntnis Apocrypher Evangelien in Zentral- und Ostasien." In Alois van Tongerloo and Søren Giversen (eds.), *Manichaica Selecta. Studies Presented to Professor Julien Ries on the Occasion of his Seventieth Birthday* (pp. 149–175). Louvain: International Association of Manichaean Studies; Center of the History of Religions; Belgian Center of Manichaean Studies.

Layton, Bentley, ed. (1987). *The Gnostic Scriptures*. Garden City, NY: Doubleday.

MacKenzie, D. N. (1979). "Mani's Šābuhragān." *Bulletin of the School of Oriental and African Studies* 42 (3): 500–534.

Marjanen, Antti (2005). "What is Gnosticism? From the Pastorals to Rudolph." In Antti Marjanen (ed.), *Was There a Gnostic Religion?* (pp. 1–53). Helsinki: Finnish Exegetical Society; Göttingen: Vandenhoeck & Ruprecht.

Müller, Friedrich Wilhelm Karl, ed. (1904). "Handschriften-Reste in Estrangelo-Schrift aus Turfan Chinesisch-Turkistan, II. Teil." *Abhandlungen der (K.) Preußischen Akademie der Wissenschaften*. Berlin.

Pearson, Birger A. (2005). "Gnosticism as a Religion." In Antti Marjanen (ed.), *Was There a Gnostic Religion?* (pp. 81–101). Helsinki: Finnish Exegetical Society; Göttingen: Vandenhoeck & Ruprecht.

Pearson, Birger A. (2007). *Ancient Gnosticism: Traditions and Literature*. Minneapolis: Fortress.

Polotsky, H. J., ed. (1934). *Manichäische Homilien*. Manichäische Handschriften der Sammlung A. Chester Beatty. Bd. 1. Stuttgart: Kohlhammer.

Robinson, James M., ed. (1988). *The Nag Hammadi Library in English*. 3rd edn. Leiden: Brill.

Rudolph, Kurt (1987). *Gnosis: The Nature and History of Gnosticism*. Trans. R. McL. Wilson. New York: HarperSanFrancisco.

Schmidt-Glintzer, H. (1987). *Chinesische Manichaica mit Textkritischen Anmerkungen und einem Glossar*. Wiesbaden: Otto Harrassowitz.

Siegert, Folker (1982). *Nag-Hammadi-Register: Wörterbuch zur Erfassung der Begriffe in den Koptisch-Gnostischen Schriften von Nag-Hammadi mit einem Deutschen Index*. Tübingen: Mohr Siebeck.

Sundermann, W. (1968). "Christliche Evangelientexte in der Überlieferung der Iranisch-Manichäischen Literatur." *Mitteilungen des Instituts für Orientforschung* 14 (3): 386–405.

Sundermann, W., ed. (1981). *Mitteliranische Manichäische Texte Kirchengeschichtlichen Inhalts*. Berlin: Akademie-Verlag.

Williams, Michael (1996). *Rethinking "Gnosticism": An Argument for Dismantling a Dubious Category*. Princeton: Princeton University Press.

Further Reading

Andreas, Friedrich Carl, and W. B. Henning, eds. (1934). "Mitteliranische Manichaica aus Chinesisch-Turkestan, III." In *Sitzungsberichte der Preußischen Akademie der Wissenschaften* 1934.27 (pp. 846–912). Berlin: Akademie der Wissenschaften.

Filoramo, Giovanni (1990). *A History of Gnosticism*. Trans. Anthony Alcock. Oxford: Blackwell.

Franzmann, Majella (1996). *Jesus in the Nag Hammadi Writings*. Edinburgh: T&T Clark.

Klimkeit, Hans-Joachim, ed. (1993). *Gnosis on the Silk Road: Gnostic Texts from Central Asia*. New York: HarperSanFrancisco.

Mack, Burton L. (1990). "All the Extra Jesuses: Christian Origins in the Light of the Extra-Canonical Gospels." *Semeia* 49: 169–176.

Marjanen, Antti and Petri Luomanen, eds. (2005). *A Companion to Second-Century Christian "Heretics."* Supplements to Vigiliae Christianae 76. Leiden: Brill.

Rose, Eugen (1979). *Die Manichäische Christologie*. Wiesbaden: Otto Harrassowitz.

Sundermann, W. (1992). "Christ in Manicheism." *Encyclopaedia Iranica* 5: 535b–539a.

Voorgang, Dietrich (1991). *Die Passion Jesu und Christi in der Gnosis*. Nag Hammadi and Manichaean Studies 33. Leiden: Brill.

Waldschmidt, E., and W. Lentz (1926). "Die Stellung Jesu im Manichäismus." *Abhandlungen der (K.) Preußischen Akademie der Wissenschaften*. Philosophisch-Historische Klasse 4. Berlin.

Williams, Michael (2005). "Was There a Gnostic Religion? Strategies for a Clearer Analysis." In Antti Marjanen (ed.), *Was There a Gnostic Religion?* (pp. 55–79). Helsinki: Finnish Exegetical Society; Göttingen: Vandenhoeck & Ruprecht.

CHAPTER 12

The Christ of the Creeds

Khaled Anatolios

Already in the New Testament, we have not only narrative material about Jesus' deeds, sayings, and sufferings, but also questions, responses, and propositional declarations about his identity and work. Some of these declarations most likely originated in liturgical settings, and thus creedal-liturgical material was in significant ways constitutive of the New Testament presentation of Jesus. As the early church came to accept the New Testament canon, at the heart of which is a fourfold presentation of the person and work of Jesus, it also found further creeds necessary to regulate the diverse strata of the scriptural witness to Jesus. Generally, the function of creeds in the early church was closely tied both to their liturgical setting and their role as hermeneutical keys for interpreting scriptural revelation. In terms of their liturgical context, the primary location of the earliest Christian creeds was the rite of baptism. These creeds generally followed a Trinitarian pattern, confessing belief in the Father, Jesus Christ, and the Spirit, with the middle section comprised of a brief christological narrative. Already with Irenaeus, in the latter third of the second century, such a Trinitarian-christological creedal formula was understood as both a manifestation of the contents of the new life initiated by the baptismal rite and simultaneously as anchoring of scriptural interpretation. Along the same lines, Athanasius defended the Nicene Creed in the fourth century as a necessary clarification of the "sense of scripture," and Augustine assured new catechumens in the fifth century that the creed is merely a "summary of scripture." Thus, over against a modern tendency to separate and compartmentalize different dimensions of the early church's experience of faith in Jesus Christ, the above considerations should rather lead us to acknowledge that the "Christ of the creeds," in the early church, was also intended to be the "Christ of the liturgy" and the "Christ of the scriptures." This chapter will presume this perspective in presenting the christological creedal content of the seven ecumenical councils, with attention to their surrounding prehistory and reception. Since these councils occurred before later divisions between

The Blackwell Companion to Jesus, First Edition. Edited by Delbert Burkett. ©2014 John Wiley & Sons, Ltd. Published 2014 by John Wiley & Sons, Ltd.

the western and eastern Greek Byzantine churches, as well as subsequent divisions within western Christianity between Catholics and Protestants, they represent a common point of reference for most Christians to this day.

The Council of Nicea (325)

The Council of Nicea, in 325 CE, is regarded as the first universal, or "ecumenical," council, not so much because of any pre-established empirical criteria pertaining to the quantity and geographical provenance of its participants, but because its doctrine was received by later tradition as foundational to the dogmatic contents of orthodox Christian belief in the identity of Jesus Christ. The controversy that led to the convening of this council erupted in Egypt ca. 318, between Alexander, the bishop of Alexandria, and Arius, an Egyptian priest. The former preached a version of Origen's doctrine of the co-eternality of the Father and the Son, while the latter insisted that the Son was created from nothing. The controversy quickly spread beyond the boundaries of Egypt and led to the convening of several councils, including the Council of Nicea. The Nicene Creed sided with Alexander and famously employed the term "*homoousios*" ("one in being" or "consubstantial") to designate the relation between Jesus Christ's divinity and that of the Father. The Nicene Creed reads as follows:

> We believe in one God, Father Almighty, Maker of all things visible and invisible.
> And in one Lord Jesus Christ, the Son of God, begotten from the Father, only-begotten, that is, from the substance of the Father, God from God, light from light, true God from true God, begotten not made, consubstantial (*homoousion*) with the Father, through whom all things came into being, those on heaven and on earth; who for us humans and for our salvation came down and was incarnate and became human, suffered and rose again on the third day, ascended into heaven, and is coming to judge the living and the dead.
> And in one Holy Spirit.
> But as for those who say, "there was once when he was not," and "before being begotten he was not," and that "he came into being from non-being," or who declare that the Son of God is of another *hypostasis* or *ousia*, or alterable or changeable, these the Catholic and Apostolic Church anathematizes. (Dosetti 1967, 226–241; author's translation)

There is a tendency in modern theology to characterize "Nicene doctrine" as a "Logos" or "incarnational" christology "from above," preoccupied with ontological, rather than functional and soteriological categories. But this tendency can be attributed primarily to the predilection of modern systematicians to read classical "conciliar" theology from within the narrow confines of creedal formulations, independently of the larger theological debates that these formulations attempted to adjudicate. In the case of the Nicene Creed, the focus of debate was not some abstract speculation on the ontological status of a free-floating "Logos," but rather the complexities and tensions within the christological biblical narrative as this was received and performed in Christian discipleship. According to this narrative, the most central fact was that Jesus Christ was in some sense "Lord," a confession that provided ground and substance to the experience of Christian worship and life. And yet this same "Lord" was also a human creature, who was subject to human limitations, suffering, and death, and was obedient to the God he called "Father." In the scriptural presentation of Jesus, he is reported to declare that "the Father is greater than I" (John 14:28) and to be exalted at the right hand of the Father. Given the complexities of this narrative, the Nicene controversy involved not merely different options for designating the ontological status of the "Logos," but rather competing narratives that were alternative construals of the biblical story of Jesus and his work. While modern historical scholarship has legitimately questioned the long-standing strategy of reducing the multiple personalities and various alliances involved in this debate in a binary framework of "pro-Nicene" and "anti-Nicene" parties, it still remains possible and helpful to sketch two broad narrative options, one of which enabled the reception of the Nicene Council as central to Christian orthodoxy and the other of which was incompatible with the Nicene formulation.

According to the latter narrative, the ultimate mystery of God is that he is unbegotten/uncaused (*agennētos*). As the crucial descriptor of the most absolute level of divinity, this designation clearly distinguished God from creation. Such a distinction was pressed both against the Hellenistic philosophical presumption that matter always existed, as well as Origen's biblical speculation that the eternal God, as eternally Almighty, must have always presided over the creation. In absolute contrast to the unbegotten God, everything else came to be from nothing through the divine will. The primacy of Christ as "Lord" consists, on the side of his divinity, in the fact that he is the first and greatest of beings who are brought into being by the Unbegotten God. Consistent with the scriptural witness, the pre-existent Christ/Word/Wisdom/Son is also Creator. Proverbs 8:22 (LXX) becomes a central text presented as evidence that the Creative Wisdom of God is itself created in order to become an instrument of God's creative activity: "He created me as the beginning of his ways for his works." For the sake of human salvation, this same Word/Wisdom/Son became incarnate, suffered, died on the cross, and was raised and exalted by the Father. His human embodiment, limitations, sufferings, and redemptive obedience are indicative of the secondary and subordinate status of his divinity in relation to the Father. Jesus is Savior because both in his pre-existent and embodied conditions he represents the ideal and exemplary relation of the creature to the unbegotten God. Christian salvation, then, consists in conforming oneself to the exemplary creaturehood of Jesus Christ, and Christian worship consists in being led into the praise of the unbegotten God through the agency of Jesus Christ.

The competing narrative, which eventually claimed the creed of Nicea as its standard, was also preoccupied with maintaining the absolute distinction between God and creation. As with the former narrative framework, the crucial descriptor of creation was that it came to be from nothing as the effect of divine willing. In this version, however, the biblical presentation of the primacy of Christ, as performed in Christian worship and life, precluded citing the relationship between the pre-existent Jesus and the Father as an instance of a Creator–creature relationship. While acknowledging the scriptural title of Jesus as "only-begotten" in contradistinction to the "unbegotten" status of the Father, this narrative insisted that the derivation of the pre-existent Jesus from the Father constituted an altogether unique (thus, *only*-begotten) relation that is qualitatively different from the relation of Creator and creature. Thus, a distinction was affirmed between the relations of generation and creation, as attested by the Nicene phrase: "begotten not made." The ultimate mystery of God was not so much the descriptor of God as "uncaused," but rather the ineffable and eternal relation of the Father and the Son, a point often made with a gloss on Isaiah 53:8, "Who shall declare his generation?" For the sake of human salvation, the eternal Word/Wisdom/Son of the Father, who has a full and unadulterated share of the divine life of the Father, became incarnate and subjected himself to the conditions of human finitude and sin in order to introduce us into his own divine mode of life. The human embodiment, limitations, sufferings, and redemptive obedience of Jesus are not in any way continuous with a secondary status of divinity but rather constitute an ineffable self-emptying (*kenōsis*) in which the divine Word takes on human possibilities, not to the diminishment of his divinity but rather to the transformation of our humanity, to the point of deification. Christian salvation consists in conforming oneself to the humanity of Jesus by which one is led into his divine life (deification), and Christian worship is directed to the Son, along with the Father.

Viewing the problematic of the Nicene controversy from this wider narrative lens enables us to see the inextricable connections in these debates between the doctrinal realms that came to be later distinguished under the rubrics of "Trinitarian theology" and "christology." The Nicene debates were simultaneously preoccupied with Jesus' relation to the God he called "Father" and to the humanity to which he was related as "the first-born of many" (Rom 8:29). Moreover, if we anachronistically project back onto the Nicene controversy a post-Chalcedonian definition of "christology" as concerned with the interrelation of humanity and divinity in Jesus Christ and with the question of how the unity of Jesus Christ may be conceived in light of the radical difference between humanity and divinity, even then we find that the Nicene debates set the framework for subsequent wrestlings with that problematic. As we saw, the Nicene version of the christological narrative insisted on the radical discontinuity between the eternal and consubstantial divinity of the pre-existent Christ and his human condition, in contrast to the opposing narrative that saw Jesus' humanity as a stage within the continuum of his secondary, creaturely "divinity." It was therefore the Nicene narrative that generated the more acute version of the christological problematic, since it was that version that insisted on the maximal difference between Jesus' humanity and unqualified divinity and thus evoked most pointedly the question of his unity. Indeed, a common and forceful complaint leveled against the Nicene position was that it did not have an intelligible conception of the unity of Christ; it was charged with positing "two Sons." Presenting an intelligible account of how Jesus Christ is both "*homoousios*" with the Father and yet fully human, while avoiding the specter of "two Sons" would be the ongoing project of subsequent early Christian reflection on the identity of Jesus Christ.

The Council of Constantinople (381)

The achievement of the Council of Constantinople is generally considered to be that of ratifying and thus "receiving" the Nicene declaration of the consubstantiality of the Father and the Son, while extending the terse Nicene confession of the Holy Spirit by identifying the Spirit as "the Lord and Life-giver, who proceeds from the Father, who is co-worshipped and co-glorified with the Father and the Son, who has spoken through the prophets." The Creed of Constantinople does not use the word "Trinity," nor indeed the vocabulary of "nature" (*ousia, physis*) and "person" (*hypostasis, prosopon*), but follows the traditional creedal and biblical pattern of confessing faith in the Father, Son, and Holy Spirit. Nevertheless, its re-endorsement of the Nicene "*homoousios*" with reference to Father and Son and its implicit acknowledgment of the full divinity of the Spirit were dependent on the clarifications provided by the Cappadocians (Basil of Caesarea, Gregory of Nazianzus, and Gregory of Nyssa), who did use that terminology. In their explication of Trinitarian faith, Father, Son, and Spirit were three distinct divine "persons" who together constituted the single divine "nature."

Considered broadly, in terms of its adjudication of surrounding theological debates, the significance of the Council of Constantinople to the ongoing creedal christological tradition can be summarized under three points: (1) its confession, in practical terms, of the full divinity of the Spirit; (2) its clarification in the christological narrative section that Christ's kingdom "will have no end"; and (3) its anathematization of the christology of Apollinaris.

The confession of the divinity of the Holy Spirit avoided applying the contentious term "*homoousios*" to the Spirit, opting for the more existential confession of the Spirit as the object of Christian worship and doxology. This declaration of the divinity of the Spirit brought to a dogmatic culmination debates about the status of the Spirit that had followed closely upon the questions about the divinity of the Son that had preoccupied the opening stages of the Alexander–Arius dispute. These debates came to a head in the 350s with the rise of groups of Christians who affirmed the full divinity of the Son but declined to extend that affirmation to the Spirit. The opposing position argued on behalf of the full divinity of the Spirit on the basis of the exalted scriptural titles of the Spirit and the scriptural descriptions of the Spirit's agency in the divine work of creation, salvation, and deification. But just as the debates about the pre-existent divinity of Jesus Christ always bore reference to the concrete scriptural christological narrative, so did discussions of the identity and work of the

Spirit involve clarifications of the relation between the Spirit and Jesus Christ. It would not be an exaggeration to designate such clarifications as amounting to a kind of "Spirit christology." In a typical version of such an approach, Jesus Christ sent the Spirit through the agency of his divinity but received the Spirit in his humanity in such a way that all humanity partakes of that reception through Jesus' humanity. The divine giving of the Spirit and humanity's reception of it are thus secured by the unbreakable unity of subject in which Jesus' divinity and humanity cohere. The Council of Constantinople's affirmation of the full divinity of the Spirit was dependent on those theologies that elaborated on the Spirit's distinct relations to both the divinity and humanity of Jesus Christ.

A second contribution that the Council of Constantinople makes is the assertion that Christ's kingdom will have no end. This short statement, which strikes modern ears as simply a pious celebration of the enduring victory of Christ, was in fact a shorthand refutation of an entire Trinitarian-christological program. The author of this program was Marcellus, bishop of Ancyra, who was a fervent supporter of the Nicene doctrine of the consubstantiality of the Father and the Son. However, Marcellus understood the "*homoousios*" to mean that Father and Son, in God's own immanent being, were simply identical and without differentiation. There is thus no duality or multiplicity of any kind in God's own being. Rather, all differentiation between the Father and his "Word" comes about in the course of God's creative activity. This differentiation reaches a maximal level in the incarnation, when the Word takes on human flesh. However, since Marcellus was committed to the absolute singularity of the divine being, he could only conceive of the fulfillment of the Christian salvific economy as a "retraction" of the divine *Logos* back into the singularity of divine being. Inasmuch as the humanity of Christ cannot be so retracted into divine being, Marcellus was reportedly constrained to say that Christ's kingdom will come to an end. That is, the kingdom of Christ will become entirely the kingdom of the Word, a conception that Marcellus articulated with reference to 1 Corinthians 15:28: "When all things are subjected to him, then the Son himself will also be subjected to the one who put all things in subjection under him, so that God may be all in all." Clearly, the salient issue in this conception is not an attempt by Marcellus to deny the endurance of the kingdom of God instituted by Jesus Christ, but rather to assert that the ultimate destiny of that kingdom is to be presided over by the Word and not by the humanity of Jesus Christ. By contrast, in insisting that the kingdom of Christ will have no end, the Council of Constantinople was really making a statement about the unbreakable and everlasting unity between the humanity and divinity of Jesus Christ. The christological content of the statement that "of his kingdom there shall be no end" is that there will never come a time when the Word will abandon the humanity of Jesus.

The third significant contribution of the Council of Constantinople is found not in its creedal statement but in its anathematization of Apollinaris, fourth-century bishop of Laodicaea. Apollinaris was also a strong supporter of the Nicene doctrine of the Son's consubstantiality with the Father, but, unlike Marcellus, he insisted on the eternally ontologically distinct subsistences of Father, Son, and Holy Spirit. Apollinaris subscribed to what we have called the "Nicene narrative," which insisted on the radical discontinuity between the unqualified divinity of the pre-existent Christ and his humanity. As we noted, this account of Christ's person and work was vulnerable to the charge of positing a divisive christology: "two Sons." Apollinaris was sensitive to this criticism and considered it justified in the case of Marcellus' loose conception of the unity of Christ's humanity and divinity, to the point where the consummation of God's kingdom seems to entail the divinity's abandoning of the humanity. For Apollinaris, a divisive christology would deconstruct the logic of both Christian worship and salvation. In terms of worship, such a christology would force Christians to distinguish the veneration rendered to the humanity from the worship granted to the divinity, while threatening to introduce a fourth object of Christian worship beyond the Trinity: "We do not say that we worship four persons: God, the Son of God, and a human being, and the Holy Spirit" (*Kata Meros Pistis* 31; Lietzmann 1904, 179). In terms of salvation, the introduction of a fully constituted human subject would fragment the integrity of the agency of salvation, since only divinity can exercise that agency and only divine immutability can secure it. Apollinaris' resolution of all these problems was to insist on the singularity of Christ's person by asserting that the divine *Logos* replaced the human spirit or mind in Christ. There is thus only a single active agency in Christ's person, exercised by the *Logos*, even if the humanity endures in the flesh over which the divinity presides. Apollinaris' radical resolution to the problems of a divisive christology came under strong attack from adherents of both the "pro-Nicene" and "anti-Nicene" narratives and it was specifically in refutation of Apollinaris that Gregory of Nazianzus penned the classic adage expressing the core principle that would underlie the soteriological thrust of orthodox christology: "What is not assumed is not healed" (*Ep.* 101:32; Gallay 1974, 50). That is, whatever part of human nature that Christ did not assume would not be reconciled to God. In its anathematization of Apollinaris, the Council of Constantinople thus implicitly affirmed that principle in rejecting the view that Christ had no human spirit or mind. In distant foreshadowing of later christological councils, it rejected an approach to christological unity that came at the cost of denying Jesus Christ's integral humanity.

The Council of Ephesus (431)

The Council of Ephesus is generally recognized for its endorsement of the title of "*Theotokos*," or "God-bearer," applied to Mary. The main protagonists in this case were Cyril, bishop of Alexandria, and Nestorius, bishop of Constantinople. Nestorius had expressed disapproval of that title, considering "*Christotokos*" or "Christ-bearer" as more appropriate, while Cyril vigorously defended it. While the appropriate veneration of Mary was one of the issues involved in this debate, it was by no means the central one. At the heart of the matter were christological concerns that were also intimately connected to issues of liturgical and homiletic language, questions about divine transcendence, conceptions of Christian salvation, and even the eucharist, not to mention personal and ecclesiastical rivalries. The Council of Ephesus, convened to settle the dispute between Cyril and Nestorius, did not issue any creed. Indeed, the calling of this council was followed by various disjointed sittings of rival alliances of bishops in the course of which Cyril excommunicated Nestorius but was himself excommunicated by the Antiochian bishops. However, according to the pattern by which earlier councils are validated retrospectively through their reception by later councils, the Council of Ephesus was received by the subsequent Council of Chalcedon as consisting in the endorsement of the Theotokos, the affirmation of Cyril's doctrine, and the rejection of Nestorius.

To gain an understanding of what was at stake at the Council of Ephesus, it is important to eschew facile dichotomies of "christology from above" versus "christology from below" or "emphasis on the divinity" versus "emphasis on the humanity." Both Cyril and Nestorius affirmed that Jesus Christ was fully human and fully divine. They both took the title of "Jesus Christ" as signifying the union of the eternal Son and Word of the Father with the humanity of Jesus, which includes body, soul, and mind. The essential disagreement between them had to do with the kind of union that obtains between the humanity and the divinity. Even more concretely, it was a disagreement about how the mystery of that unity can be rendered in Christian devotional language. Most concretely, the question was: What kind of statements succeed in rendering the contents of the gospel of Jesus Christ? For Nestorius, following an Antiochian tradition represented most notably by Theodore of Mopsuestia, this gospel is rendered successfully when the affirmation of the unique and preeminent union of Jesus' humanity with the eternal Word is balanced with maintaining the distinction between impassible divine transcendence and Jesus' humanity. As to the first point, it is affirmed that the union between Jesus' humanity and the divinity is altogether unique, such that it represents a unity whereby the honor of the Godhead is attributed to the human Jesus. As to the latter point, the transcendence of the divinity is safeguarded by insisting on the distinction between the human and divine natures. The linguistic rule that ensures the safeguarding of that distinction is that human attributes cannot be predicated directly of God; hence, it cannot be said that Mary is the "bearer of God" or that "God died on the cross." For Cyril, by direct contrast, those were precisely the kind of statements that succeeded in expressing the gospel of Jesus Christ, and anything short of such paradoxical attribution also came short of rendering the mystery of Emmanuel, God-with-us in Jesus. Over against Nestorius' concern for the maintenance of divine transcendence, Cyril saw the Christ-event as most radically a mystery of divine self-emptying (*kenōsis*), as expressed in the christological hymn of Philippians 2:6–8. Cyril also recalled the arguments against a divisive christology based on the logic of Christian worship, accusing Nestorius of reducing Christian worship to worshiping a man who was merely conjoined by honor to the divinity. On the basis of his own insistence that the humanity of Jesus was fully appropriated by the subject of the Word in a "hypostatic union," Cyril also claimed to offer a more coherent interpretation of other central aspects of Christian life and faith. Thus, the eucharist is transformative unto salvation and deification because it is the flesh and blood of God himself, while salvation itself consists in the appropriation of the human condition by God such that humanity can conversely appropriate the divine mode of life: "He took what was ours to be his very own so that we might have all that was his" (*On the Unity of Christ*; McGuckin 1995, 59). By endorsing Cyril's theology, the Council of Ephesus thus most essentially endorsed an interpretation of the gospel of Jesus Christ as comprised of this central mystery of "the wonderful exchange (*admirabile commercium*)" between God and humanity.

The Council of Chalcedon (451)

If the Council of Ephesus reaffirmed the linguistic rules for the proclamation of the gospel in terms of the paradoxical affirmation of human attributes to God and of divine attributes to humanity (*communicatio idiomatum*), it still left open the question of how such paradoxical statements enable an understanding of Jesus' humanity and divinity, their distinction and unity. In the absence of such clarity, Eutyches, the leader of a group of monks in Constantinople, attempted to bring the matter to a resolution by asserting that the incarnation was in effect the merging of two distinct natures, the humanity and divinity, into a single nature. Thus, the distinction and unity between the natures were located at different points, as it were, in the process of incarnation, with the distinction of natures conceived as a *terminus ab quo* and the unity as its concrete actualization. In 451, the Council of Chalcedon took up the matter, and the result was a christological creed that rejected this chronological separation of the distinction and unity. The Chalcedonian creed is painstaking in its adherence to a meticulous balance, modeled on the theology of Pope Leo, between Cyril's emphasis on the unity of subject in Jesus Christ and an Antiochian emphasis on the distinctions between the divine and human natures within that unity. Literarily, this balance is accomplished with an obsessive repetition of the term "the same" to emphasize the unity of subject, intermingled with repeated affirmations of the integrity of both natures. It also applied the Trinitarian terminological distinction between the language of nature (*physis, ousia*) and that of personal subsistence (*hypostasis, prosopon*) to Jesus, affirming the unity of subject to a single *hypostasis* and *prosopon*, and speaking of the humanity and divinity as "natures" (*physeis*) "consubstantial" with our humanity and the divinity of the Father, respectively. Here follows a fairly literal translation:

> Following therefore the holy fathers we all teach with one voice the confession of one and the same Son, our Lord Jesus Christ, the same perfect in divinity and the same perfect in humanity, the same truly God and truly human, having a rational soul and a body, the same consubstantial (*homoousion*) with the Father according to his divinity

and consubstantial (*homoousion*) with us according to his humanity, like us in all things except sin. The same was begotten from the Father before the ages according to his divinity and from Mary, the Virgin Theotokos, in the last days, for us and for our salvation, according to his humanity; one and the same Christ, Lord, only-begotten Son, acknowledged in two natures without confusion, without change, without division, without separation. At no point was the difference between the natures ever removed because of the union, but rather the property of each nature is preserved and concurs into one person (*prosopon*) and a single subsistence (*hypostasis*). He is not parted or divided into two persons, but is one and the same only-begotten God, Word, Lord Jesus Christ, just as the prophets from the beginning have taught us, and our Lord Jesus Christ himself, and the symbol of the fathers that has been handed down to us. (Schwartz 1914–, I, 2, 129–130; author's translation)

In 1954, Karl Rahner published a famous essay entitled "Chalcedon: End or Beginning?" (1961), in which he contested the presumption that christological questions had been conclusively settled by the Council of Chalcedon. Such a presumption is not entirely a straw man inasmuch as there is a tendency in modern christology to refer to "Chalcedonian" doctrine as an all-sufficient standard of christological orthodoxy. But the Council of Chalcedon cannot be taken in isolation from a whole series of christological councils that dealt with the unity and distinction of Christ. That series began with the Council of Ephesus, which endorsed the linguistic rules of christological predication indicated by the Marian title of "*Theotokos*." These rules presumed that Jesus Christ was a single subject to whom can be simultaneously applied two sets of predications pertaining to the humanity and the divinity. Faced with the question of whether the simultaneous distinction and unity between the humanity and divinity can be chronologically distinguished in terms of "before" and "after" the Incarnation, the Council of Chalcedon responded negatively and insisted that the unity of subject is entirely coordinate and simultaneous with the distinction of natures in the person of Christ. But the Council of Chalcedon, in turn, left behind ambiguities of its own. The Alexandrian Church, continuing the legacy of Cyril, considered the Chalcedonian "two-natures" language to be Nestorian and responded to the council by breaking communion with the churches that endorsed it. The lingering ambiguity had to do with the precise identification of the obsessively repeated "one and the same," a phrase that was clearly intended to safeguard the Cyrillian emphasis on the unity of subject. After all, it was not hard to get all parties to agree that somehow "Jesus Christ" was "one and the same." The crucial question, given the history of the Cyrillian–Nestorian dispute, was whether "the one and the same" person was in fact the eternal Son and Word who appropriated the humanity such that this eternal Word becomes the ultimate subject of even the human nature (*à la* Cyril). Or is it that the "one and same" person is constituted by an intermingling of the *honor* of divinity with the human man such that "the person of the union" is a distinct subject from the Word (*à la* Nestorius)? At least for the contemporary protagonists, Chalcedon did not adequately settle that issue, and so the christological battles raged on.

The Second Council of Constantinople (553)

The general sense that Chalcedon had not decisively settled the original questions disputed between Cyril and Nestorius was manifested in the hectic efforts to subsequently deal with Alexandrian concerns that Chalcedon had not effectively refuted the Nestorian position. These efforts came to a head with the convening of a council in Constantinople in 553. The central achievement of this council was to apply the logic of the Council of Ephesus to that of Chalcedon or, in other words, to interpret Chalcedon in a Cyrillian direction. This agenda becomes manifest in the controversial eleventh canon, which anathematizes one of the great figures of the Antiochian tradition, Theodore of Mopsuestia, along with two other notable theologians in that tradition, Theodoret of Cyrus and Ibas of Edessa, for proposing too loose a conception of the union between divinity and humanity in Jesus Christ. Positively, the crucial clarification made by Constantinople II was to interpret "the one and the same" subject of Jesus Christ, reiterated in the Chalcedonian creed, as identical with the person of the eternal Son and Word:

> If anyone understands the one hypostasis of our Lord Jesus Christ as admitting the meaning of several hypostases, and so tries to introduce into the mystery of Christ two hypostases or two persons, and after having introduced two persons, speaks of one person as regards dignity, honour and adoration, as Theodore and Nestorius have written senselessly; and if he makes the slanderous assertion that the holy Council of Chalcedon has used the term "one hypostasis" in this impious way and does not confess that the Word of God has been united to the flesh by way of hypostasis and that, therefore, there is but one hypostasis or person, and that this is the sense in which the holy Council of Chalcedon confessed one hypostasis of our Lord Jesus Christ, *anathema sit*. (Dupuis 1996, 209; revised)

Once again, it must be kept in mind that this question always had reference to the concrete life of Christian discipleship, especially the integrity of the act of worshiping Jesus Christ as Lord:

> If anyone says that Christ is worshipped in two natures, whereby he introduces two acts of worship, one proper to God the Word and the other proper to the man ... but does not venerate by one act of worship God the Word made flesh together with his own flesh, according to the Tradition received in the Church of God from the beginning, *anathema sit*. (Dupuis 1996, 211)

A vexed issue that this council introduced into subsequent christological reflection, one that particularly troubles modern interpreters, is the understanding that Jesus' human nature is "ahypostatic"; that is to say, it does not subsist in itself, thereby constituting an autonomous human "person," but rather within the hypostasis of the divine Word. It is beyond the scope of this chapter to analyze all the complex issues surrounding that problematic, at the heart of which is the question of the distinction between our modern densely psychological notion of "person" and the more objectively ontological content of the fifth-century term *"hypostasis"* as delineating a self-standing subsistence. Nevertheless, one way of understanding the content of this doctrine in modern terms is to say that it does not negate that Jesus is in fact a human person but rather affirms that his human personhood resides within and is a derivative extension of his divine personhood; conversely, the human nature of Jesus receives its ultimate self-standing from the hypostasis of the Word. One modern interpreter puts the matter aptly thus:

> In the Incarnation, the Second Divine Person, the Son, has assumed as his own a human nature so that he began to exist as man in time and history. Thus Jesus has a full human nature; however, this human nature does not subsist in itself, but in the eternal Son. Therefore Jesus' human nature lacks a corresponding human personhood. Nevertheless this does not entail a diminution of the full human reality of Jesus of Nazareth, since "person" formally does not mean any "part" of human nature but the mode of existence of a full human nature. It is the divine Person of the Son in whom the human nature of Jesus subsists as the Son's very own, and this Divine Person, in virtue of the assumed human nature, truly becomes man. (Kereszty 2002, 306)

The Third Council of Constantinople (680)

While the Second Council of Constantinople had specified the location of the "one and the same" person, or *hypostasis*, of Christ, resolutions continued to be ventured as to how the divine and human natures cohered in Christ and did not simply constitute two unrelated or even opposed and competing realities. One such resolution was to assert that the two natures of Christ coalesced into a single activity and a single will (*monothelitism*). Such an understanding seemed to flow easily from the previous council's reaffirmation that Jesus Christ was a single subject, to be identified with the divine Word who appropriated human nature to his divine subsistence. It was inferred that there was therefore a single active energy and a single will that corresponded to this single subject. Among the theologians who opposed this resolution the most illustrious was Maximos, eventually named "the Confessor" after his right hand and tongue were cut off for violating imperial orders that forbade discussion of the issue. Maximos insisted that there cannot be an integral nature devoid of its proper mode of activity and there cannot be an integral human nature devoid of the natural capacity for willing. Therefore, Jesus Christ must have two modes of activity and willing, corresponding to the two natures. Following the soteriological maxim of Gregory of Nazianzus, Maximos argued that if Christ did not assume our entire human nature intact, we would not be reconciled to God and deified. Such a salvific transformation requires that our human activity and willing be assumed by the divine person of the Word. Nevertheless, while distinct, the two wills of Christ did not make for opposition inasmuch as the human will, when untainted by sin, has a natural affinity for submitting to the divine will. Moreover, in the interactivity

of the human and divine wills of Christ, there was a hierarchy whereby the characteristic activity of the human will was precisely to submit to the divine will. The
paradigmatic manifestation of this order of divine–human interactivity was Jesus'
struggle in the Garden of Gethsemane (Matt 26:36–44 and parallels). There, Jesus
exercised a sinless human will in his disposition to affirm and preserve his human
life ("If it be possible, let this cup pass from me"), but this natural and sinless mode
of human willing was exercised in the mode of self-effacement and submission to the
divine will ("Not my will, but your will be done"). Thus, the harmonious interactivity
of the two wills of Christ are understood to be exemplary for the human person's
relation to God. Maximos died in 662, but his theological defense of the doctrine of
the two wills of Christ was vindicated by the third Council of Constantinople in 680,
which proclaimed,

> [T]he difference of natures in that same and unique hypostasis is recognized by the fact
> that each of the two natures wills and performs what is proper to it in communion with
> the other. Thus, we glory in proclaiming two natural wills and actions concurring
> together for the salvation of the human race. (Dupuis 1996, 224)

The Second Council of Nicea (787)

The Councils of Ephesus, Chalcedon, Constantinople II, and Constantinople III can
be readily seen as constituting a coherent series of meditations on the relations of
unity and distinction obtaining between Jesus' humanity and divinity, with each
successive one attempting to clarify or further interpret the preceding. The Second
Council of Nicea was less directly related to that series of successive christological
clarifications. Its presenting concern was not explicitly christological questions as
such but rather the practice of the veneration of icons. However, the theological
response advocated by that council was based on christological reasoning, and thus
the practice of praying with icons, prevalent especially in the Christian East, has
been henceforward viewed as derived from Christian faith in Jesus Christ as the
incarnate Word.

The earliest Christian art, as found in the catacombs, tended to be symbolic rather
than representational, having for its subject matter concepts and symbols pertaining
especially to the sacraments of baptism and eucharist. From these beginnings, there
developed a more representationalist art form, which by the fourth century included
more widespread use of icons in churches and public places. As the cult of saints
grew in popularity, and with the affirmation of the integral humanity of Jesus at the
Council of Chalcedon, icons representing Jesus and Christian saints became ubiquitous. Along with this growing interest came abuses, such as that implied by the
complaint of a seventh-century monk, St Anastasius of Sinai, that some people were
too busy kissing icons and not paying attention to the Divine Liturgy. Such abuses,
perhaps coupled with a defensiveness with regard to Islam's ban on images, led to a
reaction against the widespread use of icons, one that advocated a return to the

immaterial worship "in spirit and truth." This reaction became a matter of imperial policy through the agency of the emperor Leo III (717–741), who considered it to be his vocation to rid the churches of the idolatry of the veneration of icons. The campaign against icons, comprised of imperial decrees forbidding their veneration and the purging of the episcopacy from supporters of icons, was passed on from one emperor to the other until the reign of the empress Irene (780–802), who practiced the veneration of icons herself. With this change of the political tide, the Second Council of Nicea was convoked in 787. A previous council conducted by iconoclastic (anti-icon; literally "icon-breaker") bishops in 754 had forbidden icons on christo-logical grounds. The argument was that a proper understanding of the hypostatic union indicates that the humanity is inseparable from the divinity. An image of Jesus Christ must either purport to depict the humanity separably from the divinity or to depict the divinity itself, both of which were impermissible. The Council of Nicea II rejected that argument and affirmed the legitimacy of icon veneration on the basis of the referentiality of the material image to its prototype:

> Just as the figure of the precious and life-giving Cross, so also the venerable and holy images ... should be set forth in the holy churches of God ... the figure of Our Lord God and Savior Jesus Christ, of our spotless Lady, the Mother of God, of the honorable Angels, of all the saints and of all pious people. For by so much more frequently as they are seen in artistic representation, by so much more readily are people lifted up to the memory of their prototypes, and to a longing after them; and to these should be given due salutation and honorable reverence, not indeed that true worship of faith which pertains only to the divine nature ... For the honor which is paid to the image passes on to that which the image represents, and he who reveres the image reveres in it the subject represented. (Davis 1983, 310; revised)

It is commonly proposed that this conciliar legitimation of icons is based directly and simply on the logic of the incarnation: since the Word became flesh, his flesh can be depicted in visible form and, *a fortiori*, so can the bodily images of pious human beings. This style of argument indeed represents a foundational element of the christological defense of icons, one that was strongly emphasized by the iconophile bishop, Germanus of Constantinople. However, as we noted, iconoclastic bishops also put forward a christological argument based on the hypostatic union and the inappropriateness of depicting Christ's human nature inasmuch as it was inseparably united with his divinity. Nicea II's response to that argument echoes a more nuanced and sophisticated christological argument propounded by the most profound theological defender of icons, John of Damascus (675–749). While echoing the simple argument from the incarnation, the Damascene goes further in seeing the incarnation as a climactic manifestation of the ineluctably symbolic nature of reality. Iconography really begins with the divine Trinitarian being in which the Son is the icon of the Father and the Holy Spirit is the image (in Greek, image = *eikōn*) of the Son. In turn, humanity was created in the image of God, while all material reality in some way images divine ideas; even words are really audible icons. John of Damascus finally insists that the proscription of images entails the deconstruction of worship as such, since human worship can never entirely abstract from material media, which function on some level as images evoking the divine presence. As to the narrow christological question of the hypostatic union, the conundrum of whether the icon represents the divine nature itself or the human nature separated from the divine nature is transcended by the category of symbolic reference. The icon does not directly represent the divine nature, nor does it force asunder the human image from the divine nature but rather depicts the humanity of Jesus, which symbolically refers to his divinity. Analogously, the image of the saint refers to the reality of his person, which in turn refers to the source of his glorified condition, Jesus Christ.

Conclusion

As we noted at the beginning of this chapter, the early church's understanding of the "Christ of the creeds" coincided with that of the Christ of the scriptures, of worship, and of the story of salvation. If we were to form a coherent portrait of the "Christ of the creeds," we need to begin with what we have called "the Nicene narrative." According to this narrative, which purported to be a normative interpretation of scriptural revelation, there is an absolute distinction between the uncreated God and the creation that comes to be from nothing through the agency of divine willing. Even though Jesus Christ was obviously a human creature according to one aspect of his reality, he was also "Lord" and "true God" according to another aspect, as indicated by his exalted scriptural titles, his salvific work, and his status as the recipient of worship. Although his divinity was derived from the Father, that derivation belonged to the eternal perfection of the divine nature and was not created from nothing.

With this narrative in place, subsequent councils endeavored to settle disputes about the relation of humanity and divinity in Jesus Christ, intending not to explain what was considered to be the ineffable mystery of "Emmanuel/God-with-us," but rather to formulate the proper statement of that mystery, which would enable its rhetorical, liturgical, and doxological performance. Thus, the Council of Constantinople associated the divinity of the Holy Spirit with that of the Father and the Son, implicitly endorsing a "Spirit christology" that also defined Jesus' humanity as being the source of other human beings' full reception of the Spirit. It also affirmed that the union between Jesus' humanity and divinity is everlasting and constitutive of the unending kingdom of God. The Council of Ephesus insisted that the proper statement of the mystery of Jesus Christ must include the paradoxical attribution of the human attributes of Jesus to the divine subject and the divine attributes to the humanity. The Council of Chalcedon sought to balance affirmations of the single subject of Jesus Christ with those of the integrity of the two natures, while rejecting the proposition that the distinction of the natures represents merely the point of departure rather than the concrete content of the incarnation. Constantinople II reasserted that the single subject of Jesus Christ is identical with the divine person of the Son and Word. Constantinople III clarified that each of the two natures of Christ retains its own proper activity and power of willing, with the communion of the natures concretely performed through the active submission of the human will to the divine in a way that is exemplary for Christian discipleship. Finally, Nicea II saw the incarnation as the climactic manifestation of the symbolic nature of reality in which the Son images the Father and all of creation images the divine reality. Thus material elements, including most paradigmatically the humanity of Jesus Christ, refer to the divine presence, and icons represent that symbolic reference.

The guiding thread that runs through all these elaborations and clarifications was comprised of soteriological and doxological concerns. Jesus' humanity had to be an integral one, "like us in all things but sin," (cf. Heb 4:15) inasmuch as "what is not assumed is not healed"; his divinity had to be continuous with the divine nature inasmuch as only true divinity can bring about salvific healing unto deification; and the two natures must be seen to concur in a single subject for the sake of the integrity of both Jesus' salvific agency and his status as the recipient of integral and unfragmented acts of worship.

References

Anderson, David, trans. (1980). *St. John of Damascus. On the Divine Images.* Crestwood, NY: St. Vladimir's Seminary Press.

Davis, Leo Donald (1983). *The First Seven Ecumenical Councils (325–787): Their History and Theology.* Collegeville, MN: Liturgical.

Dosetti, G. L. (1967). *Il Simbolo di Nicea e di Costantinopoli.* Rome: Herder.

Dupuis, Jacques, ed. (1996). *The Christian Faith: In the Doctrinal Documents of the Catholic Church.* New York: Alba House.

Gallay, Paul (1974). *Grégoire de Nazianze: Lettres Théologiques.* Sources Chrétiennes 208. Paris: Cerf.

Kereszty, Roch (2002). *Jesus Christ: Fundamentals of Christology.* New York: Alba House.

Lietzmann, Hans (1904). *Apollinaris von Laodicea und seine Schule.* Tübingen: J. C. B. Mohr.

McGuckin, John, trans. (1995). *St Cyril of Alexandia. On the Unity of Christ.* Crestwood, NY: St. Vladimir's Seminary Press.

Rahner, Karl (1961). "Chalcedon: End or Beginning?" Revised as "Current Problems in Christology." In Karl Rahner, *Theological Investigations,* I (pp. 149–200). London: Darton, Longman & Todd; New York: Seabury.

Schwartz, Eduard, ed. (1914–). *Acta Conciliorum Oecumenicorum.* Berlin: De Gruyter.

Further Reading

Alberigo, Giuseppe, and Norman Tanner, eds. (1990). *Decrees of the Ecumenical Councils.* 2 vols. London: Sheed & Ward; Washington, DC: Georgetown.

Anatolios, Khaled (2004). *Athanasius*. Early Church Fathers Series. London, New York: Routledge.

Daley, Brian (2002). "Nature and the 'Mode of Union': Late Patristic Models for the Personal Unity of Christ." In Stephen T. Davis, Daniel Kendall, and Gerald O'Collins (eds.), *The Incarnation: An Interdisciplinary Symposium* (pp. 164–196). New York: Oxford University Press.

Grillmeier, Aloys (1975). *Christ in the Christian Tradition*. Vol. 1: *From the Apostolic Age to Chalcedon*. Rev. edn. Trans. John Bowden. Louisville, KY: Westminster John Knox.

Grillmeier, Aloys (1986–1996). *Christ in the Christian Tradition*. Vol. 2: *From the Council of Chalcedon (451) to Gregory the Great (590–604)*. Trans. John Bowden. Louisville, KY: Westminster John Knox.

Hanson, R. P. C. (1988). *The Search for the Christian Doctrine of God: The Arian Controversy, 318–381* AD. Edinburgh: T&T Clark.

Hardy, Edward, trans. (1954). *Christology of the Later Fathers*. Library of Christian Classics. Louisville, KY: Westminster John Knox.

Kelly, J. N. D. (1972). *Early Christian Creeds*. London: Longman.

Kelly, J. N. D. (2000). *Early Christian Doctrines*. 5th edn. New York: Continuum.

Louth, Andrew (1996). *Maximus the Confessor*. Early Church Fathers Series. London, New York: Routledge.

McGuckin, John (2004). *St. Cyril of Alexandria and the Christological Controversy: Its History, Theology and Texts*. New York: St. Vladimir's Seminary Press.

Meyendorff, John (1987). *Christ in Eastern Christian Thought*. Crestwood, NY: St. Vladimir's Seminary Press.

Norris, Richard, trans. (1980). *The Christological Controversy*. Sources of Early Christian Thought. Philadelphia: Fortress.

Schönborn, Christoph (1994). *God's Human Face: The Christ-Icon*. San Francisco: Ignatius.

Studer, Basil (1994). *Trinity and Incarnation: The Faith of the Early Church*. Edited by Andrew Louth. Collegeville, MN: Liturgical.

Young, Frances (1983). *From Nicaea to Chalcedon*. London: SCM.

CHAPTER 13

Jesus in Atonement Theories

Stephen Finlan

A tonement" is a word unique to English, meaning "to make one," deriving from the Middle English "at-onement" (Averbeck 2003, 709). In Christian theology, atonement usually refers to the saving effect of the death (and resurrection) of Christ. Numerous explanations of *how* Christ brought about salvation have been offered, based on ideas of sacrifice, substitution, appeasement, ransom, reconciliation, and deification. Except for the last, these have a basis in the Old Testament, so I will examine Old Testament atonement concepts before the New Testament sources of atonement theology.

Atonement in the Old Testament

The discussion of atonement generally begins with Hebrew sacrifice, which turns out to have several different functions. Ritual sacrifice can serve as a payment, a gift, or the means for obtaining blood, viewed as a purifying substance. In each case, sacrifice serves a highly practical social function.

In the mid-twentieth century, debate about sacrifice and atonement centered on the contrasting options of "propitiation" (appeasing the angry deity; Morris 1965) and "expiation" (cleansing the believer; Dodd 1935, 82–95). Propitiation seems to underlie the ancient notion of sacrificial smoke giving to God a "pleasing odor," a phrase occurring over forty times in the Pentateuch. For example, after the flood, when Noah offers "every clean animal" on an altar, the "pleasing odor" moves God to promise never again to "curse the ground" (Gen 8:20–21). Such passages presuppose that God somehow consumes the offering as a meal and that such a meal pleases him, creating in him a favorable attitude toward the one offering the sacrifice as a gift.

The Blackwell Companion to Jesus, First Edition. Edited by Delbert Burkett. ©2014 John Wiley & Sons, Ltd. Published 2014 by John Wiley & Sons, Ltd.

The priestly author, "P," (one of the authors of Leviticus) places less emphasis on the notion of God consuming the sacrifice as food, though this concept remains (e.g., Lev 3:5, 11, 16). P seems more interested in removing impurity than in persuading or feeding God. P's ritual system thus represents a move away from an anthropomorphic view of God. In its place is a technology of purification. Whenever sin was committed in Israel, it caused impurity to settle on the temple furnishings. If the impurity were allowed to remain, God would abandon the temple (Milgrom 1971, 1040). The substance used to cleanse the temple furnishings was the blood of the ḥaṭṭa't, the "sin sacrifice" or "purification offering." This cleansing went on year-round, but only on the Day of Atonement did the high priest go into the Most Holy Place and sprinkle ḥaṭṭa't blood on the kapporet, or mercy seat, cleansing the impurity caused by "presumptuous sins" (Milgrom 1983, 73, 81). The mercy seat was the golden lid of the ark of the covenant, above which the Lord was thought to dwell (Num 7:89). Thus were the people reconciled to Yahweh and the temple kept clean enough for him to remain in it.

The main Hebrew verb translated as "atone" is kippēr. In P texts, kippēr means "purify," but in many passages outside of P, kippēr still has to do with propitiating the deity, who is still viewed anthropomorphically. This becomes clear when we look at its cognate noun, kopher, "ransom." The census money that the Israelites pay to Yahweh is a kopher payment that ransoms their lives (Exod 30:12). This idea of kopher as a ransom may underlie all passages that use kippēr to speak of "averting God's wrath" (Milgrom 1991, 1082). The verb kippēr also clearly means "propitiate" in some non-cultic stories, such as that in which Jacob wants to "appease" his brother with a present of livestock (Gen 32:20). Propitiation is also present when Yahweh says that the priest Phinehas "turned back my wrath" by killing an Israelite and his foreign girlfriend (Num 25:11). Propitiation is seen in the notion of a violent God who was prepared to "consume the Israelites" until Phinehas' act of violence "made atonement for the Israelites" (Num 25:11, 13). When the Lord sends a famine because of "bloodguilt on Saul," a massacre of seven of Saul's sons expunges the bloodguilt and brings atonement (2 Sam 21:1–6). Thus, even though the primary meaning of kippēr is "purify," the word has semantic associations with the appeasement of anger. Further, the concept of substitution is implied in a payment that ransoms lives and in a killing of one party that averts wrath against another.

The sacrificial cult comes in for severe criticism by the prophets Amos, Hosea, Micah, Isaiah, and Jeremiah, expressed in negative contrasts, mockery, and frank rejection. "For I desire steadfast love and not sacrifice, the knowledge of God rather than burnt offerings" (Hos 6:6). "Will the Lord be pleased with thousands of rams, with ten thousands of rivers of oil? Shall I give my firstborn for my transgression?" (Mic 6:7). "I do not delight in the blood of bulls, or of lambs, or of goats" (Isa 1:11).

Other prophets (Ezekiel, Malachi) support the sacrificial cult. Another approach was to speak of sacrifice as a metaphor for praise or thanksgiving (Ps 50:23; 69:30–31). Christian atonement writings sometimes quote the criticisms of sacrifice, but more frequently build upon the internalization and metaphorical appropriation of the *idea* of sacrifice (Rom 12:1; Heb 13:15).

Finally, another important rite utilized in the atonement images of the New Testament is the expulsion ritual, of which the Jewish scapegoat and the Greek *pharmakos* rituals are examples. The ancient Greeks would ritually drive out a human victim, a *pharmakos*, even in classical Athens. The victim was consecrated, then ceremonially cursed and driven out of town. Such victims supposedly took a disease or curse with them (Harrison 1903, 95–104; Hengel 1981, 24–27). This ritual is not a sacrifice. The victim is not an offering, but a curse-bearer or sin-porter. The equivalent ritual in ancient Judah was that of the scapegoat, on whose head the priest put the people's sins, then "sending it away into the wilderness" (Lev 16:21), carrying away the sins.

Atonement in the New Testament

The oldest textual sources for Christian atonement theology are the letters of Paul. The gospels are all of later composition. Most scholars look to Paul for the roots of atonement theology, so the gospels will be considered after an examination of Paul.

Paul's atonement metaphors

The foundational Christian atonement idea is that "Christ died for us" (Rom 5:8), that "one has died for all" (2 Cor 5:14). This idea is probably based on the concept of "noble death," the concept of martyrdom in Greek and Latin literature, and especially in Greek-language Jewish literature, such as 2 Maccabees and 4 Maccabees. As the martyrs in these stories are killed for rejecting polytheism, they give Stoic-sounding speeches, affirming their willingness to die for the laws of Moses (2 Macc 6:28). They also ask God to use their deaths "to bring to an end the wrath of the Almighty" that had fallen on their nation (2 Macc 7:37–38); to take their blood as purification for the people and their lives in exchange for the lives of the people (4 Macc 6:28–29). They are described as a ransom for the sin of the nation, through whose blood and through whose death as an atoning sacrifice, eventually "the great Lord became reconciled" (2 Macc 5:20; cf. 7:33; 4 Macc 17:21–22). This language differs from that of Paul, who speaks of God reconciling (changing) us (2 Cor 5:18–19), not of God *being* reconciled (being changed). Still, Maccabean martyrology probably influenced Paul; these martyrs were celebrated by Hellenistic Jews, of which Paul was one.

In Paul's letters, the noble death idea is never far from the specifically Jewish concern with God's judgment of sin: "while we still were sinners Christ died for us" (Rom 5:8). "God has destined us not for wrath but for obtaining salvation through our Lord Jesus Christ, who died for us" (1 Thess 5:9–10). His only literary references are to the Jewish scriptures: "Christ died for our sins in accordance with the scriptures" and "he was raised on the third day in accordance with the scriptures" (1 Cor 15:3–4). His wording usually resembles that of the Septuagint (LXX), the Greek translation of the Jewish scriptures. His reference to God as one "who did not spare" his son (*ouk epheisato*; Rom 8:32) recalls God's words to Abraham: "you did not spare" your son Isaac (*ouk epheisō*; Gen 22:12 LXX). The scripture that speaks of Christ rising on the third day (*en tē hēmera tē tritē*) is probably Hosea 6:2 LXX, which also speaks of rising *en tē hēmera tē tritē*.

Paul uses ritual and social metaphors for the significance of the death of Christ, drawing from both the Jewish scriptures and from common Hellenistic social usages. The main metaphors are as follows.

Sacrifice   Paul utilizes several Jewish sacrificial images: "our paschal lamb, Christ, has been sacrificed" (1 Cor 5:7); "sending his own Son in the likeness of sinful flesh, and [as a sacrifice for sin], he condemned sin in the flesh" (Rom 8:3). The marginal reading of the New Revised Standard Version (NRSV), "as a sacrifice for sin," (in brackets), is to be preferred to its first choice, "to deal with sin," since the Greek (*peri hamartias*) is the Septuagint's technical term for the sin offering. Earlier in the letter, Paul had said that Christ is the one "whom God put forward as [a place of atonement] by his blood" (Rom 3:25). Again the NRSV's marginal reading, "a place of atonement," is better than its primary choice, "a sacrifice of atonement," since the term *hilastērion* never refers to the sacrificial victim but to the mercy seat (Bailey 2000, 158). The mercy seat *is* the place of atonement, the pinnacle of sacred geography, where sacrificial blood is sprinkled on the Day of Atonement (Lev 16:14, 15). In this imagery, then, Jesus is not only the sacrifice that provides the blood, but also the place where the blood is sprinkled.

Redemption   Using commercial terms, Paul indicates that salvation was *purchased* by Christ's death, in the same way that the freedom of slaves is purchased. He speaks of "the redemption [*apolytrōsis*] that is in Jesus Christ" (Rom 3:24), tells believers "you were bought [*agorazō*] with a price" (1 Cor 6:20; 7:23), and says "Christ redeemed [*exagorazō*] us from the curse of the law by becoming a curse for us" (Gal 3:13). The term *apolytrōsis* ("redemption") is commonly used for manumission of slaves or ransoming of hostages; *agorazō* ("buy") is used for ordinary purchases or for ransoming of hostages; while *exagorazō* ("buy back") may refer to freeing a slave by making a manumission payment.

Scapegoat   Galatians 3:13 also pictures what the scapegoat does, becoming cursed for the community. The scapegoat metaphor seems to be present also in the saying, "For our sake he made him to be sin who knew no sin" (2 Cor 5:21).

Justification   Several of Paul's sayings use the term "justification," a judicial metaphor, the notion of being pardoned or acquitted in one's trial before God. God's judgment is something Paul expects to happen, so such language is hardly "metaphorical" to him. Judicial terms abound in Romans 8: there is "no condemnation" for believers (Rom 8:1); "the Spirit intercedes" for us (vv. 26–27); no one can "bring any charge" or "condemn" us (vv. 33–34). The *cultic* action of Christ's death has a *judicial* result: "we have peace with God" because "we have been justified by his blood" (Rom 5:1, 9; Finlan 2007, 25–27).

Reconciliation and adoption   Thus Paul uses one judicial metaphor (justification), one commercial metaphor (redemption), and two ritual metaphors (sacrifice and scape-goat) for Jesus' death. He also uses redemption and justification to picture the death's beneficial effect upon believers, along with two other social metaphors: reconcilia-tion and adoption. The four metaphors for the beneficial effect upon believers, then, are these: those who accept the Messiah are freed (redemption), are pardoned (jus-tification), are restored to good relations (reconciliation), and are raised in social status (adoption).

    For the ancient audience, these were powerful metaphors. Reconciliation was a term used in domestic and political realms to describe the re-establishment of friendly relations after a period of estrangement. Adoption, in Greco-Roman society, did not designate the taking in of orphans, but the institution for declaring a non-relative to be one's heir. For instance, Julius Caesar adopted Octavian (later Augustus) as his heir.

Noble death   Underlying all these metaphors is the model of the noble death, some-thing that should not be called a metaphor. It is a *model of interpretation*, not a meta-phor, since it is not an image transferred from another realm. Noble death *always* has to do with the death of a principled human being, whereas "sacrifice" is an image *transferred* from the realm of ritual – a vivid and recognizable image that speaks of sudden reversal, radical forgiveness, or magical purification. Paul does not draw out the implications of purification, but he does imply propitiation in the idea of being "rescue[d] from the wrath that is coming" (1 Thess 1:10; cf. Rom 5:9).

Mixed metaphors   Paul deliberately mixes metaphors. He wants to cover several key points whenever he communicates how Jesus' death accomplished salvation; he wants to show the condemnation of sin, the acquittal of believers, and the ironic reversal that occurs in ritual. In Romans 8:3–4, he co-mingles scapegoat and sacri-ficial images in order to show judicial results: the innocent Christ took on "sinful flesh" like a scapegoat, died as a sin offering, and thus God "condemned sin in the flesh, so that the just requirement of the law might be fulfilled in us, who walk not according to the flesh but according to the Spirit." While using a variety of meta-phors, Paul rarely explains or develops any of them.

Participation, substitution   A Pauline concept that many have found hard to under-stand is that believers participate in the death and resurrection of Christ. Salvation involves "the sharing of his sufferings by becoming like him in his death if somehow I may attain the resurrection from the dead" (Phil 3:10–11). By sharing the death and resurrection of Christ, one passes from the old life (characterized by the flesh, the Law, bondage to sin, and death) into the new (characterized by the Spirit, freedom from the Law, freedom from sin, and life). Later atonement theory expands upon notions of substitution, representation, and suffering as payment (sometimes with minimal connection to Paul's teaching), but usually not on participation in the fate of the Messiah, which was an essential part of Paul's own perspective. Paul also taught the related idea of deification, the transformation of believers into the likeness of Christ, who is the likeness of God (Rom 8:29; 2 Cor 3:18; 4:4; Phil 3:21).

In former times, many New Testament scholars interpreted Paul in terms of sacrifice and interpreted Old Testament sacrifice in terms of their concept of substitutionary atonement. However, Old Testament scholarship has begun to undermine this interpretation, by showing that purification, not substitution, was the primary meaning of Levitical sacrifice. Several New Testament scholars argue that Christian atonement is not substitutionary. "Christ dies as man's representative, not his substitute"; believers still "must share his dying" (Hooker 1981, 77). Morna Hooker detects an "interchange" of conditions in Galatians 3:13 and 2 Corinthians 5:21: Christ takes on our accursed or sinful condition in order that we might take on his blessedness and righteousness (Hooker 1994, 35). Salvation depends on participation: believers "*share* his death, they *share* his resurrection" (Hooker 1994, 38). The German scholar, Otfried Hofius, agrees that the New Testament does not teach substitution, but "inclusive place-taking" – Jesus shared the human fate, died *as* a human, not displacing humans but drawing them in to his experience (Hofius 2004, 173, 180). While these scholars are right to emphasize the participatory dimension, it is doubtful that a substitutionary meaning can be fully removed from certain Pauline sayings: "Christ died for our sins"; "becoming a curse for us" (1 Cor 15:3; Gal 3:13).

Summary   To summarize, Paul teaches that Christ dies "for all," "for me," bringing new creation and pardon (2 Cor 5:15–17; Gal 2:20–21). To communicate this crucial point, Paul finds it necessary to use (and to mingle) different metaphors for the dying Christ:

- as the sin offering or Passover offering;
- as the new place of atonement;
- as becoming a curse or sin (probably a scapegoat image);
- as a ransom payment (redemption);
- as bringing reconciliation with God;
- as removing condemnation against "those who are in Christ Jesus";
- as bringing freedom, condemning sin, and enabling spiritual behavior.

Atonement in the gospels

Believers have frequently read the gospels through the lens of Pauline theology and have read atonement into every saying that refers to Jesus' death, but a closer look often shows an absence of atonement thinking. For instance, the synoptic gospels give us nine versions of Jesus' predictions of his coming passion (Mark 8:31; 9:31; 10:33–34; Matt 16:21; 17:22–23; 20:18–19; Luke 9:22, 44; 18:31–33), yet not one of them contains any notion of substitutionary atonement. Each is simply a matter-of-fact warning about what was coming.

There are two groups of passages in the gospels that do seem to speak of atonement and may show the influence of Pauline theology: the passages about the institution of the eucharist, and the ransom saying. Each synoptic gospel contains a text on the institution of the eucharist, but the earliest such text is in a letter of Paul (1 Cor 11:23–26). Mark 14:24 and Matthew 26:28 read "this is my blood of the covenant," but Luke 22:20 is even closer to Paul's "This cup is the new covenant in my blood" (1 Cor 11:25), matching it almost word for word. However, there is doubt about whether the verses in Luke 22:19b–20 were originally part of Luke, since they are absent from some manuscripts. Either Paul's atonement language was an original part of Luke (Jeremias 1966, 144, 152; Carroll and Green 1995, 69 n. 32), or a scribe added this language after the gospel was written (Westcott and Hort [1882] 1988, Appendix 63–64), probably to draw Luke into conformity with standard liturgical practice (Finlan 2004, 214–215).

Regarding the historical Jesus, two opposite interpretations emerge: that Jesus believed he was going to die a substitutionary atoning death, or that this idea was entirely the creation of early disciples. Not all the disciples had such a concept. The eucharistic liturgy in the Didache (ca. 100 CE; Richardson 1996, 161–179) contains no blood-language, but equates the wine with "the vine of David" (Did 9:2). This Jewish Christian document interprets the ritual messianically, as might be expected. The idea of drinking blood, even symbolically, would sound very strange to Jewish ears, since the Law strictly forbids the "eating" even of animal blood (Lev 7:26–27; Deut 12:16). Possibly the blood metaphor would have been more shocking to Galilean Jews or to the Syrian Jews behind the Didache than it was to more highly Hellenized Jews like Paul, who were familiar with Hellenistic allegorizing.

How one understands the eucharist yields important theological results, and the academic debate is often heated. If Jesus did not equate the wine with his blood, then he spoke only of sharing the fruit of the vine with his friends in the kingdom of God – of friendship and eschatology, but not of substitutionary atonement. It should not be surprising if Jesus did not think of his death in cultic terms. He comes into conflict with ritual purity (Mark 7:5–23), he affirms ethical over cultic meanings for Sabbath and Temple (Mark 2:27; 11:17), and he quotes anti-sacrificial prophets (Matt 9:13; 12:7; 23:23; Luke 19:46; Finlan 2005, 110–114). Without reference to cult, he establishes a spiritual family composed of those who do the will of God (Mark 3:35; Matt 23:8; Luke 6:35; John 7:17).

Besides the alternatives that Jesus had or did not have a substitutionary view of his coming death, a third possibility is that he uses the blood metaphor but without any substitutionary meaning. In this understanding, the blood language in the Last Supper passages is a metaphor referring to a covenant sacrifice, not a purification offering. In a covenant sacrifice, the blood is not expiatory, but is a self-curse on the participating parties. Jesus' emphasis would be on the covenant, not on the curse, but the latter was a recognized aspect of covenant sacrifices (cf. Jer 34:18–19). Moses sprinkles "the blood of the covenant" sacrifice on the congregation to bind them to the agreement with Yahweh (Exod 24:8). Jesus was establishing a new community, just as Moses had been, so perhaps at the Last Supper he symbolically enacted Exodus 24, just as he had enacted Zechariah 9:9 by riding into Jerusalem on a donkey. He could also be referring to Zechariah 9:11, where God liberates "because of the blood of my covenant with you." Again, blood here signifies covenant, not atonement. Then Christ's point was interpersonal, not cultic, which would be consistent with the emphasis throughout his teaching career.

The substitutionary (or representative) interpretation runs into the difficulty of its near-absence from the gospels (and Acts). The exception is the peculiar "ransom saying": "The Son of Man came not to be served but to serve, and to give his life a ransom for many" (Mark 10:45; Matt 20:28). The parallel passage in Luke has Jesus saying "I am among you as one who serves" (22:27), thus making the same point (service), but without the Pauline-looking "ransom" (*lytron*; see cognate terms in Rom 3:24; 1 Cor 1:30). The ransom idea looks out of place in the gospels, especially in Luke, which originally may have contained no atonement passages at all.

There is debate about the presence or absence of atonement in Luke. There is no doubt that Luke believed that God foreknew the Messiah's death and foretold it in scripture (Luke 24:25–27, 46; Acts 2:23; 3:18), but these do not add up to substitutionary atonement. Many passages traditionally interpreted through the lens of atonement actually work against such an interpretation. Luke 11:49–52 links the plot against Jesus with the killing of prophets, but this means that Jesus is dying a prophet's death (*not* unique, but all too familiar). Further, God did *not* will this series of deaths, but is going to punish "this generation" for them (11:50); God had hoped they would respect his son (20:13), but they did not. Jesus wept over Jerusalem (19:41) for he had tried "to gather" her children together under his "wings" (13:34).

There is an element of paradox in Luke's view, especially apparent in the sequel, the Acts of the Apostles (Carroll and Green 1995, 78). The "chief priests and scribes" brought about Jesus' death (Luke 9:22), yet it was all "according to the definite plan and foreknowledge of God" (Acts 2:23), in order to prove his status as Messiah and to fulfill the scriptural promise of the resurrection and the pouring out of the Spirit (Acts 2:16–36). The death is described as foreknown, but not as substitutionary; salvation is not actually linked to the death, but comes from recognition of Jesus as the Messiah (Acts 2:36–38; 4:10–12).

Sacrificial imagery shows up in the Gospel of John in its typology. Jesus fulfills Jewish rituals and holidays, such as Passover: "Here is the Lamb of God who takes away the sin of the world!" (John 1:29). Here a Passover image receives an expiatory interpretation. Jesus also fulfills the water-of-life and light-of-the-world images of the Sukkoth festival (7:37–38; 8:12). John has an *ironic* theology: the narrator and the enlightened reader see things from a higher level than most of the characters; for instance, attempts to humiliate Jesus only confirm his nobility; his crucifixion is his being "lifted up" (exalted) (John 3:14; 12:32). Salvation in John comes from *seeing* (believing) Jesus and his words, and accepting eternal life (John 5:20–24). John's *emphasis* is not sacrificial, but the sacrificial image is present in 1:29; 18:28; and 19:36 (Barrett 1978, 81).

Sacrificial theology is more evident in the first epistle of John: Jesus is "the atoning sacrifice [*hilasmos*] for our sins" (1 John 2:2; 4:10). This passage uses a term that (unlike *hilastērion*) can signify a sacrificial victim (Num 5:8). Interestingly, the author goes into a discussion of love after each of the *hilasmos* passages. Sacrifice is being "spiritualized": sacrificial terms are being used to signify selfless giving. This continues a process of moralizing and internalizing the language of sacrifice, a process already underway in the Old Testament (Ps 51:17; 141:2).

Atonement in Hebrews

The metaphorical appropriation of the language of sacrifice continues in the Epistle to the Hebrews, where kindly deeds, "to do good and to share," are called "sacrifices ... pleasing to God" (13:16). At the same time, Hebrews can take sacrifice very literally, analogizing at some length upon cultic details.

Unlike Paul, who uses brief and varied atonement formulas, the author of Hebrews goes on for two long chapters (9–10) with a single sacrificial metaphor. This section begins with the only mention in the New Testament, aside from Romans 3:25, of the *hilastērion*. Again unlike Paul, the author gives a physical description of "the earthly sanctuary ... the second curtain ... the ark of the covenant ... the cherubim of glory overshadowing the mercy seat" (9:1–5). Paul did not go into such details, only suggesting that Christ was the new place of atonement.

The author of Hebrews sees analogies for the death of Christ in the cultic furnishings yet also criticizes the cult for its repetition and its earthliness, compared to Christ's "once for all" offering when "he entered into heaven itself" (9:23–26). This author offers the most direct criticism of the sacrificial cult found in the New Testament, having Christ himself quote Psalm 40:6: "Sacrifices and offerings you have not desired" (Heb 10:5). Yet the author also sees the manipulation of blood as essential, both in the old cult (9:18, 22) and in Christ's replacement offering (9:12–14; 10:19). Everything in the new covenant is "better" than in the old: the promises are "better" (8:6), the sacrifices are "better" (9:23), his "sprinkled blood" is better (12:24), but everything is still *comparable* to the old. There is a tent, or sanctuary, and a redeeming death (9:11, 24, 15), accomplishing an "eternal redemption" (9:12). Even the cleansing of "our conscience" is due to the offering "without blemish" (9:14), a traditional sacrificial term. The author of Hebrews labors much harder than Paul to establish a sacrificial metaphor, possibly targeting Christians whom he feels are not making the sacrificial idea central enough, specifically in the face of their own persecution (10:23–34; 11:26).

Atonement in the Pastoral Epistles

After Paul's death, there was fierce competition for control of the Pauline tradition, one of the positions being inscribed in the Pastoral Epistles, three letters attributed to Paul but probably written a generation after his death. The Pastorals perpetuate some of Paul's atonement ideas, but in slogan-like form: there is "one mediator between God and humankind, Christ Jesus, himself human, who gave himself a ransom [*antilytron*] for all" (1 Tim 2:5–6). "He it is who gave himself for us that he might redeem [*lytrōsētai*] us from all iniquity" (Titus 2:14). The far-ranging imagery of Paul is here simplified and turned into a doctrine that enforces conformity: "exhort and reprove with all authority" (Titus 2:15).

Atonement Theories in Christian History

It seems that Paul's ideas were not widely understood (2 Pet 3:16 says as much). In the period after the New Testament we find very little specifically Pauline teaching. Several authors write confidently about salvation by works (e.g., Justin, I Apology 12; 1 Clement 30.3), seemingly unaware that Paul contrasted salvation by faith with salvation by works. The death of Christ is frequently mentioned without any specifically Pauline interpretation: it was necessary to fulfill scripture, or it was an example of obedience (e.g., 1 Clement 16.17; 7.4; Rashdall 1919, 192–193).

Ignatius of Antioch

The rarity of Pauline thought in most of the Apostolic Fathers makes the letters of Ignatius of Antioch (Richardson 1996, 74–120) all the more important, for his image of Paul as "a real saint and martyr" (*Ephesians* 12.2), and his transmission of some of Paul's atonement concepts, as wrapped up in a sacramental theology. Ignatius was *episkopos* in Antioch, capital of the Roman province of Syria (ca. 110 CE). With Ignatius, we can certainly translate *episkopos* as "bishop," in the developed sense of a figure in authority over a set ritual system. In fact, the bishop is to be respected "as you respect the authority of God" (*Magnesians* 3.1).

Ignatius has a more literal-minded understanding of the sacraments than any earlier author: "What I want is God's bread, which is the flesh of Christ ... and for drink I want his blood: an immortal feast indeed!" (*Romans* 7.3). "Break one loaf, which is the medicine of immortality, and the antidote which wards off death" (*Ephesians* 20.2). It is necessary to "believe in Christ's blood. ... The Eucharist is the flesh of our Saviour" (*Smyrnaeans* 6.1; 7.1). Thus were Paul's teachings perpetuated, reduced, and encapsulated in a sacramental form.

Ignatius writes his letters as he is being taken to Rome to be martyred, and he yearns to fulfill that fate. He prays to become "God's sacrifice. ... Let me imitate the

Passion of my God" (*Romans* 4.2; 6.2). The death of Christ is not so much interpreted as it is proclaimed, and emulated. We see this also in another second-century document, where the martyr Polycarp prays to be received "as a rich and acceptable sacrifice" (*Martyrdom of Polycarp* 14.2; Richardson 1996, 154). Reflection upon martyrdom stimulated development of the concept of Christian "sacrifice": joyous self-giving, affirmative of the unbreakable bond with Christ. Living in a world dominated by Satan, Christians might have to replicate the Savior's form of ultimate self-giving.

Irenaeus of Lyons; Aulén's theory

A more thorough interpretation of the significance of Christ's whole life (not just his death) is given by Irenaeus, the *episkopos* of Lyons, writing around 180 CE (Richardson 1996, 343–397). His soteriology is entirely centered on his idea of "recapitulation." Sin had damaged all aspects and stages of human life, but Christ lived righteously through each stage of life, restoring it: "he was made an infant for infants, sanctifying infancy; a child among children ... a grown man among the older men, that he might be a perfect teacher for all" (*Against Heresies* 2.22.4; Klager 2007, 463). Salvation is fundamentally a reorientation toward the Creator and giver of life. Affirming the goodness of the Creator, this theology rebuts the anti-cosmic views of Gnostics.

Irenaeus revives the idea of deification: "He became what we are in order to enable us to become what He is" (*Against Heresies* 5 preface; Kelly 1978, 172). It is the incarnation that made this possible: "Or how shall man pass into God unless God has first passed into man?" (*Against Heresies* 4.33.4; Finch 2006a, 99).

In an influential book on atonement, Gustaf Aulén (1931) used two terms, the "classic idea of the atonement" and "Christus Victor," to refer to all theories that center on Christ conquering the evil powers. Aulén argues that Christus Victor theology sees Sin and Death as evil powers, so its solution to the problem of sin is not "moralistic," but speaks of the defeat of the cosmic *power* of sin (1931, 41). For example, Irenaeus uses the image of ransom to describe the liberation of humanity from the "unjust" dominion of evil powers (*Against Heresies* 5.1.1; Aulén 1931, 43). The means of liberation seems to be the divine Son's deep contact with human experience, repairing everything touched by sin or death. Christ's obedience reverses the disobedience of Adam, by which the evil powers gained dominion over humanity (*Against Heresies* 3.21.10, echoing Rom 5:19).

Aulén's theory is appealing, but ultimately unsatisfying, to many scholars. His definition of the "classic" theory is broad enough to include as its proponents anyone who sees God sharing in Christ's experience, and is contrasted with the "Latin" theory, a view he attributes only to those who have a thoroughly legalistic notion of atonement as something paid to God, such as Tertullian and Anselm (Aulén 1931, 30, 98–108). He thus is able to include Luther among the "classic" theorists, despite Luther's actual preference for the language of satisfaction (Althaus 1966, 219–220). Still, Aulén did usefully draw attention to the patristic focus on Christ's triumph over evil powers.

Third and fourth centuries: Origen to the Gregories

It is easy to misinterpret Origen's position on atonement, because he uses the language of propitiation, sacrifice, and ransom payment, while his soteriology is actually dominated by ideas of God's strategy to rescue, repair, instruct, and divinize humanity. In several passages, Origen speaks of "propitiating" the sinner or the sin, by which he means "instructing" or "correcting" (*Commentary on Romans* 3.8; *Homilies on Leviticus* 5.4; 7.2; Young 1979, 170). Origen will use popular terms but change their meaning in the direction of restoration and instruction. He gives new meaning to sacrificial terms and understands the Bible to be doing the same thing. The Bible speaks of God's "anger" in the same way that parents will "put on threatening looks, not because we are angry but for the child's good" (*Homilies on Jeremiah* 18.6; Young 1979, 168). He laments that "the simpler members of the Church" actually believe in a cruel and unjust God (*On First Principles* 4.2.1; Young 1979, 186).

When Origen speaks of the death of Christ as a ransom paid to the devil, he is building on a popular belief, but changes it so that it is only an *apparent* ransom payment. In fact God is deceiving the devil, whose realm of death is conquered when Christ rises from the dead (Harnack [1900] 1961, 2:367; Kelly 1978, 185). This perspective is often called the "ransom theory" of atonement, but it might more accurately be called the *conquest theory*, since salvation did not result from the payment, which was just a ruse, but from God's conquest of the devil. In the popular mind, the ransom secured salvation. By changing the story at that point, Origen shows that God did not *actually* pay the devil anything; salvation was entirely a matter of the generosity (and cleverness) of God and Christ.

Athanasius builds on Origen but takes some of his ideas further. One gets the impression that it is the whole incarnation, not just the death of Jesus, that has a saving effect on the human race. The touch of God has changed human nature itself: "Through this union of the immortal Son of God with our human nature, all men were clothed with incorruption" (*On the Incarnation* 8; Athanasius 1998). Christ suffered in order to "invest us" with his nature (*Ad Epictetum* 6), or to "perfect what was wanting to man" (*Contra Arianos* 2.66; Finch 2006b, 118). The salvation story is not complete without the deification of believers, but this is not "automatic": one must still choose to *accept* God's plan. Athanasius revives the Pauline idea of participating in the Messiah's death, and so experiencing resurrection (*Contra Arianos* 1.41; 2.56; cf. Rom 6:5).

Sacrificial thinking is still very much present in these fathers, for whom asceticism is a necessary and beneficial sacrificial practice, with a pay-off in purification and spiritual perfecting. Sacrifice is internalized, but the old logic of a benefit to be had from painful giving is still present.

Gregory of Nyssa repeats the idea of God offering Jesus as a ransom that was really a trick, with the devil being caught like a fish on a hook when he could not hold the divine Son in his realm (*Catachetical Orations* 22–24). Gregory's friend, Gregory of Nazianzen, could not tolerate the idea of God paying a ransom to the devil. He rejected the notion of the blood of Christ as a ransom paid to anyone. God had not needed the death of Christ, but he accepted it because it meant that Christ, in his human nature, had restored humanity (*Oration* 45.22; Kelly 1978, 382–383).

Thus do we see a variety of ideas in the Greek fathers. Salvation is not described exclusively in connection with the death of Christ, nor is human sin the all-consuming problem. Salvation is deliverance from death, ignorance, and demonic powers, along with sin. Further, salvation is a re-making of believers into the likeness of Christ, who is pictured as life-giver, teacher, and revealer more often than as sacrificial lamb. Sacrifice is internalized and moralized.

Latin theologians

The real sources of the atonement doctrine as it is conceived in the West are the Latin theologians who thought primarily in terms of law. The lawyer-turned-theologian Tertullian is obsessed with sin (law-breaking) and with suffering as payment for sin. He uses the term "satisfaction" for painful forms of religious austerity by which believers need to make reparation for their sins and through which "God is appeased" (*On Penitence* 31; Bartlett 2001, 55).

Another North African, Cyprian, takes Tertullian's legalism further: Christ's suffering and death propitiated the angry God, a notion that is alien to the Greek fathers (Harnack 1961, 3:312). The important fourth-century figure, Ambrose, used many of the key terms (redemption, satisfaction, immolation, merit) that were later developed by his pupil, Augustine.

The most influential shapers of the legal concept of atonement in the first millennium were Augustine and his interpreter, Gregory the Great. Augustine emphasizes salvation by grace, not undoing the legalistic theology, but inserting grace into the legal concept. Humanity is a "mass of sin" (*massa peccati*) and of damnation (*massa perditionis*). Humans are incapable of saving themselves, but God has predestined "a fixed number" of people to benefit from Christ's atoning death, to be justified and preserved (Harnack 1961, 5:204–205). Augustine's teaching on sin and predestination has had a lasting influence. Humanity is thoroughly sinful, corrupted by Adam's sin. Lust is the characteristic sin, manifested in the sinful desire to procreate; sin is communicated to the children conceived through this lustful act (*Enchiridion* 46).

Although Augustine thinks he sees these ideas in Paul (Rom 5:12–14), most of them are "an unheard of novelty in the Church, and must be explained by reference to Manichaeism" (Harnack 1961, 5:211 n. 5), the Gnostic cult to which Augustine belonged before he became Christian, which treated sexual desire as sinful. Augustine's teachings on predestination continue to distress Christians who cannot understand why they are blamed for the sins of their ancestors, yet can be forgiven for their *own* sins – but only if God has predestined them to be among the elect. There is much that is insightful in Augustine's writings, but this teaching causes despondency among Christians who do not know whether they are predestined to be saved or damned, and so can have no confidence in their salvation.

The great popularizer of Augustinian theology was Pope Gregory the Great, who taught that only a sacrificial death could have paid for sin and "appeased the indignant Judge" (*Moral Teachings from Job* 9.54; 9.61; Dudden 1905, 2:341–342). Gregory compares God's behavior to that of a mother who beats her child although she loves him (*Homilies on Ezekiel* 1.1.18; Straw 1988, 186). Salvation comes to resemble the Roman legal process, complete with rewards, punishments, vengeance, and (fortunately!) a powerful intercessor.

In the eleventh century, an important thinker moved away from this line of thinking. Anselm of Canterbury could not accept the notion of a payment to, or negotiation with, the devil, and came up with a formulation that attributes everything to God: God was offended at human sinning, demanded punishment, and accepted the divine Son's offer to pay the penalty. Anselm aspired to think as a philosopher. God is unchangeable and is not subject to time (*Cur Deus Homo?* 1.8). This should mean that God's honor cannot be damaged, and Anselm *does* say this, yet in the same paragraph he explains atonement in terms of the logic of medieval honor: "Satisfaction or punishment must needs follow every sin" (*Cur Deus* 1.15; Deane 1962, 210). The fundamental problem with Anselm's theory is that it implies that God's honor *can* be hurt and can be reinstated by getting *satisfaction* from the offending party.

Anselm treats sin as an insult to cosmic order, but his solution comes from the feudal order: the sinner must make "some compensation for the anguish incurred. ... The honor taken away must be restored, or punishment must follow" (*Cur Deus* 1.11, 13; Deane 1962, 202, 207). The "satisfaction" that Christ makes is the *satisfactio* – a form of payment through suffering that was one of the accepted ways of paying a penalty in feudal society (Gorringe 1996, 89, 94; Finlan 2007, 57–58). The offense is so great that corrupt sinners cannot make adequate payment, yet it must be paid by man. Therefore only the God-man, Christ, could pay the debt (*Cur Deus* 2.7). Seeing that adequate satisfaction has been made, God exonerates humanity. This is the logic of payment through suffering.

The notion that sin *must* be punished permeates societies from ancient to modern times, and theories of atonement from Augustine to Anselm to the present day. God cannot just forgive, for "truly such compassion on the part of God is wholly contrary to the Divine justice, which allows nothing but punishment as the recompense of sin" (*Cur Deus* 1.24; Deane 1962, 235). The necessity of punishment is treated as a law that even God cannot break. Anselm seems to be unaware of the fact that this law limits God's free will and means that there is no real forgiveness, only a redirection of the penalty from humans to Christ. Irenaeus spoke of the incarnation accomplishing what God was always endeavoring to do (get humanity to accept forgiveness and recovery from sin), but Anselm has the incarnation – that is, the crucifixion – fulfilling a legal necessity.

It was not long before this theory found its critics. Peter Abelard was one of several theologians offended at Anselm's picture of God demanding punitive satisfaction (Gorringe 1996, 101). In opposition to Anselm, Abelard denied that God was paid off in any way. Rather, the incarnation was necessary to reveal the full measure of divine love to humans. Everything Jesus did, but especially his unselfish death, reveals love and inspires love in Christians. Some feminist theologians have detected a toxic subtext here, since this formulation makes selfless suffering a virtue to be emulated: "Abelard embeds helplessness in salvation and romanticizes and sanctifies suffering" (Brock 2006, 248). Such a perspective could be used by those in power to keep the socially weak from objecting to the injustice perpetrated against them.

Many figures in the atonement debate formulated their views in opposition to previous atonement formulations. Just as Anselm took offense at the notion that God had to deal with the devil, so did Abelard reject Anselm's punitive ideas, and so do feminists take offense at Abelard's notion that unselfish suffering is exemplary.

Abelard's ideas were mostly discussed in academic circles. Simpler atonement ideas were very influential in society at large. The Middle Ages witnessed a rise in superstitious fear of Jews, seen in the allegation that Jews were kidnapping Christian boys and draining their blood for ritual usage. Another aspect of the accusation arose after the Transubstantiation of the host was articulated at the Fourth Lateran Council in 1215. Christians now understood themselves actually to be eating the body of Christ and drinking his blood. Soon Jews were being accused of stealing and ritually abusing Christian hosts. This displays the psychopathology known as projective inversion – the projection of one's own overpowering guilt feelings onto others. In this case, Christians were projecting their anxieties about their own ritual blood-drinking (Dundes 1991: 353–355). Popes Innocent IV and Gregory X repudiated the blood libel myth, but it persisted, being a convenient avenue for expression of anxiety about ritual consumption of a "body."

The Reformers

The most influential atonement theologians were probably the great Reformers, Luther and Calvin. Martin Luther builds on Augustine's belief in predestination but heightens its cruelty: God damns some and saves some, and though "He seems unjust," we should be awed and should not expect him to seem just (*Bondage of the*

Will 19; Dillenberger 1961, 200). Luther also builds upon Anselm; in an Easter sermon he tells how "the wrath of God ... could be appeased" only by "the sacrifice of the Son of God. ... Only ... the shedding of his blood could make satisfaction. ... Well may we be terrified because of our sins" (Lenker 1983, 190–191).

Similarly, Calvin sees "the whole curse ... being transferred to him ... he by his death purchased life for us" (*Institutes* 2.16.6–7; Calvin 1975, 439–440). Human nature is totally evil (*Institutes* 2.3.2). Those theologians who are most convinced of the wickedness of all (Augustine, Luther, Calvin) are also the ones who attack the notion of free will. Luther's emphasis is to deny that people can will anything good: our wills are enslaved to Satan, and there is an "inescapability of sin" (Althaus 1966, 156). The specific formulations of Luther and Calvin (but not the similar ideas of Augustine and Anselm) are commonly called the "penal substitutionary theory" of atonement.

Critics of Penal Substitution

The penal substitutionary interpretation has become so widespread that many Christians today assume that it has always been predominant. In fact, there has never been a single dominant formula throughout the churches, nor did the ecumenical councils establish any atonement doctrine.

Reactions against penal substitutionary theology were heard in the sixteenth and following centuries. Socinus rejected the notions of original sin and collective guilt, Kant denied that guilt could be transferred to another person, and Thomas Paine likewise denied that moral justice was served by transferring punishment from a guilty party to an innocent one. But opposition to the doctrine has accelerated in the last 200 years. In the first half of the nineteenth century, William Ellery Channing attacked Calvinism for proclaiming a God who is to be dreaded. We are told to love and imitate God, but also that God does things we would consider most cruel in any human parent, "were he to bring his children into life totally depraved and then to pursue them with endless punishment" ([1820] 1957, 56). Two figures later in the century had more widespread influence: John McLeod Campbell and Horace Bushnell.

Campbell was an earnest churchman in Scotland who suffered career setbacks as a result of his writing. He stressed some long-neglected aspects of the gospel: Jesus always insisted "that those to whom He was speaking were, and ought to know themselves, God's offspring. ... We must *come to God as sons, or not come at all*" (1873, xxxii, 300). The parable of the prodigal son illustrates not some legal "fiction," but the Father's familial love, fulfilling the promise of *"bringing many sons unto glory"* (Heb 2:10; Campbell 1873, 301). Campbell retains sacrificial terms and builds on the priestly christology of Hebrews, emphasizing divine self-giving and rejecting divine vengeance.

Horace Bushnell stresses ethics and grace. The cross did not change God's attitude; it was a *revelation* of God's perpetual forgiveness and willingness to suffer (1903, 239–241; Browning 1966, 72, 81, 88). Scripture has a theology of unselfish or vicarious suffering, as in Isaiah's Suffering Servant, but not of penal substitution (Bushnell 1874, 166, 168; Browning 1966, 82). Because of these statements, Bushnell is generally considered an advocate of Abelard's moral influence theory.

Bushnell's ethical focus continues in the Social Gospel movement. Shailer Mathews sees no different meaning in Christ's death than in his life: he risked everything on trust in God and "in the practicability of love as a basis of the social order" (1930, 207). R. J. Campbell attacks "the outrageous assumption that ... His cruel death on Calvary somehow purchased Divine forgiveness" (1907, 138).

Much recent writing, even by authors who wish to defend some version of atonement, has been critical of the penal substitutionary concept. Fiddes says that Calvin distorts Paul's soteriology into a model of criminal law, picturing atonement as a "legal settlement between God the Father and God the Son in which we are not involved," a "commercial transaction" that leaves out personal transformation (1989, 98–99, 198).

Many feminists have spoken out against any theology that glorifies suffering, since that is then imposed on the socially weak. Rita Nakashima Brock describes a decline in theology from the early church's emphasis on resurrection, to an increasing emphasis on Christ's death and on sacrificial thinking from the fifth century onward (2006, 242–247). This is when we first hear that even babies deserve damnation (Augustine; Bartlett 2001, 59).

Scholars who follow the interpretation of René Girard say that "scapegoating is ... built into our religion and our politics" (Heim 2006, 64). Jesus' death exposed this structure of violence; he died not to pay a penalty but to open our eyes, "to save the people from the logic of scapegoating" (Heim 2006, 125), though Christians often fail to learn the lesson and continue to scapegoat others.

Penal substitutionary theory has its defenders. Thomas Schreiner, one of the authors in a four-way debate on atonement, insists that "God willed and planned Jesus' suffering ... propitiation is fundamental" (Boyd et al. 2006, 86 n. 61, 194). Joel Green responds that the notion of the Son dying to propitiate the Father undermines the concept of unity within the Trinity and contributes nothing to the idea of a "transformed life" (Boyd et al. 2006, 114). One defender of substitutionary theory echoes the arguments of its critics when he writes, "there is not the faintest hint in the New Testament that Jesus died to persuade God to forgive sinners" (Marshall 2007, 55).

Conclusion

Paul urges his readers to be transformed by "the renewing of your minds" (Rom 12:2). Perhaps a kind of renewal occurs through healthy debate about atonement. In any case, such debate does lead to constructive theology as the preceding survey shows.

Note

Biblical quotations in this chapter are taken from the New Revised Standard Version (NRSV), unless otherwise indicated.

References

Althaus, Paul (1966). *The Theology of Martin Luther*. Trans. Robert C. Schultz. Philadelphia: Fortress.

Athanasius (1998). *On the Incarnation: The Treatise De Incarnatione Verbi Dei*. Trans. Religious of CSMV. Crestwood, NY: St. Vladimir's Seminary Press.

Aulén, Gustaf (1931). *Christus Victor: An Historical Study of the Three Main Types of the Idea of the Atonement*. London: SPCK.

Averbeck, Richard E. (2003). "Sacrifices and Offerings." In T. Desmond Alexander and David W. Baker (eds.), *Dictionary of the Old Testament: Pentateuch* (pp. 706–733). Downers Grove, IL: InterVarsity.

Bailey, Daniel P. (2000). "Jesus as the Mercy Seat: The Semantics and Theology of Paul's Use of *Hilasterion* in Romans 3:25." *Tyndale Bulletin* 51: 155–158.

Barrett, C. K. (1978). *The Gospel According to St. John: An Introduction with Commentary and Notes on the Greek Text*. 2nd edn. Philadelphia: Westminster.

Bartlett, Anthony W. (2001). *Cross Purposes: The Violent Grammar of Christian Atonement*. Harrisburg, PA: Trinity.

Boyd, Gregory A., Joel B. Green, Bruce R. Reichenbach, and Thomas R. Schreiner (2006). *The Nature of the Atonement: Four Views*. Edited by James Beilby and Paul R. Eddy. Downers Grove, IL: InterVarsity.

Brock, Rita Nakashima (2006). "The Cross of Resurrection and Communal Redemption." In Marit Trelstad (ed.), *Cross Examinations: Readings on the Meaning of the Cross Today* (pp. 241–251). Minneapolis: Augsburg Fortress.

Browning, Don S. (1966). *Atonement and Psychotherapy*. Philadelphia: Westminster.

Bushnell, Horace (1874). *Forgiveness and Law*. New York: Scribner.

Bushnell, Horace (1903). *God in Christ*. New York: Scribner.

Calvin, Jean (1975). *Institutes of the Christian Religion*. Trans. Henry Beveridge. Grand Rapids: Eerdmans.

Campbell, John McLeod (1873). *The Nature of the Atonement*. 4th edn. London: Macmillan.

Campbell, R. J. (1907). *Christianity and the Social Order*. London: Chapman & Hall.

Carroll, John T., and Joel B. Green (1995). *The Death of Jesus in Early Christianity*. Peabody, MA: Hendrickson.

Channing, William Ellery ([1820] 1957). "The Moral Argument Against Calvinism." In Irving H. Bartlett (ed.), *Unitarian Christianity and Other Essays* (pp. 39–59). Indianapolis: Bobbs-Merrill.

Deane, S. N., trans. (1962). *St. Anselm: Basic Writings*. 2nd edn. La Salle, IL: Open Court.

Dillenberger, John (1961). *Martin Luther: Selections from His Writings*. Garden City, NY: Doubleday.

Dodd, C. H. (1935). *The Bible and the Greeks*. London: Hodder & Stoughton.

Dudden, F. Homes (1905). *Gregory the Great: His Place in History and Thought*. Vol. 2. New York: Longmans, Green.

Dundes, Alan (1991). "The Ritual Murder or Blood Libel Legend." In Alan Dundes (ed.), *The Blood Libel Legend: A Casebook in Anti-Semitic Folklore* (pp. 336–376). Madison: University of Wisconsin Press.

Fiddes, Paul S. (1989). *Past Event and Present Salvation: The Christian Idea of Atonement*. Louisville, KY: Westminster John Knox.

Finch, Jeffrey (2006a). "Athanasius on the Deifying Work of the Redeemer." In Stephen Finlan and Vladimir Kharlamov (eds.), *Theōsis: Deification in Christian Theology* (pp. 104–121). Eugene: Pickwick.

Finch, Jeffrey (2006b). "Irenaeus on the Christological Basis of Human Divinization." In Stephen Finlan and Vladimir Kharlamov (eds.), *Theōsis: Deification in Christian Theology* (pp. 86–103). Eugene: Pickwick.

Finlan, Stephen (2004). *The Background and Content of Paul's Cultic Atonement Metaphors*. Atlanta: Society of Biblical Literature; Leiden: Brill.

Finlan, Stephen (2005). *Problems with Atonement: The Origins of, and Controversy about, the Atonement Doctrine*. Collegeville, MN: Liturgical.

Finlan, Stephen (2007). *Options on Atonement in Christian Thought*. Collegeville, MN: Liturgical.

Gorringe, Timothy (1996). *God's Just Vengeance: Crime, Violence and the Rhetoric of Salvation*. Cambridge: Cambridge University Press.

Harnack, Adolf von ([1900] 1961). *History of Dogma*. 7 vols. Trans. Neil Buchanan. New York: Dover.

Harrison, Jane Ellen (1903). *Prolegomena to the Study of Greek Religion*. Cambridge: Cambridge University Press.

Heim, S. Mark (2006). *Saved from Sacrifice: A Theology of the Cross*. Grand Rapids: Eerdmans.

Hengel, Martin (1981). *The Atonement: The Origins of the Doctrine in the New Testament*. London: SCM.

Hofius, Otfried (2004). "The Fourth Servant Song in the New Testament Letters." In Bernd Janowski and Peter Stuhlmacher (eds.), *The Suffering Servant: Isaiah 53 in Jewish and Christian Sources* (pp. 163–188). Trans. Daniel P. Bailey. Grand Rapids: Eerdmans.

Hooker, Morna D. (1981). "Interchange and Suffering." In William Horbury and Brian McNeil (eds.), *Suffering and Martyrdom in the New Testament* (pp. 70–83). Cambridge: Cambridge University Press.

Hooker, Morna D. (1994). *Not Ashamed of the Gospel: New Testament Interpretations of the Death of Christ*. Grand Rapids: Eerdmans.

Jeremias, Joachim (1966). *The Eucharistic Words of Jesus*. New York: Scribner.

Kelly, J. N. D. (1978). *Early Christian Doctrines*. Rev. edn. New York: Harper & Row.

Klager, Andrew P. (2007). "Retaining and Reclaiming the Divine: Identification and the Recapitulation of Peace in St. Irenaeus of Lyons' Atonement Narrative." In Brad Jersak and Michael Hardin (eds.), *Stricken by God? Nonviolent Identification and the Victory of Christ* (pp. 422–480). Grand Rapids: Eerdmans.

Lenker, John Nicholas, ed. (1983). *The Sermons of Martin Luther*. Vol. 7. Grand Rapids: Baker.

Marshall, I. Howard (2007). *Aspects of the Atonement: Cross and Resurrection in the Reconciling of God and Humanity*. London: Paternoster.

Mathews, Shailer (1930). *Atonement and the Social Process*. New York: Macmillan.

Milgrom, Jacob (1971). "Kippēr." In *Encyclopaedia Judaica* (10:1039–1044). New York: Macmillan.

Milgrom, Jacob (1983). *Studies in Cultic Theology and Terminology*. Leiden: Brill.

Milgrom, Jacob (1991). *Leviticus 1–16*. Anchor Bible 3. Garden City, NY: Doubleday.

Morris, Leon (1965). *The Apostolic Preaching of the Cross*. 3rd edn, rev. Grand Rapids: Eerdmans.

Rashdall, Hastings (1919). *The Idea of the Atonement in Christian Theology*. London: Macmillan.

Richardson, Cyril C., ed. (1996). *Early Christian Fathers*. New York: Touchstone.

Straw, Carole (1988). *Gregory the Great: Perfection in Imperfection*. Berkeley: University of California Press.

Westcott, B. F., and F. J. A. Hort ([1882] 1988). *Introduction to the New Testament in the Original Greek with Notes on Selected Readings*. Peabody, MA: Hendrickson.

Young, Frances M. (1979). *The Use of Sacrificial Ideas in Greek Christian Writers from the New Testament to John Chrysostom*. Eugene: Wipf & Stock.

PART III

Jesus in World Religions

14 Jewish Perspectives on Jesus   215
    Michael J. Cook

15 Islamic Perspectives on Jesus   232
    Reem A. Meshal and M. Reza Pirbhai

16 Hindu Perspectives on Jesus   250
    Sandy Bharat

17 Buddhist Perspectives on Jesus   267
    Peggy Morgan

CHAPTER 14

Jewish Perspectives on Jesus

Michael J. Cook

Until the onset of the modern age, Jews' perceptions of Jesus were predominantly disparaging.[1] But the Jesus whom Jews visualized over these centuries was not the historical figure, but the anti-Jewish figure represented by the gospels. This anti-Jewish animus in the New Testament was reinforced by writings and sermons of the church fathers, church-sponsored disputations, burnings of the Talmud, and relentless missionizing campaigns. Passion plays, especially when they referred to Jews as "Christ-killers," fanned fury against Jews by the Christian masses. Such factors provided fertile ground for major historical tragedies in Jewish history, including the Spanish Inquisition, pogroms (massacres of Jews), even to a degree the Holocaust. With such horrific associations, some Jews even today tend to recoil upon hearing Jesus' name.

Beginning in the nineteenth century, however, Jewish *scholarly* assessments of the historical Jesus began to undergo substantial revision in what has come to be termed "the Jewish reclamation of Jesus" (Hagner 1984). Here the possibility was grasped that a proper sifting of the gospel materials could lead to a recovering of Jesus the man – here in the sense of Jesus the *Jew*. Conditioning this redirection, for Jewish scholars, was a dawning realization by their counterpart *Christian* academicians that the Jesus of history and the Jesus of the gospels were not one and the same, and that when late accretions to gospel traditions were stripped away a more thoroughgoingly *Jewish* Jesus emerged.

Involvement in Jesus-study by today's Jewish *populace* at large, meanwhile, lags far behind their growing number of representative scholars (e.g., Fredriksen 2000; Levine 2007). Yet interest even among this laity is accelerating, especially when it commences with learning who Jesus was *not* – that is to say, in recognizing those "gospel dynamics" by which New Testament writers enlisted, and changed, the Jesus figure so as to address problems pertaining to their own day rather than to his. Unavoidably, however, even in such sporadic efforts by Jews in general to deepen

The Blackwell Companion to Jesus, First Edition. Edited by Delbert Burkett. ©2014 John Wiley & Sons, Ltd. Published 2014 by John Wiley & Sons, Ltd.

their exposure, a characteristically Jewish mindset usually prevails: first, a detachment of sorts, because the New Testament is not scripture for the Jew; second, a disproportionate focus on gospel texts that asperse Jews and Judaism, rather than on a fuller consideration of the gospels in their broader dimensions; and, third, an indelible sadness, given the sorrows of Jewish history in which the gospels have played so generative a role.

Jesus' Ministry

Aside from Jesus' close associates, how did wider numbers of Jews of Jesus' day view him? This determination proves elusive, since his ministry (ca. 30 CE) long preceded composition of any extant written sources about him (Jewish, Christian, or other). Arguably, precisely because Jesus was a Jew, the more fully he lived and spoke as a Jew the less reason there might have been for his Jewish contemporaries to take special notice of him. While he may indeed have been a charismatic teacher of provocative parables, we nonetheless must devalue gospel assertions of Jesus' fame (e.g., Mark 1:28; Matt 9:26, 31; Luke 5:15). These match the usual mold of Hellenistic tales of wonder-workers, sagas (termed "aretalogies") that routinely aggrandized a hero's fame, words, and deeds in the interest of attracting new adherents to religious cults, including movements that (akin to Christianity) preached dying and rising savior-deities.[2]

The gospels' presentations of how Jews of Jesus' day perceived him is problematic on many other scores as well. (1) *Chronologically,* one to two generations elapsed between Jesus' ministry (ca. 30 CE) and the eventual completion of the four canonical gospels (ca. 70–100), thus inevitably obscuring any accurate recall and reportage by the four Evangelists as to how Jews had considered Jesus during his ministry. (2) *Geographically,* early Christianity expanded rapidly from the land of Israel into, and throughout, the broader Mediterranean arena. Accordingly, most adherents of new churches were unfamiliar with the very terrain, let alone the wider setting, of Jesus' ministry. Some, possibly all four, canonical gospels were completed within these Diaspora regions. So distance alone might have impeded authors' access to information about how Jews during Jesus' ministry had viewed him. (3) *Demographically,* by the time of the gospels' completion (70–100 CE), most Christians reflected Gentile rather than Jewish extraction. Recountings of Jewish views of Jesus during his ministry could well, then, have been formulated to satisfy primarily Gentile interests rather than accurately recounting Jesus' interactions with Jews of his day. (4) The problem of *bias* may here become determinative: some Gentile-Christians were not merely, as by definition, non-Jewish, but also anti-Jewish. So gospel portrayals of how Jews had perceived Jesus during his ministry could easily have become skewed by this factor alone. As a result, it is impossible to gauge, with confidence let alone precision, the extent to which Jesus' Jewish contemporaries (aside from his own followers) had viewed him positively, negatively, or even been aware of him at all.

Finally, later Jewish views about Jesus are likewise best explicable on the assumption that, from the very start, little by way of any accurate understanding of Jesus was passed on by his Jewish contemporaries to their succeeding generation – when the canonical gospels were to congeal and reach completion. This likewise, then, suggests that the Jesus to whom Jews eventually did come to react was not as much the historical figure as the gospels' later reconfigurations of him.

From Jesus' Death through 200 CE

In terms of first-century sources, aside from the Jewish historian Josephus Flavius, neither the Dead Sea Scrolls nor Philo of Alexandria (died ca. 40 CE) nor any other non-Christian intertestamental writing explicitly refers to Jesus. As for second-century Roman sources mentioning him or Christianity (e.g., Tacitus, Suetonius, Pliny),[3] they impart nothing substantive about Jesus himself – and likely themselves depended either directly on gospel testimony or on whatever formulations about him they heard emanating from Christian circles.

Respecting the two references to Jesus in Josephus' *Antiquities* (ca. 93 CE), his long paragraph about Jesus, called the "Testimonium Flavianum" (XVIII.iii.3; 63–64), is so adulatory and consistent with what we would expect of a *Christian* assessment that most scholars dismiss it as a reworking, even an outright forgery, by a later Christian hand (it was the church, not the rabbis, who preserved Josephus' writings). Further along in the same work (XX.ix.1; 197–203), Josephus describes the execution (in 62 CE) of a James whom he identifies as "the brother of Jesus who was called [or was 'the so-called'] Christ." While identifying this James *by reference to* Jesus could imply that Josephus has introduced his readers to Jesus somewhere earlier in *Antiquities* – originally, perhaps, where the later "Testimonium" now resides – this need not suggest that Jesus himself had been particularly well known to fellow Jews. After all, Josephus likewise presents other figures from Jesus' era who were unfamiliar, even unknown, to most contemporaries.

Certain Christian works indirectly attest to specifically Jewish views about Jesus during this second period. The gospel authors frame some sections of their narratives as responses to Jewish opponents of their own day (70–100 CE). We can thus comb such accounts for telltale clues as to what (non-Christian) Jews – later than Jesus' ministry – were then saying about him: for example, that since Elijah, herald of the Messiah, had himself not yet appeared, Jesus could not be the Messiah (Mark 9:11);[4] that the Messiah was supposed to triumph over Rome, not die at the oppressor's hand;[5] that he was not expected to come from Galilee (John 7:52);[6] that Jesus had not been descended from King David (John 7:40–42); that Jesus rejected or at least failed to reaffirm the Law of Moses (Mark 2:24; 7:19b; John 9:16; cf. Acts 6:13–14); that he was not genuinely resurrected from his tomb (cf. Matt 27:62–66; 28:4, 11–15; Luke 24; John 20–21); and the like.

A similar but less circuitous approach may be taken with a later (mid-second century) Christian source, Justin Martyr's *Dialogue with Trypho*. Justin specifically conveys how Christians should respond to Jewish skeptics such as the fictional "Trypho" (perhaps loosely modeled, by Justin, on Tarphon, an early second-century rabbinic opponent of Christianity). The arguments that Justin ascribes to Trypho presumably echo what Christians were then genuinely hearing from Jewish skeptics: for example, that "you Christians have all received an idle report and have formed a Christ for yourselves, for whose sake you ... throw away your lives" ("Introduction"); that the Hebrew scriptures "never acknowledge any other God than the One Creator of all things" (§55); that the idea of God becoming born in the form of a man is "incredible and almost impossible" (§68); that Christian views of Jesus rely upon an overly selective and arbitrary citation of proof-texts from Jewish scriptural passages drawn, moreover, only from the Greek translation rather than the Hebrew original (§27; 68); that the image of Jesus in Christianity heavily depends upon borrowings from Greco-Roman mythology (§67); that crucifixion is tantamount to "hanging," specifically cursed in Deuteronomy 21:23 (§89); and so forth.

On all these various bases, then, we may surmise that Jews of this second era *did* believe Jesus to have been an actual personage from Galilee who had claimed divine status and broken with the Law.[7] He had declared himself the Messiah but utterly without substantiation. Since undoubtedly many Jews at that time were disillusioned over the failure and death (135 CE) of their recent popular messianic pretender, Bar Kokhba, the fact, not to mention the mode, of Jesus' execution could have made Messianic claims on his behalf appear preposterous.

But what of views about Jesus espoused by the early "rabbis" (a new designation arising only post-70 CE)? While rabbinic literature itself belongs to the next time-frame, its oral antecedents were rooted *here*. The first rabbis had never known Jesus personally, nor had reliable traditions about him been passed down to them by their own forebears. Instead, the only Jesus of whom the early rabbis may have been aware was the anti-Jewish image of him portrayed by the gospel writers. But the rabbis had no reason to set about disengaging a real Jesus from the gospels' portrait of him – they had no mindset to suspect that there was such a disparity, nor, even if they had, any capacity to resolve it. Thus, the figure of Jesus – who both lived and died a Jew, and who neither founded Christianity nor knew of Christian theology – was processed by them as an apostate from Judaism, a profound misunderstanding that, spanning all subsequent history, prevails among many Jews even today.

As we turn now to the next two periods, we will encounter increasingly negative – even odd – descriptions of Jesus by Jews, suggesting that, until the modern age, disparagements of Jesus by Jews of any one era determined, and were intensified by, those of the next.

Early Rabbinic Literature (Third through Sixth Centuries CE)

With the age of early rabbinic literature (from Babylonia as well as the land of Israel) we begin encountering evaluations of Jesus in written *Jewish* sources per se. Yet since the Talmud, Midrash, and related rabbinic works are such vast compendia of Hebrew law and lore, their allusions to Jesus must be adjudged most strikingly sparse. These mentions are also so widely scattered that we must "hunt and peck" simply to assemble a viable portrait – combining views from different rabbis, generations, and academies.

In terms of the rabbis' cumulative understanding of Jesus, some had come to think that, while in Egypt, he had been schooled in the art of sorcery along with the charms and formulae needed to perform feats of magic. Possibly, this was how rabbis explained (or explained away) the miracles that the gospels credited to Jesus – since what were "miracles" to believers were easily dismissible by skeptics as trickery.[8] As for datings of Jesus, these are likewise puzzling. The rabbis mentioned Jesus in connection with various figures whose time-frames, when combined, spanned at least two centuries. Yet gospel testimony itself clearly assigned Jesus' ministry to Pontius Pilate's narrow tenure in Judea (26–37 CE) – when Jesus had been "about thirty" (Luke 3:23). Of course, by their later day, the rabbis – especially in Babylonia – would have had few guidelines for dating Pilate's rule either.

The Talmud allotted Jesus merely five disciples,[9] even though the gospels consistently assigned him twelve. Was it simply a rabbinic convention that often teachers had five disciples?[10] Or did the rabbis *deprive* Jesus of having "twelve" disciples so as to obstruct claims that Christianity (symbolized by these twelve) had supplanted Judaism (symbolized by twelve tribes; cf. Matt 19:28: Luke 22:28–30)? Likewise puzzling is how the rabbis could confuse Jesus' mother, Mary,[11] with Mary Magdalene.

Elsewhere, however, the rabbis seemed not only fully aligned with gospel traditions but even overly accepting of them. They naturally viewed anti-Jewish sentiments attributed to Jesus, by the gospels, as originating with him personally – rather than as retrojections by the later church. They also took for granted that Jesus had proclaimed himself divine; accordingly, any Jew worshiping him was compromising monotheism. Ironically, therefore, the same Jesus who had designated as his preeminent directive the *Shema* – "Hear, O Israel: The Lord our God, the Lord is one" (Mark 12:29, quoting Deut 6:4) – would be summarily accused of denying Judaism's cardinal teaching![12]

Mindful that some Jews had indeed been lured into Christian ranks, the rabbis denounced Jesus himself for having attempted to "entice and lead Israel astray," i.e., into apostasy and idolatry.[13] All told, accordingly, the rabbis could deem fully credible the gospel claims that Jesus underwent a Sanhedrin trial (Catchpole 1971, 1–71). These formulations cast Jesus as condemned for "blasphemy" (Mark 14:64 and parallels), an accusation consistent with how the rabbis processed Christian theology of their own day as blasphemous for exalting Jesus as more than human.

Nonetheless, while accepting these premises, the rabbis denied that Jesus' trial had been in any way speedy or unfair, for a herald (so they fancied) had announced throughout the land of Israel for forty days: "He is going to be stoned, because he practiced sorcery and enticed and led Israel astray. Let anyone who knows anything in his favor come and plead in his behalf."[14] That no one stepped forward confirmed Jesus' guilt and validated his Sanhedrin conviction.

Compounding our problems in analyzing rabbinic texts is uncertainty over whether some passages, *not* originally alluding to Jesus, became misconstrued as indeed referring to him, particularly materials mentioning the pagan prophet, Balaam (Num 22–24)[15] and otherwise unidentifiable figures (ben ["son of"] Stada, Peloni ["a certain person"], [ben] Netzer).[16] As these allusions entered into the mix of rabbinic perceptions of Jesus, they complicated, even corrupted, an already perplexing mosaic. What results is a crude kind of Jesus-composite, virtually a caricature of sorts. In such a fashion did rabbinic understandings of Jesus both grow and yet go awry.

A proper analysis of this conglomeration of traditions would be daunting, requiring, to start with, compartmentalizing these texts according to their chronological and geographical origin (Goldstein 1950, 19–139). This might clarify somewhat how rabbinic traditions about Jesus had developed. But scholars (Christian as well as Jewish) cannot agree on the degree to which the rabbis even cared to allude to Jesus, let alone on which passages were actually framed with him in mind. That is to say, varying presuppositions as to the extent to which the ancient rabbis were preoccupied with Jesus and Christianity can easily predetermine which texts might be identified and interpreted as having him in mind. Accordingly, scholars' analyses range widely from minimalists (e.g., Lauterbach 1951) – who recognize only relatively few passages that actually have Jesus in mind – to moderates (e.g., Herford [1903] 2006), to maximalists (Klausner 1943, 17–54; especially Schäfer 2007).

In any event, rabbinic texts that do refer to Jesus (however few or many) convey nothing credible about him, but do convey a flavor of how Jews of this third period viewed him. Unfortunately, the most popular Jewish-scholarly application of rabbinic literature in Jesus-study wields Talmudic capital procedures to challenge gospel reportage of Jesus' Sanhedrin trial. Yet not only may no rabbinic-like court have existed as early as Jesus' day, but Jesus arguably underwent no trial of any kind in any Jewish court. A mere Friday morning "consultation," not even involving Jesus' presence (Mark 15:1), may have been aggrandized (14:53) into an *invented* Thursday night Sanhedrin spectacle to satisfy what Christians demanded as minimally commensurate for the "Son of God" (Cook 2008, 134–140). Further, the Talmud's own and sole mention of Jesus' trial (*b. Sanh.* 43a) constitutes no independent confirmation that one occurred. Instead, the rabbis simply lifted the assumption of a formal trial from the gospels themselves (a possibility that many Jewish scholars fail to consider). That Talmudic jurisprudence is brought to bear on a trial that we cannot prove even transpired is symptomatic of why, in recent decades, Jewish scholars themselves are increasingly impatient with colleagues for accepting gospel data whose historicity many *non*-Jewish critics have dismissed long ago (Weiss-Rosmarin 1976, ix; Sandmel [1965] 2006, 63–64; cf. Hagner 1984, 67).

The Middle Ages

By holding the Jews responsible for Jesus' death, the church gave rise to the epithet "Christ-killers" (essentially amalgamated from Matt 27:25; John 8:44; Acts 3:13–15; and 1 Thess 2:14–16). During the Middle Ages especially, when the church commanded a virtual monopoly on European learning, this canard inflamed popular passions against Jews, who lived with perpetual anxiety that such accusations would become pretexts for pogroms. Such fear was not without good reason for, in conjunction with various Crusades (beginning in 1096), Christian armies, trekking through Europe to recapture Jerusalem from the Muslim "infidel," routinely ransacked Jewish communities en route and murdered the inhabitants. They justified their actions by appealing to the gospels' own assessments of Jews as Christ-killers and therefore infidels themselves.

Aside from Jewish assessments of Jesus and Christianity expressed in medieval apologetic and polemical writings (Lasker 1977; Berger 1979; Chazan 1989), we also have both Christian and Jewish testimony about publicly staged debates that pitted disputants from each side against one another (Cohen 1964). The purpose of such disputations was less to attack Jews than to win converts to Christianity and to confirm recent converts in their faith (particularly those who had become Christians under duress). Conquering "doubt" was even more important than conquering Jews.

What may we gather from purported transcriptions of the Jewish participants in such publicly staged disputations? These conceal as well as reveal. Since "winning" a debate could well jeopardize the security of the Jewish community at large, political considerations certainly entered into what Jewish disputants publicly said or refrained from saying. What we do surmise is that Jewish characterizations of Jesus from earlier centuries now surfaced as potentially embarrassing for Jewish disputants, who frequently had to soften or explain away certain Talmudic mentions of Jesus – or even to deny outright that the "Jesus" referred to within them was the Jesus *of Christianity* (it was someone else)! Official transcripts of these proceedings, moreover, might not replicate what actually transpired; in some places what they record was not the live action, as it were, but Christian polemical revision composed after the fact.

The argumentation in these texts relies on subtleties of biblical and rabbinic interpretation, philosophy, theology, and mysticism. It seems unlikely, therefore, that these materials afford us any clear reading about how Jesus was generally perceived by the wider Jewish populace. Furnishing us with a quite different kind of gauge in this fashion is a medieval Jewish tract entitled (*Sefer*) *Toledot Yeshu* – "[The Book of] the History of Jesus." Strongly denying Christian claims, this work caricatured Jesus along lines that persisted, in some circles, for centuries to come.

Unfortunately, we know neither its author(s) nor any other details of its creation (date, place of origin, etc.). The earliest references to its existence come from two

French archbishops in the ninth century, but the tract likely circulated long before surfacing to their attention. The text warrants examination because it distinctly echoes and directly extends traditions we have earlier culled from rabbinic sources, now also interweaving with them gospel motifs and, in places, even mimicking gospel style. *Toledot Yeshu*'s many versions and translations suggest that the attitudes and legends it perpetuated, embellished, or engendered had become widely disseminated on the popular level (Krauss 1938).

This parody's retelling of the life of Jesus (here severely abridged) began by introducing a chaste woman, Miriam (Mary), who lived in Bethlehem of Judea and was betrothed to a righteous man of the royal house of David. Residing nearby, however, was the disreputable Joseph Pandera (a Roman soldier?).[17] One night, pretending to be Miriam's betrothed husband, he forced himself upon her. In due course, she gave birth to Yehoshua, a name later shortened to Yeshu (Jesus). When old enough, Yeshu began Jewish schooling. But as his antecedents became publicly known, he was forced to flee to Galilee.

Later, as an adult, he returned to Judea bent on entering the Jerusalem Temple – whose foundation stone bore the letters of God's Ineffable Name (YHWH).[18] Yeshu was determined to learn the letters because their possession would enable him to perform magic (miracles). Yet the knowledge of these letters was ordinarily impossible to retain because they were guarded by lions of brass. Upon roaring, the lions induced forgetfulness. Cleverly, Yeshu smuggled a small parchment into the Temple. Upon learning the letters, he inscribed them on the parchment, which he then inserted into an open cut on his thigh. As he was leaving, the lions roared – and he promptly forgot the letters. But he later regained access to them upon finding and removing the parchment from his thigh. Thereafter, he was able to perform astounding feats to silence his opponents.

The Jewish leaders, after numerous attempts, finally managed to arrest him. They charged him with practicing sorcery and attempting to beguile and lead the Jews astray. Shortly after his execution, however, his followers told Queen Helene that they had found his tomb empty – he had been resurrected! Jewish leaders were thrown into consternation, unable to imagine how this had transpired. One upset dignitary, Rabbi Tanhuma (actually, he lived centuries later than Jesus), chanced upon a certain gardener who professed that he could explain the tomb's emptiness because *he* was responsible for it! Fearful that Yeshu's disciples would steal his body and proclaim him resurrected, the gardener himself had removed the body and buried it in his garden. (Recall here Matthew 28:15: Jews of Matthew's own day discredited the resurrection as a hoax – the disciples had taken Jesus' body, then declared him resurrected. Recall also John 20:15: Mary Magdalene initially mistook the resurrected Jesus for a gardener who she assumed had removed the body; *Toledot Yeshu* accepted and then capitalized upon Mary's original surmise.)

Toledot Yeshu is outrageous, to some disgraceful. While hardly a historical source about the person it describes, it yet accurately reflects the climate of Christian Europe, where Jews, a persecuted minority, were often under relentless pressure to convert (Troki [1851] 1970). A counter-narrative impugning gospel claims of Jesus' virgin birth, miracles, empty tomb, and resurrection, would have been potentially helpful in warding off proselytizers. Unfortunately, this kind of formulation also appears to have markedly shaped and misdirected elements of the popular Jewish mindset about Jesus for generations to come. Well into the twentieth century, European Jews were still recounting to their offspring Yiddish folkloristic tales about *Yoshke Pandre* (Yeshu [son of] Pandera)!

The Modern Era – Jewish Scholars

Because of the Jews' extensive ghetto stagnation, their exposure to modernity was relatively delayed. When, however, ghetto walls were flung open in the early nineteenth century – largely as a consequence of Napoleonic conquests – Jews exiting into Christian Europe-at-large felt directly confronted by claims about Jesus. Aiding them was a sobering undertaking, by Christian scholars, today referred to as the "Old Quest for the Historical Jesus."

Such scholars realized the importance of reconstructing Jesus' life in the light of his specifically Jewish context and thus anticipated the relevance of ancient Jewish literatures, including rabbinic, in revealing and detailing this milieu. What primarily interested them were not ancient Jewish understandings of Jesus himself, but depictions of the institutions and thought patterns that had formed the backdrop for Jesus' ministry (the Temple, Sanhedrin, and synagogues; Jewish festivals and customs; theological and ethical teachings and Pharisaic parables; liturgical elements and refrains; etc.). Jewish scholars, in turn, now became encouraged to assist their Christian counterparts in understanding especially the Hebrew and Aramaic literature that most Christian scholars felt incapable of handling by themselves. As a by-product of this reciprocity, books and lectures by Jewish historians themselves (Geiger 1864; Graetz 1867) soon began to incorporate discussion about Jesus, Paul, and Christian origins in relation to the Jewish context of intertestamental times.

Over many succeeding decades, Jewish scholars in this venture became soberingly aware of how brilliant Christian minds struggled to propose and refine new methods for determining who the historical Jesus was – only to see findings by one generation of scholars significantly modified, even overturned, by some succeeding enterprise. That "quests for the historical Jesus" – spurts of research extending decades at a time – eventually became numbered ("First Quest," "Second," "Third") revealed that interim periods were essentially calls for "time-out," for giving up the venture altogether, or possibly for reversions to earlier conventional views. Creditable (though not uniformly credible) efforts have been marshaled to show Jesus as a pacifist or militant, a prophet, reformer, liberator, apocalypticist, Pharisee, Essene, magician, charismatic, healer/exorcist, cynic-philosopher, savior, or even pure myth. And since these "Quests" insisted that the gospels also reflected church and editorial interests that overlay the original Jesus figure, it was as if multiple Jesuses were projected simultaneously on the same screen – rendering it impossible to discern and retrieve, with any certainty, the original.

If Christian scholars themselves realized, and were promulgating, that knowledge-able New Testament readers could no longer blithely accept gospel reportage at face value, such outspokenness emboldened and liberated Jewish scholars as well to speak out more freely. The collective results of such modern Jewish scholarly assessments of Jesus can be summarized in terms of at least three broad contrasts: reclaiming Jesus as a Jew, reevaluating Jesus' execution, and reassessing the influence of Paul.

Reclaiming Jesus as a Jew

During late antiquity and the Middle Ages, Jews had commonly caricatured Jesus as a sorcerer who had attempted to beguile the Jewish people and lead them astray. The modern Jewish scholarly reassessment stripped away such earlier misconcep-tions, restored respectability to Jesus' image, and then reclaimed him as a Jew who not only established no new religion but whose parables and sermons *could* have merited a rightful place in Jewish literature alongside those of other ancient Jewish sages (Friedlander [1911] 1969; Abrahams [1917] 1967; Montefiore [1930] 1970). Elements of Christianity producing its break from Judaism were now said to have arisen only after Jesus' death, with later Christian theology radically de-Judaizing Jesus of Nazareth. This was a course that Jewish scholars were enthusiastic to reverse – especially through suggesting that Jesus most likely himself had been a type of Pharisee (Cook 1978).

Indeed, it soon became typical of Jewish scholars to argue that it was Christianity's self-perception vis-à-vis Judaism that had necessitated corresponding adjustments in portrayals of Jesus' stance toward Jews and Judaism, as presented in the gospels – that Jesus' image vis-à-vis fellow Jews should be viewed *developmentally*. First, emergent Christianity, perceiving itself still within Judaism, naturally preserved or generated portrayals of Jesus as faithful to, and consonant with, Judaism. Second, with Christianity becoming more conscious of its own individuality and with most Jews still avoiding the church, Jesus' figure was adjusted by some gospel texts to reflect regret at Jews resisting Christian claims. Third, by the end of the first century, with exchanges between Christians and Jewish opponents becoming increasingly contentious, Christians' regret became supplanted by hostility toward Jews, with Jesus' figure – enlisted to support this accrued bitterness – now portrayed in some gospel passages as overtly antagonistic toward Jews. Hostility toward Jews of the Evangelists' day (70–100 CE) was retrojected to Jesus personally, not any enmity toward Jews by the historical Jesus himself forwarded.

Thus, respecting fundamental distinctions between what Jesus himself may have said and what the later church only claimed he said, a *vindictive* image of Jesus, disparaging of Jews and Judaism, became superimposed on an earlier, actual figure – with this anti-Jewishly adjusted image of Jesus being the one to which Jews of subsequent generations inevitably responded, feeding a spiral of negative inter-change within the troubled history of Christian–Jewish polemics. Here is where the dynamics of gospel composition must occupy center stage in any proper Jewish analysis: in the process of responding to challenges by Jewish opponents, emerging Christianity adjusted or added to Jesus-traditions teachings and nuances that were not authentic to Jesus' ministry. Conceiving that their own immediate problems (70–100 CE) had already originated back during Jesus' day (ca. 30 CE), and that the needed solutions must therefore be discoverable in *his* words and deeds, the Evangelists often recast Jesus' actual teachings to render them germane to later circumstances. Further, any resistance to Christians by *Jews* per se invited the shaping of gospel traditions to answer these challenges. Such a process becomes all the more obvious by study of the synoptic gospels in parallel columns, which reveals how Matthew and Luke intensified the anti-Judaism of their sources, and intimates that Mark himself likely did the same with his own. The important corollary here is that anti-Judaism (misascribed to Jesus) appears to decrease as we regress toward Christian origins.

As for passages in Jewish scripture seemingly predictive of Jesus' coming (e.g., Isa 53; Zech 9:9; Ps 22), reflective Jewish scholars came to suspect that Christianity fashioned details of Jesus' life to match texts alleged to foretell him. Accordingly, in the absence of real evidence, Christians were induced to gather "information" about Jesus by referring to the Jewish Bible for clues presumed predictive of him as Messiah. At the least, even regarding actual events in Jesus' life, recourse to Jewish scripture influenced which ones would be remembered. Thus, not only might narrators have created incidents outright that lent Jewish scriptural flavor to Christian traditions, but from incidents that did actually occur narrators dramatized those capable of echoing those scriptures.

Reevaluating Jesus' execution

Having rehabilitated and restored Jesus to respectability within the contours of Judaism, Jewish scholars had to reconsider why their Jewish forebears had seemed so resolute, even precipitous, in their decision to execute him. There now inevitably ensued a reevaluation of reasons for his arrest, eventuating in the judgment that Roman officialdom (not Pharisaic/rabbinic leadership) was primarily – if not solely – responsible for Jesus' death. Consistent with their new reconstruction, Jewish scholars also surmised the actual reason for Jesus' arrest to have been not blasphemy, apostasy, sorcery, or enticement (as per rabbinic literature and *Toledot Yeshu*), but rather Roman officialdom's suspicion that Jesus was a subversive. Presumptions of Jesus' seditious aspirations and activities, whether justified or not, had occasioned his arrest and his crucifixion not by "the Jews" but rather by Pontius Pilate, operating in conjunction with his appointee/subordinate, the high priest Caiaphas.

The gospel writers, it now became urged, must have been succumbing to pressures in their own day while shaping their narratives of Jesus' trial set decades earlier. It was their fear of Rome that had occasioned their portrait of Pilate's attempted exoneration of Jesus a generation or two before. Faced now with the urgency of establishing Jesus' loyalty to Rome (and thereby the allegiance to Rome of their own communities also), Christian writers could hardly have felt comfortable casting Rome as culpable in Jesus' execution. (Zeitlin 1946; Rivkin 1984).

Thus was blame lifted from Rome and necessarily assigned to some other quarter. Tensions with Pharisees/rabbis in the Evangelists' day encouraged this shift of responsibility for Jesus' condemnation onto the Pharisees, the "chief priests," and the Jewish Sanhedrin instead. This displacement was accomplished literarily through the notion that Jesus had private and public hearings before the Roman prefect, where the normally ruthless Pilate, supposedly convinced of Jesus' innocence, was yet pressured by Jews to crucify him.

If the placard on Jesus' cross, "King of the Jews" (signaling sedition), stigmatized later Christians as well, then defusing this accusation was imperative for their security. Useful in this regard would be Mark's account (14:53–65) – which Matthew copied (26:57–68) – of Jesus' Sanhedrin condemnation for blasphemy. Christians of the Evangelists' age, hearing themselves maligned by contemporary Jews as blasphemers for exalting Jesus as more than human, would naturally suppose (and therefore retroject) blasphemy as the charge of which Jesus himself likewise was accused. Portraying Jesus as condemned for blasphemy, a merely religious offense of concern to Jews only, would assist gospel writers in defusing notions that Jesus had entertained subversive pretensions to royalty. This facilitated portraying a Jew put to death by the Romans as a "Christian" put to death by "the Jews," thereby effectively allying Christians with Rome by presenting the Jews as enemies of both.

Reassessing the influence of Paul

In earlier centuries, the radical cleavage between Judaism and Christianity had been routinely traced to apostasy by Jesus personally. But modern Jewish scholarly opinion now generally shifted the decisive role in that parting of the ways to Paul (Jacob 1974). The various ways in which Paul's theology was construed, so it was now believed, must have influenced the gospel portraits of Jesus – both by Christians who adhered to Pauline views (whether or not interpreting Paul correctly) and by those who resisted Paul but were forced, nonetheless, to address his thinking (whether or not interpreting that thinking correctly).

The conceptualization here is that Jesus' earliest images and teachings passed through the filter of Paul's interpretation concerning the meaning of the Christ (and thus as well through the lenses of others who interpreted Paul's interpretation). The consequence of this filtering process was that Jesus' image and teachings were embellished, even transformed, with at least three decisive themes generated thereby, each bearing the impress either of what Paul himself preached or of how others construed or misconstrued that preaching: first, Jesus rejected the Law of Moses;[19] second, Christian missionaries should turn their focus from Jews to Gentiles instead;[20] and third, Jews were superseded by Gentile Christians as God's chosen people.[21]

Therefore, so many Jewish scholars came to argue, it was Pauline thought, after Jesus' lifetime, that first stimulated raising these three issues, and the church, developing and pressing them, that belatedly ascribed them to Jesus personally.

If these three motifs thus derive more from how Paul was interpreted than from what Jesus personally had advanced, then only after Paul's ministry were certain Jesus-traditions fashioned in support of Pauline views – with Christianity thereby experiencing renewal, redirection, and even radical transformation. To Jewish scholars, the very suggestion that these motifs derived more from how Paul was interpreted than from what Jesus personally had advanced opened the way to a potentially revolutionary reorientation of traditional Jewish thinking about Jesus along lines distinctly positive.

The Holocaust

Ironically, the Holocaust came to underpin rather than to undermine these profound redirections of Jewish scholarship. Deeply etched into the modern Jewish psyche was Nazism's exploitation of New Testament supersessionist theology. This theology – that Gentile Christians had displaced and replaced the Jews as God's chosen people – was manipulated by Hitler's ideologues to suggest that the persistence of Jews into the twentieth century was an anomaly, a quirk or mistake of history, that Jews were a fossil meant to have disappeared far earlier. Jewish scholars today who do not believe that the New Testament itself caused the Holocaust will likely yet insist that the Holocaust could not have occurred without it.

But sensitive Christian scholars themselves likewise felt constrained to ponder the degree to which the New Testament had lent itself to Nazi exploitation. This influenced the Second Vatican Council's Declaration, *Nostra Aetate* ("In Our Time"), in 1965, which aimed to lay to rest the Christian accusation that Jews had committed deicide. Together with its later attendant commentaries, it dismissed the notion that Jews were corporately rejected by God for complicity in Jesus' death and for failing to recognize him as Messiah then and since. Roman Catholic teaching materials were overhauled, inducing similar changes by some Protestant denominations. This watershed development stimulated an era of better Christian–Jewish feeling, typified by countless interfaith dialogues on the New Testament and Judaism by clergy and academic institutes, and manifesting new trends of thinking: such as, that early rabbinic Judaism and Christianity arose as "sibling faiths"; that the gospels' anti-Jewish vitriol originated as merely "in-house squabbling"; and that Jews and Christians could both now espouse a "two-covenant" theology, holding that God, while maintaining a covenant with Christians, also sustains a separate (and antecedent) covenant with the Jews that renders efforts to convert them unwarranted. And while these contentions continue to be vigorously debated (Cook 2008, 275–277), this new parlance made for a welcoming climate of conciliation, with many more Jews now at least openly talking about the New Testament for the first time ever.

The Modern Era – The Jewish Populace at Large

This tidal wave of change impacted Jewish scholars and clergy long before it reached the Jewish laity. As a consequence, a bifurcation developed between those relatively few Jews now willing to learn more about Jesus, and the overwhelming number still adamantly opposed even to considering doing so. While the Jewish populace at large even now remains generally unknowledgeable in this area, in recent decades growing numbers are now indeed breaking away from what had been the wary mainstream for almost two millennia. Depending on what method is applied to assist them, this new tributary could eventually widen into the dominant course.

Respecting the figure of Jesus, one approach is effectively motivating ordinarily recalcitrant Jews to study what has so profoundly alienated them. Initially, it requires them to do what their ancient rabbinic forebears could not: to disengage the gospels' portrait of Jesus from the actual figure who may underlie those texts. Entailed here for Jews is learning to ask: does such and such a gospel text reflect factual history or, instead, only early church enlistment and reshaping of the Jesus-figure for problem solving? Examples of such problems include: How to establish that Jesus was the Messiah despite his ostensible failure to fulfill Jewish expectations? How to redefine "Messiah" in view of Jesus' crucifixion – which made him appear a victim, not victor? How to account for why Jews rejected the very Messiah who allegedly came for *them*? How to persuade Rome that Jesus' crucifixion should not stigmatize his later followers as seditionists? How to shift blame for Jesus' death from Rome to another party (the Jews)? How to convey that Jesus was condemned only for "blasphemy" (of no concern to Rome)? How to disassociate Christians from the image of Jewish rebels' great revolt against Rome (66–73 CE)? How to demonstrate that Jewish scriptures predicted Jesus' coming? How to combat Jewish denials of Jesus' resurrection? How to cope with impatience, frustration, and doubt over delay in the Second Coming? And many more like these.

Whenever Jews and non-Jews alike have good reason to suspect that a given gospel tradition, ostensibly about Jesus himself, instead enlists and reconfigures him primarily to address these kinds of problems arising only well after he died, then such readers are on the trail of "gospel dynamics" (Cook 2008, 83–91, 289–292, 352–354). Increasingly, by learning to detect and explain these dynamics to themselves and their children, and ultimately to articulate them to Christian friends and to a broader Christian society, Jews are exchanging their sense of victimization by the New Testament for a strong sense of confidence that they now knowledgeably control this literature and are in such a fashion much freer from it.

Resulting Perspectives – Current and Future?

The result may then well be that fuller Jewish comprehensions of Jesus himself – or at the least less discomfort in attempting to formulate them – will be forthcoming in the future than ever in the past. Of what might such fuller comprehensions consist? The following perspectives on Jesus can fairly be claimed to represent both the fruits of Jewish scholarship and the current gradual reorientation of a well-read Jewish populace. Although no absolute consensus can yet be established, these certainly qualify as pronounced tendencies.

1   Jesus was a Jew, as were his followers. He did not found Christianity, a later movement that traced its origins to him.

2   Jesus also behaved as a Jew. Christianity's fundamental break with Jewish Law should be attributed to Paul, although Jesus may have disputed with fellow Jews on particular legal issues or on the proper emphases of legal observance.

3   Jesus was a great teacher of Jewish ethics, in some ways perhaps akin to a Hebrew prophet. But here Jesus' uniqueness may have resided more with his personality than with his originality. Since most of his teachings seem analogous to those of ancient Jewish tradition, what may most have distinguished Jesus was his charisma as a teacher.

4   Such charisma was most notably displayed through his provocative parables, which although analogous to Jewish teachings defined in a more radical degree what it meant to be truly righteous. (Yet we lack any demonstrable means of isolating the genuine core of such parables from later church accretions, or even for gauging the original context in which Jesus may have delivered them.)

5   Jesus saw his personal mission – perhaps even a messianic one – as being God's last envoy before God's imminent intervention in history. Hence Jesus' fervor to alert others to the coming of God's kingdom, which would purify the world of the evil resulting from human misbehavior and achieve places of acceptance for the poor, outcast, and lowly.

6   Jesus may even have expected to play a kind of royal role in this coming "kingdom." At the same time, he could hardly have imagined himself *divine*, for this clearly would have carried him outside the bounds of his own Jewish affiliation.

7   Nor, even if he conceived himself the Messiah in some sense or another, could he be regarded as successful since he did not bring about independence for the land of Israel from Roman oppression. (Later, Christianity redefined the Messiah's agenda – away from what Jews intended when they originated this concept – now along the new lines of bringing salvation and other sacramental benefits akin to those promised by various "mystery" cults of dying and rising savior deities.)

8   The charges on which Jesus was arrested were political, most likely that his preaching God's kingdom threatened to overthrow the Roman establishment along with its appointee, the high priest Caiaphas (and other pro-Roman elements within the Jewish priestly hierarchy).

9   Thus rounded up like other figures similarly perceived, Jesus was executed in a process whose underlying authority derived ultimately from Rome.

10   Paul and others distanced Jesus' image from the actual historical figure to such a degree as to open the way for Gentiles to remove Jesus from Judaism, both to co-opt this Jew as their own and also, eventually, to be in a position to denigrate the very people from whom they had removed "Christ-Jesus" from the start.

Notes

1   By "Jews," this essay has in mind those who have dissociated themselves from Christian affiliation and affirmation, i.e., excluding Jesus' Jewish followers, Paul, any gospel writer who might have been Jewish, also modern-day Christians who fancy themselves Jews (so-called "Jews-for-Jesus"; "Messianic Jews"; etc.), and so forth.

2   Mystery religions, named after their mythological lords (e.g., Mithras, Bacchus, Orpheus, Osiris, Tammuz, Attis, Adonis), guaranteed initiates cleansing from personal sin, protection from worldly adversities, salvation from death, and a happy immortality – attainable by undergoing intimate, sacramental reenactments of the cyclical deaths and resurrection-rebirths of cultic gods.

3   Tacitus, *Annals* xv.44; Suetonius, *On the Life of the Caesars*, "Claudius," 25; Pliny, *Letters* 10.96–97.

4   Mark 9:11; this induced the Evangelists to enlist John the Baptist as Elijah (Matt 17:13).

5   Attempted responses include Mark 10:33–34 (Jesus expected execution); Matt 26:53 (he chose not to prevent it); 26:54 (he died to fulfill scripture).

6   An accusation addressed by birth stories showing Jesus *of Nazareth* (in Galilee) born instead in *Bethlehem* (in Judea).

7   Regarding Jesus' ostensible support of the Law in Matthew 5:17–20, since this passage appears in Matthew alone we may have here but one of many Matthean devices to conform Jesus' image to Moses – meaning that the text may not authentically reflect Jesus. Arguably, Matthew also attempts here to neutralize the opposition to the Law by Paul, the possible referent of "whoever ... relaxes one of the least of these commandments and teaches men so, shall be called least in the kingdom of heaven ..." (cf. 1 Cor 15:9, where Paul terms himself *"least* of all the apostles").

8   *b. Shab.* 104b; *y. Shab.* 13d;xii,4.

9   *b. Sanh.* 43a.

10   *m. Abot* 2:8; *b. Sanh.* 14a; *b. Avod. Zar.* 8b.

11   *b. Shab.* 104b; cf. *b. Hag.* 4b.

12   Cf. *t. Shab. 13:5*; *y. Ta'an. 65b*; and late midrashic works: *Shem. Rab.* 29.5 (to Exod 20:2); *Deb. Rab.* 2:33 (to Deut 6:4).

13   *t. Sanh.* 9:7; *t. Hul.* 2:22–24; *b. Shab.* 116ab; *b. Sanh.* 43a, 67a, 103a, 107b; *b. Sotah* 47a; *b. Avod. Zar.* 16b–17a.

14   *b. Sanh.* 43a; cf. *t. Sanh.* 10:11; *y. Sanh.* 25cd;vii.16; *b. Sanh.* 67a.

15   See *m. Abot* 5:19; *m. Sanh.* 10:2; *b. Sanh* 106ab.

16   On ben Stada cf. *t. Shab.* 11:15, *t. Sanh.* 10:11, *b. Sanh.* 67a, *b. Shab.* 104b; on Peloni cf. *m. Yebam.* 4:13, *t. Yebam.* 3:3,4, *b. Yebam.* 49ab, *b. Yoma* 66b; on (ben) Netzer cf. *b. Sanh.* 43a, *b. Kethub.* 51b (also Isa 11:1).

17 Variants: Pandira, Pantera, Panthera, Pantiri, Panteri, Pantira.
18 The Tetragrammaton – the four Hebrew letters *yod, heh, vav, heh* (vocalization /
    pronunciation disputed).
19 Cf. Gal 2:16; 3:10–11, 23–26; Rom 7:1–6.
20 Cf. Gal 1:15–16; 2:7; 3:11–14.
21 Cf. Gal 4:22–30; Rom 9:6–12, 25–26, 30–32.

References

Abrahams, Israel ([1917] 1967). *Studies in Pharisaism and the Gospels*. New York: KTAV.
Berger, David (1979). *The Jewish-Christian Debate in the High Middle Ages*. Philadelphia: Jewish
    Publication Society.
Catchpole, David (1971). *The Trial of Jesus: A Study in the Gospels and Jewish Historiography
    from 1770*. Leiden: Brill.
Chazan, Robert (1989). *Daggers of Faith: Thirteenth Century Christian Missionizing and the
    Jewish Response*. Berkeley: University of California.
Cohen, Martin (1964). "Reflections on the Text and Context of the Disputation of Barcelona."
    Hebrew Union College Annual 35: 157–192.
Cook, Michael J. (1978). "Jesus and the Pharisees." *Journal of Ecumenical Studies* 15: 441–460.
Cook, Michael J. (2008). *Modern Jews Engage the New Testament: Enhancing Jewish Well-Being
    in a Christian Environment*. Woodstock, VT: Jewish Lights.
Fredriksen, Paula (2000). *From Jesus to Christ*. 2nd edn. New Haven: Yale University Press.
Friedlander, Gerald ([1911] 1969). *The Jewish Sources of the Sermon on the Mount*. New York:
    KTAV.
Geiger, Abraham (1864). *Das Judenthum und seine Geschichte*. Breslau: Schletters.
Goldstein, Morris (1950). *Jesus in the Jewish Tradition*. New York: Macmillan.
Graetz, Heinrich (1867). *Sinai et Golgotha*. Paris: Lévy Frères.
Hagner, Donald A. (1984). *The Jewish Reclamation of Jesus*. Grand Rapids: Zondervan.
Herford, R. Travis ([1903] 2006). *Christianity in Talmud and Midrash*. New York: KTAV.
Jacob, Walter (1974). *Christianity through Jewish Eyes*. Cincinnati: Hebrew Union College.
Klausner, Joseph (1943). *Jesus of Nazareth*. Trans. H. Danby. New York: Macmillan.
Krauss, Samuel (1938). "Une Nouvelle Recension Hébraique du Toldot Yesu." *Revue des
    Etudes Juives* n.s. 3: 65–88.
Lasker, Daniel J. (1977). *Jewish Philosophical Polemics Against Christianity in the Middle Ages*.
    New York: KTAV and Anti-Defamation League.
Lauterbach, Jacob L. (1951). "Jesus in the Talmud." In *Rabbinic Essays* (pp. 471–570).
    Cincinnati: Hebrew Union College.
Levine, Amy-Jill (2007). *The Misunderstood Jew*. San Francisco: Harper.
Montefiore, Claude G. ([1930] 1970). *Rabbinic Literature and Gospel Teachings*. New York: KTAV.
Rivkin, Ellis (1984). *What Killed Jesus?* Nashville: Abingdon.
Sandmel, Samuel ([1965] 2006). *We Jews and Jesus*. Woodstock, VT: Skylight Paths.
Schäfer, Peter (2007). *Jesus in the Talmud*. Princeton: Princeton University Press.
Troki, Isaac ben Abraham ([1851] 1970). *Faith Strengthened*. Trans. Moses Mocatta. New
    York: KTAV.
Weiss-Rosmarin, Trude (1976). *Jewish Expressions on Jesus*. New York: KTAV.
Zeitlin, Solomon (1946). *Who Killed Jesus?* New York: Harper.

CHAPTER 15

Islamic Perspectives on Jesus

Reem A. Meshal and M. Reza Pirbhai

In the Islamic tradition, Jesus ('Isa) was a Muslim. He was a "prophet" of the highest rank, but nothing more of the divine reposed in his being. Beyond this consensus, there is no single Jesus in Islam. The subtleties of sectarianism, not to mention the development of a variety of theological and mystical schools that tap a vast array of literary sources over a period of fourteen centuries, ensure that "Islamic christology" has been and remains a complex and dynamic field of inquiry.

This chapter attends to the complexity of Islamic christology by placing Muhammad and his message in historical context, briefly describing the primary scriptural sources employed by Muslim authors, and outlining the interpretations of these sources from various disciplinary and sectarian fields as they arose over the centuries.[1] This survey, though revealing great variety, also shows that views of Jesus in Islam are the product of two overarching factors, one external to it, the other internally generated. Regarding externality, Islamic views of Jesus are a product of the religio-cultural environment in which Muhammad lived and the Qur'an was collated, as well as the variety of relations between Muslims and Christians under which the disciplines, schools, and sects of Islam were formed following Muhammad's death, and continued to develop into the present. The internal factor is the centrality of the concept of *tawhid*, or God's "Unity," in Muslim thought, whether expressed in monotheistic or monistic forms.

Historical Contexts

Because Islamic christology is a complex and dynamic field of inquiry, developed over many centuries stretching into the present, we must outline a number of historical periods and contexts to fully identify contributing factors. Hodgson (1977) provides the periodization followed here: namely, "Muhammad's World" (ca. sixth–

seventh centuries), the "Formative Period" (ca. seventh–thirteenth centuries), the "Middle Period" (ca. thirteenth–eighteenth centuries), and the "Late Period" (ca. eighteenth century–present).

As a resident of Mecca – a local center of worship and growing hub of trade in Arabia's Hijaz region – Muhammad would have been exposed to various sources of Abrahamic doctrine (Trimingham 1979; Caetani 2008). Jewish communities, rabbinic and otherwise, were distributed throughout the area, including Jewish tribes in the Hijaz itself. Furthermore, Manichaeism was probably represented by some in the area. A substantial Christian presence in the Hijaz is not as easily verified, but there is no reason to doubt considerable Christian influence. Most obviously, the Byzantine Empire with its official Christianity loomed over the region from the north and west. Also, the "heretics" condemned by the Byzantine state-church in the fifth century – including Nestorians, Monophysites, Gnostics, and Maronites – were still active during Muhammad's time. There are also some suggestions of the presence of "Jewish Christians," such as the Ebionites and Elkesaites. Meccans were no doubt in contact with Christians through trade, while slaves, missionaries, and refugees from Byzantine persecution journeyed through and to the region.

Within a century of Muhammad's death, not only had the tribes of Arabia been unified under the banner of Islam, but also the leadership of Muhammad's companions and Mecca's old elite had forged an empire, known as the Umayyad Caliphate, which stretched from Iberia in the west to the Indus Valley in the east. As a result, the Christian and Jewish populations of such centers as Alexandria, Jerusalem, and Damascus were, by the eighth century, living under Muslim rule, many among them in the employ of the state at various ranks. The growing proximity of Jewish, Christian, and Muslim communities meant greater scrutiny of each others' doctrines and practices. In fact, scholars from each religion were now in position to debate and redefine their perspectives, and it was in the midst of this polemical relationship, furthered by the rise of the Abbasid Caliphate in 750 CE, that the dominant schools of Islamic theology, law, mysticism, and philosophy came to be established.

By the ninth century, various sects and sub-sects, multiple schools of scholastic theology, and a vast array of mystical lineages drew from the pervading Hellenism of the eastern Mediterranean (among other sources), partially as a consequence of debates with Jews and Christians of various stripes. Simultaneously, significant numbers of Jews, Christians, Zoroastrians, Hindus, and Buddhists began converting to Islam, often bringing aspects of their previous traditions to bear on the formulation of Islamic doctrines. The beginning of the "Crusades" about the tenth century added a more confrontational element to the exchange with the Roman church and western Europeans, but the systematic translation and study of non-Islamic sources, the interpretation of Qur'anic references to Jesus, and the articulation of a variety of definitions of that figure's status in Islam date in large part to this fertile phase between the ninth and thirteenth centuries, embedded in the Formative Period.

In the mid-thirteenth century, Mongol forces swept down from the Central Asian Steppes and brushed away the last vestiges of the Abbasid Caliphate, inadvertently formalizing the transfer of political authority from Arab Caliphs to non-Arab "Sultans" (lit. "rulers") that had begun in the tenth and eleventh centuries. Under the patronage of Sultans, Muslim political authority reached its zenith, extending from West Africa to South East Asia, and from western China to the southernmost reaches of the East African coast, while the disciplines, schools, and sects established in the Formative Period achieved their fullest expression, and the number of converts to Islam swelled in all regions. Although Iberia was lost to a resurgent Christian power by the end of the fifteenth century, it was also during this period that Muslim polity extended furthest into eastern and central Europe, knocking on the gates of Vienna by the early sixteenth century. In addition, the spread of western European mercantile interests in the Indian Ocean by the sixteenth century brought eastern Muslims more directly into contact with Christians and their faith, as practiced in western Europe.

By the eighteenth century, a millennium of political expansion and socio-economic development manifested itself in the rise of various vernacular classes in Muslim societies, resulting in the splintering of the Middle Period's land-based Sultanates into smaller political units. This, in turn, provided the impetus and opportunity for European powers to secure longstanding mercantile interests by imperial means, leading to the colonization of much of the Muslim world. The importance of decentralization and the reversal in the relations of power between Muslims and Christians to the understanding of Jesus in Islam, cannot be over-estimated. First, decentralization in the eighteenth century led to the rise of new movements (collectively termed "Salafism") across the Muslim world that rejected the scholasticism of the Formative and Middle Periods. Second, as European colo-nial authority grew, the institutions that had supported formal Islamic learning crumbled with Muslim polities, to be replaced by institutions promoting European learning, secular and religious, as well as by new Muslim institutions that promoted Salafism. Its redacted intellectualism provided Muslims with a convenient means of confronting or accommodating colonization and the forms of learning it carried, including for the first time Enlightenment and Protestant ideas. Furthermore, lay Muslims of the upper and middle classes, directly educated in European (rather than Islamic) systems of learning, added their voice to those representative of Salafism, the accumulated effect of which was the rise of a number of new Muslim approaches to Jesus.

As this brief history of Muslim–Christian relations suggests, a number of "exter-nal" factors must be taken into account when one assesses the figure of Jesus in Islam. These include the cultural geography of Arabia in the time of Muhammad; the rapid expansion of Muslim political power throughout the eastern Mediterranean, followed by the flowering of Islamic learning in the Formative Period; further politi-cal expansion eastwards through Asia and westward into Europe, as well as the beginnings of European mercantile interests in the Indian Ocean, during the Middle Period; and, finally, the reversal of Muslim political, economic, and intellectual for-tunes in the face of European colonial expansion during the Late Period.

Sources

Just as a number of historical contexts must be considered when outlining the "external" factors contributing to the characterization of Jesus in Islam, so too must a number of primary literary sources be taken into account for "internal" concerns to be laid bare. The latter are identified and described below, with particular reference to descriptions of Jesus.

Qur'an

The Qur'an – said to have been "revealed" to Muhammad over a period of twenty-three years – is the first source of Islamic knowledge about Jesus. It was transmitted orally and committed to loose text by the time of Muhammad's death in 632 CE. Muslim tradition records that a standard version that remains in use today was first produced under the patronage of the third Caliph, 'Uthman (d. 656). Out of the 114 chapters (suras) comprising the Qur'an, fifteen mention Jesus. He is mentioned by name, as 'Isa ibn Maryam (Jesus, son of Mary) sixteen times, and as Ibn Maryam (Son of Mary) seventeen times. He is also referred to as al-Masih (the Messiah) eleven times, nabi (prophet) once, and rasul (messenger, implying the bringer of a revealed "book") three times. Other phrases widely interpreted as references to Jesus include: (1) "among those who are close to God"; (2) "worthy of esteem in this world and the next"; (3) "blessed," a source of benefit for others; (4) "sure word"; and (5) "Servant of God."

Read as a composite without reference to order, the Qur'an portrays Jesus as follows (for specific chapters and verses, see Anawati 2004). The story begins with Mary's mother, who vowed that should God bestow a child upon her, it would live as an offering to God. Although having expected a boy, upon the birth of a girl, she sought God's protection for them both, which God delivered along with food that Mary herself claimed, in later years, was supplied by Him.

Little else is told of Mary's life, until the "annunciation," which is mentioned twice. Mary was told that she was chosen by God to deliver a son whose name was the "Messiah Jesus Son of Mary." One version says that the news was delivered by angels, but the other says that God's Spirit took the form of a man. Nowhere are details of the conception discussed, but when Mary asks how a chaste woman such as herself could bear a son, she is told in one version that God creates what He wills by simply decreeing it, and in the other she is simply informed that such things are easy for Him. Other passages allude to God's breathing His Spirit into Mary.

Jesus' birth is described as painful for Mary, but God sustains her. When she returns to her family, the baby Jesus speaks to them in Mary's defense, announcing that he is God's servant and prophet, and that he has been endowed with knowledge of the scripture. Jesus, therefore, is portrayed as a miracle-worker from birth. Other miracles or "signs" mentioned are clairvoyance, the healing of the blind and the leper, the breathing of life into a clay bird, and the serving of a feast sent by God to prove to Jesus' disciples that Jesus was a prophet.

Although the Qur'an explicitly acknowledges Jesus' mission and attributes to him miracles, knowledge of the scripture, and the strength of God's Spirit as aids to perform his task, it provides little detail of major events in his life or the specifics of his teachings. Jesus' name appears in lists of prophets, but Jesus (along with Abraham, Moses, and Muhammad) is distinguished from others as both a "prophet" (*nabi*: one inspired by God) and an "apostle" (*rasul*: the bringer of a revealed book). Jesus' book is referred to as the "Gospel" (*Injil*), a revelation of guidance that confirmed the Torah and Psalms (*Tawrat* and *Zabur*) before it and the Qur'an after it. The Qur'an also asserts that the Gospel mentioned the coming of an unlettered prophet named Ahmad (a variant of Muhammad).

Other passages in the Qur'an add that Jesus' purpose was to overcome disagreement among God's followers, make lawful some of the things forbidden to the Children of Israel, and reassert that paradise is closed to those who ascribe partners to God. It quite specifically adds that it is wrong to refer to Jesus as the Son of God, God, or one of "three" (a reference to the concept of the Trinity). In fact, in one passage, Jesus himself denies that he led humanity to believe that he or his mother were deities beside God. Furthermore, the end of Jesus' presence on earth is described. Unbelievers plotted against Jesus, so God told him that He proposed to raise him to Himself. He was not slain or crucified, but it appeared to the people that he was, while God raised him to Himself.

As this composite indicates, in the Qur'an Jesus is not only esteemed and exalted, but also placed in the highest rank of prophets as one who delivers a revealed book. The Qur'anic Jesus, in fact, closely approximates the canonical Jesus of Christianity, except for his divinity (and hence, his place in the Trinity) and crucifixion (and so, his resurrection). For historians of religion, these similarities and differences reveal the influence of the Abrahamic traditions active in the Hijaz and its environs during the lifetime of Muhammad. For example, scholars assert that the stories of the annunciation, conception, and birth of Jesus reflect the influence of the canonical gospels, and that certain miracle stories reflect apocryphal gospels. They tie the Qur'an's insistence on Jesus' humanity, its anti-Trinitarianism, its claim that Jesus was not crucified, and its idea that Jesus foretold the coming of Muhammad to the influence of various combinations of Jewish Christians (Ebionites and Elkesaites), Manichaeism, and apocryphal gospels, particularly Gnostic and docetic varieties (Robinson 1991, 17–22). For Muslims, on the other hand, these similarities and differences substantiate the Qur'an's status as a revelation of the Abrahamic God.

Hadith

The genre of literature known as *hadith* (or *akhbar* among Shi'as) appears to have been influenced by the pre-Islamic Arabian preoccupation with genealogy, and derived from the genre of *khabar* (pl. *akhbar*), a story or an anecdote that deals with a particularly remarkable figure or event in history. Given the Qur'an's reference to Muhammad's exemplary conduct and the "silent" or "living" tradition of the exemplar (the *sunna*), early Muslim scholars transformed this pre-Islamic mode of historical literature into a means by which to interpret and/or supplement the Qur'an with reports, transmitted by succeeding generations, of Muhammad's sayings and activities. Between the ninth and eleventh centuries, in fact, six collections of *hadith* achieved canonical status in Sunnism, and three gained similar status among Shi'as. These nine collections of *hadith* – each voluminous on its own – contain too many references to Jesus to catalog here, but it is important to note that while this body of literature echoes the Qur'an in much of its characterization of Jesus, it addresses the crucifixion and eschatological role of Jesus more thoroughly than the Qur'an.

Injil and Isra'iliyyat

As the Qur'an upholds the revealed sanctity of the "Gospel" (*Injil*), attributing its revelation to Jesus himself, the canonical gospels of Christianity represent another important set of writings considered by Muslim scholars in their construction(s) of an Islamic Jesus. By the Formative Period, Arabic translations of canonical gospels existed. However, Muslims argued that these gospels distorted or suppressed the true account of Jesus, later given in the Qur'an. Muslim authors, therefore, did not restrict themselves to these gospels, but also drew from various apocryphal sources.

A prime example of an apocryphal source employed by Muslims, particularly in the Late Period, is the "Gospel of Barnabas." Although such a work is mentioned in Christian lists dating to the sixth and seventh centuries, the only extant version is an Italian manuscript dating to the late sixteenth century. The earliest extant reference to the work by a Muslim author dates to the early seventeenth century. The work is particularly significant because in it Jesus predicts the coming of Muhammad (mentioned by name) and denies his own divinity, cursing those who would make such assertions. However, differences with Islamic perspectives on other points ensure that even Muslims by no means unanimously accept the work as sound (Leirvik 2002, 4–26).

The echo of the gospels, canonical and apocryphal, is also heard in a genre of literature known as *Isra'iliyyat*. Most importantly, this genre includes narratives of the lives and sayings of prophets, known as *Qisas al-Anbiya'*. These works appeared very early in the Formative Period and their tales were probably first transmitted to Muslims by Jewish and Christian communities or converts to Islam. Here, Jesus appeared along with other Abrahamic prophets, often under such topical headings as humility, repentance, and so forth. Although many such tales were not included in the "official" *hadith* collections, *Qisas* literature has flourished as a popular form, read widely by lay classes. Together, with the *hadith*s of the "official" collections, therefore, the various forms of *Isra'iliyyat* literature, such as *Qisas*, played a significant role in determining the characterization of Jesus in Islamic theology and mysticism, and in forms of popular piety (Khalidi 2001, 1–45).

The variety of literature noted above illustrates that the "Qur'anic" Jesus should not be equated with the "Islamic" Jesus. Rather, influence from *hadith* collections, the gospels (canonical and apocryphal), and *Isra'iliyyat* literature must also be considered. Together, this variety also ensures that "internal" concerns rooted in a specifically Muslim literary and cultural milieu are no less significant than the assortment of "external" factors already noted to play a role in the characterizations of Jesus in Islam.

Jesus in Islamic Theology (Kalam / Ta'wil) and Mysticism (Tasawwuf)

Our discussion of the "Qur'anic" Jesus has already illustrated the degree to which Jesus in Islam echoes the Jesus of the gospels, canonical and apocryphal. Below, therefore, only the most significant points of departure are highlighted. In addition, the differences between theological and mystical representations, as well as changes accruing over time, are the focus of discussion.

Theological representations in the Formative and Middle Periods

As outlined above, the major theological schools in Islam did not spring to life immediately upon Muhammad's death; they crystallized over a period of centuries, finally distinguishing themselves in the ninth and tenth centuries. Prior to this date, a broader spectrum of opinion on all matters theological could be heard – some opinions adhering closely to the Qur'an and the narrowing corpus of *hadith*, others drawing from the variety of sources active in the regions under expanding Muslim rule. That Jesus could have been accepted as divine by some early thinkers, therefore, is by no means beyond the realm of possibility. As theology itself became more systematized and schools that shared the tools of Aristotelian logic began to arise, the less literally grounded groups were declared *ghulat* (heretics). Thus, only the views of these later schools, Sunni and Shi'a, are outlined here.

Three theological schools are particularly relevant in this context: (1) Ash'ari, the basis of the Sunni perspective; (2) Mu'tazili, the basis of the Imami/Twelver Shi'a perspective; and, (3) Ikhwan al-Safa', the basis of the Isma'ili/Sevener Shi'a perspective (Wolfson 1976; Fakhry 1983; Corbin 1993; cf. Rissanen 1993). All three schools uphold God's Unity, or the concept of *tawhid*, but Ash'aris and Mu'tazilis define it in monotheistic terms, arguing for the "transcendence" of God, while the Ikhwan al-Safa' are monistic in their approach, making the case for the "immanence" of God. As for the basic difference between the Ash'aris and Mu'tazilis on the point of God's transcendence, the latter argued that God's Attributes (e.g., knowledge, power, etc.) must be identical with His Essence, for God's Unity would be compromised if they were not, in response to which the former argued that God's Attributes are not identical with His Essence, but "subsist" in It, for if they were the same as His Essence, one could address one's petitions to God's Attributes, rather than God Himself. As advocates of an immanent God, in a Neo-Pythagorean/Neo-Platonic sense, the most basic representation of how the Ikhwan al-Safa' dealt with the whole issue of Attributes and Essence was to argue that all multiplicity is an "emanation" of the indivisible One, just as all numbers arise from the progressive addition of one.

As much as the above representation of these theological schools does disservice to their complexity, it provides a springboard from which to dive into the first central difference between the Islamic Jesus and the canonical Christian Jesus: that is, the question of his humanity or divinity. In response to the Christian argument that Jesus' divinity can be understood as a temporal expression of the uncreated Word of God, Ash'aris in general responded that this was, in fact, the status of the Qur'an, "subsisting" in His Essence, but not identical with It. Jesus, like Muhammad and other Abrahamic prophets, therefore, shared nothing of the divine. Mu'tazilis, on the other hand, following the premise that the very distinction of Attributes and Essence compromised God's Unity, argued that the attribute of "speech" was identical with God's Essence, but that the Word "spoken" is a creation distinct from His Essence. Thus, the Qur'an, as the Word of God, is created, and Jesus, like Muhammad and other Abrahamic prophets, shares nothing of the divine. And finally, the Ikhwan al-Safa', like most monistic thinkers, argued that all souls are emanations of the Universal Soul, itself an emanation of the indivisible One. Jesus, Muhammad, other Abrahamic prophets, and all living things, therefore, share something of the divine, but are not identical with the indivisible One. From the perspective of a historian of religion, these Islamic rationalizations of Jesus' humanity, whether by means of transcendental/monotheistic or immanent/monistic theologies, are best explained as a defense of the Qur'anic version of God's Unity, which a priori defines the concept of Trinity as a form of "associationism" (shirk), in a cultural milieu rife with Christian defenders of the compatibility of Trinity and monotheism.

Another means of rationalizing Jesus' humanity employed by theologians was to argue, again in keeping with Qur'anic allusions, that canonical Christian scriptures had been misread or corrupted. Epitomizing the argument for "misreading" is a work attributed to the Ash'ari, Abu Hamid Muhammad al-Ghazali (d. 1111) (al-Ghazali 1986). In this, the author argues that a number of gospel texts imply Jesus' humanity, such as the one in which Jesus admits ignorance (Mark 13:32). Assertions of Jesus' divinity are to be read figuratively, as suggested by the fact that when Jews accuse Jesus of making himself God, he replies with the contention that Jews are referred to as "gods" in the Hebrew Bible (John 10:30–34). On the other hand, a prime example of the case for "corruption," is the work of the Zahiri (a school not mentioned above) Abu Muhammad 'Ali ibn Hazm (d. 1063), whose close comparative reading of the canonical gospels pointed to the extraordinary number of

contradictions and inconsistencies from account to account, thus calling the reliability of the entire body into question (Robinson 1991, 46–47).

Altogether, these apologetic (al-Ghazali) and polemical (Ibn Hazm) approaches
to the canonical gospels served to bolster the more metaphysical arguments outlined
above. They also proved useful in accounting for the second central difference
between the Islamic and the Christian Jesus: whether or not he was crucified. On
this point, the Qur'an states,

> ... they said (in boast),
> "We killed the Christ Jesus,
> the Son of Mary,
> the Apostle of God."
> But they killed him not,
> Nor crucified him,
> But a semblance was made to them (*shubbiha la-hum*) ...
> For a surety
> They killed him not. (4:157)
>
> Nay, God raised him up
> Unto Himself ... (4:158)[2]

That is to say, it upholds a crucifixion, but a "semblance," rather than Jesus, was its
victim. In relation to the canonical Christian perspective, therefore, the Qur'an
denies not only the crucifixion of Jesus, but also the redemption from humanity's
original sin that it and the resurrection of Jesus represent.

Indeed, original sin itself is not a Qur'anic, nor hence more generally Islamic,
precept. Rather, the Qur'an asserts frequently the favor and protection that God
offers the devout. Thus, for theologians of the Ash'ari and Mu'tazili schools, the idea
that Jesus was not crucified was consistent with their reading of the Qur'an's assurance that faith always triumphs over adversity (e.g., 22:49), and the canonical
Christian divergence could also be explained by the apologetic or polemical
approaches employed to argue for Jesus' humanity.

The Ikhwan al-Safa', however, approached the subject from a different angle
entirely. They came closest to reconciling the Qur'anic and canonical Christian
accounts by reading both through the lens of their distinction between body and
soul. According to this school, Jesus was crucified, he remained on the cross all day,
and he was stabbed with a lance. Once taken down and wrapped in a shroud, he
was laid in a tomb, only to reappear before his disciples three days later, news of
which appearance led his pursuers to open up the tomb and find his body missing.
Even so, "they did not kill him and they did not crucify him, but a semblance," while
"God raised him into his presence," as the Qur'an states, because as Robinson
explains, "the soul [*lahut*] which constitutes the personality was [already] liberated
when the body [*nasut*] – the prison of the soul – died on the cross" (Robinson 1991,
57; cf. Marquet 1982, 129–158).

By equating the "semblance" with the human body, the Ikhwan al-Safa' resolved
a question that was not so easily answered by others. For Ash'ari and Mu'tazili theo-

logians, all of whom agreed that Jesus was not crucified, the question that remained was who or what was crucified? The problem they faced in providing a definitive answer was that the Qur'an offered little further insight, unless one analyzed such terms as "semblance," while the *hadith* collections offered a mass of often conflicting reports. There are *hadiths* that report all of the following explanations. (1) When all the disciples were made to look like Jesus, his pursuers demanded that the real Jesus step forward. When one disciple stepped forward, he was crucified, and Jesus was "raised" into God's presence there and then. (2) God made a "semblance" of Jesus prior to the arrival of Jesus' pursuers. This semblance was handed to them by Jesus' betrayer (i.e., Judas) after the "last supper" and was eventually crucified. Jesus himself remained on earth for seven hours more, in which time he appeared before Mary and the eleven remaining disciples, learned of the suicide of his betrayer, and then was raised into God's presence. (3) When the disciples were asked by Jesus to volunteer as his "semblance," one complied and was killed, while Jesus himself was "raised" into God's presence. And (4) Judas or one of Jesus' Jewish pursuers was made into the "semblance" and crucified after Jesus was "raised" (Robinson 1991, 127–141).

A third and final point of divergence between Islamic and canonical Christian perspectives of Jesus – one that again illustrates the importance of *hadiths* in exegesis – concerns eschatology. The Qur'an does not explicitly acknowledge Jesus' eschatological role, but later theologians argued that it alludes to Jesus in this capacity at least twice. In one verse (4:159) that mentions belief "in him" and states that "Before his death/And on the Day of Judgment/He will be a witness/Against them," ambiguity surrounds the pronouns "him," "his," and "he." *Hadiths* referring to this passage interpret "him" in the phrase "believe in him" as either Jesus or Muhammad; they interpret "his" in the phrase "before his death" as either Jesus or the People of the Scriptures (i.e., Jews and Christians). In another verse (43:61) that speaks of a "Sign for the Hour," it is unclear whether the text states that "It" or "He" is a sign. *Hadiths*, supported by variant readings of the Qur'an, acknowledge either "It" or "He" as correct, interpreting "It" as the Qur'an and "He" as Jesus.

Formative and Middle Period exegetes considered the merits of all permutations Ultimately, however, they reached a consensus that belief "in him" refers to Jesus, that "before his death" means the death of the People of the Scriptures, and that "he will be witness against them" depicts Jesus standing as witness against the People of the Scriptures at the End Time. As for a "sign for the Hour," the verse was eventually interpreted to mean that Jesus' future descent will be a sign of the approaching Day of Judgment (Robinson 1991, 78–89, 168–170).

Clearly, the eschatological role ascribed to Jesus in Christian dogma was confirmed by Muslim theologians. However, this confirmation was not identical with the Christian perspective. Both Sunni and Shi'a *hadith* collections (though not the Qur'an) mention the appearance of the "Mahdi" (Guided One) before Jesus' descent. Although Jesus will kill the Anti-Christ (*dajjal*), the Mahdi is identified as the prime political player before the Day of Resurrection/Judgment, ushering in a period of peace and order. Jesus, in fact, will finally embrace a natural death sometime after killing the Anti-Christ. Apart from scholastic dispute on the period of the Mahdi's rule, as well as the exact time of Jesus' death, based on alternative accounts in separate *hadiths*, the only major dispute is sectarian and concerns the Mahdi's identity. Most agree, however, that Jesus will act as a judge before the Resurrection/Judgment, but even then the Mahdi will lead the prayers. Furthermore, Jesus will not be more than a witness at the Last Judgment, judgment being God's prerogative alone (Madelung 2004).

Mystical representations in the Formative and Middle Periods

As in the case of the formal theological schools, formal "orders" (*tariqas*) of mysticism did not distinguish themselves from the theological schools or each other until the ninth and tenth centuries. Much variety existed before this time. However, by the ninth and tenth centuries, the factor that most thoroughly set mysticism apart from theology was the former's "monistic" theology: that is, advocacy of an "immanent," rather than "transcendental," concept of God. Two major forms of monism, however, also divided the mystical orders of the "Sufi" mystical tradition.

One set of orders progressively came to hold the doctrine of *fana'* (annihilation), arguing that the soul, being an emanation of the indivisible One, is ultimately capable of union with the One. Another set of orders argued that the doctrine of *fana'*, as described above, compromised the uniqueness of the divine, leading them to maintain the doctrine of *baqa'* (subsistence), which allowed for no more than "inherence" of the soul in the indivisible One (Trimingham 1971; Baldick 1989; Schimmel 1975). The implications of this divide extend from theology out to the socio-ethical perspectives of their advocates.

Despite the divides between theology and mysticism, the formal orders largely agreed with theological representations of Jesus, including his humanity, the variety of approaches to his crucifixion, and his eschatological role beside the Mahdi. As monists, however, mystics interpreted these concepts in the light of an immanent, rather than transcendental, concept of divinity.

A telling example is the argument for Jesus' humanity in the work of Muhi al-Din ibn al-'Arabi (d. 1240), broadly recognized as the greatest systematizer of monism in Sufi thought. In general, Ibn al-'Arabi argued for the "Unity of Being" (*wahdat al-wujud*), meaning that all apparent differentiations are, in fact, emanations of one Reality, which is greater than the sum of its parts. As in the writings of the Ikhwan al-Safa', therefore, Jesus cannot be identified with Reality any more or less than any other human being. Thus, in his *Fusus al-Hikam*, commenting on Jesus' act of blowing life into the dead, Ibn al-'Arabi distinguishes the human Jesus' act of blowing from the divine essence or "form" that actually revived the dead (al-'Arabi 1980, 177–178). To further show that Jesus did no more than other humans could do, Ibn al-'Arabi mentions the case of a Sufi (Abu Yazid al-Bistami, d. 874) who blew life into an ant and, in that respect, was like Jesus (al-'Arabi 1980, 179).

The one respect in which al-Bistami and all others were not (and could not be) equated with Jesus, however, was the way in which Jesus was conceived. Ibn al-'Arabi's explication of this distinction begins with a monistic axiom:

> Know that it is a particular characteristic of the spirits that everything on which they descend becomes alive, and life begins to pervade it ... Now the measure of life that pervades a creature is called divine, humanity being [pre-eminently] the locus in which the Spirit inheres. (al-'Arabi 1980, 175)

Jesus' distinction is that he was conceived when "the trusty spirit, which was Gabriel, presented itself to Mary as a perfectly formed human," and "blew Jesus into her ... transmitting God's word to Mary, just as an apostle transmits His word to his community"(al-'Arabi 1980, 175). Thus "The body of Jesus was created from the actual water of Mary and the notional water [seed] of Gabriel inherent in the moisture of that blowing" (al-'Arabi 1980, 175–176). The arguments concerning Jesus' raising of the dead and his conception are then brought together in the conclusion that "Jesus came forth raising the dead because he was a divine spirit. In this the quickening was of God, while the blowing itself came from Jesus, just as the blowing was from Gabriel, while Word was of God" (al-'Arabi 1980, 176). Because of this unique conception, Jesus was born knowing the Reality, while other human beings, such as al-Bistami, have to strive to achieve that knowledge. It is ultimately on the basis of this distinction that Ibn al-'Arabi designates Jesus as the "Seal of Saints" (khatam al-awliya') (De Souza 1982), a concept modeled on the traditional designation of Muhammad as the "Seal of Prophets."

Ibn al-'Arabi's Fusus al-Hikam further illustrates that, among mystics, the theologians' emphasis on the "external" details of Jesus' being (e.g., the question of when exactly he was "raised" to God's presence, etc.), is eschewed for a concentration on the "inner" meaning of Jesus' experience.

In addition, Ibn al-'Arabi's Fusus al-Hikam is more generally representative of the mystical approach to Jesus in terms of the relationship it draws between Jesus and "sainthood" (wilayat). Although the concept of Jesus as "Seal of Saints" is specific to Ibn al-'Arabi and his followers, the entire spectrum of Sufis regarded Jesus as the epitome of sainthood. Extant ascetic works dating back to the eight century emphasize Jesus' renunciation of worldly goods and pleasures, his identification with the poor, his humility, and his patience (Khalidi 2001, 34). By the later Formative Period, "Jesus was enshrined in Sufi sensibility as the prophet of the heart par excellence" (Khalidi 2001, 42).

Late representations among the scholarly classes

The theological and mystical representations of Jesus arrived at during the Formative and Middle Periods passed into the eighteenth century largely unchanged. However, the articulation of Salafi movements in the eighteenth century and the rise of

European colonial rule in the nineteenth century had the immediate effect of transforming earlier perceptions, particularly by spurring a new round of polemical and
apologetic exchanges.

Jesus in Salafism   Works representative of Salafism include the *Kitab al-Tawhid*
(al-Wahhab 1996) of Muhammad ibn 'Abd al-Wahhab (d. 1787) – founder of
Wahhabism in Arabia – and the *Taqwiyat al-Iman* (Isma'il 1958) of Shah Muhammad
Isma'il (d. 1831) – advocate of the Tariqa Muhammadiyya in South Asia. The most
striking feature of such works is the denigration of earlier scholarship. In the opinion
of Isma'il, for example, "associationism" (*shirk*) is rampant among Muslims, because
the scholarly classes "have left the word of God [Qur'an] and the Prophet [*hadith*] to
exercise their own reason ('*aql*), and follow myths and erroneous customs (*rasum*)"
(Isma'il 1958, 13). Thus, the casting aside of Islamic sources judged to "contradict"
Qur'an and *hadith* has been a characteristic feature of the new movement in Islam.
Furthermore, non-Arabic-speaking Salafis actively promoted the translation and
printing of the Qur'an (breaking with past objections) and *hadith* collections. The
implications for the understanding of Jesus that this attitude spawned are many.

1. The widespread appeal to, and apologetic approach toward, the canonical
gospels, which argued that they had been "misread" by Christians, was more often
forsaken for a polemical stance that held them as "corrupted." As Abu al-A'la
Mawdudi (d. 1979), the founder of the Pakistani Salafi-inspired Jama'at-i Islami,
argues in his *Tafhim al-Qur'an*, the canonical gospels were written by Greek-speaking
Christians after Jesus' ascension, none before 70 CE, and were based on orally transmitted traditions from Syriac-speaking Christians. No copies earlier than the fourth
century of even the Greek gospels are extant; thus "corruption" is difficult to rule
out. The irony of the shift from apologetic and polemical approaches to the almost
wholly polemical ones represented by Mawdudi, however, is that it raised the value
of the gospels insofar as they upheld the Qur'anic and *hadith*-based depiction of
Jesus. In the same work, therefore, Mawdudi writes that the most trustworthy
account is the Gospel of Barnabas, which the church declared heretical and which
Christians have done their best to conceal (see the exegesis of *Sura al-Saff* in Mawdudi
1962–1973).

2. Despite the primary reliance on Qur'an and *hadith*s in the exegetical literature
of the Formative and Middle Periods surveyed above, the anti-scholastic bent of the
new movement prompted the stifling of variety in favor of consensus. For example,
whereas earlier theologians presented all possibilities when considering contradictory *hadith*s, then reasoned that one or another option was most sound, while
acknowledging their own fallibility in the phrase "God knows best," advocates of the
new movement either refrained from comment or argued that only the commonly
held assertions are to be considered. This also had the effect of virtually eliminating
the doctrine of *fana'* and the type of exegetical conclusions articulated by mystics like
Ibn al-'Arabi, particularly given that the majority of foundational Salafi thinkers
(including the above quoted Isma'il) were themselves Sufis who had long followed
permutations of the doctrine of *baqa'*.

3. Not even the Qur'an escaped the "dogmatic" drive of the Salafis. That variants exist was downplayed, while translations of the Qur'an often interjected definitive stands on previously acknowledged ambiguities. For example, the exegete 'Abd Allah Yusuf 'Ali, in his widely distributed translation from 1938, provides exegetical notes on the Qur'anic verses 4:157–159, concerning the crucifixion. He acknowledges earlier dispute, but states, "It is not profitable to discuss the many doubts and conjectures ... among Muslim theologians." He then cites the Gospel of Barnabas in support of the dogmatic statement that

> The Qur'anic teaching is that Christ was not crucified nor killed by the Jews, not withstanding certain apparent circumstances which produced that illusion in the minds of some of his enemies; that disputations, doubts and conjectures on such matters are vain; and that he was taken up to God. ('Ali 1989, 230 n. 663, 1337 n. 4663)

Summarized most succinctly, the overall effect of the rise of Salafism on the understanding of Jesus in most Sunni and Shi'a scholarly circles is to enshrine as dogma a view of Jesus as a book/law-giving apostle, rather than as an archetypal mystic, the details of whose past mission and future eschatological role are indisputably outlined in Qur'an and/or *hadith*s.

Influence of colonialism   Although not explicitly stated in the above explication of the rise of a dogmatic Jesus under the influence of Salafism, it should be clear that European colonialism played an important role in spurring on this new understanding, if for no other reason than that the colonized Muslim could use it as a polemical tool against the colonizers' Christian proselytizing and critiques of Islam. The full impact of European colonialism (and of European political, economic, and intellectual ascendancy more generally), however, is best illustrated by means of the rise of new forms of Muslim apologetics. Two examples will suffice to clarify the point.

Mirza Ghulam Ahmad (d. 1908) was raised and educated in the Sunni-Sufi milieu of late nineteenth century "British India," where he founded the *Ahmadiyya* movement. When confronted by the heated polemical atmosphere (inter-faith and intra-Muslim) of the time and place, he claimed to have received "revelations" from God proclaiming him a "prophet" (*nabi*, but not a *rasul*), revealing that the Day of Judgment was near and appointing him as the prophesied Mahdi and Messiah (Ahmad 1960; Friedmann 1989). That is to say, he broke with earlier Muslim tradition to collapse the distinction between the two main players of Islamic eschatology but otherwise held true to the general Islamic scheme concerning Jesus. Furthermore, regarding the life of Jesus, in his *'Isa Hindustan Mein*, Ghulam Ahmad responded to Muslim–Christian differences on the crucifixion by taking an intermediate position, arguing that Jesus was crucified but did not die on the cross. He did not ascend to heaven without bodily wounds, as is the standard Muslim argument, nor was he resurrected to ascend with bodily wounds, as in the canonical Christian version. Ghulam Ahmad contends that Jesus was rescued from the cross after approximately two hours, his wounds were healed, and he traveled to India and Tibet, where he preached until his natural death in Kashmir at 120 years of age (Ahmad 1962, 7–13).

Interestingly, Ghulam Ahmad was not alone among late nineteenth and early twentieth-century Muslims to accept aspects of the canonical Christian version of the crucifixion, although all were in the distinct minority. There was the "Nizari" branch of Isma'ili/Sevener Shi'as, which maintained the perspective of the Ikhwan al-Safa'. The crucifixion was also adopted by the Neo-Mu'tazili Muhammad 'Abdu (d. 1905) of Egypt's famous al-Azhar *madrasa*, as well as by Rashid Rida (d. 1935), leader of the Salafi-inspired Egyptian Muslim Brotherhood (MacAuliffe 1991, 141). All in the latter camp, however, argued some form of the line that Jesus' body died on the cross after his soul had already ascended to heaven. Ghulam Ahmad's version, therefore, remained closer to the common Sunni and Imami/Twelver Shi'a perspective that nothing of Jesus died on the cross, but broke with all in positing an Asian sojourn and Kashmiri bodily death. Thus, as Friedmann states, although responding to Christian missionary attacks on Islam, Ghulam Ahmad was not only "following classical Muslim tradition" in many respects, but also attempting, by claiming "affinity with Jesus," to "deprive Christianity of Jesus himself" (Friedmann 1989, 118). It should be clarified, however, that Ghulam Ahmad attempted this by turning to the canonical gospels and the literature of his Christian adversaries. His entire argument for the "short" crucifixion is based on a reading of the New Testament, which he accepts as a sound source of information that has been "misread," while Jesus' Asian sojourn is drawn from European works that argue that Jewish tribes settled in Afghanistan in pre-Islamic times and that Buddhist and Christian tenets were complementary because Jesus had traveled to India (Ahmad 1962, 21–58, 116–143).

A second apologetic strategy issued from the ranks of scholars primarily educated in the European mode, well represented in the *'Abkariyyat al-Masih* by the Egyptian essayist, 'Abbas Mahmud al-'Aqqad (d. 1964), and *Qarya Zalima* by the medical doctor and former rector of 'Ayn Shams University in Cairo, Muhammad Kamil Husayn (Husayn 1958; this summary of Husayn's and al-'Aqqad's work is drawn from Anawati 2004). The first work is a "historical" biography of Jesus, and the second is a "meditation" on the trial of Jesus, but both these authors draw their conclusions about Jesus almost exclusively from readings of the canonical gospels, whose authenticity al-'Aqqad in particular vigorously defends. The only significant manner in which they differ from canonical Christian accounts, in fact, is by avoiding all mention of the points at which the Christian canon diverges from the Islamic. Thus, the crucifixion and the issues that surround it are merely glossed over by al-'Aqqad as matters of "belief," while Husayn – whose work focuses on the events preceding it – avoids all controversy by neither denying nor affirming the event on which his entire work converges. That is to say, this mode of apologetics differs from that of the Formative and Middle Periods (represented by al-Ghazali's appeal to "misreading") insofar as no attempt is made to systematically address differences.

In sum, the Late Period is distinguished by a number of new trends spurred by the rise of Salafism and European colonial expansion across much of the Muslim world. Had these external factors not conspired to limit the variety of Middle and Late Period contributions to the characterization of Jesus – particularly those arising in the mystical context – the range of possibilities would only have grown. As it happened, however, their combined influence was to promote among the majority the dogma of Jesus as a book/law-giving apostle whose mission was indisputably outlined in Qur'an and/or *hadiths*, and among the minority, a Jesus who more closely resembled that of the canonical gospels.

Theology and mysticism: summation

This survey of the most significant points of departure between the Islamic and canonical Christian Jesus illustrates not only that theologians and mystics differed on key issues, but also that within each discipline variety is evident, particularly when considered over time. Views of the crucifixion display the greatest degree of variety, whether within one period or from one period to another. On the other hand, the humanity of Jesus and his eschatological role beside the Mahdi are almost unanimously upheld. Even in these matters, however, different approaches to divinity differently influence views of the manner and meaning of Jesus' humanity.

Conclusion

When the primary sources and theological or mystical representations of Jesus are read in historical context, it must first be said that Muhammad and the scholars who followed on his heels have mirrored the Jesus of the gospels, canonical and apocryphal, quite faithfully. From the Qur'an itself through the latest forms of apologetics, the annunciation, the virgin birth, various miracles, and even the ascension have been presented as staple features of Jesus in Islam. Some (although a minority) have even ventured as far as accepting the bodily crucifixion. The historian of religion can explain all of these similarities by considering the religio-cultural environment in which Muhammad lived, as well as the variety of relations between Muslims and Christians under which the disciplines, schools, and sects of Islam were formed, following Muhammad's death, and continued to develop into the present. However, the consistent differences between Jesus in Islamic literature and in the gospels, canonical and apocryphal, particularly on the question of Jesus' humanity or divinity, as well as his eschatological role beside the Mahdi, can only partially be explained by cultural geographies. On these points, even the historian must turn to Qur'an and *hadith* and the attempt by exegetes to align the understanding of Jesus with the concept of God's Unity, or *tawhid*, stated therein, whether approached as an expression of monotheism or monism. In the final analysis, therefore, it must be said that Jesus in Islam is the product of two overarching factors, one external to it, the other internally generated.

Notes

1   Reza Pirbhai was responsible for the section on historical contexts, while Reem Meshal prepared the section on theology and mysticism. They co-wrote the section on sources.
2   This and the following Qur'anic translations are from 'Abd Allah Yusuf 'Ali's widely published, distributed, and read version of the Qur'an ('Ali 1989). As there are multiple printings, only chapter and verse numbers are given. In the case of 4:157, however, Yusuf Ali's translation of *"shubbiha la-hum"* as "so it was made to appear to them," has been replaced with Robinson's more literal "a semblance was made to them," for clarity of exposition. See Robinson (1991, 127).

References

Ahmad, Mirza Ghulam (1960). *Ta'lim-i Islam: Islami Usul ki Falasifi*. Lahore: n.p.

Ahmad, Mirza Ghulam (1962). *'Isa Hindustan Mein*. Lahore: Nisar Art Press.

al-'Arabi, Muhi al-Din Ibn (1980). *Fusus al-Hikam*. English translation: *Bezels of Wisdom*. Trans. R. W. J. Austin. New York: Paulist.

al-Ghazali, Abu Hamid Muhammad (1986). *Al-Radd al-Jamil li-Ilahiyat 'Isa bi-Sarih al-Injil*. Cairo: Dar al-Hidayah.

al-Wahhab, Muhammad Ibn 'Abd (1996). *Kitab al-Tawhid*. Trans. A. M. Mujahid. Riyadh: Dar al-Salam Publications.

'Ali, A. Yusuf, trans. (1989). *Qur'an*. Riyadh: Islamic University of Imam Muhammad Ibn Sa'ud.

Anawati, G. C. (2004). "'Isa." *Encyclopaedia of Islam*. CD-ROM edn. Leiden: Koninklijke Brill.

Baldick, Julian (1989). *Mystical Islam: An Introduction to Sufism*. London: I. B. Taurus.

Caetani, L. (2008). *Islam and Christianity: Pre-Islamic Arabia, the Ancient Arabs*. London: Media Asia.

Corbin, Henry (1993). *History of Islamic Philosophy*. Trans. Liadain Sherrard. London: Kegan Paul.

De Souza, A. (1982). "Jesus in Ibn 'Arabi's *Fusus al-Hikam*." *Islamochristiana* 8:185–200.

Fakhry, Majid (1983). *A History of Islamic Philosophy*. New York: Columbia University Press.

Friedmann, Yohanan (1989). *Prophecy Continuous: Aspects of Ahmadi Religious Thought and its Medieval Background*. Berkeley: University of California Press.

Hodgson, Marshall G. S. (1977). *The Venture of Islam*. 3 vols. Chicago: University of Chicago.

Husayn, Muhammad Kamil (1958). *Qarya Zalima*. Cairo: Matba'at Misr. English translation: *City of Wrong: A Friday in Jerusalem*. Trans. Kenneth Cragg. London: Bles, 1959.

Isma'il, Shah Muhammad (1958). *Taqwiyat al-Iman*. Karachi: Nur Muhammad Asah al-Matabi' wa Karkhana Tijarat Kutub.

Khalidi, Tarif (2001). *The Muslim Jesus: Sayings and Stories in Islamic Literature*. Cambridge, MA: Harvard University Press.

Leirvik, Oddbjorn (2002). "History as a Literary Weapon: The Gospel of Barnabas in Muslim-Christian Polemics." *Studia Theologica* 1:4–26.

MacAuliffe, Jane Dammen (1991). *Qur'anic Christians: An Analysis of Classical and Modern Exegesis*. Cambridge: Cambridge University Press.

Madelung, Wilfred (2004). "Mahdi." *Encyclopaedia of Islam*. CD-ROM edn. Leiden: Koninklijke Brill.

Marquet, Y. (1982). "Les Ikhwan al-Safa et le Christianisme." *Islamochristiana* 8:129–158.

Mawdudi, Abu al-A'la (1962–1973). *Tafhim al-Qur'an*. 6 vols. Lahore: Maktaba-i Ta'mir-i Insaniyat.

Rissanen, Seppo (1993). *Theological Encounter of Oriental Christians with Islam during Early Abbasid Rule*. Turku: Abo Akademi University Press.

Robinson, Neal (1991). *Christ in Islam and Christianity*. Albany: SUNY Press.

Schimmel, Annemarie (1975). *Mystical Dimensions of Islam*. Chapel Hill: University of North Carolina Press.

Trimingham, J. Spencer (1971). *The Sufi Orders in Islam*. London: Oxford University Press.

Trimingham, J. Spencer (1979). *Christianity Among the Arabs in Pre-Islamic Times*. London: Longman.

Wolfson, Harry Austryn (1976). *The Philosophy of the Kalam*. Cambridge, MA: Harvard University Press.

CHAPTER 16

Hindu Perspectives on Jesus

Sandy Bharat

The Sanatana Dharma, eternal religion, or Hinduism, has no historically dateable start or single founder. It is a religion that puts experience above belief, and its multitude of practices arises from the spiritual evolution of countless *rishis* or enlightened beings through the ages. It is naturally pluralistic, not narrow or divisive, and spiritual aspirants are free to seek Truth anywhere. There is no need to convert to benefit from uplifting elements elsewhere, as they can easily be absorbed into Hinduism's eclectic mix. Mahatma Gandhi asserted that "Hinduism is not an exclusive religion. In it there is room for worship of all the prophets of the world. ... Hinduism tells each man to worship God according to his own faith or dharma, and so lives at peace with all religions" (Yogananda 1998, 509). The whole purpose of the Sanatana Dharma is to help people realize Truth, and the Vedic saying that Truth is one and the paths to it many is deeply ingrained in the spiritual psyche of a Hindu.

This openness to inspiration has enabled Hinduism to withstand the various pressures that have challenged it in India: for example, Islamic and British occupation and intense Christian proselytizing. Its ability to absorb rather than deny has similarly shaped its response to new internal religions like Buddhism. In the last century, there has been a growing diaspora, and Hinduism's influence has spread far beyond India, with significant Hindu minorities in many countries of the world. It is these two developments – historical encounter in India and Hindu expansion beyond India – that have been the main impetuses for Hindu perspectives on Jesus, all of which have been shaped by the rich religious pluralism innate in Hindu spirituality.

Jesus as an Avatar

Hindus believe in one Reality (*Brahman*), but this reality can be accessed in many different ways according to the development and inclination of each individual. The

The Blackwell Companion to Jesus, First Edition. Edited by Delbert Burkett. ©2014 John Wiley & Sons, Ltd. Published 2014 by John Wiley & Sons, Ltd.

purpose of such access is to help people return to the Source by remembering their true Selves and so be free from *avidya* (ignorance) and its conditioning. It is avidya that keeps one in the spell of *maya* (delusion) and separated from God. Most Hindus believe that, to help people return to the Source, Truth is revealed through descents of divine beings. The Bhagavad Gita, a holy scripture for Hindus, affirms that divine incarnations or *avatars* come on earth when there is need to "deliver the holy, to destroy the sin of the sinner, to establish righteousness" (4, 7–8). The Sanskrit word "avatar" means to "come down." There are different levels of avatar, from God Itself incarnating to indirect incarnations, from full to partial descents, all for particular purposes. Srila Prabhupadha, founder of the International Association for Krishna Consciousness (ISKCON), taught,

> It is not a fact that the Lord appears only on Indian soil. He can advent Himself any-where and everywhere, and whenever He desires to appear. In each and every incarna-tion, He speaks as much about religion as can be understood by the particular people under their particular circumstances. But the mission is the same – to lead people to God-consciousness and obedience to the principles of religion. (n.d., 69)

Each avatar brings with her or him a special message to help remind people who they really are so that they fulfill their spiritual destiny. Their intent is not to remain on pedestals while people get stiff necks looking up at them, but to enlighten people to the truth of their own real nature so that they become like the avatars.

Some Hindus recognize Jesus as such an avatar. As Hinduism is inherently pluralistic, the inclusion of Jesus as an avatar is not an exception to any rule, but a natural inclination. The distinct difference that Hindus bring to the concept of divine incarnation will already be apparent. While Christians traditionally have believed that Jesus is the Christ, the one and only incarnation of God on earth, for Hindus he is only one of many such divine embodiments in which God has been revealed. And such revelations will continue as long as humanity needs inspiration, guidance, and example to become Self-realized. Conventionally avatars such as Lord Krishna and Lord Rama are identified in Hindu *shruti* (revelation) and *smriti* (tradi-tion) and accepted by almost everyone, but some great gurus are also perceived by their disciples to be avatars. Others, like Buddha and Jesus, may be welcomed as avatars from outside the fold of Hinduism. Of Christ, Gandhi said, "I believe that he belongs not solely to Christianity, but to the entire world, to all lands and races" (Yogananda 1998, 510). Hindus would feel the same was true of Krishna and Rama.

Swami Prabhavananda of the Ramakrishna Mission explains how Jesus fits in this scheme according to Hindu thought:

> To worship a Christ or a Krishna is to worship God. It is not, however, to worship a man as God, not to worship a person. It is to worship God Himself, the impersonal-personal Existence, in and through the incarnation; it is to adore him as one with the eternal Spirit, transcendent, as the Father and immanent in all hearts. (1963, 42)

He quotes St. Paul's testimony to the Godhead dwelling in Jesus and the affirmation in John's gospel that the Word which was in the beginning and was God was made flesh in Jesus, in order to show that Jesus was not "a mere historical man, but ... the eternal Christ, one with God from beginningless time" (1963, 43). This concept of indwelling enables Hindus to accept Jesus as an avatar in the same way that they think of Krishna and others as such, and it makes it impossible for them to think of him as the only divine incarnation.

Just as Christians gave the title of Christ to the man Jesus, so Hindus generally distinguish between Christ and Jesus. It is the Christ aspect that is important to them; this is the universal concept applicable to all avatars. Yogananda explained:

> There is a difference of meaning between *Jesus* and *Christ*. Jesus is the name of a little human body in which the vast Christ Consciousness was born. Although the Christ Consciousness manifested in the body of Jesus, it cannot be limited to one human form. It would be a metaphysical error to say that the omnipresent Christ Consciousness is circumscribed by the body of any one human being. (1975, 297)

"Christ Consciousness" (*Kutastha Chaitanya*) is universal consciousness or omnipresent intelligence. It can also be known as "Krishna Consciousness." Swami Abhedananda put it this way:

> The word "Christ" means a state. It does not mean any particular individual. The real name of the person was Jesus. He attained to that state which is called Christ – the state of realization of Truth. So each one of us will become Christ ... when we reach that attainment of God consciousness. Then we shall be able to say boldly before the world as Jesus Christ said: I and my Father are one. (1959, 40–41)

A theological understanding of the nature of avatar has not, for the ordinary Hindu, generated the same intense debate as the human-divine nature of Jesus has for Christians. Avatars are fully divine and freely choose to incarnate to help others. However, a sense of hypostatic union and anti-docetism is affirmed by some of Hinduism's great preceptors. For example, Paramahansa Yogananda indicated that even avatars are subject to their humanity while incarnated.

> They have their weaknesses, their struggles and temptations, and then, through righteous battle and right behavior, they attain victory. ... A Christ and a Krishna created perfect by God, without any effort of self-evolution on their part, and merely pretending to struggle and overcome their trials on earth, could not be examples for suffering humans to follow. (1975, 295)

In his epochal two-volume commentary on the Christian gospels, Yogananda further emphasizes this humanity and its significance: "The eternal, omnipresent, unchanging Spirit has neither a corporeal nor heavenly form called God. Nor as the Lord God Creator does He fashion a form in which He then deigns to dwell among His creatures. Rather, He makes Himself known through the divinity in worthy instruments" (2004, 3–4).

There is the sense that the great avatars, though they have individual names and stories, are not separate human beings, since, as they all emanate from the highest Source and sole Reality, they are extensions of that one Being, incarnating in different forms and times according to human need. P. V. Nath, author of two commentaries on the Bhagavad Gita, regards

> Rama as an ideal man on earth who demonstrates all the divine qualities ... and I feel the same in the life of Christ. I do not consider Rama, Krishna or Jesus as different individuals but as the same divine appearing at different times in mankind's history. The scriptures say that all the different religions are like rivers ... that end up in the ocean losing their identities, the ocean being the Supreme Power controlling the entire universe. (Nath, personal communication. January 1, 2009)

Christian exclusivist claims, backed by colonial and contemporary mission, that Jesus Christ is the only divine incarnation and savior, have hindered Hindu–Christian dialogue and engendered negative responses to Christianity and sometimes to Jesus. When Christians think of Jesus as the only Way, the contemporary scholar Ravi Ravindra believes this is an error.

> When someone opposes other teachers and other ways, that person commits a sin against the Holy Spirit in limiting its possibilities to only one mode of expression, which the person has typically encountered through an accident of birth in a particular culture. Thus we can practice idolatry even though we may reject the idols of other people. The ever-present sense of exclusivism of the way and the savior so pervasive in Christianity is, in my judgment, based on a misunderstanding of the sacred texts. Interpreting at the surface what is spoken from the depth belittles Jesus Christ, who completely denied his self and emptied himself of any feeling of particularity, as well as distinction from God. (Luke 18.18–19; Ravindra 2004, 4)

Christian mission based on exclusivist beliefs, with the consequent impulse to convert others, continues to be extremely problematic in India. Christian missionaries may now claim to be doing humanitarian work, but distrust of them is supported by more than a century of engagement. Ram Swarup and Sita Ram Goel, two Hindu writers who studied the Christian gospels, concluded that Jesus could not be excluded from the responsibility for the type of Christian activities in India (and elsewhere). Goel even named one of his books, *Jesus Christ: An Artifice for Aggression* (Goel 1994). This polemic was based on the claims made by Jesus in the gospels, by the paucity of historical evidence to support them, and by the fundamentalist understanding of these claims that fueled aggressive proselytizing. Goel (1996, xi) quotes Dr. Radhakrishnan, scholar and former President of India, telling a missionary friend, "You Christians seem to us Hindus rather ordinary people making extraordinary claims." When the missionary explained that the claims were being made on behalf of Christ, Radhakrishnan observed, "If your Christ has not succeeded in making you better men and women, have we any reason to suppose that he would do more for us, if we became Christians?"

What has been more influential is the validation of Jesus as Christ by some of Hinduism's own great preceptors, revered as equals to Jesus. Their testimonies are more effective than those of missionaries but without narrow, divisive results. Prominent amongst these Hindu spiritual giants in India in the nineteenth century was Sri Ramakrishna Paramahansa, who, in his earliest *sadhana* (spiritual practice), famously experimented with several different types of religions, including Christianity and Islam. This is one description of his subsequent encounter with Jesus as described by Swami Prabhavananda:

> One day, while Sri Ramakrishna was seated in the drawing-room of another devotee's home, he saw a picture of the Madonna and Child. Absorbed in contemplation of this picture, he saw it suddenly become living and effulgent. An ecstatic love for Christ filled Sri Ramakrishna's heart, and a vision came to him of a Christian church in which devotees were burning incense and lighting candles before Jesus. For three days Sri Ramakrishna lived under the spell of this experience. On the fourth day, while he was walking in a grove at Dakshineswar, he saw a person of serene countenance approaching with his gaze fixed on him. From the inmost recesses of Sri Ramakrishna's heart came the realization, "This is Jesus, who poured out his heart's blood for the redemption of mankind. This is none other than Christ, the embodiment of love." The Son of Man then embraced Sri Ramakrishna and entered into him, and Sri Ramakrishna went into Samadhi, the state of transcendental consciousness. Thus was Sri Ramakrishna convinced of Christ's divinity. (1963, 15)

Of course, he did not consider this divinity exclusive to Jesus.

Not only was Ramakrishna a great teacher of his time in India, attracting western disciples and admirers as well as Hindu ones, but also his foremost disciple, Swami Vivekananda, took his master's teachings to the West for the first Parliament of the World's Religions in Chicago in 1893, seen by many today as the start of the interfaith movement. Here he laid the foundations for spiritual centers that have since flourished and can now be found worldwide. It was also Vivekananda, with fellow disciples of Ramakrishna, who founded the Ramakrishna Math and Mission on Christmas Eve in 1877. Vivekananda urged the new swamis "to become Christs themselves – to pledge themselves to aid in the redemption of the world, and to deny themselves as Jesus had done" (Prabhavananda 1963, 16).

Another significant Hindu preceptor who validated the spiritual authenticity and stature of Jesus was Paramahansa Yogananda. He was invited to the United States for a Religious Congress in 1920 and remained there for the rest of his life, except for one eighteen-month return to India in the mid-1930s. Yogananda experienced the presence of Jesus many times and described how he saw him in one vision:

> A young man, he seemed, of about twenty-five, with a sparse beard and moustache; his long black hair, parted in the middle, was haloed by a shimmering gold. His eyes were eternally wondrous; as I gazed, they were infinitely changing. With each divine transition in their expression, I intuitively understood the wisdom conveyed. (1998, 558)

He also saw Jesus and Krishna together, "walking hand in hand – the Christ who prayed by the river Jordan and the Christ-na who played a flute by the river Jamuna" (1986, 170–171). Yogananda found many parallels in the stories and teachings of Christ and Krishna and taught that both incarnated in order to be emulated not just revered. "Unless you do your part, a thousand Christs come on earth would not be able to save you. You have to work for your own salvation" (1975, 292). From a Hindu perspective, this is the real second coming of Christ, the raising of human consciousness to Christ consciousness.

So why did Jesus incarnate, from a Hindu perspective? What was his purpose? Quoting John 18:37, where Jesus says, "To this end was I born, and for this cause came I into the world, that I should bear witness unto the truth," Yogananda added, "In these few words Christ spoke volumes. A child of God 'bears witness' *by his life*. He embodies truth; if he expound it also, that is generous redundancy" (1998, 566). Swami Vivekananda has a similar message: "Look only for realization and choose the best method you can find to suit you. 'Eat the mangoes' and let the rest quarrel over the basket. See Christ – then you will be a Christian. All else is talk. The less talking the better" (1969, 135).

Avatars come then to bring a new or renewed revelation of Truth, expressed through the example of their lives. This enables people to know that they can change and become like the avatars. Getting bogged down in the teachings without the accompanying inner transformation stagnates one's spiritual development. Each revelation may be for a specific people or situation at a specific time but will have universal aspects that all may find useful in their spiritual development. The teachings, while having different emphases in different lives, will still be linked and Truth-revealing, and a Hindu generally feels no need to isolate avatars even if she may be naturally drawn to one more than another.

Sri Yukteswar, exploring parallels from Christian and Hindu scriptures, asserts that all people are destined to be Christs through *Kaivalya* or unification with God.

> In this state ... the heart becomes perfectly purified and, instead of merely reflecting the spiritual light, actively manifests the same. Man, being thus consecrated or anointed by the Holy Spirit, becomes Christ, the anointed Saviour. Entering the Kingdom of Spiritual Light, he becomes the Son of God. In this state man comprehends his Self as a fragment of the Universal Holy Spirit, and, abandoning the vain idea of his separate existence, unifies himself with the Eternal Spirit; that is, becomes one and the same with God the Father. (1972, 32)

Unification with God requires effort on the part of individuals to understand what it means and how to achieve it. The lives of the great preceptors can be inspiring and show the way to this unity.

Did Christ come to take away the sins of the world, and what might this mean to Hindus? In the sense that he hoped to enlighten people to Truth, he, like all avatars, contributed to the change of heart needed to eliminate sin or avidya, the ignorance that, for Hindus, is what keeps one from God or Self-realization. In the Bhagavad

Gita (18, 66), Lord Krishna says, "Abandoning all other duties, seek refuge in me alone. Be not grieved, for I shall release you from all sins." Sri Yukteswar gave this explanation of the text's meaning: "[Sin] is that which keeps the mind attached to sense perceptions and objects of the senses. Such attachment produces restlessness, which clouds perception of the soul" (Ghosh 1980, 177). To be free from this attachment, the devotee must use yoga (union) to lift the consciousness above these disturbances and become established in the highest state, where the mind becomes stable and fixed on God. Then the yogi will be free from sin. Swami Abhedananda confirms that, for the Hindu, sin is "nothing but selfishness and that is the result of the ignorance of our true divine nature. The moment we realize that divinity in full within us, that very moment we are divine and free from all sins" (1959, 35). No mediator is required. Explaining that the word for "sin" in the original Greek is *hamartia*, which literally means "to miss the mark," Ravindra, looking at the meaning of sin in John's gospel, wrote,

> The Son of God has come into the world to show the right path so that those who would follow his way do not miss the mark and are able to fulfil their purpose on earth. [So, if we interpret the verses in John 1:19–34] to mean that our sins have already been taken away by Jesus Christ and that we are required to do nothing to receive his teaching and to live accordingly, we fool ourselves and lull ourselves to the very sleep from which Christ came to wake us up. (2004, 24)

He strongly implies that we cannot develop spiritually through a vicarious dependence on another. Swami Vivekananda is more vehement:

> It is blasphemy to think that if Jesus had never been born, humanity would not have been saved. It is horrible to forget thus the divinity in human nature, a divinity that must come out. Never forget the glory of human nature. We are the greatest God that ever was or ever will be. Christs and Buddhas are but waves on the boundless ocean which I am. Bow down to nothing but your own higher Self. Until you know that you are that very God of gods, there will never be any freedom for you. (1969, 156)

Other Hindu Appropriations of Jesus

Not all Indians attracted to Jesus see him as an avatar. Raja Rammohun Roy was founder of the Brahmo Samaj, an organization that sought to demythologize Hinduism. In his book, *Precepts of Jesus* (1820), Roy made a compilation of moral teachings from the four Christian gospels, omitting anything that portrayed Jesus as more than a moral man, such as references to his divinity or atoning death and accounts of his miracles and prophecies. He felt that these added nothing to the impact Jesus could have and indeed could not be upheld as either exclusive to Jesus or rational. Roy's awareness of current Christian scholarship on Jesus, gained through his relationship with Unitarians, was far in advance of many of the evangelical missionaries then in India who were "greatly discomfited" by developments in contemporary biblical criticism (Young 1981, 64). Joshua Marshman, one of these evangelicals, described Roy as "an intelligent heathen whose mind is as yet completely opposed to the grand design of the Saviour's becoming incarnate" (Goel 1996, 49). Some Unitarians also found Roy's blend of Hinduism and Christianity disappointing. He did not fulfill their expectations by becoming a Christian.

Like Roy before him, Mahatma Gandhi, in the twentieth century, vexed some Christians by not converting, despite his study of and interest in Christianity. It was the *ahimsa* (nonviolence) of Jesus as well as texts like the Sermon on the Mount, radiating the kind of social justice so meaningful to him, that attracted Gandhi. He was not concerned about the historicity of Jesus, and neither did the authenticity of the texts ascribed to Jesus trouble him, as the wisdom of the latter existed, whatever their source. In response to a question asking if he felt the living presence of Christ within him, Gandhi replied, "If it is the historical Jesus surnamed Christ that you refer to, I must say I do not. If it is an adjective signifying one of the names of God, then I must say I do feel the presence of God – call Him Christ, call Him Krishna, call Him Rama" (Ellsberg 1991, 38). Nor could he think of Jesus in a Christian way, as the only Son of God and only savior for the whole of humanity. Arun Gandhi (2005) wrote that, for his grandfather, salvation was "a life of compassionate service, sacrifice and satisfaction." Jesus was more of an ideal, one example of someone dedicated to service that each of us could emulate, whereas the behavior of Christian missionaries was often far from Christ-like and generally appalled him. Gandhi once said to them that "while I am strengthening the faith of the people, you are undermining it" (Ellsberg 1991, 41).

It is not at all unusual to find images of Jesus in Hindu temples alongside those of other great saints like Guru Nanak, Buddha, and, of course, Hindu avatars like Rama and Krishna. In some Indian schools you can find saintly montages that include Jesus. Supporting this eclectic inclination of Hindus, Ravindra once wrote, "I am happy to find light wherever I can, without thereby having to deny other sources of illumination or other colors of the spectrum, which together can more fully express the glory and abundance of The Vastness than any one can alone" (2004, 6).

Many Hindu centers also commemorate Jesus' birth: for example, the Ramakrishna Missions, Sai Baba's ashrams, and Self-Realization Fellowship centers and ashrams, where an all-day meditation is held every year just before December 25. This does not mean that Hindus at these centers are becoming Christians; rather, they are remembering with devotion one of the great lovers of God and developing the aspiration that they hope will help awaken their own unconditional love for the Divine Reality. Interpreting Christmas in this way, Swami Sivananda, founder of the Divine Life Society, proclaimed, "The Call of Christmas is the Call to a new Birth in the Spirit. Its message is the lofty one of the Divine Life, the Christ-life of Compassion, Truth and Purity" (1998, 23).

The crucifixion of Jesus has also awakened reverence in Hindu hearts. Yogananda (1986, 129) called it "the mightiest miracle of love." He was referring to the fact that even in agony Jesus did not lose touch with his Christ consciousness and could forgive those who had deliberately set out to hurt him, a tremendous example of spiritual equanimity and love. Even today we see how effective such examples are in the lives of people like Nelson Mandela and the Dalai Lama, who have won human admiration worldwide for the loving and forgiving way they have dealt with those who have caused them great harm. Sathya Sai Baba, a contemporary Indian guru, argued that the crucifixion was not the greatest sacrifice Jesus offered, for then he was bound and not free. Baba (1972) suggested,

> Let us pay attention to the sacrifice that Jesus made while free, out of his own volition. He sacrificed his happiness, prosperity, comfort, safety and position. He braved the enmity of the powerful. He refused to yield or compromise. He renounced the ego, which is the toughest thing to get rid of. ... He willingly sacrificed the desires with which the body torments man. This sacrifice is greater than the sacrifice of the body under duress.

The "physical" resurrection of Jesus, so crucial to Christianity, is not a unique event for Hindus, who know of similar encounters to those experienced by Jesus' disciples after his death. For Hindus, the wisdom to be extracted from this event is the need for the Christ consciousness in each of us to be resurrected. Just as St. Paul used the language of transcendence when talking of his experience of the risen Christ, Hindus too see this as primarily a numinous rather than a physical event, one that brings about a true remembering of right relationship with God. "By following the example and teachings of the great spiritual personalities, we too can attain resurrection and everlasting life" (Satprakashananda 1975, 190).

Jesus in India

Why did Hindus begin to reflect on Jesus? What prompted Hindu–Christian encounter? For some Hindus, the first encounter with Jesus began during the "missing" years referred to in the Christian gospels, when many Hindus believe that Jesus traveled to India and there learned some of the rather un-Jewish teachings that he later took back with him to Palestine. While these beliefs may not yet be widely accepted outside of India, Jesus' ideas of family renunciation and ascetic discipleship may well be rooted in some Buddhist influence. Radhakrishnan advised, "Any interpretation of the Jewish religion which ignores the total environment in which it grew up would be dangerously narrow. Two centuries before the Christian era Buddhism closed in on Palestine. The Essenes, the Mandeans, and the Nazarene sects are filled with its spirit" (1991, 158). Paramahansa Yogananda also affirms the possibility that Jesus visited India: "The parallelisms of Christ's teachings with Yoga-Vedanta doctrine strongly supports the records known to exist in India which state that Jesus lived and studied there during fifteen of the unaccounted-for years of his life" (1975, 285).

Yogananda (2004, 81–89) recounts the testimony of some who claimed to have seen these records, including the Russian traveler, Nicolas Notovitch in 1887, Swami Abhedananda of the Ramakrishna Mission in 1922, and Nicholas Roerich in the mid-1920s. Many Hindus also think that Jesus, having survived the cross through yogic skills learned in India during those "missing" years, strengthened his bond with India by returning there accompanied by his mother and his disciple Thomas and that he is buried in Kashmir. These possibilities are all explored in more detail in the interesting 2008 film, *Jesus in India*.

Hindu–Christian Encounter

Later documented accounts show encounter between Hindus and Christian missionaries from the sixteenth century onwards. The Jesus that Hindus heard about then was the Christ of the missionaries. Many of these missionaries were not well educated, and their distaste for everything Hindu led to much denigration and destruction of temples, businesses and even communities. When the British colonized India, Christianity became closely associated with western culture, white supremacy, and military oppression. Swami Abhedananda spoke of how the early Christians came to India and persecuted Hindus by "holding a gun in one hand and the Bible in the other" (1959, 45). Satguru Sivaya Subramuniyaswami believed that Hindus converted only "to have food on the table, to gain access to schools ... or to a hospital for health care, to qualify for employment or a promotion, to protect ... lands from confiscation or ... families from harm" (2002, 50).

The missionaries were still armed with literalist interpretations of their religion and a strong desire to convert Hindus. Not many were open to dialogue or aware of the riches of Hindu spirituality and practice. The quest for the historical Jesus had not yet caused many to measure their beliefs. UK Parliamentary records show that in 1813 William Wilberforce, a Christian member of Parliament, declared that "Our religion is sublime, pure and beneficent. Theirs is mean, licentious and cruel" (Hansard XXVI, 831–832; quoted in Goel 1996, 46). Much more recently, Winston Churchill's Private Secretary, John Colville, claimed that the British prime minister was so consumed by hatred of Hindus that he wanted extraordinary destruction visited upon them. In his book *The Fringes of Power*, Colville records, "The PM said the Hindus were a foul race 'protected by their mere pullulation from the doom that is due' and he wished Bert [Bomber] Harris could send some of his surplus bombers to destroy them" (Bose 2009).

Such attitudes have left a legacy of distrust that affects Hindu response to missionaries even today, and which is agitated by ongoing defamation such as a recent call in a Baptist pamphlet to pray for and "adopt" Hindus in India because more than nine hundred million of them are considered lost in darkness, in a land overshadowed by darkness (Southern Baptist Convention 1999). Christian monastics like Bede Griffiths, much admired by liberal Christians, have caused controversy among Hindus and raised uncertainty about their true motives by creating ashrams, living and dressing as Hindu *sannyasis* (ascetics), incorporating sacred Hindu texts and symbols into the Mass, yet still preaching Jesus (Goel 1996, 386–404). The tolerance of Indian Hindu society has made such innovations tenable, but outside of India where would it be possible? I have questioned before whether it would be conceivable for Hindu swamis to live in an Italian monastery dressed as Benedictines and incorporate parts of the Mass into their spiritual practice while preaching about Krishna (Bharat 2007, 7).

Of course, Hindus were already used to the emergence of religions from within India, for example Buddhism and Sikhism, before the impact of external religions associated with occupation. Hinduism is adept at surviving such challenges. Naturally pluralistic, Hindus are easily able to absorb the most amenable aspects of other traditions and inculturate them. At its own best, the Hindu way is universal, so not easily threatened. Louis Rousselet, a French writer and photographer traveling in India in the late nineteenth century, observed the truth of this when he saw a Hindu audience remain unmoved when insulted by a Protestant missionary. He commented,

> Perhaps we should be disposed to admire the courage of the missionary if the well-known toleration of the Hindoos did not defraud him of all his merit; and it is this tolerance that most disheartens the missionary, one of whom said to me, our labors are in vain; you can never convert a man who has sufficient conviction in his own religion to listen, without moving a muscle, to all the attacks you can make against it. (Quoted in Burke 1958, 145)

Toleration is not a passive acquisition but emerges from the wisdom of direct personal awareness: "A belief comes from what you have heard or read and accepted as fact, but experience is something you have actually perceived. The convictions of those who have experienced God cannot be shaken" (Yogananda 1975, 36).

Despite a shared belief in divine incarnation, in fact because of it and the nuances that separate Hindu and Christian understanding of it, the action of Christian missionaries has often deterred positive interaction between Christians and Hindus. Dena Merriam, Convenor of the Global Peace Initiative of Women, told me of stories she had heard from an Assam delegation at a conference in India that she attended (Bharat 2007, 137). Many Christian missionaries were at work in the area, denouncing Hinduism and branding Hindus as "witches." At one school, she heard of a missionary who told the children to pray to Shiva and Krishna to see what they would give them. Nothing happened. Finally he told the children to pray to Jesus, and as they did so, he put on the overhead fan that he had earlier filled with sweets. These then fell over the children so their prayers to Jesus seemed rewarded. There are many examples of such tactics, and anti-conversion anger has often turned to interreligious violence. Sheetal Shah, Director of Development for the Hindu American Foundation, commented, "Communal harmony can truly be fostered only in an environment where practitioners of all religions respect other faiths as equally valid pathways to the Divine" (Hindu American Foundation 2008).

Nath acknowledges that Christian missionaries have done a lot of social work in deprived areas but, like most Hindus, strongly objects to conversion from one religion to another.

This does not mean I am against the idea of Christ or Christianity ... I feel it is wrong, even immoral to offer gifts that could be seen by some as bribery to the poor and ignorant with the ulterior motive of converting their religion. I do not think that anyone has the right to enforce the views of his own religion on others. How many of us really do understand fully our own religious doctrines and philosophies? When we do not know it ourselves first, we have no moral right to teach the same to others ... I believe that true service to our God/Master is not in boasting of the religion we belong to or in converting others to our religion but in putting into practice the fundamentals of love, non-injury, absence of hatred and similar divine virtues. (Nath, personal communication, January 1, 2009)

For Hindus, conversion solves nothing. The key point is how religions transform people, who can learn from them all without moving from one to another. As Swami Nikhilananda stated,

Nothing wonderful will happen to the world if the entire mankind be converted to Hinduism, Christianity, Buddhism, or Islam, or to any other religion. But assuredly, something marvellous will happen if a dozen of men and women pierce the thick walls of the church, temple, synagogue and realize the Truth. (1974, xxviii)

That Truth, Hindus believe, can be found in every being and is revealed through the lives and example of those who have understood and attuned themselves to It. Ravi Ravindra affirmed that Hindus do not object to the uniqueness of Jesus Christ but only to an exclusive claim that denies the "sacred uniqueness of all other manifestations of Divine Energy, small or great" (Bharat 2007, 123). And Swami Prabhavananda wrote, "No divine incarnation ever came to refute the religion taught by another, but to fulfil all religions; because the truth of God is an eternal truth" (1963, 43).

After Swami Vivekananda's journey to the United States for the 1893 World's Parliament of Religions, and following his establishment of spiritual centers there, other swamis also moved westward and found disciples waiting for them. These western devotees generally brought with them a Christian background and conditioning that had to be accommodated. Shaunaka Rishi Das, an ISKCON priest and Director of the Oxford Centre for Hindu Studies believes that

Abrahamic context still exists, so a need for ISKCON members to integrate, necessitating dialogue with Christianity and Judaism, is very important. The basic Christian commandment of loving our neighbour will always find difficulty in expression if we do not know who our neighbour is, or if we do not understand and respect our neighbour. (Bharat 2007, 90)

Indeed ISKCON is perhaps one of the few Hindu organizations today that actively engages in evolving Hindu (specifically Vaishnava)–Christian dialogue rather than just offering its own perspectives on Jesus.

As non-ascetic Indians also moved out of India, temples and priests were needed to look after the spiritual needs of the new communities they formed. These Indian migrants initially found themselves in predominantly Christian contexts, and, generally speaking, their pluralist perspectives enabled them to integrate quietly and effectively. Paradoxically, with the rise of religious fundamentalism, there is a now a growing impetus for Hindus to be differentiated from other religious groups and to be recognized for specific contributions to society. This, together with the need for evolving Hindu communities in the West to maintain their spiritual practices and cultural integrity in the face of deepening secularism, has encouraged a cohesiveness among Hindu communities and an accompanying level of organization that has led to national initiatives giving voice to Hinduism in a new way. Hindus no longer quietly accept misuse of things sacred to them: for example, images of Krishna or Rama on shoes, or a picture of a Hindu mother and child as a Christmas stamp, with all the implications associated with that. Nor do they passively observe Christian denigration or subversion. Many anti-mission websites now exist to educate Hindus, and during a seminar on poverty and development, part of a millennium event held at the United Nations and the Waldorf Astoria hotel in New York, I witnessed Hindu swamis and their disciples stage a planned protest against Christian mission in their homeland. They could not accept the use of aid to spread mission. As one said, "We prefer to stay poor and keep our dignity."

At the same time as these developments, expanding evangelical narrowness has heightened tensions in Hindu–Christian encounter. Recent incidents have included Christian protest at prayer led by a Hindu in the US Congress and the refusal by Christian churches to allow yoga classes to take place in church halls. Subversive attempts to convert Hindus in western universities also cause distrust. For example, the International Student Ministry researched ways to engage with Hindus and found that "the students who are most effective with Hindus are the ones that are … willing to put themselves in uncomfortable situations for the sake of the gospel." The researcher concluded that "Prayer keeps us in a solid relationship with Christ" and "that God is the only one capable of changing our friends' hearts and minds" (Stephens 2008–2009, 8–10). Here remains the insidious assumption that Hindu hearts and minds need changing. It is not surprising then that Hindus can be wary of Christian invitations to dialogue. Recently only two Hindu speakers turned up at a dialogue organized by a Christian church in the United States. Others felt that it would be "another lecture of conversion … and praising Christianity" (Masis 2007).

Some Hindus believe that the Sanatana Dharma offers the resources needed for community cohesion and interreligious harmony in our religiously diverse societies. Seetha Lakhani, author of *Hinduism for Schools*, explains why:

> It carries a unique message that is proving to become increasingly relevant for the world we live in today, i.e. religious pluralism. It states that *all* religions, and all sects within religions, are equally valid routes to the same one ultimate reality. Taking on board spiritual democracy is the only way that all world religions can live side by side with each other peacefully. (Bharat 2007, 130)

This belief does not require everyone to become Hindu, only to accept the validity of other faiths. For example, Hinduism has texts similar to those in John's gospel that seem to indicate not only the uniqueness but also the exclusively salvific nature of Krishna. Yet these assertions have never created the kind of disturbance caused by similar claims made by (or for) Jesus. They have never been understood to relate exclusively to one particular historical human individual or to give proprietary rights to any particular group. "*Ekam Sat Vipraha Bahudā Vadanti* – The truth is one; sages call it by many names. ... May we never forget that parallel streams eventually merge with the same sea" (S. Roy 2005). Perhaps too Hinduism, through yoga (from *yuj*, union), offers valuable tools to ignite the engine of intuition that can lead to direct personal perception of Christ consciousness and the relationship of Jesus with that, surely a spiritual imperative and one that could silence forever the divisiveness of misunderstanding.

> To receive Christ is not accomplished through church membership, nor by outer ritual of acknowledging Jesus as one's savior but never knowing him in reality. ... To know Christ signifies to close the eyes, expand the consciousness and so deepen the concentration that through the inner light of soul intuition one partakes of the same consciousness that Jesus had. (Yogananda 2004, 26–27)

Conclusion

As we reflect on the categories in which Hindus have primarily engaged with the figure of Jesus, it is clear that the emerging perspectives have, naturally, been very Hindu in their expressions. They have not followed the trends of western scholarship or mirrored Christian theology. Jesus has been absorbed into Hindu spirituality where prompted by preceptors considered his equal, has been framed in Hindu pluralism by some as a counter to colonialist and missionary activity, and has been acknowledged by many Hindu organizations in diaspora that have attracted and engaged with western devotees.

For there to be greater depth in the Hindu–Christian exchange, there needs to be more mutuality, less christocentrism, a broader openness to what "divine incarnation" might mean. Swami Vivekananda put the Hindu position on this topic beautifully:

> Our watchword then will be acceptance, and not exclusion. ... I accept all religions that were in the past, and worship with them all; I worship God with every one of them, in whatever form they worship Him. ... Is God's book finished? [An] infinite number of pages remain yet to be unfolded. ... Salutation to all prophets of the past, to all the great ones of the present, and to all those that are to come in the future! (1993, 45–46)

This position, one that has prevailed though occupations and evangelizations of varying types in India, is the foundation of Hindu interaction with others. In recent times it has been threatened by a more militant type of Hinduism, but because it is based on the insights and realizations of Hinduism's great rishis and sages, it is unlikely ever to be undermined, unless a time comes when these great spiritual preceptors are no longer respected or taken seriously, a time when fundamentalism or secularism wipes out their spiritual legacy. Until that time, which shall surely never come, many Hindus will respond positively to Jesus as they understand and know him and offer to Christians a way to revere him that is devotional and individual and that releases him from his lonely exclusivity. Even so, the impact of this response might be limited, for Hindu emphasis on Jesus as Christ may not resonate with liberal Christians – indeed, V. K. Gokak (1979, 59), a devotee of Sai Baba, remonstrated that the human-divine integration of Jesus by the Council of Chalcedon in 451 CE was closer to the truth than the more recent quest for the historical Jesus and "illuminates our own approach to the personality of Rama, Krishna and other Avataric figures" – while for evangelicals the concept of Jesus as one of many Christs or avatars will not be acceptable.

Perhaps too, for the majority of Hindus, Jesus, though accepted and often revered, has no special significance and does not feature regularly in their normal spiritual lives. They have no real interest in the christologies that so entrance and occupy Christian theologians. Hindus in countries where Christianity is still the major religion may have some greater awareness of Jesus because of Christmas and Easter holidays, religious laws, and so on; and Hindus in India, where some Christian mission still awakens distrust and disturbance, may even have negative feelings towards Jesus as the prompt behind missionary behavior. Rabindranath Tagore said that "When missionaries bring their truth to a strange land, unless they bring it in the form of homage, it is not accepted and should not be" (Jones 1928, 35). The connection between Jesus and Christian evangelism is inevitable, as this is the context in which most Hindus have encountered him. If missionaries showed a genuine interest in and openness to the lives of great Hindu preceptors, some transformative exchange might yet take place. From this some real trust and mutuality might emerge to uplift and enlighten and deepen Hindu–Christian encounter in the years to come. Even so it may be that Gandhi expresses the real Hindu heart. In an address to missionaries, he confessed,

> Today my position is that, though I admire much in Christianity, I am unable to identify myself with orthodox Christianity. I must tell you in all humility that Hinduism, as I know it, entirely satisfies my soul, fills my whole being, and I find a solace in the Bhagavadgita and Upanishads that I miss even in the Sermon on the Mount. ... My life has been full of external tragedies and, if they have not left any visible and indelible effect on me, I owe it to the teaching of the Bhagavadgita. (Ellsberg 1991, 34–35)

References

Abhedananda, Swami (1959). *Vedanta Philosophy*. Kolkata: Ramakrishna Vedanta Math.
Baba, Sai (1972). "54. He Whom Christ Announced." Dec 24. In *Sathya Sai Speaks*. Vol. 11. Prashanthi Nilayam: Sri Sathya Sai Books and Publications Trust. At www.sathyasai. org/search/volume11/sss11-54.pdf (accessed April 10, 2010).

Bhagavad-Gita: The Song of God (1956). Trans. Swami Prabhavananda and Christopher Isherwood. London: Phoenix House.

Bharat, Sandy (2007). *Christ Across the Ganges: Hindu Responses to Jesus.* Winchester: O-Books.

Bose, Mihir (2009). "Legacy of the Raj." *New Statesman.* April 23. At www.newstatesman. com/asia/2009/04/india-british-raj-pakistan (accessed April 10, 2010).

Burke, Marie Louise (1958). *Swami Vivekananda in America.* Calcutta: Advaita Ashrama.

Ellsberg, Robert, ed. (1991). *Gandhi on Christianity.* Maryknoll, NY: Orbis.

Gandhi, Arun (2005). "Foreword." In Sankara Saranam, *God without Religion: Questioning Centuries of Accepted Truth.* East Ellijay, GA: Pranayama Institute.

Ghosh, Sananda Lal (1980). *Mejda.* Los Angeles: Self-Realization Fellowship.

Goel, Sita Ram (1994). *Jesus Christ: An Artifice for Aggression.* Delhi: Voice of India.

Goel, Sita Ram (1996). *History of Hindu-Christian Encounters (AD 304–1996).* New Delhi: Voice of India.

Gokak, V. K. (1979). *In Defence of Jesus Christ and Other Avatars.* New Delhi: M. Gulab Singh.

Hindu American Foundation (2008). "Hindu Americans Condemn Religious Violence in India: Hate Speech and Politics to Blame." October 8. At www.hafsite.org/?q=media/pr/ hindu-americans-condemn-religious-violence-india (accessed April 10, 2010).

Jesus in India (2008). DVD. Directed by Paul Davids. Los Angeles: Universal City Studios. At www.jesus-in-india-the-movie.com (accessed April 10, 2010).

Jones, Stanley (1928). *The Christ of the Indian Road.* London: Hodder & Stoughton.

Masis, Julie (2007). "Hindu-Christian Dialog Turns out One-Sided." *India New England Online.* October 15. At www.indianewengland.com (accessed April 10, 2010).

Nikhilananda, Swami (1974). *The Mandukyopanishad with Gaudapada's Karika and Sankar's Commentary.* Mysore: Sri Ramakrishna Ashram.

Prabhavananda, Swami (1963). *The Sermon on the Mount According to Vedanta.* Hollywood: Vedanta.

Prabhupada, A. C., and Bhakivedanta Swami (n.d.). *Bhagavad-Gita As It Is.* Abridged version. Los Angeles: Bhaktivedanta Book Trust.

Radhakrishnan, S. (1991). *Eastern Religions and Western Thought.* Oxford: Oxford University Press.

Ravindra, Ravi (2004). *The Gospel of John in the Light of Indian Mysticism.* Rochester: Inner Traditions.

Roy, Rammohun (1820). *The Precepts of Jesus. The Guide to Peace and Happiness; Extracted from the Books of the New Testament; Ascribed to the Four Evangelists.* Calcutta: Baptist Press.

Roy, Sudeep (2005). "Hinduism and Christianity: Poles Apart or Parallel." *Samskar.* March 9. At www.christianaggression.org/item_display.php?type=ARTICLES&id=1136087589 (accessed April 10, 2010).

Satprakashananda, Swami (1975). *Hinduism and Christianity: Jesus Christ and His Teachings in the Light of Vedanta.* Vedanta Society of St. Louis.

Sivananda, Swami (1998). "Christmas Messages of Sri Swami Sivananda: 1945, Divinise Thy Nature!" In Swami Sivananda, *Life and Teachings of Lord Jesus* (pp. 23–24). World Wide Web edn. Divine Life Society. At www.dlshq.org/download/jesus_teach.pdf (accessed April 10, 2010).

Southern Baptist Convention (1999). *Divali: Festival of Lights. Prayer for Hindus.* International Mission Board. At www.hindunet.org/HPG.pdf (accessed April 10, 2010).

Stephens, Evelyn (2008–2009). "Training Students to Reach Hindus." *Internationals on Campus.* Winter. At www.hinduismtoday.org/archives/2009/10-12/resources/InternationalsonCampusWinter2008-09.pdf (accessed April 10, 2010).

Subramuniyaswami, Satguru Sivaya (2002). "Conversion by Conviction." *Hinduism Today.* April/May/June: 50.

Vivekananda, Swami (1969). *Inspired Talks.* Madras: Sri Ramakrishna Math.

Vivekananda, Swami (1993). *The Universal Religion.* Ramakrishna Vedanta Centre, UK. (Originally published in 1900 as *Universal Religion: Its Realization. Sermon at the Universalist Church, Pasadena.*)

Yogananda, Paramahansa (1975). *Man's Eternal Quest.* Los Angeles: Self-Realization Fellowship.

Yogananda, Paramahansa (1986). *Whispers from Eternity.* Los Angeles: Self-Realization Fellowship.

Yogananda, Paramahansa (1998). *Autobiography of a Yogi.* Los Angeles: Self-Realization Fellowship.

Yogananda, Paramahansa (2004). *The Second Coming of Christ: The Resurrection of the Christ Within You. A Revelatory Commentary on the Original Teachings of Jesus.* Los Angeles: Self-Realization Fellowship.

Young, Richard Fox (1981). *Resistant Hinduism: Sanskrit Sources on Anti-Christian Apologetics in Early Nineteenth-Century India.* Vienna: De Nobili Research Library.

Yukteswar, Swami (1972). *The Holy Science.* Los Angeles: Self-Realization Fellowship.

CHAPTER 17

Buddhist Perspectives on Jesus

Peggy Morgan

No great figure who has influenced world history and cultures is the monopoly of insiders to the worldviews that developed from such figures. It is an acknowledgment of the global city within which we all live and our increased sense of the interconnectedness of world history that members of traditions who historically may never even have heard of Jesus are now articulating their views and writing surveys of them (Barker 2005; Houlden 2003).

The plural in the title of this chapter is significant and immediately highlights an emphasis that always needs to be taken into account when considering views and practices arising from or in any religious tradition, especially in its academic study. Even though we use terms such as "Buddhism" for what Wilfred Cantwell Smith called "cumulative traditions" in his seminal *The Meaning and End of Religion* (1962), Buddhism and all other traditions are plural and range over a spectrum. At the other end of the spectrum from the cumulative tradition are the individual men and women "of faith," in Cantwell Smith's terminology – the insiders, to use another term – whose voices may or may not be representative of individual others or all parts of Buddhism. Thus there are many and various Buddhisms and Buddhists, and their multi-vocal perspectives, both historical and contemporaneous, must be noted in what is reported and described, and the scholar needs to be aware that it is never possible to be exhaustive and do more than map some views and trends.

Another way of presenting the issue is in the related question, "Who Speaks for Buddhism?" – a question that challenges both the diverse opinions of insiders and the authority of outsider scholarly voices to interpret a tradition. This debate can be mapped from a variety of authors, who focus either on the distinction between insiders and outsiders (Knott 2005; McCutcheon 1999) or on particular religious traditions: for example, Islam (Esposito and Mogahed 2007), Hinduism (Gupta 2007), or Buddhism (Jackson and Makransky 2000).

The Blackwell Companion to Jesus, First Edition. Edited by Delbert Burkett. ©2014 John Wiley & Sons, Ltd. Published 2014 by John Wiley & Sons, Ltd.

It would be my contention that outsiders' voices continue to be valuable, not least for their lack of investment in any one tradition or strand of a tradition as the "true" or "right" one and their preparedness to include those who may be marginal or controversial as individuals or who belong to the more controversial movements. Scholarly outsiders seek to understand and present the range of insiders' views with as much accuracy as possible through various means. For example, ethnographic research, participant observation, textual analysis, and the phenomenologists' use of sympathetic imagination and empathetic engagement all play their part. All of these methods I attempted to use in an earlier, much shorter overview of our subject (Morgan 2003). Engagement in dialogue may also develop empathy and an ability to portray the others' perspectives. Thus academics doing historical research (Schmidt-Leukel 2001, chs. 2, 4, and 6), those working in the field of religious studies (Grünschloss 2008), and some Christian writers (Lefebure 1993) have demonstrated insights into our theme. In an early comparative work by Ninian Smart, the insights of whose work on Buddhism was often affirmed by Buddhists, there is an emphasis on the Buddhist categories that are different from Christian ones and that we might find come into play in any Buddhist view of Jesus (Smart 1963). There are also books that include the work of scholars of Buddhism and Christianity side by side, some of whom are also practitioners (Lopez and Rockefeller 1987).

Alongside an acknowledgment of the potential variety of Buddhists' perspectives on Jesus, we need to acknowledge that there are many and varied representations of Jesus that Buddhists have encountered and to which they may relate. The variety of Christian understandings of who Jesus is and what his role and place is within the Christian cumulative tradition is vast and leads to the questions of "whose Jesus have different Buddhists encountered?" and "which Jesus is this Buddhist referring to?" Colonialist backgrounds, negative experience as a Christian before a conversion to Buddhism, a desire to distinguish the historical figure and his teaching as reflected in the New Testament from later Christian doctrinal interpretations, and Christian history all come into play here. It is intended that what follows pays attention to some of the range of methodological issues indicated above.

As well as opportunities for personal encounter through the European Network of Buddhist–Christian Studies and Dialogue, through the International Society for Buddhist–Christian Studies with its journal *Buddhist–Christian Studies*, and in many other more general international interfaith conferences and local dialogue groups, there is now a considerable amount of discussion and a substantial body of published material on the perspectives of both Buddhists on Jesus and Christians on the Buddha. It needs to be noted here that in some cases the personal name Jesus is used alongside the title Buddha. More balanced in comparative terms is to ask about attitudes to Jesus and Gautama, or more doctrinally Christ and Buddha, or more comprehensively Jesus Christ and Gautama Buddha.

My own first piece of research on this topic focused on the perspectives on Jesus of the leading figures in two Buddhist new religious movements, whose authority as Buddhists some insiders of other parts of the cumulative tradition might challenge. It was prepared over twenty years ago, for a day conference at the now closed Centre for the Study of New Religious Movements, King's College, University of London, and subsequently published in the Centre's journal *Religion Today* (Morgan n.d.). This publication was the precursor of the *Journal of Contemporary Religion*, which began in 1986. I noted there my dual reaction to being invited to explore attitudes to Jesus in Buddhist new religious movements. My first reaction was that to focus on the figure that has been most central in Christian religious history reflected a not unfamiliar North Atlantic intellectual imperialism, whether of a Christian or post-Christian variety. My second reaction was a more positive one and affirmed that I would focus attention on the attitudes of Buddhists toward the central figure in the Christian tradition because there had been less written about this subject than about Christian approaches to the "others" (often called non-Christians), their "founders," and their faiths. My own essay on this subject pre-dated the appearance of the work on the same topic edited by Paul Griffiths (1990) and more recently by Perry Schmidt-Leukel (2008). A third reaction might have been that referred to above, that these new Buddhist movements and any attitudes that were expressed from within them could be seen by many Buddhists as highly peripheral; but then most scholars focusing on new religious movements, particularly at that time and perhaps still, were well aware of their controversial nature. However, I noted in the article following the conference paper that I found I could move quite smoothly between material that I collected from Theravada, Zen, or Tibetan teachers to the comments made by members of the new movements, without any sense that something dramatically different was emerging (Morgan n.d., 11).

In addition to the now considerable amount of well documented discussion of the topic in hand, I have also encountered the following reaction by some western Buddhists. They expressed hesitation and disinclination to be involved in a discussion of their understanding of Jesus, without wanting to give any explicit reasons for their hesitation. Perhaps there is an insight into this reaction in a statement by Jiyu Kennett (Peggy Kennett), who was the founding abbot of a North Atlantic Soto Zen group of monasteries. She was reported in an *Observer* magazine article in February 1985 as saying, "I haven't any views on Christ. That would be impertinent as a Buddhist." Another possibility may lie in the comment made by one of my recent informants, who, after declining to express an opinion, indicated that he saw in my questions about his view of Jesus a possible agenda and that he assumed I wanted him to say that Buddhism and Christianity were complementary. On the other hand, to quote an example that both illustrates a readiness to respond and reflects the variety in those responses, Gross summarizes from the dialogues recorded in Gross and Muck that "Buddhists were much bolder in their comments about Jesus and their assessments of Christianity than were Christians in their comments about the Buddha and Buddhism" (2000, 12). She mentions in particular Soho Machida's challenging revisions of Christian christology and theology intended "for a global era" (Machida 2000).

When listening to or reading Buddhist practitioners' insights, it is important to understand not only in which orientation of the Buddhist world they are located but also whether they are from a Christian background in some way and converts to

Buddhism, or from a traditional Buddhist culture coming to the figure of Jesus for the first time. Both Rita Gross (2000, 32–43) and Venerable Sangharakshita, whose English name is Derek Lingwood (Morgan n.d., 12), have expressed as a problem their earlier encounters with an exclusivist, evangelical Christianity with its emphasis on sin. This has colored their view of Christianity and has led them (and other Buddhists) to make a clear distinction between the teachings of Jesus and the Christian doctrines surrounding him, such as salvation from sin, with its emphasis on guilt and on Jesus' unique and exclusive relevance for all humans. They also want to distinguish between Jesus and the religion that is rooted in and has developed from his story, and which has often been oppressive of others. This is characterized as "positive Jesus ... negative Church" by Andreas Grünschloss (2008, 253). On the other hand, Kenneth Leong (1995) is negative about all institutional religion and, in presenting Zen as a way of approaching life rather than an institutional school of Buddhism, can see Jesus as an anonymous Zen Buddhist, and Zen, understood in this way, as bringing new insights into gospel stories. With all of these perspectives, it is particularly important to know the cultural background of Buddhists, though this is something that one cannot always tell from their names without a detailed insider knowledge of the Buddhist scene.

Buddhist Bases for Inclusivism and Pluralism

As a religio-philosophical system, Buddhism is much older than Christianity and emerges on the Indian subcontinent about 500 years before the common era (BCE). Therefore neither the Pali Canon, which Theravada Buddhists claim to be the oldest textual sources, nor other early works make any reference to Jesus. Nor is Jesus mentioned in later authoritative Mahayana texts, such as the Lotus Sutra, dated at about 200 CE, nor in the writings of Nichiren, which are so important to a range of new religious movements that originated among Japanese. So in the traditions for which these texts are central, there are no explicit scriptural passages about Jesus on which Buddhists can build. But Bokin Kim, a member of a modern branch of Korean Buddhism founded in 1924 called Won Buddhism, bases his ideas on the views of the founder Sot'aesan (Chungbin Park, 1891–1943) in *The Scripture of Won Buddhism* (Pal Khn Chon 1988).

Explicit scriptural references to Jesus aside, however, Buddhists might draw on some significant texts and ideas when claiming authority within their tradition for respecting a key figure in another religion or not excluding teachings from outside Buddhism. One text relates the tradition that when Upali, a lay follower of the Jain leader Mahavira (called Nigantha Nataputta in the text), became convinced that the Buddha's teaching was the truth and wanted to become his follower, the Buddha asked him to continue to respect and support his former religious teacher in the way he used to (Upali-Sutta no. 56 of the Majjhima Nikaya in the Pali Canon; quoted in Rahula 1997, 4).

Another basis for Buddhist perspectives derives from the Edicts of the Emperor Ashoka (268–239 BCE), in which he advocates that respect given to those of another tradition brings respect for one's own. In the Twelfth Rock Edict he says, "One should not honour one's own religion and condemn the religions of others, but one should honour others' religions for this or that reason" (Rahula 1997, 4–5). And without their quoting Ashoka as the authority, if there is a general impression from conversations with and writing by Buddhists about Jesus, it is "we /I have great respect for Jesus" (Yeshe 1978, 8–9). This respect is demonstrated, and for communities of Buddhists reinforced, by the fact that both Thich Nhat Hanh and the Dalai Lama have published books focused on their appreciation of Jesus, and both emphasize tolerance, though, of course, they also read him through the perspectives of Buddhist activism and meditation (Hanh 1995; Dalai Lama 1996).

There are other general features of Buddhism that might lead to a Buddhist inclusivism or anonymous Buddhism, to use terms that have developed from Christian approaches to other religions.

Anonymous Buddhism is part of the tradition. If you take the idea of bodhisattvas for example, which means somebody who is on the path to enlightenment and is in the world working for the enlightenment of sentient beings, it says that they can appear in many different guises and forms and in fact not just in an apparently religious context, but in a totally worldly context as a being working for others. So he [sic] may not appear at all to be a Buddhist, particularly, or have any beliefs of any kind; well it is quite obvious that they could also appear within the context of another religion. It would not be a question that there was some kind of duplicity going on. They may have been born in that culture and would have the inspiration of the Dhamma in its real sense although they may not know any of its terms. So they would be imparting that as well as possible under the circumstances. (Michael Hookham in Bond 1984; Hookham now uses his Tibetan name Lama Rigzen Shikpo)

Venerable Sangharakshita describes how some Buddhists move even further into a universalist position on the basis of the ideal of the bodhisattva (a being who helps others toward enlightenment):

[I]n modern times liberal Mahayanists, especially those of Japan, have begun to wonder whether the spiritual masters of other religions whose teaching on some points coincide with the Buddha's might not be Bodhisattvas. The names of Lao-tsu, Christ, Eckhart, St. John of the Cross and Guru Nanak have been proposed in this connection. Some advocates of universalism go indeed as far as to contend that all benefactors of humanity including poets, artists, scientists, etc. ... are as much bodhisattvas as those engaged in specifically religious activities. To interpret the ideal as liberally as this might be to obscure its real meaning. (1977, 202)

An affirmation of pluralism as an appropriate approach based on the Buddhist attitude to the conditioned emptiness of "views" is expressed in Judith Simmer-Brown's insider understanding in her essay "Pluralism and Dialogue" (2000). The

Zen Kyoto School philosopher Masao Abe (1915–2006) also focuses on the possibility of religious pluralism from a Buddhist point of view (1995, 17–39). Rita Gross sees the Buddhist understanding of the nature of doctrine, based on the parable of the raft and of the idea of teachings as *upaya* or *upaya kausalya* (skillful means), as leading to a pluralist position (2000, 37–43). The test of the "fruits" of a religion might also be used by pluralists, that is, whether it is capable of, skillful in, producing people of a high ethic, in the Buddhist case, for example, people with loving kindness, compassion, sympathetic joy, and equanimity (Tanaka 2008, 76).

Elsewhere the Methodist scholar Elizabeth Harris (2008) has reflected on Buddhist voices in relation to what Christians have come to call exclusivist, inclusivist, and pluralist. Of exclusivists in Buddhism, one example is the Japanese Soto Zen master Dogen (1200–1253 CE). In his *Shobogenzo* he says only "ignorant people" see religions as ultimately one. Religions are not the same, and some religions or versions of a religion can be unacceptable. The academic Andreas Grünschloss (2008, 238–249) is critical of assumed Buddhist tolerance and introduces a variety of examples that demonstrate less inclusivist and pluralist approaches than the examples given above. These examples illustrate the diversity of views that Buddhists might unpack from scriptural texts and historical examples. Schmidt-Leukel (2001) notes in his introduction that some of the historical examples explored in chapters two, four, and six of his volume are more polemical than the more contemporary and more positive interpretations.

Images of Jesus from Buddhist Perspectives

Some images of Jesus have greater appeal for Buddhists than others. We will first consider three images that have such appeal: Jesus as a bodhisattva, Jesus as compassionate, and Jesus as a spiritual teacher. We will then consider three other images that lack such appeal: Jesus as the unique Son of God, Jesus as an object of faith, and Jesus as a savior from sin.

Jesus as a bodhisattva

Bodhisattvas are beings whose primary intention and actions are focused on helping other sentient beings toward enlightenment. This involves great compassion, generosity, patience, selflessness, and many other Buddhist virtues, the practice of which might also involve suffering. Rita Gross points out that "it is easy for Buddhists to see Jesus as a bodhisattva, as there is no dogma or assumption that all bodhisattvas belong to the Buddhist religion" (2000, 47). Two of the quotations already given identify Jesus, as well as other figures outside Buddhism, with this ideal. It is an example of a category important in one religious tradition being applied to a central figure in another and is perhaps the most commonly used Buddhist starting point for affirming the figure of Jesus.

Here I can recount the story, told to me by a friend in the Tibetan Buddhist tradition, of a Tibetan Lama who had become a refugee and while in India met a Roman Catholic Christian who, in an effort to share who he was, showed him a crucifix. The Lama's initial reaction was to recoil from such a horrible tortured image as an object of religious devotion, especially since it contrasted with the image of the Buddha, peacefully serene in meditation or even on his death bed. Of course the Roman Catholic did not leave their encounter at that point but went on to tell the Lama the story of Jesus and how he came to be stretched out in agony on a cross. As part of that, he explained that Jesus' life and death were an act of selfless love intended to help the world. The Lama's face and understanding immediately changed. "Ah!" he said, "a bodhisattva."

The Dalai Lama's reflections on Matthew 5:38–48, in a chapter called "Love Your Enemy," also strongly link the bodhisattva idea with the example of Jesus (1996, 45–52). Similarly, an early 1984 exercise in dialogue presents Buddhist understandings of the bodhisattva side by side with Christian understandings of Christ, seeing both as ideal possibilities of human nature, which operate both as liberating, redemptive forces in the lives of individuals and as sources of inspiration in the quest for a just and compassionate society (Lopez and Rockefeller 1987).

But not all Buddhists or Christians would describe Jesus as a bodhisattva. Sangharakshita finds the use of this title for Jesus rather doctrinally loose and advocates a more rigorous doctrinal comparison between the perfections of the bodhisattvas, their stages along the path, and the life of Jesus (Morgan n.d., 12–13). Another challenge to the identification of Jesus with the bodhisattva ideal can be that whereas all Buddhists can aspire to be bodhisattvas, so that there are many actual and potential bodhisattvas, Christians do not aspire to *be* Jesus, who is unique as the only incarnation of God. A response to this point might be that in Philippians 2:5–8 Christians *are* encouraged to imitate Christ, to have "the mind of Christ." However, the Christian assertion of the uniqueness of Jesus is certainly an obstacle to Buddhist understandings of him and is linked with the problem of Christian exclusivism and Christians' belief in Jesus as God incarnate, themes to which we shall return.

Jesus as compassionate

The theme of compassion follows naturally from any discussion of the ideal of the bodhisattva, and it is not difficult for Buddhists to see this quality in Jesus, though Christians have more often used the term "love" as a translation of the Greek term *agape*.

Thich Nhat Hanh, however, sees the teachings of 1 Corinthians 13 as close to Buddhist teachings on love and compassion (1995, 111). Thubten Yeshe emphasizes Jesus' "exceptionally great compassion" and that his teaching was of true love not just toward family and friends but toward all beings without discrimination (1978, 11, 13–14). The Dalai Lama, commenting on Mark 3:31–35, with its saying "whoever does the will of God is my brother and sister and mother," emphasizes that "compassion is free from attachment, free from the limitation of personal bias as a genuine compassion is to have a sense of equanimity towards all sentient beings" (1996, 67–70).

Zen Master Dae Kwang regards the compassion of the Buddha, who "left home in order to find the answer to the great question of life and death in order to ... join all human beings so the world could become one" as "not much different from the suffering of Christ. In his suffering Christ became one with all creation" (Institute for World Spirituality n.d., 7). Lily de Silva, who identifies herself as both a scholar and a practitioner of Buddhism, notes that "when we turn to the Bible we get ample testimony to the compassion of Jesus" (1990, 5).

There are fewer examples that emphasize that wisdom, which is the other great Buddhist quality, especially of bodhisattvas, is demonstrated in the person and life of Jesus, though perhaps this is more likely to be present in the reflections on him as a teacher, to which we shall return. Silva does identify his wisdom and authority as important (1990, 4) as does Buddhadâsa in the section on faith below.

Jesus as a spiritual teacher

Most Buddhists seem very happy to affirm Jesus as a spiritual teacher, though for many Christians who maintain traditional doctrinal profiles this can never be but a part of his importance. The Zen master Dae Kwang Sunim, who tells us he was raised a Christian, points out that Jesus, like the Buddha, was not a scholar or a theologian but a teacher, who went right to the heart of the matter of life and death, pointing directly to human reality (Institute for World Spirituality n.d., 12). Thubten Yeshe also emphasizes that "Jesus came to this earth and presented his teachings" "to show us how to be peaceful" and that "this is an offering made with a peaceful mind and with the motivation of true love" (1978, 3, 9, 6).

The Dalai Lama uses eight passages from Christian scripture, which Christians chose for his comment, as bases for meditative reflection from a Buddhist perspective rather than for expositions of Jesus' teaching. For example, in his interpretation of the phrase "take nothing for the journey" in Luke 9:1–6, he emphasizes that setting out on the spiritual journey is important, as is sharing with others as part of our own journey. He also says that the saying points to an important spiritual idea, simplicity and modesty, and parallels Buddhist monks' use of alms bowls (1996, 95–109). Yeshe mentions the gospel sayings that point out the distraction of material things (1978, 12).

Ajahn Candasiri, an English convert to Buddhism and a nun in the Theravada Forest Tradition, said (at a retreat entitled "Paths to Wholeness: Paths to Holiness" conducted jointly with Elizabeth West at The Abbey, Sutton Courtenay, UK from November 28 to December 1 2008) that Buddhism helped her to understand the teaching of Jesus and enhanced it. The examples of Jesus' teaching she gave were the exhortation "store not up for yourself treasure on earth" (Matt 6:19) and the parables of the kingdom, such as the pearl of great price (Matt 13:45–46).

During the retreat, the two leaders read Christian and Buddhist texts in parallel. Some of the texts read were Jesus' beatitudes in the Sermon on the Mount, paralleled with the Mangala Sutta; and 1 Corinthians 13, paralleled with the Metta Sutta. On the other hand, Ayya Khema parallels 1 Corinthians 13 and the beatitudes with "the Buddha's teaching to empty the mind, to become 'poor in spirit,' to focus the mind and attain calmness of mind. ... The phrase 'kingdom of heavens' is interpreted as alluding to such higher states of consciousness" (Grünschloss 2008, 254).

Jesus as the unique Son of God

As already indicated, for Buddhists there are many buddhas and bodhisattvas who live and teach in many forms, in many aeons and in many universes, all with their own buddha fields and messages appropriate to their contexts. What Buddhists emphasize about them is that they help sentient beings through their teaching and example. So while Buddhists can accept Jesus as a wise, compassionate, skillful, and enlightened teacher, even as a Buddha (see later), they find the Christian assertion of his uniqueness difficult, and this difficulty is increased when it is part of the Christian teaching that he is the unique incarnation of a personal creator God. This view of Jesus as the unique son of God is a major stumbling block to most Buddhists. For example, George Grimm, an early German Buddhist, is prepared to say that the son of God does not exist (Schmidt-Leukel 2001, 28).

More frequently, Buddhists try to reinterpret the terms "God" and "son of God" in a way compatible with Buddhist perspectives. The Vietnamese Zen teacher Thich Nhat Hanh, whose main center is in France, points out that "discussing God is not the best use of our energy ... in Buddhism we never talk about Nirvana," which is the Buddhist concept of an Ultimate Reality (1995, 21). But when he goes on to talk about the importance of people eating together and of the eucharist, he says that "the body of Christ is the body of God, the body of ultimate reality, the ground of all existence. We do not have to look anywhere else for it. It resides deep in our own being" (1995, 31). Further on he says, "When we look into and touch deeply the life and teaching of Jesus, we can penetrate the reality of God. ... He is the son of God" (1995, 35–36). He affirms Tillich's phrase the "Ground of Being," to which Jesus is the way, a way of understanding, tolerance and loving kindness (1995, 1–57).

Ayya Khema (1923–1997), who was a German Jewish convert to Theravada Buddhism, became a nun and pioneered work for the restoration of the full or higher ordination of Theravada nuns. She regards the God-experience of Jesus as enlightenment, which puts one in mind of some liberal protestant understandings (Schmidt-Leukel 2001, 13). She also sees God as "our true nature" or affirms that "true love can be called the Divine" (Grünschloss 2008, 254).

The Tibetan Thubten Yeshe reinterprets the Christian meaning of a God who created everything as having psychological importance and not to be interpreted literally. It can be "a very effective antidote to our false pride. Our self-attachment lessens as respect for something greater than ourselves grows. This presents us with an alternative to respecting only ourselves and taking refuge only in our own petty ego" (1978, 8). He also says that "for me, 'God' means to be without superstitions causing confusion of the mind," but he follows this by emphasizing that everyone has the power and the choice to create their own peaceful mind (1978, 20–21).

The controversial Thai teacher Buddhadâsa, on the other hand, seeking what he calls the "Dhamma-meaning," the meaning behind the words, suggests that Buddhists understand "God" to be impersonal, and he connects God and Dhamma (Santikaro 2001, 83–92), assertions for which he was criticized by the German convert Nyanaponika (Schmidt-Leukel 2001, 19–20). Yet another perspective comes from the Dalai Lama, who sees the idea that all creatures are equal – in that they are all creatures of the same God, are created in the image of God, and share a divine nature – as similar to the idea of the Buddha-nature in Buddhism (1996, 49).

Shizutera Ueda writes about ideas rooted in the highly philosophical Kyoto school of Japanese Zen, which is based on the ideas of Kitaro Nishida (1870–1945) and Keiji Nishitani (1900–1990), with influences from Nietzsche and Eckhart. Here the apophatic term "nothingness" and the phrase "immanent transcendence" for the basic structure of existence are used. So "for Nishitani Jesus is the person who lives out perfectly the link of 'into-nothingness-and-out-of-nothingness' through his death and resurrection" (Ueda 2001, 48), and the faith challenge to the Christian is to die to self and let Christ live in him/her. The prolific writer and dialoguer Masao Abe, whose background is also the Kyoto philosophical school of Japanese Zen, and who links the philosophies of East and West throughout his work, uses the term *ji* (the particular, the phenomenal) and *ri* (the universal, the noumenal) to relate the *ri* of the divine logos, the justice of God the father, to becoming *ji* and flesh, the cross of Jesus Christ (1985, 97).

A very different response to the idea of God is the "attractive and reasonable possibility" articulated by Rita Gross of seeing Jesus as one of the *yidam*, Vajrayana Buddhist deities that are "anthropomorphic personifications of enlightened activity." Gross recognizes that the problematic issue of uniqueness remains, and she accepts that her idea will seem incongruent and ludicrous to many Christians and that *yidam* are "quite different from the deities of monotheistic religions" (2000, 47–50). José Ignacio Cabezón, as a Mahayana Buddhist, is comfortable with seeing Jesus as *a*, but not *the*, manifestation of a deity, as having a divine source, which was not the God of the Hebrew Bible, which would cast "moral aspersions on the identity of Jesus," nor "the God of later Christian philosophical speculation" (2000, 25–26).

Another way that Buddhists try to affirm what they think Christians might be saying in their "God" language is to suggest that the universal Christ in a transhistorical sense is Truth, Light and Life and that of this the historical Jesus is a manifestation. This universal Truth, Light and Life is what Buddhists call the *Dharmakaya*, and Gautama is also a historical manifestation or emanation-body (*nirmanakaya*) of it. The source of both Buddha and Christ is one (Kim 2000). This line of explanation leads to an identification of the Buddhist three-body doctrine (*Trikaya*) with the Christian idea of the Trinity, with the incarnate Jesus as a *nirmanakaya* (emanation-body) of the *Dharmakaya* (God). Santikaro Bhikkhu, writing of Buddhadâsa's perspectives, says that he saw various messengers, including Jesus, as expressions of *Dhamma* or God, and that there is then resonance between the saying attributed to the Buddha in the Pali canon that "whoever sees me sees the Dhamma and whoever sees the Dhamma sees me" and Jesus' words "he who has seen me has seen the Father" (John 14:9). The Dalai Lama also comments on the resonances between these sayings in relation to his comments on John 12:44–50 (1996, 111).

But this conception does not resolve the problem that Christians regard Jesus' incarnation as unique, even when *nirmanakaya* is suggested as a possible category for Jesus, since emanation bodies in Buddhism are many (Santikaro 2001, 94–95). In another vein, when Buddhists occasionally suggest that Jesus is a Buddha, the problem then is that since Buddhists teach that there is only one Buddha for every world aeon, this is difficult to sustain doctrinally.

Jesus as an object of faith

The idea of "faith," belief in or reliance on God or Christ, is another Christian concept that most Buddhists find difficult to affirm, since most Buddhist practice does not rely on an external power to achieve enlightenment. Lily de Silva, for example, focuses on love and faith in Jesus as a contrast to Buddhism. She affirms that "His role as teacher is subservient to that of saviour" and that therefore "faith is an important value in Christianity" (1990, 24), more so than in Buddhism. For her, "Jesus Christ had to utilise mainly faith-evoking devices such as miracles as it is through faith in him that his disciples could achieve salvation" (1990, 26).

Walpola Rahula, the Sri Lankan Theravada scholar monk, in his popular *What the Buddha Taught*, also contrasts Christianity and Buddhism in this regard:

> Almost all religions are built on faith – rather 'blind' faith it would seem. But in Buddhism emphasis is laid on 'seeing', knowing, understanding and not on faith, or belief. In Buddhist texts there is a word *saddhā* (Skt. *śraddhā*) which is usually translated as 'faith' or 'belief'. But *saddhā* is not faith as such but rather 'confidence' born out of conviction. In popular Buddhism and also in ordinary usage in the texts the word *saddhā*, it must be admitted, has an element of 'faith' in the sense that it signifies devotion to the Buddha, the *Dhamma* (Teaching) and the *Sangha* (The Order).
>
> According to Asanga, the great Buddhist philosopher of the 4th century A.C. (*sic*), *śraddhā* has three aspects: (1) full and firm conviction that a thing is, (2) serene joy at good qualities, and (3) aspiration or wish to achieve an object in view.
>
> However you put it, faith or belief as understood by most religions has little to do with Buddhism.

The question of belief arises when there is no seeing – seeing in every sense of the word. The moment you see, the question of belief disappears. If I tell you that I have a gem hidden in the folded palm of my hand, the question of belief arises because you do not see it for yourself. But if I unclench my fist and show you the gem, then you see it for yourself, and the question of belief does not now arise. (1997, 8–9)

Thich Nhat Hanh's emphasis affirms much in Rahula's description, but he also goes further in linking Buddhist and Christian perceptions:

In Buddhism faith means confidence in our and other's abilities to wake up to our deepest capacity of loving and understanding. In Christianity faith means trust in God, the One who represents love, understanding, dignity and truth. When we are still, looking deeply, and touching the source of our wisdom, we touch the living Buddha and the living Christ in ourselves and in each person we meet. (1995, 12)

In a chapter on John 12:44–50 entitled "Faith," the Dalai Lama emphasizes the importance of faith in one's spiritual practice. Here he agrees with Rahula's emphasis and says that "the Tibetan word for faith is *day-pa*, which might be closer in meaning to confidence, or trust." But he then describes three different levels of the term, which he says are applicable to both Christianity and Buddhism:

I feel that all three types of faith can be explained in the Christian context as well. For example a practicing Christian, by reading the Gospel and reflecting on the life of Jesus, can have a very strong devotion to and admiration for Jesus. That is the first level of faith, the faith of admiration and devotion. After that, as you strengthen your admiration and faith, it is possible to progress to the second level, which is the faith of aspiration. In the Buddhist tradition, you would aspire to buddhahood. In the Christian context, you may use the same language, but you can say that you aspire to attain the full perfection of the divine nature, or union with God. Then, once you have developed the sense of aspiration, you can develop a deep conviction that it is possible to perfect such a state of being. That is the third level of faith. I feel that all of these levels of faith are equally applicable in both the Buddhist and Christian contexts. (1996, 112–113)

A positive evaluation of faith in the Christian sense is given by Bokin Kim. The understanding of "God" as *Dharmakaya*, as Truth, Light, and Life (see above), means that for Kim faith is "reliance on this other power" (2000, 54): "Faith as assurance is to go beyond ego-boundary and to point to the Truth, Light and Life. As Paul says 'I no longer live, but Christ lives in me' (Galatians 2:20). That is, by faith, the ego-boundary is gone and eternity is gained" (2000, 56). Kim emphasizes that Buddhists rely on self-power, while Christians go beyond the ego-boundary by relying on other-power. The terms for these distinctions, which feature largely in Far Eastern forms of Buddhism, are *tariki* (other-power) and *jiriki* (self-power). The positive attitude to Christian faith in the Korean Won movement to which Kim belongs may be linked to its founder's study of Protestant Christianity.

Jesus as a savior from sin

Most Buddhists do not agree with the Christian teaching that human beings are in the grip of original sin, from which in some way Jesus on the cross redeemed them. If there is any original condition for Buddhists, it is ignorance, which can be overcome through following the wise path of a skillful spiritual teacher.

Soho Machida does use the language of original sin but dramatically asserts that "the fact that Jesus came to be born with flesh in this world means that he chose to stand on common ground of sin with us" (2000, 59). In his view, Jesus is sinful, and his suffering and the crucifixion are to atone for his own sin. He sees the Christian idea of original sin as like the Buddhist idea of karma, so that Jesus has a "karmic body." His is perhaps the most dramatic attempt to reinterpret the Jesus figure, in his wish to move toward a new christology for a global era, and he sees the need for the visual portrayal of a "glorious figure of Christ as standing at the crossing of humanity and divinity by overcoming the eternal dichotomy of spirit and flesh, good and evil" (2000, 73).

Writing about early Buddhist–Christian controversies in seventeenth-century China, the academic Iso Kern reports that the Chinese monk Ouyi Xhixu is critical of the idea of Jesus, as the incarnated Lord of Heaven, buying back, ransoming mankind from their sins, and he identifies the law of karma, each person's responsibility for his/her actions, as the problem. Kern does, however, point out that the bodhisattvas of the *jataka* tales suffer for others and that, in the Mahayana text the *Raja-parikathara-pratnamali*, a bodhisattva vows that "the evil deeds of others will ripen as fruits of my own and that my good deeds will ripen as fruits of others" (2001, 40–41). So, as with the interpretation of the idea of faith, close investigation shows that the contrasts of Buddhist and Christian ideas are not so clear as some at first sight assert.

Parallels between Jesus and Gautama

Another way that Buddhists affirm Jesus is by noticing parallels between him and his story and Gautama Buddha. For example, the story of Asita, the wise man who gave astrological predictions about the Buddha, parallels the story of Simeon, who made predictions about Jesus (Luke 2:25–35; Hanh 1995, 45). Both Jesus and Gautama began their careers with a series of temptations, Jesus from Satan and Gautama from Mara. Ajahn Candasiri, at the Paths to Wholeness retreat mentioned above, said she thought that Jesus and the Buddha dealt in the same way with Satan and Mara. Hanh offers further parallels in that neither owned material possessions, both were healers, and both were welcoming to women (1995, 72). Various commentators also affirm the ideal of celibacy shared by Jesus and Gautama.

Buddhadâsa points out that Jesus, like the Buddha, criticized and corrected "hypocritical and superficial devotionalism, that is belief and adherence to mere beliefs, rituals and traditions" (Santikaro 2001, 94). Thubten Yeshe points out that "the thoughts and actions of highly realised beings are often contrary to those of the multitudes" (1978, 10).

Nikkyo Niwano (1906–1999), the Rissho Koseikai leader, in his interpretation of the Lotus Sutra, indicates that when Shakyamuni Buddha, Jesus Christ, and Nichiren began to preach, all were attacked by enemies and underwent religious persecution. Suffering and even persecution may be part of the life-journey of a Buddha, such as the hatred of Gautama seen in the story of Devadatta, each of whose efforts to overthrow the Buddha ended in failure.

Alongside these similarities, contrasts also appear. The story of the massacre of the innocents that accompanied Jesus' birth has no parallel in the life of Gautama. Gunananda, in the polemic of the Panadura Debate in Ceylon in 1873, saw this killing of children as indicative of the violent and capricious God whom Christians worship.

Buddhas also do not suffer a violent death as Jesus did. The life of Gautama ended peacefully, and the image of the Buddha reclining serenely at death is a central icon and an ideal for Buddhists. The central Christian icon is that at which the Tibetan Lama expressed repugnance: the image of a suffering, agonized, crucified Jesus on the cross.

Thich Nhat Hanh explains this contrast by highlighting the different contexts in which they were living, Jesus in a chaotic and the Buddha in a tolerant society. He compares the crucifixion of Jesus not with the death of Gautama, but with the self-immolation of the Vietnamese monk Thich Quang Duc in 1963. "When Jesus allowed himself to be crucified he is acting in the same way, motivated by the desire to wake people up, to restore understanding and compassion, and to save people" (1995, 81). Ajahn Candasiri, at the Paths to Wholeness retreat, also affirmed the death of Jesus, saying that Ajahn Sumedho (the senior abbot of the UK forest monasteries, administered by the English Sangha Trust) often comments on the crucifixion as an example of how we hold our ground through suffering.

Conclusion

All of these examples take us back to the general points made in the introduction. The perspectives of the individual Buddhist commentators depend very much on their own background as well as the contexts in which they are writing or speaking and their intention in those contexts. The polemic of the Panadura debate can only be fully understood against the story of missionary and colonialist encounters in Sri Lanka (Harris 2006). An increase in face-to-face dialogue and a sense of the need for understanding and harmony between those with a spiritual orientation means that the contemporary examples and comments by Buddhists on Jesus are usually of a different kind, though not without questions. Many are very well informed. They are also challenging, in the very different perspectives they bring to the figure and the sense that christologies, just as they always have, emerge anew in new cultural contexts. These are provided by the contemporary arenas of both the academic study of religions and interfaith dialogue.

References

Abe, Masao (1985). *Zen and Western Thought*. London: Macmillan.

Abe, Masao (1995). *Buddhism and Interfaith Dialogue*. London: Macmillan.

Barker, Gregory A., ed. (2005). *Jesus in The World Faiths: Leading Thinkers from Five Religions Reflect on His Meaning*. Maryknoll, NY: Orbis.

Bond, C. (1984). "Religious Encounters: A Practical Exercise in Dialogue." Unpublished dissertation. Westminster College, Oxford.

Cabezón, José Ignacio (2000). "A God, but Not a Savior." In Rita M. Gross and Terry C. Muck (eds.), *Buddhists Talk About Jesus: Christians Talk About The Buddha* (pp. 17–31). New York, London: Continuum.

Dalai Lama (1996). *The Good Heart: A Buddhist Perspective on the Teachings of Jesus*. Boston: Wisdom Publications.

Esposito, John L., and Dalia Mogahed (2007). *Who Speaks for Islam?* New York: Gallup Press.

Griffiths, Paul. J., ed. (1990). "*Buddhist Perceptions of Christianity in the Twentieth Century*." In *Christianity Through Non-Christian Eyes* (pp. 135–190). Maryknoll, NY: Orbis.

Gross, Rita M. (2000). "Meditating on Jesus." In Rita M. Gross and Terry C. Muck (eds.), *Buddhists Talk About Jesus: Christians Talk About The Buddha* (pp. 32–51). New York, London: Continuum.

Gross, Rita M., and Terry C. Muck, eds. (2000). *Buddhists Talk About Jesus, Christians Talk About The Buddha*. New York, London: Continuum.

Grünschloss, Andreas (2008). "Buddhist-Christian Relations." In Perry Schmidt-Leukel (ed.), *Buddhist Attitudes to Other Religions* (pp. 237–268). St. Ottilien: EOS.

Gupta, Ravi (2007). "Who Speaks for Hinduism?" *Oxford Magazine* 267 (Michaelmas): 10–11.

Hanh, Thich Nhat (1995). *Living Buddha, Living Christ*. New York: Riverhead.

Harris, Elizabeth J. (2006). *Theravada Buddhism and the British Encounter*. London: Routledge.

Harris, Elizabeth J. (2008). "Buddhism and the Religious 'Other.'" *Interreligious Insight* 6 (3; July): 32–39.

Houlden, Leslie, ed. (2003). *Jesus in History, Thought, and Culture*. 2 vols. Santa Barbara, CA: ABC-Clio.

Institute for World Spirituality (n.d.). *The Buddhist-Christian Retreat, July 1996*.

Jackson, Roger, and John Makransky, eds. (2000). *Buddhist Theology: Critical Reflections by Contemporary Buddhist Scholars*. London: RoutledgeCurzon.

Kern, Iso (2001). "Buddhist Perception of Jesus and Christianity in the Early Buddhist-Christian Controversies in China during the 17th Century." In Perry Schmidt-Leukel (ed.), *Buddhist Perceptions of Jesus* (pp. 32–41). St. Ottilien: EOS.

Kim, Bokin (2000). "Christ as the Truth, the Light, the Life, but a Way?" In Rita M. Gross and Terry C. Muck (eds.), *Buddhists Talk About Jesus: Christians Talk About The Buddha* (pp. 52–58). New York, London: Continuum.

Knott, Kim (2005). "Insider/Outsider Perspectives." In John R. Hinnells (ed.), *The Routledge Companion to The Study of Religions* (pp. 243–258). Abingdon and New York: Routledge.

Leong, Kenneth S. (1995). *The Zen Teachings of Jesus*. New York: Crossroad.

Lefebure, Leo D. (1993). *The Buddha and the Christ*. Maryknoll, NY: Orbis.

Lopez, Donald S. Jr., and Steven C. Rockefeller, eds. (1987). *The Christ and the Bodhisattva*. Albany: SUNY Press.

Machida, Soho (2000). "Jesus, Man of Sin: Toward a New Christology in the Global Era." In Rita M. Gross and Terry C. Muck (eds.), *Buddhists Talk About Jesus: Christians Talk About The Buddha* (pp. 59–73). New York, London: Continuum.

McCutcheon, R. T., ed. (1999). *The Insider/Outsider Problem in the Study of Religion: A Reader*. London: Cassell.

Morgan, Peggy (n.d.). "Buddhist Movements and Jesus." *Religion Today: A Journal of Contemporary Religions* 5 (1 & 2): 10–15.

Morgan, Peggy (2003). "Buddhism." In Leslie Houlden (ed.), *Jesus in History, Thought, and Culture* (pp. 1:142–146). 2 vols. Santa Barbara, CA: ABC-Clio.

Pal Khn Chon, trans. (1988). *The Scripture of Won Buddhism*. Iksan, Korea: Won Buddhist Publishing.

Rahula, Walpola ([1959] 1997). *What the Buddha Taught*. Oxford: One World.

Sangharakshita (1977). *The Three Jewels*. Windhorse Publications.

Santikaro Bhikkhu (2001). "Jesus and Christianity in the Life and Work of Buddhadâsa Bhikkhu." In Perry Schmidt-Leukel (ed.), *Buddhist Perceptions of Jesus* (pp. 80–105). St. Ottilien: EOS.

Schmidt-Leukel, Perry, ed. (2001). *Buddhist Perceptions of Jesus: Papers of the Third Conference of the European Network of Buddhist-Christian Studies (St. Ottilien 1999)*. In cooperation with Thomas Josef Götz and Gerhard Köberlin. St. Ottilien: EOS.

Schmidt-Leukel, Perry, ed. (2008). *Buddhist Attitudes to Other Religions*. St. Ottilien: EOS.

Silva, Lily de (1990). Essay with no title. *Dialogue* (Tulana Institute) 17: 1–28.

Simmer-Brown, Judith (2000). "Pluralism and Dialogue." In Roger Jackson and John Makransky (eds.), *Buddhist Theology: Critical Reflections by Contemporary Buddhist Scholars* (pp. 312–330). London: RoutledgeCurzon.

Smart, Ninian (1963). "The Work of the Buddha and the Work of Christ." In S. G. F. Brandon (ed.), *The Saviour God* (pp. 160–173). Manchester: Manchester University Press. Reprinted in J. Shepherd (ed.), *Ninian Smart on World Religions*. Vol. 1, Sect. 4. Abingdon: Ashgate, 2009.

Smith, Wilfred Cantwell (1962). *The Meaning and End of Religion*. New York: Macmillan.

Tanaka, Kenneth (2008). "Buddhist Pluralism: Can Buddhism Accept Other Religions as Equal Ways?" In Perry Schmidt-Leukel (ed.), *Buddhist Attitudes to Other Religions* (pp. 69–84). St. Ottilien: EOS.

Ueda, Shizutera (2001). "Jesus in Contemporary Japanese Zen. With Special Regard to Keiji Nishitani." In Perry Schmidt-Leukel (ed.), *Buddhist Perceptions of Jesus* (pp. 42–59). St. Ottilien: EOS.

Yeshe, Thubten (1978). *Silent Mind, Holy Mind: A Tibetan Lama's Reflections on Christmas*. Ulverston: Wisdom Culture.

PART IV

Philosophical and Historical Perspectives on Jesus

18   Skeptical Perspectives on Jesus' Resurrection   285
Michael Martin

19   The Quest for the Historical Jesus: An Overview   301
David B. Gowler

20   The "Jesus" of the Jesus Seminar   319
Robert J. Miller

21   The Quest for the Historical Jesus: An Appraisal   337
Helen K. Bond

CHAPTER 18

Skeptical Perspectives on Jesus' Resurrection

Michael Martin

Skeptics typically attack two traditional beliefs about Jesus: the historicity of Jesus and the resurrection of Jesus. Some skeptics have maintained that the best account of biblical and historical evidence is the theory that Jesus never existed; that is, that Jesus' existence is a myth (Wells 1999). Such a view is controversial and not widely held even by anti-Christian thinkers. In any case, it will not be considered here. The most widely criticized Christian belief and the one evaluated here is that Jesus arose from the dead. Obviously any critique of this view must assume that Jesus was a real person.

Background of the Question

Orthodox Christianity assumes that Jesus was crucified on the order of Pontius Pilate and was then resurrected. Thus the Apostles' Creed proclaims that Jesus "suffered under Pontius Pilate, was crucified, dead, buried; he descended into hell; the third day he rose again from the dead." The Nicene Creed maintains that Jesus "was crucified also for us under Pontius Pilate; He suffered and was buried; and the third day he rose again according to the Scriptures." Furthermore, the resurrection has been considered by Christians to be a crucial element of Christian doctrine. For example, nearly 2000 years ago, Paul proclaimed, "If Christ has not been raised, then our preaching is in vain and your faith is in vain. We are even found to be misrepresenting God. ... If Christ has not been raised, your faith is futile" (1 Cor 15:14–17). Many contemporary Christians seem to agree. Hugh Anderson, a New Testament scholar, writes,

> With all assurance we can say that, save for Easter, there would have been no New Testament letters written, no Gospels compiled, no prayers offered in Jesus' name, no

The Blackwell Companion to Jesus, First Edition. Edited by Delbert Burkett. ©2014 John Wiley & Sons, Ltd. Published 2014 by John Wiley & Sons, Ltd.

Church. The Resurrection can scarcely be put on a par with certain other clauses in the Apostles' Creed – not if the New Testament is our guide ... Easter, therefore, is no mere addendum to other factors in the story of Jesus Christ; it is constitutive for the community's faith and worship, its discipleship and mission to the world. (1964, 186–187)

Terry Miethe, a Christian philosopher at Oxford, has maintained that " 'Did Jesus rise from the dead?' is the most important question regarding the claims of the Christian faith" (1987, xi).

Despite the importance of the resurrection to Christianity, expressions of skepticism concerning it existed at the very beginning of Christianity and have continued to this day (Avolas 2007). In late antiquity, expressions of unbelief regarding the resurrection appeared in the New Testament itself: Jesus' enemies spread the rumor that his body was stolen (Matt 28:13–15); Thomas doubted at first that Jesus had risen, though later was convinced (John 20:24–29); and Jesus ate food to convince his followers of his bodily resurrection (Luke 24:36–43). Gnostic Christians who denied the bodily resurrection of Jesus maintained that Jesus as he was usually pictured was a fiction and that the real Jesus was pure spirit. In 248 CE, Origen, a distinguished father of the church, wrote *Contra Celsus*, attacking the anti-resurrection arguments of Celsus, a pagan philosopher. Anti-resurrection arguments in the Middle Ages and Renaissance appeared in Europe in Jewish sources, and in Arabia in Islamic literature. In the eighteenth century, Herman Samuel Reimarus (1694–1768), a German scholar, critically examined evidence for the resurrection, such as that of the Roman guard in the Gospel of Matthew and the other Christian testimony. In the nineteenth century, David Friedrich Strauss (1808–1874), another German scholar, extended Reimarus' criticisms. In the twentieth century, the criticisms of Celsus, Reimarus, and Strauss were refined, elaborated, and combined with new methods of textual analysis and archeological findings, producing even more powerful arguments. In the later part of the century, the Jesus Seminar, formed by Robert Funk and consisting of a group of liberal Bible scholars, voted on the probable historicity of individual New Testament passages. Passages about the resurrection were usually given a low probability rating (Jesus Seminar 1998).

Nevertheless, philosophical apologists such as William Lane Craig (Copan and Tacelli 2000), Steve Davis (1993) and Richard Swinburne (2003) still defend the resurrection. Since Swinburne's defense is the most philosophically sophisticated, let us examine the case against the resurrection and what Swinburne can say in its defense.

The Improbability of the Resurrection

One strong argument against belief in the resurrection of Jesus is the following (Martin 2002, 291–292):

1   A miracle claim is initially improbable relative to our background knowledge.
2   If a claim is initially improbable relative to our background knowledge and the evidence for it is not strong, then it should not be believed.
3   The resurrection of Jesus is a miracle claim.
4   The evidence for the resurrection is not strong.

---

5   Therefore, the resurrection of Jesus should not be believed.

While premise 2 is a self-evident proposition, and premise 3 is a definition, premises 1 and 4 require further justification.

Premise 1: the initial improbability of miracle claims

Why suppose that the resurrection, as a miracle claim, is initially improbable? Traditionally a miracle is defined as a violation of a law of nature caused by the intervention of God. The improbability of miracle claims in the traditional sense can be understood in the following way. Let us suppose for the sake of the argument that theism, belief in the existence of God, is true. Can we then expect God to intervene in the natural course of events and violate a natural law? We cannot. If theism is true, then miracles in the sense of divine intervention are *possible*, since there is a supernatural being who *could* bring them about, but it does not follow that such miracles are more likely than not to occur. Indeed, God would have good reasons for never using miracles to achieve his purposes. Consider that this kind of a miracle cannot be explained by science and, indeed, is an impediment to a scientific understanding of the world. Consider also that great difficulties and controversies arise in identifying miracles. Whatever good effects miracles might have, then, they also impede, mislead, and confuse. Since an all-powerful God would seem to be able to achieve his purposes in ways that do not have unfortunate effects, I conclude that there is actually reason to suppose that the existence of miracles is initially improbable even on a religious worldview (Overall 2003).

However, for the sake of the argument, let us assume with Christian apologists like Richard Swinburne (1992, 71–72) that miracles in the sense of divine intervention are probable given God's existence. This assumption is perfectly compatible with the thesis that in any particular case a miracle is unlikely. Consider the following analogy. It is overwhelmingly probable that in a billion tosses of ten coins all ten coins will turn up heads at least once, but it is extremely unlikely that in any given case all ten coins will come up heads. In the same way, even if Swinburne were correct that, given the existence of God, some miracles are probable, it would be extremely unlikely that in any given case a miracle has occurred.

So far I have argued that miracle claims are initially improbable even on the assumption of theism. From the perspective of atheists and believers alike, miracles are rare events. In addition, from a historical point of view, religious believers themselves have often rejected miracle claims understood as violations of laws of nature. Even thoughtful believers in miracles admit that *most* miracle claims turn out to be bogus on examination; that in most cases of alleged miracles, no law of nature has been violated, and no action of God need be postulated. Even believers say that relatively few claims ultimately withstand critical scrutiny. Thus, for example, although the Catholic Church has investigated thousands of claims of miraculous cures at Lourdes, it has rejected most of these as unproven. Indeed, the number of officially designated miracles at Lourdes is less than eighty (Martin 1990, 202–207). Inductively, therefore, any new claim made at Lourdes is initially likely to be spurious as well. The same is true of other miracle claims: sophisticated religious believers consider most to be invalid. Thus, for example, Steve Davis, a well-known Christian philosopher and apologist and believer in miracles, argues that "naturalistic explanations of phenomena ought to be preferred by rational people in the vast majority of cases" (1993, 13). His position is perfectly compatible with both the existence of miracles and the possibility of obtaining strong evidence for them. It does imply, however, that, even on the assumption of theism, *initially* any given miracle claim is incredible and that to overcome this initial improbability strong evidence must be produced.

The resurrection and God's purpose

So far, I have shown that, in general, particular miracle claims are initially unlikely even in a theistic framework. Is the claim that Jesus arose from the dead an exception to this rule? Could God have had special purposes that made it necessary to cause the resurrection? Could it be the case that, although any ordinary given miracle claim is initially unlikely, the claim that the resurrection occurred is initially likely? What special purpose of God would make the resurrection initially likely?

According to Swinburne, it is likely that God would make it possible for human beings to atone for their sins and, consequently, it is likely that God's son would become incarnated as a human and would die in order to do this (1992, 71–72). I have argued in detail elsewhere that all the historically important theories of the atonement either fail to explain why God sacrificed his son for the salvation of sinners or else make the sacrifice seem arbitrary (Martin 1991, 252–263). An all-powerful God could have us atone for our sins in many ways that would not involve his son at all or without his son's death and resurrection. So it is not as clear as Swinburne thinks that God incarnate would die to atone for human sins.

But for the sake of the argument, let us suppose that it is likely that God would sacrifice his son for the redemption of humanity. Still it would not follow that the incarnation and the resurrection are themselves likely, for these are *particular* historical events that occurred at *particular* times and places. However, God could have become incarnate and died for sinners on an indefinite number of other occasions.

There does not seem to be any a priori reason to suppose that he would have been incarnated, or would have died, at one particular time and place in one particular way rather than at many other times and places in many other ways. Consequently, even if *some* incarnation and resurrection or other is likely, there is no a priori reason to suppose that he would have become incarnate and would have died as Jesus in first-century Palestine on a cross and would have been resurrected in relative obscurity. Indeed, given the innumerable alternatives at God's disposal, it would seem a priori unlikely that the incarnation and resurrection would have taken place where and when and how they allegedly did.

Consider the following analogy, which I adapt from one used by Swinburne (1992, 71). Suppose a parent has decided to pay her child's debt. Suppose that this parent can do this in an enormous number of different ways and that there is a wide time span in which the parent can act. Suppose we know of no reason why the parent might use one of these ways rather than another or act at one time rather than another. Although it is likely that, given the parent's decision, she will pay her child's debt in some way at some future time, it is unlikely that she will settle her child's debt by a cash payment on July 8 of this year. Indeed, it is initially improbable that she will do so. Similarly, given all of God's options, it is initially unlikely that his son would have become flesh and then have died in the way he is portrayed to have done in the scriptures.

Premise 4: the general insufficiency of most of the evidence

Although it is not widely recognized, Jesus' resurrected body was supposedly transformed into a living supernatural body. Thus all of the following statements are supposed to be true:

1. Jesus is unable to be injured at any time after 33 CE
2. Jesus is unable to die at any time after 33 CE
3. Jesus is unable to age at any time after 33 CE
4. Jesus is unable to be sick at any time after 33 CE
5. Jesus is able to move at will instantaneously from place to place at any time after 33 CE
6. Jesus is able to walk through solid walls at any time after 33 CE

Let us call Jesus' being brought back to life with these attributes the strong sense of resurrection, and being brought back to life without supernatural attributes the weak sense of resurrection. Most of the evidence cited for Jesus' resurrection, even if free from other problems, gives no support to the resurrection in the strong sense. For example, appeals to the empty tomb, the conduct of the disciples, many of the post-resurrection appearances, and the rise of Christianity at best support resurrection in the weak sense. Indeed, the only relevant evidence apologists can give for resurrection in the strong sense seems to be descriptions of Jesus' post-resurrection appearances in which he is alleged to have manifested supernatural abilities at some particular time and place.

This means that the entire burden for the claim that Jesus was resurrected in the strong sense rests on these few descriptions. But even if such descriptions were accurate, Jesus' resurrection in the strong sense would not be proven. For example, suppose one had reason to believe that Jesus was not injured by some event that injured his disciples. This would not be adequate to support statement 1, that "Jesus is unable to be injured at any time after 33 CE." In order to do that, one would need either to infer this statement from some well-established general theory or to produce evidence of Jesus not being injured in a wide range of circumstances after 33 CE that normally injury people (Cavin 2005). But no such theory is available, and this sort of evidence is lacking.

The lack of relevant evidence for the resurrection in the strong sense would alone be a devastating objection to believing that it actually happened. But when it is combined with our previous argument, that the resurrection is initially improbable, it seems like conclusive grounds for skepticism.

I now turn to the evidence for the resurrection in the weak sense, as this is presented by Swinburne. I will consider whether a case can be made against the resurrection even in the weak sense and show that it can. The reason is simple. Although the relevant evidence for the resurrection in the weak sense is stronger than the relevant evidence for the resurrection in the strong sense, it is not strong enough to overcome the initial improbability of the resurrection.

Swinburne's Argument Expanded

In *The Resurrection of God Incarnate* (2003), Swinburne clarifies and expands his argument for the resurrection. I will now show that his argument fails, without assuming the strong sense of resurrection; that is, I will only assume that he claims Jesus was resurrected in the weak sense.

Swinburne makes it clear that his defense is based on what he considers the rather modest background assumptions that he defended in his earlier work. Among these are the assumptions that God's existence is as probable as not and that, given his existence, God's incarnation and resurrection are as probable as not (2003, 211). Swinburne maintains that these assumptions, when combined with the failure of alternative explanations, certain epistemological principles, and historical evidence, yield the near certain conclusion that Jesus is the resurrected incarnated God. The evidence he has in mind consists of Jesus' "perfect" moral life, Jesus' post-resurrection appearances, and the empty tomb. By alternative explanations, Swinburne means explanations such as hallucinations or fraud. He assumes the epistemological principle—what he calls the principle of testimony – that "other things being equal we should believe what others tell us that they have done or perceived – in the absence of counter-evidence" (2003, 12–13).

The probability that God exists

Swinburne makes it clear that, when one considers the probability of the resurrection, it is important to address the question of the probability of God and the question of how likely it is that God would intervene (2003, 202–203). For without making modest background assumptions about the probability of God and the incarnation, the historical evidence might not make the resurrection probable. There is good reason, however, for rejecting Swinburne's background assumption that God exists: his concept of God is incoherent (Martin 1990; 1997). Swinburne's God does not know the future, is disembodied, and is all-knowing. There are at least three conceptual problems with this view of God. (1) One is that if God cannot know anything about the future, he consequently cannot know if anything is morally right or wrong. (2) Another is that if God is disembodied, he cannot be all-knowing. (3) And a third is that if God is all-knowing, he cannot be morally perfect (Martin 2005, 454).

1. According to Swinburne, although God is all-knowing, it is logically impossible for him to know what human beings will freely do. Unfortunately, this view of God's all-knowingness both limits God's knowledge far more than Swinburne acknowledges and creates problems about the moral nature of God (Martin 1990, 297–302). Not only can God not know what human beings will freely do, he cannot know what he himself will do. This means that God cannot know whether any physical event will take place, since he always has the option of intervening in the workings of natural law. Consequently, he cannot know now whether *any* particular event will occur in the future. Thus he cannot know what the future free actions of his creatures will be; he cannot know what his own future actions will be; and he cannot know if any event governed by natural laws will occur, since he cannot know now if he will intervene in the natural course of events. This seems to cover all possible future events.

But if God cannot know anything about the future, he cannot know if his past actions were morally correct – given any moral theory that takes the future consequences of a decision at least *partly* into account – for their correctness will depend (at least in part) on what happens in the very distant future. No matter how good an action seems to be up to time t_1, new consequences after t_1 can change the assessment. It is difficult, then, to see how Swinburne can continue to think of God as morally perfect. As I have argued elsewhere, a morally perfect being is not just a being that never does anything wrong. A morally perfect being's action must be based on the being's knowledge (Martin 1990, 299). So Swinburne's God is not morally perfect, let alone all-knowing, unless he adopts an extreme deontological moral theory: that is, a moral theory in which consequences play no role. Swinburne gives us no reason, however, to suppose that he embraces such a theory.

2. In addition, Swinburne's assumption that God is disembodied conflicts with his assumption that God is all-knowing (Martin 1990, 286–292). If God is disembodied, he does not know, for example, how to swim, since only embodied beings have such knowledge.

3. Moreover, Swinburne's assumption that God is all-knowing conflicts with his assumption that God is morally perfect. To be all-knowing, God would have to possess, for example, the knowledge by acquaintance that a sadist derives from torturing children. In order to be all good, however, God cannot have this knowledge (Martin 1990, 286–292).

While Swinburne has defended the coherence of theism at considerable length elsewhere, he has not addressed either the second or third objection that I have raised. As for the first, Swinburne has failed to answer my objection that his concept of omniscience limits God's knowledge far more than he acknowledges and creates problems about the moral nature of God (Martin 1990, ch. 12).

Furthermore, additional arguments against the coherence of Swinburne's God have been published elsewhere that he does not consider (Martin and Monnier 2003). Swinburne takes it for granted that God thinks and that God is an agent. However, Matt McCormack has shown in "Why God Cannot Think" (2003b) that an omnipresent God cannot be aware of us, or have thoughts, or relate to people. McCormack has also shown in "The Paradox of Divine Agency" (2003a) that God cannot act and yet must act to be worthy of religious devotion.

The probability of the incarnation and resurrection of God

Swinburne estimates that, if God exists, then it is as probable as not that God would be incarnated, die, and be resurrected. But this estimate is too high. According to Swinburne, God wants us to form our own character and to help others do the same. This is why he gave us free will (Swinburne 2003, 35). Swinburne maintains that God's becoming incarnate, dying, and being resurrected would assist us in using our free will to make the right choices. In his view, there are three basic ways the incarnation would help: it would help us atone for our sins, it would enable God to identify with our suffering, and it would show us and teach us how to live.

1. According to Swinburne, we humans are not in a very good position to atone properly for sins. We need help, which God provides by offering a perfect human life as reparation, a life led by God himself. Only the sacrifice of God himself, that is God incarnate, would be adequate reparation. However, there are many serious problems with this theory (Martin 1991, 254–256; 2002, 258–260). Here I will mention three of them.

First, it is not clear why providing atonement by means of the incarnation would be a good thing for God to do. Swinburne admits that one alternative is "for God to insist on our making considerable atonement ourselves and then forgiving us in the light of this" (2003, 43), but he rejects this alternative because it would make obtaining divine forgiveness "very difficult for most of us" (2003, 43). Given Swinburne's stress on the exercise of free will, however, it is hard to see why this would be a problem. Working out one's own salvation, hard as it might be, surely would build more character than receiving it through Jesus' death.

Second, it is not clear why the death of the God-Man is the best means of providing satisfaction for a wrong against God's honor. Why would not some other punishment be preferable? If God's honor is infinitely wounded by human sin, why could it not be appeased more effectively by the eternal punishment of Jesus? Why the death penalty? It would seem more commensurate with the sin committed against God to inflict suffering on Jesus for eternity than to kill him after only relatively little suffering. Even if one argues that death has a harshness that no pain can match, it is important to recall that Jesus was dead for only a short time. It would have been a punishment more commensurate with human sin if Jesus had remained dead.

Third, one must wonder why it took God so long to offer atonement via the sacrifice of his son. Humans had been sinning for tens of thousands of years before the incarnation.

Although Swinburne (2006) objects to my interpretation of his theory, he makes no effort to answer my main criticism, namely, that no matter what theory of atonement is at issue, the incarnation, death, and resurrection of God are not necessary for the atonement of sins. An all-powerful God has many ways to allow humans to atone. Given these alternatives, the incarnation, death, and resurrection of God are a priori unlikely.

2. Swinburne also argues that the incarnation enables God to share in the suffering of humanity. Again there are problems. First, why did this sharing come so late? For tens of thousands of years God did not share in this suffering. It is important to note that Swinburne argues that there is only one incarnation – none before or since the incarnation in first-century Palestine. Why did God decide to share only 2,000 years ago? Second, why did God have to die to experience human suffering? If Jesus had been tortured but not killed, he would have shared in human suffering, and no resurrection would have been necessary.

3. Swinburne's last reason for God's incarnation is that it shows human beings what a perfect life is like, providing paradigmatic examples of moral goodness. This, according to Swinburne, is necessary to supplement the propositional moral revelation given to human beings (2003, 48). But is it? First, the propositional moral revelation can be supplemented by the example of lives of excellent but less than perfect moral teachers, such as Buddha, Confucius, and various saints. Why is perfection necessary for paradigmatic examples of moral goodness? Second, it seems logically possible for moral teachers to lead perfect moral lives without being God incarnate. Third, even if it were true that the incarnation was needed to provide a concrete example of moral goodness, this would provide no justification for the death

and resurrection of God. It is possible for God incarnate not to be executed. I see no reason to accept Swinburne's view that a perfect moral life "must end in death, plausibly the hard death of execution" (2003, 49). God could be incarnated and not die or could die and not be resurrected. But Swinburne's supposition is not true. An all-powerful God would have many ways to provide concrete moral examples. Incarnation is just one way.

In the light of these problems, it seems overly optimistic to suppose that, if God exists, it is as probable as not that God would become incarnate, die, and be resurrected.

The probability of Jesus being the incarnate God

If we grant the assumption that there is or will be an incarnate God, how probable is the evidence used to support the thesis that Jesus is in fact the resurrected God incarnate? Not very probable. Indeed, Swinburne himself believes that the probability is small – 10 percent (2003, 212). But even this figure seems high.

According to Swinburne, it is probable that Jesus is the incarnated God because he led a perfect life. However, I have elsewhere cited some of Jesus' teachings and behavior that are hardly perfect (Martin 1991, ch. 6). Swinburne dismisses these as either historically inaccurate or as, on reflection, perfect after all (2003, 91). Suggesting that we ought not to judge Jesus' actions by ordinary human moral standards (2003, 89), he argues that Jesus can perform actions that according to these standards would be immoral and still lead a morally perfect life. Thus, for example, Swinburne considers whether Jesus can be said to have lived a morally perfect life despite the harsh punishment he inflicts on the wicked in the afterlife. Downplaying the traditional view that such punishment will be eternal, he defends Jesus' action as morally justified. However, he admits that "anyone not sympathetic [with my argument] will have reason to believe that Jesus was not God incarnate" (2003, 95).

In *The Resurrection of God Incarnate*, Swinburne completely ignores what seems to me to be the hardest case of apparent moral imperfection to explain away: Jesus' tacit approval of slavery (Martin 1991, 168). In a later work (2006), he unconvincingly dismisses my claim that Jesus was not morally perfect because he tacitly approved of slavery. He writes,

> Jesus is not recorded as having said anything about slavery, but I think it extremely unlikely that he would have not endorsed the Old Testament teaching about slavery – that (as regards Hebrew slaves) it ought to end after 6 years (and so not really be slavery at all) – see (e.g.) Deuteronomy 15:12–18.

He seems to suppose that since Jesus never spoke of slavery, this counts against the view that he was imperfect – but just the opposite is true. A morally perfect being would have spoken out against it. Thus Jesus' silence, far from exonerating him, condemns him.

In addition, Swinburne seems to grant that Jesus would have allowed for involuntary servitude so long as the practice followed the teaching of Deuteronomy 15:12–18. Apparently Swinburne supposes that since the servitude was only for six years, Jesus had no obligation to oppose it. Indeed he seems to maintain that involuntary servitude of just six years is really not slavery. I note, however, that dictionaries do not construe slavery in this limited way; and in any case, a perfectly moral being would speak out against six years of involuntary servitude, call it what you will. Furthermore, Jesus' life in other respects was hardly morally perfect (Martin 1991, ch. 6).

Jesus exhibited not only moral imperfection, but also imperfection in knowledge. He was completely mistaken that he would return within the lifetime of his followers (Matt 16:28; Mark 9:1). His inaccuracy is more probable on the assumption that he was not God incarnate than on the assumption that he was.

The credibility of the evidence for the resurrection

What is the credibility of the evidence for the resurrection, given the assumptions that God exists and became incarnate as Jesus? Here I will discuss just two of the relevant factors that lower it (see also Martin 2005; 2006).

First, we lack independent confirmation of the resurrection from either Jewish or pagan sources (Martin 2002, 311–313). Moreover, other parts of the New Testament fail to support the details of the resurrection story. The genuine Pauline epistles, not to mention the earlier non-Pauline letters, provide no details about the death, burial, and resurrection of Jesus. The writers seemed to be ignorant of how Jesus died, where he died, and when he died, as well as of his moral teachings, his family, his miracles, and so on.

Swinburne denies the importance of the fact that neither Paul nor early non-Pauline letter writers confirm details of the death, burial and resurrection of Jesus. According to Swinburne, Paul did not write of these things because he took them for granted. This is highly implausible, however, since in many cases it would have been to his advantage to bring them up. For example, Paul does not refer to Jesus' teachings as stated in the gospels even when it would seem to support his case. Thus when Paul advocates blessing those who persecute you (Rom 12:14), protracted celibacy (1 Cor 7), and the doctrine that resurrected bodies will be of an imperishable form, he does not refer to Jesus' teachings (Luke 6:27–28; Matt 19:12; Mark 12: 25). Indeed, sometimes he goes against them. For example, Jesus instructed his disciples to baptize men everywhere (Matt 28:19), but Paul says that "Christ did not send me to baptize" (1 Cor 1:17); Jesus warned his followers to "go nowhere among the Gentiles" (Matt 10:5–6), whereas Paul claims that he was called by God "to be a minister of Christ Jesus to the Gentiles" (Rom 15:16); Jesus said, "judge not, that you be not judged" (Matt 7:1–2), but Paul says that he has "pronounced judgment in the name of the Lord Jesus" on the sexual immorality of a man who was living with his father's wife (1 Cor 5:1–5); and Paul's advice on paying taxes (Rom 13:6–7) conflicts with Jesus' advice to Peter on the same subject (Matt 17:25–27).

Second, the type of evidence that we do have is unreliable. Swinburne holds the principle of testimony that, other things being equal, we should believe what others tell us that they have done or perceived, in the absence of counter-evidence that would give us reason to doubt it (Swinburne 2003, 12–13). But we often do have such counter-evidence. In the light of well-known evidence from psychological experiments, we are aware that eyewitness testimony is often unreliable. Eyewitness testimony is influenced by what psychologists call "post-event" and "pre-event" information. In the case of Christianity, for post-event information we can read "early Christian beliefs," and for pre-event information we can read "prior messianic expectations." Moreover, we know from other religious movements, such as that of Sabbatai Sevi, that eyewitnesses in such movements tend to be unreliable (Scholem 1973; Loftus 1979). Why should we expect the situation to be different in the case of Christianity?

Swinburne disagrees that the credibility of the evidence for the resurrection is low. He believes that the fact that "Jews (all the immediate followers of Jesus) who believed in the resurrection inevitably became Christians" provides confirmation. On the contrary, the fact that Jews who immediately followed Jesus converted to Christianity shows only that they believed that the resurrection took place. It provides no independent support for the truth of the resurrection. To suppose otherwise would permit one to argue that the fact that the converts to Mormonism who were the immediate followers of Joseph Smith believed in the story of the golden tablets provided independent confirmation of that story, or that friends of Betty Hill who came to believe her UFO abduction story provided independent confirmation of her story.

The probability of alternative explanations

Could the empty tomb and the post-resurrection appearances be explained by alternative hypotheses, such as that witnesses were experiencing hallucinations or that some person or persons were perpetrating a fraud? According to Swinburne, these alternative explanations are highly improbable (Swinburne 2003, 213). But he neither gives evidence to support this view nor refutes *prima facie* defenses of alternative accounts (Carrier 2005b; Lowder 2001).

Swinburne's view that alternative accounts of the resurrection story, such as the theft theory, are extremely improbable is unjustified (Carrier 2005a). Let us grant his claim that one must evaluate the probability of Jesus' entire life against alternative accounts. This point by itself hardly shows that alternative accounts are extremely improbable. Indeed, some alternative accounts seem more likely than the view that Jesus' was God incarnate. Considered from a moral point of view, the case for the divinity of Jesus' life is so weak that the theft theory seems strong in comparison.

Swinburne accepts the theory that Jesus was buried according to the scriptural tradition and rejects alternative accounts (Swinburne 2003, 175). But what historical accuracy do these traditional stories have? Given Roman crucifixion customs, the prior probability that Jesus was buried is low. Even if Jewish customs were followed, his enemies probably buried Jesus ignominiously and permanently in a graveyard for criminals on Friday. Still another plausible scenario is that Joseph of Arimathea temporarily stored Jesus in Joseph's own tomb on Friday and then, in order to conform to Jewish law, Jesus was buried in a criminals' graveyard on Saturday (Lowder 2001; Carrier 2005a).

Swinburne rejects the theory that Jesus' post-resurrection appearances could be based on hallucinations shared by a number of witnesses, on the grounds that it is hard to document that such cases occur (Swinburne 2003, 185) and because Jesus not only appeared to groups of people, but also was involved in a continued conversation with them. Swinburne claims there are no recorded examples of these sorts of hallucinations. But in fact, there have been several well documented cases of hallucination shared by a number of people (Parsons 2005; Martin 1990, ch. 7).

Swinburne really does not seriously consider the view I have suggested elsewhere, that the resurrection and post-resurrection appearances of Jesus are based on legend (Martin 2002, 304–306). Given the prior probability that Jesus was not buried in accordance with the traditional story, the legend view, when combined with an assumption of widespread hallucination, would go some way toward making sense of the resurrection accounts.

Given all these problems, Swinburne's belief that the resurrection is nearly certain seems unjustified, and rational doubt is justified.

Davis's Apology

Steve Davis (2006) has defended Swinburne's argument for the resurrection against my criticisms, by raising two relatively minor critical points while ignoring my major criticisms. Thus, he says nothing about my critique of Swinburne's defense of Jesus' post-resurrection appearance, and he does not discuss the fact that Swinburne ignored Jesus' false prediction of the second coming, or the difficulties of maintaining that Jesus is perfect (Martin 2005). Instead Davis says that my arguments that the concept of God is incoherent can all be answered, some answered fairly easily, but he supplies no references to where they have been.

Davis also supports Swinburne's defense of the traditional account of Jesus' burial and maintains that Rome often allowed local customs to prevail. Let us suppose it did and that Rome allowed for Jewish burial customs to prevail. But, as essays in *The Empty Tomb* point out, if Jewish custom was followed, his enemies probably buried Jesus ignominiously (and permanently) in a common grave, in which case the traditional account is still probably mistaken (Carrier 2005b; Kirby 2005). Indeed, my claim that Swinburne is on shaky ground in defending the traditional account is not very controversial. Many New Testament scholars agree with the general idea that where Jesus is buried is unknown (Jesus Seminar 1998, 231–232; Carrier 2005a). So even if one grants Davis's claim that it is probable that Jesus was buried, there is reason to suppose that the location was not known, and he provides no evidence to the contrary. Hence, my critique of Swinburne's belief that the traditional biblical account of the empty tomb is true remains intact.

Summary of the Case Against the Resurrection

The probability of the resurrection is initially low. Although God could bring about miracles there is reason to suppose that at the very most he would do so rarely. Even if one assumes that God would use a miracle to save humanity, there are many ways he could do this without sacrificing his son and resurrecting him. Moreover, even if he chose incarnation, death, and resurrection, there is no reason to think this would take place when and where and how it is alleged to have taken place.

Since the resurrection is initially improbable, the evidence for it must be very strong, but it is not. Jesus was supposedly resurrected in the strong sense, that is, brought back to life transformed into a being with supernatural attributes. However, the usual evidence cited, for example the empty tomb, is irrelevant to establishing that Jesus had these attributes. Moreover, the kind of evidence that is required is unavailable.

Moreover, even if one assumes that Jesus was resurrected in the weak sense, the evidence is not strong enough to overcome the initial improbability. This is shown by Swinburne's defense of the resurrection. Based on his estimates of the probability (1) that God exists, (2) that the incarnation would occur if God did exist, (3) that Jesus was God incarnate if the incarnation occurred, (4) of the relevant evidence, and (5) of alternative explanations of the resurrection, he argues that the resurrection is nearly certain. But we have seen that his estimates of (1), (2), and (3) are too high and that they are too low for (4) and (5). Once these estimates are corrected, the view that the resurrection occurred is at the very least uncertain and even unlikely.

This suggests a final skeptical argument. If the resurrection actually occurred, it would not be uncertain that it did: God would have made it an event beyond rational doubt. A similar argument is given by J. L. Schellenberg (1993), who argues that the existence of reasonable disbelief is evidence against the existence of God. Thus the great theological importance of the resurrection is incompatible with its epistemic uncertainty (cf. Kirby 2005, 256).

References

Avalos, Hector (2007). "Resurrection." In T. Flynn (ed.), *The New Encyclopedia of Unbelief* (pp. 657–660). Amherst, NY: Prometheus Books.

Anderson, Hugh (1964). *Jesus and Christian Origins*. New York: Oxford University Press.

Carrier, Richard (2005a). "The Burial of Jesus in the Light of Jewish Law." In R. M. Price and J. J. Lowder (eds.), *The Empty Tomb* (pp. 369–392). Amherst, NY: Prometheus Books.

Carrier, Richard (2005b). "The Plausibility of Theft." In R. M. Price and J. J. Lowder (eds.), *The Empty Tomb* (pp. 349–368). Amherst, NY: Prometheus Books.

Cavin, Robert Greg (2005). "Is There Sufficient Evidence to Establish the Resurrection of Jesus?" In R. M. Price and J. J. Lowder (eds.), *The Empty Tomb* (pp. 19–42). Amherst, NY: Prometheus Books.

Copan, Paul, and Ronald K. Tacelli (2000). *Jesus' Resurrection: Fact or Fiction? A Debate between William Lane Craig and Gerd Lüdermann*. Downers Grove, IL: InterVarsity.

Davis, Stephen T. (1993). *Risen Indeed*. Grand Rapids: Eerdmans.

Davis, Stephen T. (2006). "The Counterattack of the Resurrection Skeptics: A Review Article." *Philosophia Christi* 8 (1): 39–63.

Jesus Seminar (1998). "Voting Records: The Passion Narrative." *Forum* n.s. 1 (1, Spring): 227–233.

Kirby, Peter (2005). "The Case Against the Empty Tomb." In R. M. Price and J. J. Lowder (eds.), *The Empty Tomb* (pp. 233–260). Amherst, NY: Prometheus Books.

Loftus, Elizabeth F. (1979). *Eyewitness Testimony*. Cambridge, MA: Harvard University Press.

Lowder, Jeffery Jay (2001). "Historical Evidence and the Empty Tomb: A Reply to William Lane Craig." *The Journal of Higher Criticism* 8 (Fall): 251–293.

Martin, Michael (1990). *Atheism: A Philosophical Justification*. Philadelphia: Temple University Press.

Martin, Michael (1991). *The Case Against Christianity*. Philadelphia: Temple University Press.

Martin, Michael (1997). "Trying to Save God." *Free Inquiry* 17 (4): 58–61.

Martin, Michael (2002). *Atheism, Morality, and Meaning*. Amherst, NY: Prometheus Books.

Martin, Michael (2005). "Swinburne on the Resurrection." In R. M. Price and J. J. Lowder (eds.), *The Empty Tomb* (pp. 453–468). Amherst, NY: Prometheus Books.

Martin, Michael (2006a). "On Swinburne's Reply." *The Empty Tomb*. At http://theemptytomb.googlepages.com/martin2.pdf (accessed April 10, 2010).

Martin, Michael (2006b). "Reply to Davis." *The Empty Tomb*. At http://theemptytomb.googlepages.com/Martin.pdf (accessed April 10, 2010).

Martin, Michael, and Ricki Monnier, eds. (2003). *The Impossibility of God*. Amherst, NY: Prometheus Books.

McCormick, Matt (2003a). "The Paradox of Divine Agency." In Michael Martin and Ricki Monnier (eds.), *The Impossibility of God* (pp. 313–320). Amherst, NY: Prometheus Books.

McCormick, Matt (2003b). "Why God Cannot Think: Kant, Omnipresence and Consciousness." In Michael Martin and Ricki Monnier (eds.), *The Impossibility of God* (pp. 258–273). Amherst, NY: Prometheus Books.

Miethe, Terry (1987). "Introduction." In Gary Habermas and Antony G. N. Flew, *Did Jesus Rise From The Dead? The Resurrection Debate* (xi–xvi). Edited by Terry Miethe. San Francisco: Harper & Row.

Overall, Christine (2003). "Miracles as Evidence Against the Existence of God." In Michael Martin and Ricki Monnier (eds.), *The Impossibility of God* (pp. 147–154). Amherst, NY: Prometheus Books.

Parsons, Keith (2005). "Peter Kraft and Ronald Catelli on Hallucination Theory." In R. M. Price and J. J. Lowder (eds.), *The Empty Tomb* (pp. 433–452). Amherst, NY: Prometheus Books.

Schellenberg, J. L. (1993). *Divine Hiddenness and Human Reason.* Ithaca, NY: Cornell University Press.

Scholem, Gershom (1973). *Sabbatai Sevi: The Mystic Messiah.* Princeton: Princeton University Press.

Swinburne, Richard (1992). *Revelation.* Oxford: Clarendon.

Swinburne, Richard (1993). *The Coherence of Theism.* Rev. edn. Oxford: Oxford University Press.

Swinburne, Richard (2003). *The Resurrection of God Incarnate.* Oxford: Clarendon.

Swinburne, Richard (2006). "Martin's Misgivings: On Swinburne and the Resurrection." *Tektoniks.* At www.tektonics.org/tomb/martinm11.html (accessed April 10, 2010).

Wells, G. A. (1999). *The Jesus Myth.* La Salle, IL: Open Court.

CHAPTER 19

The Quest for the Historical Jesus: An Overview

David B. Gowler

The Jesus portrayed in the gospels transcends human abilities and categories. For most of Christian history, this transcendence posed little difficulty, but the rise of the historical method during the Enlightenment ensured that some would seek for a Jesus who was explicable within the limits of human history. So began the quest for the historical Jesus. In this overview of the quest, we will investigate the sources for the quest, the reasons for the quest, the history of the quest, various criteria of authenticity that historical Jesus scholars utilize, and some recent portraits of Jesus that have emerged from the quest.

To a large degree, the quest has been determined by the question, "For whom are you looking?" (John 20:15). The Johannine Jesus asked Mary Magdalene this question outside the empty tomb. Mary, the gospel reports, did not recognize Jesus and supposed him to be the gardener. In some respects, Mary's (mis)perception of Jesus can be a metaphor of the quest for the historical Jesus: the Jesus for whom we look, because of our presuppositions, determines to an extent the Jesus we find, as well as the aspects of Jesus that we overlook or even misconstrue. As we search for the historical Jesus, how and where we begin influences where we go, and what we look for influences what we see.

Sources for the Quest

Unlike Mary, we do not have Jesus standing before us; instead we have to sift through sometimes problematic historical evidence. Outside the canonical gospels, this data is limited.

The Jewish historian Josephus provides some evidence, but sections of those references include later Christian interpolations. In his *Antiquities* (mid-90s CE), Josephus refers to Jesus as a "wise man," a "doer of startling deeds," and a "teacher of people"

The Blackwell Companion to Jesus, First Edition. Edited by Delbert Burkett. ©2014 John Wiley & Sons, Ltd. Published 2014 by John Wiley & Sons, Ltd.

who gained a following from both Jews and Gentiles. He also relates that Pontius Pilate condemned Jesus to death and that the "tribe of Christians" still existed (*Antiquities* 18.63–64; cf. Dunn 2003, 141). A later chapter in *Antiquities* refers to James, "the brother of Jesus who is called the Christ" (*Antiquities* 20.200).

Information about Jesus in non-Jewish sources is even sparser. Pliny the Younger (ca. 111 CE) notes that Christians worshiped "Christ as god" (*Epistles* 10:96) but relates no information about Jesus' life or teachings. The Roman historian Tacitus (ca. 116–117 CE) says that Jesus was executed "in Tiberius's reign by the procurator of Judea, Pontius Pilate" (*Annals* 15.54). The Roman historian Suetonius (ca. 121 CE) only mentions that the emperor Claudius "expelled from Rome the Judeans who were constantly rioting at the instigation of a certain Chrestus" (*Life of Claudius* 25.4). What these sources mainly reveal about Jesus is that he was executed by Pilate and that his followers continued after his death.

Most apocryphal gospels are dependent on the canonical gospels, with the Gospel of Thomas being a possible exception. In some instances, Thomas' wording seems closer to the voice of Jesus than the parallel synoptic traditions (e.g., Thomas 20; 31; 65). Other apocryphal gospels reveal much about the Christians who wrote them, but little about the historical Jesus. Most stories are clearly legendary, such as that in which a five-year-old Jesus makes clay sparrows and then brings them to life (*Infancy Gospel of Thomas*) or that in which a vegetarian Jesus refuses to eat lamb at Passover (*The Gospel of the Ebionites*).

Outside of the four gospels, the rest of the New Testament gives minimal evidence about Jesus' life and teachings. The earliest source, the apostle Paul, relates that Jesus was born a Jew (Gal 4:4); that he had brothers, including one named James (1 Cor 9:5; Gal 1:19); and that he had twelve disciples (1 Cor 15:5). Paul rarely cites an explicit teaching of Jesus, but he does refer to Jesus' saying against divorce (1 Cor 7:10–11), his saying that preachers should receive payment (1 Cor 9:14), and his words instituting the Last Supper (1 Cor 11:23–25). Explicit references in other parts of the New Testament are also rare (e.g., "it is more blessed to give than to receive," Acts 20:35).

Reasons for the Quest

The quest for the historical Jesus is necessary because of historical questions raised by our primary sources, the New Testament gospels. The similarities among the gospel portraits of Jesus, especially among Matthew, Mark, and Luke, are striking, but so are the differences. This fact did not escape even early commentators, yet they did not usually raise serious questions about whether the gospels were reliable historical narratives.

The focus on the Bible during the Reformation by such scholars as Erasmus prepared the way for the detailed investigations it would receive during the Enlightenment from such scholars as David Friedrich Strauss. Strauss's analysis, for instance, of the differing versions of the resurrection narratives demonstrated that the gospels' numerous discrepancies could not be papered over (1994, 705–744). The gospels included not just minor inconsistencies, but also important differences in how Jesus was understood and therefore portrayed.

Scholars could no longer take it for granted that the traditions in the gospels that are attributed to Jesus are authentically from him, because the gospels are the result of a complex process of oral tradition and written composition. The gospels were not written by the earliest disciples of Jesus (cf. Luke 1:1–4); the traditions were passed on orally to a later generation, and the first gospel (Mark) was not written until at least 65 CE. Some changes in the tradition took place during the time of oral transmission, and the gospel authors creatively reworked the traditions as well. Ancient authors were free to vary the wording, details, and dynamics of their stories according to their theological and rhetorical interests (Gowler 2006).

To a large extent, then, the necessity of the quest for the Jesus of history comes from the nature of our sources. The gospels are not unbiased historical narratives; they are religious texts that were written to inculcate and nurture belief in Jesus as the Son of God (cf. John 20:31).

After Easter, the primary focus for many followers of Jesus shifted from the message *of* the historical Jesus – the proclaimer of the kingdom of God – to the message *about* the risen Jesus – the proclaimed Christ, Son of God, and exalted Lord. The Easter experience thus led many of Jesus' followers to focus on the implications of his death and resurrection. What little interest the apostle Paul shows in Jesus' life and teachings, for example, is often connected to Jesus' salvific death (e.g., 1 Cor 11). The later creeds of the church, such as the Apostles' Creed and the Nicene Creed, share this focus by omitting the details of Jesus' life and skipping straight from the virgin birth to Jesus' death and resurrection. The quest for the historical Jesus, however, reorients the focus from what Marcus Borg calls the "post-Easter Jesus" (the risen Jesus/Christ of Christian experience) to the "pre-Easter Jesus" (the historical Jesus who lived in first-century Palestine; Borg 1994, 195).

Since the gospels are more concerned with the "post-Easter Jesus" than the "pre-Easter Jesus," we must reconstruct the historical Jesus by carefully evaluating our sources. Such reconstruction is difficult, and the great historical, social, and cultural chasms between us and first-century Mediterranean peoples are difficult to bridge. The quest for the historical Jesus is thus both necessary and difficult, as the great number and diversity of published volumes about Jesus demonstrate. Since the deluge of books about the historical Jesus continues almost unabated, a brief survey of the major developments in the modern quests for Jesus will help put these studies into perspective.

Brief History of the Quest

The following history of the quest is adapted from Gowler (2007, 1–30).[1] Other helpful summaries may be found in Tatum (1999); Dunn (2003); Borg (1994); Wright (1996); and Powell (1998).

The rise of critical scholarship

Most summaries of the quest for the historical Jesus begin with Hermann Samuel Reimarus (1694–1768), but in fact Reimarus's work was anticipated by Spinoza and Pierre Bayle, and his views on Jesus were indebted to such English Deists as Edward Herbert, Thomas Woolston, and Matthew Tindal (Brown 1985, 36–55).

Reimarus had circulated a 4,000-page manuscript anonymously among some of his friends, but after his death, his friend Gerhard Lessing anonymously published seven fragments of that manuscript from 1774 to 1778 (Talbert 1970). According to Reimarus, Jesus believed that he was the Messiah, and he proclaimed the imminent coming of the kingdom of God that would liberate the Jews from Roman oppression. Instead, he was crucified by the Roman governor, Pontius Pilate. Because Jesus' disciples did not want to return to their former lives, they probably stole his body from the tomb, fabricated stories about his resurrection, and invented the message of his atoning death and future return in glory.

Reimarus' historical reconstructions did not gain many followers, but his work raised critical issues, such as the irreconcilable differences between gospel accounts (e.g., in the resurrection narratives). In addition, Reimarus made an important methodological assumption: it was both methodologically possible and theologically necessary to (re)discover the historical Jesus and his message (Tatum 1999, 94).

Strauss's *Life of Jesus* (1835–1836) also rejected the view that the gospels present accurate, historical portraits of Jesus, but he disagreed with Reimarus and other "rationalists," who explained miraculous elements in the gospels in a naturalistic way. For example, the "miracle" of the loaves and fishes occurred by Jesus' shaming people into sharing their hidden food. For Strauss, such attempts to preserve the "historicity" of these accounts by excising all miraculous elements ignored the true significance of the narratives. He argued that Christian *myth* was found throughout the gospels: "the representation of an event or of an idea in a form which is historical, but, at the same time characterized by the rich pictorial and imaginative mode of thought and expression of the primitive ages" (1994, 53).

Ernest Renan's *Life of Jesus*, published in 1863, was a "biography" that portrayed Jesus the human being: "Jesus was born at Nazareth. ... He proceeded from the ranks of the people [i.e., not of the lineage of David]. His father, Joseph, and his mother, Mary, were people in humble circumstances, artisans living by their labor" (1927, 80–83, cf. 18–19). With these three sentences, Renan rejected Jesus' birth in Bethlehem, his Davidic lineage, the virgin birth, and the incarnation. The novelistic style and flowery language of Renan's book imbued it with an aesthetic power that seemingly made first-century Palestine come alive. Yet the artistic prose was not matched by historical accuracy.

The usual assumption was that the earliest sources would offer the most reliable data to reconstruct the historical Jesus, so scholars explored the gospels' dates of composition, their sources, and the literary relationships among them. The work of Karl Lachmann (1835) and Heinrich Julius Holtzmann (1863) convinced most scholars that Mark was the oldest gospel and that Matthew and Luke utilized a (non-extant) "sayings collection" called "Q." Mark's gospel thus became more important for reconstructing Jesus' life, thought, and "inner development."

The "Liberal Quest" for Jesus

After Strauss demonstrated the irreconcilable differences between the gospels, scholars could no longer view them as unvarnished historical narratives. Foundational to the Liberal Quest, however, was the belief that one could establish through historical-critical methodology the authentic teaching and historical person of Jesus. This reconstructed historical Jesus was the legitimate object of faith – not the traditional Jesus of creedal orthodoxy – and his teaching should be learned and imitated.

Liberal Protestant theologians, such as Albrecht Ritschl (1900) and Adolf Harnack ([1901] 1978), thus sought to free the historical Jesus from the dogma of the church. Harnack, for example, emphasized that Christianity is a way of life, not a system of beliefs, dogma, or doctrine. Jesus proclaimed God as Father, the brother and sisterhood of human beings, the infinite value of the human soul, and the "love commandment": to love God, ourselves, and other human beings, including our enemies.

With the work of William Wrede, a crack appeared in the foundation of the Liberal Quest. Many nineteenth-century Lives of Jesus assumed that Mark's gospel, as the earliest source, was basically historical. Wrede's 1901 book, *The Messianic Secret*, however, demonstrated that certain motifs in Mark were not simply historical observations. Mark's theme of Jesus keeping his messiahship a secret, the "Messianic Secret," was a theological construction that stemmed primarily from Mark and the early church, so Mark's gospel could not be used to reconstruct the historical "inner development" of Jesus' messianic consciousness. Wrede's work thus reinforced skepticism about both the likelihood of success, and theological value of, a historical reconstruction of the life of Jesus (Wrede [1901] 1971).

The re-emergence of eschatology

Another blow to the liberal Jesus was the (re)emergence of eschatology. In 1892, Johannes Weiss, for example, argued that Jesus' message of the kingdom was apocalyptic – the end of the world was imminent – and could not be equated with ethical conduct or the Christian community envisioned by liberalism ([1892] 1971).

Albert Schweitzer's 1906 book, *The Quest of the Historical Jesus*, argued that this imminent eschatology determined "the whole course of Jesus' life" ([1906] 2001, 212). Jesus was obsessed with the apocalyptic expectation that the kingdom of God would immediately erupt into human history to bring the world to an end. Jesus also was deluded into thinking that God had designated him as the messiah, the agent to bring about that end (1968, 103, 111). Schweitzer's reading of Matthew 10:23 was that Jesus did not expect to see the Twelve return from their missionary journey on which he sent them, because the *parousia* (arrival) of the Son of Man would "take place before they have completed a hasty journey through the cities of Israel to announce it" (2001, 327). Because the kingdom did not arrive before the Twelve returned, Jesus reflected on the Suffering Servant in Isaiah 53, became (erroneously) convinced that God would spare others from suffering if he suffered and died (1968, 119–120), and deliberately sought his own death. Jesus was mistaken again; he died, and the kingdom did not come.

The partial eclipse of the historical Jesus

Schweitzer's classic book also decisively demonstrated that scholars, because of their presuppositions, inevitably project a bit of themselves into their portraits of Jesus. After Schweitzer, in fact, some scholars decided that it was methodologically impossible to reconstruct the historical Jesus and theologically unnecessary to base one's faith on the uncertain results of historical research. Rudolf Bultmann, for example, distinguished the historical Jesus from the historic Christ, the true object of Christian faith, because faith is independent of tendentious historical research. In addition, the gospels are products of the preaching (*kerygma*) of the early church and are not reliable sources for a "Life of Jesus." All we can or need to know about the historical Jesus is his understanding of existence that can be gleaned from his teachings (Bultmann 1934; [1921] 1963).

Bultmann's era is often labeled the "no quest period," which brought "the eclipse of the historical Jesus." In reality, though, it was only a partial eclipse, especially in British and American scholarship, because the quest for Jesus continued with the publication of numerous Lives of Jesus. Even in Germany the quest was not completely abandoned (e.g., Jeremias 1971).

The "New Quest" for the historical Jesus

This partial eclipse of the historical Jesus lasted until Bultmann's own students proposed a way in which the study of Jesus could emerge from his shadow.

Ernst Käsemann's 1953 lecture to a reunion of Bultmann's former students inaugurated a "New Quest" for the historical Jesus. In contrast to Bultmann, Käsemann thought that it was methodologically possible to reach certain historical conclusions about Jesus of Nazareth and theologically necessary to do so, because there is some continuity between the historical Jesus and the Christ of faith (Tatum 1999, 101). Jesus of Nazareth meets us in the New Testament, *not* "as he was," but as "Lord of the community which believes in him." The gospel authors paint different portraits of Jesus, but they all agree that "the life history of Jesus was constitutive for faith, because the earthly and the exalted Lord are identical" (Käsemann 1969, 33–34).

In 1956, Günther Bornkamm, another former student of Bultmann, published *Jesus of Nazareth*, in which he argued that it is possible to arrive at a reliable understanding of Jesus' thought and teaching, to achieve a sound picture of the type of person Jesus was, and to understand what he was trying to accomplish. The gospel traditions, despite their limitations, are concerned with the pre-Easter Jesus. Therefore, the sources permit Bornkamm to "compile the main historically indisputable traits and to present the rough outlines of Jesus' person and history" (1960, 14).

According to Bornkamm, Jesus was a Jew from Galilee. His family lived in Nazareth, his father was a carpenter, and we know the names of four of his brothers. We know much about his teaching, conflicts with opponents, and healing activities; we know that he gathered disciples, that people flocked to him, and that his enemies arise and increase. The decisive turning point in his life was the trip to Jerusalem with his message of the kingdom of God. He ended up on a Roman cross (1960, 53–55).

Jesus' message was apocalyptic: the day of judgment would soon dawn violently, although he was reticent to speak of the day or hour. The kingdom's imminent arrival was evident in Jesus' words and deeds – the blind see, lepers are cleansed, and the dead are raised. He called people to repent and accept God's invitation in light of this dawning of God's reign. Jesus never claimed to be the messiah, but "the Messianic character of his being is contained *in* his words and deeds and *in* the unmediatedness of his historic appearance" (1960, 66–67, 82–83, 178).

Norman Perrin was not a student of Bultmann but was influenced by his work and the work of his students. A major contribution of his *Rediscovering the Teaching of Jesus* (1976) was to define some of the major criteria to determine the authenticity of the sayings of Jesus (see below). Perrin tried to "reconstruct major aspects of the teaching of Jesus beyond reasonable doubt" in three areas: the parables, kingdom of God sayings, and Lord's Prayer (1976, 47). All aspects of Jesus' ministry, such as the ethical teachings, disputes over the law, and welcoming of sinners, have to be understood in the context of Jesus' proclamation of the kingdom. Jesus offered forgiveness of sins and a resulting new relationship with God and one's fellow human beings. Perrin decided, though, that Jesus never predicted the future arrival of an apocalyptic Son of Man. This concept, Perrin argued, was not found in ancient Judaism, and all such passages in the synoptics stem from Christian reflection on passages such as Daniel 7:13, Psalm 110:1, and Zechariah 12:10 (1976, 164–183).

The New Quest developed and flourished primarily among Bultmannian scholars, so it possessed a homogeneity that other quests lack. The gap between the historical Jesus and the risen Christ was bridged through the *kerygma*, the preaching of the church. In addition, history was envisioned as "event" not a "sequence of facts," and New Questers focused primarily on the *teachings* of Jesus, since the nature of gospels precludes a biographical approach.

The continuing "Third Quest" for the historical Jesus

In 1985, historical Jesus scholarship entered a new phase with two important events. First, E. P. Sanders published *Jesus and Judaism*, which attempted to answer how Jesus could live totally within Judaism and yet be the origin of a movement that separated from Judaism (1985; cf. 1993). Second, Robert Funk convened the first meeting of the Jesus Seminar, a group of scholars that met twice a year for several years to compile a list of words and deeds attributed to Jesus and to determine their authenticity.

The conclusions reached by Sanders and the Jesus Seminar were very different, but they both claimed that their primary interest was historical, not theological. There is less explicit theology in these and many other current works, but as Albert Schweitzer demonstrated over a hundred years ago, ideological positions underlie all investigations of the historical Jesus, despite protestations to the contrary.

Most scholars designate this current phase of the quest with N. T. Wright's term, the "Third Quest," but they have defined it in different ways (Neill and Wright 1988, 379–403; Wright 1996, 83–85). The best description comes from Gerd Theissen and Annette Merz, who include all current Jesus research as part of this Third Quest and see certain common elements tending to emerge: (1) "sociological interest" replaces "theological interest"; (2) Jesus is situated within Judaism rather than distinct from Judaism; and (3) many scholars are open to using non-canonical sources (Theissen and Merz 1996, 10–11). Other distinctive elements of recent historical Jesus research include: (4) attention to questions broader than the authenticity of individual sayings; (5) frequent critiques of New Quest methodology, including the criterion of dissimilarity; (6) placing the "Jewish Jesus" into a wider first-century context; (7) openness by many scholars to interdisciplinary approaches; and (8) greater recognition of the "political character" of Jesus' public works (Telford 1994, 57–58; Herzog 2000, 24).

The Third Quest has produced a wide range of approaches and results (see below), and many of the differences stem from the fact that they begin with different assumptions and utilize different methodologies. As with the New Quest, debates over which types of criteria for authenticity should be used still dominate many discussions.

The Quest for Reliable Criteria of Authenticity

Historical Jesus scholars utilize various criteria to determine "authentic" Jesus traditions. One such criterion is the age of the tradition. As a general rule, it is likely that earlier traditions give us better data about the historical Jesus than later ones. Using the criterion of age, the writings of Paul, though limited in data, are of the most value, followed by Q and Mark, and then our other sources. The results of this criterion, however, greatly depend on one's judgments about the dating (and existence, in the case of Q) of sources.

The criterion of dissimilarity (or difference) was perhaps the most important criterion during the New Quest period. To ascertain whether a saying of Jesus was "authentic," it must be demonstrably different in content from conceptions current in Judaism before Jesus or in the early Christian communities after Jesus. If that is the case, the tradition almost certainly stemmed from the historical Jesus. Ernst Käsemann argued that the criterion of dissimilarity was the only one that provides "more or less safe ground under our feet" (1969, 37), whereas Norman Perrin believed that all reconstructions of the teaching of Jesus must build upon this criterion (1976, 39).

Many scholars, however, object to this criterion. There obviously is some continuity between Judaism, Jesus, and early Christianity, and we do not know enough about the various streams of first-century Judaism and Christianity to determine exactly what might be "dissimilar." In addition, by focusing on what is different or unusual, one necessarily ends up with a historical Jesus who is different and unusual, a slanted portrait of Jesus in contrast with that of his fellow Jews. Hence a subtly non-Jewish or even anti-Jewish historical Jesus can result. Because of these and other difficulties, some scholars have abandoned this criterion (see Theissen and Winter 2002).

The criterion of embarrassment states that scholars should look for sayings or actions of Jesus that would have created embarrassment for the early Christian church, because the church would not create such "difficult" traditions. Jesus' baptism by John the Baptist, for example, was problematic: how could the early church explain why the sinless Son of God was baptized by John the Baptist, a ritual that signified the forgiveness of sins (e.g., Matt 3:13–17)? These "embarrassing" events are few in number, but they belong to bedrock traditions about Jesus. One difficulty, though, is determining whether we can actually know what would have been embarrassing for the early church.

Norman Perrin's version of the criterion of multiple attestation argues that material may be authentic if it is found widely in all (or most) of the "sources which can be discerned behind the synoptic gospels" (1976, 45). Other scholars, such as John Meier, have expanded its use to include literary forms: Meier focuses on both Jesus' sayings or actions "that are attested in more than one independent literary source" (e.g., Paul, Q, Mark, M, L, John, Gospel of Thomas) and/or in "more than one literary form or genre" (e.g., parable, aphorism, miracle story), especially if material is found in both independent sources *and* multiple literary forms (e.g., Jesus' words at the Last Supper; Meier 1991–2009, 1:174). Since authentic traditions may be located in only one independent source, this criterion should primarily be used to include materials, not exclude them.

The criterion of coherence states that a tradition may be accepted as authentic if it coheres in some way with material already established by other criteria as authentic. Norman Perrin, for example, argues that the saying in Thomas 82 ("He that is near me is near the fire; he that is far from me is far from the Kingdom") is authentic, because it coheres with other authentic sayings (e.g., Mark 9:49; 12:34; 1976,

44–45). As Meier notes, this criterion should be used to add traditions that cohere with previous data, not to eliminate data that does not cohere (1991–2009, 1:176). We cannot assume that all of Jesus' sayings and actions were entirely coherent or systematic.

Several criteria focus on the *language* of the sayings in the Jesus tradition. Some scholars explore forms of language that most likely stem from oral tradition, such as memorable sayings of short enough length to be remembered and transmitted, humor and exaggeration (e.g., Matt 23:24), or shocking elements (e.g., Luke 9:60). One needs to be careful, however, not to assume *a priori* that the teachings of Jesus took a particular form and then, so that the assumption becomes self-fulfilling, evaluate traditions as "authentic" that fit within that form.

Other scholars, such as Matthew Black, Geza Vermes, and Joachim Jeremias, try to recover the "voice" of Jesus by attempting to delineate traces of Aramaic in the sayings tradition, including types of speech typical of Palestinian Judaism, such as rhythmic two, three, or four beat patterns; semitic hyperbole; the divine passive; or alliteration, paronomasia, or assonance that appears when sayings are translated "back" into Aramaic (see, for example, Jeremias 1971, 3–29). The problem with this approach, however, is that (assuming Jesus taught in Aramaic) Jesus' early followers also would have spoken Aramaic and most likely used similar forms of language. So distinguishing between the words of Jesus and the words possibly created or added by his Aramaic-speaking followers in Palestine is problematic.

The criterion of environmental (Palestinian Jewish) appropriateness traditionally functions as a negative one: certain traditions can be determined to be inauthentic if they reflect settings other than the Palestinian Jewish environment in which Jesus lived. Mark 1:12, for example, which assumes that a woman could divorce her husband, seems to reflect a later Hellenistic context. The authentic saying in Mark 1:11, however, assumes the Jewish context in which a man might divorce his wife, but a wife could not divorce her husband. The primary difficulty with this criterion, however, is whether we can tell the difference between life under Herod Antipas and Pilate, and life in Palestine ten, twenty, or even thirty years later.

Gerd Theissen and Annette Merz suggest the criterion of historical plausibility: "Whatever helps to explain the influence of Jesus and at the same time can only have come into being in a Jewish context is historical in the sources" (1996, 116). Theissen and Dagmar Winter state it this way: "What we know of Jesus as a whole must allow him to be recognized within his contemporary Jewish context and must be compatible with the Christian (canonical and noncanonical) history of his effects" (2002, 212).

Theissen, Merz, and Winter use this criterion in conjunction with other ones, such as multiple attestations of substantial motifs and subject matter. The criterion of historical plausibility, though, seeks to make sure that Jesus' words and actions are plausible for a first-century Jewish charismatic, but it also takes into account the fact that Jesus and other Jewish charismatics were prophetically critical of many of their contemporaries. Unlike the criterion of difference, it does not stress alleged uniqueness; it focuses on *individuality*: Jesus is not removed from or placed against his Jewish context. Instead, Jesus "stands out from it" with "a peculiarity which is bound up with the context" (Theissen and Merz 1996, 118).

N. T. Wright's criterion of double similarity (and dissimilarity) is similar: when something can be seen as credible (even if subversive) within first-century Judaism *and* credible as the implied starting point of something in early Christianity, there "is a strong possibility of our being in touch with the genuine history of Jesus" (1996, 132, 149). Unlike Perrin, who declared that the burden of proof was on those who wished to demonstrate the authenticity of a tradition (1976, 39), Wright places the burden of proof on those who wish to demonstrate inauthenticity (1996, 132–134).

In the New Quest, some scholars were more confident than others about the possibility of removing redactional additions to the Jesus traditions and getting back to more authentic traditions. Joachim Jeremias, for example, attempted to recapture the teachings of Jesus from the developments added by the early church by postulating "certain definite principles of transformation" (Jeremias 1972, 23). Such "principles" (in parables) included a switch from eschatological emphasis to exhortation that often resulted in allegorization. Gospel authors also have distinctive theological tendencies, such as Matthew's focus on a higher standard of righteousness. As always, however, one's presuppositions often influence one's conclusions. The actual transformations in the Jesus traditions seem to be more complex and less regular than Jeremias and others sometimes make them appear to be (Gowler 2000, 8–10).

The use of criteria of authenticity is an art, not a science, and scholars' presuppositions – such as an image of Jesus already in mind – can determine to a large extent how these criteria are used and what conclusions are reached by applying them. That is one reason why the application of these criteria – although certain agreements about Jesus exist – has not led to uniform results or consensus.

A more basic question is whether the application of criteria is the best way to proceed in the first place. Is this process of investigating the traditions about Jesus like solving a puzzle, where the individual pieces of tradition have to be examined one by one to see if they fit in the larger puzzle and, if so, where? E. P. Sanders suggests a quite different metaphor: using these criteria can be seen as a quagmire from which a historical Jesus scholar can never truly emerge. As Sanders noted, we have "*very good* knowledge of Jesus at a somewhat general level" (1993, 56), but "the quagmire is produced by treating the synoptic Gospels as if ... by sufficiently careful attention to what they say one can discover with precision and nuance what Jesus thought" (1985, 131).

Recent Portraits of Jesus

Major debates still swirl in historical Jesus scholarship, such as questions of method or the role of eschatology in the teachings and actions of Jesus. Consequently a wide range of portraits of Jesus has emerged in recent scholarship. Any attempt to categorize these is necessarily imprecise, but we can observe some general trends. Some portraits present Jesus primarily (though not exclusively) as an apocalyptic figure, oriented toward the imminent arrival of God's kingdom. Others present him primarily (though not exclusively) as a non-apocalyptic figure, who began a renewal movement oriented toward reforming Jewish society or religion. Others attempt to provide a more inclusive view of Jesus, and still others argue for the basic historicity of the synoptic portraits of Jesus.[2]

Jesus as primarily an apocalyptic figure

E. P. Sanders envisions Jesus as a prophet of Jewish restoration. Jesus operated within first-century Jewish "covenantal nomism," the concept that God is loyal to the covenant with Israel and expects Israel's response of gratitude and faith to include showing loyalty by obeying God's law (Sanders 1985). Sanders builds his case on "almost indisputable facts" about Jesus. For example, he was baptized by John the Baptist, he engaged in controversy about the temple, and he was crucified by the Roman authorities. Sanders argues that the temple controversy means that Jesus publicly predicted or threatened the imminent destruction of the temple and probably awaited the establishment of a new temple from heaven (1985, 71). This "restoration eschatology" places him in the category of a prophet of Jewish restoration, and it included such events as Jesus' calling of twelve apostles, which points to the hope for the restoration of the twelve tribes of Israel (1985, 103).

Jesus taught about a future and imminent kingdom; he was executed as a would-be king; and the disciples, after his death, expected him to return to establish the kingdom. These points are "indisputable." Jesus' self-claim was great indeed, and he may have thought of himself as "viceroy-to-be" (1985, 240). This self-evaluation possibly led to discussions of him as messiah in his lifetime and definitely led to this title being ascribed to him after the resurrection. Jesus thus was not misunderstood by the Jewish aristocrats and the Romans: what he claimed for himself was tantamount to claiming kingship (1985, 322).

Dale Allison pictures Jesus as a millenarian ascetic. He agrees with Sanders that Jesus proclaimed the restoration of Israel, but he differs significantly by arguing that Jesus (a) rejected covenantal nomism and (b) called for repentance (1987). Allison instead places Jesus within the larger category of millenarian movements. Jesus' negative attitude toward wealth (e.g., Luke 9:58) and his sexual asceticism (e.g., Matt 19:10–12) were integral parts of his eschatological urgency as a millenarian ascetic (1998).

For John Meier, Jesus is a complex "fusion of *eschatological prophet, baptizer, exorcist, miracle-worker and healer, and rabbinic teacher of the law*" (1991–2009, 2:453–454; emphasis added). Meier believes that Jesus proclaimed the definitive coming of God in the near future to establish God's rule. Yet unlike other eschatological prophets, Jesus did not set a timetable for the kingdom's appearance. Since regular miracle-working by an itinerant prophet in northern Israel would conjure up thoughts of Elisha and Elijah, Jesus was "clothed in the aura of Elijah," the eschatological prophet "par excellence." Jesus acted as the eschatological prophet who proclaimed the imminent coming of God's rule, and he made God's rule a present reality through his healings and exorcisms, as well as by welcoming tax collectors and sinners into table fellowship (1991–2009, 2:132–133; 350–351). Jesus also taught ethical imperatives (e.g., love and forgiveness) and gave his followers concrete instructions on how to observe the Law of Moses. Meier thus concludes that "the historical Jesus is the halakic Jesus"; that is, Jesus, as a pious first-century Jew, was involved in vigorous debates about the Law of Moses and questions about the practice of following it (1991–2009, 4:8).

Gerd Theissen and Annette Merz portray Jesus as a homeless itinerant preacher with a message of the Jewish God who would soon bring deliverance to the poor, weak, and sick. Jesus required a renunciation of home (Matt 8:20), family (Luke 14:26), and possessions (Mark 10:17–25). He proclaimed the saving message of God's rule as both imminent and as already present; everyone had a chance to escape the coming judgment, including toll collectors and sinners (1996, 217, 240, 265). The kingdom of God thus stood at the center of Jesus' preaching; healings and exorcisms formed the center of his activity. People flocked to this charismatic healer, and he saw these healings as signs that the kingdom of God was already beginning. Jesus' healings and exorcisms thus have eschatological significance: "As an apocalyptic charismatic miracle-worker, Jesus is unique in human history" (1996, 281, 309).

Jesus combined elements from both wisdom and eschatology in his ethics, but, as a good Jew, all his teachings remained grounded in the Torah – with the commandment to love God and neighbor at the center (1996, 348, 381). He radicalized this ethic, however, by making love applicable to strangers, outcasts, and even one's enemies. A distinctive feature of the Jesus tradition is that the powerless, persecuted, and humiliated are to show the generosity and renunciation of power that God demands from the powerful, an active, nonviolent resistance of the powerless with the aim of revealing injustice and overcoming it (1996, 343, 393).

Jesus as primarily a non–apocalyptic figure

In contrast to the scholars mentioned above, Marcus Borg makes a "temperate case" for Jesus as a non-eschatological figure, a charismatic wisdom teacher. For Borg, however, "non-eschatological" does not mean that Jesus never said anything about eschatology; it means that "imminent eschatology is not to be the interpretive context for reading the Jesus tradition" (1994, 88; cf. 1986). Borg's historical Jesus is a "Spirit-filled person in the charismatic stream of Judaism" similar to other Jewish holy men such as Honi the Circle-Drawer and Hanina ben Dosa. Jesus was a healer and exorcist, but he is most like the classical prophets of Israel. As such, he had a multifaceted role within the socio-political life of his people: He was a sage, a teacher of an "alternative wisdom," who pointed to a way of transformation. In addition, Jesus was a revitalization movement founder, who wanted to renew Israel with a charismatic, itinerant movement grounded in the Spirit, centered on him, focused on a call to repentance, and marked by joy and compassion, especially for the poor, outcasts, and sinners (1987, 124–140).

In 1989, Robert Funk described the Cynic-sage Jesus that was emerging from the Jesus Seminar's work: Jesus' precise words were unrecoverable, because oral transmission hopelessly obscured them, but we know that his characteristic speech included aphorisms, parables, and challenge-riposte exchanges; his language was pithy, vivid, and often humorous with caricature, hyperbole, or paradox (1989, 11–15).

The Seminar's reliance on what they viewed as the earliest layers of the tradition (Q and Thomas) led to their conclusion that Jesus did not expect the world to end soon. Jesus thus used the term "kingdom" more like a Cynic-sage than an apocalyptic prophet; apocalyptic elements are later additions (e.g., from Mark). Although Jesus regarded himself as anointed with the spirit, he did not believe himself to be the messiah. Jesus proclaimed the presence of "God's empire" in both deeds and words (e.g., Luke 11:20), and the lifestyle in God's empire is conditioned by reciprocity, radical almsgiving, and other "outrageous" standards of behavior (e.g., turning the other cheek; 1989, 12).

In 1998, Funk reported the Seminar's conclusions about the "acts" of Jesus. For example, Jesus' father was Joseph or some other male who seduced or raped Mary. Jesus was seen as a healer, but he only cured psychosomatic maladies and did not perform any "nature miracles." He did not claim to be the messiah, was executed as a public nuisance, and did not rise bodily from the dead (1998, 462, 533).

John Dominic Crossan argues that Jesus was a rural peasant Jewish Cynic who proclaimed a "brokerless kingdom" and lived in a system of open commensality that served to rebuild peasant community (1991, 262). Jesus proclaimed an "ethical eschatology" and a present kingdom in contrast to the apocalyptic eschatology of John the Baptist (1998, 282–304).

Jesus was a marginalized peasant trying to survive as a rural artisan or landless laborer. His voice cried out "from below," and his program united the destitute landless (itinerants) and the poor landed ones (householders) to rebuild the peasant community ripped apart by commercialization and urbanization (1991, 350–353). Jesus' strategy involved free healing and common eating, a religious and economic egalitarianism of the brokerless kingdom of God (1991, 421–422). He used such meals to signify unity, symbolize that God was present in the meal, and proclaim that everyone should have equal shares of both God and food. It is a present, sapiential kingdom of "nobodies" and the "destitute" – the unclean, degraded, and expendable (1991, 269, 273). Jesus, as an exorcist and a healer, offered an alternative means to God than those sanctioned by the dominant religious institution (1991, 309), and his healings demonstrated what God's kingdom looked like (1991, 332).

Bruce Chilton portrays Jesus as a *rabbi* or master of Jewish oral traditions, a teacher of the Kabbalah, and a practitioner of a Galilean form of Judaism that emphasized direct communication with God (2000, xix). A crucial element of Jesus' development is his identity as a *mamzer* (an "Israelite of suspect paternity") in Nazareth and the resulting ostracism from his community (2000, 3–22).

Richard Horsley depicts Jesus as a social revolutionary. He argues that Jesus formulated and led a program of renewal for the Jewish people. As a social revolutionary, Jesus actively opposed violence, especially institutionalized violence. Among various forms of Jewish resistance (e.g., rebellion, tax resistance, mass protests, and apocalypticism), Jesus advocated nonviolent social revolution in anticipation of the political revolution being effected by God (1987). This social revolution began when Jesus established alternative communities of covenant renewal that opposed the "Pax Romana" through exorcisms and healings. Similar to other prophetic leaders, Jesus proclaimed and enacted the Israelite tradition of God's judgment on oppressive rulers and an egalitarian renewal of the Jewish people. Jesus also proclaimed judgment on the temple, its leadership, and Roman rule (2003).

Toward a more inclusive view of Jesus

Other scholars, from perspectives that have not yet received a fair hearing, are more explicit about acknowledging their own ideological stances and depict Jesus in light of those perspectives.

Elisabeth Schüssler Fiorenza believes the Jesus movement was grounded in the experience of God's all-inclusive love, one that had a dream of liberation for every wo/man in Israel. Jesus stressed the goodness and mercy of God, and this emancipatory kingdom-of-God Jesus movement, as a discipleship of equals, most likely understood itself as a "prophetic movement of Sophia-Wisdom." Jesus as the prophet of Sophia sought to abolish the patriarchal family and rejected Jewish purity. Jesus' first followers then were "*Jewish wo/men* ... [who] followed a vision of liberation for every wo/man in Israel" (1994, 89–94).

African biblical scholars explore at least four major issues: (1) mission and colonialism, because they are acutely aware of being "evangelized"; (2) suffering and liberation, in light of the difficulties that Africa faces; (3) faith, in which the church is more important than the academy; and (4) the African cultural context, especially since similarities exist between the biblical cultural contexts and African contexts today (LeMarquand 1997, 165–167).

African scholars provide important new areas of dialogue, such as the image of Jesus as life-giver and healer, the one who restores life wherever it has been diminished (Stinton 2004, 103). Jesus also is envisioned as victorious over evil forces and thus becomes the protector, liberator, and leader (Bediako 2004, 21–22). A particularly important contribution is the image of Jesus as a "loved one," a member of a family and community who "actually shared in the life of the people" (Stinton 2004,

171). For western scholars who often focus on Jesus as an individual, this family/group-oriented nature of Jesus' historical context is a much-needed corrective.

The "synoptic Jesus"

Some third-quest interpreters defend the basic authenticity of the traditions of or about Jesus. Richard Bauckham stresses the presence of eyewitness testimony in the gospels (2006), while others focus on the reliability of oral traditions. James Dunn, for example, assumes that the characteristic features of the Jesus tradition – the structure, identifying elements, and key words – were treasured and formulated by the disciples *before* Easter and had already "become firm and established" (2003, 26, 121). Even Q "was given its lasting shape *prior to Jesus' death*," and the community's "corporate memory" protected oral performances from varying too much (2003, 27, 55).

Wright's criterion of double similarity and dissimilarity (see above) also assumes the general reliability of the Jesus traditions. Wright admits that there was some flexibility in the oral tradition but argues that the whole community knew the tradition well enough to prevent serious innovation (1996, 134).

Wright's signal contribution to the more conservative perspective is that he is able to affirm those traditions that portray Jesus as an apocalyptic prophet but to do so in a way that also allows Jesus to succeed – not incorrectly to predict an imminent end of the world. Wright accomplishes this by claiming that Jesus' apocalyptic language was not meant to be taken literally; it was a "complex metaphor-system," through which many ancient Jews expressed their aspirations for "social, political and above all theological liberation" (1996, 103). Jesus saw himself as the focal point of the returning-from-exile Israel. He was the true interpreter of the Torah, the true builder of the new, restored temple, and the true spokesperson for Wisdom. He also was the king through whom God was restoring Israel. In his redefinition of his role as the messiah, Jesus felt called by God to evoke the traditions promising God's return, enact those traditions in Jerusalem, and thereby to embody God's return. The kingdom was coming in and through his ministry and would be accomplished through suffering (1996, 651–652).

Thus, in practice, the historical Jesus of Dunn, Wright, Bauckham, and other such interpreters primarily takes the form of the Jesus portrayed in the synoptic gospels. One is left, however, with the problem that the gospels themselves give us varying portraits of Jesus, so we have almost come full circle.

Conclusion

In John 20:15, Mary Magdalene supposed Jesus to be the gardener, a foreshadowing perhaps of the many different conceptions of Jesus that developed throughout the centuries. These differing perceptions of Jesus certainly can be disconcerting; how can such a wide range of portraits result from such limited data? How can these portraits be diametrically opposed, such as whether Jesus was an apocalyptic prophet or a non-apocalyptic teacher of wisdom? The answer, once again, depends upon us as much as on our sources, and that is one of many reasons why the quest for the elusive but compelling Jesus of Nazareth will never truly end.

Notes

1   Used with permission: www.paulistpress.com.
2   This section is adapted from Gowler (2007, 31–190). Used with permission: www. paulistpress.com.

References

Allison, Dale C. Jr. (1987). "Jesus and the Covenant: A Response to E. P. Sanders." *Journal for the Study of the New Testament* 29: 57–78.

Allison, Dale C. Jr. (1998). *Jesus of Nazareth*. Minneapolis: Augsburg Fortress.

Bauckham, Richard (2006). *Jesus and the Eyewitnesses: The Gospels as Eyewitness Testimony.* Grand Rapids: Eerdmans.

Bediako, Kwame (2004). *Jesus and the Gospel in Africa*. Maryknoll, NY: Orbis.

Borg, Marcus J. (1986). "A Temperate Case for a Non-Eschatological Jesus." *Foundations and Facets Forum* 2 (3): 81–102.

Borg, Marcus J. (1987). *Jesus: A New Vision*. San Francisco: Harper & Row.

Borg, Marcus J. (1994). *Jesus in Contemporary Scholarship*. Harrisburg, PA: Trinity.

Bornkamm, Günther (1960). *Jesus of Nazareth*. New York: Harper & Row.

Brown, Colin (1985). *Jesus in European Protestant Thought 1778–1860*. Durham, NC: Labyrinth.

Bultmann, Rudolf (1934). *Jesus and the Word*. New York: Scribner.

Bultmann, Rudolf ([1921] 1963). *History of the Synoptic Tradition*. New York: Harper & Row.

Chilton, Bruce (2000). *Rabbi Jesus: An Intimate Biography*. New York: Doubleday.

Crossan, John Dominic (1991). *The Historical Jesus: The Life of a Mediterranean Jewish Peasant*. San Francisco: HarperSanFrancisco.

Crossan, John Dominic (1998). *The Birth of Christianity*. San Francisco: HarperSanFrancisco.

Dunn, James D. G. (2003). *Jesus Remembered*. Grand Rapids: Eerdmans.

Funk, Robert W. (1989). "The Emerging Jesus." *The Fourth R* 2 (6): 1, 11–15.

Funk, Robert W., and the Jesus Seminar (1998). *The Acts of Jesus: The Search for the Authentic Deeds of Jesus*. New York: HarperCollins.

Gowler, David B. (2000). *What Are They Saying About the Parables?* Mahwah, NJ: Paulist.

Gowler, David B. (2006). "The Chreia." In Amy-Jill Levine, John Dominic Crossan, and Dale C. Allison Jr. (eds.), *The Historical Jesus in Context* (pp. 132–148). Princeton: Princeton University Press.

Gowler, David B. (2007). *What Are They Saying About the Historical Jesus?* Mahwah, NJ: Paulist.

Harnack, Adolf ([1901] 1978). *What is Christianity?* Gloucester, MA: Peter Smith.

Herzog, William R. II (2000). *Jesus, Justice, and the Reign of God: A Ministry of Liberation*. Louisville, KY: Westminster John Knox.

Holtzmann, Heinrich J. (1863). *Die Synoptischen Evangelien*. Leipzig: Engelmann.

Horsley, Richard A. (1987). *Jesus and the Spiral of Violence: Popular Jewish Resistance in Roman Palestine*. San Francisco: Harper & Row.

Horsley, Richard A. (2003). *Jesus and Empire*. Minneapolis: Fortress.

Jeremias, Joachim (1971). *New Testament Theology*. Part 1: *The Proclamation of Jesus*. London: SCM.

Jeremias, Joachim (1972). *The Parables of Jesus*. 2nd edn. New York: Scribner.

Käsemann, Ernst (1969). *New Testament Questions of Today*. London: SCM.

Lachmann, Karl (1835). "De Ordine Narrationum in Evangeliis Synopticis." *Theologische Studien und Kritiken* 8: 570–590.

LeMarquand, Grant (1997). "The Historical Jesus and African New Testament Scholarship." In William E. Arnal and Michael Desjardins (eds.), *Whose Historical Jesus?* (pp. 161–180). Waterloo, Ontario: Wilfred Laurier.

Meier, John P. (1991–2009). *A Marginal Jew: Rethinking the Historical Jesus*. 4 vols. New York: Doubleday; New Haven: Yale University Press.

Neill, Stephen, and Tom Wright (1988). *The Interpretation of the New Testament, 1861–1986*. 2nd edn. Oxford: Oxford University Press.

Perrin, Norman (1976). *Rediscovering the Teaching of Jesus*. New York: Harper & Row.

Powell, Mark Allan (1998). *Jesus as a Figure in History*. Louisville, KY: Westminster John Knox.

Renan, Ernest (1927). *The Life of Jesus*. New York: Random House.

Ritschl, Albert (1900). *The Christian Doctrine of Justification and Reconciliation*. Edinburgh: T&T Clark.

Sanders, E. P. (1985). *Jesus and Judaism*. Philadelphia: Fortress.

Sanders, E. P. (1993). *The Historical Figure of Jesus*. London: Penguin.

Schüssler Fiorenza, Elisabeth (1994). *Jesus: Miriam's Child, Sophia's Prophet*. New York: Continuum.

Schweitzer, Albert (1968). *The Kingdom of God and Primitive Christianity*. New York: Seabury.

Schweitzer, Albert (2001). *The Quest of the Historical Jesus*. Minneapolis: Fortress. (Originally published in 1913 as *Geschichte der Leben-Jesu-Forschung*.)

Stinton, Diane B. (2004). *Jesus of Africa*. Maryknoll, NY: Orbis.

Strauss, David Friedrich (1994). *The Life of Jesus Critically Examined*. Ramsey, NJ: Sigler.

Talbert, Charles H. (1970). *Reimarus: Fragments*. Philadelphia: Fortress.

Tatum, W. Barnes (1999). *In Quest of Jesus*. Rev. edn. Nashville: Abingdon.

Telford, William R. (1994). "Major Trends and Interpretive Issues in the Study of Jesus." In Bruce Chilton and Craig A. Evans (eds.), *Studying the Historical Jesus* (pp. 33–74). Leiden: Brill.

Theissen, Gerd, and Annette Merz (1996). *The Historical Jesus: A Comprehensive Guide*. Minneapolis: Fortress.

Theissen, Gerd, and Dagmar Winter (2002). *The Quest for the Plausible Jesus: The Question of Criteria*. Louisville, KY: Westminster John Knox.

Weiss, Johannes ([1892] 1971). *Jesus' Proclamation of the Kingdom of God*. Philadelphia: Fortress.

Wrede, William ([1901] 1971). *The Messianic Secret*. Cambridge: James Clarke.

Wright, N. T. (1996). *Jesus and the Victory of God*. Minneapolis: Fortress.

CHAPTER 20

The "Jesus" of the Jesus Seminar

Robert J. Miller

To speak of a "Jesus" as a reconstruction or portrait is to acknowledge that such a representation is a crafted object, an artful assembly of parts. The mission and achievement of the Jesus Seminar was to exercise critical control over what parts might legitimately be taken up into credible portraiture of the historical Jesus.

The Jesus Seminar was established in 1985 by Robert Funk, with the dual goals of bringing scholars together to collaborate on historical Jesus research and communicating the findings of these scholars to the public. The present writer has participated in the Seminar since 1986. The task undertaken by the Seminar was ambitious: to assess the historicity of anything attributed to Jesus in any Christian source from the first three centuries. This task was tackled in two phases: the words of Jesus first, then his deeds (see McGaughy 1996). The Seminar's assessment of the sayings encompassed 518 sayings (1,553 if different versions of the same saying are counted). That phase of the Seminar's work was more or less complete by 1991 and the results were presented in 1993 in *The Five Gospels*. That volume offers a substantive introduction and the full texts of Mark, Matthew, Luke, John, and Thomas, with each saying color-coded, to indicate the degree of probability that it was spoken by the historical Jesus, and annotated, to explain the Seminar's rationale for each determination. In 1991, the Seminar turned to the deeds of Jesus, completing that work in 1997. Those results were published in *The Acts of Jesus*, which gave the four-color treatment to the narratives of the four canonical gospels, along with those of the Gospel of Peter and the brief narratives in Q. In short, the Seminar provided a database for crafting a historical portrait of Jesus.

This chapter describes the Seminar and its procedures, reviews the results of its work and their implications for historical Jesus research, and analyzes some difficulties in understanding the Seminar's conclusions. I briefly engage some of the critics of the Seminar, having done so at length elsewhere (Miller 1999).[1] I also explain my

The Blackwell Companion to Jesus, First Edition. Edited by Delbert Burkett. ©2014 John Wiley & Sons, Ltd. Published 2014 by John Wiley & Sons, Ltd.

own dissatisfactions with a few aspects of the Seminar's flagship publication, *The Five Gospels.*

The Seminar agreed to make decisions collectively by voting on the historical accuracy of items in the gospels. To report its findings, the Seminar sought to adapt the custom of red-letter editions of the New Testament, with the initial aim of printing in red only those words that Jesus "really" said. Fellows of the Seminar would vote for red if they judged a saying to be authentic or for black if they did not. This experiment died quickly when members balked at this either/or option and called for a way to accommodate more nuanced distinctions. Thus, two intermediate colors (pink and gray)[2] were added, and definitions of the four colors were adopted:

- Red: Jesus undoubtedly said this or something very like it;
- Pink: Jesus probably said something like this;
- Gray: Jesus did not say this, but the ideas contained in it are close to his own;
- Black: Jesus did not say this; it represents the perspective or content of a later or different tradition.[3]

Of the New Testament scholars invited by Robert Funk and co-chair Dominic Crossan, about two dozen attended the initial meetings. Membership in the Seminar was open to anyone who could read Greek and held a PhD or its equivalent in New Testament or a cognate discipline. No one with those credentials has ever been denied membership. Over the years, some members have resigned, and many others have joined. I estimate that most meetings had 30–40 Fellows in attendance, with many more on a few occasions. If everyone who participated at least once is counted, there have been about 200 Fellows; 74 consented to be named in the roster of Fellows in *The Five Gospels* and 79 in *The Acts of Jesus.*

The Seminar met twice a year to work through an ambitious agenda. A position paper, which included a voting recommendation, was prepared on each agenda item and pre-circulated. Meeting time was devoted entirely to discussion and debate, with votes taken at the end of each session. As a check on hasty decisions, the Seminar allowed reconsiderations. Any Fellow could call for a reconsideration of any vote at a future meeting and was given the opportunity to make a case for a different color. This happened on occasion, and some items received new colors on second votes.

The Seminar expressed the results of its votes by means of a weighted average. This process is far more democratic than a winner-takes-all system, which in any case is impractical when there is no majority among four options. By weighting the average, every vote is reflected in the outcome. The weighted average is calculated by assigning numerical values to the colors and applying a simple mathematical formula. An item is colored pink, for example, if its weighted average falls within the numerical range assigned to pink.[4] The Seminar reports its votes by giving both the color and the weighted average so that readers can see where the vote for each item falls within its color range.[5]

Fellows quickly discovered that there was little agreement among them on methodological issues. An early attempt to hammer out a consensus on method went nowhere. Most believed such an effort to be futile. Even if it had succeeded, members were worried that it might become a standard of academic orthodoxy within the Seminar. Members came to agree that the Seminar did not need a uniform method. Fellows would assess the historicity of the sayings according to whatever methods and criteria each judged most appropriate.

The Seminar's Conclusions about the Sayings

The Seminar found 15 red sayings in the gospels, of which 8 come from the sermon on the mount/plain: the beatitudes on the poor, hungry, and sorrowing, and the admonitions about the other cheek, coat and shirt, love of enemies, giving to beggars, and the second mile. "Give to Caesar" and Jesus' addressing God as *abba* are also red, as are the parables about leaven and mustard, the Samaritan, the shrewd manager, and vineyard laborers. There are 75 pink sayings, 13 of them falling only a Fellow's vote or two short of red. Among these "almost red" items are the parables about found treasure, lost sheep, a lost coin, a corrupt judge, a prodigal son, and a friend at midnight. Parables, aphorisms, and other wisdom sayings are well represented in the 90 red and pink items, which also, among many other sayings, include parts of the Lord's Prayer, the birds and lilies discourse, and the mission discourse.

Most of the pink and red sayings come from the Q material shared by Luke and Matthew. Mark has only 1 red saying (God and Caesar) and 17 pink ones. John has no red and only 1 pink saying (a prophet gets no respect at home, John 4:44).

Of the 518 sayings on the Seminar's agenda, 90 (or 17.4 percent, for some reason rounded up to 18 percent) of them are red or pink. This figure of 18 percent has been used by critics to emphasize how skeptical the Seminar was. But the percentage needs to be understood (and should have been much better explained in *The Five Gospels*) for what it is: 18 percent of the sayings in *all* Christian texts from the first three centuries, including non-canonical gospels colored black both by the Seminar and presumably also by its critics. As for John, my sense is that most scholars outside the Seminar would agree that few, if any, of its sayings are demonstrably authentic. So, if we consider the sayings in Mark, Matthew, Luke, and Thomas, and if we keep in mind that some of the gray material can be included (with the appropriate reservations – see the definition of gray in note 3 below), then the percentage of sayings admitted into the database would be significantly higher.

The Gospel of Thomas

The Seminar's work on Thomas attracted much attention. A number of critics assailed the Seminar for its consideration of this gospel, some attributing ideological motives to the Seminar's work on it (e.g., Johnson 1996, 19–20; Wright 1999, 107 n. 49), although no one offered any reasons why historical Jesus scholarship should *not* assess the authenticity of the sayings in Thomas. Criticism focused on the view prevalent within the Seminar that Thomas does not show literary dependence on canonical gospels. Most of the Fellows were convinced that some sayings in Thomas are as early as their canonical parallels. The Seminar worked with the hypothesis that the earliest layer of the Thomas tradition is as early as the earliest layer in the synoptic tradition, something most critics concede.[6] It is especially noteworthy that the Seminar's critics did not actually dispute its findings on Thomas.

The Seminar found only 3 red sayings in Thomas: the beatitude on the poor, the parable about the mustard seed, and the saying about God and Caesar (Thomas 54, 22, 100). The Seminar found 32 more sayings in Thomas that it colored pink. Of these 35 red and pink items, 33 have canonical parallels. Of the sayings unique to Thomas, the Seminar traced only 2 to Jesus: the parable about an assassin and the parable about an empty jar (Thomas 97 and 98). These results need to be empha-sized: of the sayings unique to Thomas none is red and only 2 are pink. The Seminar's verdict is therefore that Thomas tells us virtually nothing about Jesus that we did not already know from the synoptics.

However, seen from another angle, the Seminar's work shows Thomas to be a valuable resource for assessing Jesus' teaching. The Seminar takes Thomas to be an independent source. If that is correct, then Thomas provides multiple independent attestation for many otherwise singly attested sayings. By my count there are 33 such cases. The Seminar's analysis of Thomas therefore has the result of increasing our confidence in the historicity of a good deal of canonical material.

Some Implications of the Black Material

Much of the black material bears directly on salient issues in historical Jesus scholar-ship. Here is a quick, impressionistic outline of the types of reconstructed historical Jesuses that are incompatible with the Seminar's exclusion of its roster of black sayings.

The Seminar's work gives no support to reconstructions of a historical Jesus whose self-understanding matches up to later orthodox christology: a Jesus, for example, who believed and proclaimed (or coyly hinted) that he was the messiah; who identified himself with a supernatural Son of Man or personified Wisdom; who predicted his own passion; who saw himself fulfilling prophecy or believed that Israel's covenantal history was reaching its culmination in him; or who saw his death as a human sacrifice.

The Seminar's findings do not cohere with a Jesus who put himself at the center of his message and demanded that people "believe in" him, nor with a Jesus who insisted that loyalty to his person determined one's post-mortem status.

Although the Seminar's findings imply a Jesus who clashed with religious author-ities, virtually all the "woe to you" (which the Seminar de-euphemizes as "damn you") sayings are black;[7] the Seminar believes they originated in the polemics of early followers of Jesus against the Jewish authority figures of their own day.

The Seminar's work also rules out a Jesus who recruited the Twelve as a surrogate for Israel, left instructions for his church to carry on after his death, delegated his supernatural authority to apostles, or instituted the eucharist.

What proved most controversial among scholars is the Seminar's denial that Jesus was an apocalyptic prophet – the apocalyptic discourse, references to the *parousia*, warnings about eschatological judgment, for example, are all black. This issue has been one of the flash points in historical Jesus scholarship, and here the Seminar bucked the reigning paradigm.[8] The debate over whether Jesus taught and acted within an apocalyptic mentality probably cannot reach a consensus resolution, given the nature of the evidence. The best we can hope for is spirited and respectful debate, from which all can learn.[9]

Problems in Understanding the Seminar's Work

Careful readers of *The Five Gospels* and *The Acts of Jesus* face two difficulties. First, the color scheme is more complex than it might seem at first glance; the same color can sometimes have different meanings. Second, the two books provide only summary explanations of why the votes came out the way they did.

The four-color scheme

The four-color scheme is readily intelligible as a spectrum of judgments about historical probability. However, the interpretation of these colors requires some comment.

Red Red votes were rare, and inevitably so. To vote red, a member had to be convinced that a saying pre-existed any of its literary sources and that it had survived both the oral tradition and the composition of the gospel without being modified in any way that matters. Red results require a strong majority of red votes, because it takes only a few black votes to pull the average down to pink.

Black Black results likewise represent a wide agreement; a few red or pink votes can offset a majority of black ones to average out into gray. Black votes are not always as clear-cut as red ones, however. A black vote might reflect high confidence that a saying did not originate with Jesus. But a black vote might just as well reflect a high level of uncertainty: a consensus that there is no good evidence that a saying comes from Jesus. Many Fellows voted black not only when they were reasonably sure that a saying did not come from Jesus, but also when they could not make even a small case that it did. If a certain saying "sounds Christian," as a great deal of gospel material does, many (I hope most) critical scholars start with an initial presumption that it did not originate with Jesus. Given that starting point, a vote of any color other than black requires some countervailing evidence that, despite a saying's Christian overtones, it goes back to the Jewish Jesus. Thus a black vote on a saying can mean *either* that there are strong reasons to think a saying did not originate with Jesus *or* that there is no good reason to think that it did.

The black votes on most of the sayings in which Jesus quotes scripture merit some comment. Since the followers of Jesus used the scriptures to express their beliefs about him, most Fellows voted black on a given scriptural quotation attributed to Jesus unless there was some reason to think that it reflected his own teaching.[10] Here is where the ambiguity of black is most acute, for observers might infer from all the black ink that the Seminar does not believe Jesus used the scriptures in his teachings. Such an inference is understandable, but it is a mistake. I know of no Fellow who holds that Jesus avoided quoting scripture. The black results indicate that the Seminar could not make the case that the specific quotations attributed to Jesus did not originate with early Christians.

Pink   Pink and gray results are inherently more ambiguous than red or black ones, because, while the latter require consensus, the former might not. A pink designation can reflect broad agreement that "Jesus probably said something like this," but it can also reflect broad disagreement among the Fellows.[11] Even so, a pink result requires a healthy majority of red/pink votes, or at least a near majority of red/pink with very few black.

Gray   Gray is the most troublesome color to interpret, and the Seminar periodically debated its significance. The trouble is inherent in its definition, which contains two statements that pull in opposite directions: "Jesus did not say this, but the ideas contained in it are close to his own." Depending on which statement one emphasizes, a gray vote could be either an essentially negative or basically positive assessment. Fellows never achieved consensus on this matter.

Gray votes were often cast when there were good arguments on both sides and members could not decide. (An informal meaning eventually adopted for gray is, "Well, maybe.") A gray verdict was sometimes not the result of indecision, but, like its pink partner, of sharp disagreement within the Seminar. The mathematics of weighted averages also produced a few statistical anomalies: a few items with a majority of red and pink votes are colored gray.[12] The oddest example is the parable about the sower in Luke 8:5–8, which received no gray votes at all (21 percent red, 43 percent pink, 36 percent black). In this case the gray result is counterintuitive in light of the 64 percent red/pink. But gray is the correct calculation because (decisive) votes for red and black carry more mathematical weight than do (less decisive) ones for pink and gray.

Reasons for the votes

The second problem that complicates understanding the Seminar's findings is that there are limits to what can be known about the reasoning behind the members' votes. Three factors contribute to this problem.

1. The sheer number of votes taken by the Seminar[13] entails that the explanations for them are necessarily condensed. The commentary in *The Five Gospels* and *The Acts of Jesus* focuses on the major reasons for the colors in which each item is printed. In cases where there was a wide range of votes, as there often was, minority positions are given shorter shrift. Important nuances in the debates are sometimes not reported. Unfortunate as this state of affairs might be, the limitations of publishing – each volume extends to more than 550 pages – made it impossible to do otherwise.

2. Even if there were unlimited space for reporting the Seminar's deliberations, a full accounting would still be unattainable, because the Seminar is a collective entity. Strictly speaking, the Seminar does not have positions or even cast votes – only its members do. Statements like "the Fellows voted this saying gray because XYZ" need to be understood for the generalizations they are. Fellows who voted the same color might have done so for quite different reasons. Hostile critics of the Seminar who insinuate that its members marched in some kind of ideological lockstep need only to have attended a meeting to witness the diversity of views around the table.

Furthermore, different Fellows attended different meetings. It is entirely plausible – and in a few cases I am convinced it is certain – that a given item would have received a different color if it had been on the agenda of a different meeting.

3. The protocols of the Seminar ensure Fellows' confidentiality. Members judge the evidence by whatever standards they deem most appropriate at the time. Although Fellows often revealed during debates how they were inclined to vote, all voting was secret, and there was no expectation that anyone declare how he or she had voted or why.

So-called "Rules of Evidence"

A major portion of the Introduction to *The Five Gospels* (Funk and Hoover 1993, 16–34) is devoted to "Rules of Evidence." Much of this section is a skillful methodological primer to the historical assessment of the gospels, but parts of it are seriously flawed. Here I must register the most serious of my short list of criticisms of the book. But I want to make it clear that I do so within the far more encompassing gratitude and admiration I have for the erudition and prodigious intellectual labor that the authors generously lavished on *The Five Gospels*.

Most of the "rules" are basic principles of traditional gospel scholarship. Here are four examples:

- the evangelists frequently group sayings or parables in clusters and complexes that did not originate with Jesus (1993, 19);
- the evangelists often revise or edit sayings to make them conform to their individual language, style, or viewpoint (1993, 21);

- the evangelists frequently attribute their own statements (e.g., Mark 1:15) to Jesus (1993, 23);
- sayings or parables that are attested in two or more independent sources are older than the sources in which they are embedded (1993, 26).

Some of the "rules," however, are of a quite different character; they are generalizations about the speech of Jesus that are (and can only be) derived after a good bit of historical sifting has already occurred. For example,

- Jesus' sayings and parables cut against the social and religious grain (1993, 31);
- Jesus' sayings and parables surprise and shock: they characteristically call for a reversal of roles or frustrate ordinary, everyday expectations (1993, 31).

Obviously, there is an element of question-begging here, for one cannot know this about Jesus' words unless one has already determined which sayings come from the historical Jesus. Something similar must be said for the following:

- words borrowed from the fund of common lore or the Greek scriptures are often put on the lips of Jesus (1993, 22).

This is not a rule of evidence in the sense that it can be used as a criterion; it is a generalization entailed by the criterion of distinctiveness: that Jesus' characteristic speech must have been distinctive – and hence distinguishable from common lore – or else people would not have bothered to remember what he said. As a generalization, the principle is true enough. Yet it is useless as a criterion inasmuch as "often" allows for an exception in any specific case.

Finally, some "rules" are actually characterizations of the historical Jesus. Consider the following:

- Jesus rarely makes pronouncements or speaks about himself in the first person (1993, 32);
- Jesus makes no claim to be the messiah (1993, 32).

While the former of these can be taken as a reasonable description of the synoptic Jesus, one has to rule out the historicity of the Fourth Gospel for the description to stand as is. While the two statements could be defended as emergent from the criterion of coherence, calling them simply "rules of evidence" can confuse general readers and give scholars the false impression that the Seminar had already agreed on a portrait of the historical Jesus *before* it started its historical assessment of the gospels. In fact, statements like these were actually *results* of the Seminar's work, not the basis for it. Neither of the two statements can or did serve as a criterion for authenticity. They emerged as hypotheses for testing. Thus, to label them "rules of evidence" was seriously misleading.

Critics and Criticisms

A number of extremely critical reviews of the Seminar and its work appeared after the publication of *The Five Gospels*. Some of the most aggressive criticism of the Seminar has been exactly that, criticism of the group itself rather than of its academic work: impugning Fellows' integrity, belittling their academic positions, and accusing them of perpetrating fraud. Having previously analyzed and responded to these insults, I will here only list some of them and make the briefest of rejoinders.

1 The Seminar's membership is "self-selected." (True; membership is wide open to qualified scholars. What is wrong with that?)
2 Fellows do not teach on the faculties of prestigious institutions. (Mostly true, but so what?)
3 The Seminar was hungry for media attention. (What is wrong with courting publicity? And why would that count against the Seminar's findings?)
4 The Seminar deceptively claimed to speak on behalf of most scholars. (This charge is not supported by evidence: see Miller 1999, 66–67.)

Other criticism has been directed at the Seminar's procedures for voting and calculating its colors. Most critics have taken issue with the Seminar's treatment of the Gospel of Thomas, and some go to the heart of the historical Jesus debate by contesting the Seminar's finding that Jesus was not an apocalyptic prophet (see above for both issues). Many objections to the Seminar's work are not actually criticisms, but merely disagreements with its conclusions. That someone disagrees with a position is a fact, not a criticism.

The most acerbic of the criticisms of the Seminar's work is the most interesting, because it is the most puzzling: that the Jesus of the Seminar is not Jewish. This charge was clearly intended to be incendiary but turns out to lack content. The only "Jesus" of the Jesus Seminar is the implied speaker of the 90 red and pink sayings and the implied doer of the red and pink deeds. For this Jesus to be non-Jewish can mean only that those 90 sayings are outside the bounds of Judaism. In the absence of arguments why those sayings are non-Jewish, the charge of a non-Jewish Jesus must be regarded as vacuous rhetoric. The unmistakable passion and moral outrage with which this accusation has been made surely points to some underlying anxiety over the issue of Jesus' Jewishness (see Arnal 2005).

There is another point raised by critics that coincides with my own (and some other Fellows') disappointment in how the Seminar presented itself: the positivistic tone in which some spokespersons for the Seminar have occasionally represented its work to the public. Critics are right to protest on this point. All minimally competent scholars know well that all historical accounts are reconstructions, that the evidence for the historical Jesus is fragile, that strict objectivity is impossible, and that historical findings are matters of degrees of probability rather than certainty.

The Seminar should have done a much better job of communicating those crucial nuances.

There is also an element of truth in the critics' point that the positivism with which the Seminar's work is sometimes presented was a function of an anti-fundamentalist agenda. About that agenda the Seminar had no secret. It was a stated aim of the Seminar to open up a viable alternative to fundamentalism in public discourse about the Bible in North America. It does seem that in pursuing that laudable goal, the Seminar, both as a group and through its spokespersons, sometimes expressed itself in the positivistic rhetoric of the literalism it opposed. Not a few Fellows have winced at the "What Did Jesus Really Say?" on the front cover of *The Five Gospels*.

Although the Seminar finished its work on the gospels in 1998, some recent Jesus books for general readers still warn against it. Two examples will suffice. Thomas Rausch's *Who is Jesus?* (2003) has a brief, hostile treatment of the Seminar that impugns its members' motives[14] and tries to shock by insinuating that the Seminar maintains that Jesus was "accidently crucified" (2003, 10), a charge contradicted by the Seminar's finding that Jesus' temple incident led to his arrest (see below). Rausch's tone is unmistakably dismissive, but he offers no reasons why the Seminar's positions are wrong. Rausch assures the reader that "[f]ew scholars take the work of the Jesus Seminar seriously" (2003, 19), without, however, explaining how he knows this.

Catherine Murphy's *The Historical Jesus for Dummies* (2008) treats the Seminar in less than one page, most of it misinformation.[15] After giving the false impression that the Seminar has only thirty members, Murphy uncritically reports several criticisms of the Seminar, most of them inaccurate or misleading: for example, that the Fellows "aren't all trained scholars" (2008, 60) and that the Seminar relies heavily on the criterion of dissimilarity (the term "dissimilarity" is, I believe, absent from the Seminar's two big books). None of this shows evidence that Murphy actually read the Seminar's publications. Murphy's brief polemic, like Rausch's, obviously aims to assure readers that they too can safely dismiss the Seminar's work without examining it.

The Seminar and the Deeds of Jesus

Assessing the deeds of Jesus led the Seminar to affirm a number of his general practices. But specific instances of those practices were challenging to confirm. Two nested methodological problems had to be confronted that were not encountered in assessing Jesus' words.

The first had to do with an implication of the obvious and inevitable fact that the Jesus tradition was transmitted in language, which entails a fundamental distinction between how his words and deeds were transmitted: words can be repeated, while deeds must be reported. Jesus' words could have been, and in a few cases certainly were, remembered nearly verbatim and repeated for others to hear. His deeds, on the other hand, even if carefully remembered by eyewitnesses, had to be put into words and converted into stories. This process necessarily turns traditors into narrators, involving them in a series of choices of which the narrators are seldom fully aware: which details to include; how to describe the setting, characters, and actions; whether to pose as an omniscient narrator, and, if so, how much omniscience to assume; and so on.

Second, a fundamental distinction within the verbal art of narrative that impinges directly on the historian is the literary distinction between "recounting" an event and "enacting" it, or between "telling" and "showing." In recounting/telling, the narrators report events on their own authority: "this is what happened; take my word for it" (Funk 1998, 3). In enacting/showing, narrators verbally stage the event for the audience to "see" and hear what happened. Consider, for example, the story of Jesus' baptism in Mark 1:9–11. Verse 9 tells what happened (Jesus was baptized in the Jordan by John), while verses 10–11 show us what happened (the skies are torn open, the spirit descends like a dove, a voice from the sky is heard and quoted) (Funk 1998, 27). Historical assessment of this passage has to take up two distinct questions: how probable is it that (a) John baptized Jesus in the Jordan, and (b) the skies were opened, a presumably invisible spirit came down on Jesus "like a dove," and a voice spoke from the sky? The Seminar split the difference; it voted red on Mark 1:9 and black on 1:10–11, affirming the event of Jesus' baptism, but attributing the sights and sounds to the narrator's imagination.

These structural differences between how the sayings and the deeds of Jesus were preserved necessitated a modification in the definitions of the four colors. When voting on the deeds, the historical assessment goes to the information contained in a given gospel report rather than to its wording. Thus,

- Red: The historical reliability of this information is virtually certain. It is supported by a preponderance of the evidence.
- Pink: This information is probably reliable. It fits well with other evidence that is verifiable.
- Gray: This information is possible but unreliable. It lacks supporting evidence.
- Black: This information is improbable. It does not fit verifiable evidence; it is largely or entirely fictive.

The Jesus tradition passed on its memories of his deeds as stories (mostly anecdotes), not as a list of facts. As a result, there are a good number of scenes in the gospels that look like typifications. These stories bear so many traces of having been shaped by the oral tradition and/or composed by the evangelists that, assessed individually, they cannot be certified as reports of actual events. However, when similar stories are taken as a group, they may well point to an authentic memory about the kind of things Jesus did.

The exorcism stories are a case in point. The four gospels contain six exorcism stories, as well as several narrative reports and summaries of Jesus' exorcisms. The

Seminar voted five of those six stories gray and one of them black. Yet the memory of Jesus as exorcist is so firmly and widely rooted in the tradition that the Seminar was unsatisfied with those individual results. It therefore voted red on the statement "Jesus drove out what were thought to be demons." (The "what were thought to be" language seeks to disembed the act from its ancient interpretation.) The Seminar thus concluded that Jesus' contemporaries accepted him as an exorcist, but that the individual exorcisms in the gospels do not relate specific historical events.

The practice of distilling historical statements derived from the gospel accounts, though not actually contained in them, led the Seminar to a series of (red) affirmations:

- Jesus was an itinerant preacher in Galilee;
- Jesus preached in the synagogues of Galilee;
- Jesus cured some sick people;
- Jesus enjoyed a certain amount of popularity in Galilee and surrounding regions;
- Jesus practiced prayer in seclusion;
- Some who saw Jesus thought he was mad;
- Some who saw Jesus thought he was an agent of Beelzebul;
- Jesus consorted openly with social outcasts and was criticized for it.

In addition, the Seminar voted pink on the following:

- Jesus was a disciple of John the Baptizer;
- Some of John's disciples became followers of Jesus;
- The crowds who came to hear Jesus expected a sign related to the coming of God's kingdom, but Jesus refused to provide heavenly signs.

Jesus the healer

The Seminar's treatment of the healing stories illustrates well the complexity of assessing the deeds tradition. Of the nineteen cures or resuscitations in the gospels, the Seminar found that six are probably based on real events. That is, the Seminar voted pink on the "core stories" in the healings of Peter's mother-in-law (Mark 1:29–31), a leper (Mark 1:40–45), a paralytic (Mark 2:1–12), and a woman with vaginal bleeding (Mark 5:24–34), as well as two stories of Jesus restoring sight to the blind (Mark 8:22–26 and 10:46–52). A brief review of the assessment of three of these stories shows how the Seminar distinguished a core story from its narrative embellishments or determined that there was no core story.

1. In the healing of the bleeding woman (Mark 5:25–34), the core event is contained in vv. 25, 27, 29. These are colored pink, based on a reconstructed gist of the story: a woman suffering from a flow of blood touched Jesus' cloak and her bleeding

stopped instantly. The background explanation in v. 26 (she had suffered at the hands of many doctors who had taken her money but only made her worse) was voted gray. The rest of the narrative elements were voted black, because they were judged to be imaginative details (including the omniscient narration of the woman's interior monologue in v. 28) invented by storytellers. The result is a three-colored story.

2. In analyzing the Seminar's assessment of the healing of Bartimaeus, it is useful to include the different versions of the story. The whole of Mark 10:46–52 is pink, except for the gray introduction and conclusion. The introduction in v. 46 provides the geographical setting (outside Jericho), the audience (disciples and a crowd), and the name of the patient along with its explanation. The conclusion, "he started following him on the road," reflects Markan interests, especially Mark's *hodos* (road) theme. Both verses were voted gray (possible but unreliable) rather than black (largely or entirely fictive), because their details were deemed plausible.

Matthew's version of this story (Matt 20:29–34) is printed entirely in gray, because Matthew has transformed it into a healing of two blind men (as in Matt 9:27–31).

Luke's version (Luke 18:35–43) is colored the same as Mark's, except for the redactional touch at the end: the healed man starts to follow Jesus, "praising God all the while; everyone who saw it gave God the praise" (Luke 18:43b). This report reflects a favorite Lukan theme, praising God as an appropriate response to a miracle, and so it earned a black designation.

John's story of the man born blind (John 9:1–7) is a distant parallel to the Bartimaeus story. The only action statements in the story are John 9:6–7. The Seminar voted them gray, but agreed that the story "might well have been colored pink had the author not so completely adapted it to the controversy in which it is now embedded. Gray indicates the Fellows' recognition that what is left may yet harbor the memory of an actual event" (Funk 1998, 404). The Seminar reached similar conclusions about three other Johannine miracles (all gray): the healing of the official's son (John 4:45–54), the healing at Bethzatha (John 5:1–9), and the raising of Lazarus (John 11:33–34).

3. To round out this sampling of the Seminar's treatment of healing stories, it is instructive to examine one which is all black: the raising of the widow's son in Luke 7:11–17. Among the factors pointing to the fictional nature of this story are that it is: (a) found only in Luke, (b) modeled on the story of Elijah and the widow of Zarephath (1 Kings 17:17–24) – Luke being the most keen of the evangelists to portray Jesus as a prophet, and (c) situated just prior to Jesus' reply to John the Baptizer (Luke 7:18–23), in which Jesus quotes Isaiah's celebration of divine miracles, specifically that "the dead are raised" (Luke 7:22). It is also relevant that, unlike other resuscitation stories, in which it is unclear whether the victim is truly dead (as in 1 Kings 17:1; Luke 8:52; Acts 20:10), this story is unambiguous ("a man who had died," Luke 7:12), thus providing an unmistakable instance of the fulfillment of Isaiah's prophecy, as well as proof that "God has visited his people" (Luke 7:16).

Nature wonders

The Seminar joined a solid majority of historical Jesus scholarship in a skeptical judgment about the seven nature wonders narrated in the gospels: stilling the storm, feeding the four thousand and the five thousand with a few loaves and fish, walking on water, withering a fig tree, the miraculous catch of fish, and transforming water into wine. No doubt worldviews about the reality of supernatural miracles played a part in the Fellows' judgment, as they necessarily do for all scholars.

Passion narratives

The passion narratives present their own problems for historians. Four considerations loomed large in the Seminar's deliberations. (1) For many of the events in the passion narrative, it is difficult to imagine there having been eyewitnesses. Who would have witnessed and then reported, for example, the meeting between Judas and the authorities, Jesus' prayer in Gethsemane, or what happened at Jesus' "trials"? (2) The scenes in the passion narrative do not function as remembered anecdotes; they make sense only within a connected, plotted narrative. These episodes are therefore not the kind of material suited for oral transmission. (3) The strong influence of prophecy and psalms on the formulation of the stories in the passion narrative points to its scribal origins, further evidence that the narrative did not travel to the evangelists through the oral tradition. (4) All our versions of the passion narrative "exhibit a single, relatively coherent narrative," suggesting they all derive from a single source (Funk 1998, 132–133).

These considerations made it necessary for the Seminar to confront the issue of the source(s) of the passion narrative. Fellows agreed that Mark's was the earliest written passion narrative. Given the likely date of Mark's composition and the lack of evidence for prior individual oral anecdotes about the passion, the Seminar proceeded on the hypothesis that "scripture and theological imagination contributed to the contours and details of the story" (Funk 1998, 133). The Seminar took up each episode in the passion narrative separately, but the results were nearly always the same: black. The passion narrative in its entirety is colored black, except for a few bits which contain information the Seminar judged reliable: the temple incident precipitated Jesus' arrest (pink); Jesus alone was arrested – his disciples were not arrested (pink); the disciples fled when Jesus was arrested (pink); Jesus appeared before the high priest (pink); the priests turned Jesus over to Pilate (pink); Pilate had Jesus flogged and crucified (red); some female followers witnessed his death at a distance (pink).

The Seminar voted gray on two further details in the passion narrative: that Jesus was crucified as "King of the Judeans" and that Judas betrayed Jesus. The Seminar concluded that some disciple betrayed him, but there were doubts whether Judas was a real person.

The Seminar gave full consideration to the Gospel of Peter. Every verse in it was voted black.

Resurrection

Historical assessment of the resurrection by New Testament scholars has been beset by especially thorny problems, because of the intertwining of historical and theological issues. Although the question of whether Jesus was raised from the dead is theological, not historical, two questions are amenable to solution by assessing gospel texts: (1) did certain followers of Jesus experience visions of him after his death, and (2) are the empty tomb stories reports of an actual event? The issues and arguments on all sides of these questions are well known to New Testament scholarship, and the Seminar added nothing new to them. In considering the appearance tradition, the Seminar reached beyond the gospels to include Paul's testimony in his own writings and the stories about his visions in Acts. The Seminar reached the following non-black conclusions about appearances experienced by specific persons: red for the appearance to Paul (but gray for the stories in Acts: yes, Paul had a vision of Jesus, but those three stories are Lukan fictions); pink for that to Peter; red for that to Mary of Magdala (though the story in John 20 is gray); gray for that to the Twelve; and gray for that to James.

As for the empty tomb stories, the Seminar affirmed the traditional judgment of New Testament scholarship that they "represent a later development of the appearance stories" (Funk 1998, 466). The Seminar voted all these stories black.

The Seminar's "Jesus"

The Seminar accomplished what it set out to do. The task took twelve years of dogged effort. Participants can remember more than one dark day when the project seemed doomed. Able leadership and committed members collaborated to see this momentous adventure through to its goal. The Seminar's achievement is unprecedented: a detailed critical assessment of the entire Jesus tradition, complete with lucid commentary in language accessible to the public.

And yet this achievement has limitations. The Jesus Seminar did not reconstruct a historical Jesus. It did not try to – hence the hesitation in the title of this present chapter flagged by the scare quotes around the name of Jesus. What the Seminar produced is a database from which a historical Jesus can be reconstructed. Especially if one keeps in mind the ambiguous nature of the large fund of gray material, this database is malleable enough to support a range of diverse and even clashing portraits of Jesus. Only the black material is in principle excluded. It is fairly easy to see what kinds of Jesuses are ruled out by avoiding the black material – see the quick partial list above. It is far more challenging to take the Seminar's findings and (re)construct a coherent and credible historical Jesus. To do that, one needs to call upon a considerable repertoire of knowledge and practices, such as a hermeneutical framework, a parable theory, a robust description of first-century religion, politics, and economics in Judaism and the Roman Empire, a sociological model of Galilean society, and a fair grasp of the relevant archeology, to name only some.

The Seminar challenged its Fellows to employ its database and sketch their individual understandings of the historical Jesus. The best of these essays, too brief to be full portraits of Jesus and hence termed "profiles," are available in *Profiles of Jesus* (Hoover 2002), which includes contributions from Robert Funk, James Robinson, Marcus Borg, Dominic Crossan, Stephen Patterson, Kathleen Corley, Charles Hedrick, Bernard Brandon Scott, Robert Fortna, and others.

Notes

1   Portions of the present chapter are excerpted and adapted from that book.
2   Because the pink and gray inks are quite faint, for the two major volumes, the publisher opted for more vivid approximations: magenta and a soft blue.
3   An alternative set of definitions was also official, but in my estimation was seldom used by the Fellows: "I would include this item unequivocally in the database for determining who Jesus was (Red); I would include this item with reservations (or modifications) in the database (Pink); I would not include this item in the database, but I might make use of some of the content in determining who Jesus was (Gray); I would not include this item in the primary database (Black)."
4   The values are 3 for red, 2 for pink, 1 for gray, and 0 for black. The number of votes cast is divided by the sum of the numerical values of all the votes. The result is a weighted average between 0 and 1, which is then matched to a color according to a scale marked off into four equal regions: 0–.250 for black, .251–.500 for gray, .501–.750 for pink, and .751–1.00 for red. For example, consider a vote with the following result: 10 red, 15 pink, 10 gray, 5 black. The number of votes cast is 40 and the sum of their values is 70 (30 for the ten red votes + 30 for the fifteen pink + 10 for the ten gray + 0 for the black). The weighted average is .58 (40/70), which is pink.
5   *The Five Gospels* and *The Acts of Jesus* report the weighted averages only for the red and pink items. Full results for all votes on the sayings, which include the percentage of the votes for each color, are reported in exhaustive detail in *Forum* (the journal of Westar Institute), volumes 6 and 7 (1990 and 1991).
6   Critics object, and rightly so, to *The Five Gospels'* reference to an early "first edition" of Thomas, dated to the 50s. The existence of such an edition is controversial and does not have wide support. A controversial theory should not be presented as if it were a well established position.
7   Only one woe saying, Luke 11:43, came out pink.
8   For most critics of the Seminar, a non-apocalyptic Jesus is not just a historical error, it is beyond the pale of reason. Some critics found this aspect of the Seminar's work so offensive that they could not imagine it being the result of honest inquiry. *The Five Gospels* unwisely exposed the Seminar to this type of polemic by describing "the

liberation of the non-eschatological Jesus of the aphorisms and parables from Schweitzer's eschatological Jesus" as one of the "pillars of scholarly wisdom" (Funk and Hoover 1993, 4). This perspective on Jesus might indeed be a wise one, but presenting it as if it were a secure consensus was unhelpful to the Seminar and seriously misleading to the public.

9   This is the goal in *The Apocalyptic Jesus: A Debate* (Miller 2001), which features a productive exchange among Dale Allison and Dominic Crossan, Marcus Borg, and Stephen Patterson.

10 In four cases (Mark 10:6–8; 10:19; 11:17; 12:29–31; and all their parallels, including John 2:16), enough members had reasons to attribute these quotations to Jesus to produce a gray result.

11 For example, the saying about the powerful man's house in Luke 11:21–22 is printed in pink because the vote was 24 percent red, 41 percent pink, 17 percent gray, and 17 percent black. The most polarized vote for a pink saying, the one about saving your life by losing it, in Luke 17:33, was 46 percent red, 0 percent pink, 18 percent gray, and 35 percent black – in this anomalous case, a pink saying received *no* pink votes.

12 N. T. Wright complains that a "voting system that produces a result like this ought to be scrapped" (1999, 95), which is easy enough to say – until one tries to devise a fairer system. In fact, however, this "problem" is rare. Of the 518 sayings the Seminar analyzed, 15 (less than 3 percent of all sayings) with majorities of red and pink are printed gray.

13 For example, 380 votes were taken on the sayings in Luke. Separate votes were often held on different parts of the same saying, especially in sayings that contain redactional additions.

14 "[W]hether or not 'high scholarship' is the goal of the Seminar is highly debatable" (Rausch 2003, 17).

15 The bibliographic page in Murphy's book contains an astonishing disclaimer in bold print: "The publisher *and the author* make no representation or warranties with respect to the accuracy or completeness of the contents of this work" (italics added).

References

Arnal, William (2005). *The Symbolic Jesus: Historical Scholarship, Judaism and the Construction of Contemporary Identity*. London: Equinox.

Funk, Robert W., Roy W. Hoover, and the Jesus Seminar (1993). *The Five Gospels: The Search for the Authentic Words of Jesus*. New York: Macmillan.

Funk, Robert W., and the Jesus Seminar (1998). *The Acts of Jesus: The Search for the Authentic Deeds of Jesus*. San Francisco: HarperSanFrancisco.

Hoover, Roy W, ed. (2002). *Profiles of Jesus*. Santa Rosa, CA: Polebridge.

Johnson, Luke Timothy (1996). "The Jesus Seminar's Misguided Quest for the Historical Jesus." *Christian Century* (January 3–10): 16–22.

McGaughy, Lane (1996). "The Search for the Historical Jesus: Why Start with the Sayings?" *The Fourth R* 9 (5/6, Sept/Dec): 17–25. Reprinted in Brandon Bernard Scott (ed.), *Finding the Historical Jesus: Rules of Evidence (ch. 8)*. Santa Rosa, CA: Polebridge, 2008.

Miller, Robert J. (1999). *The Jesus Seminar and its Critics*. Santa Rosa, CA: Polebridge.

Miller, Robert J., ed. (2001). *The Apocalyptic Jesus: A Debate*. Santa Rosa, CA: Polebridge.

Murphy, Catherine (2008). *The Historical Jesus for Dummies*. Hoboken, NJ: John Wiley & Sons, Inc.

Rausch, Thomas (2003). *Who is Jesus? An Introduction to Christology*. Collegeville, MN: Liturgical.

Wright, N. T. (1999). "Five Gospels but not Gospel: Jesus and the Seminar." In Bruce Chilton and Craig A. Evans (eds.), *Authenticating the Activities of Jesus* (pp. 83–120). Leiden: Brill.

CHAPTER 21

The Quest for the Historical Jesus: An Appraisal

Helen K. Bond

The dominant view today seems to be that we can know pretty well what Jesus was out to accomplish, [and] that we can know a lot about what he said. (Sanders 1985, 2)

The figure of Jesus has always aroused interest and inquiry, both from the devoted and from his detractors. It is only since the Enlightenment and the rise of biblical criticism, however, that it has been thought possible and even worthwhile to attempt to separate the "historical Jesus" who walked the Galilean hills from the "Christ of faith" preached by the Christian church. With this development, the "Quest for the Historical Jesus" was born, manifesting itself in a number of distinctive phases over the last two centuries. The aim of this chapter is to offer an assessment of the quest, particularly its most recent phase. What are the distinguishing features of modern ("Third Quest") Jesus research? What are the most disputed areas? Where is the quest most open to criticism? And what are the ways forward for future research? First, though, a few words about the quest as a whole.

Quest or Quests? Messiness and Disorder

The quest, as any introductory textbook will verify, is usually divided into four broad periods: the Old Quest (from Reimarus to Schweitzer, 1778–1906); the period of No Quest (from Schweitzer to Käsemann, 1906–1953); the New Quest (from Käsemann, 1953 to roughly 1985); and the Third Quest (roughly from 1985 to the present). As an initial orientation, this scheme is certainly useful in mapping the broad contours of research into the life of Jesus. Yet, it is clearly an over-simplification, and like all over-simplifications there comes a point when the fourfold schema may begin to obscure rather than to clarify – as a few examples will illustrate.

The Blackwell Companion to Jesus, First Edition. Edited by Delbert Burkett. ©2014 John Wiley & Sons, Ltd. Published 2014 by John Wiley & Sons, Ltd.

First, it is well known nowadays that the quest did not really start as a "bolt from the blue" with Reimarus; rather he developed and synthesized views already current elsewhere, particularly among the English Deists (Brown 1985). It is true that Schweitzer began his highly influential book *The Quest of the Historical Jesus* (1906) with the Hamburg professor, but Schweitzer was writing very much from his own late nineteenth-century German context and took little interest in scholarship outside his native land (Bowman 1949, Gathercole 2000).

More problematic is the period designated "No Quest." This title ignores the works of eminent scholars such as T. W. Manson, C. H. Dodd, and Joachim Jeremias, all of whom published works on Jesus in the early twentieth century, not to mention important books by Jewish scholars such as Joseph Klausner (1925), whose work in some respects foreshadowed a number of third-quest assumptions. Furthermore, it quietly draws a veil over highly dubious scholarship from the Nazi era, some of it arguing for an Aryan Jesus (a topic to which we shall return below). The majority of New Testament researchers may well have been more interested in studying the composition of the gospels and the creativity of the early church at this period, but the broad label "no quest" is, at best, misleading (Marsh 1997).

And we also have the problem of the "Third Quest": who is included and who is not? N. T. Wright, who coined the phrase (Neill and Wright 1988), redefined it some years later to include only those who presented an *apocalyptic* Jesus (Wright 1996); the non-apocalyptic Jesus presented by the Jesus Seminar and those associated with it (Crossan, Borg) was not included, an assessment shared by the Seminar itself, which seems to locate its work more within the New Quest. Most historical Jesus scholars, however, use the term much more inclusively to refer to everyone involved in historical-critical reconstruction of the life of Jesus of Nazareth, though some prefer "Life of Jesus Research" (Telford 1994) or simply "Jesus Research" (Charlesworth 2006). In what follows, I shall use all these terms interchangeably, simply to refer to the most recent surge of interest in Jesus since the mid-1980s.

Second, it is also important to note that the usual, linear trajectory gives the rather misleading impression that research is moving in a straight line, and that there is a sense of "progress." In fact, things are much more cyclical than this (Carleton Paget 2001). Strauss' thoroughgoing use of "myth" in relation to the gospel stories anticipated the work a century later of Bultmann; Schweitzer's apocalyptic prophet was recreated to some extent in the work of Sanders; and some see in the work of certain members of the Jesus Seminar a return not so much to the New Quest as to the liberal Lives of Jesus of the nineteenth century (Dunn 2003). In any analysis of the various quests, it is as important to stress the continuity and parallels between the various phases as what distinguishes them.

Third, "the Quest" also suggests a unity of purpose and goal, which cannot be assumed for its contributors over the centuries. The Old Quest grew out of Enlightenment rationalism and had a distinct anti-dogmatic motivation; the New Quest, arising from a post-Bultmannian desire to recover the core of Jesus' teaching, had a much more theological agenda; and the Third Quest (as we shall see later) encompasses a diverse group of people, aims, and methods. Each phase of the quest was clearly interested in the first-century man from Nazareth, but the motivations and presuppositions behind this interest diverged significantly from one to another.

Fourth and finally, Jesus research clearly cannot be viewed in isolation, as if it existed in a vacuum distinct from western culture as a whole. The liberal Lives of the nineteenth century were clearly influenced by the artistic Romantic movement; the devastating legacy of two world wars in the early twentieth century left its impact on many aspects of Jesus scholarship; and the proliferation of profiles and methods in the most recent phase of research can hardly be unrelated to postmodern culture. Jesus research, like any discipline in the humanities, mirrors its historical and sociological setting. Changes in the landscape of New Testament studies have also left their mark: for example, archeological discoveries (such as the Dead Sea Scrolls or the Nag Hammadi library) and greater scholarly receptiveness to insights from the social sciences.

The story of the quest needs constant revision. Decisions need to be taken over what is included and what is not, and where to locate significant turning points and new trajectories, which are often observable only in retrospect. Useful evaluations include Telford (1994), Wright (1996), Marsh (1997), Powell (1998), Meier (1999), Carleton Paget (2001), du Toit (2001), and Evans (2006). What is abundantly clear, though, is that the last thirty years or so have seen a new and exciting phase in Jesus research, characterized by diverse methods and an almost bewildering array of reconstructions. What, then, does all this work have in common? What is it that allows us to see this new phase of scholarship as something distinct from what has gone before?

Distinguishing Features of Recent Jesus Research

The modern quest as a historical enterprise

One of the most striking features about modern Jesus research is its resolutely historical nature. While earlier phases of the quest were driven by theological or ecclesiastical concerns, the "historical Jesus" is now seen as a legitimate area of scientific enquiry, subject to the same constraints and methods of historical reconstruction as any other great figure from the past (e.g., Alexander the Great or the Emperor Augustus). Undoubtedly the main factor here has been the movement of the center of Jesus study from German theological faculties to secular university settings in North America (and, to a lesser extent, the British Isles). Contributors are no longer drawn from exclusively Protestant circles (though they still predominate), but now include Catholics, Jews, agnostics, and secularists. A Christian agenda can no longer determine the questions (still less the outcomes), and the only language permitted is that of historical-criticism.

Of course, the appeal to "history" rather than "theology" is not quite as straightforward as it might at first appear. Scholars have widely different conceptions of what "history" actually is, and the methods employed are as diverse as the contributors.

Still, the essentially historical rather than theological nature of the endeavor is now assumed. (We shall return later to some of the implications of this assumption).

The Jewishness of Jesus

For many observers, the leading characteristic of third-quest research is the insistence that Jesus was a Jew (Casey 2005). This is not an entirely new phenomenon: earlier scholarship had acknowledged Jesus' Jewishness but had either regarded it as having little relevance (so the liberal Lives) or had used it to show Jesus' inability to transcend the limitations of his own time and place (Reimarus and Schweitzer). Bultmann's demythologizing approach tended to reduce the specifics of Jesus' historical location in favor of a timeless, existentialist challenge, while the form-critical assumption that much of the gospels derived from the creativity of the early church directed attention toward nascent Christianity rather than the religion of its founder. The New Quest accepted that Jesus was a Jew, but was seriously hampered by the "criterion of double dissimilarity," which maintained that only material demonstrably at variance with both the Jewish milieu and the early church could be regarded as genuinely from Jesus (Perrin 1967). Not surprisingly, as many have observed, this criterion produced a Jesus strangely at odds with his Jewish environment (not to mention the church that followed him!).

What is distinctive about the Third Quest is its insistence that Jesus needs to be seen not *against* his Jewish environment, but very much as belonging to it, as someone *within* the first-century Jewish world and its structures. Part of the spur here was the fact that scholars came to appreciate more fully the diversity of Second Temple Judaism in the wake of the discovery of the Dead Sea Scrolls. The surge of interest that these scrolls awakened led to the breakdown of the division that scholars had erected between Judaism and Hellenism, the end of the assumption that rabbinic attitudes could be read back into the first century, and the publication of a number of significant works challenging the characterization of Judaism as legalistic (most notably Sanders 1977). While New Questers presupposed a "normative," monolithic Judaism of works-righteousness against which Jesus stood out, the Third Quest imagines Jesus operating within an extremely complex and diverse understanding of Second Temple Judaism. The question now is not so much "Was Jesus a Jew?" (the affirmative answer is assumed), but to which of the many branches of first-century Judaism did Jesus belong: apocalyptic, sapiential, prophetic, or sectarian (Essene, hasidic, Pharisaic, nationalist)? In other words, "What *kind of a Jew* was Jesus?" If the criterion of dissimilarity has not been entirely abandoned by recent research, it is used much more cautiously, while some prefer to replace it with a "criterion of plausibility," in which the significant question is whether Jesus' actions make sense within a Palestinian setting (Theissen and Winter 2002).

In view of the importance of Jesus' context, reconstructing the Jewish world of the first century is now central for Jesus scholars. It is necessary to know details not only of religious observance, but also of the social, cultural, economic, and political strands of life so intertwined in an ancient setting. Studies of Galilee in particular have proliferated, detailing the degree of Hellenization in the region, the extent and effect of Antipas' urbanization policies, relations between village and city, settlement patterns, taxation, and so on (see L. Levine 1992; Meyers 1999; Reed 2000; Chancey 2002; Jensen 2006). Interdisciplinary approaches are particularly popular, often drawing on sociological models developed by cultural anthropology and the social sciences more generally in an attempt to understand peasant societies, honor and shame, purity, patron and client relationships, and millenarian movements (so Oakman 1986; Horsley 1987; Crossan 1991; Borg 1998; Allison 1998). Archaeological excavations, too, have played a crucial role: historical Jesus scholars now take an interest in site reports from a variety of locations throughout Israel – Jerusalem, Caesarea Maritima, Sepphoris, Capernaum, and Bethsaida (Charlesworth 2006). The social and religious lives of women, along with the reconstruction of gender in the first century, have also become important (see, e.g., Ilan 1996; Kraemer and D'Angelo 1999).

Literary texts continue to occupy a central position in historical reconstruction, but Jesus scholars now move beyond the information furnished by the gospels alone and consult a much wider range of contemporary literature. Recent decades have seen more sophisticated studies of Josephus (Freyne 1988; Mason 2003) and Jewish sectarian literature (Charlesworth 1982; Sanders 1985; Rowland 2002), particularly the Dead Sea Scrolls (Vermes 1997), the targums (Chilton 1984), and the New Testament Apocrypha and Pseudepigrapha (Schneemelcher 1991–1992; Robinson 1988). Although not all the authors mentioned in the last two paragraphs would regard themselves primarily as "Jesus scholars," their work has provided invaluable guidance in situating Jesus within a realistic first-century environment. And this interest in the Jewish environment, and Jesus' place in it, leads to our third distinguishing feature of third-quest research: its preference for what we might call the "larger picture."

Focus on the larger picture rather than sayings

The New Quest focused all its attention on the *sayings* of Jesus; this was perhaps only to be expected, given the high store set by Protestants on "the Word" and the tendency of the form critics generally to regard narrative sections of the gospels as "legendary compositions." While some still prefer to start with sayings (e.g., the Jesus Seminar; Crossan 1991; Meier 1991–2009), a striking feature of the majority of modern Jesus scholars is their confidence that it is possible to present a much more rounded picture of Jesus, his role, and his significance in his ancient setting. The search for the actual words of Jesus (the *ipsissima verba*) has now given way to broader questions: What were Jesus' aims? Where do we locate him within first-century Judaism? How did he relate to his contemporaries (social outcasts, women, the Jewish leadership, and the religiously impure)? Why did he die? And how can we explain the movement that followed him?

The approach of Sanders (1985) may be considered paradigmatic. Sanders starts with a reconstruction of both first-century Judaism and what he regards as "indisputable facts" relating to Jesus' life. These include baptism by John, calling of the Twelve, preaching the kingdom of God, the demonstration in the Temple, and crucifixion. Sanders sees the Temple controversy as central, so he starts his investigation at this point, interpreting Jesus' actions within the wider setting of Jewish restoration eschatology. Jesus, for Sanders, was an apocalyptic prophet, announcing the establishment of a new Temple and the restoration of the twelve tribes of Israel. It is only once this broader picture is in place that various gospel sayings, after some analysis, are placed into the framework. Most recent Jesus work has followed this basic pattern. There is still an interest in criteria for determining which sayings of Jesus are most authentic (multiple attestation, coherence, and embarrassment are popular), but this is very much secondary to establishing the broader context.

This general concern to establish the "larger picture," however, is as far as the agreement goes. To a large extent, whichever aspect a scholar emphasizes in Jesus' context determines the resultant portrait of Jesus. Where healing is seen as central, Jesus is presented as a magician (M. Smith 1978) or a charismatic healer and exorcist in the line of Honi the Circle-Drawer or Hanina ben Dosa (Vermes 1973). If apocalyptic eschatology is the defining element, Jesus is characterized as an eschatological prophet of restoration (Sanders 1985; Meier 1991–2009, vol. 2). Where teaching takes center stage, Jesus is seen as a sage or rabbi (Flusser with Notley 2007; Chilton 1984), a Pharisee (Maccoby 2003), a wisdom teacher preaching a radical egalitarianism (Schüssler Fiorenza 1983), a subversive sage (Borg 1998), or a social revolutionary (Horsley 1987). And those who argue for a strong Hellenistic influence on Galilee often categorize Jesus as a Cynic teacher (Downing 1992; Mack 1993; Crossan 1991). Despite their different emphases, however, all these reconstructions represent attempts to situate Jesus firmly within his Jewish environment, and to show his significance within that setting.

It is already apparent, however, that historical Jesus scholars are far from reaching a consensus on who Jesus was. Once we go beyond the three broad areas that I have highlighted – a commitment to the historical method, the certainty that Jesus was a Jew, and a concern to present the larger picture within a Jewish context – division and diversity reign. We shall now explore some of the main areas of disagreement.

Disputed Areas

Sources for the study of Jesus

Until the nineteenth century, it was assumed that all four gospels were equally valid sources for the life of Jesus. Two events, however, shattered this confidence. First was Strauss' forceful presentation of the theological nature of John's gospel and his consequent insistence that historical reconstructions should utilize only the synoptic gospels (1835). Second, this was followed by a growing acceptance of the "two document" hypothesis, in which Mark was regarded as the earliest gospel and seen as the source (along with another document, Q) behind both Matthew and Luke (Streeter 1924). Although it had to be admitted that Mark, like all the gospels, had a theological agenda, the question of sources had been raised, and the assumption made that the earliest (and least obviously theological) was to be preferred. The New Quest, consequently, confined itself to analyses of the synoptics; even Dodd's valiant attempts to unearth historical traditions in the Fourth Gospel failed to have much of an impact (1963).

Today, however, the question of sources has been reopened and debated like never before. This springs, partly, from a general revival of scholarly interest in apocryphal (non-canonical) literature but is also fueled, in some circles, by a desire to move away from what is seen as the constraints of an ecclesiastically determined canon (Hedrick 1988) or, for some, a desire to embrace it. The (hypothetical) document Q, believed by some to be from Galilee and to date to the 50s, has been analyzed and stratified into three literary layers (sapiential, apocalyptic, and a final redaction), each with a discernible theology (Kloppenborg 1987). While some take the first of these layers as early evidence for the historical Jesus (e.g., Crossan 1991), Kloppenborg himself warns against such naive assumptions (1996), and still others doubt the possibility of redactional analysis on a non-extant document (Van Voorst 2000; Dunn 2003).

Most divisive of the non-canonical gospels is the Coptic *Gospel of Thomas*, a copy of which was found in the Nag Hammadi library. While the majority date it to the second century, and regard it as both Gnostic and in all probability dependent on the canonical gospels, others argue that it may preserve more authentic traditions than the canonical gospels (Patterson 1993). Crossan vigorously defends the "Cross Gospel," a passion narrative he dates to the 40s and finds embedded within the second-century *Gospel of Peter* (1988). Less controversially, the historicity of the Fourth Gospel has been reopened, with a number of scholars accepting John's more complex relationship between Jesus and the Baptist, his longer three-year ministry, his Jesus who regularly attends Jewish feasts in Jerusalem, his more realistic depiction of Jesus' Jewish interrogation, and his dating of Jesus' death on the Day of Preparation (D. M. Smith 2001; Anderson et al. 2007).

It is impossible to underestimate the importance of sources in this whole enterprise: the sources on which a scholar bases his or her reconstruction will fundamentally determine what kind of Jesus emerges. In general terms, the more liberal the scholar, the more likely s/he is to seek to use material beyond the four gospels. It is hardly an accident that the Jesus of Sanders, Wright, or Dunn looks and sounds very much like the synoptic Jesus on which their reconstructions are exclusively based. Bringing John into the matrix (so Meier 1991–2009; Fredriksen 2005) creates a subtly different picture, but one still very much in continuity with older reconstructions and recognizable in ecclesiastical circles. Once precedence is given to other sources, however, whether a putative earliest strand of Q or sayings from the *Gospel of Thomas* (so Crossan 1991; Mack 1993; and the Jesus Seminar generally), the reconstructed Jesus begins to look rather different. His death and its significance become much less prominent, since neither Q nor the *Gospel of Thomas* have passion narratives or give any explicit importance to Jesus' crucifixion; and the apocalyptic element so central to many synoptic texts gives way to a portrait of Jesus as a slightly Gnostic wisdom teacher. In fact, the whole question as to whether the apocalyptic sayings in the tradition go back to the historical Jesus or to the early church is a particularly divisive issue in modern Jesus studies, and one to which we shall now turn.

Did Jesus preach an apocalyptic eschatology?

Following Schweitzer (1906), it was taken for granted that Jesus was an apocalyptic prophet who expected the imminent intervention of God in a decisive cosmic cataclysm that would sweep away this world and inaugurate a new creation. The centrality of theologies of hope after the devastation of the Second World War reinforced this understanding (Kloppenborg 2005), as did the vivid apocalyptic eschatology revealed in the Dead Sea Scrolls. Although it was accepted that there was an element of the "here and now" in Jesus' kingdom language (see in particular Dodd's "realized eschatology," 1935), the stress throughout the New Quest continued to be on the imminent future arrival of God's kingdom, and the view that Jesus was an apocalyptic prophet is still the dominant position today (see, e.g., the reconstructions of Sanders 1985; Wright 1996; Allison 1998; Ehrman 1999; Fredriksen 1999; Meier 1991–2009; Dunn 2003). Proponents of this view stress the flourishing of apocalyptic and millenarian beliefs within some strands of contemporary Jewish thought (such as 1 Enoch, the *Sybylline Oracles*, and the *Testament of Moses*). They argue that since both Jesus' predecessor, John the Baptist, and his earliest followers (including Paul) held an apocalyptic outlook in which Jesus would return to herald God's judgment, it seems only logical that Jesus himself held such a view. They also stress the centrality of certain key passages within the tradition (such as Mark 9:1; 13:30; Matt 10:23). Other arguments can be brought too: Amy-Jill Levine (2005) suggests that Jesus' teaching on sexuality (followed by Paul and the early church) assumes that his is the last generation and that the world is about to end.

Since the 1980s, however, a number of scholars, particularly in the United States, have begun to challenge this position (in particular, the Jesus Seminar and many of its members: Crossan 1991, Borg 1998, Mack 1993). Was Jesus' teaching really apocalyptic, or was the stress rather on the present and on what humans need to do to bring about the kingdom of God in their own lives? Many would still regard Jesus as "eschatological" (in that he had some sense of the end of things, of the establishment of the kingdom) but reject the view that he was an apocalyptist preaching the imminent end of the world through the decisive action of God. A great deal depends on what is counted as primary material. Do the sayings that predict the future vindication of the "Son of Man," for example, originate with Jesus or with the post-Easter church? How much weight should be given to reconstructions of Q that suggest that the earliest layers of tradition lacked apocalyptic orientation? And are the apocalyptic-sounding kingdom passages to be understood literally or metaphorically? Did Jesus break with John the Baptist on the question of apocalyptic eschatology (as he did in other areas, such as his rejection of John's ascetic lifestyle), only for it to be reinstated by the post-Easter fervor of the early church? And does Jesus' love of celebration sit awkwardly with an apocalyptic message in which the world is about to pass away (so Funk 2000)?

Decisions on (the degree of) Jesus' apocalypticism color scholars' assessments of his teaching. In general terms, the more Jesus is seen as an apocalyptic prophet, announcing the imminent end of the world, the more he is seen as an otherworldly figure and the less interest he appears to have with worldly concerns or social reform. If, however, one rejects the apocalyptic Jesus, this-worldly issues become more prominent, and Jesus emerges as a social prophet with a specific program. It is largely (though not exclusively) among those advocating a non-apocalyptic Jesus, therefore, that the greatest attention is paid to Jesus as a social reformer, or even revolutionary, as we shall see below.

A social and political revolutionary?

Precisely which aspects of society are targeted by Jesus' critique depends to a large extent on scholars' analyses of the "problems" of first-century Galilean and Judean society, though there are several areas of overlap.

Borg (1998), for example, argues that Jesus set himself against the "politics of holiness" that permeated first-century society. Like the Hebrew prophets before him, he preached instead the unmediated compassion of God. For Schüssler Fiorenza (1983), the problem was society's oppressive patriarchy; she sees Jesus as the leader of a Jewish renewal movement, a "discipleship of equals" based on inclusivity, egalitarianism, and a rejection of all forms of hierarchy and control. Horsley (1987) presents Jesus as a (nonviolent) political rebel and revolutionary; his Jesus set himself not only against Roman imperialism (as to varying extents did the Jesus of Reimarus, Schweitzer, and Brandon 1967), but also against deeper societal injustices: political oppression, hierarchical structures, and unequal distribution of power, privilege, and wealth (see also Oakman 1986). Crossan (1991), too, regards Jesus as a counter-cultural Cynic teacher inaugurating a "brokerless kingdom of God," a social and political revolutionary promoting religious and economic egalitarianism through free healing and common eating.

Most of these presentations reconstruct a Galilee in which heavy Herodian taxation and urbanization, coupled with priestly oppression, contributed to debt, land loss, and the rise of brigandage. Jesus' message, therefore, was one of hope to the economically and politically oppressed. Not surprisingly, perhaps, those who argue for an apocalyptic Jesus often tend to have a more positive assessment of conditions under Antipas (e.g., Sanders 1985; Meier 1991–2009; Dunn 2003). Although there were clearly injustices in contemporary society, and Jesus spoke out against them in his parables and other teaching, they were not the central concern for the apocalyptic Jesus. Once again, the way in which a scholar reconstructs the first-century context plays an important role in determining the resulting portrait of Jesus and his role within society.

Critique of the Quest

We have now looked at both some shared features of modern Jesus research and some areas of considerable divergence. Is this lack of consensus a problem? And does the lack of secure results undermine the whole project? In this final section, we shall look at critiques of the quest, both from Jesus researchers themselves and from outside observers.

It has to be acknowledged at the outset that the quest is open to criticism on a number of grounds. It is often said to be too western, too white, too bourgeois (Georgi 1992), and too male (aside from Schüssler Fiorenza, Fredriksen, and Corley 2002, very few women write "Jesus books"). The quest has also been criticized for not taking into account the reconstructions of liberation theologians and third-world scholars, who often do not work within traditional historical paradigms. The lack of any kind of clear and agreed-on methodology is also a difficulty for some, not to mention the lack of consensus as to how this might be rectified. The Jesus Seminar's reliance on a wider group of sources has been criticized by their opponents (Johnson 1996; Meier 1999; Bock 2002); many question the existence of Cynic traditions in Galilee in the first century; and even the use of sociological models is not uncontroversial (see the critique in Sawicki 2000). And the tendency of some Jesus scholars to court media attention, while beneficial in ensuring popular interest in the founder of Christianity, has the less advantageous effect of promoting more sensational views.

Perhaps the best known criticism of the quest, however, is its subjectivity. It is often said that those who look for the historical Jesus end up seeing only their own reflection at the bottom of a deep well. In the following paragraphs, I shall focus on this critique. Is it true? Can it be avoided? And *should* it be avoided?

One of Schweitzer's most powerful arguments against the liberal Lives was that they had made Jesus into a nineteenth-century German who provided a relevant example for their own day. The charge that researchers make Jesus in their own image, and concerned with their own concerns, is a persistent and important one. It is also one that is much easier to see in others than oneself. Ironically, even Schweitzer's Jesus, whom he categorized as a "stranger and an enigma," served his own purposes of liberating the "spiritual Christ" rather well (Bowman 1949). As

Kloppenborg (2005) notes, it is not so much that scholars construct a Jesus whom they *like*, as that there is a tendency to conceptualize a Jesus who accords with (or fails to accord with) their worldviews.

A few examples will illustrate this. One of the most glaring cases of agenda-driven research comes from Nazi Germany. Jesus books from this period exhibit an appalling anti-Semitism. An early example was the popular and bestselling work of Chamberlain (1899, in its twenty-ninth German edition by 1944), which argued that Jesus belonged to the mixed ethnic group brought into Galilee after the Assyrian deportation, and that he might possibly be of Aryan stock. More academically, Grundmann (1940) similarly argued that Jesus was probably not racially a Jew, even though his family held to the Jewish "confession," and that he stridently opposed the Judaism of his day. Grundmann's views, though completely discredited now, are a particularly good example of how assumptions and biases arising from a scholar's own situation can influence his portrait of the historical Jesus (see discussion in Heschel 2008; Head 2004; Casey 2005).

At the opposite extreme, the Jesus of Vermes and Sanders has been criticized for downplaying the opposition between Jesus and his co-religionists to such an extent that it becomes difficult to account for his death (so, e.g., Casey 2005). The implicit criticism here is that these scholars have produced a Jesus who is too Jewish, that they are so concerned to move away from outdated pictures of "normative Judaism" that they have blurred distinctions and disputes between Jesus and his fellow Jews. In a similar vein, Holmén (2001) notes that third-quest researchers emphasize Jesus' Jewishness while the new understanding of the diversity of first-century Jewish belief renders such assertions meaningless. What does it actually mean to say that Jesus was Jewish? And at what stage, in the variegated landscape, might a researcher argue that he was not Jewish? Jesus is held to a greater conformity to "common Judaism" (to use Sanders' well-known phrase) than any other first-century Jew. Not surprisingly, perhaps, several researchers (Holmén 2001; Arnal 2005) see the Third Quest's insistence on Jesus' Jewishness as a reaction to the Holocaust, as a reflection of (predominantly Christian) guilt, and an attempt at atonement. This may also account for the fact that Jesus is nearly always presented as someone who looks broadly like a Jew today: despite scholarly awareness of the diverse character of first-century Judaism, Jesus is rarely seen as anything other than Torah-observant and upholding the traditions of Israel. Indeed, as Arnal notes, those who stress a Hellenized, Cynic teacher often find themselves accused of presenting a non-Jewish Jesus. The simple phrase "Jesus the Jew," then, while clearly historical at a basic level, may stand as a cipher for a whole host of modern concerns – from scholarly and societal guilt to the construction of Jewish and Christian religious identity.

The Jesus Seminar and the works of those associated with it have been particularly criticized for producing a Jesus curiously attractive to modern concerns (see Johnson 1996). Their Jesus – a "hippy in a world of Augustan yuppies," who challenged hierarchy and "organized religion" – is deeply unpalatable to those of a more fundamentalist or conservative persuasion, yet he appeals to many modern people, particularly those outside the church, for whom the greater stress on social action coupled with a reduced role for dogma and the supernatural is attractive. Just because a presentation has contemporary relevance, of course, does not automatically mean that it is unhistorical, but it should make an interpreter stop and consider.

Most Jesus scholars today, informed by postmodernism, are very much aware that historical reconstruction is culturally embedded. No one can ever be "neutral"; the situation and interests of scholars, not to mention those of the communities to which they belong, have an effect on their reconstructions. While many still aspire to some degree of "objectivity," there is a growing sense that Jesus research needs to take postmodernism much more seriously (see the discussions in Wright 1996; Crossan 1991; Dunn 2003). Crossan in particular declares himself striving after "attainable honesty" rather than "unattainable objectivity" (1991, xxxiv). One of the advantages of the wider participation of scholars in the Third Quest is that assumptions and preconceptions not demonstrably arising from ancient sources can quickly be highlighted and challenged.

But is it always wrong to allow modern concerns to influence our reconstructions, particularly when the focus of our scholarly endeavors is the founder of a faith that still has enormous significance today? The answer to this question seems to be mixed. Some would say that imputing one's own concerns to Jesus is inadmissible. The "historical Jesus" is a scholarly construct, a term to denote our best attempt, on the basis of available sources, to reconstruct the life of Jesus of Nazareth. The "real Jesus" of Christianity, or the Christ of faith, though clearly connected to this construct, is a different matter altogether. Christians are free to assign to the "real Jesus" whatever values and concerns they deem theologically appropriate, but the same freedom does not apply to the "historical Jesus." The construction of ethically useable portraits of Jesus (to say that he was egalitarian or that he had a social agenda) is of particular concern to Jewish scholars, who realize that too much stress on Jesus as a reformer potentially suggests that such concerns were not prevalent within contemporary Jewish society at large. An example of such stress is the feminist emphasis on Jesus' egalitarian attitude toward women. The more Christian feminists emphasized Jesus' egalitarian agenda, the bleaker the portrait of contemporary Jewish attitudes toward women became, creating a dichotomy between a "good and liberating Christianity" and a "bad and restricting Judaism" (Fredriksen 2005, A.-J. Levine 2005).

Those approaching the historical Jesus from a broadly Christian perspective, however, are perhaps unlikely to have modern issues far from their minds. Although it is criticized for its "modern" picture of Jesus, one of the *intentions* of the Jesus Seminar was to reform Christianity, to present its founder as a social activist with relevance to the secular world rather than as the Christ of dogma (the implications of this are spelled out in Jesus Seminar 2000). Nonwestern theologians might specifically promote the work of those scholars who see a strong socio-political agenda in Jesus' message, arguing that it speaks more powerfully to the needs of people in the third world who may similarly be confronted with issues of debt, land tenure, and exploitation (Sugirtharajah 1990). And from a feminist perspective, Schüssler Fiorenza (2000) argues that the focus on Jesus as the unique "genius" fails to give enough significance to the groups of disciples who remembered him, revered him as God incarnate, and formed the earliest Christian communities. Only by focusing on the *movement* rather than its founder can the many contributions of women and marginalized men come to the fore and offer an alternative to Christianity's deeply patriarchal traditions.

What is needed in all this, besides honesty and self-reflection, is something between historical positivism (the view that there is some kind of objective, recoverable "truth") and an irresponsible desire to modernize Jesus – though the path between the two is extremely difficult to navigate.

Future Inquiries

All indications suggest that Jesus studies are set to continue well into the twenty-first century. The "historical Jesus" is a credible and lively area of study, within both secular and, increasingly, more traditional settings. Several features of the Third Quest are now clearly established: the need for interdisciplinary approaches (some of the older sociological models may have been challenged, but others will doubtless take their place); the centrality of archaeology and the Galilean context; and the study of first-century Judaism and Jesus' place within it. Detailed studies of the political situation of Judea, the villages of Galilee, and the people associated with Jesus are now possible and, even indirectly, will shed light on the man from Nazareth. Sources and methods will continue to attract debate, as will the apocalyptic orientation of Jesus, though I doubt, in the end, whether there will be much consensus. Perhaps an area of growth will be the study of the transmission of the traditions, fine tuning older form-critical analyses through attention to studies of orality (Bailey 1991; Weeden 2004) and memory (Schüssler Fiorenza 1983; Crossan 1999; Dunn 2003; 2005). Ultimately, historical Jesus studies, though based on a scholar's most accurate and tested set of "hard facts," will always involve some leap of imagination. What new portraits of Jesus will emerge in the coming decades, only time will tell.

References

Allison, Dale C. (1998). *Jesus of Nazareth: Millenarian Prophet*. Minneapolis: Fortress.
Anderson, Paul N., Felix Just, and Tom Thatcher, eds. (2007). *John, Jesus and History*. Vol. 1: *Critical Appraisals of Critical Views*. Atlanta: Society of Biblical Literature.
Arnal, William (2005). "The Cipher 'Judaism' in Contemporary Historical Jesus Scholarship." In John S. Kloppenborg and John W. Marshall (eds.), *Apocalypticism, Anti-Semitism and the Historical Jesus: Subtexts in Criticism* (pp. 24–54). Edinburgh: T&T Clark.
Bailey, Kenneth E. (1991). "Informal Controlled Oral Tradition and the Synoptic Gospels." *Asia Journal of Theology* 5: 34–54.

Bock, Darrell (2002). *Studying the Historical Jesus: A Guide to Sources and Methods*. Grand Rapids: Baker Academic.

Borg, Marcus J. (1998). *Conflict, Holiness, and Politics in the Teachings of Jesus*. New edn. Harrisburg, PA: Trinity.

Bowman, John W. (1949). "The Quest of the Historical Jesus." *Interpretation* 111: 184–193.

Brandon, S. G. F. (1967). *Jesus and the Zealots: A Study of the Primitive Factor in Early Christianity*. Manchester: Manchester University Press.

Brown, Colin (1985). *Jesus in European Protestant Thought, 1778–1860*. Durham, NC: Labyrinth.

Carleton Paget, James (2001). "Quests for the Historical Jesus." In Markus Bockmuehl (ed.), *The Cambridge Companion to Jesus* (pp. 138–155). Cambridge: Cambridge University Press.

Casey, Maurice (2005). "Who's Afraid of Jesus Christ? Some Comments on Attempts to Write a Life of Jesus." In James G. Crossley and Christian Karner (eds.), *Writing History, Constructing Reality* (pp. 129–146). Aldershot: Ashgate.

Chamberlain, Houston S. (1899). *Die Grundlagen des Neunzehnten Jahrhunderts*. Munich: Bruckmann. English translation: *The Foundations of the Nineteenth Century*. London: Lane, 1910.

Chancey, Mark A. (2002). *The Myth of a Gentile Galilee*. Cambridge: Cambridge University Press.

Charlesworth, James H. (1982). "The Historical Jesus in Light of Writings Contemporaneous with Him." *Aufstieg und Niedergang der Römischen Welt* 2.25.1: 451–476.

Charlesworth, James H., ed. (2006). *Jesus and Archaeology*. Grand Rapids: Eerdmans.

Chilton, Bruce (1984). *A Galilean Rabbi and His Bible: Jesus' Own Interpretation of Isaiah*. London: SPCK.

Corley, Kathleen E. (2002). *Women and the Historical Jesus: Feminist Myths of Christian Origins*. Santa Rosa, CA: Polebridge.

Crossan, John Dominic (1988). *The Cross that Spoke: the Origins of the Passion Narrative*. San Francisco: Harper & Row.

Crossan, John Dominic (1991). *The Historical Jesus: The Life of a Mediterranean Jewish Peasant*. San Francisco: HarperCollins; Edinburgh: T&T Clark.

Crossan, John Dominic (1999). *The Birth of Christianity: Discovering What Happened in the Years Immediately after the Execution of Jesus*. Edinburgh: T&T Clark.

Dodd, C. H. (1935). *The Parables of the Kingdom*. London: Nisbet.

Dodd, C. H. (1963). *Historical Tradition in the Fourth Gospel*. Cambridge: Cambridge University Press.

Downing, F. Gerald (1992). *Cynics and Christian Origins*. Edinburgh: T&T Clark.

Dunn, James D. G. (2003). *Christianity in the Making*. Vol. 1: *Jesus Remembered*. Grand Rapids: Eerdmans.

Dunn, James D. G. (2005). *A New Perspective on Jesus: What the Quest for the Historical Jesus Missed*. Grand Rapids: Baker Academic.

du Toit, David S. (2001). "Redefining Jesus: Current Trends in Jesus Research." In Michael Labahn and Andreas Schmidt (eds.), *Jesus, Mark and Q: The Teaching of Jesus and its Earliest Records* (pp. 82–124). Sheffield: Sheffield Academic Press.

Ehrman, Bart (1999). *Jesus, Apocalyptic Prophet of the New Millennium*. New York: Oxford University Press.

Evans, Craig A. (2006). "Assessing Progress in the Third Quest of the Historical Jesus." *Journal for the Study of the New Testament* 4: 35–54.

Flusser, David, with R. Steven Notley (2007). *The Sage from Galilee: Rediscovering Jesus' Genius.* 4th edn. Grand Rapids: Eerdmans.

Fredriksen, Paula (1999). *Jesus of Nazareth, King of the Jews: A Jewish Life and the Emergence of Christianity.* New York: Knopf.

Fredriksen, Paula (2005). "Compassion is to Purity as Fish is to Bicycle, and Other Reflections on Constructions of 'Judaism' in Current Work on the Historical Jesus." In John S. Kloppenborg and John W. Marshall (eds.), *Apocalypticism, Anti-Semitism and the Historical Jesus: Subtexts in Criticism* (pp. 55–67). Edinburgh: T&T Clark.

Freyne, Sean (1988). *Galilee, Jesus and the Gospels: Literary Approaches and Historical Investigation.* Dublin: Gill & Macmillan.

Funk, Robert W. (2000). "The Once and Future Jesus." In Jesus Seminar, *The Once and Future Jesus* (pp. 5–25). Santa Rosa, CA: Polebridge.

Gathercole, Simon J. (2000). "The Critical and Dogmatic Agenda of Albert Schweitzer's 'The Quest of the Historical Jesus.'" *Tyndale Bulletin* 51: 261–283.

Georgi, Dieter (1992). "The Interest in Life of Jesus Theology as a Paradigm for the Social History of Biblical Criticism." *Harvard Theological Review* 85: 51–83.

Grundmann, Walter (1940). *Jesus der Galiläer und das Judentum.* Leipzig: Wigand.

Head, Peter M. (2004). "The Nazi Quest for an Aryan Jesus." *Journal for the Study of the Historical Jesus* 2: 55–89.

Hedrick, Charles W. (1988). "The Tyranny of the Synoptic Gospels." *Semeia* 44: 108.

Heschel, Susannah (2008). *The Aryan Jesus: Christian Theologies and the Bible in Nazi Germany.* Princeton: Princeton University Press.

Holmén, Tom (2001). "The Jewishness of Jesus in the Third Quest." In Michael Labahn and Andreas Schmidt (eds.), *Jesus, Mark and Q: The Teaching of Jesus and its Earliest Records* (pp. 143–162). Sheffield: Sheffield Academic Press.

Horsley, Richard A. (1987). *Jesus and the Spiral of Violence: Popular Jewish Resistance in Roman Palestine.* San Francisco: Harper & Row.

Ilan, Tal (1996). *Jewish Women in Greco-Roman Palestine.* Peabody MA: Hendrickson.

Jensen, Morten Horning (2006). *Herod Antipas in Galilee: The Literary and Archaeological Sources on the Reign of Herod Antipas and its Socio-Economic Impact on Galilee.* Tübingen: Mohr Siebeck.

Jesus Seminar (2000). *The Once and Future Jesus.* Santa Rosa, CA: Polebridge.

Johnson, Luke Timothy (1996). *The Real Jesus: The Misguided Quest for the Historical Jesus and the Truth of the Traditional Gospels.* New York: HarperCollins.

Klausner, Joseph (1925). *Jesus of Nazareth: His Life, Times and Teaching.* New York: Macmillan. (Hebrew original 1922.)

Kloppenborg, John S. (1987). *The Formation of Q: Trajectories in Ancient Wisdom Collections.* Philadelphia: Fortress.

Kloppenborg, John S. (1996). "The Sayings Gospel Q and the Quest for the Historical Jesus." *Harvard Theological Review* 89: 307–344.

Kloppenborg, John S. (2005). "As One Unknown, Without a Name? Co-opting the Apocalyptic Jesus." In John S. Kloppenborg and John W. Marshall (eds.), *Apocalypticism, Anti-Semitism and the Historical Jesus: Subtexts in Criticism* (pp. 1–23). Edinburgh: T&T Clark.

Kraemer, Ross Shepard, and Mary Rose D'Angelo, eds. (1999). *Women and Christian Origins.* New York, Oxford: Oxford University Press.

Levine, Amy-Jill (2005). "The Earth Moved: Jesus, Sex and Eschatology." In John S. Kloppenborg and John W. Marshall (eds.), *Apocalypticism, Anti-Semitism and the Historical Jesus: Subtexts in Criticism* (pp. 83–97). Edinburgh: T&T Clark.

Levine, Lee, ed. (1992). *The Galilee in Late Antiquity*. New York: Jewish Theological Seminary of America.

Maccoby, Hyam Z. (2003). *Jesus the Pharisee*. London: SCM.

Mack, Burton (1993). *The Lost Gospel: The Book of Q and Christian Origins*. Shaftesbury, UK: Element.

Marsh, Clive (1997). "Quests of the Historical Jesus in New Historical Perspective." *Biblical Interpretation* 5: 403–437.

Mason, Steve (2003). *Josephus and the New Testament*. 2nd edn. Peabody, MA: Hendrickson.

Meier, John P. (1991–2009). *A Marginal Jew: Rethinking the Historical Jesus*. 4 vols. New York: Doubleday; New Haven: Yale University Press.

Meier, John P. (1999). "The Present State of the 'Third Quest' for the Historical Jesus: Loss and Gain." *Biblica* 80: 459–487.

Meyers, Eric M., ed. (1999). *Galilee Through the Centuries: Confluence of Cultures*. Winona Lake, IN: Eisenbrauns.

Neill, Stephen, and Tom Wright (1988). *The Interpretation of the New Testament 1861–1986*. 2nd edn. Oxford, New York: Oxford University Press.

Oakman, Douglas E. (1986). *Jesus and the Economic Questions of his Day*. Lewiston, Queenston: Edwin Mellen.

Patterson, Stephen J. (1993). *The Gospel of Thomas and Jesus*. Sonoma, CA: Polebridge.

Perrin, Norman (1967). *Rediscovering the Teaching of Jesus*. London: SCM.

Powell, Mark Allan (1998). *Jesus as a Figure in History*. Louisville, KY: Westminster John Knox.

Reed, Jonathan L. (2000). *Archaeology and the Galilean Jesus: A Re-Examination of the Evidence*. Harrisburg, PA: Trinity.

Robinson, James M., ed. (1988). *The Nag Hammadi Library*. 3rd edn. Leiden: Brill.

Rowland, Christopher (2002). *Christian Origins: The Setting and Character of the Most Important Messianic Sect of Judaism*. 2nd edn. London: SPCK.

Sanders, E. P. (1977). *Paul and Palestinian Judaism: A Comparison of Patterns of Religion*. London: SCM.

Sanders, E. P. (1985). *Jesus and Judaism*. London: SCM.

Sawicki, Marianne (2000). *Crossing Galilee: Architecture of Contact in the Occupied Land of Jesus*. Harrisburg, PA: Trinity.

Schneemelcher, Wilhelm, ed. (1991–1992). *New Testament Apocrypha*. 2 vols. Rev. edn. Louisville, KY: Westminster John Knox.

Schüssler Fiorenza, Elisabeth (1983). *In Memory of Her: A Feminist Theological Reconstruction of Christian Origins*. London: SCM.

Schüssler Fiorenza, Elisabeth (2000). *Jesus and the Politics of Interpretation*. New York: Continuum.

Schweitzer, Albert (1906). *Von Reimarus zu Wrede: Eine Geschichte der Leben-Jesu Forschung*. Tübingen: Mohr. English translation: *The Quest for the Historical Jesus: A Critical Study of its Progress from Reimarus to Wrede*. 3rd edn. London: Black, 1954.

Smith, D. Moody (2001). *John Among the Gospels*. 2nd edn. Columbia: University of South Carolina Press.

Smith, Morton (1978). *Jesus the Magician*. London: Harper & Row.

Strauss, David F. (1835). *Das Leben Jesu, Kritisch Bearbeitet*. 2 vols. Tübingen: Osiander.

Streeter, B. H. (1924). *The Four Gospels: A Story of Origins*. London: Macmillan.

Sugirtharajah, R. S. (1990). "Jesus Research and Third World Christologies." *Theology* 93: 387–391.

Telford, William R. (1994). "Major Trends in Interpretive Issues in the Study of Jesus." In Bruce Chilton and Craig A. Evans (eds.), *Studying the Historical Jesus: Evaluations of the State of Current Research* (pp. 33–74). Leiden: Brill.

Theissen, Gerd, and Dagmar Winter (2002). *The Quest for the Plausible Jesus: The Question of Criteria*. Louisville, KY: Westminster John Knox.

Van Voorst, Robert E. (2000). *Jesus Outside the New Testament: An Introduction to the Ancient Evidence*. Grand Rapids: Eerdmans.

Vermes, Geza (1973). *Jesus the Jew: A Historian's Reading of the Gospels*. London: Collins.

Vermes, Geza (1997). *The Complete Dead Sea Scrolls in English*. Complete edn. New York: Allen Lane, Penguin.

Weeden, Theodore J. Sr. (2004). "Theories of Tradition: A Critique of Kenneth Bailey." *Forum* 7 (1): 45–69.

Wright, N. T. (1996). *Jesus and the Victory of God*. London: SPCK.

PART V

Modern Manifestations of Jesus

22 Modern Western Christology   357
    John P. Galvin

23 Christology in Africa, Asia, and Latin America   375
    Veli-Matti Kärkkäinen

24 Jesus in American Culture   394
    Paul Harvey

25 The Black Christ   410
    Kelly Brown Douglas with Delbert Burkett

26 Feminist Christologies   427
    Lisa Isherwood

27 The "Gay" Jesus   443
    Theodore W. Jennings Jr.

28 Modern Mystifications of Jesus   458
    Per Beskow

CHAPTER 22

Modern Western Christology

John P. Galvin

The purpose of this chapter is to provide a succinct survey of modern christology, defined for present purposes as western (European and North American) christology since the Enlightenment. Christology itself, of course, has a history reaching back nearly two millennia, but only a relatively recent segment of that history will be examined here.

While the Enlightenment itself is a complex intellectual (and political) development, with major centers in Scotland, France, and Prussia, a description of the Enlightenment provided by Immanuel Kant (1724–1804) can serve as a guide to its impact on religion and theology. In a famous essay entitled "What Is Enlightenment?" (1783), Kant asked if we now live in an enlightened age. He answered,

> No, but we do live in an age of enlightenment. That people, as things stand now, taken as a whole, would already be in position or could be placed in position to use their own reason in matters of religion surely and well without direction of another, for that much is still lacking. But we do have clear indications that now the field is being opened to them, and that the obstacles to general enlightenment, or of emergence from their self-caused immaturity, are gradually becoming fewer. In this respect, this age is the age of enlightenment. (Schupp 1974, 5)

Compressed in this brief citation are characteristic elements of Enlightenment thought: the optimism about the present, particularly in contrast to the past; the emphasis on proper use of one's own reason and confidence in its possibilities, in distinction to control by another; the comparison of the relationship of past and present with growth from childhood to maturity; and the non-historical approach to reason. Also to be noted is the anthropocentric turn to the subject, a concentration on the human person, which is common in typically modern thought. These characteristics reflect both values (emphasis on personal freedom and critical inquiry) and dangers (individualism, underestimation of tradition) and need to be assessed in all their complexity.[1]

The Blackwell Companion to Jesus, First Edition. Edited by Delbert Burkett. ©2014 John Wiley & Sons, Ltd. Published 2014 by John Wiley & Sons, Ltd.

In Kant's judgment, knowledge of God is associated with the presuppositions of practical reason and thus with the moral law. "Subjectively considered," he wrote, "religion is the recognition of all our duties as divine commandments" (Kant [1788] 1997, A233). Operating within this framework, he developed a conception of *Religion within the Limits of Reason Alone* ([1793] 1960), which accents the ethical dimension of religion and presents Jesus as "the ideal of moral perfection and the founder of a moral community" (Welch 1972, 47). The result is a conception that tends to equate religion in general and Christianity in particular with individual morality (Schupp 2003).

Our chief interest here is not in Kant in himself, but rather in Kant as background for modern christology. Adapting analyses of Claude Welch (1972, 47–48) and Karl Barth ([1946] 1973), we may distinguish four possible avenues for theology to pursue in view of Kant's thought: (1) following Kant in adoption of moral categories (nineteenth-century liberal Protestantism); (2) questioning the validity of Kant's restriction of human knowledge of God to practical reason (in quite different ways, German Idealism [Hegel] and modern Catholic Neo-Scholastic philosophy and theology); (3) accepting this self-limitation of reason in religious matters, but turning entirely to revelation and faith instead of remaining within the boundaries imposed by reason (Barth); and (4) searching for an alternative point of reference within human beings, more basic than either intellect or will, for pursuit of the question of God (Schleiermacher). As we shall see, each of these options has been developed in considerable detail during the past two centuries.

The following pages will consider in sequence nineteenth-century Protestant christology (Friedrich Schleiermacher, and research on the historical Jesus); nineteenth-century Catholic christology (neo-scholastic theology); twentieth-century Protestant christology (Karl Barth, Paul Tillich, and Wolfhart Pannenberg); and twentieth-century Catholic christology (Karl Rahner, Edward Schillebeeckx, Roger Haight, and Raymund Schwager). While christology has not been a traditional area of conflict between Catholics and Protestants, divergent positions on the relationship of reason and revelation and on the relationship of scripture and tradition have had an impact on the development of christology in both churches and make it advisable to consider each separately.

As is evident, this presentation is by no means exhaustive; it seeks only to provide basic information about selected major authors and developments in thinking about Christ. It will, however, supply a framework in which the work of individual theologians can be viewed in an appropriate context.

Nineteenth-Century Protestant Christology

Friedrich Schleiermacher

Friedrich Schleiermacher (1768–1834) was the major Protestant systematic theologian of the nineteenth century. A long-term colleague of the noted philosopher G.

W. F. Hegel at the University of Berlin, Schleiermacher developed a conception of religion and theology that differed significantly from both Kant's philosophical assessment of religion and Hegel's speculative reflections. In his first major work, *On Religion: Speeches to Its Educated Despisers* (Schleiermacher [1799] 1967),[2] he located the human basis for religion in feeling, or immediate self-consciousness, rather than either theoretical or practical reason. Religion is characterized by a feeling (consciousness, not a transient emotion) of utter dependence, and God is the One upon whom one utterly depends. Within the multiplicity of human religions, Christianity is classified as a religion of redemption; it includes the antithesis of sin and grace, with the additional specific characteristic that in Christianity everything is related to Jesus of Nazareth.

Schleiermacher's chief systematic work, *Der Christliche Glaube* ([1830–1] 1960), develops this conception of human religion with detailed analysis of its Christian component. Christian self-consciousness, always conceived as that of members of a church and not of isolated individuals, refers its immediate consciousness of forgiveness of sin (grace) to its historical source in the Redeemer, Christ. Christ's person and his salvific work are treated as a unity, and his unique relationship to God is conceived, in the words of Martin Redeker (1973, 134), as "the uninterrupted power of his God-consciousness." In the words of Schleiermacher's own Thesis 94, "The redeemer is thus like all human beings by virtue of the sameness of human nature, but different from all through the constant power of his consciousness of God, which was a genuine being of God in him" (1960, 2:43). In biblical terms, Schleiermacher's language is more reminiscent of Paul's statement that "God was in Christ reconciling the world to himself" (2 Cor 5:19) than of the Johannine assertion that "the Word became flesh and dwelt among us" (John 1:14).

Research on the historical Jesus

A second strand of Protestant christology, which in its original form reached its peak during the nineteenth century, consisted of critical research into the historical Jesus. Such research continues, in new forms, today, and is conducted by Catholics as well as Protestants. But the stage with which we are concerned at this point was primarily a Protestant undertaking. Most (though not all) of its practitioners were liberal Protestants who envisioned the Jesus of history as an ethical teacher and an inspiring example of how to live; they saw him as a figure quite different from the dogmatic christology of the ecumenical councils of the fourth and fifth centuries, which defined Christ as truly God and truly man, one person in two natures. Here we shall consider the main stages through which this research developed and the theological objections that led to its (temporary) termination.

At the start of this movement stands Hermann Samuel Reimarus (1694–1768), a rationalist philosopher and professor of Semitic languages. Reimarus composed a lengthy defense of his rationalist views entitled *Apologie*, but this was not published in full until more than two centuries after his death. Between 1774 and 1778, however, G. E. Lessing published seven long excerpts from Reimarus' work (Talbert 1970), two of which concerned the aims of Jesus and his disciples and the story of the resurrection.

In Reimarus' judgment, Jesus' aims differed greatly from those of his disciples after his crucifixion. Jesus saw himself as Messiah in a nationalistic, political sense: a royal Son of David who would overthrow Roman rule and liberate his people. After achieving some initial success in developing a following, he ultimately failed and was executed by his enemies. He died in an attitude of despair as reflected in his last words: "My God, my God, why have you forsaken me?" (Matt 27:46).

While Jesus' disciples shared his views during his lifetime, they were unable to continue to think in these terms after his death. Instead of abandoning matters entirely, they drew upon a different element of Jewish messianic expectation. Drawing on Daniel 7:13, an apocalyptic form of messianic hope looked for a Son of Man who would come twice, once in weakness and once in heavenly glory. From this new perspective, Jesus' public life could easily be interpreted as the messiah's first coming. To pave the way for proclaiming their new message, the disciples stole Jesus' body (cf. Matt 28:11–15, where this charge is refuted), waited fifty days (until Pentecost; Acts 2:1–42), and then began to preach Jesus' resurrection and imminent return in glory. The gospels were eventually written to express the disciples' new views, but enough of what actually had happened still remains in the text to make possible exposure of their deliberate deception.

While Reimarus' positions, especially his political interpretation of Jesus' aims and his accusation of fraud on the part of the disciples, are open to serious objection, his sharp disjunction of what would later be called the Jesus of history from the Christ of faith raised issues that remain important for theology to this day.

The next major figure in the history of this research is David Friedrich Strauss (1808–1874), whose two-volume *Life of Jesus Critically Examined* was originally published in 1835–1836 (Strauss [1835–6] 1972). A student of Hegel's philosophy, Strauss sought to promote his own "mythical" interpretation of the gospels by closely examining each scene in the four texts. Both traditional attempts to harmonize the texts and modern rationalist attempts to eliminate the miraculous were rejected as inadequate to the texts themselves. Strauss then argued that the texts are best understood as the expression of early Christian ideas, especially messianic concepts derived from the Old Testament, which early Christians applied to the life of Jesus. The gospels provide some basic information about Jesus, though less than formerly thought, but are primarily Christian thought presented in historical form. For Strauss, Jesus is simply the vehicle used to express the ideas, a human being of no more importance than anyone else. The ideas expressed in mythical form in the gospels must now be applied to the human race as a whole, for no individual can be the full expression of an idea. His recasting of christology into anthropology is evident in his claim that "humanity is the union of the two natures – God become man" (Strauss [1835–6] 1972, 780).

While Strauss hoped to influence Christian thought through his speculative theology, his chief impact resulted from his critical historical analysis of the gospels. Though his conclusions were rarely favorably received, he exercised a strong influence on subsequent scholarship by directing attention to questions concerning the historical relationship of Jesus' public life to the portrayal of that life in the New Testament. The chief weakness of Strauss' approach lies in his failure to recognize the importance of the person of Jesus and the actual events of his life for the development of early Christian religious ideas. Christians did indeed draw on the Old Testament in their efforts to understand Jesus, but their use was selective: Jesus himself was the criterion by which Old Testament ideas were adopted and adapted to fit their new purpose.

During the rest of the nineteenth century, Lives of Jesus predominated in historical-critical circles. Drawing almost exclusively on the synoptic gospels, and gradually coming to a recognition of the priority of Mark rather than Matthew, these biographies rejected traditional christology as a distortion of Jesus' actual life. Their reconstructions presented Jesus as a moral teacher who proclaimed the kingdom of God as an interior reality, present within human hearts, and whose own life provided an inspiring example for us to follow. Such approaches to christology direct their attention almost entirely to Jesus' public life.

The most important example of liberal Protestant christology was not, however, a biography, but rather a series of lectures on the essence of Christianity delivered at the University of Berlin by Adolf von Harnack in 1899–1900. Convinced that "the Gospel, as Jesus proclaimed it, has to do with the Father only and not the Son," Harnack saw Jesus as the gospel's "personal realization and its strength, and this he is felt to be still" (Harnack 1986, 144, 145). The basic content of Jesus' teaching is the coming of God's kingdom (understood as an ethical reality), the understanding of God as a loving Father, and the command to love God and neighbor. Gospel passages that present the kingdom of God as a cosmic transformation of present reality expected in the near future (e.g., Mark 13:1–37) are dismissed as remainders of contemporary Jewish apocalypticism, unimportant for modern Christians.

In the last decade of the nineteenth century and the first decade of the twentieth, views such as those of Harnack were subjected to serious challenges from a variety of perspectives. Taken together, these criticisms eventually contributed to the demise of liberal Protestantism's reductionist portrayal of Christ.

Two exegetical works called into question fundamental elements of liberal Protestant interpretation of the New Testament. In a study of Jesus' understanding of the kingdom of God, Johannes Weiss argued that Jesus' message of the kingdom was fundamentally eschatological in character; the prevailing interpretation of his preaching as concerned with an interior, ethical reality was inaccurate (Weiss [1892] 1971). Investigating a different New Testament topic, Wilhelm Wrede examined in 1901 the theme of the messianic secret in the gospels (stories in which Jesus performs messianic deeds but strives to keep his true identity hidden) and concluded that the structure of Mark's gospel, on which modern Lives of Jesus were inevitably based, was an invention of the evangelist, unsuited as a basis for composing a historical biography of Jesus (Wrede [1901] 1971). While both Weiss and Wrede exaggerated some of their judgments, their studies did undermine the foundations upon which the liberal Lives of Jesus were based.

Further objections to the liberal reconstructions of Jesus' public life were also registered from other vantage points. In 1892, Martin Kähler, a more traditional Lutheran dogmatic theologian, argued that, in view of the limitations of our sources and the nature of our theological interests, historical research is an unsuitable method for reaching Jesus. Our goal should rather be to comprehend the Christ of faith, since "the real Christ is the Christ who is preached" (Kähler 1964, 66). Finally, in 1906, Albert Schweitzer (a later recipient of the Nobel Peace Prize) surveyed the history of research from Reimarus to Wrede and concluded that its results failed to serve the purposes that most of its protagonists sought. In Schweitzer's judgment, most of the authors he examined had unwittingly read their own modern theological positions back into Jesus' life as part of an effort to use "the Jesus of history as an ally in the struggle against the tyranny of dogma" (Schweitzer 1911, 4). In fact, however, the actual Jesus was an apocalyptic preacher who mistakenly expected the world to be brought to an end in the very near future. Biographies portraying Jesus in these terms would, in Schweitzer's opinion, have little or no religious value.

Nineteenth-Century Catholic Christology

While many nineteenth-century Protestant theologians broke with the christology of the past, Catholic theologians typically sought greater historical continuity. Over the course of the nineteenth century, and especially during its final decades, Catholic theology was increasingly dominated by a deliberate promotion and restoration of medieval Scholastic philosophy and theology, especially in the form of Neo-Thomism (cf. McCool 1977). A five-volume work *Die Theologie der Vorzeit* [The Theology of the Past] by the German Jesuit theologian Josef Kleutgen (1853–1870) provided detailed information on medieval authors and defended their thought as superior to modern alternatives. The most significant expressions of Neo-Scholasticism, however, came in the form of textbooks, or manuals, which covered the major dogmatic treatises.

Neo-Scholasticism was not an exact replica of its medieval ancestor. In the intervening centuries, the new discipline of fundamental theology (then often termed apologetics) had been inserted into Catholic theological curricula between philosophical studies and the study of dogmatics (Niemann 1983). Fundamental theology sought first to establish on the basis of historical information and logical argumentation the credibility of Christian revelation; building on this foundation, it then examined the theology of the church, with particular emphasis on the church's teaching authority, or magisterium. Dogmatic theology, as a later stage, was then positioned to appeal to this authority as its own chief method of argumentation. Of primary interest for present purposes is the way in which christological themes were assigned places in the overall system.

The central christological topics – incarnation, public life, crucifixion, and resurrection of Jesus – were studied in three distinct parts of the Neo-Scholastic edifice. Both Jesus' public life and his resurrection were examined in fundamental theology as a decisive part of the treatment of revelation. His public life raised a personal claim to be God's legate, and his fulfillment of prophecy, his performance of miracles, and above all his resurrection from the dead constituted convincing evidence of the credibility of his message. The incarnation, in contrast, was treated in a course on christology (in the narrow sense of the word, as a course on the person of Christ, often known by its Latin title, *De Verbo Incarnato*); in practice, this course concentrated on the teaching of the ecumenical councils of the fourth and fifth centuries regarding the person and natures of Christ, as it examined the content and implications of that doctrine. Finally, a course on soteriology (from the Greek *soteria*, salvation) studied the salvific work of Christ, with almost exclusive concentration on the theology of the crucifixion.

The system of thought outlined here had several strengths, most notably its provision of an overview of important historical material. It occupied a position of great prominence in Catholic thought from the middle of the nineteenth century to the middle of the twentieth. However, Neo-Scholastic theology tended to isolate matters better viewed in close relationship to each other, as can be seen in the facts that neither Jesus' public life nor his resurrection find much space within dogmatic theology and that the crucifixion is interpreted in isolation from both. As we shall see after looking at twentieth-century Protestant theology, more recent Catholic christology typically strives to provide a unified portrayal of Christ in which the concerns and topics of both fundamental and dogmatic theology are addressed in a unified manner.

Twentieth-Century Protestant Christology

While twentieth-century Protestant christology is a large and wide-ranging field, I will restrict myself here to three major authors with distinctive positions on the subject: Karl Barth, Paul Tillich, and Wolfhart Pannenberg.

Karl Barth

Karl Barth (1886–1968), a Swiss Reformed theologian, studied theology under the guidance of liberal Protestant theologians. Though favorable to their thought during his student years, he later vehemently rejected liberal Protestantism. While a radical first expression of his thought in the form of a theological commentary on Paul's Epistle to the Romans (1922) attracted much attention, Barth later moderated his thinking and gave it a strongly christocentric focus in his multi-volume *Church Dogmatics* (1932–1965). I will concentrate on selected major characteristics of his christological thought.

As early as the second edition of his commentary on Romans, Barth gave clear expression to his option for the Christ of faith rather than the historical Jesus. Commenting on Paul's reference to "God's Son, who was descended from David according to the flesh and designated Son of God in power according to the Spirit of holiness by his resurrection from the dead, Jesus Christ our Lord" (Rom 1:3–4), Barth observes,

> This is the significance of Jesus: the installation of the Son of man as *Son of God*. What he is apart from this installation is as important and as unimportant as everything temporal, material, and human can be. "Even if we have known Christ according to the flesh, we know him that way no longer" [2 Cor 5:16]. Because he *was*, he *is*; but because he *is*, what he *was* lies behind him. (Barth 1922, 6)

Christ's true significance lies not in the past, in the preaching and example of Jesus' public life, but in the present, in his exalted status as Lord.

Barth's mature presentation of his christology is to be found in the first three partial volumes of Volume IV of his *Church Dogmatics*, a volume whose topic is the doctrine of reconciliation. In structuring his christology, Barth creatively and fruitfully organizes his treatment of the person and the work of Christ into a unified whole by combining categories of patristic christology (one person, two natures) with the post-Reformation concept of the threefold office of Christ as priest (or judge, in Barth's preferred vocabulary), king, and prophet. In keeping with his general theological principles, he presents a descending christology, or a christology from above: his starting point is God, who always takes the initiative in matters concerning salvation.

The first third of this account of christology considers Jesus Christ as true God (Son of God), who emptied and lowered himself in the incarnation (cf. Phil 2:5–8) and thus reconciled the world with God (cf. 2 Cor 5:18–19). In showing himself as servant, the Lord reveals that his divinity is not what we would be inclined to expect it to be, but something quite different. Exercising his office as high priest or judge (*munus sacerdotale*), Christ is judged in our place.

Against this background, the second third of Barth's presentation turns to the same Jesus Christ but views him now in his humanity as true man (Son of Man). Reversing the perspective of the first part, the servant is now seen as elevated by God and thus as Lord. Now exercising his office as king (*munus regale*), Christ reveals our true humanity as exalted far above our own conceptions of human existence.

Finally, a third perspective considers Jesus Christ as the one person who is both divine and human. No new material is added here, but reflection on the unity of the Son of God and Son of Man reveals the irrevocable reality of the reconciliation of the human race. Christ thus exercises his office as prophet (*munus propheticum*) and shows himself to be the guarantor and witness of reconciliation.

Paul Tillich

Paul Tillich (1886–1965), a German-born Lutheran theologian, spent most of his teaching career in the United States, teaching at Union Theological Seminary, Harvard, and the University of Chicago. His chief work is a carefully structured *Systematic Theology* (Tillich 1968), written in English and divided into three volumes and five parts (originally published in 1951, 1957, 1963). Volume I contains Parts I and II; it considers respectively Reason and Revelation, and Being and God. Volume II is devoted entirely to Part III, Existence and the Christ. To conclude the trilogy, Volume III includes Parts IV (Life and the Spirit) and V (History and the Kingdom of God).

As is easily seen above, Tillich's subtitles always consist of two terms joined by the conjunction "and." In each case, the first half consists of the elaboration of a human problem, while the second half recounts the divine answer. Tillich calls his procedure the method of correlation and describes what he terms the theological circle by writing, "God answers man's questions, and under the impact of God's answers man asks them" (1968, 1:69). Tillich notes that he is interested here in questions implied in human existence, not in issues that happen to be in the foreground of attention at a particular time. "Man is the question he asks about himself, before any question has been formulated" (1968, 1:69). Given this understanding, he judges that a correlation of question and answer is strictly necessary in theology: "the answers implied in the event of revelation are meaningful only insofar as they are in correlation with questions concerning the whole of our existence, with existential questions" (1968, 1:69). Aware that Barth had rejected this method (with reference to earlier writings of Tillich) as infringing on divine freedom, Tillich responded that while God is in principle independent of creatures, "God in his self-manifestation to man is dependent on the way man received his self-manifestation" (1968, 1:68).

Applying this method to christology, Tillich analyzes the human experience as a condition of estrangement. It is the function of the Christ to be the bearer of the New Being and to bring redemption from the old.

More specifically, Tillich distinguishes between our essential being (what we should be) and our existential being (what we in fact are). Our actual situation is marked by a threefold estrangement. Estrangement from God, or unbelief, is an act by which the entire person turns away from God, who ought to be the center of our existence, and turns instead toward self and world. Estrangement from self, hubris or pride, is a self-destructive effort to constitute oneself as the center of existence. Finally, concupiscence is a disordered relationship to the world, in which one tries to possess all and to dominate others. These overlapping dimensions of estrangement contradict the structure willed by God and tend toward destruction.

The divinely given answer to the problem of existential estrangement is the presence of the Christ, the bearer of the New Being. In him the gap between essential being and existential being is overcome. The New Being is manifest in Christ's words, his actions, and his suffering; his death is the consequence of the inevitable conflict between the powers of existential estrangement and Christ as the bearer of the New Being. Explicitly criticizing liberal theology, Tillich suggests that Jesus is not just "a man in whom God was manifest in a unique way," "but a man whose being was the New Being and who was able to conquer existential estrangement" (1968, 2:168). As far as classical creeds (Nicea, Chalcedon) are concerned, Tillich judges that "the christological dogma saved the church, but with very inadequate conceptual tools" (1968, 2:161). His own formulations seem to fall short of the creeds' full content.

Wolfhart Pannenberg

Wolfhart Pannenberg (b. 1928), a German Lutheran, is the most significant Protestant systematic theologian of the generation after Barth and Tillich. The author of *Jesus – God and Man* (1968) and the three-volume *Systematic Theology* (*Systematische Theologie* 1988–1993), he has made an original contribution to christology while steadfastly pursuing an overall theological program based on an understanding of revelation as history.

In Pannenberg's judgment, the central theological question in the modern world (since the Enlightenment) is the question of the truth of the Christian faith (1988–1993, 1:11–72). While agreeing with Barth's opposition to liberal Protestant theology, Pannenberg held that Barth's refusal to address the issues pursued in Catholic fundamental theology (not necessarily in the same way) left unanswered foundational questions of major importance. To address these questions requires careful attention to history, both to individual historical events and to the meaning of history as a whole. Since the latter can only be determined when history is complete, the future necessarily occupies a prominent role in Pannenberg's thinking.

Pannenberg's christology, first expressed in 1964 and presented in mature form (but substantially unchanged) in the second volume of his *Systematische Theologie* (2:315–511), clearly reflects these basic theological positions. Unlike Barth, Pannenberg begins his christological argumentation with the historical figure of Jesus of Nazareth (an object of renewed attention by New Testament exegetes from the mid-1950s to the present) and develops his thought as a christology from below. Jesus' office was to call people into the kingdom of God – a reality expected in the future, but one also beginning to be present in and through Jesus' own activity. Implicit in this message is a claim to be God's definitive representative, to stand in unity with God while still being distinct from the one he called Father. Thus the truth of Jesus' message stands or falls with the validity of his personal claim.

Nothing in Jesus' public life suffices (or could suffice) to establish Jesus' implicit claims; his public life serves only to raise them. What is needed is divine confirmation, of the sort that would be forthcoming with the full advent of God's kingdom, at the end of the world. As it is, however, the truth of Jesus' claim remained an open question during his lifetime; it was then further undermined by his shameful death on the cross.

Were that the end of the matter, christology (and Christian faith in general) would lack any legitimate foundation. But Pannenberg turns here to the second part of what he sometimes terms Jesus' twofold fate: death and resurrection. He argues that the resurrection appearance tradition, as reported by the eyewitness Paul in 1 Corinthians 15:3–8, is historically reliable, even though the same cannot be asserted of the detailed appearance narratives of the gospels. Beyond this, the emptiness of Jesus' grave can also be established as historical, for otherwise the early Christians would not have been able to preach in Jerusalem, soon after Jesus' crucifixion, that Jesus has been raised from the dead. (Pannenberg does not argue for the historicity of the gospel stories of the discovery of the empty tomb.) While neither an appearance nor an empty grave is the resurrection itself, they do require an explanation – and the only viable explanation is that the crucified Jesus has been raised from the dead.

Developing his christology further, Pannenberg argues that the resurrection fulfills several essential theological functions. First, it provides the needed divine confirmation of Jesus' message and of his implicit personal claims to unity with God. Second, because Jesus' individual resurrection is an anticipation of the general resurrection awaited at the end of the world in the full coming of God's kingdom, it provides us with the vantage point needed for assessment of history as a whole. Finally, it sheds new light on the religious significance of the cross and makes it possible and necessary to interpret Jesus' death in salvific terms.

Twentieth-Century Catholic Christology

The final section of this chapter will review major twentieth-century Catholic contributions to the study of christology. We will begin with two authors who published important texts between 1950 and 1980 (Karl Rahner and Edward Schillebeeckx), and conclude with two more recent theologians of the next generation (Roger Haight and Raymund Schwager).[3] As we shall see, the approaches of these modern Catholic theologians vary widely.

Karl Rahner

The German Jesuit theologian Karl Rahner (1904–1984) wrote extensively on christology throughout his long career. Among his more significant works are a lengthy programmatic essay originally published in 1954 and now entitled "Current Problems in Christology" (1961) and a lengthy summary of christology in his *Foundations of Christian Faith* (1978, 176–321). My intent in these pages is to present Rahner's main christological concerns and to outline the manner in which he sought to address them. I will not seek to examine the development of Rahner's christological thought over the course of his life.

First, like many other Catholic theologians of his generation (cf. Galvin 1994), Rahner was concerned with what he diagnosed as an under-emphasis on the humanity of Christ. In his judgment, the balanced teaching of the Council of

Chalcedon (one person, two natures) was often unconsciously abbreviated in a crypto-monophysite direction. Emphasis on Christ's humanity, often through concentration on the earthly Jesus, is thus one characteristic of his thought.

Second, Rahner wishes to underscore here as elsewhere the universality of God's salvific will (cf. 1 Tim 2:4), which is addressed to all human beings of all times and all places, and which elevates and fulfills human nature by enabling all human beings to participate in God's own life. He is therefore anxious to make sure that reference to the particularity of Jesus' life and death does not undercut this universality, which is a major theme of Rahner's theology of grace.

Third, Rahner also wishes to articulate the universal salvific significance of Jesus. In his judgment, a major christological concern is to reconcile the importance of Jesus in all his particularity with the universality of God's salvific self-gift in the offer of grace to all.

In response to this assessment of major issues in christology, Rahner developed a conception that incorporates an understanding of the incarnation, public life, death, and resurrection of Jesus and is summarized in the designation of Jesus as the eschatological, or definitive, savior. God's self-gift in grace is addressed to all aspects of human existence. As such, it has both an interior, individual dimension (universal) and a public, historical aspect (particular). The incarnation, considered in tandem with the life-history that it initiated, is the climax of this public, historical dimension of God's self-gift. Only with Jesus' death, which he freely accepts "at least as the inevitable consequence of fidelity to his mission and as imposed on him by God" (1978, 248) is his lifelong exercise of freedom complete; only then is the human acceptance of God's gift definitive. This death leads of itself to resurrection, so that the salvific meaning of Christ's death and resurrection can only be understood when the two inseparable realities are taken into consideration together (1978, 266).

Edward Schillebeeckx

In contrast to Rahner, who stresses God's gracious perfection of an already good creature, the Flemish Dominican theologian Edward Schillebeeckx (1914–2009) develops his christology as an account of the divine response to the universal human experience of evil, concretized in the history of human suffering. His major christological works, *Jesus: An Experiment in Christology* (1979) and *Christ: The Experience of Jesus as Lord* (1980), were composed relatively late in his career. They reflect continuity with his earlier work, which is characterized by the influence of Thomism and an emphasis on the theme of personal encounter with God. But they also reflect new developments in his thinking: a concentration on christology and detailed engagement with biblical exegesis and with critical theory.

Taking the problem of evil as his starting point, Schillebeeckx holds that the proper response to this universal human concern is opposition to it: "the only adequate response is via a practical exercise of resistance to evil, not a theory about it" (1979, 620). But such resistance is itself in need of direction and support if it is to be sustained and effective. This consideration leads Schillebeeckx to advocate a narrative method: "People do not *argue* against suffering, but tell a story" (1980, 698). The specifically Christian response to unjust suffering is to retell "the life-story of the man Jesus as a story of God" (1979, 80). This story inevitably has two aspects, since "The starting point of the Christian movement was an indissoluble whole consisting on the one hand of the offer of salvation through Jesus and on the other of the Christian response in faith" (1980, 66). Our interest here lies primarily in the first of these aspects.

In keeping with his option for narrative, Schillebeeckx presents at length Jesus' public life as a sustained offer, in word and in deed, of definitive salvation from God. In a context marked by suffering, Jesus presents God as the radical opponent of all suffering and proclaims the arrival of God's kingdom as a state in which all evil will be overcome. In Schillebeeckx's judgment, the source of Jesus' confident preaching can only be his own personal experience of God, since nothing in visible history would support such a message. To describe Jesus' experience Schillebeeckx draws on Mark 14:36, Romans 8:15, and Galatians 4:6 to coin the term "Abba-experience," based on the Aramaic word for father. As far as Jesus himself is concerned, his followers identified him initially and most fundamentally as the long-awaited eschatological prophet, the prophet like Moses (cf. Deut. 18:15–20) with whom God speaks face to face, the definitive representative of God.

In fact, however, Jesus' message was on the whole rejected, and rejection of his message inevitably led to rejection of his person as well. He faced death with unbroken assurance of salvation (cf. Mark 14:25), but left it, in great part, for others to interpret later on the basis of his life. Schillebeeckx notes with approval some such interpretations of Jesus' death: as the death of a prophet-martyr; as part of the divine plan of salvation; as an atoning, redemptive sacrifice. However, he also insists strongly on preserving the memory of the negativity of Jesus' death in terms of the unjust suffering he underwent. On this basis, he maintains that "first of all, we have to say that we are not redeemed *thanks to* the death of Jesus but despite it" (1980, 729), though he does immediately add that the expression "despite it" does not say enough. His more direct points of reference for his theology of salvation remain the public life of Jesus and his resurrection.

As might be expected against this background, Schillebeeckx does not share Rahner's conception of the unity of Christ's death and resurrection, but envisions the resurrection over against death's negativity, as a distinct event after death, which confers new meaning upon the crucifixion. The revelation of the resurrection to Jesus' followers (not the resurrection itself) is located tentatively in "conversion experiences" on the part of his followers, who experience after Jesus' death a renewed divine offer of forgiveness of sin through Jesus and reassemble at the initiative of Peter.

Insisting that "there is no gap between Jesus' self-understanding and the Christ proclaimed by the Church" (1979, 312), Schillebeeckx argues that the foundational identification of Jesus as the eschatological prophet soon diversified into the variety of christologies and christological titles reflected in the New Testament. In principle, this diversity is to be welcomed, but one-sided concentration on any single aspect of Jesus' history must be avoided. In the long run, the ultimate criterion for assessing the validity of any interpretation of Jesus of Nazareth is Jesus of Nazareth himself (1979, 43).

Roger Haight

Roger Haight, a contemporary American Jesuit theologian, is the author of *Jesus Symbol of God* (1999), a monograph that was preceded by several essays studying individual themes of christology and Trinitarian theology, and of *The Future of Christology* (2005). He has also written extensively on ecclesiology and on the theology of grace, but those studies are beyond the scope of this chapter.

Writing consciously for an educated audience of the third millennium, Haight adopts a pluralist theology of religions and develops a christology from below, which begins with the historical Jesus, that is, with Jesus "insofar as he has been reconstructed by the historian" (1999, 31). As suggested by the title of his major book, his own preferred category for understanding Jesus is that of "symbol," more precisely of "concrete symbol" or "an entity which reveals and makes present something else" (1999, 197). In this sense, he conceives of Jesus as "the mediation of God's presence to Christianity," since, "for Christians, Jesus is the concrete symbol of God" (1999, 14). Haight pays considerable attention to Jesus' public life, especially as far as his mediation of God is concerned, and to his resurrection, which he understands as a transcendent and eschatological exaltation and glorification of God, not requiring the assumption of Jesus' physical corpse (1999, 123–126). He pays surprisingly little attention to the crucifixion, in view of its importance in Jesus' life and in subsequent theology.

Haight's detailed accounts of biblical christologies and of later christologies, both classical and modern, strongly accent their pluralism. He devotes special attention to the christological teachings of the Councils of Nicea and Chalcedon; in his judgment, both councils have relied excessively on the framework of Johannine Logos-christology (cf. John 1:1–18) and have misread its poetic language in literalist fashion (1999, 173–178, 273–298). The conciliar decrees should be read in symbolic terms. In sum, "the meaning of Nicaea is that no less than God was and is present and at work in Jesus" (1999, 284), while "Chalcedon reasserts his integral human existence" (1999, 298).

Haight's christology has understandably stimulated considerable theological discussion, especially in North America. Questions have been raised about the adequacy of his presentation of Jesus and of his interpretation of the councils of the fourth and fifth centuries. In this regard, it should be noted that Haight's thought has been criticized in an official *Notification* of the Vatican's Congregation for the Doctrine of the Faith (2004).

Raymund Schwager

A christological perspective quite different from Haight's approach has been developed by Raymund Schwager (1935–2004), a Swiss Jesuit professor of theology at the University of Innsbruck. In his three major works, *Must There Be Scapegoats?* (1987), *Der Wunderbare Tausch* (1986), and *Jesus in the Drama of Salvation* (1999), Schwager has presented a dramatic soteriology that presents the story of Jesus as marked by distinct stages and developments.

Drawing fruitfully on the thought of René Girard, a cultural anthropologist and literary critic with a strong interest in religious themes, Schwager devotes particular attention to the problem of violence, especially to the question of the relationship of violence to God, an issue that remains unresolved within the Old Testament and raises questions about the relationship between the two testaments (1987). In addition, he is concerned to examine the tension between Jesus' message of forgiveness and his threat of eternal condemnation, and the apparent opposition between Jesus' proclamation of the kingdom, on the one hand, and the attribution of salvific necessity to Jesus' crucifixion, on the other.

Influenced by the Swiss Catholic theologian Hans Urs von Balthasar (1905–1988), but adapting von Balthasar's structure to ascribe greater significance to Jesus' public life, Schwager chose to present his christology in the form of a drama. He divided his presentation into five distinct acts.

Act I begins with the start of Jesus' public life, when he presents Israel with an offer of unconditional divine forgiveness and salvation: "The time is fulfilled, and the kingdom of God is at hand" (Mark 1:15). This initial divine offer of salvation initiates a dialogue; its appeal to human freedom requires acceptance and conversion for the full presence of the kingdom to ensue.

Act II presents both the negative response to Jesus' offer of salvation and Jesus' own reaction to his initial failure to evoke the desired reaction. It is here that Schwager locates Jesus' threats of eternal damnation, which Schwager understands as exposing the far-reaching consequences inherent in failure to accept Jesus' word, not as extrinsic retaliation. Like the first act, Act II also remains inconclusive, as neither Jesus himself nor his adversaries have reached the end of what they have to say and do.

In the central Act III, matters come to a head. Jesus' foes unite against him, and his disciples remain weak and irresolute, so that the fate of the promised kingdom now rests on Jesus alone. While his opponents plot his demise, Jesus reacts in keeping with his own message by intensifying his love and offers his life to God in atonement for human sin. While the judgment imposed upon him is a human misdeed, Jesus, in a new development, identifies himself with all victims of the power of sin and in this sense bears the sins even of his persecutors. Act III concludes at this new and decisive stage, but with a further question still open. How will God react to the execution of his son? Will he take the part of Jesus against his foes (cf. Mark 12:1–12)? Or will his reaction be of a significantly different nature?

In Act IV, these questions are resolved as God's gradual historical revelation of his love reaches a new and previously unexpected climax. In passing judgment on behalf of Jesus by raising him from the dead and thus overturning the sinful human condemnation of Jesus, the Father takes the part of Jesus who gave himself in death for his enemies. This judgment takes the part of both Jesus and his enemies, thus displaying a degree of mercy greater than anything previously conceived. Through this decisive act, the incompatibility of God and violence finally becomes apparent.

Act V brings the presentation to a close with an account of the descent of the Holy Spirit and the gathering of the church. Sent by the Father as a further dimension of his response to Jesus' condemnation, the Spirit acts internally to transform sinful human hearts.

Some aspects of Schwager's historical reconstruction have been questioned by biblical scholars, and questions remain about the precise relationship of Jesus to his foes in his act of atonement. Nonetheless, his dramatic account of Jesus' life, death, and resurrection provides fresh insights into these important topics.

Conclusion

This chapter has surveyed selected major contributions to christology on the part of Protestant and Catholic theologians of the past two centuries. The theologians who produced these christologies have responded in quite different ways to the shifts in perspective introduced by the Enlightenment. Some have embraced Kant's goal of "religion within the limits of reason alone," seeking an understanding of Jesus that is credible within those limits yet still relevant for Christian faith. Among these, liberal Protestants followed Kant in adopting moral categories to understand Jesus as a teacher and model of ethics. Proceeding from a different perspective, Schleiermacher portrayed Jesus as differing from other human beings chiefly in his uninterrupted consciousness of God. Tillich saw Jesus as the one who overcame the gap between what we are and what we should be. For Haight, Jesus is the concrete symbol of God for Christians. Other theologians, both Catholic and Protestant, have moved further from the limits imposed by Kant. Much nineteenth-century Catholic christology looked back to medieval Scholastic philosophy and theology, defending the thought of medieval authors as superior to modern alternatives. Barth opted for the Christ of faith, not the Jesus reconstructed by historians. Pannenberg proposed an ascending christology, with strong emphasis on historical knowledge of Jesus' public life, death, and resurrection. Rahner sought to develop christology within the context of an overarching conception of a history of salvation and revelation. Finally, Schillebeeckx and Schwager, in different ways, have developed their christologies in response to their distinct perceptions of the problem of evil. This survey, while far from exhaustive, provides an overview of major options that have been pursued in modern western christology.

Notes

1 The Enlightenment's blind spots have led some recent theologians, such as Johann Baptist Metz (1977, 2006), to call for a creative reassessment of major Enlightenment categories.
2 The original publication was anonymous, as the form of a "speech" was a literary device.
3 Mention should also be made of Walter Kasper, whose *Jesus the Christ* (1976) is the most representative recent textbook of Catholic christology.

References

Barth, Karl (1922). *Der Römerbrief*. 2nd edn. Zurich: EVZ-Verlag.

Barth, Karl (1932–1965). *Kirchliche Dogmatik*. Zurich: Evangelische Buchhandlung.

Barth, Karl ([1946] 1973). *Protestant Theology in the Nineteenth Century: Its Background and History*. Valley Forge, PA: Judson.

Galvin, John P. (1994). "From the Humanity of Christ to the Jesus of History: A Paradigm Shift in Catholic Christology." *Theological Studies* 55: 252–273.

Haight, Roger (1999). *Jesus Symbol of God*. Maryknoll, NY: Orbis.

Haight, Roger (2005). *The Future of Christology*. New York: Continuum.

Harnack, Adolf von ([1900] 1986). *What Is Christianity?* Philadelphia: Fortress.

Kähler, Martin (1964). *The So-Called Historical Jesus and the Historic, Biblical Christ*. Philadelphia: Fortress.

Kant, Immanuel ([1793] 1960). *Religion within the Limits of Reason Alone*. New York: Harper Torchbooks.

Kant, Immanuel ([1788] 1997). *Critique of Practical Reason*. Cambridge: Cambridge University Press.

Kasper, Walter (1976). *Jesus the Christ*. New York: Paulist. (German original 1974.)

Kleutgen, Josef (1853–1870). *Die Theologie der Vorzeit*. 5 vols. Münster: Theissing.

McCool, Gerald A. (1977). *Catholic Theology in the Nineteenth Century: The Quest for a Unitary Method*. New York: Seabury.

Metz, Johann Baptist (1977). *Glaube in Geschichte und Gesellschaft*. Mainz: Matthias-Grünewald.

Metz, Johann Baptist (2006). *Memora Passionis*. Freiburg: Herder.

Niemann, Franz-Josef (1983). *Jesus als Glaubensgrund in der Fundamentaltheologie der Neuzeit: Zur Genealogie eines Traktats*. Innsbrucker Theologische Studien 12. Innsbruck: Tyrolia.

Pannenberg, Wolfhart (1968). *Jesus – God and Man*. Philadelphia: Westminster. (German original 1964.)

Pannenberg, Wolfhart (1988–1993). *Systematische Theologie*. 3 vols. Göttingen: Vandenhoeck & Ruprecht.

Rahner, Karl (1961). "Current Problems in Christology." In Karl Rahner, *Theological Investigations*, 1 (pp. 149–200). Baltimore: Helicon.

Rahner, Karl (1978). *Foundations of Christian Faith*. New York: Seabury.

Redeker, Martin (1973). *Schleiermacher: Life and Thought*. Philadelphia: Fortress.

Schillebeeckx, Edward (1979). *Jesus: An Experiment in Christology*. New York: Seabury. (Dutch original 1974.)

Schillebeeckx, Edward (1980). *Christ: The Experience of Jesus as Lord*. New York: Seabury. (Dutch original 1977.)

Schleiermacher, Friedrich ([1830–1] 1960). *Der Christliche Glaube*. 2nd edn. 2 vols. Berlin: De Gruyter.

Schleiermacher, Friedrich ([1799] 1967). *Über die Religion: Reden an die Gebildeten unter ihren Verächtern*. Göttingen: Vandenhoeck & Ruprecht.

Schupp, Franz (1974). *Auf dem Weg zu einer Kritischen Theologie*. Quaestiones Disputatae 64. Freiburg: Herder.

Schupp, Franz (2003). *Geschichte der Philosophie im Überblick*. Band 3: Neuzeit. Hamburg: Meiner.

Schwager, Raymund (1986). *Der Wunderbare Tausch: Zur Geschichte und Deutung der Erlösungslehre*. Munich: Kösel.

Schwager, Raymund (1987). *Must There Be Scapegoats?: Violence and Redemption in the Bible*. San Francisco: Harper & Row. (German original 1978.)

Schwager, Raymund (1999). *Jesus in the Drama of Salvation: Toward a Biblical Doctrine of Redemption*. New York: Crossroad. (German original 1990.)

Schweitzer, Albert (1911). *The Quest of the Historical Jesus: A Critical Study of Its Progress from Reimarus to Wrede*. London: Black.

Strauss, David Friedrich ([1835–6] 1972). *The Life of Jesus Critically Examined*. Philadelphia: Fortress.

Talbert, Charles, ed. (1970). *Reimarus: Fragments*. Philadelphia: Fortress.

Tillich, Paul (1968). *Systematic Theology*. Combined volume. Digswell Place, UK: Nisbet.

Weiss, Johannes ([1892] 1971). *Jesus' Proclamation of the Kingdom of God*. Philadelphia: Fortress.

Welch, Claude (1972). *Protestant Thought in the Nineteenth Century*. Vol. 1: *1799–1870*. New Haven: Yale University Press.

Wrede, Wilhelm ([1901] 1971). *The Messianic Secret*. Cambridge: Clarke.

CHAPTER 23

Christology in Africa, Asia, and Latin America

Veli-Matti Kärkkäinen

If any single area of theology is especially poised to raise questions about the nature and practice of inculturation, it is surely christology. The fact of the Incarnation itself places us already on a series of boundaries: between the divine and the human, between the particular and the universal, between eternity and time. (Schreiter 2001, xi)

Interpretations of Christ from Latin America

"The other Spanish Christ"[1] at the time of the Conquista

At the end of the fifteenth century, when South America was discovered under the leadership of Christopher ("The-Christ-Bearer") Columbus and taken over by the *conquistadors* (Spanish soldiers), the figure of Christ was introduced to the first nations of the continent. There is no denying the fact that the Christ presented to the Indios erred on the side of the Powerful and the Ruler. This was the beginning of the long suffering of the Indians, as they "have been economically exploited, culturally destroyed and alienated, and raped in matters of religion" (Wessels 1990, 61). In too many cases, the figure of Christ presented from the point of view of the power holders served the interests of oppression and suppression.

While the figure of the suffering and dying Christ, so dramatically displayed and represented in Catholic folk piety even centuries afterwards, consoled those oppressed, it did not necessarily elicit the hope that would inspire people to rise to the occasion.

> The two images [of Christ presented to the Indios] are to some degree two sides of the one coin of colonialist propaganda. The dying or dead Christ is an offer of identification in suffering, without arousing hope – the resurrection is distant. Even today, in the popular Catholicism of Latin America, Good Friday is the greatest day of celebration.

The Blackwell Companion to Jesus, First Edition. Edited by Delbert Burkett. ©2014 John Wiley & Sons, Ltd. Published 2014 by John Wiley & Sons, Ltd.

The other side, Christ the ruler, is embodied in the Spanish king and the colonial rulers, to whom the Indios are to bend the knee in veneration. In both cases the christology degenerates into an instrument of oppression. At an early stage resistance against it grew. (Küster 2001, 42)

The Spanish Dominican priest and social activist Bartolomé de Las Casas set out to defend the Indians after he himself had been an *encomendero* (landowner), part of the colonial system, and had witnessed a horrible massacre of people in Cuba. In 1514, Las Casas experienced "his conversion to the Indios, the poor of Jesus Christ" (Küster 2001, 44). From then on, Bartolomé began to see the Indios of the Americas as the poor whom Jesus Christ of the Gospel loved so dearly. No wonder contemporary Liberationists from Latin America, such as Gustavo Gutiérrez, hail the man of Sevilla as the first Liberationist (Gutiérrez 1993). The following citation from Las Casas' *Tears of the Indians* reflects the change of heart of the former colonialist:

> Now Christ wanted his gospel to be preached with enticements, gentleness, and all meekness, and pagans to be led to the truth not by armed forces but by holy examples, Christian conduct, and the word of God, so that no opportunity would be offered for blaspheming the sacred name or hating the true religion because of the conduct of the preachers. (Cited in "Bartolome de Las Casas")

The often quoted story behind the popular cult of Guadalupe illustrates the neglect of the first people of South America over against the conquerors. The Virgin appeared to Juan Diego, a poor and unlearned Indian, and gave him certain instructions to be handed over to the bishop of Mexico. The bishop, of course, did not want to listen to the man until he was forced to do so by a miracle that assured him that the Virgin had really manifested herself to the poor man. "Thus the Virgin of Guadalupe became a symbol of the affirmation of the Indian over against the Spanish, of the unlearned over against the learned, of the oppressed over against the oppressor" (González 1990, 61).

It took several centuries for Christians in South America to bring to full(er) fruition the Liberationist intentions and inspirations brought about by Las Casas and other like-minded individuals. That struggle of the poor and oppressed set the stage for much of the contemporary Latin American interpretation of Christ.

The emerging liberation consciousness

Speaking of his own frustration as a *Mexicano*, Catholic student of theology Virgilio P. Elizondo reminisces about his frustrations when studying theology in the United States:

> [We] shared the scandal, the outrage, and the anger at our respective churches ... with ... orthodox theologies ... [with] no knowledge of the suffering of the millions of Lazaruses

all around them. We shared the frustration with schools of theology and theologies ... who ignore the needs for the poor and dispossessed of this world and continue to read Scripture and the Christian tradition from within the perspective of the rich, the nicely installed, and the powerful of the world. (1990, 10–11)

Yet, as Elizondo forcefully argues, it is this *mestizo*[2] tradition that can enrich the predominantly Euro-North American theology, "because it is the Christian religious expression of the millions of poor, oppressed, and marginated peoples of the Americas" (1990, 13).

It is often said that whereas African theology begins with a shout of joy, in Latin America theological reflection starts from a cry of despair. As much as that saying is a generalization – and as such must be handled with care – there is no denying the fact that theological reflection in South America wrestles with social and political issues. A number of factors have contributed to the rise of the theme of liberation as the key to theology, such as massive poverty and injustice, the history of oppression and colonization, as well as what has been called "anthropological poverty,"[3] meaning that alien languages were imposed on the "natives" (Spanish or Portuguese) and their own cultures denigrated.

The rise of liberation theologies owes a debt to the development of liberation consciousness by the Roman Catholic church in the aftermath of the transformative effect of Vatican II (1962–1965; see, e.g., Chenu 1977, 56–61). Roman Catholic Liberationists – followed by many Protestants – have come to see Christ as identified with the poor and oppressed and have focused on the self-understanding of the church "from underneath." The socio-political reality – what it is to be the poor, the despised, the marginalized – is understood as the "praxis" of theology.[4] The "preferential option for the poor" is not only a practical result of all theology; poverty, suffering, and death also form the right methodological guide to discerning God and doing theology. "The faith experience of the poor and oppressed that bursts into our theology is the vital context, the historical and social setting [for] ... a reflection on the God of biblical revelation" (Gutiérrez 1991, xiii).

The hermeneutics of liberation

Critical analysis not only of theological ideas but also of the political and socio-economic implications of theology lies at the heart of liberation theologies. Juan Luis Segundo presents his methodological starting point in the famous idea of a "hermeneutical circle" (1976, 9; 1973, 27):

1 Our way of experiencing reality leads to ideological suspicion.
2 The next step is the application of our ideological suspicion to the whole ideological superstructure in general and to theology in particular in order to expose those latent assumptions and interpretations that guide theology.

According to Segundo, traditional western theology is a textbook example of a theology adapted to the particular ideological interests of the dominant social classes.

3   A new way of experiencing theological reality leads to the exegetical suspicion that the prevailing interpretation of the Bible has not taken important pieces of data into account.

4   The final result is a new hermeneutic, a new way of interpreting the scripture with the new elements at our disposal.

This hermeneutical circle – or perhaps, spiral – "keeps on moving on to an ever more authentic truth that is to be translated into ever more liberative praxis" (Segundo 1976, 97).

In other words, the term *theology* for Latin American and other liberation theologians has a different connotation than in classical theology. Medieval scholastic theology attempted to construct a finished theological system in which the language is more or less stable and in which all of the major doctrines have been examined. Theology in the liberation style bears marks of its pragmatic nature, in the spirit of Karl Marx's argument that his aim was not to explain the world but to change it. The advocates of the liberation theologies argue for the epistemic nature of praxis, which means that praxis is not only functional, it is also epistemic: committing ourselves to the betterment of the society is itself a means of gaining reliable knowledge of reality. This is the insight of a new epistemological style, often called the "sociology of knowledge," according to which knowledge is never neutral or value-free but betrays the influence of the context and circumstances.

The importance of the Jesus of history

Liberation christology is "theology from below." Rather than taking its point of departure from the lofty titles of Christ, such as "the Lord," found in the New Testament and early christology, Liberationists begin with the historical Jesus. Understandably, it is a great resource for a Liberationist framework to reflect on the meaning of the historical Jesus, who lived a real life under real human conditions. Not surprisingly then, the synoptic gospels and especially Luke, with its interest in the poor and marginalized, and Mark, with its portrait of a humble, suffering Servant, lie at the center of attention. Matthew's christology, while echoing key synoptic voices, also reflects to many Liberationists the interests of the reign of the kingdom, with its dark side of ruling and power.

Naming the Latin American Liberationist christology "theology from below" must not be confused with the theology from below of classical liberalism's Quest of the Historical Jesus. Whereas for Liberals, the historical *facts* of the life of Jesus were the main focus in their desire to reconstruct the life of Jesus, for Liberationists the key is the need to understand the *relevance* of the history of Jesus to the struggles in Latin America. "*Understanding* Jesus, as opposed to recovering Jesus, requires holding together in creative fusion two distinct horizons: the historical Jesus of the Gospels and the historical context of contemporary Latin America" (Pope-Levison and Levison 1992, 31).

From the point of view of the importance and relevance of Jesus' history, Leonardo Boff has investigated the question of the meaning of the ascension for liberation christology. Incarnation and ascension seem to be on opposite sides of the meaning of the history of Jesus. In Boff's vision, the risen and ascended Christ has penetrated the world in a much more profound manner – now ever-present according to his own promise (Matt 28:20). Boff also refers to the Pauline idea of Christ as the "pneumatic body," spirited body (1 Cor 15:44). The resurrection has revealed the cosmic dimension of Christ, for in him all creation has come into existence and he is the goal of all. From this perspective, the significance of the incarnation comes into a new light. For Boff, the main focus of incarnation is the completion of creation rather than the remedy for sin, which has been the focus of classical theology. "The eternal person of the Son was always acting in the world from creation, but his presence was concentrated in Christ and was spread throughout the cosmos after the resurrection. Jesus is portrayed as the focal being in whom the total manifestation of God takes place within creation" (LaDue 2001, 175).

Jesus – the liberator

According to Justo L. González, the celebrated Cuban-born Hispanic American church historian, early in Christian history the interpretation of Christ became tuned in with the wishes and hopes of the ruling class, and the role of Christ as the one who identifies with the outcasts, the poor, and the oppressed lost its dynamic. He traces this tendency not just to the time of the *conquistadors* but all the way back to the rise of Constantinian Christendom:

> Great pains were taken to mitigate the scandal of God's being revealed in a poor carpenter. His life and sayings were reinterpreted so as to make them more palatable to the rich and powerful. Innumerable legends were built around him, usually seeking to raise him to the level that many understood to be that of the divine – that is, to the level of a superemperor. Art depicted him as either the Almighty Ruler of the universe, sitting on his throne, or as the stolid hero who overcomes the suffering of the cross with superhuman resources and aristocratic poise. (1990, 140)

This kind of Christ who supports the ruling elite has little to offer in terms of liberation. This elicits the question, what, then, is the vision of liberation in liberation christologies? In keeping with classical theology but differing in emphasis, Liberationists connect the liberative work with the central New Testament concept of the kingdom of God. Jesus' announcement of the coming of the kingdom – attested to by healings, exorcisms, welcoming of those outside the covenant-community, and the forgiveness of sins – signaled the coming of the rule of God. The coming of God's righteous rule was heralded in a "world in which the creative plan of God is finally fulfilled; where hunger, poverty, injustice, oppression, pain, even disease and death have been definitively overcome; it is a world from which evil has been rooted out forever" (Bonino 1979, 41).

In his programmatic work, *Jesus Christ Liberator*, the Brazilian Liberationist Leonardo Boff (1978) complains that the originally revolutionary message of Christ has been reduced in many cases to a decision of faith by individuals without much relation to the social and political aspects of life. Boff argues that the liberation proposed by Jesus relates to the public realm as well as the personal sphere. He even contends that, over the years, "the church has fallen into the temptation of adopting the customs of pagan society, with authority patterns reflecting domination, and with the use of lofty and horrific titles by those in positions of power over others" (as explained by LaDue 2001, 170). By doing so, the church is hiding its true identity as the community of Christ.

While few liberation theologians would go as far as Camilio Torres, once a priest and then a guerilla fighter, who claimed that "I am revolutionary because I am a priest" and that therefore "revolutionary action is a Christian, a priestly struggle" (cited in Bonino 1975, 43–44), there is a definite socio-political aspect to their vision of salvation. While Christian salvation is "spiritual," it is not spiritual in a reductionist sense, ruling out the harsh realities of injustice, oppression, and poverty; rather it is a holistic, all-encompassing liberation. Gutiérrez brings home this holistic vision with his conclusion that the Christian sense of salvation as liberation involves three interrelated facets:

- personal transformation and freedom from sin;
- liberation from social and political oppression; and
- liberation from marginalization (which may take several forms, such as unjust treatment of women and minorities).

The church that follows Christ in pursuing this vision "finds its full identity as a sign of the reign of God to which all human beings are called but in which the lowly and the 'unimportant' have a privileged place" (Gutiérrez 1988, xlii).

Interpretations of Christ from Asia

The "European" and "Asian" faces of Jesus

It was largely colonization and evangelization in tandem that brought and propagated the western understanding of Jesus in Asia. Not only was it foreign to Asia, it was also an understanding which was polemical against non-Christian religions, disrespectful of indigenous cultures and insensitive to the injustices which colonialism brought about. (de Mesa 2001, 1)

The shadow of the "European Jesus" superimposed by the colonialists of the past centuries is a continuous challenge to Asian theologians as they are in the process of rediscovering the "Asian Faces of Jesus" (cf. Sugirtharajah 1993) – and this in the midst of religious plurality and rampant poverty. In the words of the Sri Lankan Aloysius Pieris, "The Asian context can be described as a blend of a profound religiosity (which is perhaps Asia's greatest wealth) and an overwhelming poverty" (Pieris 1980, 61–62).

Yet, "It was on a hill in Asia, at the far western edge of the continent," Samuel H. Moffett reminds us, "that Jesus said to his disciples, 'Go ye into all the world and preach the gospel' (Mark 16:15)" (Moffett 1992, 4). Jesus was Asian – western Asian, to be more precise – rather than European! This is to say that the roots of the Christian church go deep in Asian soil. At the same time, it is also true that "It was in *Roman* Asia that Jesus Christ was born." Like the Greeks before them, the Romans were intruders in the continent (Moffett 1992, 6). This means that the figure of Jesus Christ in the largest continent of the world has most of the time stood in the matrix and junction of many cultures and many powers.

The Nestorian and Monophysite christologies

Two christological "schools" have played a formative role in the history of the church in Asia: namely, Nestorianism and Monophysitism. While the former was denounced at the (First) Council of Ephesus in 431 and the latter at Chalcedon twenty years later, the influence of both in Asian Christianity surpasses description. The details of the historically and theologically complicated dispute between the two eastern theological centers, Alexandria and Antioch, which produced these two "heresies," belong to the history of christology before Chalcedon; suffice it to say here that whereas for Nestorianism the tendency was not only to distinguish but also to separate the divine and human natures of Christ, Monophysites erred on the opposite side, having a hard time in making a distinction with their emphasis on the divine nature.

Nestorianism was *the* theological cause for the division between the East and West, Europe and Asia, after the patristic era. The Nestorian "two-nature" christology was greatly interested in the human nature of Christ, allegedly because "[i]t had long been known for its care for the poor and hungry" and therefore saw it fitting to "emphasize Christ's humanity, for only a completely human Christ could be an ethical and moral example" (Moffett 1992, 171).

To China, Christianity was introduced by the Nestorians in the first half of the seventh century, when the land was ruled by the powerful Tai Tsung of the Tang dynasty. The "two-nature" christology was preached in the most influential country of that time until the mid-ninth century, when an imperial edict virtually banned Christianity (and Buddhism) (Latourette 1975, 324–325). While a number of Christian communities in central and East Asia fell under the power of the Mongols, and thus Islam, the Christian church slowly established itself in many places in central Asia and India and returned to China – again with the Nestorians

– in the eleventh century (Latourette 1975, 401–402). In the thirteenth century, the Nestorians had an archbishop in Peking (the then Mongol capital), and early in the fourteenth century the Nestorian patriarch is reported to have had twenty-five metropolitans in China, India, Turkestan, Kashgar, and elsewhere (Latourette 1975, 591). This is all to say that the Nestorian interpretation of Christ has been immensely influential in the history of the largest continent of the world.

The other "heresy" in the eyes of the advocates of the Chalcedonian Creed, Monophysite christology has similarly exercised a significant role in many parts of Asia. An instrumental role in the later consolidation of Monophysitism was played by the West Syrian Jacobite churches in the eighth and ninth centuries. While having their earliest strongholds in Africa (Egypt and Ethiopia), Monophysites soon gained influence beyond Syria in such Asian regions as the powerful church of Armenia, and even in Persia, as the influence of Nestorianism began to fall off in Persian Asia. Monophysitism also found its way to India in the seventeenth century, in the form of the (Jacobite) Syrian Orthodox Church.

The Christ of the Hindu Renaissance

Perhaps unexpectedly, during the heights of the colonial enterprise beginning from the end of the nineteenth century in the huge land of India, there emerged a new wave of interpretations of Christ that were deeply rooted in the religious (Hindu) soil of Asia and that pointed to an authentic Asian christology. It was part of the so-called Indian Renaissance or neo-Hindu reform. The contemporary Indian theologian Stanley J. Samartha, one of the ablest interpreters of this Renaissance, describes the Christ acknowledged by Neo-Hinduism as an "unbound" Christ (1980). By that he means that while many Indians attached themselves to the person of Jesus Christ – who reflects the features of a Hindu *avatara* (an incarnation of a Hindu god such as the famous *Krishna* of *Vishnu*) – they also detached that person from the institutional church, which for them did not represent the quintessence of Christ's religion (Dupuis 1991, 15).

For Keshub Chunder Sen, the nineteenth-century Hindu teacher (Scott 1979), Christ was regarded as the focus of personal devotion (*bhakti*). Jesus was no stranger to Asians, but rather one of them. Sen summed up his christology as a "doctrine of the divine humanity." The essential component of Christ's divinity is his oneness with the Father. Christ is "as a transparent crystal reservoir in which are the waters of divine life ... The medium is transparent, and we clearly see through Christ the God of truth and holiness dwelling in him" (cited in Dupuis 1991, 24).

Several Hindu writers were turned on by the social teachings of Christ without making a personal commitment to him. Mahatma Gandhi's Jesus is an ethical teacher who expresses the ideal of a new community and way of life in the beatitudes and other teachings. In those teachings, Gandhi saw the same principles that guided his own pacifistic fight for the liberation of the Indian people, namely *satyagrapha* (the search for truth) and *ahimsa* (nonviolence). As deeply as Gandhi was committed to the teaching of Jesus, especially the Sermon on the Mount, he was never ready to make a personal commitment to the person of Christ, let alone the community of the Christian church (Gandhi [1940] 1963).

Finally, there are Hindus who have become Christians but insist that they have remained Hindus. The best known of these is Brahmabandhab Upadhyaya, who became a Catholic by way of first receiving an Anglican baptism. Upadhyaya's spirituality is based on a deep personal experience of the person of Jesus the Son of God, who becomes at once his *guru* and his friend. Whether Jesus was divine or not is not the point; what matters is that Christ claimed to be the Son of God. As a monk, Upadhyaya also understood Jesus Christ in terms of *advaita*, the Hindu mystical experience (Kavunkal 2008, 28–30).

The creativity and potential of the christological portraits in neo-Hindu reform is beautifully reflected in the different, yet complementary titles of current interpreters: Raimundo Panikkar's *The Unknown Christ of Hinduism* (1964) and M. M. Thomas' *The Acknowledged Christ of the Indian Renaissance* (1969). Yet another facet of the Indian portrait of Christ – in keeping with Roman Catholic theology – is offered by the title of a book written by the famous missionary John N. Farquhar, *The Crown of Hinduism* (1913), in which he presented a case for Christianity as something complementary to rather than exclusive of Hinduism.

Silhouettes of Jesus in current Asian theologies

Jesus of the poor   The Sri Lankan Jesuit Aloysius Pieris links Asia's poverty and spirituality to Jesus' "double baptism" in "the Jordan of Asian religions and the Calvary of Asian poverty." This is Jesus' immersion in the Asian context and life. Jesus pointed to the ascetic John as the archetype of the true spirituality of the kingdom of God and denounced the striving for the accumulation of wealth and trust in mammon. Jesus' radical social program led him finally to the cross, executed by the power elite. The powerful crucified him at "a cross that the money-polluted religiosity of his day planted on Calvary with the aid of a colonial power (Luke 23:1–23). This is where the journey, begun at Jordan, ended" (Pieris 1988, 49).

The Korean *minjung* ("masses of people") interpretation of Jesus is another Asian Liberationist christology. Byung Mu Ahn argues vocally that it is time for Christian theology to free "Christology of the Kerygma" from western enslavement and put the living Jesus in contact with the common people. The "real" Jesus lived with the poor, the sick, and the women, healing them, feeding them, and defending them. Unlike the "Christ of the Kerygma," Jesus does not remain seated, immovable on his unshakable throne within the church (Ahn 1993; see further Chung 2006).

Another Asian Liberationist force, the Indian Dalit christology, represents a liberation movement for people at the very bottom of the society; the term itself refers to a group of people (particularly in South India) regarded as "untouchables" or outcasts. A. P. Nirmal, who coined the term "Dalit theology" in the beginning of the 1980s, argues that Jesus himself was a Dalit and identified himself with the

"Dalits" of his day. In Jesus' "Nazareth Manifesto" (Luke 4:16–18), he promised liberation for the prisoners (Küster 2001, 168–173).

Jesus in the yin–yang interpretation   The Korean Methodist Jung Young Lee begins Trinitarian theology from christology: "I will begin with God the Son because the dual nature of Christ is a key to understanding the divine Trinity. Moreover, God the Son represents the fulfillment of the trinitarian principle through the incarnation" (Lee 1996, 19). Behind this move is the employment of the ancient Asian concept of *yin-yang*, which is a way to go beyond the typical western either/or dualism; in the *yin-yang* complementarity, feminine and masculine, light and darkness, heaven and earth, matter and spirit are both distinguished and united. This principle helps Lee to inquire into the mystery of the incarnation, a profound event in which seemingly opposite entities come together, without separation and without confusion: "The relationship between Christ's divinity and humanity is the relationship between *yin* and *yang*. Just as *yang* cannot exist without *yin* nor *yin* without *yang*, the humanity of Jesus cannot exist without the divinity of Christ nor the divinity of Christ without the humanity of Jesus" (Lee 1979, 98). The *yin-yang* symbolic helps negotiate the mystery of fullness and emptying evident in passages such as the hymn in Philippians 2:5–11, to which Lee finds parallels in Taoist philosophy (Lee 1996, 73–74).

A cosmotheandric view of Christ   The often quoted autobiographical comment, according to which he "left" Europe as a Christian, "found" himself as a Hindu, and "returned" as a Buddhist, fittingly illustrates the diverse background of Raimundo (Raimon) Panikkar (1978, 2). A Catholic priest and theologian, born to a Spanish Roman Catholic mother and a Hindu father, Panikkar places himself at the confluence of the four rivers: Hindu, Christian, Buddhist, and secular (Panikkar 1964, 30).

Whereas the Korean Lee employs the inclusive concept of *yin-yang* in his Asian interpretation of Christ and the Trinity, Panikkar uses the neologism *cosmotheandrism*. Parsing the term reveals three interrelated components: namely, *cosmos* (world), *theos* (God), and *anthropos* (human). Briefly defined, "The cosmotheandric principle could be stated by saying that the divine, the human and the earthly – however we may prefer to call them – are the three irreducible dimensions which constitute the real, i.e., any reality inasmuch as it is real" (1993, ix). Important to Panikkar is the insight that this is not only – and certainly not exclusively – a statement from the perspective of Christian theology but also holds true for the whole of reality (1973, viii).

In his highly acclaimed small book, *The Trinity and the Religious Experience of Man*, Panikkar produces a highly constructive – and in many ways idiosyncratic – christology, employing resources from various religious traditions of Asia. Whereas the Father is best described as "Nothing," echoing the apophatic refusal to name the Mystery and paralleling the (*Mahayana*) Buddhist notion of *sunyata* ("emptiness"), the "being of the Father" is "the Son." In the incarnation, which is *kenosis* (self-emptying), the Father gives himself totally to the Son. Thus the Son is "God" (1973, 45–47, 51). Panikkar believes this understanding is the needed bridge between Christianity and Buddhism as well as advaitic Hinduism. What *kenosis* is for Christianity, *nirvana* and *sunyata* are for these two other religions. "God is total Silence. This is affirmed by all the world religions. One is led towards the Absolute and in the end one finds nothing, because there *is* nothing, not even Being" (1973, 52).

Christ among religions

First published in 1964 and significantly revised in 1981, Panikkar's christology, as presented in the above-mentioned *The Unknown Christ of Hinduism*, took a definitely pluralistic bent. Panikkar seems to reject all notions of Christianity's superiority over or fulfillment of other religions, by arguing that the world and our subjective experience of the world have radically changed since the Christian doctrine concerning Christ was first formulated. Panikkar's revised christology also builds on the cosmotheandric principle. Christ represents an intimate and complete unity between the divine and the human. The meaning of the confession "Christ is God the Son, the Logos" is that Christ is both symbol and substance of this non-dualistic unity between God and humanity.

Another theologian from India, S. J. Samartha, argues in his main work, *One Christ – Many Religions: Toward a Revised Christology* (1991), that "Christocentrism" is applicable only to Christians; it cannot be the norm by which the various religious traditions are valued. All various approaches to the divine have their validity. Samartha firmly believes that "wherever two or three Hindus and Christians are gathered together in his name, there one need not doubt the presence of the living Christ in the midst of them" (1980, 146).

Samartha greatly appreciates the process of seeking new ways of understanding the relationship of Jesus Christ to God and humanity. In his terminology, there is a shift from the "normative exclusiveness" of Christ to what he calls the "relational distinctiveness" of Christ. The term *relational* refers to the fact that Christ does not remain unrelated to neighbors of other faiths, while *distinctive* denotes the recognition of the distinctiveness of the great religious traditions as different responses to the Mystery of God. A key concern behind Samartha's pluralistic orientation is the significance of the Mystery; the Divine, God, is a Mystery to be approached with reverence, openness, and tolerance.

This Mystery, the Truth of the Truth (*Satyasya Satyam*), is the transcendent Center that remains always beyond and greater than apprehensions of it even in the sum total of those apprehensions. It is beyond cognitive knowledge (*tarka*), but it is open to vision (*dristi*) and intuition (*anubhava*). It is near yet far, knowable yet unknowable, intimate yet ultimate, and according to one particular Hindu view, cannot even be described as "one." It is "not-two" (*advaita*), indicating thereby that diversity is within the heart of Being itself and therefore may be intrinsic to human nature as well (Samartha 1993, 110–111).

Several other metaphors, images, and symbols of Jesus Christ from Asian soil could be added to enrich and complement this brief presentation, such as those of Jesus the Guru, Jesus the Satyagrahi (Mahatma Gandhi's word for "truth"), and Jesus the Avatar, that is, incarnation of the Divine (Amaladoss 2006).

African Christologies

Jesus in the history of Africa – was he there?

Two seemingly opposite observations mark the beginning of any consideration of distinctively African interpretations of Christ. On the one hand, as recently as the latter part of the twentieth century, several leading African theologians – from the Kenyan John S. Mbiti to the Ghanain Kofi Appiah-Kubi to the Botswanan Gabriel Setiloane – have lamented the lack of *African* christology (Mbiti 1972, 51; Appiah-Kubi 1977, 56; for Setiloane, see Wessels 1990, 109–110). On the other hand, "Jesus was in Africa even before the rise of Christianity" in that his family found a hiding place in Egypt and one of the first converts was Ethiopian, among other early allusions (Wessels 1990, 98–99). Furthermore, much of early Christian theology in general and christology in particular was shaped by North African theologians such as Tertullian, Cyprian, and Augustine.

True, by the time of the Islamic invasion in the seventh century, both Christian theology and churches had virtually disappeared from African soil, and it took until the beginning of the modern missionary movement in the nineteenth century to reintroduce Christianity on any significant scale back to Africa.

Like Christians in Asia and Latin America, Africans have struggled to discover and make legitimate their distinctive interpretations of Christ: "For too long, embracing Christ and his message meant rejection of African cultural values; Africans were taught that their ancient ways were deficient or even evil and had to be set aside if they hoped to become Christians" (Schreiter 1991, viii). This task is even more important in light of the centrality of christology to all theology in Africa. Christology stands at the center of African theology: "If it is true that Christology is at the very heart of all Christian theology, it is particularly true for African Christian theology" (Onaiyekan 1997, 356). Furthermore, today, as is well known, Africa is the "most" Christianized continent, with the significant presence of not only traditional Christian churches but also African Instituted (or Initiated) churches with highly contextualized spirituality as well as rapidly growing Pentecostal/Charismatic movements. Unfortunately, the emerging theological interpretations of these two latter Christian families are seldom recorded in academically accessible sources; thus, even our survey of current African views of Jesus is biased toward "mainstream" and academic-theological interpretations.

The context of African theological reflection on Christ

The cultural and religious context of Africa forms the background of an emerging reflection on Christ (Kärkkäinen 2004, 245–246; for a concise survey, see Dyrness 1990, 43–52). In Africa, unlike the Global North, "there is no formal distinction between the sacred and the secular" or between "the spiritual and material areas of life" (Mbiti 1969, 2). Religion permeates all of life. Consequently, the reality of spirits is affirmed all over in Africa (Adeyemo 1998, 130–131). All of life, not just the "spiritual," is governed by God, the ancestors, and (other) spirits (see further, Kapolyo 2005). Consequently, healing and deliverance are an important part of the culture and looked upon as the works of the Divine (see further, Wessels 1990, 97–98).

Alongside God and heavenly beings, ancestors are greatly venerated throughout Africa. These "intermediaries" are not as much part of the kingdom of the dead as they are of the realm of the living.

One of the most striking features of African life is communality and participation (see further Kapolyo 2005, 40–44). "Communality, relationality, and fundamental interconnection underlie the African mode of seeing and being in the world" (Ogbonnaya 1994, 1). This is succinctly brought home in the famous statement of Mbiti, "I am because we are, and since we are, therefore I am" (Mbiti 1969, 106).

The importance of African traditional religions and religiosity cannot be overstated. While in Africa, the living faiths such as Hinduism, Buddhism, Taoism – with the exception of Islam – are marginal, the distinctively *African* religiosity permeates all of life and has also significantly shaped African Christianity. Anton Wessels goes so far as to claim that "African religiousness has attached itself in one way or another both to Christianity and Islam, so that it may even be asked which has had the greater influence on which" (Wessels 1990, 94; cf. Sanneh 1983).

Christus victor

The African theological Grand Old Man J. Mbiti has worked tirelessly in trying to find parallels and connections between the biblical and historical views of Christ and the African traditional worldview and beliefs (Mbiti 1986; Nyamiti 1991). The ancient idea of *Christus Victor*, the powerful Christ who rose from the dead and defeated the opposing powers, is obviously relevant to the African search for power. What is also distinctively African about the *Christus Victor* is his ability to overcome the spell and threat of spirits, magic, disease, and death.

The idea of Jesus Christ as the Son of God in Mbiti's interpretation corresponds with several tribal beliefs, since the title "Servant of God" can be found in some African societies. Several other key christological titles, such as Redeemer, Conqueror, and Lord, also have parallels in African cultures.

Like the Kenyan Mbiti, the Nigerian Roman Catholic bishop John Onaiyekan claims that several traditional titles that the New Testament applies to Christ make sense in the African context. The title "Son of God" makes good sense for a culture used to divinities and the Supreme Being. The title "Lord" denotes authority and power in the same way as the title "Oluwa l'oke," the "Lord on the hills" of the people of Kabba, one of the Yoruba tribes. Even though the idea of "Savior" is less common in African cultures, it is not totally foreign either. The Yorubas' expectation of the divinities (*Orisha*) to save them echoes the same theme, and the "Redeemer" is welcomed as he who rescues us from the enslavement of the evil forces that surround us (Nyamiti 1991).

Christ as ancestor

While the theme of ancestry is not limited to theologies from Africa, a distinctive feature of African theologies in general and christologies in particular is the use of ancestors as a theological resource (Bediako 1990; 1995, 84–86; Kabasélé 1991; Vähäkangas 1997). This is simply because "In many African societies ancestral veneration is one of the central and basic traditional and even contemporary forms of cult" (Nyamiti 1993, 14; cited in Vähäkangas 1999, 171 n. 106).

Charles Nyamiti, author of the widely acclaimed *Christ as Our Ancestor* (1984), succinctly summarizes the significance of the ancestor theme for the African context (1996, 41):

- kinship between the dead and the living kin;
- sacred status, usually acquired through death;
- mediation between human beings and God;
- exemplarity of behavior in community;
- the right to regular communication with the living through prayer and rituals.

All these traits are more or less relational. An important characteristic about the sacred status of the ancestor is also the possession of "superhuman vital force" deriving from the special proximity to the Supreme Being. That gives the ancestor the right to be a mediator. Christ as "Brother Ancestor" is the means by which God communicates with humanity (Nyamiti 1984, 74–76).

The Ghanaian Kwesi Dickson reminds us of the significance of the role of ancestors in representing the sense of community and the "concept of corporate personality," a theme familiar from the Old Testament (Dickson 1984, 170, see also 172–174). The ancestors, as well as those not yet born, are regarded as part of the community, and by their presence they express the solidarity of the community. The spirits of the ancestors use their power for the well-being of the community; this is consistent with the fact that not all dead become ancestors, but primarily those who have lived a good, virtuous life or served as the leaders of the community. Ancestors are certainly lower in status than God, but higher than humans. They are called upon at the important moments of life (Fulljames 1993, 47).

For Benezet Bujo of Zaire, the fact that in Africa the *gesta* ("deeds [and lives]") of ancestors are constantly reenacted through ritual, and that consequently the human being is able to conform his or her conduct to them, serves as the cultural starting point for reflection on the mystery of Christ as a "Proto-Ancestor," the unique ancestor, the source of life and highest model of ancestorship (Bujo 1992, 79–121; cf. 1998, 23–27). According to Bujo, the idea of Jesus as the Ancestor, rather than being a superficial concession to the existing culture, is a legitimate way to bring home the central idea of the Word becoming flesh (John 1:14; Bujo 1992, 83). Ancestorship helps explain not only the role of Christ but also that of the whole Trinity: "The Father has the fullness of eternal life and begets the Son. They live for each other in a total and vital union, mutually reinforcing their common life. The vital power goes out from the Father to beget the Son and finally returns to the Father." This vital union, which produces the interaction between Father and Son, is nothing else than the Holy Spirit, the bond between the Father and the Son (Bujo 1992, 86).

Christ the healer

Among the several titles appropriate for Jesus Christ in the African culture along with the Ancestor – or, for example, the Chief (see, e.g., Wessels 1990, 11–12) – one is certainly that of the Healer. In Africa, health not only means lack of sickness, but also well-being in a holistic sense. Sickness is not primarily a result of physical symptoms but more of a deeply spiritual malady. Unlike their counterparts in the West, African Christians reject both the secularist worldview as well as missionaries' western conceptions of reality and spirit. "Orthodoxy" has left Christians helpless in real life, and so an alternative theology has been needed that relates to the whole range of needs, which includes the spiritual but is not limited to abstract, otherworldly spiritual needs. Indeed, for many African christologists, healing is the central feature of the life and ministry of Jesus Christ. A parallel can be found between the figure of Jesus of the Gospel as the Itinerant Healer and the traditional African medicine man. Both practice a holistic form of healing on the physical, mental, social, and even environmental levels (see further Kolié 1991, 128–150).

Of all Christian traditions, Pentecostalism and later Charismatic movements have focused on the role of Jesus Christ as the Healer. A rapidly growing "Pentecostalization" is going on in Africa, with many traditional churches adopting Pentecostal-type worship patterns, prayer services, and healing ministries. A major attraction for Pentecostalism in African contexts has been its emphasis on healing. In these cultures, the religious specialist or "person of God" has power to heal the sick and ward off evil spirits and sorcery. This holistic function, which does not separate the "physical" from the "spiritual," is restored in Pentecostalism, and indigenous peoples see it as a "powerful" religion to meet human needs (see further, Anderson 1999).

Notes

1   The heading is taken from McKay ([1933] 1979).
2   North Americans of Hispanic/Latino origin – most of whom are *mestizos*, persons of mixed race – are often looked down on by the dominant White population in North America for not being American enough and by South Americans and Mexicans for not being true Latino/as.
3   Term coined by John Parratt (2004, 5), though Parratt does not apply this concept to the Latin American context alone.
4   Some liberationists, but not all, were also inspired by several Marxist ideas and the tools of social analysis. See further Dussel (1993, 85–103). Liberation theologians who have not resorted to Marxist resources are, for example, Leonardo Boff in Latin American and Justo L. González in the United States.

References

Adeyemo, Tokunboh (1998). "Unapproachable God: The High God of African Traditional Religion." In Aida Besançon Spencer and William David Spencer (eds.), *The Global God: Multicultural Evangelical Views of God* (pp. 127–145). Grand Rapids: Baker.
Ahn, Byung Mu (1993). "Jesus and People (Minjung)." In R. S. Sugirtharajah (ed.), *Asian Faces of Jesus* (pp. 163–172). Maryknoll, NY: Orbis.
Amaladoss, Michael (2006). *The Asian Jesus*. Maryknoll, NY: Orbis.
Anderson, Allan H. (1999). "The Gospel and Culture in Pentecostal Missions in the Third World." *Missionalia* 27 (2): 220–230.
Appiah-Kubi, Kofi (1977). "Jesus Christ: Some Christological Aspects from African Perspectives." In J. S. Mbiti (ed.), *African and Asian Contributions to Contemporary Theology* (pp. 51–65). Geneva: WCC Ecumenical Institute.
"Bartolome de Las Casas, Missionary, Priest, Defender of the Oppressed, *17 July 1566*." At http://elvis.rowan.edu/~kilroy/JEK/07/17.html (accessed March 8, 2009).
Bediako, Kwame (1990). *Jesus in African Culture – A Ghanaian Perspective*. Accra: Asampa.
Bediako, Kwame (1995). *Christianity in Africa: The Renewal of a Non-Western Religion*. Edinburgh: Edinburgh University Press; Maryknoll, NY: Orbis.
Boff, Leonardo (1978). *Jesus Christ Liberator*. Maryknoll, NY: Orbis.
Bonino, José Miguez (1975). *Doing Theology in a Revolutionary Situation*. Edited by William H. Lazareth. Philadelphia: Fortress.
Bonino, José Miguez (1979). *Room to Be People*. Philadelphia: Fortress.
Bujo, Benezet (1992). *African Theology in Its Social Context*. Maryknoll, NY: Orbis.
Bujo, Benezet (1998). "The Two Sources of Life: The Eucharist and the Cult of Ancestors in Africa." *African Christian Studies* 4 (1): 67–85.
Chenu, M. D. (1977). "Vatican II and the Church of the Poor." In Norbert Greinacher and Alois Muller (eds.), *The Poor and the Church* (pp. 56–61). New York: Seabury.
Chung, Paul S., ed. and trans. (2006). *Asian Contextual Theology for the Third Millennium: Theology of Minjung in Fourth-Eye Formation*. Co-edited by Kim Kyoung-Jae and Veli-Matti Kärkkäinen. Eugene: Pickwick; Wipf & Stock.

de Mesa, José M. (2001). "Making Salvation Concrete and Jesus Real: Trends in Asian Christology." *Exchange: Journal of Missiological and Ecumenical Research* 30 (1): 1–17. Posted in *The Network for Strategic Missions.* Article 07429. At www.strategicnetwork. org/index.php?loc=kb&view=v&id=07429&mode=v&pagenum=1&lang=   (accessed March 16, 2009).

Dickson, Kwesi (1984). *Theology in Africa.* London: Darton, Longman & Todd.

Dupuis, Jacques (1991). *Jesus Christ at the Encounter of World Religions.* Maryknoll, NY: Orbis.

Dussel, Enrique D. (1993). "Theology of Liberation and Marxism." In Ignacio Ellacuria and Jon Sobrino (eds.), *Mysterium Liberationis: Fundamental Concepts of Liberation Theology* (pp. 85–102). Maryknoll, NY: Orbis; San Francisco: CollinsDove.

Dyrness, William (1990). *Learning about Theology from the Third World.* Grand Rapids: Zondervan.

Elizondo, Virgilio P. (1990). "Foreword." In Justo L. González, *Mañana: Christian Theology from a Hispanic Perspective* (pp. 9–20). Nashville: Abingdon.

Farquhar, J. N. (1913). *The Crown of Hinduism.* Reprinted New Delhi: Oriental Books Reprint Corporation, 1971.

Fulljames, Peter (1993). *God and Creation in Intercultural Perspective: Dialogue between the Theologies of Barth, Dickson, Pobee, Nyamiti, and Pannenberg.* Frankfurt, New York: P. Lang.

Gandhi, Mohandas K. ([1940] 1963). *The Message of Jesus Christ.* Bombay: Bharatiya Vidya Bhavan.

González, Justo L. (1990). *Mañana: Christian Theology from a Hispanic Perspective.* Nashville: Abingdon.

Gutiérrez, Gustavo (1988). *A Theology of Liberation.* Rev. edn. Maryknoll, NY: Orbis.

Gutiérrez, Gustavo (1991). *The God of Life.* Maryknoll, NY: Orbis.

Gutiérrez, Gustavo (1993). *Las Casas: In Search of the Poor of Jesus Christ.* Maryknoll, NY: Orbis.

Kabasélé, François (1991). "Christ as Ancestor and Elder Brother." In R. J. Schreiter (ed.), *Faces of Jesus in Africa* (pp. 116–127). Maryknoll, NY: Orbis.

Kapolyo, Joe M. (2005). *The Human Condition: Christian Perspectives through African Eyes.* Downers Grove, IL: InterVarsity.

Kärkkäinen, Veli-Matti (2004). *The Doctrine of God: A Global Introduction.* Grand Rapids: Baker Academic.

Kavunkal, Jacob (2008). "The Mystery of God in and through Hinduism." In Sebastian C. H. Kim (ed.), *Christian Theology in Asia* (pp. 22–40). Cambridge: Cambridge University Press.

Kolié, Cécé (1991). "Jesus as Healer?" In R. J. Schreiter (ed.), *Faces of Jesus in Africa* (pp. 128–150). Maryknoll, NY: Orbis.

Küster, Volker (2001). *The Many Faces of Jesus Christ: Intercultural Christology.* Maryknoll, NY: Orbis.

LaDue, William J. (2001). *Jesus among Theologians: Contemporary Interpretations of Christ.* Harrisburg, PA: Trinity.

Latourette, Kenneth Scott (1975). *A History of Christianity.* Vol. 1: *Beginnings to 1500.* Rev. edn. New York: Harper & Row.

Lee, Jung Young (1979). *The Theology of Change: A Christian Concept of God in an Eastern Perspective.* Maryknoll, NY: Orbis.

Lee, Jung Young (1996). *The Trinity in Asian Perspective.* Nashville: Abingdon.

Mbiti, John S. (1969). *African Religions and Philosophy.* London: Heinemann.

Mbiti, John S. (1972). "Some African Concepts of Christology." In Georg F. Vicedom (ed.), *Christ and the Younger Churches: Theological Contributions from Asia, Africa and Latin America* (pp. 51–62). London: SPCK.

Mbiti, John S. (1986). *Bible and Theology in African Christianity*. Nairobi: Oxford University Press.

McKay, John A. ([1933] 1979). *The Other Spanish Christ: A Study in the Spiritual History of Spain and South America*. Wilmington, DE: International Academic.

Moffett, Samuel Hugh (1992). *A History of Christianity in Asia*. Vol. 1: *Beginnings to 1500*. San Francisco: HarperSanFrancisco.

Nyamiti, Charles (1984). *Christ as Our Ancestor: Christology from an African Perspective*. Gwero: Zimbabwe.

Nyamiti, Charles (1991). "African Christologies Today." In R. J. Schreiter (ed.), *Faces of Jesus in Africa* (pp. 3–23). Maryknoll, NY: Orbis.

Nyamiti, Charles (1993). "African Ancestral Veneration and Its Relevance to the African Churches." *African Christian Studies* 9 (3): 14–35.

Nyamiti, Charles (1996). "The Trinity from an African Ancestral Perspective." *African Christian Studies* 12 (4): 38–74.

Ogbonnaya, A. Okechukwu (1994). *On Communitarian Divinity: An African Interpretation of the Trinity*. New York: Paragon House.

Onaiyekan, John (1997). "Christological Trends in Contemporary African Theology." In William R. Barr (ed.), *Constructive Christian Theology in the Worldwide Church* (pp. 355–368). Grand Rapids: Eerdmans.

Panikkar, Raimundo (1964). *The Unknown Christ of Hinduism*. London: Darton, Longman & Todd.

Panikkar, Raimundo (1973). *The Trinity and the Religious Experience of Man: Icon-Person-Mystery*. Maryknoll, NY: Orbis; London: Darton, Longman & Todd.

Panikkar, Raimundo (1978). *The Intrareligious Dialogue*. New York: Paulist.

Panikkar, Raimundo (1993). *The Cosmotheandric Experience: Emerging Religious Consciousness*. Edited by Scott Eastham. Maryknoll, NY: Orbis.

Parratt, John (2004). "Introduction." In John Parratt (ed.), *An Introduction to Third World Theologies* (pp. 1–15). Cambridge: Cambridge University Press.

Pieris, Aloysius (1980). "Western Christianity and Asian Buddhism." *Dialogue* 7 (May–Aug): 49–85.

Pieris, Aloysius (1988). *An Asian Theology of Liberation*. Maryknoll, NY: Orbis.

Pope-Levison, Priscilla, and John R. Levison (1992). *Jesus in Global Contexts*. Louisville, KY: Westminster John Knox.

Samartha, Stanley J. (1980). "Unbound Christ: Towards Christology in India Today." In Douglas J. Elwood (ed.), *Asian Christian Theology: Emerging Themes* (pp. 145–160). Philadelphia: Westminster.

Samartha, Stanley J. (1991). *One Christ – Many Religions: Toward a Revised Christology*. Maryknoll, NY: Orbis.

Samartha, Stanley J. (1993). "The Cross and the Rainbow: Christ in a Multireligious Culture." In R. S. Sugirtharajah (ed.), *Asian Faces of Jesus* (pp. 104–125). Maryknoll, NY: Orbis.

Sanneh, Lamin (1983). *West African Christianity: The Religious Impact*. Maryknoll, NY: Orbis.

Schreiter, Robert J. (1991). "Introduction: Jesus Christ in Africa Today." In R. J. Schreiter (ed.), *Faces of Jesus in Africa* (pp. vii–xiii). Maryknoll, NY: Orbis.

Schreiter, Robert J. (2001). "Foreword." In Volker Küster, *The Many Faces of Jesus Christ: Intercultural Christology* (pp. xi–xiii). Trans. John Bowden. Maryknoll, NY: Orbis.

Scott, D., ed. (1979). *Keshub Chunder Sen*. Madras: Christian Literature Society of CISRA and United Theological College.

Segundo, Juan Luis (1973). *Our Idea of God*. Maryknoll, NY: Orbis.

Segundo, Juan Luis (1976). *The Liberation of Theology*. Maryknoll, NY: Orbis.

Sugirtharajah, R. S., ed. (1993). *Asian Faces of Jesus*. Maryknoll, NY: Orbis.

Thomas, M. M. (1969). *The Acknowledged Christ of the Indian Renaissance*. London: SCM.

Vähäkangas, Mika (1997). "Trinitarian Processions as Ancestral Relationships in Charles Nyamiti's Theology: A European Lutheran Critique." *Revue Africaine de Théologie* 21: 61–75.

Vähäkangas, Mika (1999). *In Search of Foundations for African Catholicism: Charles Nyamiti's Theological Method*. Leiden: Brill.

Wessels, Anton (1990). *Images of Jesus: How Jesus Is Perceived and Portrayed in Non-European Cultures*. Grand Rapids: Eerdmans.

CHAPTER 24

Jesus in American Culture

Paul Harvey

Jesus dominates American culture. With roots in the colonial era, but taking shape primarily in the nineteenth century, the American Jesus has since become the most important religious figure and icon in American life. When asked who was his favorite philosopher, the presidential candidate George W. Bush in 2000 responded immediately: "Jesus. Because He changed my life." Bush's own conversion experience, facilitated through the evangelist Billy Graham (himself an instrumental figure in formulating twentieth-century popular evangelical ideas of Jesus), saved him from his earlier problems with alcoholism and gave him a purpose, eventually helping to launch him into the governorship of Texas and then to the presidency. Simultaneously instinctive and calculated, Bush's response arose from a long history of very personal American appropriations of Jesus as man, symbol, and savior. Jesus has been in America, and his presence here has created the American Jesus: a Savior who is all things to all people, who is infinitely adaptable, pliable, and merchandisable. The American Jesus is the product of evangelicalism, but he has spread beyond Christian evangelical roots to take hold in numerous other religious venues.

And yet Jesus Christ in America has not always been so ubiquitous or so personal. Protestants in the early years of North America, especially the Puritans, emphasized God's divinity more than Christ's kingship. Certainly Jesus was not unknown in the colonial era, but those groups who emphasized Christ's divinity (such as the Moravians) were considered strange and perhaps a little heretical. By the time of the American Revolution, Enlightenment views of Jesus Christ as a moral paragon, but not necessarily as a divine son of God, had spread through the American intelligentsia. As Thomas Jefferson wrote in a letter to Philadelphia physician Benjamin Rush,

> To the corruptions of Christianity I am indeed opposed; but not to the genuine precepts of Jesus himself. I am a Christian, in the only sense in which he wished any one to be;

The Blackwell Companion to Jesus, First Edition. Edited by Delbert Burkett. ©2014 John Wiley & Sons, Ltd. Published 2014 by John Wiley & Sons, Ltd.

sincerely attached to his doctrines, in preference to all others; ascribing to himself every human excellence, and believing he never claimed any other.

But he cautioned Rush against making his ideas *too* public, fearing the "malignant perversions of those who make every word from me a text for new misrepresentations and calumnies" (Fox 2004, 164). During Jefferson's years in the White House, he took his scissors to the Bible, literally cutting out the portions he considered unreliable or *posthoc* add-ons but retaining those relatively fewer sections that he thought might lead people to a purer human-built moral code. References to Jesus' divinity did not survive being swept off Jefferson's cutting-room floor.

Jesus' rise to a supreme place in the American divine pantheon took off mostly in the nineteenth century, during the years of the Second Great Awakening. The evangelical revolution, the democratization of Christianity, and the explosion of Protestant sects personalized religious experience and brought Jesus to people's everyday lives. Once religious experience was personalized, made available to all, and seen as central to one's own destiny, then the mediating figure between God and humanity could become the central icon of religious devotion.

Albeit ubiquitous in American culture, Christ's image has played an especially significant role in the nation's profound struggles over race. From the colonial era to the present, Americans have crafted an assortment of images of Christ in their efforts for control, community, autonomy, individual identity, group rights, political power, economic security, and international authority. As the human embodiment of Christianity's God, Jesus has been racialized time and again in American culture to serve a host of aims. A white Christ has been the dominant image, one that has been inseparable from America's long history as a white Republic; yet red, black, and brown Christs have rivaled his supremacy and challenged America's racial hierarchies at every turn.

In tracing how the United States became a "Jesus nation" and how the American Jesus moved from being an "abstract principle into a concrete person, and then into a personality, a celebrity, and finally an icon," Stephen Prothero's *American Jesus: How the Son of God Became a National Icon* (2004) is the single most readable and accessible text, tracing the career of Jesus through American history from the Revolutionary era to the present. Prothero's lively text serves as a primary influence on this chapter. Focusing especially on evangelicals, but also looking at how Jews, Asian Americans, Mormons, and others have appropriated the Savior, Prothero shows how "evangelicals liberated Jesus first from Calvinism and then from creeds," retaining Jesus' divinity but emphasizing most his humanity, and thus

> transforming him from a distant god in a complex theological system into a near-and-dear person, fully embodied, with virtues they could imitate, a mind they could understand, and qualities they could love. In the process, they emboldened their Jesus to rise up and overthrow his Father as the dominant person in the Trinity. (Prothero 2004, 12–13)

Through the nineteenth and twentieth centuries, the liberation of Jesus from text and tradition continued. He was loosed from the Bible, and then even from the Christian tradition itself, to roam the land as a free-ranging icon.

As a result, Jesus came to be claimed by everyone. He comforted slave-holders and empowered slaves alike; he inspired black churchmen and Ku Klux Klansmen; he was the subject of Protestant hymns and American Buddhist chants; and he showed up in American art and popular culture in everything from Warner Sallman's ubiquitously reprinted *Head of Christ* to Andrew Lloyd Webber's smash hit *Jesus Christ Superstar* to Andres Serrano's infamous painting *Piss Christ* (which depicted the Crucifix sitting in a vase of urine). Evangelicals and groups such as "Jews for Jesus" claimed him as their own, to be sure, but so did the Japanese Buddhists who sang "Buddha loves me, this I know/For the Bible tells me so." And so did religious radicals from Thomas Jefferson to Thomas Merton, who sought to liberate Jesus from the confinements of stultifying tradition and see him as an "enlightened sage" or a holy man whose power could not be contained by doctrinal creeds.

Jesus' rise to prominence made him as close to a universal figure as any in American history. As Prothero concludes, "Jesus became a major personality in the United States because of the ability of religious insiders to make him culturally ines-capable. He became a national icon because outsiders have always felt free to inter-pret him in their own fashion" (2004, 16). The fashion of distinguishing between the "religion of Christianity" and the "religion of Jesus" allowed Jesus to serve as a free-ranging religious symbol, meaning that "Everyone is free to understand Jesus in his or her own way." In short, the American Jesus has been at once central, ubiquitous, and malleable. If America is a "Jesus nation," it is because Americans have made Jesus as multivalent, polyglot, racialized, diverse, and commercial as themselves.

Jesus in Early American History

Stephen Prothero's *American Jesus* begins the story with Jesus as Thomas Jefferson's enlightened sage. He then follows the popularization of Jesus as comforter, friend, and even manly savior through the nineteenth and early twentieth centuries. Alongside Prothero's short and readable text, Richard Wightman Fox's lengthier and more scholarly *Jesus in America: Personal Savior, Cultural Hero, National Obsession* traces the story back through the colonial era. Scattered other sources suggest that Jesus' rise to prominence in American history may date earlier than Prothero sug-gests. In particular, while English Protestants stressed God the Father and relegated Jesus the Son to a distinctly secondary or even tertiary place in the religious pan-theon, other groups in early America found room to exalt Jesus symbology as reli-giously powerful.

The significance of Jesus appears, for example, in the encounter between the Jesuits and the natives whom they converted. The Jesuits recorded their wanderings through the land and wonderings about the Indians in New France in over seventy volumes of the *Jesuit Relations*. Sent home as missionary and fundraising propaganda through the seventeenth century, the *Relations* recorded the Jesuits' efforts to explain the figure of Jesus to the natives among whom they missionized. Jesus' practical power came through in the Jesuit literature, and so did Jesus' power to bless the overseas imperial ventures of the Europeans. When Jesuits came to Canada in 1611, an early Jesuit historian related, they celebrated their role in the story of bringing Christ to the new land: "The figure of Christ, covered with a canopy, was carried about with the greatest possible ceremony, and he came auspiciously into the possession, so to speak of the happy land" (Fox 2004, 33). Jesus blessed the European possession of the land.

The natives in this encounter understood Jesus as a man-god, a figure familiar to them in their own religious symbology, and also sometimes took Jesus as an immediately practical spirit that might intervene in important functions of everyday life, especially hunting. Like most Indian peoples, the Huron incorporated Christian teachings into the context of their own culture, using them as they proved to be of practical value or discarding them as they seemed to lead to even more trouble, disease, or conflict. In the winter of 1633–1634, Jesuit Father Paul Le Jeune reported on two Montagnais who said that Jesus had offered to help them on their hunt: "I have seen thy Manitou [a spirit], and I thy Jesus ... Oh what a good year he promised us! What Beavers, what Elks!" In turn, in the dream Jesus expected obedience in recompense for his assistance. As historian Kenneth Morrison concludes of the incident, "Jesus turned out to be a hitherto unknown, but extremely powerful, Master of the Animals" (2002, 127).

A second encounter in which Jesus symbology played a major role was that between the Franciscans and the Pueblo Indians. The power represented in images and material artifacts of Jesus and the cross might be adopted or resisted, but they represented power to all. The powerful symbolism of Jesus came through as well to the Pueblo Indians of New Mexico, then being missionized and converted by Spanish Franciscans in the upper northern reaches of the Spanish empire in the New World. Sent to establish outposts in Nuevo Mexico in the late sixteenth century, the Franciscans deliberately mixed stories of Jesus' power together with Puebloan symbology, especially of rain gods. But Jesus was far from omnipotent, for he could be overturned and his symbols desecrated. Natives in New Mexico in 1680 led the most successful revolt in American history against European conquerors and their Jesus: the Pueblo Revolt of 1680. The Pueblo rebels brilliantly used iconoclasm as a symbol for their rejection of Spanish ways and their drive to recapture the power of tribal gods and customary ways. In one Indian village in the New Mexico mountains near Taos, some icons buried by the Spaniards in an attempt to protect them "had been opened by the apostates and the images taken out"; in the sacristy "was found a crown of twigs and two pieces of the arm of a holy image of Christ; and in the cloister were the skeletons of two dead persons." In the plaza of this pueblo rested the "entire thigh, leg, and foot of a holy image of Christ, in one piece, all the rest of the divine image being burned to charcoal and ashes; also some bases of other images and many pieces of burned crosses" (Wilson 1942, 2.204–205).

A third encounter, with a different focus on Jesus, occurred between the Moravians of the Middle Colonies and the Mohicans. Unlike the Protestant Puritans and the Franciscans in New Mexico, the Moravians identified personally with their Indian subjects and followed religious practices more akin to native ways than to English or Spanish "civility." The Moravians espoused a "blood-and-wound" theology emphasizing the bodily presence of Christ and his humanity. Their "Litany of Wounds," introduced in 1744 in Bethlehem, Pennsylvania, went, "Hail! Lamb of God. Christ, Have mercy! Glory to the side wound! ... Powerful wounds of Jesus, so moist and gory, bleed on my heart so that I may remain brave and like the wounds" (Wheeler 2008, 99).

The Mohicans among whom the Moravians successfully evangelized adapted the blood-and-wounds theology in ways fitting their emphasis on proper ritual practice. The parallels between Jesus, the man-god to whom individuals could appeal and receive higher powers, and the Mohican conception of the *Manitou* (an individual spirit) allowed the Mohicans to adopt the Moravian conception of Jesus. Jesus was physically present. Mohicans saw Jesus sitting in trees, guiding hunts, and bleeding his love literally and profusely. One Mohican woman, christened Rachel by the Moravians and married to Moravian missionary Christian Friedrich Post, imagined feeding her child with the Savior's blood. When her child was stricken with a cough and other illnesses for which she had no cure, Rachel worried over the child, who died a year later: "I wish our savior did make her well again. I can't help her at all. The Savior must do everything." She imagined feeding her child the Savior's blood rather than breast milk: "[W]hen I give my child suck and I think about the blood and wounds of our Savior I feel my heart sometimes very wet and so I think my child sucks the blood of our Savior and I feel the angels look after me and my child." She prayed that the Savior would give fellow villagers a "feeling of his blood and wounds in their hearts" (Wheeler 2008, 144).

In upstate New York and Canada with the Jesuits, in New Mexico with the Franciscans, and in Delaware and Pennsylvania with the Moravians, Jesus became a potent symbol of the colonial encounter. Whether as a practical diviner showing the way to animals, as a symbol of colonial power targeted for desecration in anti-colonial revolts, or as a new divine presence whose physical suffering spoke to the human suffering and struggles of those in the colonial encounter, Jesus was present in the colonial world. He was not there for everyone in some popular or democratized sense. But once we stretch our lens beyond English Protestants on the East Coast, Jesus appears as a prominent figure in early American history. And yet he was a very different figure from the Jesus of the Protestant evangelicals, who became the central religious figure of America in the nineteenth and twentieth centuries.

Jesus of the Awakening

In the mid-eighteenth century, with the Great Awakening, Jesus emerged in English Protestant conceptions as well. From such conceptions originated the democratized Jesus who swept through the American religious imagination of the nineteenth century. This was a Jesus for the ordinary American – energetic, restless, personal, and entrepreneurial. As Richard Wightman Fox puts it, "The Puritan Jesus was lodged in a transcendently stable and hierarchical Father-Son relation. The revivalist Jesus blew like an invisible wind, while planting himself securely in each believer's heart. This Jesus was as mobile and energetic as the American populace" (2004, 117).

Betokening his later appeal to ordinary folk in the evangelical revolution, Jesus appeared especially to the female pious, to African Americans, and to dissenting evangelical groups (such as the Baptists). He appeared, for example, to the pioneering female exponent of the Great Awakening in New England, Sarah Osborn. Raised with Puritan conceptions of piety, Osborn's diary entries show the transition to the evangelical Awakening ideas about the infilling of Jesus' spirit. "O dear Jesus! Still look me into deeper repentance. Look me into faith. Look me into flaming love and zeal. Look me into constant and universal obedience" (Hambrick-Stowe 1992, 133). In the act of the Lord's Supper, she "saw a crucified Saviour pouring out his precious blood to redeem his people from their sins." She later reflected, "When feeding upon his broken body, I was filled with astonishment. ... His blood was sweet to me, as it was shed for the remission of sins" (Hambrick-Stowe 1992, 134). Osborn's language of piety and her personal identification with Jesus prefigured the explosions of awakenings in the nineteenth century.

Moving beyond the more distant and formal Jesus of the Puritans, and directly contradicting the enlightened sage of Jefferson's Bible, Osborn's love of a physically and emotionally present Savior came closer to the Moravian theology of a human Jesus than to the Christ preached by Puritan divines and Anglican elites. It was this Jesus of the Awakening who dominated much of American Protestant Christianity over the next two centuries.

The Evangelical Jesus Rises

Jesus' central role in American popular culture took off in the nineteenth century, during the time described by scholar Nathan Hatch as the "democratization of American Christianity" (Hatch 1991). Some have also emphasized the transformation of theology during this time, from a more stringent Calvinism of the colonial Puritans to a "softer," gentler Jesus increasingly adopted by Protestants of the antebellum era. One should not exaggerate this transformation too much. Rich theological debate between Calvinists and "Arminians" (who emphasized the universal promise of salvation) still characterized theological fights of the antebellum era, and during that time as well many objected to a "feminized" Christ who softened and sentimentalized the manly Master.

Evangelical imagery and hymnology illustrate especially well the evolution of Jesus' role in American religious life during the nineteenth century. Beginning in the 1820s and 1830s, evangelicals deployed the latest of technologies (such as steam printing presses, an innovation of the antebellum era) in spreading what they understood to be the "old, old story, of Jesus and his love" (Morgan 1998). In the twentieth century, for example, this meant that evangelical preachers appeared on the radio almost as soon as there was publically broadcast radio, that they preached on commercially sold audio recordings from the very inception of the music industry, and that they pioneered the use of television shows to broadcast their message from the early days of television. In the earlier nineteenth century, it meant widely disseminated tracts, periodicals, lithographs, and commercially produced images. The result was that, from the early days of the Second Great Awakening, stories of personal encounters with Jesus exploded through the new technologies that allowed for quick, cheap, and relatively easy reprinting and selling of tracts, periodicals, and books. In this way, evangelicals played a key role in the creation of the modern publishing industry, just as they did with the electronic broadcasting industry in the twentieth century (Brown 2004). They made the message of Jesus as accessible and universal as possible. The virtual cult of personality permeating the figure of Jesus annoyed intellectuals of the antebellum era, especially the Transcendentalists, who were more inclined to see the divine in everyone than locate it specifically in Jesus. "You name the good Jesus until I hate the sound of him," Ralph Waldo Emerson complained, adding that he thought it his duty to "spit in the face of Christ as a sacred act of duty to the Soul." Emerson's carping against the ubiquity of Jesus demonstrated that this was in fact the age of Jesus in America (Prothero 2004, 53).

As ordinary Americans moved gradually away from doctrine and toward devotion, from the intellectual abstractions of religion to the practices of emotionally engaging worship, Jesus' appearance in biography, imagery, and song increasingly characterized American popular religious culture. The enlightened Jesus of Thomas Jefferson's Bible was an axiom-spouting moral teacher, a sage who taught moral truths. In the 1830s, David Friedrich Strauss' *Life of Jesus* further demystified Jesus by casting doubt on the historical authenticity of a good deal of the Bible. Conversely, even as intellectuals took the divine out of Jesus, popular religious thought located it squarely in him. Henry Ward Beecher's *The Life of Jesus, the Christ*, from 1871, illustrated a Jesus who was not a distant appendage to the Father, nor an enlightened sage, but instead a "sweet savior" who modeled the virtues of gentleness and goodness for humanity. As Beecher wrote of his theology, "[W]hen I found out that it was Christ's nature to lift men out of weakness to strength, and out of impurity to goodness, out of everything low and debasing to superiority, I felt that I had found a God" (Prothero 2004, 60). This was the Jesus pictured in the popular Christmas carols authored during this era, when "Christmas" took on its current-day trappings as a religious and commercial holiday. "It Came Upon a Midnight Clear" and "O

Little Town of Bethlehem," among many other Christmas carol classics, came out of this era. Meanwhile, the Currier & Ives Company, which pioneered the marketing of popular art prints, distributed hundreds of religious lithographs, many featuring either baby or grown-man Jesus. Jesus could be envisioned, in stunning color detail, feeding the multitudes, walking on water, and instructing children. He was closer than ever, because he could be seen, conversed with, and understood.

And Jesus could be seen and heard in the hymns of the era as well. By the mid to late nineteenth century, evangelical hymns, especially those authored by the gospel songwriters Ira Sankey, Fanny Crosby, and others, gave themselves over to Jesus. "All Hail the Power of Jesus' Name" was the most printed hymn of the era, while Dwight Moody's mass revivals of the era often concluded with altar calls with the sweet tones of hymns such as "Come to Jesus" beckoning people to surrender their lives to the Savior. In other hymns, such as "I Surrender All," singers pledged, "all to thee, my blessed Savior, I surrender all." Even more compelling, "What a Friend We Have in Jesus," first printed in 1875, told of how Christians could carry all their burdens to God in prayer, through the intervention of Jesus, the closest and best friend man could ever have.

Popular gospel hymnology continued to trumpet the Savior as the primary focus of religious devotion. Black gospel hymnists drew in part from the tradition of the spirituals, combining that with their experience listening to the Moody/Sankey gospel hymns of the late nineteenth century. The result was a potent musical mix that fed into black gospel music, or the "gospel blues," pioneered by hymnwriters such as Charles Albert Tindley and Lucie Campbell, and then put into popular musical form by Thomas Dorsey and his legion of gospel followers. Dorsey authored the great classic of black gospel music, "Precious Lord, Take My Hand," in which the power of God represented in Jesus leads the believer "through the storm, through the night." Later, Dorsey's classic "If You See My Jesus" instructs his dying friend to tell Jesus in heaven that "I am on my way." Black gospel writers took a tradition that had been collective and anonymous, resulting in the spirituals, and imprinted them with highly personalized voices, resulting in copyrighted songs and lyrics, to bring black Protestant music as well as African American conceptions of Jesus squarely into the twentieth century.

The popular Protestant Jesus of the gospel hymns of the era from the Civil War to World War I spread through text, imagery, and song. Charles Sheldon's novel *In His Steps*, first published in 1896, introduced Jesus as a social gospeler. The minister from Topeka, Kansas, first popularized the phrase "What Would Jesus Do." In the novel, "one character after another imitates 'Christ' by imitating reigning Protestant norms," especially the norms of a then nascent but growing Social Gospel (Fox 2004, 281). Walking through the streets of America, seeing crime, corruption, poverty, and violence everywhere, Jesus was ashamed. "What would Jesus do," Sheldon asked his readers, placing Jesus as a social reformer back into the mix of Jesus imagery. In later years, Sheldon's social-gospel catch phrase became an acronym – WWJD – stamped on innumerable items of clothing, consumer products, and jewelry worn by evangelical youths later in the twentieth century. By then, the "WWJD" phrase had been co-opted by conservative evangelicalism, often used then for purposes precisely the opposite of what Sheldon had intended in his proto-Christian-Socialist text.

What Jesus would do, of course, depended almost entirely on what social position one held in society. Even groups suspicious of organized Christianity, or critical of its complicity in the growing corporate capitalist order, adopted Jesus as their icon. For them, Jesus would rectify the manifest injustices in the social order as experienced by working-class people. Iron workers meeting in 1896, for example, scorned any mention they heard of churches (identified as institutions funded and controlled by the industrial class) but cheered when the name "Jesus" was mentioned. An organizer for the largest labor group of the era, the Knights of Labor, asserted that "Christ must have been a true Knight of Labor, being a carpenter's son. He was a master of His Father's trade. And this proves all Knights of Labor should be Christlike" (Fox 2004, 281).

From biographies to fictionalizations to rock operas to T-shirts, the popularization and commercialization of Jesus exploded during the twentieth century. The crudity of some of this imagery came through most clearly in Bruce Barton's bestselling text of the 1920s, *The Man Nobody Knows.* "He picked up twelve men from the bottom ranks of business and forged them into an organization that conquered the world," wrote Barton, a minister's son and corporate public relations specialist. The parables of Jesus were not only pearls of wisdom but also the "most powerful advertisements of all time" (Barton 1925, 107). Barton was one of numerous authors who sought to recapture the "manliness" of Jesus, this time in the guise of a virile businessman. While scorned and parodied by intellectuals, his portrayal found its way into the hearts of Americans of the 1920s and after, for readers hungered for texts that presented a Jesus they could imagine in their human everyday struggles.

But the single most influential depiction of Jesus in the twentieth century, and probably for all of American history, came from a previously unknown graphic artist from Chicago in 1940. Warner Sallman produced his famous painting *Head of Christ* in the year before America entered World War II. Over the next sixty years, his work would be reprinted over 500 million times. *Head of Christ* appeared in every conceivable form and shape and on every imaginable product. Sallman professed to be inspired by a dream and by a teacher at Moody Bible Institute in Chicago who told him to "[m]ake him a real man. ... Make Him strong and masculine, so people will see in His face that He slept under the stars, drove the money changers out of the temple, and faced Calvary in triumph" (Prothero 2004, 118). His dream and this advice first eventuated in a charcoal drawing in 1924 and then in the epochal *Head of Christ* in 1940. Drawing from their spectacularly successful distribution techniques pioneered in the antebellum era, evangelicals found myriad ways to distribute *Head of Christ* during World War II, and received the blessings of General Dwight D. Eisenhower and J. Edgar Hoover of the FBI in doing so. In the second half of the twentieth century, it was almost impossible not to encounter *Head of Christ* at some point in one's life, and many saw it every week in their church. When they saw the painting, many believed they really saw Jesus, or "an exact likeness of our Lord Jesus Christ," as one believer expressed it (Prothero 2004, 118). The simple depiction of Jesus – divorced from any biblical context, as if Jesus had sat in the studio for a portrait – became "the best picture available in a culture that increasingly longed for a glimpse of his true face" (118). The nineteenth-century evangelical publishers who pioneered the mass production and distribution of tracts, pamphlets, and books blazed a trail that led directly to *Head of Christ*. And perhaps to their astonishment, or perhaps to their delight, in the post–World War II years they could have seen the natural extension of their work in the merchandising of Jesus, "the real thing."

What Color Was Jesus? Christ in the South

In a society as riven by race as was (and is) the United States, Jesus inevitably was given a race, either implicitly or explicitly. Jesus' race took form in the nineteenth century, just as he was popularized in word and image (Callahan 2006). He entered American popular culture bathed in the imagery of whiteness, which spread rapidly through the commercial imagery of the twentieth century, from *Head of Christ* to Johnny Cash's 1973 Jesus bio-pic *Gospel Road: The Story of Jesus* (Blum and Harvey, forthcoming).

African Americans also saw Jesus as a "little white man," coming in brightness, shining with the light of God. Their religious imagery adopted some of the symbolism of the whiteness of Jesus (Johnson 1960). And yet, as the trickster of the trinity, Jesus' purity, symbolized by whiteness, condemned racializing ideas of the divine. The black Jesus may have appeared as white in imagery and symbolism, but he became a black Southerner in the act of suffering: an oppressed slave, a victim of a crucifixion-lynching, a poor migrant, a fellow-sufferer on the front lines of civil rights battles. Long before the rise of black theology in the civil rights era, slaves and freed African Americans imagined, painted, sermonized about, and musically portrayed a black Jesus who was a figure of liberation. For them, Jesus' white imagery belied his black sympathies.

In the 1810s, a black woman named in the records only as "Aunt Katy" attended a North Carolina Methodist gathering. In the midst of a revival service, she felt the spirit, and "with many extravagant gestures, cried out that she was 'young King Jesus'" (Heyrman 1997, 36). Black worshipers knew that she was filled with the spirit; she was channeling the voices of the ancestors through the language of Jesus.

Stories of Jesus suffused the evangelical South. He often materialized in a blaze of bright glory or riding a milk-white horse. "If you want to find Jesus, go in the wilderness," so the slave spiritual went. For slaves, the life of Jesus was itself an example of how the powerless could overcome the powerful, through parable and poetry.

Jesus' humble birth, miraculous deeds, gruesome execution, and glorious resurrection often came through the words of white ministers and missionaries. Soon enough they could be found everywhere in the black southern imagination, often retold and re-envisioned in ways that freely mixed biblical characters from different time periods and appealed to slaves who sought both to escape from Egypt and to achieve salvation. Slaves encountered Jesus when they retreated to the woods seeking conversion experiences, in times of extreme turmoil, during the middle of whippings and beatings, and in their own dreams and visions. A young slave in South Carolina in 1850 saw Jesus, he insisted, in a vision. In heaven, he observed the "Lord Jesus, a sittin' behind de door an' a reading his Bible." In moments of transfiguration, slaves observed the physical presence of God or Christ. One said, "I looked away to the east and saw Jesus ... I saw God sitting in a big arm chair." Another saw him "when he freed my soul from hell"; still another related his encounter with Jesus in a "snow-white train," moving as quick as lightning, Jesus on board as the conductor. "I saw the Lord in the east part of the world," said another believer; "he looked like he had been dipped in snow and he was talking to me" (Levine 1997, 36–37).

Disillusioned by their abandonment and by the surge in racist violence in the late nineteenth century, black ministers, activists, and politicians combed religious texts for explanation and counter-theologies. The racialization of Christ since the Civil War demanded radical counter-theologies. Jesus had to return again, this time not in the guise of the Union Army but in the voices of black men. Henry McNeal Turner enunciated the idea best in his paper *Voice of Missions*, a sheet promoting African American missionary work in and emigration to Africa. "We have as much right Biblically and otherwise to believe that God is a Negro as you buckra, or white, people have to believe that God is a fine looking, symmetrical and ornamented white man," wrote Turner, whose tumultuous time as a Reconstruction state legislator in Georgia embittered him toward the prospects of equality for black Americans. "For the bulk of you, and all the fool Negroes of the country, believe that God is a white-skinned, blue-eyed, straight-haired, projecting-nosed, compressed-lipped and finely robed white gentleman, sitting upon a throne somewhere in the heavens." As did the Marcus Garveyites of the next generation, and a number of relatively unknown black ministers of his own generation, Turner understood that the racialization of the divine devastated freed people already imprinted with the stigma of slavery. Turner reshaped God in the image of blacks. He reasoned that every other race of people had re-imagined an abstract divine in their own color and culture:

> Every race of people since time began who have attempted to describe their God by words, or by paintings, or by carvings, or by any other form or figure, have conveyed the idea that the God who made them and shaped their destinies was symbolized in themselves, and why should not the Negro believe that he resembles God as much so as other people? We do not believe that there is any hope for a race of people who do not believe that they look like God. (Turner [1898] 1971, 176)

Black religious folk artists, entrepreneurs, literary figures, and essayists picked up on Turner's themes in the early twentieth century. They wove black Christs into textiles, pictured him through paintings, wrote about him in literary works and theological treatises, and theologized about him in new churches and religious institutions. From David Walker to Henry Turner and W. L. Hunter, black theologians excoriated the white God, represented on earth by a lily-white Jesus. This perspective found its twentieth-century expressions in works such as *Jesus Christ Had Negro Blood in His Veins*, in the black Jesuses installed by George MacGuire of the African Orthodox Church, in the "blackening" of Jesus through the rise of the gospel blues, and in fine and vernacular artists who envisioned black Christs before there was anything called black theology. W. E. B. Du Bois expressed it best in 1913, in his vision of what Jesus would do:

> Jesus Christ was a laborer and black men are laborers. He was poor and we are poor; He was persecuted and crucified and we are mobbed and lynched. If Jesus Christ came to America he would be associated with Negroes and Italians and working people; He would eat and pray with them, and He would seldom see the interior of the Cathedral of St. John the Divine. (Fox 2004, 360)

Jesus was the buckle on America's Bible Belt, which in the later nineteenth century the South became. The need to understand slavery in a liberal democracy, and then the Confederacy's loss in the Civil War, proved central in implanting conservative evangelicalism as the dominant religious motif of whites in the region. In many senses, Jesus became a Southerner. White southern ministers frequently analogized the suffering South to the dying Christ. Just as Jesus was pierced by a crown of thorns before he was fitted with a crown of glory, so Southerners would endure their suffering in a Christ-like way and emerge victorious over those who would do them evil. Christian symbology pervaded the Confederate camps and revivals late in the war, and thereafter underlay the theology of the "religion of the Lost Cause." In the hundreds of Confederate monuments setting in biblical relief the major southern war heroes, in the addresses at yearly meetings of Sons of Confederate Veterans and United Daughters of the Confederacy, and in the inscriptions on the monuments themselves, Jesus sanctified a unified white southern people who had fought for Him. In the process, whites reclaimed Jesus (in part), for now his suffering was akin to that of the white South rather than to the black servants of the slave South.

Thus the southern war heroes, especially Robert E. Lee, were described in Christ-like language. John William Jones' *Christ in the Camp*, first published in 1887, identified the southern cause with Christ, and more than anything else claimed that the success of revivalism in the southern army camps proved the righteousness of the cause. Such revivalism presented a Christ who identified with nobly struggling soldiers. To receive Jesus prepared southern soldiers to fight for "freedom"; and, for them, to see Jesus was to see victory in the here and the hereafter. "Jesus *was* in our camps with wonderful power, and ... no army in all history – not even Cromwell's 'Roundheads' – had in it as much of the real, evangelical religion and devout piety as the Army of Northern Virginia" (Jones 1887, 344). Thomas Wentworth Higginson had made the same contention for his black northern troops in his *Army Life in a Black Regiment* ([1870] 1971), showing how much both sides during the Civil War claimed the support of Jesus.

And thus, too, the Ku Klux Klan identified itself with Jesus. Klan publications in the 1920s adopted "the living Christ" as the "Klansman's criterion of character," as went the opening prayer of the officially prescribed Klan ritual of the 1920s. Klansmen were to emulate the Savior's example, for Jesus himself "was a Klansman," one Texan proclaimed. The Klan's cross, uniting faith and nation in one symbol, had been "sanctified and made holy nearly nineteen hundred years ago by the suffering and blood of the crucified Christ, bathed in the blood of fifty million martyrs who died in the most holy faith."

The white robes of the Klan in *Birth of a Nation*, the epochal 1915 film adapted from the stories in southern minister Thomas Dixon's novels, became a centrally produced and regulated uniform for the Second Ku Klux Klan. The careful way in which Klan leaders selected and monitored the production of the Klan's official white uniforms suggests how the "white robe" itself bore the "righteousness of Christ." Jesus himself was on the Klansman's body; a Klansman wore "this white robe to signify the desire to put on that white robe which is the righteousness of Christ, in that Empire Invisible, that lies out beyond the vale of death." Thus the Klan became a real-life realization of an Empire Invisible that was now visible in public parades and spectacles (Baker 2007, 40, 44, 58).

The Klansman's Jesus met his match in the mid-twentieth-century civil rights struggle. The moral force of the civil rights movement, empowered with the rhetoric and music from black churches, overwhelmed the deep legacy of religious justifications for a racialized America. Even the black Protestants who led the movement, however, had to deal with the legacy of America's racialized Jesus.

"Why did God make Jesus white, when the majority of peoples in the world are non-white?" someone wrote to ask Martin Luther King in an advice column in 1960. Martin Luther King's answer fascinatingly suggests the juxtaposition of the white Christ and the black Jesus in American history. King initially dismissed the relevance of the query. "The color of Jesus' skin is of little or no consequence," he reassured his readers, because white or black skin "is a biological quality which has nothing to do with the intrinsic value of the personality." Jesus, of course, transcended race. His significance lay "not in His color, but in His unique God-consciousness and His willingness to surrender His will to God's will. He was the son of God, not because of His external biological makeup, but because of His internal spiritual commitment." King unconsciously referred back to the triumph of the white Christ in American history, probably without meaning to do so, even while claiming the white Jesus for African Americans. Jesus, he said, "would have been no more significant if His skin had been black. He is no less significant because his skin was white." Not all of King's readers were satisfied with this rather confusing conclusion. One follow-up query came from a reader "disturbed" by King's apparent acceptance of the belief that Jesus was white. "I believe, as you do, that skin color shouldn't be important, but I don't believe Jesus was white. What is the basis for your assumption that he was," this reader challenged the civil rights icon. There is no record of a reply (Carson 2005, 279–280).

Entering the era of the modern civil rights movement, the black birth and white rebirth of Jesus left a conflicted legacy. African Americans inherited contending images of Jesus as subversive savior and Jesus as the living representative of the white man's God. Overcoming the racialization of the divine proved an emotionally fraught struggle for many during the years of the civil rights revolution. The white Christ of American history, which had given divine imprimatur to ideas of white supremacy, met the black Jesus of the African American tradition. The conflicting imagery could be seen on the walls of countless black churches and homes, where Sallman's *Head of Christ* as well as white political heroes mixed with images from heroes of black history. Jesus was a comforter to the afflicted, but could be a salve that took a generation's eyes off the prize. The critique coming from the black secular left as well as from Black Muslims condemned as hopelessly outdated those who would sing, "You may have all the world, but give me Jesus." With minds "stayed on Jesus," could minds be focused on freedom? Then too, Jesus could be an avenger, the one calling the chickens home to roost. The black appropriation of the southern evangelical Christ, and His re-emergence as the white Christ of southern racial power, clashed in the twentieth century. For African Americans, Jesus had to be saved. Doing so involved a re-imagination of the same evangelical culture of salvation and segregation that was part of his creation.

The centuries-long interplay between a universal savior and a racially defined Jesus came to a head in the twentieth-century South. Even with the seeming triumph of the subversive savior in the civil rights years, and the apparent discrediting of a Christ invoked to bless white supremacy, the white Jesus of American history was not dead yet, as the term "Christian" increasingly connoted evangelical, white, and southern, in modern American terminology. Even after the civil rights movement, the black Christ remained something of an outsider.

Jesus Christ Superstar

Jesus Christ is one of the most important political, social, and cultural symbols in American history. Presidents have pledged their full devotion to him, the nation has invaded other countries in his name, and his image was used vigorously on all sides during the Civil War. Pacifists claim Christ's mantle as readily as the war hawks do, while millions flock to motion pictures about him. Paintings of Christ adorn homes, sanctuaries, and businesses, and it seems that every generation looks to Jesus for answers to their problems. During the 1990s, millions of Americans looked back to a nineteenth-century novel and asked themselves "What would Jesus do?" Then they actually tried to do likewise. In early 2004, Mel Gibson's *The Passion of the Christ* was a box office hit as it raised issues of anti-Semitism in American Catholicism and culture. Christ even dominates professional and amateur sports. If one listens to NASCAR drivers, ball players, and track stars, Jesus seems to control race cars, curve balls, and times in the hundred-meter dash.

Perhaps most importantly, Jesus has furthered the image Americans have carried of themselves as a chosen people. With Jesus, Richard Fox concludes,

> [Americans] could get divine sanction for making all things new while believing that they honored their most precious inheritance of all, Christ himself. They could see themselves as a chosen people ... but a people chosen now for free-spirited development as individuals. Jesus, the chosen Son, provided vital underpinning for *novus ordo Seclorum* (new order of things): a nation of individuals embarked on an open-ended journey of territorial expansion, economic innovation, and social experimentation. As a symbolic figure, Jesus could offer moral support for that journey while also raising moral objections. (2004, 13)

As well, Jesus held together a nation both materialistic and deeply religious, both Christian and diversely religious, and both freewheeling and doctrinal. Intellectual and artistic critics of American life, including Richard Niebuhr in his well-known text *Christ and Culture*, consistently have lamented and lampooned the American talent for manipulating, commercializing, and diluting Jesus Christ into a figure that suits virtually any purpose. These critiques matter little to ordinary Americans, who have incorporated Jesus successfully into their own self-made religious traditions. They know what Jesus would do, what he would drive, and how he would respond to personal situations and religious crises. Like the Doobie Brothers, they know that "Jesus is just alright with me."

References

Baker, Kelly J. (2007). "The Gospel According to the Klan: The Ku Klux Klan's Vision of White Protestant America, 1915–1930." PhD dissertation, Florida State University.

Barton, Bruce (1925). *The Man Nobody Knows*. Indianapolis: Bobbs-Merrill.

Blum, Edward, and Paul Harvey (forthcoming). *Jesus in Red, White, and Black*. Chapel Hill: University of North Carolina Press.

Brown, Candy (2004). *The Word in the World: Evangelical Writing, Reading, and Publishing in America, 1790–1880*. Chapel Hill: University of North Carolina Press.

Callahan, Allen (2006). *The Talking Book: African Americans and the Bible*. New Haven: Yale University Press.

Carson, Clayborne, et al., eds. (2005). *The Papers of Martin Luther King*. Vol. IV: *Threshold of a New Decade*. Berkeley: University of California Press.

Fox, Richard Wightman (2004). *Jesus in America: Personal Savior, Cultural Hero, National Obsession*. San Francisco: HarperOne.

Hambrick-Stowe, Charles (1992). "The Spiritual Pilgrimage of Sarah Osborn (1714–1796)." *Church History* 61 (Dec): 408–421. Reprinted in Jon Butler and Harry Stout, *Religion in American History: A Reader* (pp. 130–141). New York: Oxford University Press, 1997

Hatch, Nathan (1991). *The Democratization of American Christianity*. New Haven: Yale University Press.

Heyrman, Christine Leigh (1997). *Southern Cross: The Beginnings of the Bible Belt*. Chapel Hill: University of North Carolina Press.

Higginson, Thomas Wentworth ([1870] 1971). *Army Life in a Black Regiment*. New York: Norton.

Johnson, Clifton (1960). *God Struck Me Dead: Religious Conversion Experiences and Autobiographies of Ex-Slaves*. Philadelphia: Judson.

Jones, John William (1887). *Christ in the Camp; or, Religion in Lee's Army*. Richmond: B. F. Johnson.

Levine, Lawrence (1977). *Black Culture and Black Consciousness: Afro-American Folk Thought from Slavery to Freedom*. New York: Oxford University Press

Morgan, David (1998). *Protestants and Pictures: Religion, Visual Culture, and the Age of Mass Production*. New York: Oxford University Press.

Morrison, Kenneth (2002). *The Solidarity of Kin: Ethnohistory, Religious Studies, and the Algonkian-French Religious Encounter*. Albany: SUNY Press.

Prothero, Stephen (2004). *American Jesus: How the Son of God Became a National Icon*. New York: Farrar, Strauss, & Giroux.

Turner, Henry McNeal ([1898] 1971). *Respect Black: The Writings and Speeches of Henry McNeal Turner*. Edited by Edwin Redkey. New York: Arno Press.

Wheeler, Rachel (2008). *To Live Upon Hope: Mohicans and Missionaries in the Eighteenth-Century Northeast*. Cornell: Cornell University Press.

Wilson, Charles Hackett (1942). *Revolt of the Pueblo Indians of New Mexico and Otermin's Attempted Reconquest, 1680–1682*. 2 vols. Albuquerque: University of New Mexico Press.

CHAPTER 25

The Black Christ

Kelly Brown Douglas with Delbert Burkett

In a 1963 interview, Malcolm X stridently proclaimed, "Christ wasn't white. Christ was a black man" (Haley 1963). More recent black scholars and church leaders have repeated Malcolm's proclamation. Various black church leaders have urged black churches to destroy images of Christ with white skin and features and to replace them with images of a Christ with black skin and features. This, they claim, will help to nurture the kind of black self-esteem needed to mitigate the murderous or suicidal self-hate that is apparently present in various segments of the black community.

Although Jesus' ethnicity and dark-skinned complexion are certainly important aspects of Christ's blackness, to call Christ black points to more than simply ancestry or biological characteristics. Throughout black religious history, black people have believed that Christ identified with the black struggle against the tyrannies of a white racist society. To call Christ black affirms this identification.

The present chapter surveys the development of both aspects of Christ's blackness. For a more detailed presentation, see the book *The Black Christ* (Douglas 1994), on which this chapter is based.

Roots of the Black Christ

The Christ of slave Christianity

The roots of the Black Christ can be traced to slavery. Black Christian slaves developed a conception of Jesus that contrasted with the Jesus preached by white Christian slaveholders.

The white slaveholders placed little or no emphasis on the ministry of Jesus to the poor and oppressed. They emphasized instead that he did not speak directly against slavery. One proslavery minister made his case for slavery this way:

Our Lord repeatedly spoke of slaves, especially in several of his parables, without the slightest intimation that he condemned slavery, and in such a way as plainly showed that he considered it lawful. ... We are told, Matt. 8:23–35, that a Centurion came to Jesus beseeching him to heal his sick servant. ... If the holding of slaves had been sinful, Jesus would, we doubt not, have so informed [the Centurion]. (How 1856, 24)

This Christ of the white slaveholders not only approved slavery, but also failed to condemn the cruelty with which they treated their slaves.

While some Christian slaves accepted this slaveholders' Christianity, many others did not. These held clandestine church services in the slave quarters or brush arbors (Raboteau 1978, 177, 212). From this slave Christianity emerged a different view of Jesus, a Christ who identified with black people in their oppression.

This Christ of the black slaves was a living being with whom the slaves had an intimate relationship. Thus the enslaved could sing that "Jesus is my bosom friend" or that a "little talk with Jesus makes it right." To the slaves, Jesus was a trusted companion who understood their pain, sufferings, and sorrows. In arriving at this understanding of Jesus, the slaves focused on Jesus' ministry to the oppressed. They reasoned that if Jesus helped the oppressed of his own time, he would surely do the same for them. Even more so, the crucifixion of Jesus demonstrated his solidarity with them. They saw the suffering of Jesus on the cross as their own suffering. The crucifixion confirmed to slaves that they were one with Jesus, and more importantly, that Jesus was one with them (Cone [1972] 1991, 54). The resurrection of Jesus revealed to the slaves that Jesus was not dead and could therefore meet their needs. It also revealed that oppression was not the last word. Jesus' deliverance from the death of the cross meant that they would be delivered from the death of slavery. Black people testified in song that "Jesus Christ, He died for me, Jesus Christ, He set me free."

While an emphasis on Jesus' ministry opened the slaves to an intimate relationship with Christ, it also radicalized some of them to fight for their freedom. Although some slaves adopted the notion that Jesus offered freedom only in "heaven," many others did not completely spiritualize the concept of freedom. They regarded the freedom offered by Jesus as a reality to be attained on earth. Their concept of freedom was shaped in particular by the story of the exodus, in which God sent Moses to deliver the Israelite slaves from bondage in Egypt. As Moses delivered the Israelites from bondage, so Jesus would deliver the slaves (Raboteau 1978, 318).

The Christ of the slaves also made them aware of the contradiction between Christianity and the cruelty of slavery. They saw that to enslave and brutalize others betrayed the example that Jesus set and contradicted what it meant to be a Christian. The Christ of slave Christianity made it possible for black people to be Christian without worshiping a Christ that ravaged Africa, fostered slavery, and accepted the rapes of black women. The slaves' conception of Christ contested the slaveholders' understanding of Christ as one who supported and suborned slavery. It revealed such an understanding as heretical. It made clear that slave ships named "Jesus" blasphemed the Christian God.

The Christ of the slaves made God real for them. Christ was the presence of God in the lives of enslaved men and women as they navigated the harsh and dehumanizing realities of their enslavement. Their Christ was a fellow sufferer, a confidant, a provider, and a liberator. Yet, while slave Christianity emphasized that Christ was on the side of black people in their daily struggles, it did not address the matter of "color." In retrospect we can call the Christ of the slaves black. But this blackness had to do with Jesus' identification with the oppressed black slaves, not with the color of Jesus' skin. If black Christians were not to be shamed by a Christ "whose skin color was so obviously not their own" (Harding 1979, 37), something more had to be said about the Christ's blackness. The actual pigmentation of Christ was addressed as black people began to overtly and consciously connect the fact of their biological givens, especially their skin color, with their oppressive social condition.

The Black Christ of black nationalists

As early as the antebellum period and throughout black people's historical struggle against racial oppression, black nationalist thinkers have been in the forefront in recognizing the color component of black oppression. They have been clear that according to the white supremacist ideology that undergirds the oppression of black people, blackness signals inferiority and hence unwarranted suffering. In an effort to affirm the positive value of blackness and thus to sever the link between blackness and inferiority, black nationalists have promoted a variety of programs and concepts that suggest racial pride, if not racial chauvinism. One of the most significant efforts to affirm blackness and contest any notion of it as a sign of defect has been the recognition of God and Christ as literally black. For many nationalists, identifying God and Christ as black fosters black people's self-esteem by allowing them to worship a God in their own image and by signifying that blackness is not to be disdained. On the contrary, it is sacred. It reflects not only an experience that the divine affirms, but also a color that the divine takes on.

Black nationalists have made this point throughout history in various ways. For instance, Robert Alexander Young calls Christ "black" in his "Ethiopian Manifesto" (Young 1829). He begins this manifesto by arguing that enslavement of black people is against God's will. He explains that black people are created by God, just like white people; thus whites have no right to prevent black men and women from enjoying the freedom that God grants to all people. Based on this claim that God intends for black people to be free, Young argued that God would send for a messiah – born of a black woman – who would liberate black people from bondage. Young's version of the Black Messiah echoes themes of slave Christianity in stressing that God is against slavery.

Henry McNeal Turner, in an 1898 speech, presented a model of the Black Messiah that did not explicitly link God's blackness to God's opposition to oppression. Turner emphasized, instead, the importance of black people's ability to image God and Jesus in their own likeness. He argued that if other peoples of the world, especially white people, have a right to image God in their likeness, so too do black people (Redkey 1971, 176). Later, in the twentieth century, Marcus Garvey agreed with Turner that black people had every right to envision God as black. Going further than Turner, he also argued that Jesus actually was black. He said that as a Jew from the line of Jesse, Jesus had "Negro blood" running through his veins. Accordingly, he often admonished black audiences to "never admit that Jesus Christ was a white man" (Burkett 1978, 53).

The Black Christ in early black literature

The early twentieth century was an era in which black literature also reflected an emphasis on the Black Christ. Langston Hughes, for instance, portrayed Christ as a southern "nigger" in his poem entitled "Christ in Alabama." In the final stanza of this poem, Hughes writes,

> Most holy bastard
> Of the bleeding mouth,
> Nigger Christ
> On the cross
> of the South. (1969, 37)

Countee Cullen, reflecting more of an existential struggle to relate Christ to black people, wrote an epic poem in 1928 entitled "The Black Christ." In his book *Color*, Cullen had already published the poem "Heritage," in which he described the comfort that would come from knowing that Christ, too, was black. He wrote,

> Ever at Thy glowing altar
> Must my heart grow sick and falter,
> Wishing He I served were black,
> Thinking then it would not lack
> Precedent of pain to guide it,
> Let who would or might deride it,
> Surely then this flesh would know
> Yours had borne a kindred woe. (1925, 36–41)

Finally, John Henrik Clarke wrote a short story entitled, "The Boy Who Painted Christ Black." Clarke relates the dramatic account of a little boy who got in trouble with a white school supervisor for painting a picture of a Black Christ. But the story also tells of the heroic black principal of the school who lost his job for daring to stand up for the boy. Clarke represents the principal as saying,

I don't think the boy is so far wrong in painting Christ black. The artists of all other races have painted whatsoever God they worship to resemble themselves. I see no reason why we should be immune from that privilege. After all, Christ was born in that part of the world that had always been predominately populated by colored people. There is a strong possibility that he could have been a Negro. (1972, 163ff.)

The Black Christ in the Black Struggle

The Black Christ came to maturity in the 1960s during the era of black consciousness that accompanied the civil rights and Black Power movements. This era was characterized by black people demanding, from the white community as well as their own, a respect for blackness – not only for the color of their skins, but also for their heritage, music, art, and culture. Many black people in America, especially the young, donned symbols of blackness, wearing African dashikis, styling their hair in Afros, and hanging African carved statues (Tikis) around their necks. A popular song of the era expressed their mood: "Say it loud, I'm Black and I'm Proud!"

This spirit of black consciousness had religious and theological implications. Could Jesus Christ have meaning for a people determined to be free and proud of their blackness? Two individuals in particular addressed this question most clearly. Martin Luther King Jr. continued the tradition of the Black Christ of slave Christianity, as he linked black freedom to the Christian gospel. At the same time, Malcolm X continued the nationalist tradition, as he pointed out the absurdity of black people worshiping a Christ who looked like their white oppressors.

Martin Luther King Jr. challenged the view of Christ held by many white Christians. This view emphasizes the divinity of Jesus but minimizes the significance of his liberating ministry. White church leaders with this perspective did not voice a concern for racial justice, feeling that the minister's task was to "save souls," not to engage in social protest. Such passivity, however, implied that Jesus was not concerned with black oppression, and it permitted white racism to go unchallenged. King strongly opposed such a view of Christianity, one that could lead to silence in the face of injustice. He questioned the view of God and Jesus held by many southern white clergy: "Who is their God? Is their God the God of Abraham, Isaac and Jacob? And is their Savior the Savior who hung on the cross at Golgotha?" (Washington 1986, 345).

In contrast, King's own theological perspective formed the foundation for his participation in the black freedom movement. This perspective, which he undoubtedly encountered in the black church as he grew up, reflected the religion of the Black Christ of slave Christianity. It did so in at least three areas: the relationship between black people and God, the meaning of freedom, and the compatibility between Christianity and protest activity.

While King sometimes spoke about God without referring to Jesus, what he said about God was rarely divorced from his understanding of Jesus. His understanding of the relationship between black people and God began with his recognition that they were as much God's children as any other human beings. They were therefore entitled to the same rights as other humans, and God cared about them just as God cared about all people. Specifically, he believed that God identified with them in their struggle to be free and that God sustained them during that struggle. King saw the Israelites' exodus from Egypt as evidence of God's liberating activity in history (1963, 76–85). Like the black slaves before him, he believed that God identified with black people as God had identified with the Israelites. What God did for the Israelites in Egypt, God would do for the oppressed blacks in the United States.

Consistent with this emphasis on God's activity in history, King's understanding of Christian freedom focused on liberation in this world. Like his slave ancestors, he did not completely spiritualize the concept. While the freedom that Jesus offered may have had "heavenly implications," King did not consider it limited to heaven. Through his protest activity and his public addresses, he expressed his belief that the freedom offered by God through Jesus could be experienced as an earthly possibility. This perspective was also expressed in the "freedom songs," which King called "the soul" of the civil rights movement. Many of these came from slave spirituals, which civil rights protesters revised to fit their contemporary situation. If the meaning of Christian freedom was sometimes ambiguous in the spirituals, it was clearly an earthly hope in the versions reshaped and sung by the black protesters. For this view of freedom, King found support in the prophetic narratives of the Old Testament, especially those of the prophet Amos. He equated Jesus' freedom with Amos's call for "justice to run down like waters and righteousness like an ever-flowing stream" (Amos 5:24).

In line with these views, King saw a compatibility between Christianity and protest activity. If God sustained black people in their struggle for freedom and through Jesus offered them a freedom attainable in history, then it was appropriate – if not required – for Christians to rebel against any social barrier to the freedom of black people. In his first public speech during the Montgomery bus boycott, he articulated the affinity between being a Christian and protesting against racial injustice. He accented the fact that the boycotters were Christian and proclaimed, "[W]e are not wrong in what we are doing. ... If we are wrong God Almighty is wrong. If we are wrong Jesus of Nazareth was merely a utopian dreamer and never came down to earth" (King 1955). King's image of Jesus as a social reformer was shaped in part by Jesus' sermon at Nazareth, to which King referred on many occasions:

> The spirit of the Lord is upon me
> because he has anointed me;
> he has sent me to announce good news to the poor,
> to proclaim release for prisoners
> and recovery of sight for the blind;
> to let the broken victims go free,
> to proclaim the year of the Lord's favor. (Luke 4:18–19)

These words, King said, illustrated that "Christianity is itself a protest" (1958, 93). Thus King's liberating Jesus contrasted with the disengaged Jesus of some white Christianity. Jesus' liberating ministry, especially his teachings, challenged all Christians to protest any form of social oppression, in this case racial injustice. Like the slave religion before him, King's words and actions demonstrated how Christianity can become a critique of a white racist status quo.

But just as slave religion did not make the color of Christ an issue during the antebellum period, King did not do so during the 1960s black freedom movement. Again, black nationalists would be the ones to articulate the need for a physically Black Christ. No contemporary nationalist raised the issue of Christ's color more forcefully than the Black Muslim, Malcolm X.

While King and many white clergy disagreed over the relation of Christianity to the black struggle, Malcolm X vociferously proclaimed that Christianity itself was detrimental to black freedom. It was a religious tool used by the slaveholders to keep black people "happy go lucky" on earth with their "eyes fixed on pie in the sky and heaven in the hereafter" (Haley 1965, 200–201). By emphasizing Christianity's turn-the-other-cheek ethic, slaveholders kept their slaves passive and content on earth (Malcolm X 1957a). For Malcolm, King's movement, with its nonviolent strategy and emphasis on love for the enemy, was merely an example of the "slave-holder's religion" in practice.

Malcolm's most penetrating critique of Christianity focused on the color of Jesus' skin. He realized the irony of black people worshiping a Christ who looked just like the white people who oppressed and terrorized them. He observed that while religions of other people made them proud of who they were, Christianity "was designed to make [black people] feel inferior." It achieved this purpose by giving black people a "blond, blue-eyed, pale-skinned 'god' ... to worship and admire" (1957b). Malcolm regarded the loyalty of black people to a white Christ as a betrayal of their own black heritage and culture and as a severe impediment to their freedom.

Theological Development of the Black Christ

A more comprehensive understanding of the Black Christ would develop with the 1970s emergence of the black theological movement. With a few exceptions, white theologians followed the pattern that southern white clergy maintained: they remained silent on issues of racial injustice. Their silence suggested that Christ was unconcerned with black oppression. They saw no connection between blackness and the gospel of Jesus. A group of black theologians saw something different. They believed that the Christian gospel and blackness were inextricably related. James Cone, James Deotis Roberts, and Albert Cleage, each in his own way, pronounced that Christ was black. They provided three different models for understanding the meaning of Christ's blackness.

James Cone

James Cone taught at Adrian College, a traditionally white college about seventy miles outside of Detroit. After the 1967 Detroit riot, in which forty-three people were killed in the struggle for black freedom, he felt he could no longer remain silent about God's relationship to black people. He was outraged, not only at the silence of white theologians concerning racial injustice, but also at those white theologians and ministers who condemned black violence while saying nothing about the daily systemic violence perpetrated against black people. In response, he sought to interpret the significance of Christ for the struggle of black people.

Cone developed a view of Christ as symbolically black, a perspective reflecting the black faith tradition of slavery. In Cone's version, blackness does not refer to Jesus' ethnic characteristics. It is a symbol for Christ's existential commitments to the oppressed in general and to the black oppressed in particular.

In developing his argument, Cone borrowed from Paul Tillich's definition of ontological symbols. Such a symbol points beyond itself to the divine, which finite human beings cannot adequately express or capture in words. With Cone's version of the Black Christ, black is literal in relationship to the human reality of black-skinned people in America, but symbolic in relationship to the divine. He explained: "Through my particular experience of blackness, I encounter the symbolic significance of black existence and how that existence is related to God's revelation in Jesus Christ" (Cone and Hordern 1971, 1084).

Cone defined blackness in relation to the oppression experienced by black people in America, arguing that discrimination against black people was primarily connected to the color of their skin ([1970] 1986, 213). Christ was symbolically black because he identified with the oppressed during his own time. Cone argued that Jesus' commitment to the oppressed characterized what it meant for him to be the Christ. For Cone, then, Christ's blackness is predicated on Jesus' identification with the oppressed in his own time and on the fact that in a white racist society black people are the oppressed ones. Cone makes clear that "Christ is black ... not because of some cultural or psychological need of black people, but because and only because God *really* enters into the world where the poor, the despised and the oppressed are" (1975, 136).

Like slave Christianity, Cone saw the exodus of the Israelites from Egypt as the revelation of a God "whose will is identical with the liberation of the oppressed from social and political bondage" (1975, 64). He goes on to argue that Jesus came to fulfill God's covenant with the Israelites. Cone makes a distinction between the Jesus of history and the Christ of faith. Jesus was a Jew who came to help free the Jews and to make them into a nation. But the Christ who was crucified and resurrected revealed that liberation was not restricted to first-century Jews. The Christ of faith existed beyond the first century and was present in the black struggle for freedom.

In that context, Christ had to be black, because he identified with the oppressed, and the oppressed were black. As he put it, "If Jesus Christ is in fact the Liberator whose resurrection is the guarantee that he is present with us today, then he must be black, taking upon his person and work the blackness of our existence and revealing to us what is necessary in our destruction of whiteness" (1970, 1087).

Cone found the Black Christ best represented by the Black Power movement that Malcolm X spawned. In his perspective, "Black Power, even in its most radical expression, is not the antithesis of Christianity, nor is it a heretical idea to be tolerated with painful forbearance. It is rather, Christ's central message to twentieth century America" (1969, 1). Cone argued that the Black Christ, whose primary concern was for the freedom of black people, did not prescribe a particular strategy to effect this freedom, whether violence or nonviolence. In practice, this perspective translated into the philosophy of Black Power that freedom should be achieved, in the words of Malcolm X, "by any means necessary."

James Deotis Roberts

James Deotis Roberts taught at Howard University, a historically black university in Washington DC, at the time of the Black Power and black consciousness movements. He came to black theology from an interest in the study of world religions, which made him acutely aware of the diversity of religions as well as the diversity within Christianity. As a black theologian, he could not teach in a black university without addressing the concerns about Christianity and the white Christ that were raised by the young advocates of Black Power and black consciousness. He presented another model of Christ's blackness that stressed its symbolic meaning. Unlike Cone, however, Roberts stressed Christ's universal identity with all humanity as opposed to his particular identity with the oppressed.

Roberts argued that in becoming incarnate, becoming Christ, God identified with all humans. But for Roberts, this identification was particular as well as universal. He goes on to explain that because Christ identified with all people, Christ identified with each person in his or her own particularity.

This understanding of the universal Christ, who identified with humans in their particularities, provided the foundation for Roberts' recognition of Christ's blackness. Roberts argued that if the universal Christ came to all people in their particular historical context, then all people had a right to define Christ through their particular experience and thus to image Christ in their own likeness. Black people, therefore, had as much right to see Christ in their own likeness as did white, red, yellow, and brown people. Roberts recognized the importance for black people of being able to image Christ as black. He said, "If [the Black man] can accept his Blackness, be proud of it and find meaning for his life, he can know true inner freedom. This is where Jesus, as the Black Messiah, comes in. The Black Messiah enables the Black man to stand up to life" (1971a, 16).

Roberts saw a particular and a universal aspect not only in Jesus' incarnation, but also in his ministry, aspects that he associated with the Jesus of history and the Christ of faith, respectively. The Jesus of history revealed God's concern for the liberation of the oppressed, while the Christ of faith revealed God's concern for the reconciliation of all people to each other. Roberts proclaimed that Jesus meant freedom but Christ meant reconciliation.

This Christ who suffered unmerited oppression on the cross so that humanity might experience reconciliation called oppressed peoples to become agents of reconciliation as well. God chose the Israelites not just to reveal that he liberated the oppressed, but also to reveal that those who suffered unjustly were called to carry forth a mission of reconciliation (Roberts 1971b, 29, 59). Similarly, God called black Christians, who had endured unmerited suffering through the years, to carry on a ministry of reconciliation between races and nations (Roberts 1974, 152).

Roberts saw the best embodiment of Christ's reconciling ministry in Martin Luther King Jr., who was concerned not just with liberation, but also with reconciliation between blacks and whites (Roberts 1974, 182). Like King, Roberts excluded violence as a means to liberation. Violence might lead to the liberation of black people, but it would not lead to reconciliation with whites (Roberts 1971b, 191–192).

Albert Cleage

Albert Cleage had ties to black nationalists, such as his close friend and associate Malcolm X. Yet he was not willing to give up his Christian heritage. He pastored a black church in the heart of Detroit's black ghetto during the height of Detroit's racial rebellions. In line with black nationalist thought, however, he saw the black church as a barrier to black freedom because of its slaveholding religion and worship of a white Jesus. He sought to free black people from this enslavement by presenting Jesus as a Black Messiah. He put forth a model of Christ's blackness based on his claim that Jesus of Nazareth was ethnically black. He explained,

> When I say Jesus was black, that Jesus was the black Messiah, I'm not saying "Wouldn't it be nice if Jesus was black?" or "Let's pretend that Jesus was black," or "It's necessary psychologically for us to believe that Jesus was black." I'm saying that Jesus WAS black. (Poinsett 1969, 176).

Cleage based this claim on his understanding of Jesus' bloodline, which he traced through Jesus' mother, Mary. According to Cleage, Mary was a member of the Israelite tribe of Judah, which consisted of a "non-white black people in the same sense that Arabs were black people, in the same sense that Egyptians were black people" (Cleage 1969, 42). Cleage supported this view by claiming that the Israelites were a "mixture of Chaldeans, Egyptians, Midianites, Ethiopians, Kushites,

Babylonians and other dark peoples, all of whom were already mixed with black people of Central Africa" (1969, 4). Therefore "Jesus was a Black Messiah born to a Black woman" (1969, 42).

When Cleage called Jesus black, he was referring to more than just the color of Jesus' skin. He was also referring to Jesus' actual ancestry. Hence, Cleage was able to suggest that Christ was of African ancestral heritage and had an actual genealogical relationship to black Americans.

For Cleage, not only Jesus but also God was black. He argued,

> But if God created man in his own image, then we must look at man to see what God looks like. There are black men, there are yellow men, there are red men and there are a few, a mighty few, white men in the world. If God created man in his own image, then God must be some combination of this black, red, yellow and white ... we must think of God as a Black God. ... In America, one drop of black blood makes you black. So by American law, God is black. (1969, 42–43)

Cleage regarded the Black Christ as one stage in a long history of the Black God's attempts to build an independent black nation. God took the first step toward building this nation by delivering the Israelites, a black people, from their Egyptian oppressors into the promised land. But after the Israelites received their freedom, they turned away from the teaching of their Black God. God therefore sent Jesus, the Black Christ, to redeem the black nation. Jesus, a member of the revolutionary group the Zealots, attempted to free the black Israelites from the rule of Rome, a white nation, and to rebuild an independent black nation. After Jesus' death, his disciples at first carried on this task but, like the earlier Israelites, again lapsed into fragmentation. This continued until Jesus' goal for a black nation was resurrected by Malcolm X.

While Cleage did not directly advocate violence, his version of the Black Christ suggested that it might be appropriate, not only for self-defense, but also as a method of protest. Since Cleage's Jesus was a revolutionary, this Black Christ did not condemn, and perhaps even preferred, the use of violence as a means for overthrowing a white racist regime. According to Cleage, Jesus' teaching to "turn the other cheek" was directed to members of the black nation in relation to each other, not in relation to their oppressors.

A critical assessment

The strength of the Black Christ, as it emerged in black theology, is that it embraces black people in their blackness. It affirms not only what it means to be physically black, but also black experience, heritage, and culture. It fosters a sense of self-esteem and pride in black people as they come to understand that who they are is not abhorred, but valued by the divine being. They are able to see themselves in Christ.

The Black Christ of theology, however, also has its limitations. First, it remains identified primarily with the academy – universities and seminaries. Though the

Black Christ was born out of black faith, it ironically has not made significant inroads in black churches. Many black churches continue to display images of a white Christ. Some critics trace this lack of impact to a shortcoming of black theology itself: it fails to address the pastoral concerns of black Christians, the spiritual and personal aspects of Christian faith (Wilmore 1986; West 1988, 273–280).

A second limitation is that the theology of the Black Christ presents a one-dimensional understanding of social oppression. Calling Christ black explicitly indicates Christ's opposition to white racism, but it is not apparent that it is concerned with eradicating other forms of oppression. Skin color is not the only barrier to black liberation, and racism is not the only form of persecution visited upon the black community. Black people live in a society that is also sexist, classist, and heterosexist. There are persons in the black community who suffer and are discriminated against because of their gender, economic status, or sexual preference. And some of this oppression comes not only from white people, but also from other black people. To call Christ black does not address either the problem of black-on-black oppression or the different types of oppression to which black people are subjected. Essentially, the Black Christ was such a thorough response to the 1960s black freedom struggle that it was impotent in dealing with concerns beyond racism. It, like the movement that called it forth, was grounded in a social analysis focused solely on race.

This limitation becomes most apparent when one considers the failure of the Black Christ to address the particular form of oppression experienced by women. Black women were a significant part of the civil rights and Black Power movements out of which the Black Christ emerged. Yet black women were rarely afforded the opportunity to hold leadership roles in national organizations or even to be national spokespersons for those organizations. As black women gave tirelessly to the black freedom struggle, it became clear that a significant segment of the black community was plagued by more than white racism. Black women suffered under the yoke of gender exploitation as well as racial oppression. Yet all three versions of the Black Christ ignored the plight of women. In part, this failure may be due to the fact that black women did not draw attention to their peculiar experience. Many feared that raising the issue of sexism might subvert the black freedom movement. Another part of the explanation was the perspective of the theologians themselves. Cleage, Cone, and Roberts were not unlike other black men during that period. They too had been socialized into a sexist society. Consequently, they remained focused solely on the problem of racist oppression, as this was understood from a black male perspective.

A Womanist Approach to the Black Christ

As black women recognized the contradiction of participating in freedom-fighting organizations that discriminated against them, and as black men continued to display sexist attitudes and behaviors, what can now be called a "womanist" consciousness began to emerge. This term, which originated with Alice Walker (Walker 1983), refers to a form of feminism specific to black women, one that seeks to address the unique oppression connected to being both black and female in the United States.

From womanists who are also Christians has emerged womanist theology. Black women began to be aware of discrimination against them not only in secular organizations and the black community, but also in the black church. Many black churches continue to refuse black women ordination or other roles in leadership, despite the fact that around 75 percent of the membership is female. As black women began to criticize the black church, they also began to criticize black theology. Jacquelyn Grant initiated this criticism in 1979, charging that by ignoring the experiences of black women, black theologians rendered black women invisible in their theologies (Cone and Wilmore 1993, 1:418–443). Furthermore the feminist movement that developed out of the 1960s black freedom struggle failed to rectify this problem. As a struggle of primarily white women against patriarchalism, it failed to recognize the difference that race makes in relation to patriarchalism. Unfortunately, the theological manifestation of the women's movement, feminist theology, also disclosed a neglect of black women. While black theology expressed the perspective of black men, feminist theology expressed the perspective of white women. It remained for womanist theology to address the concerns of black women. The rest of this chapter illustrates one particular womanist theology, with a special focus on the Black Christ (Douglas 1994, 97–117).

Laying a womanist foundation

A womanist theology has as its goal the welfare of the black community as a whole, not just one segment of it. To this end, it includes an analysis of society and politics. This analysis is multidimensional. That is, it seeks to understand how various dimensions of society – race, gender, class, and sexual oppression – interact in the oppression of black people, especially black women. This analysis is also bifocal. That is, it seeks to understand racism, sexism, classism, and heterosexism not only as they impinge upon the black community from without, but also as they are nurtured within that community. Such an analysis challenges the black community to eliminate anything that prevents black people from being whole, liberated individuals and from working together as a whole, unified community. It also challenges the black community to move toward wholeness not only as individuals and as a community, but also in relation to other oppressed communities, especially people of color around the world.

A womanist theology also includes an analysis of black religion and culture. It affirms those aspects of black religion and culture that sustain and liberate black people, but disavows those aspects that do not. Positive aspects of black religion and culture include the "spirituality of resistance" that has allowed black women to transcend the negative, dehumanizing images that society has maintained of them. This spirituality, which black women have nurtured and passed on to their children, provides a sense of heritage and nurtures a connectedness to God. Not everything that is "black," however benefits the black community. Negative aspects of black religion and culture include those forms of "rap" music that perpetuate abuse of women and other destructive behaviors or images. Also included are the ways in which the black church uses the Bible in the oppression of women, gays, and lesbians.

The Black Christ in womanist theology

A womanist theology affirms that for the black community, Christ is black. That is to say, Christ has black skin and features and is committed to the black community's struggle for life and wholeness. Such an assertion affirms the need for black people to be able to see themselves in the image of Christ. A womanist theology, however, moves beyond the question of Jesus' color.

The womanist Black Christ does more than to endorse black people in their struggle against white racism. The womanist Christ is not just a sustainer and liberator, as in black theology, but also a prophet. That is, Christ not only sustains and liberates the black community, but also criticizes it, challenging it to rid itself of anything that divides it against itself and to renounce any way in which it oppresses others.

A womanist theology does not regard Jesus' maleness as central in determining what it meant for him to be the Christ. For example, womanist theologian Jacquelyn Grant says that the important factors were his humanity and his liberating actions on behalf of the oppressed (1986; 1989). Grant affirms that, today, "Christ, found in the experience of black women, is a black woman" (1986, 210). However, for a womanist theology that seeks the wholeness of the black community, it seems preferable not to restrict the image of Christ to that of a woman. The image of the Black Christ can be found in the faces of all those in whom this Christ is present, all those who promote life and wholeness for the black community, whether women or men. The face of the Black Christ can thus be found in the faces of black heroines and heroes of the past, in the faces of black people currently engaged in the struggle for wholeness, and in the faces of the poorest black women.

A womanist perspective on the Black Christ may not include certain traditional ideas about Christ. Most Christians believe that Jesus died on the cross in place of sinful human beings. According to Delores Williams, this conception of Jesus as "the ultimate surrogate figure" is problematic for black women, since inhumane and denigrating patterns of voluntary and coercive surrogacy have been part of their reality (1991). For example, black female slaves were forced to substitute for the slave owner's wife in nurturing white children and to substitute for white women in satisfying the male slave owner's sexual desire. An understanding of Christ as a substitute therefore cannot be liberating or life-affirming for black women who need to be set free from oppressive forms of surrogacy. Williams further concludes that such an understanding wrongly emphasizes Jesus' death instead of his life and ministry. Humanity's redemption is to be found in life, not death.

Likewise the Nicene and Chalcedonian creeds have no normative significance for the Black Christ of womanist theology. The Nicene confession of faith moves directly from the incarnation of Christ to the crucifixion and resurrection. It ignores completely Jesus' sustaining, liberating, and prophetic ministry. In addition, these creeds emphasize the uniqueness of Christ's metaphysical nature, making what it means to be Christ inaccessible to ordinary Christians. There becomes little reason to strive to be an example of Christ in the world, because to be Christ requires a divine incarnation, which happened only in Jesus. In contrast, in a womanist understanding of the Black Christ, Jesus was Christ because of what he did for others, particularly the poor and oppressed. Such an understanding encourages others to be an example of Christ in their own lives. The Black Christ can thus be seen in the faces of black women and men as they strive to promote life and wholeness.

Conclusion

Like Malcolm X, a womanist theology affirms that Christ is black. But in affirming Malcolm's claims, and similar claims before and after him, it does so with a womanist eye on what is required if the Black Christ is to compel the black church to advance wholeness for black women and men.

In Alice Walker's Pulitzer-Prize-winning novel, *The Color Purple*, one of her female characters, Shug Avery, reminds the main protagonist, Celie, that God is present inside her. Shug simply says, "Here's the thing. ... The thing I believe. God is inside you and inside everybody else" (Walker 1982, 177). For a womanist Black Christ, "here's the thing." Christ is inside of black women and men as they fight for life and wholeness.

References

Burkett, Randall K. (1978). *Garveyism as a Religious Movement*. Metuchen, NJ: Scarecrow.

Clarke, John Hendrik (1972). "The Boy Who Painted Christ Black." In Gloria M. Simmons and Helene D. Hutchinson (eds.), *Black Culture: Reading and Writing Black* (pp. 163–167). New York: Holt Rinehart & Winston.

Cleage, Albert (1969). *The Black Messiah*. Kansas City: Sheed & Ward.

Cone, James H. (1969). *Black Theology and Black Power*. New York: Seabury.

Cone, James H. ([1970] 1986). *A Black Theology of Liberation*. Maryknoll, NY: Orbis.

Cone, James H. (1970). "Black Theology and Black Liberation." *The Christian Century* 87 (September 16): 1084–1088.

Cone, James H. ([1972] 1991). *The Spirituals and the Blues*. Maryknoll, NY: Orbis.

Cone, James H. (1975). *God of the Oppressed*. New York: Seabury.

Cone, James H., and Gayraud S. Wilmore, eds. (1993). *Black Theology: A Documentary History*. 2 vols. Maryknoll, NY: Orbis.

Cone, James H., and William Hordern (1971). "Dialogue on Black Theology." *The Christian Century* 88 (September 15): 1079–1085.

Cullen, Countee (1925). "Heritage." In Countee Cullen, *Color* (pp. 36–41). New York: Harper.

Douglas, Kelly Brown (1994). *The Black Christ*. Maryknoll, NY: Orbis.

Grant, Jacquelyn (1986). "Womanist Theology: Black Women's Experience as a Source for Doing Theology, with Special Reference to Christology." *Journal of the Interdenominational Theological Center* 13 (2, Spring): 195–212.

Grant, Jacquelyn (1989). *White Women's Christ and Black Women's Jesus: Feminist Christology and Womanist Response*. Atlanta, GA: Scholars.

Haley, Alex (1963). "The Playboy Interview: Malcolm X Speaks with Alex Haley." *Playboy* (May).

Haley, Alex (1965). *The Autobiography of Malcolm X*. New York: Ballantine Books.

Harding, Vincent (1979). "Black Power and the American Christ." In Gayraud S. Wilmore and James H. Cone (eds.), *Black Theology: A Documentary History, 1966–1979* (pp. 35–42). Maryknoll, NY: Orbis.

How, Samuel D. (1856). *Slaveholding Not Sinful: Slavery the Punishment of Man's Sin, Its Remedy, The Gospel of Christ*. New Brunswick, NJ: Terhunes. Reprinted Freeport, NY: Books for Libraries, 1971.

Hughes, Langston (1969). *Panther and the Lash: Poems of Our Times*. New York: Knopf.

King, Martin Luther, Jr. (1955). "Address to the Initial Mass Meeting of the Montgomery Improvement Association" (Holt Street Baptist Church, December 5). King Center Archives.

King, Martin Luther, Jr. (1958). *Stride Toward Freedom: The Montgomery Story*. New York: Harper & Row.

King, Martin Luther, Jr. (1963). *Strength to Love*. Philadelphia: Fortress.

Poinsett, Alex (1969). "The Quest for a Black Christ." *Ebony* 24 (March): 170–178.

Raboteau, Albert J. (1978). *Slave Religion: The "Invisible Institution" in the Antebellum South*. New York: Oxford University Press.

Redkey, Edwin, ed. (1971). *Respect Black: The Writings and Speeches of Henry McNeal Turner*. New York: Arno.

Roberts, James Deotis (1971a). "Black Theology and the Theological Revolution." *Journal of Religious Thought* 28 (1): 5–20.

Roberts, James Deotis (1971b). *Liberation and Reconciliation: A Black Theology*. Philadelphia: Westminster.

Roberts, James Deotis (1974). *Black Political Theology*. Philadelphia: Westminster.

Walker, Alice (1982). *The Color Purple*. New York: Washington Square Press, Pocket Books.

Walker, Alice (1983). *In Search of Our Mothers' Gardens*. New York: Harcourt Brace Jovanovich.

Washington, James M., ed. (1986). *A Testament of Hope: The Essential Writings of Martin Luther King, Jr.* New York: Harper & Row.

West, Cornel (1988). *Prophetic Fragments*. Grand Rapids: Eerdmans; Trenton, NJ: Africa World Press.

Williams, Delores S. (1991). "Black Women's Surrogacy Experience and the Christian Notion of Redemption." In Paula M. Cooey, William R. Eakin, and Jay B. McDaniel (eds.), *After Patriarchy: Feminist Transformations of the World Religions* (pp. 1–14). Maryknoll, NY: Orbis.

Wilmore, Gayraud S. (1986). "Pastoral Ministry in the Origin and Development of Black Theology." *The Journal of the Interdenominational Theological Center* 13 (Spring).

X, Malcolm (1957a). "God's Angry Men." *New York Amsterdam News* (April 27): 18.

X, Malcolm (1957b). "God's Angry Men." *New York Amsterdam News* (May 18): 5.

Young, Robert Alexander (1829). "The Ethiopian Manifesto." New York. Reprinted in Sterling Stuckey (ed.), *The Ideological Origins of Black Nationalism* (pp. 30–38). Boston: Beacon, 1972.

CHAPTER 26

Feminist Christologies

Lisa Isherwood

As the early proponents of feminist theology strove to understand the exclusion of women and women's experience in church practice and theological reflection, they were increasingly faced with the realization that it may be the very fabric of Christianity that caused the exclusion. Traditional belief held that Christ's incarnation and subsequent death and descent into hell were to enable the divine to experience all and therefore redeem all. If Christ could not experience being female, then the question arose as to whether the female state could be redeemed. This was not a new question, and it had occupied the minds of the church fathers for many generations. Many of them just could not believe that women, the descendents of Eve, had been saved in the same way as men.

It goes without saying that feminist theologians approached the question of Christ's role as a savior for women in a radically different way than the church fathers. Instead of problematizing women through the question, they were exposing the flaws in Christianity (Isherwood 1999). Here was a religion that declared universal salvation yet denied women full participation in all aspects of its life, and did so on the basis of a questionable philosophical and theological past. As Elizabeth Johnson so succinctly puts it,

> [T]he idea that the Word might have become female flesh is not even seriously imaginable, so thoroughly has androcentric Christology done its work of erasing the full dignity of women as christomorphic in the community of disciples. ... [A]s a logical outcome ... women's salvation is implicitly put in jeopardy, at least theoretically. (Johnson 1992, 151)

Rosemary Radford Ruether was concerned to examine where the denial of the female first infiltrated a religion that declared a new social order. She found that the denial of the feminine originated in the Hellenistic Neo-Platonism and apocalyptic Judaism out of which Christianity was born. Here we find the combination of a

The Blackwell Companion to Jesus, First Edition. Edited by Delbert Burkett. ©2014 John Wiley & Sons, Ltd. Published 2014 by John Wiley & Sons, Ltd.

male warrior God with the exaltation of the intellect over the body. The alienation of the masculine from the feminine is the basic sexual symbol that sums up all the other dualisms, which are mind and body, subjective self and objective world, individual and community, autonomous will (male) and bodily sensuality (female), and the domination of nature by spirit. The Hellenistic influence has shaped concepts such as Logos and Christ in devastatingly androcentric ways (Radford Ruether 1998, 82). While Christianity has never claimed that God was literally male, its Hellenistic underpinning has led to many assumptions about the nature of God and normative humanity. There has been in it an unspoken, yet enacted, androcentric bias, which has reduced the place of women and men in the world, holding them as it does to very outmoded and reductive notions of humanness.

Women, under this scheme, are not the full creation that God intended. It follows as a matter of logic from these ideas, that the Savior had to be male and that this has certain implications for women. At each turn in the Christian narrative, women are systematically excluded or defined as inferior. Indeed, much of the Christian story depends on the "truth" of women's inferiority, since the logic of many of the doctrines, such as atonement and redemption, spring from an understanding of Eve and so-called Original Sin. Without the weakness and deceit of the original woman, there would be no need for a redeeming savior. God's secondary act of creation, Eve, brought about the need for a whole new creation, which was initiated through the perfect son of God, the God/man. How then can woman be redeemed? The question is a real one, and the answers over the centuries have been varied and have carried a variety of consequences for women, from the grotesque to the merely ludicrous. Simply by refusing to believe the rhetoric of the innate inferiority of women, feminist theologians brought into question the entire androcentric/patriarchal logic that had to date underpinned christological debates.

However, that was in many ways a western debate, since in certain cultures it was seen as a positive advantage that Jesus, a man, could concern himself with women at all. For example, some Filipino women do not find the maleness of Jesus to be a problem in their christology. Indeed, born, as he was, a male, he was in the best position to challenge the male definition of humanity and male privilege. He could offer a more effective challenge to men to change their ways.

Monica Melancton also gives a hint as to how some Indian theologians deal with the problems of the maleness and male identification of Jesus. This, she says, is part of the historical Jesus, but it does not mean that it is an essential ingredient of the risen Christ who is dwelling in the redeemed order (1990, 18). This risen Christ transcends all particularities. Therefore the maleness of Jesus can no longer dictate how all women for all time may be female; he becomes the symbol of a new humanity rather than a model of gender enactments.

Many feminist theologians who have no wish to be shackled by the assumptions of essentialism nevertheless argue that human nature is not androgynous and that many of the differences that we see displayed between the sexes have redemptive significance in themselves. Of course there is always the danger that, in claiming

Jesus as the model of "humanity," we have "maleness" yet again turned into a universal way of being.

Indian women are demanding that the churches should be countercultural, as they believe Jesus was, and support them in their struggle for dignity in a patriarchal society. They also hope that rape and physical abuse both inside and outside the family will decrease. Of course, Christ will not do this through magic but through people realizing that Jesus thought that women were human too and deserved the dignity and celebration attached to all God's creation. It is the Christ who, as a male, acted against "male culture" who gives hope to many women in India. The message of women's dignity is, within that culture, more powerfully heard when spoken by a man. Jesus then is the male advocate par excellence, and his gender is less of a problem than his colonial crown.

Post-Christian Feminist Perspectives

For many feminist theologians, then, the "scandal of particularity" is no scandal at all. There are other feminist theologians, such as Mary Daly, who would not accept this approach. For Daly, Christianity is irredeemably patriarchal, and so for her the notion that women should wish to be redeemed through it and within it is a mystery beyond all comprehension. Not only is it a mystery, it is impossible. Patriarchy rests on the premise, so beautifully expressed by Daly herself, that "If God is male, then male is God" (1986, 71). Why would men wish to give up such privilege? Therefore, in a western mindset that finds it hard to go beyond woman as passive space, to go beyond God the father and the world of the sons that he spawns requires more than the addition of women to the equation. Daly proposes the castration of Christianity through the removal of the products of supermale arrogance: namely, the myths of sin and salvation. Both hold women captive, and both lend themselves to scapegoating not only Jesus, but also those who fail to model themselves on this illustrious hero.

Daly uses some of the language and ideas inherent in the Christian story but characteristically develops the meaning in a gynocentric way. She looks forward to the Second Coming, which will be not the return of the Christ, but the emergence of female presence. This presence, through female pride and self-affirmation, will "liberate the memory of Jesus" (1986, 71) into a place of contagious freedom. This freedom will extend to all and not make female experience into a metaphysical absolute. In rejecting a male savior for women, Daly introduces the notion that Jesus may need women to redeem him from the chains of male arrogance.

The image of a son sacrificed to his father in order that good may come of it is a common theme in masculinist mythology. Not unsurprisingly, women have struggled in this heady world of male bonding and have found themselves alienated by the story or victimized by it. Women have found not that sacrifice and suffering are salvific, but that they crush the very humanity they strive to rejoice in.

Black feminist (womanist) theologians were among the first to engage critically with the notion of glorious sacrifice. Coming as they do from a situation where slavery is a recent memory, they were suspicious of doctrine that appeared to justify suffering and death. Delores Williams (1993) is adamant that the cross legitimizes the surrogacy experience of black women: it makes it legitimate for some to bear the burdens of others, when in fact it is inhumane. She says, "The cross is a reminder of how humans have tried throughout history to destroy visions of right relationships that involve transformation of tradition and transformation of social relations and arrangements sanctioned by the status quo" (1991, 12).

Daphne Hampson is concerned about the male Christ for reasons beyond that of biological determinism. For her the central question is one of maturity. She puts it clearly: "[T]o be a Christian is to be placed in a heteronomous position. Feminists believe in autonomy" (1996, 23). To be ruled by another is, in her opinion, to be in the role of a child. Women, she believes, have been in such a position, under the rule of clerics and husbands, because of the way in which Jesus is imaged as Savior. It is a disempowering image and one that leads to lack of personhood in relationships. Feminism, Hampson declares, stands for the full adult equality of women.

Like Daly, Hampson believes that Christianity will never be able to provide such equality, because it is based on a sexist and patriarchal past. Hampson understands Christianity to be a historical religion, in the sense that events from the past influence present-day matters. This constant reference to the past makes Christianity a non-viable religion in the present: it is not moral enough for the modern day, a time when the equal rights of women are acknowledged and the full humanity of all people is championed. As long as issues to do with women are always considered in the light of a man who lived 2,000 years ago, the way ahead for women is gloomy. Hampson accepts that Christianity has changed over the centuries, but remains sure that the revelation-point in history will always be of significance and therefore always highly problematic for women. By giving our autonomy away in favor of this moment of revelation, we are flying in the face of a feminist way of life. In giving such power to a revelation, we are also giving power to those who claim to understand it most fully, the churches. In ways that are quite contrary to feminist thinking, women are placing themselves in unequal power relationships with churches and clerics. Hampson finds this almost unbelievable, since feminist ways of relating are quite different.

For Hampson, then, Christianity's attachment to the historical moment of revelation as universally salvific means that women cannot be saved by the male Christ that is portrayed. We do not find our own salvation through giving away our autonomy to the historical person of Jesus or to the churches. Hampson's position highlights how male hierarchical thinking, for example the view of Jesus as Lord, excludes women from declaring Christ a savior just as much as the male gender of Jesus. When feminists consider whether or not a male savior can save women, the question goes beyond the maleness of the man and embraces the male who has been created by generations of fathers and sons in an attempt to gain a firmer hold on power in the world.

Feminists' initial questioning about the maleness of Jesus opened up issues of power. Since some feminists, such as Daly and Hampson, felt these issues could not be resolved by Christian theology itself, they opted for other routes. The views of both Daly and Hampson are called post-Christian, though each is rather different from the other. However, many other feminists believed that only a continued engagement with this dysfunctional tradition could make a difference in the world, and it is this engagement that has given rise to a rainbow of christologies by women of different races, cultures, genders, sexual orientations, faith positions, and economic situations.

Feminist Liberation Christologies

Inevitably the initial christologies were those based squarely in a liberation theology context, with scholars such as Ruether asking that we take seriously the liberation strand in our traditions. For her, as for most feminist theologians, christology is ethical: that is, it calls for the end of injustice through an understanding of how that injustice is created and lived (Radford Ruether 1988, 18). This emphasis inevitably gives feminist christology a partial feel, since it is clear that we continue to live in a world riddled with injustices. And so Christ becomes a paradigm for hoping and aspiring to a liberated form of humanity. Rita Brock is concerned about this approach, seeing it as yet again making Jesus the hero, and by extension the rest of humanity passive and disabled. Like Hampson she is also concerned about a focus on one historical moment and person, but for her it is because the event is made too narrow. Brock wishes christology to be a much broader tent, one that encompasses communities, which she calls "Christa" communities (1988, 36).

The Christ who burst out among feminists in Latin America was not simply the classical liberation Christ of the poor. Women have brought new dimensions – such as color, race, and ecology – to understandings of liberation. Elsa Tamez (1989) from Costa Rica focused on the need for Christianity to understand indigenous spirituality rather than to adopt a superior position, as it has done since its imposition in Latin America. She is working toward a theology of liberation that takes liberating aspects from both traditions, while condemning those parts of both traditions that have been perverted and lead to moral enslavement. Tamez then is looking for the Christ who can critique and be critiqued by the traditions that came before his conquering soldiers. This is quite a radical move, and one that feminists worldwide should pay heed to. There is still an unforgivable tendency by some to see Jesus as the one who put all the previous wrongs right and saved women from stifling cultures.

The Mexican theologian Maria Pilar Aquino is clear that, for feminists to succeed in their struggle, they must thoroughly understand the way in which gender oppression operates. Such understanding requires a critical analysis of race, class, and culture, as well as economics. Aquino (1995) images Jesus as the one who wished liberation for all, and, for her, the followers of Jesus have to expose, and quickly, the fact that the current economic system is not the democratizing force that it claims to be. The truth is that it enslaves and dehumanizes a large percentage of the world's population. Aquino wants the "dehumanized" to find a common voice and expose the grand lie.

When womanists drew on the liberating strand in christology, an interesting issue arose. While the Christ of liberation was a powerful figure for many of their foremothers who suffered slavery, contemporary African American women were realizing that this was not the whole picture. For Kelly Brown Douglas (1994) and Jacquelyn Grant (1989), the whiteness of Christ just enforced their own sense of "otherness," and the notion that a black woman should kneel before this figure simply emphasized the subordinate position of black women. Furthermore, these womanists highlighted the many layers of oppression that black women experienced within a christological system: oppression based not only on race, but also on gender, economic status, and sexual preference. A more nuanced christology began to emerge from the complex reality of black lives in America.

Feminist Biblical Christologies

Over the years, feminist christology has not always looked to the scriptures for its starting point, and so it is interesting to consider a type of feminist christology that at one and the same time looks to scripture and to the lives of women.

Elisabeth Schüssler Fiorenza (1994) approaches feminist christology in a slightly different way than many of her feminist sisters. She sets out to explore the theoretical frameworks of various discourses about Jesus rather than to write a revolutionary biography or a post-patriarchal christology. Feminist movements seek to intervene in the struggle over the control and commodification of knowledge, and they try to keep the knowledge of radical equality alive in the eyes of the disenfranchised. This is a hard struggle in the reality of global systems and requires global analysis, and Schüssler Fiorenza believes that theology has to play its part, or religion in general and christology in particular will be a dangerous weapon in the hands of those who wish to reinstate conservative and oppressive regimes. In such a context, women must not give up the power of naming by respecting conservative claims to owner-ship of the texts. Feminist theologians should seek to destabilize the center by speak-ing both the language of our intellectual theological fathers and the dialects of our feminist sisters. Feminist christology is a political practice, aiming not only at per-sonal change, but also at structural change. As so many women collude with the structures, feminist theology has to tackle the self-hatred that so many women have, and confront cultural disrespect for women. Redemption, then, within feminist christology is about liberation. Therefore it involves struggle against oppression as well as struggle for personal integrity and human freedom; it is about wholeness and transformation. It involves not just personal journeys, but also societal journeys, which redeem impoverished visions and heal a damaged planet. We all have to recover a sense of self-worth; "being redeemed in Christ" is not enough.

Schüssler Fiorenza's own approach is to search for divine Wisdom or Sophia, a feminine personification from the Jewish tradition. This is a difficult task, since traces of her are buried in masculinist christological traditions. The Christian scriptures, particularly the Johannine literature, highlight a stage when Jesus is given the attributes of Sophia. Some of the earliest traditions of the Jesus movement understood Jesus as the prophet of Sophia who was to make the realm of God available to the poor and marginalized. As a child of Sophia, he also made the message experientially available to all through ministry and miracles. One of the earliest Jesus sayings states that "Sophia is justified by her children" (Luke 7:35), which signifies that Sophia is with all her children and is made just in and by them. The statements that have been hijacked to proclaim Jesus' atoning death can be seen in a different light, as confirming that Jesus was the prophet of Sophia. For example, "Therefore also the Wisdom [Sophia] of God said 'I will send them prophets and apostles, some of whom they will kill and persecute'" (Luke 13:34).

Such passages suggest that the earliest reflections on the nature of Jesus were sophialogy, not christology. Schüssler Fiorenza wants to argue that Jesus does not close the Sophia tradition by being the last and greatest prophet – to do so would be a contradiction of the tradition. Rather he opens it yet further. He stands in a long line of Sophia prophets, both men and women, who have been killed for the message they bring. Their deaths were not willed by Sophia; indeed they are lamented (Luke 13:34).

Elisabeth Johnson (1992) also develops her christology in terms of Jesus-Sophia. She is convinced that the early church used many of the traditions about personified Wisdom in order to come to an understanding of who Jesus was. For Johnson, the identification of Jesus with personified Wisdom does a number of things. It illustrates the importance of everyday living in the unfolding of the kingdom, and it offers female metaphors for part of the divine process (Johnson 1993, 122). It also makes inclusion the central element of salvation. Jesus, as the child of Sophia, gives hope for the establishment of right relations across all boundaries. For Johnson, the stories of resurrection illustrate how Sophia rises again and again in unimaginable ways; the gift of life cannot be overcome even by extreme torture and death. Further, personified Wisdom is at work all over the world and in many different traditions, and so Christianity can no longer claim special revelation. Sophia is also inherent in the world and so demands a far greater ecological awareness and striving for balance and right order in the natural world.

Johnson argues that once the emphasis is removed from the once-and-for-all Christ, then the story of Christ Sophia is no longer a single event in Jesus, but an ongoing process involving all other children of Sophia as well. The story of Christ Sophia thus has to include the story of others besides Jesus who were also engaged in this process. Many of these were women. In this way then, the stories of women become part of the salvific narrative, and the women become not mere bystanders, but participants with Sophia. Not only were the women active in the life of Jesus, but they continued the life of Sophia beyond his death. Mary Magdalene witnessed the resurrection, and women were hubs of the early groups; they continued to be the embodiment of Sophia when the male disciples questioned the vision by running away and doubting. Women then remained the source of Sophia; they remained her faithful actors.

Johnson is mystified as to how the church has so successfully trivialized the doctrine of the incarnation. They have, she argues, reduced it to petty disputes about gender and human superiority, all of which fall into insignificance next to a real understanding of the power of incarnation. The inner dynamic of incarnation speaks of embodiment and the profound relatedness of all humans (and non-humans) in a passionate striving for liberation (Johnson 1993, 168). This liberation depends on both the universality of love and the particularity of love. The friendship of God, which pervades the cosmos, nevertheless needs to be made manifest in acts of inclusion and justice-making. Johnson is clear that while Sophia strives for the flourishing of the world and those who live in it, she is also radically distinct from the world. She remains always in herself, yet her essence is relatedness.

Mary Grey engages with Sophia in the hope of finding revelation for today. She sets out a dialogue between two myths, those of Logos and Sophia. The former is shown to create a hi-tech and disembodied rule-driven world of universal "executives" while the latter is "a dark haired woman telling stories by ... glowing embers" (1993, 7). Her tales are of freedom and courage, and she responds to loneliness and despair with tales of hope. Grey presents us with a compelling picture that speaks from deep mythological roots yet addresses the issues of today. She appeals for Sophia to be central to decision-making processes within and outside the churches, since the Logos Christ simply reinvents the mistakes of the past by re-entrenching hard, cold logic over the lived experiences of women and men. Sophia, on the other hand, is shouting "epiphanies of connection" in a broken world.

All three women believe that the time is long overdue for an embrace of Sophia and the interconnections that She embodies, for an embrace of the wisdom that is in stark contrast to the cold logic of a patriarchal, hierarchical world based on separation.

Feminist Christologies of Embodiment

The concept of connection and relatedness has been central to much feminist christology right from the start and has been applied to it in radical ways. It has meant a move from the dualistic and highly metaphysical view of the purpose of Christ to one of embodiment as the purpose and significance of the Christic event. This understanding is seen clearly in the work of Elisabeth Moltmann-Wendel, Rita Nakashima Brock, and Carter Heyward.

Among those who envisage an embodied Christ is Elisabeth Moltmann-Wendel. For her, the stories about Jesus and women are less androcentrically edited than the rest of the gospels, and she feels that here, through touch and interconnection, we see something of the true dynamics of Jesus and the emerging Christ (Moltmann-Wendel 1986). In the gospel stories, Christic power is something that emerges in a relationship between Jesus and others. He touches people's bodies, engages with them, anoints them, gives them food, and nurtures them. However, by the time of the second generation of Christians, Jesus loses his earthly sensual touching character and "the Christ" becomes a set of cerebral beliefs.

Carter Heyward and Rita Brock are two feminist theologians associated with the notion of Christ as erotic power. Brock believes that when speaking of Jesus as powerful, we have to be quite clear about what type of power we are speaking of, and for her it is erotic power. This understanding leaves us in no doubt about where the source of this power lies. It is not an abstract concept but is deeply embedded in our very being and is part of our nature, residing there as our innate desire to relate with each other, not just for the benefit of the individual self, but for the justice and growth of the whole cosmos. This kind of power is wild and cannot be controlled, and living at this level saves us from sterility that comes from living by the head alone. Christianity has always encouraged *agape*, a type of love that Brock sees as heady and objective and therefore not as something that will change the world. *Eros* on the other hand will engage us and so can change the world. Brock is convinced that erotic power redeems both the world and Christ.

Therefore, our christology needs to begin in our deepest form of connectedness and our ability to create and sustain relationships; we have to allow ourselves to feel. We have been encouraged to look the wrong way. Brock (1988) refers to this misdirection as the broken heart of patriarchy, as we have been encouraged to rip ourselves away from what is dear to us: feeling, the earth, others, ourselves. She believes that "heart" is the original grace and that, in exploring the depth of our hearts, we find incarnate in ourselves the divine reality of connection. The divinity that we find lies in the heart's fragility. We are vulnerable creatures, and it is this openness to the world that makes us both vulnerable and redeemers of the world. We are, as Jesus was, broken-hearted healers.

The major christological implication in this thinking is to reject Jesus as a static figure, a victim who had to be delivered to some outside force and placed in an abstract realm where he dwells in non-present reality as the redeemer. Women have not found the victim role to be redeeming and so question how Jesus could have found it so for himself, let alone for anyone else. Brock is suggesting that in giving back power to Jesus and refusing to see him as the victim, we are also seeing the Christ as an image of shared power, which increases in the sharing rather than disappearing as a once-and-for-all event in the person of Jesus. She illustrates the implications of this shared power through reflecting on the exorcisms, performed by Jesus not because he has the power to forgive but because he has experienced those same demons and so has been empowered by his own experience to release others. They show a wounded healer who understands vulnerability and inner oppression. Brock claims the same is true of us: once we name our own demons, we have the power to help others claim their erotic power. In this way, erotic power is not only political but also relational (1988, 82).

Heyward's starting point for seeking to understand God is taking human experience seriously. She says, "We are left alone, untouched, until we choose to take ourselves – our humanity – more seriously than we have taken our God" (1982, xix). Her emphasis is on experiencing God as a living reality, not as a plausible abstract concept. The way in which we do this is to connect with God's creative power, which is the power to love and to be loved. Heyward declares it was this incarnate, loving, dynamic, relating God that Jesus made visible and that the church lost. She thinks that in the development of Greek christology, the ultimacy of the voluntary character of the divine–human covenant was lost (1982, 3). To preserve the unity of divinity and humanity in Jesus, Chalcedon compromised the possibility of a voluntary union between a human Jesus and the divine God and opted for a hypostatic or essential union of the two natures. The acceptance of such a doctrine changed the emphasis on justice. Instead of being something people worked for, it became something God granted as a gift in the form of natural justice.

Heyward believes it is a crippling mistake to see Jesus as a divine person "rather than as a human being who knew and loved God" (1982, 23). It is crippling because it prevents people from claiming their own divinity. She does not deny the possibility of incarnation; indeed, if God is a God of relation, then incarnation is bound to be not just a possibility, but a desirable necessity. She is not devaluing the reality of incarnation but rather exposes the limits of exclusivity. By re-imaging the incarnation of Jesus, she also re-images human beings by realizing that the amazing power and relation that lies dormant in human nature is also the power of incarnation. Heyward therefore re-images divinity as something we grow toward by choice and activity.

This shift requires her to look critically at the notions of authority and power. She is anxious to move away from the idea that authority is something that is exercised over us by God or state and to come to an understanding of it as self-possessed. Heyward notes that two words for power are used in the gospels. One is *exousia*, which denotes power that has been granted, whereas *dunamis*, which is raw power, innate, spontaneous, and often fearful, is not granted but inborn. And this is the authority that Jesus claims. By acting with *dunamis*, we, just like Jesus, act from both our human and divine elements. Heyward's Christ is one who meets us where we are, between the "yet" and the "not yet" of embodying that erotic birthright, and impresses upon us not so much the nature of the Christ, but the meaning of who we are (1982, 163). Therefore, "God's incarnations are as many and varied as the persons who are driven by the power in relation to touch and be touched by sisters and brothers" (1982, 164). Most of all, Heyward's christology is fully embodied, sensuous, and erotic, seeking vulnerable commitment, alive with expectancy and power.

Feminist theologians are not afraid to deal with the fleshy reality of Jesus and connect it with their own lives. An example from Latin America can be found in the work of Maria Clara Bingemar (1994), who argues that women's bodies are eucharistic. She extends the divinely creative actions of women's bodies beyond that of giving birth to toiling in the fields and factories in order to provide life for others. Most of all, the bodies of women in Latin America are placed in the struggle for liberation. She says, "Woman's body, eucharistically given to the struggle for liberation, is really and physically distributed, eaten and drunk by those who will – as men and women of tomorrow – continue the same struggle" (1994, 317). Bingemar moves the christological debate forward many steps when she equates the bodies of women with the eucharistic body of Christ, not least because these are real bodies that experience the pleasures and pains of being fully incarnate. These women laugh, cry, love, hate, make love, are raped or beaten, are violated by the system, and often abuse others. What is raised here, in a striking way, is the notion that incarnation and perfection do not sit easily together. The Christ of otherworldly, yet enfleshed, perfection is taken to task and found lacking. What good is such a Christ to women whose compromised flesh needs liberation?

Marcella Althaus-Reid (1999) proposes an indecent theology, which she develops from her background in Argentina, where women were defined through the concept of decency. Women on the margins of this tightly regulated society rebelled against decency, either through choice or necessity. That is, the category of decency did not fit their lived experience. They were unable to be defined and contained by imperial inventions, and in their "indecency" found new life-giving ways. Women who worked in factories or took part in revolutionary struggle were defined as indecent and were seen as sexually available. Through the embodiment of these women, Christ is indecent, the one who expands the edges of categories and seeks life. For this reason Althaus-Reid engages with Coya women, those who wear no underwear, carry their children on their backs, and let their sexual smells blend with their surroundings as they work and pray. The bodies of these women are starting points for christology, just as the body of Jesus was. Indeed, as the poorest women, liberation theology is bound to start with them.

Althaus-Reid critiques the way in which male liberation theologians have almost romanticized christological images. We have the Christ who embraces the poor, and Christ the Peruvian peasant on the cross. For Althaus-Reid, this romanticizing is not even half the story, as it does not shift the christological core far enough. If the truly poor are to be embraced, then we should be imaging Christ as a young girl prostituted by two men in a public toilet in Buenos Aires (1999, 41). This is too strong an image for many liberation theologians, but it is the very stuff of indecent theology, as it tells the truth about women's lives. She argues that a new understanding of Christ is needed, one that moves away from the Christ as the fetish of Christianity, and away from the patriarchal discourse that underpins it. By challenging the gendered construction of Christ, we are also challenging the hierarchy of power and releasing Christ into a freer and more empowering relationality. By telling indecent sexual stories, those that are the reality of people's lives, we destabilize normative rules that cripple people. Telling such stories is, then, a Christic act. Althaus-Reid offers a very challenging image of Christ as Xena, warrior princess: a "leather woman" hanging on a cross, declaring love into eternity for the woman she loves. She is courageous and transgressive, just as Jesus of Nazareth was. She is the sort of Christ that women need, one who will free them from preconceptions and be the death of stereotypes.

The enfleshed nature of emerging feminist christology has taken theologians into many areas of embodiment, from disability to size, with interesting and challenging results for traditional christology. Nancy Eiesland (1994) is one of the first theologians to attempt to develop a theology of disability (cf. Stuart 2001). It is thought that there are about 600 million people who are disabled worldwide, and malnutrition is the cause of at least 20 percent of it. A theology of disability therefore calls for relief from the causes of the pain. In addition, there is a pacifist agenda, which wishes to eliminate disability caused by the body-ripping realities of war. It is the disabled Christ who sits at the center of this theology, who acts as the moral imperative to strive for these things. God became flesh, and flesh, as we know, comes in all shapes and sizes and with a wide range of ability and disability. For Eiesland, it is the resurrected Christ who is a theological starting point, since in the resurrected Christ, those who witnessed the resurrection "saw not the suffering servant for whom the last word was tragedy and sin, but the disabled God who embodied both impaired hands and feet and pierced side and the imago Dei" (1994, 99). The disabled Christ highlights the necessity for mutuality and interdependence, the latter being a condition of many disabled people. Our society perpetuates the myth that the truly capable person needs no one and moves beyond interdependence; the disabled model challenges this and draws us back to humanity. Above all else, the disabled Christ is a symbol "of rightly ordered interpersonal and structural relations."

Body size has increasingly taken a role in the production of female identity, worth, and subjectivity over the last century. Slenderness has come to signify beauty, a perception that has created a hierarchy of beauty based on physical difference, in which those at the top of the hierarchy gain the supposed fulfillment of material privilege. On the other side of the equation, we have the fat body, which has increasingly been viewed with suspicion and even disgust, as a deeply morally flawed form of embodiment, chaos-driven and lacking control. Fat phobia also holds in place many social structures, and the fat bodies of women have under certain circumstances come to carry economic and racial overtones (Isherwood 2007). Fat women are loathed and even feared, because they function as the abject in our society. That is fat bodies take up the burden of representing the horrors of the body itself for the culture at large. They are the walking reminder of corporeality, which the West with its Christian roots has always found difficult. So perhaps putting a self in a fat body is the kind of act of heresy that a Fat Jesus would commit, because doing such a thing would require that society think again about the way in which the fat body is "abjected," ejected from the self as unthinkable and intolerable. Christology of the fat female body is a call to society to heal the split between body and mind. It also requires that we look again at food distribution, the sexual commodification of women, sacramentality, and even Tribulation theologies (Isherwood 2007). It is an example of the multilayered realities of women's lives opening up multidimensional challenges to traditional christology.

Ecofeminist Christologies

Feminist christologies have not just stopped at the human when considering the nature of incarnation. Ecofeminism has found expression in many parts of the feminist world and has a very important part in Asian theology. However, Kwok Pui-Lan is one of the few Asian theologians to explicitly tackle the implications of ecology for christology. She is keen to show that she places ecology and christology together not because she is overly focused on Christ, but because she believes that the West has been too anthropocentric (Kwok 1997, 116). Kwok argues that this does not have to be the case, because there is enough biblical evidence to create "an organic model" of Christ. He calls himself the vine and the disciples the branches, while the breaking of bread together is also an organic paradigm (1997, 121). Kwok claims that an organic model of Christ makes plain the interrelatedness of humans and the cosmos. Further, from an Asian point of view, if Jesus is seen as wisdom, much of that wisdom would be to do with the earth.

Ivone Gebara from Brazil has different motivations in searching for christological models in the ecological crisis. She wishes to show the connections between pollution, hunger, and unemployment and the patriarchal image of God (1999, 1). Ecojustice for her is grounded in an affirmation that our bodies are part of the sacred body of the earth and that all is christological. Gebara's general framework poses interesting questions for christology. She declares that the place that Jesus occupies in the Christian community should no longer be understood as an absolute dogmatic reference point, but that he should be seen in a more participatory way, more dialogical and open (1999, 178). We have to discard dogma since it is dogma that took a conversation by a well, a shared meal, and a caress and turned them into disembodied systematic reason (1999, 176). Jesus demonstrates a practical wisdom based on connection, touch, and the here and now. Gebara argues that the ecological crisis demands just such practical wisdom. The earth has been enslaved by economic exploitation, and so it has to become the subject and object of salvation. The principles we see at work in Jesus and his relationship with people need to be extended to the earth, not in order that he becomes its redeemer, but that we may act with it in divine solidarity. Christ is, for Gebara, a symbol and, as such, moves beyond the man from Nazareth and becomes a possession of the community of followers, a path to meaning. The man of Nazareth was constrained by cultural expectations and understandings, but the symbol can move far beyond historical moments and is a dialogue partner in which we include ourselves and by definition our own time and space. Gebara is not arguing in the classical sense about the Jesus of history and the Christ of faith. She is instead finding practical christology for a world in ecological crisis.

She considers that a Christ who provides enough symbolism for life-giving and flourishing of dignity gives the collective authority to speak in different ways about our experiences of Jesus. Christ is a symbol of orthopraxis.

Conclusion

Many of the feminist christologies that are emerging appear to suggest that embodiment and not metaphysics is the foundation of the life of Christ, and this is why many Christians would not even consider engaging with feminist christologies. But what are we left with if we ditch metaphysics? Well strangely enough, Christian theologians are left with what the early message declared: flesh and blood, incarnation. We are asked to consider the divine reality of embodiment. Incarnation calls us to deep connection rooted in bodies not metaphysics. The Jesus narrative enables the flesh to become word and is not "the Word" made flesh (Isherwood 2008). The body emerges as a place of revelation and moral imperatives, as the place through and between which incarnation continues to unfold. There are any number of examples of how this transforms the landscape of our lives. Those who are starving present themselves not as cases for pity, but as moral imperatives for the rest of us, as challenges to redress the imbalances in food distribution. Those who are poisoned by toxic waste challenge the ethics of business and profit, and call into focus the integrity of the planet as well as people. And those who labor under the genocidal reality of advanced capitalism present their bodies as a moral challenge to find alternative economic systems. When the flesh is word, these questions cannot be hidden in delayed *parousias* or reward for the faithful; they press on the incarnate flesh of the Christ between and within us. Taking the flesh as word also demands that absolutes be placed to one side and that listening take the place of unilateral dictation. The flesh made word speaks, not just from the head, but through the whole body, and it is this voice that returns power to people. Our praxis becomes fueled by an enfleshed hermeneutic, and we must become experts in "reading the body." This involves a variety of tools, from psychology to economic theory, since what goes on in people is as important as what happens to them under the weight of advanced capitalism (Isherwood 2007).

Our bodies, so foundationally part of the incarnational drama, tell stories, very complex and challenging stories. It is in the living of these complex realities that we embody co-creation and redemption. It is in the struggling flesh that the utopian vision is embodied and the redeeming action plays out. A post-metaphysical christology appears to be possible. Indeed it may be the reality of incarnational theology, since it gives us little option but to engage with the unfolding of our godding through the telling of our lives in the light of a communal story. The utopian visions that metaphysics allowed for have not been lost in feminist christologies; they have rather been relocated to the incarnate flesh we share and the world we are so innately part of. They will be realized when we have the courage to move beyond, to transcend, the narrow boxes we place ourselves in, so that a fuller and more abundant life may be the reality for all in this world.

Feminist christologies have yet further to go, but they have traveled a great deal of theological distance since the question was asked about how a male savior can save women.

References

Althaus-Reid, Marcella Maria (1999). "On Wearing Skirts without Underwear: Indecent Theology Challenging the Liberation Theology of the Pueblo; Poor Women Contesting Christ." *Feminist Theology* 20: 39–51.

Aquino, Maria Pilar (1995). "Directions and Foundations of Hispanic/Latino Theology: Toward a Mestiza Theology of Liberation." In Arturo J. Bañuelas (ed.), *Mestizo Christianity: Theology from the Latino Perspective* (pp. 192–208). Maryknoll, NY: Orbis.

Bingemar, Maria Clara (1994). "Women in the Future of the Theology of Liberation." In Ursula King (ed.), *Feminist Theology from the Third World: A Reader* (pp. 308–318). London: SPCK.

Brock, Rita Nakashima (1988). *Journeys by Heart: A Christology of Erotic Power.* New York: Crossroad.

Daly, Mary (1986). *Beyond God the Father: Towards a Philosophy of Women's Liberation.* London: The Women's Press.

Douglas, Kelly Brown (1994). *The Black Christ.* Maryknoll, NY: Orbis.

Eiesland, Nancy L. (1994). *The Disabled God: Toward a Liberatory Theology of Disability.* Nashville: Abingdon.

Gebara, Ivone (1999). *Longing For Running Water: Ecofeminism and Liberation.* Minneapolis: Fortress.

Grant, Jacquelyn (1989). *White Women's Christ and Black Women's Jesus.* Atlanta, GA: Scholars.

Grey, Mary (1993). *The Wisdom of Fools? Seeking Revelation for Today.* London: SPCK.

Hampson, Daphne (1996). *Swallowing a Fishbone? Feminist Theologians Debate Christianity.* London: SPCK.

Heyward, Isabel Carter (1982). *The Redemption of God: A Theology of Mutual Relation.* Lanham, MD: University Press of America.

Isherwood, Lisa (1999). *Liberating Christ: Exploring the Christologies of Contemporary Liberation Movements.* Cleveland: Pilgrim.

Isherwood, Lisa (2007). *The Fat Jesus: Feminist Explorations of Boundaries and Transgressions.* London: DLT.

Isherwood, Lisa (2008). "Jesus Past the Posts: An Enquiry into Post-Metaphysical Christology." In Lisa Isherwood and Kathleen McPhillips (eds.), *Post-Christian Feminisms: A Critical Approach* (pp. 201–211). Aldershot: Ashgate.

Johnson, Elizabeth A. (1992). *She Who Is: The Mystery of God in Feminist Theological Discourse.* New York: Crossroad.

Johnson, Elizabeth A. (1993). "Redeeming the Name of Christ." In Catherine Mowry LaCugna (ed.), *Freeing Theology: The Essentials of Theology in Feminist Perspective* (pp. 120–134). New York: Harper.

Kwok Pui-Lan (1997). "Ecology and Christology." *Feminist Theology* 15: 113–125.

Melancton, Monica (1990). "Christology and Women." In Virginia Fabella and Sun Ai Lee Park (eds.), *We Dare to Dream: Doing Theology as Asian Women* (pp. 12–22). Maryknoll, NY: Orbis.

Moltmann-Wendel, Elisabeth (1986). *A Land Flowing with Milk and Honey: Perspectives on Feminist Theology*. London: SCM.

Radford Ruether, Rosemary (1988). *To Change the World: Christology and Cultural Criticism*. New York: Crossroad.

Radford Ruether, Rosemary (1998). *Introducing Redemption in Christian Feminism*. Sheffield: Sheffield Academic Press.

Schüssler Fiorenza, Elisabeth (1994). *Jesus, Miriam's Son, Sophia's Prophet*. New York: Continuum.

Stuart, Elisabeth (2001). "Disruptive Bodies: Disability, Embodiment and Sexuality." In Lisa Isherwood (ed.), *The Good News of the Body: Sexual Theology and Feminism* (pp. 166–184). Sheffield: Sheffield Academic Press.

Tamez, Elsa (1989). *Through Her Eyes: Women's Theology from Latin America*. Maryknoll, NY: Orbis.

Williams, Delores S. (1991). "Black Women's Surrogacy Experience and the Christian Notion of Redemption." In Paula M. Cooey, William R. Eakin, and Jay B. McDaniel (eds.), *After Patriarchy: Feminist Transformations of the World Religions* (pp. 1–14). Maryknoll, NY: Orbis.

Williams, Delores S. (1993). *Sisters in the Wilderness: The Challenge of Womanist God-Talk*. Maryknoll, NY: Orbis.

CHAPTER 27
The "Gay" Jesus

Theodore W. Jennings Jr.

The idea that Jesus may have been in some sense "gay" or might be represented in this way is a source of considerable anxiety, controversy, and, sometimes, rage. When my book, *The Man Jesus Loved* (Jennings 2003), was published, the loudest voices, whether on the internet or on "shock radio" or among the religious right in the United States, gave full vent to the rage that such a suggestion can provoke. Even six years later, the seminary where I teach was subjected to a demonstration organized by some of the most notorious homophobes in the United States. There have been similar reactions to productions of the drama *Corpus Christi* (McNally 1998). Of course, it is not only the presumed depiction of a gay Jesus that can provoke highly charged controversy, as the response to such films as *Jesus Christ Superstar* and *The Last Temptation of Christ* or even *The Da Vinci Code* can attest. Although the eroticism of these depictions is resolutely heterosexual, many seemed appalled at the mere suggestion that Jesus may have felt or reciprocated any sexual desire or attraction at all. Thus the reaction to the suggestion that Jesus might be depicted as in some sense "gay" is but a subset, if an especially charged one, of the dismay that many seem to feel at the suggestion that Jesus might be connected to any sort of sexual feeling or practice.

As we approach this theme, it may be helpful, if not to resolve, then at least to indicate the complexity that is hidden in the term "gay Jesus." On one level, this might mean simply how it is that people who are identified as gay understand or depict Jesus, much as we might ask about an Islamic Jesus or an Indian Jesus. Or we might be asking about whether Jesus may be depicted as "gay" in contemporary renditions of the Jesus story or in ancient or even canonical versions of the same story. Or we might be asking about the Jesus who presumably stands behind any such representation, the "Jesus of history," as it were.

Now if we refer to the Jesus of two millennia ago, or even the representations of Jesus that come down to us from antiquity (in the gospels, for example), then we

The Blackwell Companion to Jesus, First Edition. Edited by Delbert Burkett. ©2014 John Wiley & Sons, Ltd. Published 2014 by John Wiley & Sons, Ltd.

come up against another level of complexity: the extent to which it is or is not misleading to use a term and concept (what it means to be "gay") to apply to ancient persons or texts that simply did not organize sexuality in the ways we do. In order to reduce the levels of confusion that might arise if we did not take these complexities into account, I would suggest that the term "gay" as in "gay Jesus" be confined to contemporary depictions or representations and that for ancient sources (and persons) we might speak of "same-sex love" instead, with the term "homoeroticism" serving as a way of referring to both ancient and modern depictions. Thus it makes more sense to ask whether the Gospel of John depicts Jesus as being involved in a same-sex relationship, while a contemporary novel might depict Jesus as gay. One way this approach may help to clarify things is that for most people today the supposition that one is gay precludes erotic or sexual relations with a person of the opposite sex. In the Greco-Roman world within which the New Testament took shape, a person who had same-sex relationships might well be imagined to have heterosexual relations as well. Today we have invented a separate category for this: bisexuality.

I have referred to the Gospel of John, and this is indeed the springboard for most of the questions about the "gayness" of Jesus, while much of the speculation about the relationship of Jesus to the women associated with his movement (Mary Magdalene or Salome, for example) comes from extra-canonical sources. In addition to the Gospel of John, some have also pointed to what Morton Smith identified as the "Secret Gospel of Mark" as also carrying suggestions about a homoerotic relationship between Jesus and another "youth."

In what follows, I will first indicate some of the earlier intimations that Jesus was viewed as one who had a homoerotic relationship with another man (usually the beloved disciple). I will then summarize the analysis that I provided in *The Man Jesus Loved*, supplementing this with some additional material. This will be followed by a summary of views from scholars associated with the study of religion. A subsequent section will turn to a variety of artistic and literary representations of what might be more properly termed a gay Jesus, before concluding with reflections on the possible theological ramifications of such a notion: does such a depiction of Jesus run afoul of basic Christian doctrine regarding the humanity and divinity of Christ?

Intimations

Perhaps the earliest interpretation of biblical materials as indicating something like a homoerotic relationship between Jesus and the beloved disciple comes in the work of the first great medieval theologian of love and friendship, Aelred of Rievaulx (1977). While his contemporary, Bernard of Clairvaux, gave expression to the relationship between the (male) believer and Jesus as an erotic one – depicting the relationship to Jesus as a sequence of kisses (of feet, hands, and lips), as the ascent of a ladder of love toward greater intimacy with Jesus – it is Aelred who famously suggested that the relationship between Jesus and the beloved disciple be interpreted as a "marriage bed," which indeed may be construed as a pattern even for what we might term the heterosexual relationship between a man and a woman. In spite of the suggestiveness of Aelred's interpretation, it is doubtful that he supposed that the eroticism of this relationship was expressed or mediated by what we might recognize as sexual practices. For Aelred, the expression of intimacy reaches a certain apex in what he speaks of as the sharing of secrets. While Aelred's perspective may be understood, as John Boswell suggests (1980), as an expression of a sort of gay renaissance in early medieval Europe, this flowering was soon to be stamped out as Europe turned relentlessly homophobic in the later Middle Ages.

A perhaps premature sign of awareness of the possibly homoerotic character of Jesus' relationship to the beloved disciple comes in the Elizabethan Renaissance, in the allegation that the playwright Christopher Marlowe had suggested that Jesus and John were "bedmates" (Karlen 1971, 116–117). However, this allegation, together with others, was offered as a defense for those accused of assassinating Marlowe. Scarcely an encouragement to pursue this suggestion any further!

Nonetheless, the great philosopher and legalist Jeremy Bentham seems to have drawn the conclusion that the relationship between Jesus and "John" should be viewed as homoerotic (Crompton 1985, 278–283). Moreover, Bentham seems to have supposed that this relationship should be construed as entailing sexual practice, since his interpretation of the relationship is embedded in an argument for the decriminalizing of "sodomy." Although Bentham's interpretation of New Testament texts was not published until the late twentieth century, his case for the decriminalization of same-sex sexual practices as an essential part of rational legal reform did become influential in Europe and in many parts of Latin America as the influence of the so-called "Napoleonic Code" spread.

In the wake of the psychoanalytic revolution associated with Freud, one of the most innovative of Freud's associates, Franz Groddeck, wrote in his reflections on the "Id" that homosexuality is actually primary and that heterosexuality is learned behavior that distorts and displaces this primary homosexuality. In the course of this argument, he points to the relationship between Jesus and the man he loved as being a perfectly obvious homosexual relationship that cultural tradition had rendered virtually invisible despite the fact that it is "right there before our eyes" (Groddeck 1949, 263).

While the intimations I have pointed to above are treated more extensively in *The Man Jesus Loved*, there is at least one more to which somewhat more attention should be given here. This is the work of George Steiner, one of the best known interpreters of literature of our era. In a collection of essays, *No Passions Spent* (1996), Steiner's last two essays deal with certain parallels that he sees in narratives concerning Jesus and Socrates. The last essay ("Two Suppers") highlights the homoerotic aspects of love in the last chapters of the Fourth Gospel and the Symposium of Plato. He writes, "These two nights, both in the spring, respectively in the two seminal cities in our western identity, Athens, Jerusalem, generate the lineaments of desire, of the dialogue between body and soul, flesh and spirit, in unnumbered nights of love to follow" (1996, 404). Steiner goes on to refer to "the disciple whom Jesus loves both in the spiritual, 'carative' sense proclaimed by Paul and in the more general, everyday connotations of loving affection, of friendship and intimacy modulating into love" (1996, 414).

In a subsequent book, Steiner again takes up a reflection on the Gospel of John's depiction of the Last Supper, in the context of a reflection on the vicissitudes of the erotic bond between teachers (masters) and their students or disciples. Here Steiner focuses particular attention on the jealousy of Judas, who may be seen as one who desired intimacy with Jesus but sees that intimacy on display with another disciple: "Judas has been compelled to witness Jesus' election to manifest love of one whom tradition will designate as 'John' and whom some mystical hierarchies will set above Peter" (2003, 38). Accordingly, he reads Judas' betrayal as an act of jealous rage. In all this, what is remarkable is that Steiner reads the relation between Jesus and "John" (and even Judas) as plainly homoerotic. This reading does not seem to have anything to do with using the Bible for "culture war" purposes. Rather it is that, for one who is trained to read literature with an eye toward character and motivation, the homoerotic element supplies the key to make sense of the narrative. In this sense, the philosopher, the literary critic, and the psychoanalyst are driven to see the homoerotic tone of the relationship between Jesus and the man he loved.

The Gospel of John

It is important then to turn to the text of the Gospel of John in order to see what it is exactly that may serve to provoke or underwrite such a homoerotic reading.

Certainly the Gospel of John is replete with accounts of Jesus' special relationships with several of his followers. This focus upon relationships is one of the distinguishing features of the text. Moreover, unlike the other gospels, this narrative places special emphasis upon the theme of love, alternatively employing the verbs *phileō* and *agapaō* in ways to make them equivalent or at least complementary. Indeed the five chapters of this text devoted to Jesus' last meal and discourse with his disciples is notable for its emphasis on love.

It is within this context that the reader first encounters one who is simply termed "the disciple Jesus loved." The narrator points him out not only as the man Jesus loved but also gives concreteness to that love by indicating that he is the one who was lying in Jesus' lap. The action of the scene is set in motion by Jesus' assertion that one of these friends will betray him, and the beloved is beckoned out of his intimate repose by Peter, who wants to know to whom Jesus is referring. The beloved then reclines, this time on Jesus' chest, in order to discreetly ask, "Who is it?" Jesus, rather than replying directly, asks the man he loves to watch who dips his bread in the gravy. While one might miss the intimacy of the scene by focusing attention upon the dramatic announcement of impending betrayal or upon the astonishing level of intimacy and commitment between Jesus and this band of "friends" in the scene of foot washing that precedes it, it is nonetheless a startling picture. Although Jesus loves all his disciples with a love that would abase itself for love of the other or even die for them, there is one who is singled out as the one he loved. And this love is precisely that signified by physical intimacy, the intimacy of those who appear to be, in our terms, "lovers." Now to this it might be objected that this posture of reclining at table together was the normal way of sharing meals and fellowship in the Greco-Roman world. And this is to a certain extent true. But as any number of depictions left to us on vases and cups of antiquity make quite clear, this posture of physical intimacy (in the lap, on the chest) was not customary, save in situations marked by erotic, indeed sexual, intimacy. (It is not after all a posture that facilitates eating, drinking, or even general conversation.) People recline yes, but not on one another. This is also true of narrative depictions. Thus in the Symposium of Plato, when Socrates sits on Agathon's mat or couch, much is made of the erotic nature of the posture through sexual innuendo. When Scipio Aemilianus, who was consul in 143 BCE, accuses another of being a cinaedus (boy-toy), he accuses him as one "who when he was a young man reclined at banquets next to his lover" (Halperin 2004, 125).

This supper is the first appearance of the man Jesus loved, and it is by far the one that is most often referred to not only in literature but also in art. But it is not his last appearance in the gospel. While there is an unknown disciple who lets Peter into the scene of Jesus trial, he is not referred to explicitly as the one Jesus loved. But the one he loved does appear at the foot of the cross accompanied by several women, including Jesus' mother and aunt and also Salome and Mary Magdalene. As at the supper so also here in the midst of dramatic events, we see a scene of remarkable intimacy. Jesus says to his mother, "Woman, behold your son," and to the beloved, "Behold your mother." In spite of the attempt to read this episode as an occasion for mother's day sentimentality, it must be recalled that in this narrative Jesus has nowhere evinced any particularly filial regard for his mother. Here as before he addresses her as "woman," as he also does the Samaritan woman. Moreover, it is not the mother's welfare that is the object of concern here, since the gospel suggests that Jesus has many brothers and so she is by no means alone in the world. Rather it is the welfare of the beloved that seems to be at stake. Those who are here in grief at the death of the lover of one of them and the son of the other are directed to care for one another. Since the Gospel of John came to be regarded as an antidote to those who denied the bodily suffering and death of Jesus, the scene emphasizes the presence of one who was mother according to the flesh and one who was beloved, perhaps also according to the flesh. Of course, if Jesus had instead addressed himself in this way to Mary Magdalene and his mother, we would immediately conclude that the Magdalene was his wife or betrothed. The dying man commends his mother and his beloved to one another's care. It is the same-sex character of the love displayed here that has made this scene so difficult to appropriate in exegesis.

The man Jesus loved is next encountered with Peter, as the Magdalene reports that the tomb is empty. They race to the tomb, but the beloved waits outside for Peter to catch up and enter first. That they are found together reminds the reader that Peter chose to ask the beloved about Jesus' meaning when he had spoken of betrayal. Whatever the relationship between Jesus and the beloved, it is one that Peter seems to accept, perhaps even approve of. And who else would be able to console the one who had denied Jesus than the one who was his beloved?

The last scene comes at the end of the narrative, when the disciples are out fishing. A mysterious stranger is recognized (by the beloved) as Jesus returned from the dead. There ensues a long conversation between Jesus and Peter, in which Peter is charged to take care of Jesus' followers. Peter notices that the beloved is there waiting patiently in the background and asks, "What about him?" Jesus tells Peter not to worry about the beloved. Unlike all the others, he remains Jesus' personal responsibility. It is here that we are again reminded of the posture of physical intimacy that had characterized their relationship (the one who had been lying in his lap).

Such is the material in the Gospel of John that is evocative of the depiction of Jesus as the lover of another man. To what extent is this depiction compatible with the remainder of this text? Some might argue that Jesus, as a Jew, could not possibly be regarded as one who had a relationship that is plainly prohibited by Leviticus as an integral part of the Law of Moses. But Jesus' attitude toward the Law of Moses in this and in other texts that have come down to us is one of, at best, marked ambivalence. He reduces the entire law to the question of love for the other. He is vigorously attacked by the proponents of this law as a sinner and a blasphemer. He blatantly disregards the law when it suits his purposes, as, for example, in his refusal to allow the plain requirement of the law to be carried out with respect to the woman taken in adultery. He gives his opponents to understand that his way supersedes the way marked out by Moses and the law. There is then nothing in the text that would suggest that Jesus would automatically adopt the law as placing restrictions upon his love.

What then of the suggestion that even if there were an erotic attachment between Jesus and another man this would have to be understood in a spiritual sense? To be sure, the gospel often goes to great lengths to emphasize the "spiritual" meaning of certain expressions (water from the well, rebirth, and so on). But it is also the case that the text emphasizes, in quite graphic ways, the physical, bodily character of many episodes and sayings. It is in this gospel that Jesus mixes his own spit with dirt to apply to the eye of the blind man; it is in this text that Jesus turns bath water into wine, and weeps at the death of a friend, and so emphasizes the quasi-cannibalistic undertones of "eat my flesh" as to have opponents and disciples leave in disgust. Indeed what characterizes this text is the tension between the "spiritual" and the fleshly, a tension that is signaled in the very beginning of the text in the assertion that "the word became flesh."

One might wonder why, if the desire was to portray Jesus as one with us in the flesh and so as sharing desire for and delight in physical intimacy, he is not portrayed as having an erotic relation with a woman? As we shall see, there are attempts to depict Jesus in this way, sometimes making him appear, in modern terms, bisexual. But there is another reason why the depiction of Jesus as having a homoerotic relationship may have commended itself to the writer of this text while an erotic relationship with a woman may not have. In all the gospels, Jesus is depicted as having a very critical attitude toward what are today called marriage and family values. In some of the texts, the language can be exceedingly harsh: "anyone who does not hate father, mother, spouse, child ... cannot be my disciple" (Luke 14:26). What could account for this apparent hostility? It would seem that the institutions of marriage and family could be perceived as deeply destructive of the values that Jesus sought to inculcate; not only because marriage and family are the places where the negative values of xenophobia or acquiescence in the economic or political status quo are learned; not only because here is where the structures of patriarchy are most deeply embedded (although all of this counts heavily). It is also because these structures are built upon dominations of various kinds and upon possession of one human by another. Indeed in antiquity if one wanted to point to a relationship of mutual respect and care in general, one pointed to same-sex rather than heterosexual relationships. To depict Jesus in this context as being the lover of a woman would all too easily have made him into a justification for, or legitimation of, those structures of domination. As it was, in the early centuries of Christianity, one of the most compelling features of Christianity that accounted for its growth was precisely that it liberated people from these structures. Thus into the fourth century, congregations were heavily populated by the unmarried, the virgins (of both sexes) who were released from the obligations of marriage and family structures. Indeed some of "orthodox" Christianity's strongest competitors (Marcionites, Encratites, and others) were those who forbade marriage completely.

So far we have been attending to the Gospel of John and the depiction of a relationship between Jesus and one he loved. There are a few quasi-historical questions that might be dealt with in this connection. Does all this entail any claim about whether or not Jesus had sex? Not exactly. This narrative, like almost all "love stories," leaves out of sight the specific practices that may have mediated this love. In general, the sexual mediation of relationships that are most known to us must still be inferred; it is not made explicit. We are simply presented with certain public features of a relationship: Joe and Bill are always together, sit and sleep together, exchange tender glances, and so on; Mary and Sue live together, raise a kid together, even self-identify as lesbian; Frank and Elizabeth have been living together for three years, they seem to deeply enjoy one another's company. Now are any of these people "having sex?" On one level, we do not know, perhaps do not even want to know. On another level, we may tacitly assume that they are, since the relationships look like relationships that we otherwise suppose are expressed, at least occasionally, sexually. With respect to the relationship depicted between Jesus and the man he loved, we may be in a similar situation. What one tacitly supposes about sexual mediation will have much to do with how comfortable one is with such practices, either in one's own life or in that of others.

In this discussion, I have emphasized the narrative text of the Gospel of John, and that simply points to one more layer of ambiguity. To say that Jesus was depicted in this way in this text does not necessarily mean that we can therefore conclude that Jesus, as more than a character in this narrative, Jesus as the historical person to whom the text seems to be referring, had such a relationship. That conclusion would entail a whole set of suppositions about the historical accuracy of the portrayal of Jesus in this text. Conservative Christians, the very ones most likely to be offended by a "gay Jesus," are the very ones least likely to entertain any doubts at all about the historical veracity of this text. But modern scholars tend to be more suspicious about this text in terms of its reliability as a source for the historical Jesus, or the Jesus of history. On this point, as it bears upon this particular feature of the Gospel of John, I have no strong opinion. But if one wanted to claim that something other than community or personal memory is the source for this characterization of Jesus' relation to the beloved disciple, then it would be necessary to identify a plausible motive for the apparent invention of a homoerotic relationship.

Religious Perspectives

As I have indicated, the Gospel of John contains the episodes that are most evocative of something like a homoerotic Jesus. But this is not the only text that has provoked such speculation. The Gospel of Mark has also been read in this way. Already Jeremy Bentham had remarked upon the curious episode of the youth in the Garden of Gethsemane, whose nudity was at first covered by a linen cloth and then, as he escaped capture, fleetingly glimpsed by the narrator. Bentham actually wonders about a same-sex tryst or even whether the lad was a prostitute. The episode has certainly puzzled interpreters. Why is the reader introduced to a naked lad fleeing the arrest of Jesus on that fateful night? In some church tradition, the episode is decently clothed in the supposition that the lad is none other than the author of the gospel. Others point to a connection to the clothed youth in the tomb and wonder about a baptismal significance (sharing in the death and resurrection for example).

In 1973, Morton Smith published a fragment of a letter from Clement of Alexandria, who was a Christian teacher at the end of the second century CE. In that letter, Clement seems to refer to two versions of an episode from the Gospel of Mark that had disappeared from the commonly circulated text. One, according to Clement, is authentic and speaks of a youth who comes to Jesus at night for instruction in the reign of God. The other version (ascribed to heretics) specifies that Jesus and the lad were, for purposes of that instruction, "naked with naked and so on." The "and so on" seems, given Clement's expressed outrage, to suggest sexual practices.

This fragment has been accepted by many scholars as an early text that may shed light on the formation of the Gospel of Mark. Others have maintained deep suspicion about the circumstances surrounding its discovery and publication. But an interesting book by Will Roscoe, who has specialized in noticing "gay" features of Native American and related cultures, uses this text as a jumping-off point to enter into a wide-ranging discussion of *Jesus and the Shamanic Tradition of Same-Sex Love* (2004). The book surveys a multitude of mystery (orphic) and shamanistic practices that in his view shed light on what might be meant by a baptismal practice that results in intimate relationship with Jesus. Following up on clues suggested by Morton Smith in the books that publicized the discovery of the fragment, Roscoe argues for a relationship between same-sex love and a queer spirituality that would validate the place of same-sex love within the domain of spirituality. The Jesus presented in this text may not be in most senses gay as we typically understand the term but is a figure whose baptismal practice erases the boundary between the erotic and the spiritual. The relationship between the believer and Jesus then would be homoerotic if the believer were male and hetero-erotic if the believer were female (an option not strongly thematized in this book). On the other hand, given the gender ambiguity of some shamanistic antecedents, the situation might be more complex. The point thus seems to be that same-sex love is not incompatible with the spirituality that is focused upon Jesus.

A somewhat less ambiguous portrait is suggested by William Bramley, who, in the course of offering a number of alternative portrayals of Jesus, devotes one chapter to Jesus as a "Gay Man" in his *Jesus Goes to Hollywood* (2005). However, he does suggest that bisexuality would also be a possible construal and even that, whether or not Jesus was "gay," the alleged biblical support for homophobia is based upon a misreading of the texts. Despite the moderate views actually espoused in this chapter, it is headed by a warning that persons offended by explicit sexual discussion should skip it, an indication again of the explosiveness of even the barest suggestion in the direction of a gay Jesus.

A book that seeks to explore what might be termed the "bisexuality" of Jesus, both in terms of the erotic connection to Jesus and in terms of Jesus' own comportment, is Jeffrey Kripal's *The Serpent's Gift* (2007). In a chapter entitled "The Apocryphon of the Beloved," Kripal takes as his starting point the view presented by *The Man Jesus Loved* and adds to it the early Christian echoes of a special (and erotic) relationship between Jesus and Mary Magdalene. He suggests the possibility that, in its haste to rid orthodoxy of Mary Magdalene (a tension visible in the quite early Gospel of Thomas), the church of Peter re-gendered her to become the male beloved of Jesus. Another possibility would seem to be that Jesus was, as we would now say, bisexual, in having two erotic relationships, one with a male, the other with a female. In antiquity, no special category was needed for this sexual orientation, since it seems to have been widely assumed that all men would be attracted to both male and female partners and that at least many, even most, would act upon that attraction. But the main point that Kripal is interested in making is that the study of religion, in this case Christianity, is, at its best, subversive of rigid orthodoxies as well as of such binaries as the erotic or the scholarly, gay or straight, even male or female. The study of religion does not leave one unaffected but rather offers "the serpent's gift" of knowledge, in which the erotic, the spiritual, and the scholarly join together to awaken a more profound and disturbing consciousness. Certainly the various ways of representing a "gay" Jesus constitute one way of validating such a claim.

While students of religion have in different ways and to differing degrees found it possible to present something like a gay Jesus, there has been more reluctance to do so within areas more closely related to theology. Here things are more often tentative and allusive. One of the first to point in this direction was Hugh Montefiore (1968). In a sermon and in a subsequently published essay, Montefiore explored the significance of the hypothesis that "Jesus was a homosexual," noting that this might explain his celibacy and recalling that those he was said to have loved were male. Montefiore did not suggest that Jesus was what was then called a "practicing homosexual" and did emphasize that he in no way intended to impute sin to Jesus. This was of course long before the Vatican determined that homosexuality, even as a bare tendency, was an "objective" tendency to sin (a position not endorsed by Montefiore's Anglican communion). In 1984, perhaps in recognition of Montefiore's controversial position, the United Reformed Church referred to the suggestion that "Jesus may have been homosexually inclined" (Melton 1991, 245).

The most elaborate attempt to make the case that Jesus was "gay" comes in the book by Robert Williams, *Just As I Am*, published in 1992. Williams develops a sort of composite of biblical and other evidence to maintain that the man Jesus loved was Lazarus. Other writers who adopt a gay or queer stance are generally more allusive in their treatments. Robert Goss (2002), for example, while referring to Montefiore and Williams, is more concerned to develop the notion of Jesus as embracing a more general eroticism and thereby effacing the boundary between the erotic and the spiritual. More recently Dale Martin's book *Sex and the Single Savior* makes a strong case for the validity of many ways of reading texts of the New Testament, but in the title chapter he devotes less than a full page (2006, 99–100) to the possibility of reading New Testament texts as pointing to a gay Jesus, even if he does point out a number of ways Jesus may be regarded as "queer."

The Arts

For most people, the scholarly discussions of, or pointers to, a gay Jesus may have little purchase. The arts broadly conceived may have a more immediate, even if sometimes subliminal, impact in depicting Jesus as the lover of another man or as the object of that love. One of the ways this may come across is in the standardized depiction of the "Four Evangelists" in many churches and cathedrals. While Matthew, Luke, and even Mark are typically portrayed as middle-aged men, with girth, beard and (often) receding hairline to match, John is inevitably represented as a comely youth, what might be supposed to be the conventional object of the male erotic gaze. Since by tradition "John" is both the author of the Fourth Gospel and the beloved of Jesus, it would seem that church artists were influenced by the erotic possibilities of the relationship and thereby subliminally transmit it to all who view the works they create. Similarly, many of the works of art that depict the Last Supper may also subliminally convey a certain eroticism in the postures of Jesus and "John."

In a book of contemporary art entitled *Art That Dares* (2007), Kittridge Cherry has assembled a number of works that reflect feminist and also gay sensibilities. Some of these works depict a Jesus who is the object of gay male adoration. That is, it is the followers of Jesus rather than Jesus himself who are iconically "gay." Others depict a crucified Jesus with signs that identify him with victims of lethal homophobia. That Jesus should be depicted as one of the victims of legal and religious persecution is, of course, theologically appropriate. It stands in line with such famous paintings as the Matthias Grünewald Isenheim altar, one of Karl Barth's favorite paintings, which represented a crucified Jesus as afflicted with the same sort of suffering as the patients in the hospital where it was designed to be displayed. In the case of images by Becky Jayne Harrelson, however, we do get images that are suggestive of a gay Jesus, particularly in *Study for The Last Supper* (Cherry 2007, 46).

In addition to the art book, Kittridge Cherry has also written two novels that explore the sexuality of Jesus as erotically engaged with both John (the beloved disciple) and Mary Magdalene. Her novels, *Jesus in Love* (2006) and *At the Cross* (2008), thus depict a Jesus who in conventional terms might be termed bisexual. This eroticism is depicted as itself dependent on the omni-erotic vitality of the Spirit, who appears to be Jesus' true lover, most often represented as feminine. These novels then comport more precisely with the suggestive work of Kripal (2007, noted above) than with the depiction of a more specifically homoerotic relationship that characterizes my own study of the Gospel of John. However, the relationship with John becomes the most sexually charged of Jesus' many erotic relationships with human characters.

A theatrical work that has generated considerable controversy is *Corpus Christi* (1998) by acclaimed dramatist Terrence McNally. The play is constructed as a sort of modern morality play in which Jesus/Joshua as well as his disciples are represented as gay while still being quite recognizably engaged in the mission of enacting and announcing the reign of love. It is both a powerful retelling of the story of Jesus in a contemporary way and an exercise in a certain gay sensibility. Since its initial performance in New York in 1998, it has been the object of considerable controversy as well as acclaim. Although vigorously denounced by the religious right, it has also been performed in churches and thus has become the most popular presentation of a gay Jesus. In so far as Jesus is depicted as having a lover, it would seem to be Judas, although this is not made explicit.

A final novelistic depiction is found in John Henson's *The Gay Disciple* (2007), which depicts a strongly homoerotic relationship between Jesus and Lazarus, who also is conflated with the "rich young ruler" from the Gospel of Mark who was the object of Jesus' intent and loving gaze (Mark 10:21).

Theology

The hesitancy of Christian interpreters to develop the idea of a gay Jesus may owe at least in part to a hesitancy to undertake a depiction that would undermine basic Christian doctrine. What would a gay Jesus mean for Christian theology? Would the very idea of a gay (or homosexual or bisexual or even queer) Jesus entail a repudiation of the basic tenets of Christian tradition?

Of course, there is no doctrinal problem when persons who have been marginalized or persecuted see in the figure of Jesus one who shared their fate. There is a long and honorable tradition of precisely this sort of identification with Jesus and the identification of the figure of Jesus with the class of the oppressed or humiliated.

Nor does it seem at all untoward that the relationship of the believer to Jesus should be cast in erotic terms or that expressions of devotion to Jesus should have a more or less strong erotic current. To deny this would be to deny much mysticism as well as folk hymnody and piety. This has the effect that male devotion to Jesus may be expected to have a more or less strong current of homoeroticism, however much sublimated.

However uncomfortable these aspects of a "gay" Jesus might make some who have rather highly developed homophobic tendencies, they seem in general to pose no basic problem for theological or christological reflection.

But what of the stronger sense in which the idea of a gay Jesus might be entertained, namely that Jesus be understood, as the Gospel of John suggests, as the lover of another man and that this love be supposed to be one that may have found sexual expression? Would this be a repudiation of basic christological claims that have defined orthodox Christianity? Many claimed that my own book was, in some such sense as this, blasphemous. Even supposing I had made the claim about Jesus having been, in the quaint phrase of another generation, a "practicing homosexual," would that entail a denial of basic christological claims? I think not.

It is important to recall that the basic issue for the emerging shape of christology had been set by the prologue to John's gospel: the Word became flesh. This becoming flesh of the divine received its basic shape in the argument of Athanasius' treatise "On the Incarnation of the Word," in which the claim had to be made that it was not unseemly for God to become fully human even to the point of assuming mortality. As Athanasius claimed, the opponents of Christianity had nothing to argue against the faith except the cross. He then goes to great lengths to show that, since God is the creator of creatures and of humanity, there can be nothing unseemly in God coming to his own. Thus the becoming human of the Word is established. The taking on of both birth and death is then understood to be the way in which the divine demonstrates its benevolence toward humanity and bestows upon humanity an overcoming of corruptibility and mortality. It is by taking on the fullness of humanity and not simply an idealized or "spiritual" humanity that the act of God in Christ has real efficacy with respect to redemption. This position is amplified in important ways by Athanasius' younger contemporary, Gregory Nazianzen, who maintained that any aspect of humanity that is not taken on, or assumed, by divinity in Christ is not saved. In this way, he sought to emphasize that the Divine not only becomes human spirit, or even soul, but body as well.

A further step is undertaken by Augustine, who maintains that the humanity created by God necessarily includes sexuality, as this is an essential aspect of the good creation of God. The consequence of taking this seriously would be to maintain that the divine assumes or is incarnate as a sexual human being. That is, in so far as sexuality is regarded as an essential aspect of humanity, then that must be attributed to the God-human of orthodox christology. The humanity assumed by the "Son" or "Word" then is not only the humanity that can suffer and die but is also the humanity that yearns for and delights in the intimate companionship that includes sexual expression. To deny any sort of sexuality to Christ, then, is to destroy the very idea of incarnation and so the very bedrock of orthodoxy.

Now, it may be claimed that this does not mean that Jesus had to have had sexual experience in order to have been fully human. And to a certain point this is no doubt true. The essentiality of erotic desire and delight does not entail the necessity for any particular form of sexual practice. It merely means that such practice cannot be ruled out in advance as unthinkable or as incompatible with the incarnation (any more than eating and drinking could be ruled out).

But what about same-sex sexuality? Is this not by definition sinful, and thus would it not be ruled out for one who was, as Paul says, in every way like us except for sin? What does the sinlessness of Christ mean and what does it require?

First, it is important to note that there is a difference between the claim of the divinity of Christ and his sinlessness. The sinlessness belongs not to the divinity but to the humanity. Put another way: sinless human beings would not therefore be divine. This is obvious in the case of the image of Adam and Eve prior to the Fall. But it also is the case that various "Holiness" movements within Christianity, including the Wesleyan revival, supposed that it was possible, indeed necessary, for human beings to come to be without sin. That was taken to mean not that they would cease to be creatures or humans, only that in that way they would be renewed in the image and likeness of God.

So what then about sinless humanity? What does it mean that Jesus was without sin? Certainly this does not mean that one could count up all the laws in Exodus and Deuteronomy and Leviticus and see if Jesus checked them all off in an unblemished manner. The people who thought that way about the law were the ones who condemned Jesus. He did not seem to honor his parents, he did not seem to honor the Sabbath, he disregarded the rules regarding purity, he even stopped the imposition of the law in the case of the woman taken in adultery. And not only so, but he was also responsible for a movement of people who similarly disregarded much of the law of "Moses." That is, his law-breaking became contagious. This is entirely consist-ent with his own message about the law being fulfilled in the love of God and neigh-bor rather than in scrupulous attention to the proliferation of rules.

Thus when Paul refers to the sinlessness of Jesus, he is not claiming that he knows that Jesus followed all the rules. In fact, he is clear that he knows little or nothing about Jesus "according to the flesh." What he is pointing to instead is the way God vindicates one who was condemned according to the law: Jesus is vindicated through the resurrection from the dead. Thus those who measure sin in accordance with obedience to a multitude of laws found Jesus to be anything but sinless. But the resurrection demonstrates that God judges sinlessness in terms of that justice that consists in loyalty to the divine desire to re-create human beings as a new creation by following the way, not of violence, but of concrete service to the other – that is, the way of love.

Thus only if same-sex love (whether sexually expressed or not) was a violation of the love of the neighbor would it contravene the biblical idea of sinlessness. The same would be true of "cross-sex" love. Thus it would turn out that there is nothing in the notion that Jesus may be thought of as "gay" (in any of the senses that we have explored in this chapter) that would contravene the claim that his humanity was without sin, still less the claim that he was united inseparably with God as "the only begotten son."

Viewed in this way, then, the representation of Jesus as "gay" may actually serve to clarify what is (and is not) at stake in the claims of even the most orthodox christology.

The hypothesis of a gay Jesus, then, is not an arbitrary fantasy. It is deeply rooted in fundamental aspects of the gospel. It underlines the character of Jesus' mission and ministry as placing him on the side of all who are despised and outcast. It sug-gests a way of including the erotic within the incarnation and hence within the core of human being, without making Jesus complicit with patriarchal domination embedded in the structures of marriage and family values. It may root itself in a common-sense reading and interpretation of the relevant New Testament texts, without distorting those texts in accordance with a legalistic ideology. And it helps to clarify (rather than deny) what is truly at stake in even the most orthodox chris-tological formulations.

However much this suggestion has seemed to many to be subversive or even blasphemous, it is no more subversive than the ministry and mission of Jesus, no more blasphemous than the assertion that God and humanity come together in the incarnation without separation or confusion.

References

Aelred of Rievaulx (1977). *Spiritual Friendship*. Trans. Mary E. Laker. Kalamazoo, MI: Cistercian Publications.

Boswell, John (1980). *Christianity, Social Tolerance, and Homosexuality*. Chicago: University of Chicago Press.

Bramley, William (2005). *Jesus Goes to Hollywood: The Alternative Theories About Christ*. Modesto, CA: Dahlin.

Cherry, Kittridge (2006). *Jesus in Love: A Novel*. Berkeley, CA: AndroGyne.

Cherry, Kittridge (2007). *Art That Dares: Gay Jesus, Woman Christ, and More*. Berkeley, CA: AndroGyne.

Cherry, Kittridge (2008). *At the Cross*. Berkeley, CA: AndroGyne.

Crompton, Louis (1985). *Byron and Greek Love: Homophobia in Nineteenth Century England*. Berkeley: University of California Press.

Goss, Robert E. (2002). *Queering Christ: Beyond Jesus Acted Up*. Cleveland: Pilgrim.

Groddeck, Georg Walther (1949). *The Book of the It*. Trans. V. M. E. Collins. New York: Vintage.

Halperin, David M. (2004). *How to Do the History of Homosexuality*. Chicago: University of Chicago Press.

Henson, John (2007). *The Gay Disciple: Jesus' Friends Tell it Their Own Way*. Winchester, UK: O-Books.

Jennings, Theodore W., Jr. (2003). *The Man Jesus Loved: Homoerotic Narratives from the New Testament*. Cleveland: Pilgrim.

Karlen, Arlo (1971). *Sexuality and Homosexuality*. New York: W. W. Norton.

Kripal, Jeffrey J. (2007). *The Serpent's Gift: Gnostic Reflections on the Study of Religion*. Chicago: University of Chicago Press.

McNally, Terrence (1998). *Corpus Christi: A Play*. New York: Grove.

Martin, Dale B. (2006). *Sex and the Single Savior: Gender and Sexuality in Biblical Interpretation*. Louisville, KY: Westminster John Knox.

Melton, J. Gordon (1991). *The Churches Speak: On Homosexuality*. Detroit: Gale Research.

Montefiore, Hugh (1968). "Jesus the Revelation of God." In Norman Pittenger (ed.), *Christ for Us Today* (pp. 101–116). London: SCM.

Roscoe, Will (2004). *Jesus and the Shamanic Tradition of Same-Sex Love*. San Francisco: Suspect Thought.

Smith, Morton (1973). *Clement of Alexandria and a Secret Gospel of Mark*. Cambridge: Harvard University Press.

Steiner, George (1996). *No Passion Spent: Essays 1978–1995*. New Haven: Yale University Press.

Steiner, George (2003). *Lessons of the Masters*. Cambridge: Harvard University Press.

Williams, Robert (1992). *Just As I Am*. San Francisco: Harper.

CHAPTER 28

Modern Mystifications of Jesus

Per Beskow

Within Christian circles, there has always been literature that attempts to supplement the narratives of the gospels and to reinterpret the events in the life of Christ. These apocryphal writings were abundant during the first centuries CE, and there was a new wave of them in the nineteenth century, in response to biblical criticism. These writings often originated with groups that wished to picture the person and life of Christ differently than the gospels do, and they were often presented as radical challenges to established Christianity. I once wrote a book about these modern alternative gospels, *Strange Tales about Jesus* (Beskow 1985), in which I described some of them and explained their origins and tendencies (see also Goodspeed 1956).

These narratives are pure fictions, but they generally claimed to be genuine documents from the past, and they were accompanied by accounts of how they were discovered in formerly unknown manuscripts. They were downright forgeries and could usually be unmasked as such. In most cases it was also possible to identify the authors and to establish the purpose of their falsifications. These Jesus apocrypha reflect tendencies that were in fashion during the period when they were published. For example, Christ would be depicted as an Indian sage, as a faith healer or – in some cases – as an extraterrestrial visitor to earth.

Twenty-five years have passed since *Strange Tales* was published, and meanwhile the whole character of this apocryphal literature has radically changed. Jesus apocrypha of the "classical" type do not seem to appear any more and have been replaced by new ways of conveying disinformation, which I prefer to classify as mystifications. The reason for this change is obviously to be found in our new relations to written and printed texts. When I wrote *Strange Tales*, I performed my work in a university library with huge piles of books on my desk. Today I am sitting in front of my computer seeking information on the internet.

As long as we inhabited the Gutenberg galaxy, to speak with Marshall McLuhan, the printed book had a prestige that it no longer holds. The mere fact that something

The Blackwell Companion to Jesus, First Edition. Edited by Delbert Burkett. ©2014 John Wiley & Sons, Ltd. Published 2014 by John Wiley & Sons, Ltd.

was printed gave an impression of credibility. Today, authoritative texts are no longer the starting points for a formation of opinions. Contemporary revisions of the story of Jesus therefore do not often start with the forgery of an ancient text. Nor or they directed to small, esoteric societies. Today, information is more widely available than in times past. It is in free circulation, produced by many independent actors in a constant interchange. Accordingly, new Jesus myths are not directed toward closed groups of people with mutual interests but disseminated as widely as possible through modern media. In postmodern culture, the veracity of a claim may be of less interest than its appeal to the audience. The border between reality and fiction has been more and more dissolved, a development that also affects the shape of these new Jesus myths. They make a common pool of stories and ideas where anyone can pick the parts that suit his or her own fancy.

Recent Discoveries

In recent years, some real finds have been made and have been exploited by the media as significant for revising the story of Jesus. Very often they are said to be revolutionary and shocking for most Christians, but with no real ground. One example is the *Gospel of Judas* (Kasser et al. 2006), a Sethian Gnostic writing from the second century, in which Jesus asks Judas to betray him. According to the National Geographic Society, which took care of its publication, this writing would have a great impact on Christianity. However, interest in it soon faded. As a matter of fact, this writing is more or less unreadable for the non-specialist, and its religious message is not understandable for people of today. Another example is a stone tablet with a Hebrew text, the so-called "Gabriel's Revelation," on which the Israeli professor Israel Knohl thought that he could find a reference to a death and resurrection within three days, but related to a historical person living before Jesus (Knohl 2009). Few scholars seem to have found this interpretation convincing. The so-called family tomb of Jesus, in which Jesus and other members of his family were purportedly found buried, was made known to the public in 2007. It has also been used for a great deal of sensationalism (Jacobovici and Pellegrino 2007), and it will certainly be the subject of further debate. These are real finds from antiquity, but the interpretations of them are doubtful, and the media's interest in them has too often been motivated by the wish to rewrite the history of Jesus.

There is one case, mentioned in *Strange Tales*, where there is still no decisive answer to the question of whether this is an ancient Christian writing or a modern forgery. I refer to the *Secret Gospel of Mark*, about which the debate is still going on. The manuscript was found in 1958 by Professor Morton Smith in the Mar Saba monastery in the Judean desert (Beskow 1985, 96–104). The text had been written on the two last blank pages of a bound volume from 1646 and on a page inserted by the binder. The Greek handwriting is of a kind used in the middle of the eighteenth century. Smith himself took pictures of the manuscript and published the text (Smith

1973a; 1973b). After this time, nobody seems to have had a closer look at the manuscript. Its text purports to be a letter from Clement of Alexandria, including a fragment from an unknown gospel, called by Smith the *Secret Gospel of Mark*.

From the very beginning, there were doubts about the authenticity of the text. In the first edition of *Strange Tales* (published in 1983), I did not directly take sides in the debate, but I mentioned that there were reasons to be skeptical of its genuineness. This statement had unexpected consequences. Professor Smith got upset about what I had written, threatening to sue for one million dollars in damages if the book was not immediately withdrawn, and the publisher yielded to the threat. A new edition was published in 1985 with some slight changes in the chapter in question, which Smith seems to have accepted. The content of the chapter was more or less the same as in the first edition, but in the new version I emphasized that I did not accuse Morton Smith of having forged the manuscript (1985, 104).

My curiosity had, however, been aroused, and I learned that the manuscript had been moved from the Mar Saba monastery to the library of the Greek Patriarchate in Jerusalem. In autumn 1984, I went there in the hope of seeing the manuscript, and I also obtained permission from the Patriarch. But then my effort came to a sudden stop, for the librarian refused to let me into the library. The manuscript had been sprayed with insecticides, he said, and nobody was allowed to come near it. I was not quite convinced by his explanation, for a colleague of mine, looking for another manuscript in the same library six months earlier, had been refused with the same excuse. That is all that I have learned about it. I have heard that the pages with the text have been removed from the volume, but I have not had this confirmed.

I do not render the content of the text here – it can be read in *Strange Tales* (1985, 97–98) – but its greater part seems to be a kind of paraphrase of the narrative about the raising of Lazarus in John's gospel. According to Smith, there are hints in the text that Jesus was a homosexual. However, this reading is not evident for the reader of the text but arises from Smith's interpretation of it. It would have been expressed more clearly if this were the purpose of a possible forgery.

The debate ceased after the death of Morton Smith in 1991, but some criticism has been resumed from time to time. Jacob Neusner, who was once Morton Smith's devoted disciple, has been very outspoken about it, declaring that the *Secret Gospel of Mark* is "the forgery of the century," and recounting the suspicions of many that Smith himself faked the manuscript (1993, 27–31, esp. 28). Other scholars have put forward similar arguments for the view that the text is a fake. Personally I still have doubts about its authenticity, but I prefer to regard this as an open question.

Mystifications

All such discoveries – genuine or not – are fairly rare, and the public interest in them is generally short-lived. Of quite another kind are the mystifications, unverified speculations about Jesus, which are rapidly spread in printed publications and in the media, and not least on the web. It is sometimes difficult to distinguish between new and daring theories about Christian origins and these mystifications, fanciful legends based on ungrounded assumptions far from reality. These stories are constantly being told and retold, and new material is brought forward, giving fuel to further speculations.

Jesus in Kashmir

The first one of these new myths had its heyday already in the 1970s. At that time, there was a widespread rumor in the media that the tomb of Jesus was to be found in Srinagar, the capital of Kashmir. This story was presented as a venerable oriental tradition, and for a while it forcefully penetrated into the western world and was believed by many to be a hidden truth now revealed. Its main propagandist in the West was Andreas Faber-Kaiser with his book *Jesus Died in Kashmir* (1978), where he uncritically reproduced the entire legend with its many details. It is dealt with in *Strange Tales* (Beskow 1985, 57–64).

According to this legend, Jesus survived the crucifixion. He only apparently died, and his disciples revived him. Jesus then left Palestine and traveled along the Silk Road together with his mother Mary and his disciple Thomas. They passed Nisibis and Taxila, and in Murree, north of Rawalpindi, Mary died and was buried – obviously a play on the similarity of Mary to Murree. Jesus and Thomas continued their route toward Kashmir and Srinagar. Here Jesus lived to the age of 120, and his tomb remains in Mohalla Khaniyar.

What was not always explicitly told was that this legend had been created by one person only, the Indian Mirza Ghulam Ahmad from Qadiyan (1833/1839–1908), founder of the Ahmadiyya movement. This is still a considerable movement in the Orient with about ten million members; it has spread to the West and has a huge mosque in London. Ahmadiyya is often described as an Islamic movement, but this categorization is denied in statements issued by top-level Islamic authorities.

In part, the legend was based on forgeries about Jesus, such as *The Essene Letter* and the *Life of Issa*. The former is an alleged letter from an Essene elder telling his readers how Jesus survived the crucifixion. It was first printed in German in 1849 (Beskow 1985, 42–50), and several American translations have followed; the most recent one is named *The Essene Elder's Letter* (Dallison 1993). The *Life of Issa* is an alleged Tibetan document, which the journalist Nicolas Notovitch (1894) pretended to have found in the monastery of Himis in Ladakh. This claim, however, was severely refuted by the famous orientalist Max Müller (1894), who had himself visited Himis and had interviewed its abbot (Beskow 1985, 57–63). Far more important for Ahmad's arguments are several obscure and misunderstood oriental sources in Arabic, Persian, and Sanskrit. The story of the myth's origins was too complicated to be included in *Strange Tales*, where there is only a short summary (Beskow 1985,

63–64), and therefore I wrote a separate book about it, *Jesus i Kashmir* (1981, only in Swedish), where I tried to unravel its many tangled threads.

Mirza Ghulam Ahmad was a Muslim and gained a certain reputation as a defender of Islam in his book *Barahin-i-Ahmadiyya* (1955 [1880–1905]). Many regarded Ahmad as a reformer (*mujaddid*) of Islam, but one could also discern a certain tendency to rely on private revelations, and he includes several prophecies about himself in the book. Ahmad gathered a circle of disciples around himself, and in 1889 he appeared as both Messiah and *mahdi*, an eschatological savior expected in Islam. When his book *Fath-i-Islam* was published ([1890] 1923), it became evident that his teachings deviated widely from the teachings of Islam. In this book, he declared that Jesus had not been taken up into heaven with body and soul; instead he had died on earth, and Ahmad was the real Messiah.

In 1899 Ahmad put forward his complete Jesus legend in his book *Masih Hindustan mein* (in Urdu), known in the West as *Jesus in India* ([1899] 1989). He now appeared openly in his messianic role and declared to the Hindus that he was also an avatar of Vishnu. But his time as a revealer and wonder-worker would be short, for he died during a cholera epidemic in 1908. His movement has since then been governed by elected caliphs, often descendants of Ahmad. One part of the movement separated in 1914 and established its center in Lahore. It rejects the highest pretensions of Ahmad but nevertheless sticks to his Jesus legend.

Ahmad never mentions *The Essene Letter* in his writings, but the idea that Jesus survived the crucifixion must have been taken from this writing, directly or indirectly. Strangely enough, he does refer to the Muslim *Gospel of Barnabas* and must have been aware of it before Lonsdale and Laura Ragg brought it into light by publishing an English translation in 1907. This apocryphal writing, published in Italy or Spain in the Middle Ages (Beskow 1985, 11–15; Cirillo and Fremaux 1977), relates that angels lifted Jesus up into heaven before his enemies arrived to arrest him; but as we have seen, Ahmad taught that Jesus died and was buried here on earth. Probably Ahmad had heard about the *Gospel of Barnabas* but had not been sufficiently informed about its content.

Ahmad also knew about Notovitch's *Life of Issa* and about Max Müller's devastating criticism of this fake, but he seems not to have understood the gravity of the latter, and his teaching is not consistent with Notovitch's story. According to this writing, Jesus visited India in his youth, while Ahmad taught that he arrived in India after his crucifixion. Only later did Ahmad's disciples invent the compromise that Jesus had been twice in India.

Ahmad's primary source is a legend, known in the West as the tale of Barlaam and Josaphat. It was widely read all through the Middle Ages as an edifying Christian legend, but it originated as a Buddhist tale, to which some Christian elements were added (Lang 1957). It was probably written in the fourth or fifth century CE and is a paraphrase of the well-known story of the Buddha's path to enlightenment, how he realized the role of suffering in human life and left his father's palace. Yuzasaf, as the principal character is named in Urdu, is helped on his way by the wise Bilhawar, who arrives in the royal court in disguise and instructs the prince about deliverance from suffering. Already at an early stage, the Christian elements were added to the story, such as the parable of the sower (Mark 4:1–9).

The legend was first written in Sogdian, which indicates a Central Asian origin, and from there it spread all over the Islamic and the Christian world. The name "Yuzasaf" is derived from *bodhisattva*, a future Buddha who abstains from entering nirvana in order to be a helper for the unenlightened. During the transmission of the legend, this name underwent several changes: to Budhasaf, Yudasaf, and finally Yuzasaf. In Greek, his name is Ioasaph; in Latin, Josaphat, the name of one of the kings of Israel. Ahmad divided Yuzasaf in two: Yuz Asaf. He declared that Yuz signified Jesus (who is not called by that name in any language) and that Asaf was the Hebrew verb for "gather." Yuz Asaf would then be "Jesus the Gatherer."

In an Arabic version of the legend, *Kitab Bilawhar-wa-Budhasaf* (published in Bombay 1888–1889), there is an addition, which tells how Budhasaf came to Kashmir with his disciple Ababid (= Ananda), and how he died and was buried there. This very addition is the origin of the legend of Yuz Asaf's arrival in Srinagar and of his tomb in Mohalla Khaniyar. Ahmad referred to a Persian inscription on a Hindu temple near the city, which had already then been obliterated, but where Yuz Asaf was said to have been mentioned. Ahmad's disciples have gathered other "evidence" from local traditions in Kashmir. A literary source, often mentioned in Ahmadiyya literature, is supposed to have been written by a certain Mulla Nadiri, but the only manuscript is said to have been lost for many years, and what remains is only some blurred photos of a page. It is imperative that a source text be available and readable, or at least well documented, to be taken seriously. This manuscript has the same problem as the *Secret Gospel of Mark*, although the latter is available in its original language and has been photographed in its entirety.

As evidence for the legend, the Ahmadiyya often use a further source. It is the *Bhavishya-Purana*, a collection of Hindu traditions from different times, printed in Bombay in 1910 (Winternitz 1963, 497). It is here told that a king of the Shaka people went to "the snow-covered mountain." There he had a vision of a shining white-clad figure who presented himself as the son of the Lord (*ishaputra*) and as one born of a virgin (*kumarigarbhasambhava*). This vision seems to refer to Jesus, but it is mixed with elements of Iranian sun-worship. While this event occurs in a vision, seen in the mountains, in the Ahmadiyya version it has been brought down to the vicinity of Srinagar and turned into an ordinary encounter. The original story, however, does not support the Ahmadiyya claim that Jesus journeyed to the East.

As already mentioned, Ahmad's legend had a strong impact on western media, and for a time many accepted it as a serious alternative to the gospel narratives of the death and resurrection of Jesus. Its connection with Ahmad and his messianic pretensions was often obscured. This whole episode shows how easily a loose combination of uncertain or fictional claims can gain credibility in a setting where any reinterpretation of the gospels is appreciated. This legend, however, differs remarkably from those mystifications that are being spread in the media of today. This one was promoted out of religious conviction without any commercial considerations, and today it may seem old-fashioned.

Descendants of Jesus and Mary Magdalene

The new kinds of Jesus myths are far more nebulous than their predecessors and are therefore more difficult to refute. Each such story involves a network of pretended sources and discoveries, including historical persons, places, and symbols connected with Jesus. By combining these, the mythmakers create new and fictitious universes. This kind of mythmaking belongs to the much wider category of systematic misinformation now often designated as "counterknowledge," which embraces such cultural phenomena as pseudo-history and conspiracy theories (Thompson 2008).

Earlier but similar forms of mythmaking are found in various kinds of esotericism, vividly pictured in Umberto Eco's novel *Foucault's Pendulum* (1988). There is, however, a great difference between these make-believe worlds from the past and the modern mystifications. Those esoteric speculations developed in order to edify closed circles of initiates, while the new mystifications prove profitable and spread openly all over the world in books, films, and television programs, and on the internet. The most successful of these modern myths is that generally associated with Dan Brown's novel *The Da Vinci Code* (2003; film: 2006). This myth has a long and complicated history, which I will try to summarize here. Most observed and discussed has been the thesis that Jesus and Mary Magdalene were married and that some of their descendants are still among us, conscious of their descent. There are, however, many other elements in the myth that have to be considered.

The Da Vinci Code has aroused more attention than it really deserves, and my intention here is not to analyze the novel, but to untangle various threads that the author has used as elements in his story. The novel's success largely depends on its mixture of exciting adventures and surprising historical assertions, which have obviously appealed to many readers. Many such readers have had their understanding of Jesus thoroughly revised by acquaintance with "Leigh Teabing's" expositions, in which he totally rewrites early Christian history. Brown's novel is certainly pure fiction, but it has evident pretensions to be a source of trustworthy information. At the beginning of the book, there is a list titled "Fact" where we read, "All descriptions of artwork, architecture, documents and secret rituals in this novel are accurate." The author does not mention here all the faked elements in his story, but any claim for the novel's accuracy is discredited by his depiction of the documents of the Priory of Sion and the art and architecture of Rosslyn chapel – treated below.

As is well known, the themes of the novel are not Brown's own inventions but are almost entirely based on earlier mystifications. The main contribution comes from *The Holy Blood and the Holy Grail* by Michael Baigent and Richard Leigh (1982), renamed *Holy Blood, Holy Grail* in the United States. These authors were not pleased with Brown's use of their material for his novel and sued him for plagiarism, though with no success. Their attitude is revealing, for if they claimed to be spreading the truth, they would rather be thankful for his assistance. By talking of plagiarism, they confirmed themselves that their work is fiction and thereby their literary property.

The two books of Baigent and Leigh, *Holy Blood, Holy Grail* and *The Messianic Legacy* (1986), were written in cooperation with the actor and journalist Henry Lincoln (a pseudonym of Henry Soskin). In each, the long and winding exposition concludes with the story of the bloodline supposedly carried by many generations from Jesus and Mary Magdalene to our time. According to the authors, the knowledge of this bloodline has been carefully preserved by a secret organization, the Priory of Sion, which is said to have existed since the Middle Ages. The documents of this organization, we are told, have been preserved in the Bibliothèque Nationale in Paris. These give the Holy Grail, well known from medieval romance, a new interpretation as *sang real*, "royal blood": Mary Magdalene's body is the sacred vessel in which the holy blood has been carried to the West. It is not evident which language is intended; in French it should be *sang royal*, in Spanish *sangre real*.

All information about the Priory of Sion derives from one single person, the Frenchman Pierre Plantard (1920–2000), who spent his whole life in a world of imagination. Already as a child, he dreamt of being of royal descent, and he gradually built up a myth around himself. As a teenager, he was drawn to royalist and rightwing circles in France and was also a member of the secret and anti-Semitic order Alpha Galates. During the Second World War, this organization had close relations with the Vichy regime, and at the end of the war it was dissolved.

Plantard's doings after the war are somewhat obscure, but in 1953 he was sentenced to six months in prison for breach of trust. In 1956 he founded a new society with the now well-known name of *Prieuré de Sion*, Priory of Sion. He took its name from a medieval order, but, in his own version of the priory, it did not refer to the Holy City of Zion, but to a certain Mont Sion near Annemasse, where he lived at that time. The priory was a little friendly society without any special purpose, and it was dissolved the following year.

At the beginning of the 1960s, the castle in Rennes-le-Château in Southern France came into the picture. Plantard had gotten into contact with the hotelier Noël Corbu, owner of an estate that had formerly belonged to the Catholic priest Bérenger Saunière. This man had acquired a greater fortune than is generally expected of a Catholic priest, and he had also built a tower, Tour Magdala, on his estate. Corbu and Plantard concocted the myth that his wealth had come from a large treasure, which he had found buried somewhere in Rennes-le-Château, sometimes said to be the temple treasure from Jerusalem. Gradually Plantard created another element of the myth: when Saunière restored his church, he found documents hidden in a hollow Visigothic pillar. This pillar, which can now be seen in the local museum, is neither Visigothic nor hollow. Plantard claimed that the documents contained the secrets about the descendants of the Merovingian king Dagobert II, of which Plantard considered himself to be one. In 1967 he revived the Priory of Sion, as the guardian of the documents, in the hope of a future *coup d'état* that would make him the king of France. As we may understand, this was not a very realistic project.

In this task of linking himself to royalty, Plantard was aided by another creative mythomaniac, Philippe de Chérisey, who constructed the history of the priory and made up a list of its grand masters. This included Leonardo da Vinci, Isaac Newton, Victor Hugo, Claude Debussy, and Jean Cocteau, for de Chérisey was also interested in surrealism. The whole list can be seen in *The Da Vinci Code*. Plantard and de Chérisey wrote together about fifteen "secret documents" of the priory and deposed them in the Bibliothèque Nationale. They were not meant to be read, but their presence in the library could be used as an argument for their authenticity. De Chérisey also produced two parchment sheets with a text composed by himself. The journalist Gérard de Sède published a book, *L'Or de Rennes* (1967), following Plantard's instructions, and here the relationship between the Priory of Sion and Rennes-le-Château was presented for the first time. During a conflict over the royalties from the book, de Chérisey declared that the deposed documents were not originals, only copies, but he never indicated the whereabouts of the originals.

In 1975 Plantard began to call himself Plantard St.-Clair. This Norman noble name connected him with the Scottish family Sinclair and thus with Rosslyn Chapel near Edinburgh and its "mysteries," well known to any reader of *The Da Vinci Code*. Great numbers of visitors have come to this church but have left it with disappointment, as the symbols described in the novel have never existed there.

So far this romance had nothing to do with Jesus. But the story entered a new phase when Plantard got into contact with Henry Lincoln, who was busy with writing the text of two television programs about Rennes-le-Château on BBC, shown in 1971. With Plantard's help, Lincoln got into contact with esoteric groups in Paris. Here he became acquainted with Robert Ambelain, the last "patriarch" of the Gnostic Church, a tiny and obscure society with roots in French occultism of the nineteenth century. Already in the 1960s, Ambelain had lost his Gnostic faith and wrote several books that depicted Jesus as a false messiah. In one of these books, Ambelain told a story about a love affair between Jesus and his female disciple Salome, a woman mentioned in the gospels. Lincoln found this story useful but understood that it would fit better into Plantard's myth if he changed Salome to Mary Magdalene. He could then more easily connect Jesus' supposed lover with France, the Merovingians, and the Priory of Sion, and so he did (Introvigne 2005).

According to a widespread medieval legend, Mary Magdalene and some other personalities from the gospels had traveled by boat to the south of France and had landed in the Rhône delta at a place later called Saintes-Maries-de-la-Mer. According to the Lincoln myth, she gave birth to her child in France and thus gave rise to the Merovingian dynasty and finally to Plantard himself. Thus Plantard, as the supposed heir of the Merovingians, became a descendant of Jesus and Mary Magdalene, with the Priory of Sion preserving the documents that authenticated this bloodline.

Baigent and Leigh incorporated this story into their mystification as it was presented in books and on television, and the bloodline from Jesus and Mary Magdalene soon became its main point. But Plantard was not happy with it, and it created a breach between him and Lincoln. In 1986 he also dissociated himself from de Chérisey's version of the Priory of Sion and created an entirely new story. This time it had been founded in Rennes-le-Château in 1681. Plantard discarded the former list of grand masters and produced another list, which included Roger-Patrice Pelat, a friend of president Mitterrand. This was an unlucky choice, for shortly afterwards Pelat was arrested as a central figure in a great corruption scandal, and Plantard was suspected of being part of it. The judge had his house searched, and all the papers were found with his claims to the French throne. He was never prosecuted but received a sharp admonition and withdrew from public life. I later saw a television program on the Discovery channel, in which Henry Lincoln once more tried to interview him, but Plantard refused to let him in and gave only evasive answers through the chink of the door.

These events are of general interest for the study of modern Jesus tales, for they give us rich information about the patterns according to which modern myths are being created. This myth was from its very beginning the outcome of a private person's vanity and desire for royal honor, and, after all changes and additions, it ended up as something totally different, a theory of the relationship between Jesus and Mary Magdalene. Themes arise and are mixed, they appear and disappear in new combinations as in a kaleidoscope, and there is no final result that may be anticipated.

Mary Magdalene as a feminist symbol

Dan Brown understood that his American readers would not take an interest in French royalist speculations and therefore excluded these from his novel. On the other hand, he introduced some feminist themes that do not appear in the original myth. He derived this material from two American writers, Margaret Starbird and Lynn Picknett, who depend on Baigent, Leigh, and Lincoln. A kind of feminist branch of this ramified mystification has therefore appeared, centered on the figure of Mary Magdalene.

Mary from Magdala plays an important role in the gospel tradition, as the first witness of the risen Jesus (Mark 16:9; John 20:11–18). The gospels mention her twelve times, more than any other woman except the mother of Jesus, but they give few details about her life. They do say that Jesus delivered her from seven demons, that she stood at the cross together with other women, and that she was among those women who first saw the empty tomb. They say nothing about her age. That she was young and beautiful is an invention of Renaissance art; she may just as well have been an old woman. The common view of her as a converted prostitute is a medieval construction, created by identifying her with other women in the gospels.

The feminists of today have taken a great interest in Mary Magdalene and have generously given her new roles in Christian history. In reaction against the dominance of males in the apostolic church, from the twelve apostles and forward, they have attempted to find traditions according to which women would have had a greater importance in the first Christian communities. It is generally recognized that women are given more prominent positions in the genuine Pauline letters than in the somewhat later pastoral letters of the New Testament, so this quest for female influence is certainly a legitimate trace to follow.

But the New Testament evidence is unfortunately scarce, and many feminist theologians have therefore turned their attention to post-apostolic Gnostic litera- ture, to writings such as the *Gospel of Mary* (= Mary Magdalene) and the *Gospel of Philip*, where Mary Magdalene has a prominent place. This evidence has then been used to argue that women played a more leading role in early Christianity, at least in some branches of it, and that this social order was thwarted by their adversaries, led by the apostle Peter.

Such speculations still belong to the area of scholarly theories, and they may therefore be considered legitimate, although they are disputed. As a side effect, however, they have inspired a number of fictitious writings about Mary Magdalene, totally independent of any scholarly criticism. This development is noticeable in some books by Margaret Starbird and Lynn Picknett, already mentioned. These works show up in *The Da Vinci Code*. When Sophie Neveu visits Leigh Teabing – whose name is an allusion to Leigh and Baigent – he tells her that "the royal blood- line of Jesus Christ has been chronicled in exhaustive detail by scores of historians." Teabing then runs his finger down a row of several dozen books while Sophie scans the list of titles (Brown 2003). The titles that she sees are first, *The Templar Revelation: Secret Guardians of the True Identity of Christ*; second, *The Woman with the Alabaster Jar: Mary Magdalene and the Holy Grail*; and third, *The Goddess in the Gospels: Reclaiming the Sacred Feminine*. Teabing then adds what is "perhaps the best-known tome," *Holy Blood, Holy Grail*.

This is the only passage in the novel where Dan Brown openly discloses his sources. *The Templar Revelation* is written by Lynn Picknett and Clive Prince (1997), the other two books by Margaret Starbird, all adherents of the Mary Magdalene myth. They are certainly not historians.

The subtitle of *The Woman with the Alabaster Jar* (1993) clearly indicates the source of its inspiration: *Mary Magdalene and the Holy Grail*. It is totally dependent on Baigent's and Leigh's story. As Starbird tells us in the introduction to this book, her reading of *Holy Blood, Holy Grail* caused a total change in her view of life. She left the Catholic church and now professes "the Grail heresy," the myth of a bloodline from Jesus and Mary Magdalene. In her second book, *The Goddess in the Gospels* (1998), and in *Magdalene's Lost Legacy* (2003), she develops her idea of a sacred union between Jesus and Mary Magdalene as "the Bride of Christ" and regards it as a way of awakening "the Sacred Feminine." She supports her idea with supposed coded messages, "symbolic numbers," in the gospels.

A more freewheeling elaboration of this theme is *The Templar Revelation* by Lynn Picknett and Clive Prince (1997). Here we learn that Mary Magdalene was an

Egyptian priestess dedicated to the Osiris cult. Jesus came to Egypt as her adept, and they practiced sexual rites together. This tale may be compared with the secret rite witnessed by Sophie Neveu in *The Da Vinci Code*. From being regarded as a common whore, the poor Mary Magdalene has now gone the whole way round to become a posh temple prostitute. This book is also based on *Holy Blood, Holy Grail*, but in Picknett's version Jesus and Mary Magdalene are not married. In a later book, *Mary Magdalene: Christianity's Hidden Goddess* (2003), written by Lynn Picknett on her own, she repudiates the tales of the Priory of Sion and of Rennes-le-Château, but at this time *The Da Vinci Code* had already been published.

Other writers, such as Lionel Fanthorpe (2004) and Laurence Gardner (1996; 2005; 2008), have latched on to the same theme but apparently for commercial reasons without any ideological motivation. I cannot see that they deserve our attention, as they do nothing to lead the mystification into new tracks worth noticing.

The story continues

There is a continuing stream of literature focused on the Priory of Sion, on Rennes-le-Château, and on Rosslyn Chapel, in which Mary Magdalene is only of secondary importance. Some of these books may be classified as Jesus apocrypha. Most notable is *The Tomb of God* by Richard Andrews and Paul Schellenberger (2005), with the astounding theory that Jesus was buried in Rennes-le-Château. Their argument is based on nothing more than an inscription on a gravestone that once stood on private ground in the neighborhood but that has now been destroyed. A tomb with the same inscription appears on a painting by the French artist Nicolas Poussin (1594–1665), and it is part of the myth that Poussin had this monument in mind when he made his painting. This is, however, not very likely, as the gravestone seems not to have been erected until 1932.

The inscription, *Et in arcadia ego*, "I [= death] am also in Arcadia," has been given various interpretations in the myths surrounding Rennes-le-Château. Andrews and Schellenberger suggest that it is an anagram for *arcam dei tango iesu*, understood as "I touch the tomb of God, Jesus," and they draw the conclusion that this grave is his burial-place. The sentence, however, is not as unique and mysterious as they claim but has a long and well-known history. Lest the reader waste time with the different interpretations of the inscription, I recommend the excellent essay with the same title by Erwin Panofsky ([1955] 1993). Not unexpectedly, a team is now preparing to dig in search of the tomb of Mary Magdalene in the same area. Rennes-le-Château has become a place of pilgrimage for those who are eager to learn about "unsolved mysteries." A sound evaluation of this entire complex is carried out in a book by Bill Putnam and John Edwin Wood (2005).

Picknett and Prince have since then published several pseudo-historical books on similar themes. In *The Sion Revelation* (2006), they put forward a theory that the

Priory of Sion was a secret political organization, completely misunderstood by Plantard. In *The Masks of Christ* (2008) they have trodden in the footsteps of nineteenth-century biblical critics, uncovering the gospel narratives as lies and distortions. The final truth found under the many masks is, not unexpectedly, the relationship between Jesus and Mary Magdalene.

The bestselling author Tim Wallace-Murphy, specializing in Knights Templar and freemasonry, continuously publishes a flood of books about Rennes-le-Château, Rosslyn, and Lincoln's Grail myth, often written in cooperation with other writers. Most noticed is *Rex Deus* (2000), in which he develops the idea that the bloodline of Jesus and Mary Magdalene was derived from a priestly hierarchy in Jerusalem. More disclosures are likely to follow.

On facts and theories

As already noted, there is an obvious difference between earlier forgers of written sources and the new mythmakers, who pick up their arguments wherever they can find them. There is, however, also a difference between the old and the new world. Manuscripts from biblical times are mostly found in the Middle East or in European archives, and consequently forged Jesus apocrypha have generally been created in Europe. The *Book of Mormon* (Beskow 1985, 31–41) and Levi Dowling's *Aquarian Gospel* (Beskow 1985, 75–80) were both written in the United States, but neither of them included the alleged find of an ordinary manuscript. Joseph Smith's golden plates were revealed by an angel, who then took them back; Dowling never claimed that he had access to a manuscript. The *Secret Gospel of Mark*, whatever can be said about its authenticity, was found in Palestine, and the documents of the Priory of Sion were allegedly discovered in France. The forgers thus imitate the researchers, but instead of analyzing ancient manuscripts they produce their own writings.

The myths produced in the United States are generally of a different character and often based on published texts, authentic or not. This difference can be regarded as a funhouse mirror, in which the distinction between European and American research is distorted and revealed. In European university libraries and archives, there are still numerous unpublished manuscripts from antiquity and the Middle Ages. They are just lying there, waiting to be published or to become the subject of a doctoral dissertation. Most editions of such manuscripts never reach the general public but are only discussed in academic seminars. Sometimes a new find of a manuscript may arouse an interest in the media, but no scholar can expect such a happy discovery. The sensational manuscript text, rocking the world, remains a dream. The scholar's editing work is laborious and time-consuming, and it seldom receives attention outside the academic world. The European confusion of languages also limits the dissemination of the research. A French scholar has difficulties reaching a German audience and vice versa.

In the United States it is different. There is no great supply of old manuscripts, for European archives have always been unwilling to part with them. Most research has to be based on works that have already been edited and published. This situation saves the scholars the labor of deciphering the original documents and gives them a chance to theorize for themselves about given texts. A great part of antique and medieval literature is now available on the net and in CD versions. Such texts are therefore easily read in the original languages with critical notes, but they are still editions and not original manuscripts. There are well-known American scholars who specialize in paleography; some of them took part in the debate about the *Secret Gospel of Mark*. Nevertheless they are a minority in the vast academic world of the United States.

In the American academic world – increasingly also in European universities – students live under a constant pressure, forcing them to demonstrate their academic efficiency by publishing scholarly works. One road to success is constructing new and bold theories around a given text. This method attracts attention, leads to academic success, and may attract a wider public. Such a procedure may lead to the misuse of source material in order to sustain an already given theory. This tendency of propagating instead of analyzing may tomorrow be taken over by quite a different ideology, which turns out to be selling.

In the footsteps of the academic theorists the mythmakers follow, writers like Margaret Starbird and Lynn Picknett, who appear with pseudo-academic pretensions and freely create new myths in a mixture of private imagination and pure falsification. Face to face with these myths, the old forgeries fade away as ineffective. The border between fact and fiction is blurred, and it is understandable how a thriller like *The Da Vinci Code* could be believed by many to be a historical authority outdoing generations of scholarly research.

It is a common goal among serious scholars to distinguish between given facts, which may be dull, and theoretical constructions, which may be fascinating, and to always stick to the factual basis of their scholarly work. By doing this they may also counteract that new and less serious universe of imagination taken over in the media and in the public consciousness.

References

Ahmad, Mirza Ghulam ([1890] 1923). *The Triumph of Islam (Fath-i-Islam)*. Trans. Basheer Ahmad Sayeed. Madras: Guardian Press. At http://aaiil.org/text/books/mga/triumphislamfathislam/triumphislamfathislam.shtml (accessed April 11, 2010).

Ahmad, Mirza Ghulam ([1880–1905] 1955). *Barahin-i-Ahmadiyya*. Trans. Mirza Masum Beg. Lahore: Ahmadiyya Anjaman Ishaat-i-Islam. At http://aaiil.org/text/books/mga/barahinahmadiyya/barahinahmadiyya.shtml (accessed April 11, 2010).

Ahmad, Mirza Ghulam ([1899] 1989). *Jesus in India*. Leyton, UK: Islam International.

Andrews, Richard, and Paul Schellenberger (2005). *The Tomb of God: Unlocking the Code to a 2000-Year-Old Mystery*. London: Little, Brown.

Baigent, Michael, Richard Leigh, with Henry Lincoln (1982). *The Holy Blood and the Holy Grail*. London: Jonathan Cape. Published in the U.S. as *Holy Blood, Holy Grail*. New York: Delacorte, 1982.

Baigent, Michael, Richard Leigh, with Henry Lincoln (1986). *The Messianic Legacy*. London: Jonathan Cape.

Beskow, Per (1981). *Jesus i Kashmir* (in Swedish). Stockholm: Proprius.

Beskow, Per (1985). *Strange Tales about Jesus*. 2nd edn. Philadelphia: Fortress.

Brown, Dan (2003). *The Da Vinci Code*. New York: Doubleday.

Cirillo, Luigi, and Michel Fremaux (1977). *Évangile de Barnabé*. Paris: Beauchesne.

Dallison, Jaydee, ed. (1993). *The Essene Elder's Letter: The Crucifixion and the Resurrection of Jesus by an Eyewitness*. Cary, NC: J. Dallison.

Dowling, Levi (2002). *The Aquarian Gospel of Jesus the Christ*. London: Daniel.

Eco, Umberto (1988). *Foucault's Pendulum*. Harcourt Brace Jovanovich.

Faber-Kaiser, Andreas (1978). *Jesus Died in Kashmir*. London: Gordon & Cremonesi.

Fanthorpe, Lionel, and Patricia Fanthorpe (2004). *Mysteries of Templar Treasures and the Holy Grail: The Secrets of Rennes-le-Château*. York Beach, ME: Red Wheel/Weiser.

Gardner, Laurence (1996). *Bloodline of the Grail: The Hidden Lineage of Jesus Revealed*. Shaftesbury, UK: Element.

Gardner, Laurence (2005). *The Magdalene Legacy: The Jesus and Mary Bloodline Conspiracy*. New York: Barnes & Noble.

Gardner, Laurence (2008). *The Grail Enigma: Hidden Heirs of Jesus and Mary Magdalene*. Harper Element.

Goodspeed, Edgar J. (1956). *Modern Apocrypha*. Boston: Beacon.

Introvigne, Massimo (2005). *Gli Illuminati e il Priorato di Sion*. Milan: Piemme.

Jacobovici, Simcha, and Charles R. Pellegrino (2007). *The Jesus Family Tomb: The Discovery, the Investigation, and the Evidence That Could Change History*. San Francisco: Harper.

Kasser, Rodolphe, Marvin Meyer, and Gregor Wurst, eds. (2006). *The Gospel of Judas*. Washington, DC: National Geographic Society.

Knohl, Israel (2009). *Messiahs and Resurrection in "The Gabriel Revelation."* New York: Continuum.

Lang, David Marshall (1957). *The Wisdom of Balahvar: A Christian Legend of the Buddha*. London: Allen & Unwin; New York: Macmillan.

Müller, Max (1894). "The Alleged Sojourn of Christ in India." *The Nineteenth Century* 36 (April): 515–516.

Neusner, Jacob (1993). *Are There Really Tannaitic Parallels to the Gospels? A Refutation of Morton Smith*. Atlanta, GA: Scholars.

Notovitch, Nicolas (1894). *La Vie Inconnue de Jésus-Christ*. Paris: Paul Ollendorf.

Panofsky, Erwin ([1955] 1993). "*Et in Arcadia Ego*: Poussin and the Elegiac Tradition." In *Meaning in the Visual Arts* (pp. 340–367). Harmondsworth: Penguin.

Picknett, Lynn (2003). *Mary Magdalene: Christianity's Hidden Goddess*. New York: Carroll & Graf.

Picknett, Lynn, and Clive Prince (1997). *The Templar Revelation: Secret Guardians of the True Identity of Christ*. New York: Simon & Schuster.

Picknett, Lynn, and Clive Prince (2006). *The Sion Revelation: The Truth about the Guardians of Christ's Sacred Bloodline*. New York: Simon & Schuster.

Picknett, Lynn, and Clive Prince (2008). *The Masks of Christ: Behind the Lies and Cover-ups About the Life of Jesus*. New York: Simon & Schuster.

Putnam, Bill, and John Edwin Wood (2005). *The Treasure of Rennes-le-Château: A Mystery Solved*. Stroud, UK: The History Press.

Sède, Gérard de (1967). *L'Or de Rennes*. Paris: René Julliard. English translation: *The Accursed Treasure of Rennes-le-Château*. Trans. Bill Kessey. Worcester Park, Surrey: DEK, 2002.

Smith, Morton (1973a). *Clement of Alexandria and a Secret Gospel of Mark*. Cambridge: Harvard University Press.

Smith, Morton (1973b). *The Secret Gospel: The Discovery and Interpretation of the Secret Gospel According to Mark*. New York: Harper & Row.

Starbird, Margaret (1993). *The Woman with the Alabaster Jar: Mary Magdalene and the Holy Grail*. Rochester, VT: Bear.

Starbird, Margaret (1998). *The Goddess in the Gospels: Reclaiming the Sacred Feminine*. Rochester, VT: Bear.

Starbird, Margaret (2003). *Magdalene's Lost Legacy: Symbolic Numbers and the Sacred Union in Christianity*. Rochester, VT: Bear.

Thompson, Damian (2008). *Counterknowledge*. London: Atlantic Books.

Wallace-Murphy, Tim, Marilyn Hopkins, and Graham Simmans (2000). *Rex Deus: The True Mystery of Rennes-le-Château*. Nelson, New Zealand: Element.

Winternitz, Maurice (1963). *A History of Indian Literature*. 1.2. 2nd edn. Calcutta: University of Calcutta.

Further Reading

King, Karen L. (2003). *The Gospel of Mary of Magdala: Jesus and the First Woman Apostle*. Santa Rosa, CA: Polebridge.

Picknett, Lynn (2006). *The Secret History of Lucifer and the Meaning of the True Da Vinci Code*. New York: Carroll & Graf.

Puech, Henri-Charles, and Beate Blatz, eds. (1992). "The Gospel of Mary." In Wilhelm Schneemelcher (ed.), *New Testament Apocrypha*. Vol. 1: *Gospels and Related Writings* (pp. 391–394). Trans. R. McL. Wilson. Louisville, KY: Westminster John Knox.

Schenke, Hans-Martin, ed. (1992). "The Gospel of Philip." In Wilhelm Schneemelcher (ed.), *New Testament Apocrypha*. Vol. 1: *Gospels and Related Writings* (pp. 179–208). Trans. R. McL. Wilson. Louisville, KY: Westminster John Knox.

Smith, Wilfred Cantwell (1960). "Ahmadiyya." In *Encyclopedia of Islam*. 2nd edn. Leiden: Brill.

Wallace-Murphy, Tim, and Marilyn Hopkins (2000). *Rosslyn: Guardian of the Secrets of the Holy Grail*. Nelson, New Zealand: Element.

PART VI

Jesus in Art, Fiction, and Film

29   Jesus in Christian Art   477
     Robin M. Jensen

30   Jesus Novels: Solving Problems with Fiction   504
     Zeba A. Crook

31   Jesus in Film   519
     Adele Reinhartz

CHAPTER 29

Jesus in Christian Art

Robin M. Jensen

The Orthodox defender of icons, John of Damascus, justified making an image of Christ by arguing that as God incarnate Jesus had a visible bodily appearance. Denying Christian followers a physical likeness of Christ, if only in art, deprived them of the chance to gaze upon Christ's suffering and to marvel at God's condescension to human form and the holiness reflected in it. Such denial was, in his view, inspired by a jealous devil, the hater of humankind (John of Damascus, *Apol.* 2.6). John's concern was not only for the depth and quality of Christian devotion, but also for the very heart of Christian dogma – the Savior was born to a human mother and, as a bodily being, appeared to followers, onlookers, enemies, and even innocent bystanders in the thirty-plus years of his earthly sojourn. He had a face, and people could see him.

Asserting Christ's visibility is a counterpart of the equally Orthodox claim that the eternal Godhead is inaccessible to ordinary, mortal human gaze. Moses was denied a glimpse of God's face (Ex 33:20), even though the Bible records that both Abraham and Jacob were afforded such sight (Gen 18:1; 32:30), and both Isaiah and Ezekiel were granted visions of God (Isa 6:1; Ezek 1:1). John of Damascus, along with other iconophiles, nevertheless clearly articulated the difference between the invisible, eternal Godhead and the incarnate one, who (as such) manifests the Divine Nature to mortal sight. It is impossible, he said, to make an image of the uncircumscribable Godhead; it is sinful even to try (*Apol.* 2.5). Jesus, however, was not only the visible incarnation of the divine Word, but also the perceptible icon of the invisible God (Col 1:15).

Despite the fact that Christ had a visible body while on earth, the writers of the four canonical gospels never described his physical appearance. Furthermore, according to them, his post-resurrection appearance must have been unrecognizable, since his disciples failed to identify him in the garden (John 20:14), on the beach (John 21:4), or along the road to Emmaus (Luke 24:16). Moreover, the fact that

The Blackwell Companion to Jesus, First Edition. Edited by Delbert Burkett. ©2014 John Wiley & Sons, Ltd. Published 2014 by John Wiley & Sons, Ltd.

Christ bore a physical body and visible appearance does not necessarily justify making artistic representations of his likeness. Many early Christian writers (e.g., Tertullian, Clement, and Origen) expressed anxiety about idolatry – confusing a human-made artifact for its departed model and offering it homage or adoration. This was, in their view, a demonic attempt to seduce devotees to worship sensible creation rather than the transcendent Creator (Jensen 2005, 9–10).[1]

Yet even those who most strongly repudiated the making of idols did not define visual art as intrinsically idolatrous. So long as viewers were not tempted to worship objects manufactured from base materials (paint, wood, stone), visual representations could serve useful purposes, as Gregory the Great argued (*Ep.* 9.105; 11.13). And, in fact, among the earliest material evidence for Christianity are artworks that depict figures from both testaments of the Bible (e.g., Adam and Eve, Abraham, Daniel, and Jonah) along with New Testament scenes of Jesus teaching, healing, and working wonders.

Such images reminded Christian viewers of the sacred narratives they had heard read in the assembly or retold (with their meanings expounded) in homilies or catechetical lessons. Pictures of this sort adorned tombs, church walls, and even ordinary household objects (e.g., lamps and bowls). Eventually, as the Christian community became more materially and politically secure, such images also adorned grand basilicas and liturgical furnishings and illuminated sacred books.

At the beginning, Christian visual art represented Jesus more or less symbolically, in the guise of a caretaking shepherd. By the end of the third century, he was depicted as a teacher and then later as a miracle-worker. Works of art showing certain events of his life – his infancy and baptism – also date to the late third and early fourth century. By the mid-fourth century these scenes included Christ riding into Jerusalem on a donkey, being arrested, and standing before Pilate. Significantly, the single most common image in Christian art – the crucifix – emerged only much later.

In contrast to images of the Greco-Roman gods, these compositions were not designed to invite veneration. They were, for the most part, two-dimensional visual presentations of particular scripture episodes. By the early fifth century, however, portraits of Christ emerged (along with likenesses of the Virgin Mary, the apostles, saints, and angels). Unlike earlier narrative iconography, these frontally composed likenesses directed the viewer to contemplate Christ's physical appearance as such and even to experience a kind of face-to-face engagement. As a focus for prayer or meditation, the development of the icon inevitably led to renewed concern about idolatry, both in the eastern iconoclastic debate and the Protestant Reformation critique of visual art.

Through this historical process, diverse presentations of Jesus evolved, most of them reflecting their particular culture, sect, or era. Theological stances are visually expressed in how communities depict (or do not depict) Jesus. They may portray him as a king upon a throne, a mild and thoughtful teacher, a worker of miracles, the giver of a new law, a suffering figure upon a cross, a beautiful savior, a judge separating the saved from the damned, or the creator of the cosmos, just to list a few of his personae in visual art (see Pelikan 1997; MacGregor 2000). Most recently, artists have presented Jesus as a liberator, as a superhero, as having different racial traits or ethnicities, or even as a woman.

Some Christians would deem all visual depictions insufficient, while others accept all of them as manifesting some degree of truth. What is certain is that the variations have been – and always will be – reflections of the beliefs about Jesus by different groups of Christians in different times and places. This chapter examines the emergence of Christian depictions of Jesus as well as certain overarching themes in Christian iconography of Christ, particularly as they emerge in antiquity and, to a lesser degree, as they are developed or transformed during the Middle Ages and Early Modernity.

Earliest Depictions of Jesus

Surviving evidence for the earliest Christian art dates to the late second or early third century, belongs mostly to the environs of Rome, and comes largely from a funereal context, that is, the paintings and relief sculpture found in underground burial tunnels and chambers known as the catacombs. Although an unknown (but certainly vast) body of evidence has been lost or remains undiscovered, the significant exceptions to this dominance of Roman, sepulchral material tend to demonstrate a certain degree of consistency of motif, if not style, in the canon of early Christian iconography.

These earliest surviving Christian artworks depict Jesus as Good Shepherd and Teacher of True Philosophy. Adaptations of contemporary Greco-Roman iconographic themes, these two figures emphasized the Christian Savior's attributes as a loving caretaker and source of true wisdom.

Jesus as Good Shepherd

The image of Jesus as a Good Shepherd was as commonplace in the early church as it is today. It appears more than 120 times in extant Roman catacomb frescoes alone (see figure 1). It also appears in relief on sarcophagi, in funerary epitaphs, as small statuettes, in mosaics, and on lamps, gems, and metalwork. It also appears in baptismal chambers as, for example, over the font of Dura Europos' house church, and among the ceiling mosaics of the late fourth-century baptistery of San Giovanni in Fonte in Naples.

Two distinct reasons may account for the shepherd's popularity. First, the Bible frequently employs the figure as a symbol of God's provident care. Among the best known of these references are the shepherd of Psalm 23 and Jesus' self-identification as the Good Shepherd in John 10:1–19. Other biblical texts include Isaiah 40:11 ("He will feed his flock like a shepherd, he will gather the lambs in his arms"), Ezekiel 34:31 ("You are my sheep, the sheep of my pasture, and I am your God"), and Matthew 18:12–14 (the parable of the lost sheep).[2]

Figure 1 Jesus as the Good Shepherd. Catacomb of Peter and Marcellinus. © The International Catacomb Society. Photo: Estelle Brettman.

Second, the figure of a shepherd with a sheep or ram over his shoulders was a well-known Greco-Roman motif, often representing Hermes as a guide for departed souls.

Given its biblical basis and pre-existing popularity, Christians naturally viewed the faithful shepherd as a figure of Jesus. The visual image had parallels in early Christian literature, including the second-century visions of Hermas, the *Hymn to Christ the Shepherd* (attributed to Clement of Alexandria), and the epitaph of Abercius, a second-century bishop of Hierapolis who described himself as a "disciple of the pure shepherd who feeds his flock on hills and plains" (see Jensen 2000, 37–41).

By the late fourth century, the shepherd also became identified with the clergy (thus not only with Christ). As the administrator of baptism and the earthly care-taker of the flock, the bishop was particularly associated with the shepherd, whose crook became the episcopal crosier – a symbol of his rank and role.

Gradually, a single lamb came to represent Christ as the "Lamb of God," which symbolized his atoning sacrifice (cf. John 1:29; Rev 5:6–10). Both images – Jesus as shepherd and as sacrificial lamb – endured. One of the best-known examples of recent centuries is Bernhard Plockhorst's 1930s illustration of Jesus as Good Shepherd, reprinted in countless Sunday school texts, funeral programs, and church bulletins. Much as it did in antiquity, the shepherd image has particular resonance with those who understand Christ as a tender, faithful, and protective guardian of his flock.

Jesus as Teacher of True Philosophy

A late third-century sarcophagus fragment, now in Rome's Palazzo Massimo, shows Jesus surrounded by his disciples and wearing the traditional *pallium* (a kind of rec-tangular stole) of the Greek philosopher. His beard, bare chest, and sandaled feet add to this identification. His left hand grasps a scroll while his raised right hand, palm forward with two fingers raised indicates that he is speaking.

Somewhat similar images appear a decade or two later, in Rome's catacomb of Domitilla and in the Via Anapo Catacomb. In these instances, Christ sits in a high-backed chair flanked by his apostles. Here, however, rather than bearded and bare-chested, Christ is beardless and dressed in the recognized garb of a Roman citizen of senatorial rank – a white tunic decorated with two vertical purple stripes. Despite their differences, these images portray Jesus as a teacher like Socrates or Plato – but better (since his is the true philosophy).

This image accords with the writings of early Christian apologists, who presented Christ as the divine Logos who reveals true wisdom, and Christianity as the sur-passingly worthy philosophical school (Mathews 1993, 109–111).[3] Portraying Christ as the eternal Word or Reason also reflects their efforts to make Christianity appeal to an intellectual elite who might otherwise have viewed it as a superstitious cult.

The image of Jesus as teacher lost popularity in the early medieval West, although eastern icons of Jesus holding an open book and offering a blessing are often identi-fied as "Christ the Teacher." However, with the emergence of Renaissance human-ism, followed by the emphases and values of the Protestant Reformation and, finally, in line with Enlightenment attitudes, artists recast Jesus as a preacher and peda-gogue – a giver of parables, humanistic values, and exhortations to do good works – more than as a wonder-worker or sacrificial victim.

Examples of this renewed stress on Christ as teacher include representations of Jesus blessing the children or defending the woman taken in adultery, such as those

Figure 2   "Christ Healing the Sick." Rembrandt Harmensz van Rijn, ca. 1647. British Museum, London. Photo credit: © The Trustees of the British Museum/Art Resource, NY.

by Lucas Cranach the Elder (a close associate of Martin Luther). Depictions of the young Jesus in the Temple conversing with the rabbis (e.g., *Christ among the Doctors* by Albrecht Dürer) portray him as an adolescent prodigy. One of the most popular images of the seventeenth century was Rembrandt's etching of Christ preaching (1647–1649), often known as *The Hundred Guilder Print* (see figure 2). Based on the episode of the rich young man (Matt 19:16–22), Rembrandt presents Jesus exhorting a socially diverse audience, including wealthy burghers and supplicants seeking his healing touch.

Jesus as Healer and Wonder-Worker

From the late third through the mid-fourth century, New Testament narrative scenes appear that, for the most part, depict Christ's works – his miracles and wonders – as a way of visually expressing his divine power and status rather than simply his character (i.e., attentive shepherd) or attributes (teacher of divine Reason). Probably reflecting the popularity of certain gospel pericopes that were retold, elaborated, and interpreted in sermons, hymns, or prayers, the images present Christ

Figure 3 Jesus as healer and wonder-worker. Sarcophagus of Marcia Romania Celsa, Musée départemental Arles antique. Photo credit: Author (used with permission).

healing the sick and the lame, raising the dead, multiplying loaves of bread, and changing water to wine. These acts reveal him to viewers as a Savior God who rescues people in distress – the ill, the hungry, the dying, and the mourning.

The miracle episode that appears most frequently in early Christian art is of Jesus multiplying loaves and fishes. Following this in frequency are three episodes that are unique to or prominent in the Fourth Gospel: Jesus changing water to wine at Cana, Jesus calling Lazarus from his tomb, and Jesus healing the man born blind. Next most frequent are depictions of Jesus healing the paralytic, Jesus healing the hemorrhaging woman, Jesus meeting the Samaritan woman at the well, and Jesus raising other dead individuals (e.g., Jairus' daughter). In many of these, particularly in scenes that show him multiplying loaves, changing water to wine, or raising the dead, Jesus wields a staff (see figure 3, left side). Historians sometimes describe this as a magician's wand, but it probably is more appropriately likened to the miracle-working rods of Aaron and Moses (cf. Ex 7:8, 17, 20 etc., and Ex 17:5–6) (see Mathews 1993, 54–61). By contrast, in most of the healing scenes, Jesus performs the act by an imposition of his hand (see figure 3, right side).

Although representations of Christ as healer appear with some frequency in illuminated manuscripts and on luxury objects of ivory or precious metal (as well as in the monumental mosaics in the twelfth-century Cathedral of Monreale), they are relatively less common in the early Middle Ages, possibly because of the increasing importance of saints (and their relics) as sources of miraculous cures. Then, when the miracle depictions regained popularity in the Renaissance, they served more as evidence of Jesus' compassion for the suffering or needy than as signs that reveal his power and glory. Some of these episodes belong to narrative cycles of Christ's life, such as those in Duccio di Buoninsegna's great altarpiece known as the *Maesta* (1308–1311).

Others artists likewise depicted Christ as a benevolent caregiver or effective wonder-worker, but as one who often went unnoticed in bustling urban settings. El Greco's several compositions of Christ healing the blind man (ca. 1567–1575) show the event as taking place among a distracted crowd. Paintings of the marriage at Cana became opportunities for colorful depictions of everyday life, with boisterous wedding guests, servants, tables heaped with food, and even dogs and cats scrounging for scraps, rather than a simple visual record of Christ's first miracle. Those who observe are astonished, but the frame is also filled with a great many who miss the miracle.

Episodes from Christ's Life in Visual Art

Exceptions to the early Christian visual emphasis on Jesus as healer and wonder-worker are depictions of his birth and earthly life, especially the relatively popular images of the adoration of the Magi and of John baptizing him in the Jordan. Extremely rare scenes of Christ walking on water or stilling the storm appear in the baptisteries of Dura Europos and San Giovanni in Fonte, Naples. Episodes from the passion, including Christ entering Jerusalem and his trial before Pilate, appear in the fourth century, but Christ's crucifixion and resurrection are not depicted before the fifth century, and not commonly before the ninth or tenth century. The Last Supper is almost entirely absent in early Christian art before the sixth century. By the early Middle Ages, however, images of the nativity, of Christ bearing his cross, and his death by crucifixion became far more dominant than representations of him as teacher or healer.

The nativity and the adoration of the Magi

Contrary to the art of later centuries, for which the nativity is a prominent theme, only a few depictions of Jesus in the manger appear in early Christian art. Of these, most show Mary and often include the ox, ass, and shepherds, but rarely Joseph. One exception to this occurs on the throne of Archbishop Maximian of Ravenna (ca. 550).

The adoration of the Magi is the most common nativity scene in early Christian art. The earliest examples (late third century) show the Christ child, in profile, sitting

Figure 4 Madonna and Child, mid-sixth century. From the Basilica of Sant'
Apollinare Nuovo, Ravenna. Photo credit: Author.

on his mother's lap receiving the visitors. The Magi, normally three in number, are
identical in dress and age, and come forward single file to present their gifts. As
before, Joseph is usually absent from the setting, possibly in order to stress the Virgin
Mary's singular role in the story of salvation.

The adoration image may have been intended to express certain theological arguments about the nature of the child. In early Christian exegesis, the three gifts specifically indicate that the baby is simultaneously king (gold), God (incense), and
doomed to die in order to overcome death (myrrh).[4] The story of the Magi was also
taken as a sign that the covenant was extended to the Gentiles (thus their exotic
foreign dress) and that Christ came to destroy pagan magic and idolatry.[5]

Later Christian visual art presents innumerable images of the nativity that harmonize the Lukan and Matthean infancy narratives. Mary and Joseph, along with midwife, shepherds, angels, animals, Magi, and servants are often shown all gathered together in a richly elaborated setting, adoring the helpless infant Jesus lying in his manger. Even more common are later images of Christ as a child in his mother's arms, which only began to appear in the fifth century but became one of the most beloved Christian icons from any time or place (see figure 4).

Other scenes from Christ's infancy (e.g., the flight into Egypt, the circumcision, or the presentation in the temple) rarely appear before the early Middle Ages. These episodes quickly became enormously popular in Christian art, possibly due to their inclusion in cycles celebrating the life of the Virgin Mary, and to the growing devotion to Christ's mother in both East and West. Tellingly, perhaps the earliest example of the presentation appears in the triumphal arch of Rome's Basilica of Santa Maria Maggiore, dedicated just after the Council of Ephesus declared Mary to be Mother of God (ca. 435).

Jesus' baptism by John the Baptist

In the earliest baptism iconography, Jesus nearly always appears as a young, nude child. John, who ordinarily wears some identifiable garb (e.g., a tunic made of animal skin), lays his right hand on Jesus' head. A dove descends from above. Witnesses or angels sometimes show up as well. A somewhat enigmatic addition to the composition is a figure who personifies the Jordan River, usually holding a jug that produces the stream, but in some instances shown partially submerged and witnessing Christ's baptism or turning away as if to flee from the scene.

The presentation of Jesus as a child probably demonstrates an aspect of the baptismal ritual – to return the initiate to the innocence of a newly born child – rather than indicating a common practice of infant baptism at this time. On the other hand, Christ's nakedness conforms to the practice of nude baptism, and John's gesture reflects the consecratory action of the bishop (imposition of hands for confirmation) immediately after the neophyte emerges from the bath. Later images of Christ's baptism depict him as an adult, yet also nude (see figure 5). The dove is always present, as is John the Baptist, but in certain later examples God the Father appears as a bearded elderly man, looking down from the sky. These representations of Christ with the Holy Spirit dove and God the Father were one way that artists depicted the Trinity, albeit as three visible figures.

Transfiguration

The first visual representation of the transfiguration appears in the apse of Sant' Apollinare in Classe, outside of Ravenna. An unusual composition, the mosaic (ca.

Figure 5   Baptism of Christ, late fifth or early sixth century. From the Arian Baptistery, Ravenna. Photo credit: Author.

549) shows a gemmed cross with a small, central bust portrait of Christ, floating in a starry sky that appears to be seen through a round opening in the apse. To the right and left of this window are Moses and Elijah. Below Peter, James, and John are depicted as lambs.

Almost simultaneously, the more traditional transfiguration composition emerged and is exemplified by the mid-sixth-century apse mosaic at St Catherine's Monastery in Sinai. Here Christ stands within a blue mandorla, rays of light beaming through his body. Moses and Elijah stand to each side, while Peter, James, and John kneel before the vision (see figure 6). This repeatedly copied image became, for Orthodox Christians, a way of demonstrating the validity of the icon as such, since Christ's divine nature became manifestly visible in this moment to his three disciples.

Entrance to Jerusalem

Jesus riding a donkey into Jerusalem first appeared in the art of the mid to late fourth century and quickly became one of the most popular of early Christian visual motifs, especially on Roman sarcophagi (see figure 7). As in other depictions of that time,

Figure 6 Transfiguration. Portable mosaic from Constantinople, ca. 1200 CE. Louvre Museum, Paris. Photo credit: Réunion des Musées Nationaux/Art Resource, NY.

Jesus wears a *pallium* draped over a tunic, has sandals on his feet, is beardless, and has long curling hair. He holds his staff in left hand and with his right makes a gesture of blessing. Someone places a cloak on the ground before him, and another figure is often shown above, in the branches of a tree, perhaps cutting boughs to cover his path (cf. Matt 21:8).

Slightly later Byzantine depictions of this same episode include angels and illustrate Christ as riding sidesaddle rather than straddling the donkey (see Mathews 1993, fn. 30, p. 41). The significance of this presentation is unclear, although at

Figure 7 Jesus' entry into Jerusalem, last quarter of the fourth century. Sarcophagus from the Vatican Museo Pio Cristiano. Photo credit: Author (used with permission).

least one scholar has argued that showing Jesus not only on a donkey but also riding sidesaddle entirely undercuts the identification of this image with an imperial *adventus* ceremony. Rather than showing Christ as a worldly king, it depicts him as a humble bringer of peace (Mathews 1993, 45, quoting John Chrysostom). Another possible explanation for Jesus' riding sidesaddle is that here the donkey is a throne rather than merely a means of transport.

Last Supper

Although scenes of diners at a table occur in the Roman catacombs and on early Christian sarcophagi, they cannot be identified as depictions of the Last Supper. Rather, they are more likely to be representations of a funerary meal, given the number of diners (usually seven) and the context (a tomb). Beginning in the sixth century, however, the image becomes more prominent, and usually depicts Jesus and the twelve seated on one side of a table set with bread and wine, along with platters of fish (see figure 8). In the earliest examples, Jesus reclines at the head of a semicircular table in the traditional Roman manner; his apostles also recline.

Figure 8   Last Supper, early sixth century. From the Basilica of Sant' Apollinare Nuovo, Ravenna. Photo credit: Sacred Destinations Images.

Later compositions, like the famous *Last Supper* of Leonardo da Vinci (1495–1498), tend to arrange the diners around three sides of a rectangular table, with Christ at the center, although Judas (identified by his money bag) often sits by himself at the foreground side. These later compositions also frequently depict the Beloved Disciple resting his head upon Jesus' breast – an image that was frequently presented by itself in the Middle Ages.

Arrest and trial

Significantly before images of Christ's crucifixion appeared with any frequency, scenes of the events that led up to his death – his arrest, trial before Pilate, crowning with thorns, and bearing of his cross – turned up first in fourth-century relief sculpture and then in sixth-century mosaics and manuscript illumination, thus creating a kind of preliminary passion cycle (see figure 9). These episodes usually occur adjacent to other events from the last days of Christ's life (e.g., his entry into Jerusalem,

Figure 9   Arrest and trial of Jesus, ca. 350. Sarcophagus from the Vatican Museo Pio Cristiano. Photo credit: Author (used with permission).

washing the disciples' feet, and Last Supper) or depictions of Peter and Paul going to their martyrdom, along with Old Testament figures such as Adam and Eve, Cain and Abel, or Job and his wife, as well as Abraham about to slay Isaac.

The scene of Christ before Pilate is especially notable in these compositions, particularly on the fourth-century sarcophagi from Rome. In most, Pilate is shown turned away from Christ, preparing to wash his hands. Featuring this particular episode may have signaled Pilate's exoneration as the one who condemned Christ. Unlike later passion iconography, which emphasizes Christ's flagellation, crowning with thorns, and mockery, these first compositions do not show Christ as suffering either pain or degradation. In fact, in an early image of Christ being crowned by a Roman soldier, he receives a wreath of laurel rather than of thorns – an indication of his victory rather than his humiliation (cf. figure 9). Likewise, the other images allude to his resurrection more than to his death –an association strengthened by the common inclusion of a central, empty cross.

Jesus on the cross

The image of Christ upon the cross is commonly assumed to be the most ancient and universal of Christian visual icons. Yet, however ubiquitous this image was in later centuries, it did not exist from the beginning and, in fact, was not at all common before the seventh or eighth century.

Certain rare early versions present controversial images, including the famous graffito found in Rome and now in the Palatine Museum that depicts a crucified donkey-headed figure being saluted by a man, along with the caption "Alexamenos worships his god." Some gems with carved images of the crucifix are usually dated to the fourth century. Apart from these are two small crucifixion scenes that date to the early fifth century, one of them a small wood panel from the doors of Rome's basilica of Santa Sabina (422–432; see figure 10), the other being one of four ivory

Figure 10   Jesus crucified, ca. 432. Panel from the wooden doors of Santa Sabina, Rome. Photo credit: Lee Jefferson.

panels that formed part of a small casket – the Maskell ivories – now in the British Museum.

The Santa Sabina image shows Christ with two smaller figures on either side (the two thieves). All three appear to be standing on the ground with their hands outstretched in the prayer (*orans*) posture more than being nailed or tied to crosses. The Maskell casket panel shows Christ upon the cross with the plaque over his head that announces that he is *REX IUD*, that is, "King of the Jews" (John 19:19). Mary and John stand on his right, looking downcast; a Roman soldier, looking up at Christ and making a gesture of awe, stands on his left (cf. Mark 15:39). To the left of the crucifixion scene Judas appears, hanging from a tree and creating a stark contrast with the living, almost vigorous body of Jesus on the cross.

The next oldest surviving images of Jesus on the cross come from the East: one from a sixth-century illumination in the gospels of Rabbula and others found on small tokens or holy-oil vials (*ampullae*) made for pilgrims to the Holy Land. The Rabbula gospel image shows Christ dressed in a sleeveless purple robe with two golden stripes (*colobium*). The two thieves on either side are nude apart from knotted undergarments (*perizomata*). Surrounding figures include Mary and John, the three witnessing women (John 19:25), Roman soldiers casting lots (John 19:24), and the two soldiers, traditionally named Longinus and Stephanus, holding a spear and a sponge dipped in vinegar (John 19:29, 34). These latter images, however, tend to show only a bust of Christ, floating above a cross, rather than depicting his actual crucifixion.

Scholars have suggested different reasons for this paucity of visual portrayals of Jesus' crucifixion, including the fact that such an image was initially scandalous. It may also have been too sacred a subject to allow visual depiction (Jensen 2007). That the crucifixion was a relatively unimportant subject for popular reflection is an untenable suggestion given the emphasis on Christ's passion narrative in homilies, poetry, and hymns of the early church. Furthermore, Abraham's offering of Isaac seems to have served as an alternative figure of the crucifixion, as it is often included in compositions that portrayed Jesus' arrest and trial. It seems most likely that a visual portrayal of Christ's death was too graphic for the sensibilities of early Christians, even though Roman art was not reticent about depicting violent, grue-some, or cruel acts (e.g., the flaying of Marsyas or depictions of gladiatorial games). The lack of crucifixion images may even be a reaction to this kind of iconography. Noteworthy too is the lack of martyrdom scenes, compared to the textual descriptions of martyrdom.

Although the first images show Jesus as nude or nearly nude upon the cross, wearing only a loincloth, later images show him dressed either in a royal purple robe (and sometimes crowned) or with a knotted undergarment. Whereas earlier images tended to show him as still alive and even passively enduring, beginning in the tenth century the iconography begins to emphasize his agony and death: his body slumps, his head sinks onto his chest, and his eyes are closed. This transformation might be aligned with a shift of emphasis from Jesus' divinity (and glory) to his humanity (and bodily suffering).

In time, the suffering image came to dominate, possibly in response to certain external events (the plague or the violence of war) or perhaps as a visual counterpart to the emotionally charged and imaginative character of high medieval piety, espe-cially as promoted by the mendicant orders. Along with this development, artists began to emphasize the grief of the bystanders – Jesus' mother and Mary Magdalene in particular. Images of deposition were especially colored by pathos and included weeping angels along with the agony of the Christ's followers.

Jesus resurrected, his post–resurrection appearances, and ascension

The empty cross or empty tomb appeared earlier than the crucifixion, possibly indi-cating that visual depictions of Christ's resurrection were more acceptable than presentations of his suffering, but also probably a way of showing the conclusion or triumphant, happy ending of the narrative. This is, arguably, why a resurrec-tion scene is often presented near to the earliest depictions of the crucifixion (e.g., the Santa Sabina doors, the Maskell ivory, the Syrian Rabbula gospels, and the pil-grimage *ampullae* from Palestine). The earliest presentations of the empty tomb are

Figure 11   Christ resurrected, Fra Angelico, 1438. Museo di San Marco, Florence. Photo credit: Erich Lessing/Art Resource, NY.

prototypes for many of the later examples, especially in their depiction of an aedicule tomb that must have looked something like the shrine that was constructed inside the Anastasis Rotunda attached to the Basilica of the Holy Sepulchre in Jerusalem.

   Unlike early Christian examples, later depictions of the resurrection include the figure of Christ, rising out of or floating above the tomb (see figure 11). These include works of the Renaissance masters Fra Angelico (1440–1441) and Piero della Francesca (1463), as well as one of the wings of Matthias Grünewald's famous Isenheim altarpiece (1510–1516). Other images present Christ harrowing Hell and, in particular, lifting Adam and Eve up from the depths while striding over a broken cross and bound figure of Satan. These images, known in the East as "Anastasis" (resurrection) icons appeared first in the seventh century and quickly became central to Orthodox iconography (Kartsonis 1986).

However, while resurrection images do not necessarily depict Jesus, images of his post-resurrection theophanies require his appearance. Some of the first images of Christ's post-resurrection appearances are included in the passion cycle of mosaics in Ravenna's Basilica of Sant' Apollinare Nuovo, while one of the wooden panels on the doors of Santa Sabina depicts Jesus within a circular wreath, surrounded by the four living creatures. Below, two males and one female gaze up at him while the sun and moon fill the intermediary space.[6] The ascension also appears in the Syrian gospels of Rabbula (ca. 586). This example, however, more closely follows Ezekiel's vision (Ezek 1:4–21), which became more standard in the East, as it portrays the four living creatures as a tetramorph with four faces and two pairs of eye-covered wings. Below, the Virgin Mary stands among the apostles, her hands raised in the posture of prayer.

Christ's post-resurrection epiphanies, especially to Mary Magdalene and to his disciples at Emmaus, became far more popular in later Christian works of art, some of which constitute great masterpieces of western art, including Titian's painting of Jesus appearing to Mary Magdalene, *Noli Me Tangere* (1510–1515), and Caravaggio's *Supper at Emmaus* (1606).

Dogmatic Themes

In the past, art historians tended to view early Christian art as primarily narrative or devotional; they did not see it as intrinsically engaged with dogmatic claims about God or salvation (Grabar 1968, 112). Yet, when certain early works represent the Trinity, or God the Father, it is difficult not to notice their doctrinal implications. Thus, at least one famous sarcophagus in the Vatican Museum is traditionally labeled the *Dogmatic Sarcophagus*, largely because it portrays the Trinity creating Adam and Eve (cf. figure 12, discussed below). Furthermore, all artworks depicting Jesus necessarily reinforce particular beliefs or reflect arguments that were circulating in the contemporary milieu among all classes of Christians.[7] Among the contended issues were the relationship of the Father and the Son, the role of the Son as creator, the Son's establishment of a new covenant with the church, and the Son's status as judge at the end of time.

Christ as one of the Trinity

In Rome's Domitilla catacomb, a rare, early Christian mosaic rises behind a tomb. Probably made during the third quarter of the fourth century, it shows Christ enthroned within a bright green aureole or mandorla. Peter and Paul sit slightly

Figure 12   Trinity creating Adam and Eve, mid-fourth century. Sarcophagus from the Vatican Museo Pio Cristiano. Photo credit: Author (used with permission).

below on either side, between them a container of scrolls. Above, a mosaic legend reads, *Qui filius diceris et pater inveneris* ("The one said to be the Son but revealed to be the Father"). Presumably, then, the mosaic depicts the moment when the disciples became fully aware of Christ's transcendent glory in order that they might proclaim it in their preaching and writing (indicated by the scrolls between their feet).

This mosaic was, perhaps, inspired by Jesus' words to Philip in the Gospel of John. In reply to Philip's request, "Lord, show us the Father and we will be satisfied," Jesus counters, "He who has seen me has seen the Father" (John 14:8–9). However, given the probable date of the composition, it may have been prompted by debates about the nature and person of Christ – whether he was God, fully, or rather a unique human being, especially chosen by God to be the Savior. The glowing green orb along with the Latin legend implies the former but also tends toward the heresy of monarchianism, which protected the unity of the divine being at the expense of asserting a Trinity of divine persons. The Son does not simply reveal the Father, but is revealed *to be* the Father.

Showing Christ as one of the Trinity occurs in rare, early depictions of God creating Adam and Eve (see figure 12). Attempts at depicting the Trinity in later medieval and Renaissance art included some compositions that showed the Holy Spirit as a dove hovering above God the Father, who holds the crucified Son in his arms, and others that showed both Father and Son crowning Mary as Queen of Heaven, with the dove fluttering between or over them. Diego Velázquez's altarpiece, *The Coronation of the Virgin* (1645) is an exceptionally good example of the latter. Traditional Orthodox icons of Abraham receiving his three visitors at Mamre (Gen 18) do not actually depict the Trinity but show three angels who symbolize the Triune Godhead.

Christ as creator

The prologue to the Gospel of John describes the Logos as he through whom all things came into being (John 1:3). This proclamation, that the eternal Word was not only present at creation but was active as creator was affirmed in early Christian teaching and in early Christian visual presentations of Jesus with Adam and Eve in the Garden of Eden.[8] In some of these images, Jesus-as-Logos appears even to look like Adam, perhaps a way to stress his role as "New Adam." In many he presents them with the symbols of their labors in the world outside Eden (cf. figure 12).

Showing Jesus as creator, and as present with Adam and Eve at their creation, fall, and expulsion was even more typical of medieval art, where it appeared in frescoes, illuminated manuscripts (e.g., the Canterbury Psalter), panel painting (Giovanni di Paolo, 1445), and mosaics (e.g., the Creation cupola in Venice's Cathedral of San Marco). As in the earlier iconography, these images underscore the role of Christ (pre-incarnation) as creator, in some instances even showing him holding the tools of an architect (e.g., a compass).

Christ as giver of the new covenant

Around the mid-fourth century, several new iconographic motifs appear in Christian wall paintings, mosaics, sarcophagus reliefs, gold glasses, ivories, and metalwork. One of these new motifs depicts Christ either seated or standing, passing a scroll to Peter (and sometimes to Paul). The composition is usually referred to as the *traditio legis* (the handing over of the law). According to many art historians, one of the earliest monumental versions of this image was created for the apse of St. Peter's Basilica in Rome (ca. 340) (see Hellemo 1989, 65–89). Early versions also appeared in the mausoleum of Santa Constanza (see figure 13) and in the early Christian baptistery of Naples.

Scholars have proposed several different interpretations of this composition. Long interpreted as a depiction of Jesus commissioning Peter as the rock of the church

Figure 13   Christ giving the new law to Peter and Paul, ca. 350. Mosaic from an apse of Santa Constanza (Mausoleum of Constantina), Rome. Photo credit: Author.

(cf. Matt 16:18–19), the scene also has been viewed as showing Christ returning to earth in his second coming. Many historians have asserted the influence of imperial iconography on the image, seeing its parallels in scenes of the emperor delegating officials to act on his behalf. In any case, Christ is clearly shown as no longer "on earth" but as the ascended Lord and lawgiver, either enthroned in heaven, poised upon an orb of the cosmos, or standing on a small rocky mount that represents Calvary and Eden simultaneously. Certain additional details provide evidence for this view, including the inclusion of red-tinted heavenly clouds (cf. Matt 24:30), palm trees (symbols of victory) and a phoenix (a reference to Christ's resurrection).

A related composition, in the apse of Santa Pudenziana in Rome (ca. 400) shows Christ seated on a throne, surrounded by his apostles and in front of a cityscape that represents the New Jerusalem. Above, in a sunrise-streaked sky, are a gemmed cross and the four living creatures (Rev 5:6–8). Christ holds a book in his left hand that declares him to be the "Protector of the Church of Santa Pudenziana." Other fifth- and sixth-century apse images show him seated on a throne or the orb of the world and flanked by archangels, saints, or the four living creatures (e.g., in Hosios David in Thessalonica, Ss Cosmas and Damian in Rome, and San Vitale in Ravenna).

Figure 14   Last Judgment, ca. 1230. Tympanum of west portal, Notre Dame Cathedral, Paris. Photo credit: Sacred Destinations Images.

Christ at the final judgment

Christ as judge constitutes another version of the second coming image. Early depictions of this are rare and tend to present Christ as separating the sheep from the goats (cf. Matt 25:31–46). This image appears on at least one fourth-century sarcophagus and in a mosaic in Sant' Apollinare Nuovo (early sixth century), as well as in a textual description of an apse image by Paulinus of Nola (*Ep.* 32.17). The judgment scene becomes more central, however, as it appears in medieval sculpture, often in the tympanum over the west door of a gothic cathedral (see figure 14), and on altarpieces (e.g., Rogier van der Weyden's *The Last Judgment*, 1443–1451) as well as frescoes, including the famous version designed by Michelangelo for the Sistine Chapel (1537–1541). In these later images, souls are being raised from their graves, judged (often by means of a scale held by the archangel Michael), and either found worthy and lifted up to heaven, or condemned and sent down to eternal perdition.

The Image and Likeness: Jesus' Portrait in Christian Art

With only a few exceptions, third- and fourth-century art shows Jesus as a youthful figure. He is beardless and has long curling hair, delicately rendered features, and an almost feminine figure (cf. figure 3). As such, Jesus is physically different from other men (witnesses, disciples, soldiers) who appear with him, a fact that makes his appearance even more remarkable. Some scholars have noted his physical similarity to contemporary representations of Apollo, Dionysus, Hermes or other youthful, savior gods (Mathews 1993, 115–141; Jensen 2005, 131–172). His beauty and youth are especially emphasized in portrayals of him as caretaking shepherd and in scenes of his healing or wonder-working activities that he shared with some of those Greco-Roman gods.

Since none of the canonical gospels describe Jesus' appearance, artists had to rely upon such associations and thus produced a type that they must have thought appropriate. At least one early Christian writer, following the description of the suffering servant in Isaiah 53:3, asserted that Jesus was probably physically unattractive, while others seem to have thought that his divinity ought to have ensured that he was surpassingly beautiful (cf. Ps 45:2).[9]

However, by the end of the fourth century, a different type emerged, which showed Jesus as more mature, with a full beard. Although this facial type, combined with a bare chest and sandaled feet in earlier iconography, presented him as a teacher of philosophy, these later representations showed him enthroned and wearing royal robes. Thus, he came to look less like Socrates or Apollo and more like Greco-Roman portrayals of majestic Jupiter.

Around this time another development emerged – a composition that showed only Christ's likeness, lacking a specific narrative context. Whereas earlier images of Jesus typically showed him performing some act and surrounded by followers, by the early fifth century he began to appear alone, in a front-facing pose, making direct eye contact with the viewer. This new composition, like earlier images of the Greco-Roman gods, invited veneration. The timing is significant, coming as it does at the time when the Christian emperors began to outlaw the cult of these gods, and theologians engaged in controversial debates about how two natures (human and divine) could be joined in a single, incarnate person.

For a time, the two different presentations (the beardless and the bearded mature types) appeared, sometimes in close proximity. In certain instances, this may have been intended to express the Savior's two distinct natures. Such dual presentations occur in Rome's mid-fourth-century Mausoleum of Santa Constanza in Rome, and in Ravenna's sixth-century churches of Sant' Apollinare Nuovo and San Vitale. In each case, the two different representations were produced at almost the same time and probably by the same artists' workshop. Their contradictory co-existence demonstrates that a single, consistent portrait type was not deemed necessary at the time. A polymorphous appearance may even have seemed more faithful, or less idolatrous, in its implication that even Christ's image cannot be entirely comprehended.

Such variations were noted in certain non-canonical scriptures. The author of the *Apocryphon of John* claims that the Lord appeared to him in the form of a child, an old man, and even a figure with three distinct forms (Father, Mother, Son) that appeared sequentially (*Apoc. John* 2:4–8). Origen argued that Christ appeared to

Figure 15   Portrait of Christ, mid-sixth century. From the Basilica of San Vitale, Ravenna. Photo credit: Author.

individuals differently according to their need or ability to understand him (*Cels.* 2.64). Even the canonical stories of the transfiguration or of Christ's post-resurrection appearances show that Christ's appearance might change, or that his disciples could fail to recognize him until he chose to reveal himself.

Nonetheless, by the sixth century, Christ's bearded likeness had become standard. Strikingly consistent through the centuries in both eastern and western art, this type shows Jesus with long reddish-brown, wavy hair, parted in the middle and reaching to his shoulders (see figure 15). His beard comes to a point, his almond-shaped eyes are set under dark brows, and his nose is long and narrow. Although he almost needs no further identifying attributes, his halo usually incorporates a cross, later often inscribed with the Greek letters *omicron, omega,* and *nu* to indicate his title "*ho ōn*" (= "the one who is"), and flanked by the Greek letters IC XC ("Jesus Christ") or *alpha* and *omega*.

Some Christians have claimed that this standard portrait is validated by an actual likeness made during Jesus' earthly life. One of these traditions, dated to the mid-fifth century, recounts the story of King Abgar of Edessa, whose servant brought him a miraculous image of Christ, imprinted upon a linen cloth that Christ placed over his own face. A similar, but later (twelfth-century), legend tells of the woman Veronica, whose veil retained an impression of Jesus' face when she held it up to wipe Jesus' brow as he carried his cross on the way to Calvary (Belting 1994, 208–224; MacGregor 2000, 85–96; Jensen 2005, 135–139).

Each of these stories has numerous representations in visual art, demonstrating the influence of these miraculous, made-without-hands portraits. Other such holy images include the Holy Face of Lucca (Italy) and even the Shroud of Turin. The consistency of Christ's features in these images as well as in their copies demonstrates the perceived value of a "true likeness" of Christ in visual art, no later than the early Middle Ages.

The face of Christ in Christian art remained largely the same, at least in certain basic respects, through the centuries. Jesus nearly always wears a beard and has shoulder-length hair of a dark brown to chestnut hue. Whether shown as a healer, teacher, sacrifice, or ascended or enthroned king, Jesus usually wears a loving and compassionate expression. During the first half of the twentieth century, critics who thought the presentation not masculine enough objected to the traditional portraits. Later others argued that the traditional portrait falsely represented Christ as a European (and Caucasian), rather than as a Jewish man from the first century, which would, ostensibly, be a more historically accurate rendering (Morgan 1998, 97–123). At the turn of the twenty-first century, a quest was launched for a new image of Jesus in art, an image that would reflect the ethnic, racial, socio-cultural, and theological diversity of Christian believers (Jensen 2003). Almost as if returning to the gospel reluctance to describe or define his appearance, Jesus could look like anyone – even appear as a female.

Thus, the way Jesus is represented in art continues to express the different ways that Jesus' person and message have been viewed through the centuries, by different kinds of Christians and in different parts of the world. Each image of Jesus is, itself, a theological statement as much as an aesthetic one. Often these visual messages are as or more effective than the verbal ones, since they transcend language barriers and now, unlike earlier centuries when artworks were precious and unique commodities, can be widely disseminated through print and electronic media. In the age of the icon, whether on screen, in print, or displayed upon museum or church walls, the face of Jesus will undoubtedly continue to form and conform to various and divergent beliefs about who he was and what he did.

Notes

1   Examples of ancient texts include Tertullian, *Pud.* 10 and *Idol.* 8; Clement, *Prot.* 4; and Origen, *Cels.* 3.76 and 4.31.
2   Quotations of the Bible in this chapter are from the New Revised Standard Version.
3   Ancient sources include Justin Martyr *1 Apol.* 12–13, 21; *2 Apol.* 8,10; *Dial.* 8; Clement of Alexandria, *Paed.* 1.7, 9; Tertullian, *Apol.* 46; and Origen, *Cels.* 7.41.

4   See Irenaeus, *Haer.* 3.9.2; Prudentius, *Carm.* 12.28; and Leo I, *Serm.* 33.2; 36.1.
5   See Justin Martyr, *Dial.* 77.4; 78.1; Origen, *Cels.* 1.60; Tertullian, *Idol.* 9; Augustine *Serm.* 202.2; and Caesarius of Arles, *Serm.* 195.
6   This also might be an image of the second coming.
7   On this point see Gregory of Nyssa, commenting on ordinary people debating the relation of the Father to the Son, *Deit.*, PG 46.557.
8   Ancient sources include Justin Martyr, *2 Apol.* 6; and Irenaeus, *Haer.* 2.2.4–5; 5.6.1.
9   See Justin Martyr, *Dial.* 14; Origen, *Cels.* 6.75–77, for examples.

References

Belting, Hans (1994). *Likeness and Presence: A History of the Image before the Era of Art.* Trans. E. Jephcott. Chicago: University of Chicago Press.

Grabar, André (1968). *Christian Iconography: A Study of its Origins.* Princeton: Princeton University Press.

Hellemo, Geir (1989). *Adventus Domini: Eschatological Thought in 4th Century Apses and Catecheses.* Leiden: Brill.

Jensen, Robin (2000). *Understanding Early Christian Art.* London: Routledge.

Jensen, Robin (2003). "Jesus up Close." *Christian Century* (Sept. 20): 26–30.

Jensen, Robin (2005). *Face to Face: Portraits of the Divine in Early Christianity.* Minneapolis: Fortress.

Jensen, Robin (2007). "The Passion in Early Christian Art." In Christine Joynes (ed.), *Perspectives on the Passion* (pp. 53–84). London: T&T Clark.

Kartsonis, Anna (1986). *Anastasis: The Making of an Image.* Princeton: Princeton University Press.

MacGregor, Neil (2000). *Seeing Salvation: Images of Christ in Art.* New Haven: Yale University Press.

Mathews, Thomas (1993). *The Clash of Gods: A Reinterpretation of Early Christian Art.* Princeton: Princeton University Press.

Morgan, David (1998). *Visual Piety: A History and Theory of Popular Religious Images.* Berkeley: University of California Press.

Pelikan, Jaroslav (1997). *The Illustrated Jesus through the Centuries.* New Haven: Yale University Press.

CHAPTER 30

Jesus Novels: Solving Problems with Fiction

Zeba A. Crook

Novels about Jesus have been around for almost as long as the novel itself. Though not a straightforward conclusion, it is widely accepted that Daniel Defoe's *Robinson Crusoe* (1719) is the first English-language novel. Given this, it is significant that the first English Jesus novel appears a mere fifty years later, in the form of John Cameron's *The Messiah: In Nine Books* (1770). Since then, almost 300 Jesus novels in English have been published. No less significant, the frequency with which Jesus novels have appeared has more or less increased through each decade of the twentieth century: the 1990s saw a record high of fifty Jesus novels, and the first decade of the twenty-first century has seen thirty-seven thus far. Despite the longevity of this type of novel, it is surprising how little scholarly attention has been paid to it. This lack of attention contrasts with the attention paid to films about Jesus, which have a much shorter history but no shortage of recent public and scholarly interest.

As with all questions of genre, what counts as a "Jesus novel" depends on how one defines the genre. A Jesus novel is not a short story or a novella. Though admittedly arbitrary, the line between a novel and a novella lies at one hundred pages. The point is that the work must be a long and sustained fictional account of the life of Jesus. Other criteria that I would set are that a Jesus novel must have Jesus as a main character, must be set in the first century, and must attempt to cover most of his life. A Jesus novel might look like the Gospel of Mark, in that it lacks a birth narrative and post-death accounts, but as long it purports to cover most of the rest of his life, I consider it a Jesus novel. I do not include in the category of Jesus novel a work that imports the character Jesus into a foreign setting (such as twentieth-century Los Angeles) or one in which Jesus appears only at the fringes of the story.

The most interesting aspect of reading a Jesus novel is that you always know how it ends (plot spoiler alert: the hero dies). There are a few surprises in these fictional accounts, but not many. Despite that, no two novels are exactly alike. They are like

The Blackwell Companion to Jesus, First Edition. Edited by Delbert Burkett. ©2014 John Wiley & Sons, Ltd. Published 2014 by John Wiley & Sons, Ltd.

the canonical gospels in that regard: they tell largely the same story, but each in a unique way.

Most Jesus novels are harmonized versions of the canonical gospels. Gospel harmonies and harmonized "lives" of Jesus represented Christians' first attempts to deal with the differences among the gospels. A harmonized life of Jesus would take the four canonical gospels and splice them together into one "authoritative" story. The guiding assumption here was that since the gospels were the inerrant and inspired word of God, they must all report what actually happened. Thus, since John has the cleansing of the temple at the start of Jesus' career and Matthew, Mark, and Luke have it at the end, that event must have happened twice. Likewise, since Luke has Jesus' rejection by his own townspeople at the start of Jesus' mission, and Matthew and Mark have it midway through, it too must have happened twice. To their credit, most Jesus novels are less dogmatic than this in their harmonization, even those by evangelical Christian authors. None, for example, has the temple cleansing happening twice. The harmonizing tendencies of Jesus novels are more general: features unique to John such as the adulterous woman, Jesus as the "lamb of God," the "I am" statements, and characters like Nicodemus are commonly spliced into the synoptic storyline, which typically is extended to three years (in keeping with the Gospel of John).

In addition, few novels rely solely on gospel material. Almost all of them take material from historical sources, such as Josephus and Philo, including stories about Pilate and Judean life under Roman occupation, as well as stories of other rebels and messianic figures. Some novels also take stories and sayings of Jesus from noncanonical Christian sources, most commonly the Gospel of Thomas and the Infancy Gospel of Thomas. Anne Rice draws on the latter for her "infancy gospel," which is surprising for two reasons: first, one would expect such a staunchly orthodox Christian to avoid "heretical" sources like this; second, that she uses this gospel implies it has some historical value, a type of judgment characteristic of the historical Jesus scholarship she so despises (2005, 313–314). Other novels draw upon historical Jesus scholarship in order to create a "historical" Jesus novel, though this is not common.

All novels are highly selective of the gospel material they include, but not in a systematic way. Authors take the stories they like, or feel are most representative of the historical Jesus, or that most fit the character they are constructing, as most historical Jesus scholars themselves do. Very commonly, however, the selection of material reflects a hermeneutic of suspicion: generally, and this includes even some novels written by evangelical authors, Jesus novels reflect suspicion concerning official or traditional church versions of the story. This can be seen very often in how novelists deal with Judas Iscariot, but also in how Jesus himself is portrayed – often as a complicated character, moody, evasive, and almost always irascible.

It is difficult to know always how authors intend their Jesus novels to function. Sometimes authors make explicit that they wish to retell the greatest story ever told, and thereby (ideally) attract people to Jesus. Sometimes it seems that the writing of the novel is cathartic in some manner. Perhaps the novel is a way of dealing with the problem generated by having four different accounts of the life of Jesus in the New Testament, and others that are extra-canonical. Thus the novelist's creation of a single account eliminates that problem.

But there are other, more local problems novelists can address in their works of fiction. For example, most modern Christians are troubled by the portrayal of the Jews in the trial narratives, and by the history of Christian anti-Semitism that derives from them. It is common for novels to reduce the culpability of the Jews in the death of Jesus, either by making explicit that only a few were responsible, or by suggesting that Jews were not involved in Jesus' death at all. Miracles also present a "problem" that most modern novelists address in some way. On a more mundane level, an author might seek to explain how Jesus could have had "brothers and sisters" if Mary remained ever-virgin, or why Jesus appears to have rejected his family. In what follows, I shall draw attention to how modern novelists use fiction to solve such "problems" presented by the gospels. In doing so, I will break up the life of Jesus into six sections – birth and youth, mission, miracles, betrayal, trial, and post-death appearances.

Birth and Youth

The main problem that a novelist must contend with is the divergent and historically dubious nature of the narratives concerning Jesus' birth. From four gospels, we have only two infancy narratives, and they are almost completely unlike one another. One of the details on which they agree is important, because it gives us a glimpse into the problem with which Matthew and Luke were struggling. They both believe that Jesus *of Nazareth* was the Messiah, who by virtue of that status must have been born *in Bethlehem*. The problem is that neither knows how this came about, so each creates a narrative to explain it.

Matthew has Mary and Joseph living in Bethlehem; when Jesus is born, he is, fittingly, born in a house (2:11). But then Matthew has to explain how Jesus of Bethlehem came to grow up in Nazareth, which he does by creating a story about the slaughter of innocent children by a tyrant Herod. This story, notably uncorroborated by any other ancient witness (Jewish or Christian), is Matthew's way of explaining how Jesus came to be raised in Nazareth (though it also serves his "new Moses" motif that informs his first five chapters). Luke likewise struggles: he takes a historical event – a census under a Syrian governor in 6 CE – and moves it ten years earlier, adding the nearly comical requirement that people were expected to return to their ancestral villages, even if the ancestor concerned lived a thousand years previously, as in Joseph's case.

Concerning Jesus' youth, Matthew is silent. Luke offers one story, set deliberately at the next stage in maturity (twelve years old), of a precocious Jesus sparring ably with the Temple priests. To their credit, Matthew and Luke are remarkably restrained in their speculation on these lost years (that same restraint, for instance, is absent in gospel speculation concerning what happened after Jesus died). In striking contrast, the Infancy Gospel of Thomas is less restrained about these "missing" years. It offers some fantastic stories that speculate on what it might have been like to grow up with the divine power of life and death.

The most common method for solving the problem of these divergent narratives is harmonization. Harmonization works only up to a point, since there always details that cannot be easily harmonized. An alternative response here is to choose one version over the other. This is the approach of Walter Wangerin Jr. (2005), who takes over Luke's birth narrative and completely ignores the uniquely Matthean elements of the story. Another approach is to have a character or narrator address the problem directly. Anthony Burgess (1979) cannot harmonize Matthew's flight to Egypt with Luke's purification at the Temple, so he has a narrator allude to Luke's story and discount it as fabrication. This use of meta-narrative, in which the author assumes the authority of most of the material (implied in the act of harmonization) while having the narrator question the historicity of what cannot be harmonized, is one of the most interesting – and most common – features of modern Jesus novels.

Rice (2005) takes a different approach. Rather than use a character to discount questionable material, she has a character defend historically questionable material. Luke's census is a problem historically, so Rice suggests that Joseph and Mary had to return to Bethlehem not because the census forced people to return to their ancestral villages, but because Joseph happened to own property there.

The parentage of Jesus is another problem, both for gospel writers and novelists. Of course all the gospel writers agree that Jesus is the "son of God," but what exactly does that mean to them? Israelites, as part of the Hellenistic world, had long known sons of God, which is what they called exceptional men. Mark does not try to explain the term; in fact, no human father of Jesus is ever named in Mark. Matthew and Luke explain it by introducing an impregnating holy spirit, but then they do something quite odd. They both give Jesus a genealogy that is traced through Joseph, a human father. It seems Matthew and Luke agree that something significant happened but do not understand the mechanics of it.

Burgess tells the story that Joseph was an old man whose testicles had been crushed in a carpentry accident; Mary is a fourteen-year-old virgin sworn to celibacy. For Burgess, Joseph *cannot* have been the father of Jesus (this feature of the story also helpfully explains how Mary remained "ever virgin," something Anne Rice is also interested in defending). When it comes to the many New Testament references to James the brother of Jesus, Burgess (raised Catholic) must ignore those, while Anne Rice explains them in the common Catholic manner: they were children from a previous marriage of Joseph (before his testicles were crushed), as well as cousins who were like brothers and sisters to Jesus.

Other novelists seek a more human depiction. Rolf Gompertz (1977) implies a normal and loving conception for Jesus. Nino Ricci (2002) conjures up that old canard that Jesus was the product of rape by a Roman soldier. It is not mere slander here, as it was for Celsus. For Ricci, this strained beginning explains the strained relationship that Mary and Jesus have (Mark 3:21, 31–35). José Saramago (1991) and Nikos Kazantzakis (1960), on the other hand, both mix the profane and the divine. Saramago has Mary and Joseph as sexually active as any young couple would be, yet during one act of love-making, God surreptitiously replaces Joseph's seed with his own, and thus was Jesus conceived the son of God. Kazantzakis does not say much, but the implication is that Jesus was born of normal means. However, when Matthew the scribe sits to write the story of Jesus' beginning, the Holy Spirit takes control of the pen and forces a reluctant Matthew to write something he knows is not true (the virgin birth).

Matthew's slaughter of the innocents might be a problem for historians, but not for novelists, who are drawn to the drama. Two novelists in particular have worked with this story in a powerful way, Anne Rice and José Saramago. Rice's *Out of Egypt* (2005) is an infancy gospel all its own; in it we follow Jesus as he ages from seven to twelve years old. Along the way, he learns there is a family secret, something everyone knows but will not share with him. Slowly he realizes that something happened when he was born, that it had to do with him, and that it was the reason they went to Egypt. At the end of the novel, Jesus is at the temple, and he asks an elder rabbi what happened in Bethlehem twelve years prior. The rabbi tells him that Herod had every child in Bethlehem under two years old killed because of the birth of one. Jesus' world falls apart around him in what is the strongest narrative feature of Rice's novel. Saramago (1991) has the same question, but he asks it in quite a different way: what kind of God would let twenty-five children die in order to save just one? In this account, Joseph overhears Herod's plan from two passing soldiers; he runs himself ragged to save his son but is for the rest of his life wracked by guilt for not attempting to let the other families know. Saramago's God is narcissistic and pathological; he leaves the people (Joseph and the other families) alone in their grief.

Mission

Early Christian writers struggled with a few issues pertaining to Jesus' career. They all believed he was significant but could not agree on why exactly. Christian readers are taught to focus on what is common among the gospel portraits of Jesus, especially major theological themes: that he was the Messiah and Son of God, that he died, and that he was raised by God to glory. But this approach misses the fact that each author presents his own portrait of Jesus, and by extension his own interpretation of the significance and identity of Jesus. For instance, the synoptic Jesus is notoriously coy about his identity. He is made to allude to his identity as Messiah, but never once explicitly makes that claim himself. This suggests that the gospel writers were perhaps dealing with a gap in their own material: they believed Jesus to be the Messiah and Son of God but did not have any sayings from him stating this explicitly. No one takes this as far as Mark, where Jesus goes out of his way to hide his identity, a feature all the more striking in contrast to the Gospel of John, in which

Jesus could not be more explicit about his identity. And then there are the non-canonical interpretations of Jesus' identity.

One of the thorniest problems with which scholars of the historical Jesus wrestle concerns the mission of Jesus. What was he up to? Did he focus on healing or on teaching about the kingdom of God? If these activities were related, how so? Who were his primary opponents – the "Jews" or the rich? In other words, was the core of his mission religious or socio-economic? Did he think he was the Messiah, and if he did, what *kind* of Messiah? In other words, what would that title have meant to him and to his followers?

The Jesus of Daniel Bliss (1994) discovers his messianic identity only at his baptism, but even then he is directionless. Only very late in his ministry does Jesus discover that he has been sent for all people. The essence of his message is love and mercy; he teaches that people should get along, help each other, and never victimize each other; he teaches that they should not judge each other but should see the good in each other; he teaches that people should not feel sad or alone, because God is everywhere and with them always. Likewise, Gompertz's Jesus preaches love but explains at great length to Judas that love is not an emotion and is not romantic. Love is God, and God is love. Jesus acknowledges that practicing love is an uphill battle. People either like their lives or they do not but are too married to their routines to change. But he argues that love is that one thing that can change what is inside a person. Love can change everything.

The problem with overly emphasizing Jesus' message of love is explaining how or why he was killed. Bliss's Jesus illustrates the love he is talking about by healing on the Sabbath, which of course angers some, but killing Jesus on account of that is an overreaction, to say the least. Bliss makes Jesus likeable and harmless, but in the process he fails to account for why he was killed.

Others do a better job of rationalizing Jesus' death. In Gompertz's novel, the people who initially liked Jesus start to see contradictions in his teachings and actions, even hypocrisy. Jesus claims that not one part of the Law can be altered until heaven and earth cease, and yet he himself violates the law continuously. He thereby loses public support. Burgess' Jesus likewise loses the support of the people and makes enemies of powerful people. The Pharisees reject Jesus because they find his claim to have the authority to interpret the Torah individually to be arrogant, hubristic even. On the other end of the spectrum, the Zealots consider Jesus a traitor. Even though he never said he was with them, they had great hope in his teaching about the kingdom. When they learn that this kingdom is as much for Romans as for Jews, they are incensed. So Jesus is caught between these two powerful groups and dies as a consequence.

Kazantzakis has a more realistic portrayal of a radical Jesus. Jesus' message is unrelentingly opposed to the rich. Jesus has been attacking the rich and telling parables, but late in the novel he offers his first sermon, which involves more railing against the rich. The people dislike being attacked by Jesus and they attack back. Gompertz's Jesus enjoys the support even of most Pharisees, but that changes when his attacks on them ("woes against the Pharisees") become too random and savage. Ricci's Jesus likewise has a sharp edge. This Jesus knows that he is a bastard and thus lacks the authority to teach and heal. But he does so anyway, and in a way that constantly seeks out the attention of the authorities, though, as we shall see later, the death of Ricci's Jesus is something of an accident.

Finally, Saramago has the most creative and theologically moving explanation for Jesus' mission. In a meeting with both God and Satan in a boat on the Sea of Galilee, Jesus learns that God's plan is to create a religion not just for the Jews but for the whole world; he yearns to be worshiped by the whole world. So he creates a son to start a new religion. But that son *must* die for this plan to work. And Jesus learns that the bloodshed and suffering will not end there. God reveals to Jesus the future of Christianity, with its grisly martyrdoms, inquisitions, and crusades. Jesus then takes it upon himself to thwart God's unholy plan. Jesus decides that if he can die as a messianic pretender, *not* as the Son of God, then maybe God's plan will not work. He hopes to do this quickly, while God is looking the other way, but to no avail. Jesus dies, realizing that he was a pawn and that God was in control all along. Thinking on the rivers of blood that will flow from this event over the coming centuries, Jesus' last words are "Men, forgive Him, for He knows not what He has done" (Saramago 1991, 377).

Parables have been a problem for Christian writers from the start. All synoptic authors agree on the obfuscating quality of parables, even if they may disagree with Mark that obfuscation was the goal (Mark 4:12). The rise of the allegorical method attests that Christians found this to be the easiest way to make sense of these puzzling stories. And it is no wonder: the parables as we have them often invite more questions than they answer. The point and application of some parables may be perfectly clear; for instance, the parable of the Good Samaritan is a powerful illustration of who is one's neighbor. But others are not so clear. In Matthew, for instance, there is a wedding banquet to which none of the invitees come. We are told that people were then invited at random off the street to the feast. These people were probably feeling quite lucky, until the king enters and sees a man who is not dressed for a wedding and he is thrown out roughly. The point, according to Matthew, is that "many are called, but few are chosen." But this would be a much clearer story had the man been rejected by God (the king) for something within his control. Apparently the moral of the story is that we are to wear wedding attire everywhere we go, just in case.

Parables, and the problem of teaching in parables, feature in many novels. Nino Ricci's presentation of them is perhaps the most cynical: Jesus teaches in parables because he is being purposely evasive, either because he does not want to answer a question directly, or because he himself does not know the answer. The parables allow Jesus to make people think he is answering their question with wisdom and insight, when in fact this is an illusion. The educated can see through the ruse, but the uneducated masses of the Galilee are awed by the parables.

If Ricci's portrayal of the parables is cynical, that of Christopher Moore (2002) is the most humorous. Moore's Jesus is well-intentioned but just does not understand that his uneducated disciples cannot understand him. Biff, Jesus' best friend in this novel, tries to illustrate Jesus' method to him. Biff will save Mary Magdelene from a bad marriage by having her fake a demon possession, which will compel her husband to part with her. When Jesus wonders whether this plan is ethical, Biff tells him that "faking demon possession is like a mustard seed." When Jesus expresses confusion, Biff says, "You don't know, do you? Doesn't seem at all like a mustard seed, does it? Now you see how we all feel when you liken things unto a mustard seed? Huh?" (Moore 2002, 358–359).

Miracles

The "problem" with miracles is different from the other "problems" I have addressed thus far. None of the gospel writers had a problem with miracles. They believed that Jesus had a power that came from God, and they knew that miracles were common. Great Emperors (Vespasian) and lowly holy men (Honi the circle-drawer) performed them. Miracles were a signifier of greatness, of proximity to the gods. Of course, early Christian writers elaborated even within this tradition. The story from John of Jesus giving sight to a man born blind (interpreted in some Christian communities as having been born without eyes) obviously functions as a form of symbolic one-upmanship: this fellow was not just recently blind, and definitely not psychosomatically blind, but had been born blind!

The problem with miracles sits entirely at the modern end of the spectrum. The enlightenment and rise of scientific rationalism created a crisis for Christianity. The problem of miracles is what seems most to have motivated the so-called "Old Quest" of historical Jesus scholarship, but though the focus of the subsequent quests changed, the problem of miracles for modern biblical scholars has not disappeared. The most recent stage has evangelical scholars appropriating postmodernism to argue for the historicity of the miracle tradition.

This same range of responses to miracles is reflected in modern fiction and largely follows denominational fault lines. On the most conservative end, you have the evangelical Walter Wangerin. Wangerin's Jesus is not only superhuman in his power over nature and in his ability to heal people and raise them from the dead (consistent with the gospel stories), but he can even climb steep mountains without breaking a sweat or huffing and puffing like those around him. Even on the flat, he walks faster than anyone else and never seems to tire. This augmentation of powers is also a feature of Anne Rice's adult Jesus (2008): he knows everyone's name before he meets them, reads minds, and has superhuman hearing. Christopher Moore shares with Wangerin the practice of supplementing canonical miracles with new miracles. The effect is that although Moore's novel is satirical and profane, his depiction of Jesus is almost completely orthodox. In a creative twist on the canonical miracle tradition, Saramago has Jesus performing all the gospel miracles, but these miracles are a curse put upon Jesus by a God who wants to attract worshipers.

The approach of Norman Mailer (1997) to the miracles might appear surprisingly traditional, but it is more complex than that. Mailer's Jesus turns water into wine at Cana, heals Peter's mother-in-law, heals withered hands and leprosy, raises people, and is himself raised from the dead. And yet, the miracles take a very heavy toll on Jesus. Single miracles leave Jesus completely drained, but when he performs two miracles in short succession (the hemorrhaging woman and Jairus' daughter), it wipes him out emotionally and physically.

More commonly, novelists treat miracles with suspicion. Sometimes they do this somewhat awkwardly. For example, Burgess affirms the central miracles of the Christian tradition (the virgin birth, the resurrection, the raising of Lazarus), yet "lesser" miracles are questioned. For instance, Jesus claims that miracle stories cannot be trusted: "Cure a man of a fever, and your enthusiastic chronicler will convert that into a resurrection from the grave" (1979, 223). The irony is that ten pages later Jesus raises a man from the dead. Kazantzakis delivers his skepticism more subtly: miracles in his novel are only reported, not narrated, and are never evaluated. In other instances, gospel miracle stories are retold without miraculous content: for example, Peter walks on water only in a dream (1960, 342).

In other cases, the miracles produce an ambiguity regarding Jesus' identity. After one of the few miracle stories in Gompertz's novel, people exclaim, "Blessed be thou, O Lord our God, king of the Universe, who creates miracles daily" (1977, 103). It is not at all clear who is being addressed here: Jesus or God. The prayer is a typical Jewish prayer to God, but neither God nor Jesus is clearly identified as the recipient of the praise.

The most complex treatment of miracles comes from Nino Ricci. Over and over, Jesus is presented as a non-supernatural healer. He correctly diagnoses human illness and deals with it unsuperstitiously. What is more, it is made clear that grandiose stories of Jesus' healings are grossly exaggerated, something that derives as much from Jesus' supporters (hoping to promote him) as from his enemies (hoping to discredit him). And yet, for all that, Ricci is unwilling wholly to deny metaphysical possibilities. Jesus is called to heal a man who was clubbed in the head by a Roman soldier. Simon of Gergesa, watching by firelight, reports that Jesus seemed to insert his whole hand right into the man's head and pull something out, which he throws into the fire. Simon is not overly superstitious, but even he wonders whether it was a demon that was thrown into the fire. Even though Jesus tells the people that this procedure was nothing more than medicine, they think he is being modest. As Eleazar recovers, Jesus asks him, "Do you know who I am?" and Eleazar replies, "You must be the son of god himself, if you brought me back from the dead" (Ricci 2002, 402). In the narrative, everyone laughs long and hard at that response, including Jesus. Ricci's "historical-critical" approach to the miracles is echoed by Daniel Bliss, who offers no miracles at all but plenty of healings. A withered hand is healed with massage, a demon-possessed boy suffers from split personality disorder, and a blind man is healed by washing away scabrous tissue from over his eyes.

Betrayal

The narrative problems with the gospel stories of Judas Iscariot are notorious. Of course there are smaller problems, such as who Judas was, what he actually did, how he set it all up, and how he died, but the most serious problem of all is what motivated Judas. This problem persists regardless of how one translates *paradidōmi*: to "hand over" or to "betray." Mark is the first to put the event into a narrative, though he does so without commenting in any way on Judas' motivation (Mark 14:10). It is possible that Matthew implies a motivation by adding a detail to the material he takes over from Mark. To the story immediately preceding Judas' decision to betray Jesus – the wasteful anointing of Jesus' feet with an ointment worth a year's wages – Matthew adds that it was not just "some people" who objected but "the disciples." *Then* Matthew's Judas leaves to betray Jesus (Matt 26:14–15).

Luke on the other hand has a much more transparent explanation for what motivated Judas: Satan entered into him (Luke 22:3). John offers the most developed narrative on Judas' motivations. In the story of the wasteful anointing, it is Judas alone (not nameless characters and not "the disciples") who objects to the wastefulness. He claims to be concerned for the poor (John 12:5), but John tells us that in fact his concern was greed, as Judas had been known to steal from the group's common purse, which he controlled. Oddly enough, in John, the wasteful anointing does not explain Judas' actions, since that story appears in a different part of the gospel. As in Luke, Satan enters into Judas. Explaining what Judas did and why he did it is exceedingly difficult, as even the gospel writers attest.

Modern novelists seem at their most creative when working with the Judas tradition, perhaps because the gospels provide them with so little coherent material. Every writer seeks to explain what Judas did, and the effect, almost without fail, is that Judas is to some extent rehabilitated. Sometimes Judas only does what Jesus tells him to do (as the Gospel of John implies). Christopher Moore's Judas, though underdeveloped as a character, claims to have been told by Jesus to do what he did, though in this novel we are not privy to that conversation. Kazantzakis is more explicit: when Jesus decides that he must die in order for the world to be saved, he sends Judas to Caiaphas to make the necessary arrangements. He even promises Judas that his death will only be temporary. And Saramago's Judas is used by Jesus as a tool to thwart God: Jesus hopes that if he can die a simple human, an enemy of Rome, and not as the divine Son of God, then perhaps God's plan for world domination can be averted. Walter Wangerin's Judas is a childish and simple-minded teenage zealot who *thinks* Jesus has arranged to get inside the center of power by having him hand Jesus over.

Other novelists solve the Judas problem in the gospel narratives by suggesting that he was tricked into betraying Jesus. This Judas is always, therefore, naïve. He trusts the authorities, whom he thinks he has converted, and therefore lets them know where Jesus is hiding out. So, Burgess' Judas is persuaded by an old friend on the Sanhedrin that Jesus must be taken into protective custody, for his own good and so they can learn more about him. Likewise, Gompertz has Caiaphas persuade Judas that God would never let anything bad happen to his Messiah. Caiaphas of course knows that Jesus is not the Messiah, but Judas, full of faith, hands Jesus over. Gompertz and Wangerin both have Judas believe that by doing so he is accelerating the arrival of the kingdom.

These authors all agree that Judas did what the gospels say he did; their goal is to seek to understand that action. Only Nino Ricci wholly exonerates Judas of all guilt. Ricci's Judas is a rebel hiding from the Romans among Jesus' disciples. Jesus is arrested and executed not because Judas betrays him, but because a follower of Jesus divulges that the rebel Judas was a disciple of Jesus. Jesus is guilty by association, but he is not exactly betrayed by Judas. Nonetheless, Judas is so disliked by the disciples because he is different from them (and quite dislikable) that he comes to bear sole responsibility in the death of Jesus.

Interestingly, no author takes the opposite approach, by making Judas purely evil. In fact, Mailer makes Judas the most principled disciple of them all. Judas tells Jesus bluntly one day that he does not believe any of Jesus' claims about the arrival of the kingdom of heaven. Judas follows Jesus only because he believes that Jesus' message gives hope to the poor. Jesus asks whether he would lose the support of Judas were he (Jesus) to reduce his efforts for the poor even by a little. Judas replies, "I would turn against you. A man who is ready to walk away from the poor by a little is ready to depart from them by a lot" (Mailer 1997, 139). When Judas is eventually rebuked for objecting to the anointing of Jesus' feet with ointment that could have been sold, he abandons Jesus. In Mailer's story, it is not Judas who betrays Jesus, but Jesus who betrays Judas.

Many authors also feel compelled to understand Judas' character, which can also function in his rehabilitation. Often Judas is depicted as highly educated (Ricci, Kazantzakis, Burgess, Mailer). He is also often fiercely independent (Ricci, Mailer, Kazantzakis). This is all significant, because Judas is always then very different from the other disciples. Ricci's Judas, for example, can speak to Jesus in a way the other disciples cannot follow. They become resentful of the relationship Judas has with Jesus. The most common claim about Judas is that he was a Zealot. Sometimes this is current (Ricci, Kazantzakis), sometimes it is in Judas' past (Gompertz, Moore), and sometimes Judas simply exhibits zealot tendencies but is not technically a Zealot. These characteristics taken together, Judas is almost always depicted as the outsider. Jesus likes him, usually adores him, but the others distrust Judas as the foreigner to the group.

Trial

The trial of Jesus invites historical query. In the same way that one must wonder who heard the prayers of Jesus in the darkened Garden of Gethsemane (since apparently those in nearest proximity to Jesus were sound asleep), one must wonder which of the followers of Jesus could have heard the trial exchanges. Unlike modern trials, ancient trials were not open to the public, let alone to rabble from the back-country. But far more pressing for many modern Christian readers is the culpability of the Jews in the death of Jesus.

Since the Holocaust, Christians have been trying to distance themselves from Christianity's anti-Semitic past. The first step toward this was to acknowledge the anti-Jewish polemical tendencies of the gospels. These tendencies (depicting the Pharisees as plotting against Jesus from the very beginning of his mission, woes against the Pharisees and scribes, hurling insult after insult at "the Jews") appear throughout the gospels, but predictably they hit a climax in the trial narrative, especially in the Gospel of Matthew. All the gospels agree on shifting the blame for the death of Jesus from the Romans to the Jews. This is accomplished first by Mark, who offers us a ridiculously unhistorical portrait of a dithering Pilate, who knows that Jesus is innocent but feels compelled to satisfy a mob. Matthew increases the blame on the Jews exponentially. First, he has Pilate publicly and ritually exculpate himself from all responsibility for the death of Jesus, and then "the people as a whole" call a blood curse upon themselves and their descendents (Matt 27:24–25). John and Luke resemble Mark more than Matthew in their trials, but the point remains clear: Jewish misanthropy and corruption lead them to bloodlust and deicide.

Novelists deal with this problem in three ways. The first is to have characters speak reasonably and rationally against Jesus' teaching. For instance, the story of Jesus healing a man with a withered hand is often reproduced from a Jewish perspective: of course one is allowed to save a life on the Sabbath (Mark 3:4), but a withered hand (however unfortunate that might be) is hardly life-threatening. In Norman Mailer's novel, several of Jesus' Jewish opponents are shown to be reasonable in their concern about Jesus' teaching, and not hypocritical. These opponents do not attack Jesus but simply wish to talk to him. For example, a polite scribe reminds Jesus that many Jews suffered and died struggling to observe the Law when foreign rulers made it illegal for them do so. This scribe asks Jesus whether his relaxed attitude to the Law might not dishonor the deaths of those martyred Jews, and whether that might not explain the offense some are taking to him. Jesus tries to express the idea that he has not come to end the Law but to fulfill it, but the subtlety of the scribe's point appears to be lost on him.

Likewise, Anthony Burgess shows how reasonable it was for Jesus' contemporaries to be troubled by his (in this novel at least) changing Judaism from a "national religion" to one open even to Greeks and Romans. Burgess also suggests that the idea of the Messiah is a symbolic and ritual idea; it is not a real and active hope. It cannot be, Burgess' elite Jewish characters claim, for what would become of "Judaism" if the Messiah actually came? What would be left? Belief in the Messiah must be an ongoing belief; it cannot be a fulfilled belief.

A second way that the anti-Judaism of the gospels is rewritten in novels is by reducing the role of "the whole people" and increasing the role of a few powerful elites. So, Christopher Moore lays the blame entirely at the feet of a fictional character, Jakan. Jakan was a bully as a boy in Nazareth and grew up to be a power-hungry bully of a Pharisee, and he goes after Jesus for personal reasons. The far more common solution, however, is to blame the high priest Caiaphas and his close circle of other high priests and to leave "the people" out of it. This is the approach of Wangerin and Bliss, who ascribe to Caiaphas an irrational hatred of Jesus and have him railroad other members of the Sanhedrin into convicting Jesus. Gompertz does something creative here: he suggests that it is Pilate who wants Jesus dead, but Pilate bullies Caiaphas into doing it. Pilate warns Caiaphas that there will be much worse bloodshed than the death of just one man if Caiaphas cannot get this done. Gompertz and Bliss also draw attention to the fact that there was not even unanimity among elite Jews on the Sanhedrin against Jesus. Not only, then, are the Jewish people not responsible for the death of Jesus, but neither even are all elite Jews.

A few writers go even further in removing all Jewish culpability for the death of Jesus. Nino Ricci's Jesus is at the wrong place at the wrong time, is arrested in a sweep, and is executed by a Roman governor eager for approval from Rome for appearing to have executed a rebel. At Ricci's trial, the highest-ranking Jew even speaks in Jesus' defense. Similarly, Wangerin (in part) and Saramago (wholly) blame Jesus for his own death. Both authors draw on the gospels to do this, in that Jesus says nothing in his own defense at any version of the trial; it is as if Jesus *wants* to die.

Post-Death Appearances

The post-death appearances of Jesus pose the same problem for modern Christians that the miracles in general do. But what sets this miracle apart from the others is the centrality of it to Christian doctrine, and indeed to Christianity as a whole. Christians ancient to modern – from Paul and Augustine to N. T. Wright and Michael Bird – have claimed that Christianity is empty if there is no resurrection. No less, the very survival, growth, and rise of Christianity are commonly cited as *proof* of the reality of the resurrection. How else, these conservative Christian scholars challenge, can we explain this success of Christianity if there was no resurrection?

Such a claim ignores the rather complex nature of earliest Christian thinking about the fate of Jesus. Paul does indeed claim that belief in the resurrection of Jesus is a non-negotiable element of his movement, but what *is* resurrection to Paul? First Corinthians 15 offers as an analogy the process of a seed becoming a plant. The seed is transformed into a plant; yet the plant and the seed are clearly not the same, related though they may be. Paul would seem here to be arguing for resurrection, not resuscitation, and the two are clearly not interchangeable. What is sown is the physical body; what is raised is a spiritual body (1 Cor 15:44). This view appears to cohere with Luke's view of resurrection: on the road to Emmaus, the disciples perhaps do not recognize Jesus because the sown physical body is not the same as the raised spiritual body.

What is more, Mark does not narrate a resurrection at all but rather offers only an empty tomb at the end of the story. One might claim that this omission is insignificant, but an early Christian scribe did not think so: he found this troubling enough that he wrote a resurrection narrative for Mark. It might be harder to argue the significance of Q's lack of a resurrection narrative, since it more or less lacks narrative entirely, but one recent study suggests that the absence of a Jesus resurrection motif anywhere in Q is made significant by the presence of a post-death vindication motif in Q (Smith 2006). In other words, a comparison of Paul and Luke with Mark, Q, and Matthew suggests that early Christians themselves did not agree on what resurrection entailed, or even whether it was really all that central to the story they were telling.

Modern novelists do not tend to do very surprising things with the resurrection: they either affirm it, or they offer an alternative explanation. Nino Ricci describes a scene in which one of his narrators witnesses people paying off a guard and leaving the tomb with a body. He cannot tell if it is Jesus they are leaving with because it is dark and he is a ways off, but he assumes so later when he hears about the empty tomb and claims of a resurrection. Daniel Bliss' narrator, a follower of Jesus, hears claims about a resurrection but is not convinced. He himself knows, after all, that when he remembers Jesus' teachings, Jesus is with him. Then later, we learn what happened to Jesus' body: Joseph of Arimathea, fearing the body would be desecrated, stole it under cover of darkness. Jesus was buried honorably in an unmarked grave in the corner of Joseph's garden. Conversely, Saramago affirms the resurrection (though it is implied earlier in a promise God makes to Jesus, rather than narrated), as do Wangerin, Mailer, and Moore. Some novelists even strengthen the claim. Anthony Burgess, for example, has the empty tomb discovered not only by the women, Peter, and the Beloved Disciple, but also by a group that includes soldiers, high priests, and disciples. Burgess' resurrected Jesus is more than corporeal: not only does he eat (as in Luke), but he pays for dinner! Apparently money resurrects too!

Conclusion

Who writes Jesus novels? They are written by Christians, Jews, atheists, and agnostics; fervent Catholics, lapsed Catholics, Protestants, evangelical Protestants, and Maronite Christians; men and women; North American, European, and Asian writers; big-name writers seeking to apply their trade to retelling a well-known story, and first-time writers who likely see their work as an act of piety.

It goes without saying, given this range of authors, that not all novels are of equal quality as novels. A Jesus novel can attempt historical reconstruction (Ricci, Bliss, Mailer, Gompertz), undertake pious/canonical retelling (Wangerin, Rice, Burgess), or create a literary work of art all its own (Saramago, Kazantzakis). As a rule, authors sacrifice art for a liberal-historical or conservative-theological agenda; the more historical or theological the novel, the fewer its literary qualities. This goes even for literary greats such as Norman Mailer and Anthony Burgess. Nino Ricci's *Testament* comes closest to combining historical and literary aspirations; it is beautifully written, tells a complex story, and is historically plausible. Conversely, Anne

Rice's Jesus novels (two installments of her trilogy have now appeared) share the same literary quality as her erotica (originally published under the pseudonym A. N. Roquelaure). The prose of Bliss' novel is tortured in places, and his Jesus sounds strangely like Guru Pitka (a character played by Mike Myers in the 2008 comedy *The Love Guru*).

Yet, despite the fact that not all Jesus novels are equally literary, they all offer something interesting and unique to this familiar story. Mailer's novel is narrated in the first person by the resurrected Jesus, who has a few problems with the gospel accounts of his life; Wangerin's novel is narrated by the Beloved Disciple, and it depicts the accurate transmission of Jesus stories aided by a close relationship between the family and disciples of Jesus; Bliss' novel, narrated by a fictional follower, suggests that many of Jesus' parables came from the real-life stories of other people; Gompertz depicts a spineless Caiaphas who has been blackmailed by Pilate to seek the execution of Jesus; Burgess presents Judas as a faithful follower of Jesus who is fooled into revealing where Jesus is hiding; Kazantzakis has a Jesus troubled on the cross by his own life decision; Ricci questions the reliability of individual perception and memory in the transmission of Jesus stories; Saramago's novel depicts a Jesus fully immersed in the real and sensual world. As I indicated above, Rice has us consider how learning about the slaughter of the innocents would have impacted the boy Jesus. And for something completely different, Christopher Moore's novel strives neither for art, history, nor apology. As "absurdist fiction," it is in a class of its own, and despite its humor and profanity, it has received a surprisingly warm reception among Christian readers.

References

Bliss, Daniel (1994). *Jeshua: The Gospel According to Benjamin*. Monmouth: Monmouth Press.

Burgess, Anthony (1979). *Man of Nazareth*. New York: McGraw-Hill.

Cameron, John (1770). *The Messiah: In Nine Books*. London: Robinson & Roberts.

Defoe, Daniel (1719). *Robinson Crusoe*. London: W. Taylor.

Gompertz, Rolf (1977). *My Jewish Brother Jesus: A Different Biblical Novel*. North Hollywood: Word Doctor.

Kazantzakis, Nikos (1960). *The Last Temptation of Christ*. Trans. P. A. Bien. New York: Simon & Schuster.

Mailer, Norman (1997). *The Gospel According to the Son*. New York: Random House.

Moore, Christopher (2002). *Lamb: The Gospel According to Biff, Christ's Childhood Pal*. San Francisco: HarperCollins.

Ricci, Nino (2002). *Testament*. Toronto: Random House.

Rice, Anne (2005). *Christ the Lord: Out of Egypt*. New York: Knopf.

Rice, Anne (2008). *Christ the Lord: The Road to Cana*. New York: Knopf.

Saramago, José (1991). *The Gospel According to Jesus Christ*. Trans. G. Pontiero. San Diego: Harcourt Brace.

Smith, Daniel A. (2006). *Post-Mortem Vindication of Jesus in the Sayings Gospel Q*. London, New York: T&T Clark.

Wangerin, Walter Jr. (2005). *Jesus: A Novel*. Grand Rapids: Zondervan.

CHAPTER 31

Jesus in Film

Adele Reinhartz

By the late first century, when the gospels were written, Jesus had been absent from the world for more than four decades. At that time, and for the subsequent nineteen centuries, those with an interest in Jesus have not been able to see Jesus directly. Their situation is anticipated in Jesus' parting words to doubting Thomas in John 20:29. When the disciples told Thomas that they had seen the risen Lord, Thomas refused to believe without seeing and touching Jesus for himself. Jesus returns to oblige Thomas but then remarks, "Have you believed because you have seen me? Blessed are those who have not seen and yet have come to believe."

The Fourth Gospel here explicitly praises a faith that is not based on sight. Yet these words have by no means alleviated the longing of believers to see Jesus for themselves. Until the late eighteenth century, the doubting Thomases of the community of believers fulfilled their desire through visual art and live drama, thereby creating an artistic legacy of painting, sculpture, manuscript illumination, and theater that remains compelling to this day. With the birth of the cinema in the late nineteenth century, however, a new and highly appealing medium for seeing Jesus became available to anyone who could afford the low price of admission. Of course, the celluloid Jesus is not "really" Jesus, just as the Jesus of art and drama is not the man or messiah himself. It is nevertheless the case that the movies bring Jesus to life in a way that no other medium can.

The ongoing desire to see Jesus, and the suitability of cinema to fulfill that desire, has spawned hundreds of Jesus movies in numerous countries, from the earliest years of the movie industry to the present. In general terms, these films belong to the genre of biographical film, commonly known as the "bio-pic" (Custen 1992, 144). Bio-pics are feature films that are set in a specific historical time and place and whose subjects are historical figures. Bio-pics generally combine historical narrative with fictionalized elements; while they usually adhere to the known biographical facts of their subjects, they freely invent narrative, characters, and dialogue.

The Blackwell Companion to Jesus, First Edition. Edited by Delbert Burkett. ©2014 John Wiley & Sons, Ltd. Published 2014 by John Wiley & Sons, Ltd.

The Jesus movies are almost always set in early first-century Galilee, Samaria, and Judea (even if they are rarely filmed there); most, including the epics such as *The Greatest Story Ever Told* (1965) and *Jesus of Nazareth* (1979), tell Jesus' entire life story from the nativity through to the resurrection appearances. Others, such as Gibson's *The Passion of the Christ* (2004), focus on specific parts of that story, most commonly the events leading to Jesus' death. With the notable exception of Pasolini's *The Gospel According to Saint Matthew* (1964) and Philip Saville's *The Gospel of John* (2003), filmmakers do not focus on a single gospel but make use of the events and dialogue from all four canonical gospels.

Historical Accuracy versus Invention

Perhaps the most salient characteristic of this genre is the fact that it simultaneously makes a claim to historical accuracy while undermining that very claim. Claims to accuracy may take the form of explicit comments, as in the silent movie *From the Manger to the Cross* (1912), which introduces itself as "a review of the saviour's life according to the gospel-narrative." These claims may also be made more subtly, by referring to dates and events in a sonorous and authoritative voiceover, as in the introduction to the 1961 film *King of Kings*, narrated impressively by Orson Welles.

While claiming accuracy, those who make Jesus films undermine that claim by creating scenes, dialogue, and even characters that fill in the gospels' gaps in order to create a coherent and compelling film. Filmmakers draw on numerous sources to flesh out their portrait of Jesus. They use the writings of Josephus, the first-century Jewish historian, for example, to add detail to the social and political contexts of Jesus' life, and the apocryphal gospels (e.g., the Infancy Gospel of Thomas) to add events to Jesus' early life. They may draw on fictional accounts such as *Ben-Hur* or *The Last Temptation of Christ* to create a fictional framework within which to situate their portraits of Jesus; similarly, they may use the passion play tradition to explore the events surrounding his death, and other Jesus movies to pay homage to certain iconic images and scenes.[1] Nicholas Ray's film *King of Kings* (1961) links Judas and Barabbas, placing them among the leadership of a militant Jewish group that seeks to exploit Jesus' charisma for the good of the revolution. Robert Young adds romantic interest to his made-for-TV movie, *Jesus* (1999), avoiding controversy by having the youthful savior fall in love with Mary of Bethany but renounce marriage in order to pursue his destiny as the Messiah.

Most obviously, filmmakers create the visual and aural elements that no written text can convey fully, such as the physical appearance of the characters, the tone and quality of their voices, the sounds and images of their settings, and their body movements and gestures. Some of these elements come from the art tradition. For example, many films include a brief scene in which Jesus' mother Mary cradles her dead son in her lap, in homage to Michelangelo's *Pieta*, and many also arrange their Last Supper scene to imitate Leonardo's famous fresco.

Related to the ambiguity regarding historical accuracy is the tension between "faithfulness" – to the gospels and/or to Christian theology – and relevance to the present day. The Jesus movies are not only a medium through which viewers can "see" Jesus, but are also a vehicle through which to consider Jesus' ongoing relevance to modern society. For this reason, they address the concerns and anxieties of their own time. For example, as overt anti-Semitism became less acceptable, the Jesus movies began to shift focus away from the role of the Jewish people in Jesus' death to lay the blame on Rome (*The Miracle Maker*, 2000), Caiaphas (*The King of Kings*, 1927) or even a fictional character (the scribe Zerah, in *Jesus of Nazareth*, 1979). Similarly, the changing role of women in society and in some streams of Christianity is reflected in the prominence that more recent films give to Jesus' mother (*Il Messias*, 1975), Mary and Martha of Bethany (*Last Temptation of Christ*, 1988), and Mary Magdalene (*Jesus of Montreal*, 1989; *The Passion of the Christ*, 2004).

The Jesus movies not only interpret the gospels but also bow to the conventions of their era and genre. Cecil B. DeMille's magnificent film, *The King of Kings* (1927) has the spectacle, near-nudity, romance, and circus animals that were *de rigueur* in the silent movie era. Nicholas Ray's *King of Kings* (1961) and George Stevens' *The Greatest Story Ever Told* (1965) have the majestic scenery, symphonic music, and large casts of famous actors that characterized the epic genre in the period after World War II. David Greene's *Godspell* (1973) and Norman Jewison's *Jesus Christ Superstar* (1973) are rock operas that share many features with other famous productions such as Ken Russell's *Tommy* (1975) and Milos Forman's *Hair* (1979). Mel Gibson's 2004 film *The Passion of the Christ* owes much to the spiritual memoirs of Anne Catherine Emmerich (1833) but even more to the contemporary action movie genre to which Gibson himself has contributed.[2]

The Jesus of Jesus Movies

While they make ample use of the cinematic conventions of their genre and era, the Jesus films also testify to fundamental tensions in New Testament depictions of Jesus. Though the Jesus movies, like other bio-pics, explicitly claim some degree of historicity and authenticity, they are in fact expositions of theology, with a particular emphasis on christology.

Humanity and divinity

The gospels present Jesus as a human being who is also the son of God. The synoptic traditions include stories that accentuate Jesus' human nature, including the nativity and infancy narratives (Matt 1–2; Luke 1–2). The Gospel of John, by contrast, relentlessly focuses on Jesus' identity as the Son of God, by emphasizing his pre-existence (1:1–18), his role as God's representative in the world and God's agent of salvation, and even his equality to God (10:30).

As early as 1912, the British Board of Film Censors banned the visual representation of Jesus, thereby deemphasizing his humanity. American films that were slated for British distribution had to conform to this standard (Telford 1998, 130). The American Motion Picture Production Code of 1930, also known as the Hays Code, stipulated that "Ministers of religion in their character as ministers of religion should not be used as comic characters or as villains" (Section 8.2). These requirements had an inhibiting influence on Jesus bio-pics.

One of the significant challenges in making a Jesus movie is the belief that Jesus of Nazareth did not grow into his role as the Messiah but was free from sin at birth and perhaps even before he was born. This belief puts a serious constraint on films that represent themselves as historical or in other ways faithful to the gospels and to Christian faith. Most films, including bio-pics, depict the protagonist as undergoing some sort of change or development. Character development is not possible, however, in the case of a hero who is already perfect in every way. Jesus, in contrast to the subjects of most other bio-pics, cannot be shown as subject to the faults, doubts, or concerns of ordinary human beings.

One way that Jesus movies compensate for this limitation is to develop more fully some of the other characters of the gospels, particularly Judas and Mary Magdalene. Both of these figures are amenable to dramatic development. As the disciple who handed Jesus over to the enemy, Judas moves from devotion to betrayal. As a woman with a reputation for promiscuity, Mary Magdalene moves from sinfulness and demon possession to faith.

Another, more radical, solution is to humanize Jesus by depicting him as a man who grows into his salvific role as the Son of God. The films *Last Temptation* and *Jesus of Montreal* combine these two approaches to create narratives that are the furthest removed from the gospel accounts but at the same time present arguably the most compelling, engaging, and thought-provoking Jesus figures of the entire genre.

The only film, however, to show Jesus as a figure who never does quite measure up to the expectations of those around him is *Jesus Christ Superstar* (1973). This Jesus, as the film's name implies, is concerned not so much with his divine mission but with celebrity. In the Last Supper scene, Jesus turns the solemn institution of the eucharist into a complaint about his disciples' devotion:

> For all you care this wine could be my blood
> For all you care this bread could be my body
> The end! ...
> I must be mad thinking I'll be remembered – yes
> I must be out of my head!
> Look at your blank faces! My name will mean nothing
> Ten minutes after I'm dead!

The film is not a critique of Christianity, however, but a polemic against society's preoccupation with celebrities, to whom it then attributes superhuman powers and saintly qualities.

Most Jesus films do not ascribe any negative qualities to their hero. At the same time, given the generally realistic nature of the bio-pic genre, it is easier for filmmakers to portray Jesus' human aspects than his divine nature. High christology is often depicted only indirectly, as reflected in the rapt responses of those around Jesus, both their facial expressions and their words. Perhaps the most memorable moment of this sort occurs at the end of the scene of Jesus' crucifixion in *The Greatest Story Ever Told*, in which a Roman centurion played by John Wayne drawls, "Truly this man was the Son of God!" More subtly, techniques such as lighting and camera angles as well as aspects of the setting (e.g., "big sky") and soundtrack ("big music") help to convey the divine aspect of Jesus' identity.

Jesus' miracles pose a major challenge. Many films avoid depicting many of Jesus' healings and exorcisms directly on the screen, making use of verbal descriptions instead. In the opening scene of *The King of Kings*, Mary Magdalene's suitors tell her about a certain carpenter from Nazareth who, it is said, heals the sick and raises the dead. In *The Greatest Story Ever Told*, Pilate is informed of Jesus' miracles through a formal report read aloud by one of his officials. This device relieves the filmmaker of the responsibility of depicting the miracles visually. To be sure, the most spectacular events, such as the raising of Lazarus, are still portrayed, but overall the miracles are much less prominent in the Jesus movies than in the gospels themselves. In general, it is Jesus the teacher, not Jesus the miracle-worker, who comes to the fore in the Jesus movies.

The cinematic emphasis on Jesus' human dimensions also emerges in other aspects of his depiction. In *The Gospel According to Saint Matthew* (1964), Pasolini's Jesus is a young man whose anger is directed not so much at the spiritual ills of his society but at the Roman state machine. As in the First Gospel, this Jesus cuts his ties with his biological family, but he quietly sheds a tear when he walks past his mother's home without acknowledging her presence. Both his anger and his tears draw attention to his human aspects far more than to his divine nature.

Another film that focuses on the human Jesus is Arcand's 1989 film *Jesus of Montreal*. This film depicts a group of actors who are commissioned to do a passion play in Montreal and thereby sets the passion story itself into a contemporary fictional narrative framework. As in most films of this type – other examples are *He Who Must Die* (*Celui Qui Doit Mourir*, dir. Jules Dassin, 1959) and *The Master and Margareth* (dir. Yuri Kara, 1994) – the character who plays Jesus in the passion play gradually takes on aspects of Jesus' persona in the narrative framework. Daniel Coulombe, the "Jesus" of Montreal, does not perform any supernatural miracles, yet he has a profound and perceptible impact on those around him. Through his personality and encouragement, he transforms the lives of the actors who work with him, and even, to some extent, those who oppose him or attempt to degrade his work.

The tension between Jesus' human and divine characteristics is the central theme in Scorsese's *The Last Temptation of Christ* (1988). In contrast to most other Jesus films, Scorsese's offering does not claim to be historical; rather, as indicated in the scrolling text that opens the film, the film is an adaptation of Nikos Kazantzakis' novel by the same name. In exploring Jesus' subjectivity, this film reflects upon what Scorsese (and Kazantzakis) call the "eternal conflict" between the spirit and the flesh. Scorsese's Jesus is tortured by insecurity and self-doubt. He is ashamed of his occupation – a carpenter, he specializes in making the crosses for Roman crucifixions – and driven by fits and voices to engage in behaviors whose source – the devil? God? – he cannot identify. Scorsese's Jesus eventually comes to understand that he is indeed God's son, but this knowledge does not strengthen him or allow him to defeat the forces of evil in the world. Until his final breath, he struggles against this knowledge and the destiny that it dictates. At the moment of his death, however, he is truly transformed into the Son of God, in a scene that is perhaps the most exultant, and therefore evinces the highest christology, of any in the Jesus movie genre. The eternal conflict between spirit and flesh has now finally been won, and Jesus' doubt about himself in his relationship with God has been resolved.

The most incoherent and conflicted presentation of christology is to be found in Mel Gibson's 2004 blockbuster, *The Passion of the Christ*. The film opens with a scrolled text quoting from Isaiah 53: "He was wounded for our transgressions, crushed by our iniquities; by His wounds we are healed" (cf. Isa 53:5). By introducing the film in this way, Gibson implies that Jesus fulfills the prophecy of the suffering servant messiah and attaches salvific significance to the terrible crushing of Jesus' body that is the major theme of the film. The film emphasizes Jesus' suffering and the forbearance with which he endured it. This portrayal may be intended to underscore Jesus' divine nature, as the suffering exceeds what a mere human being could endure. Yet visually, Gibson's Jesus is reduced not to his humanity but to his physicality; he does not resemble a god or even a man, but a hunk of raw flesh. This portrayal erases not only Jesus' divine identity but his human one as well.

Sexuality and ethnicity

If some aspects of Jesus' humanity, such as his compassion and his physical suffering, are easy to depict, two other elements – his sexuality and his ethnicity – are more problematic. The Fourth Gospel's portrayal of Mary Magdalene, who apparently is ready to embrace the risen Lord (John 20:17), has from the beginning suggested the possibility that Mary had a special role in Jesus' life (Reinhartz 2007). The gospels are silent with regard to Jesus' sexual or romantic liaisons and even, it must be said, with regard to his celibacy or asceticism. In Christian tradition, however, Jesus was understood to be celibate, and sexual asceticism became a very important part of his identity. Young's *Jesus* (1999), to be sure, does portray him as having a romantic interest in Mary of Bethany, which he abandoned reluctantly as being incompatible with his larger mission.[3] But the cinematic Jesus is generally celibate and even asexual. There has to date been no mainstream film in which Jesus is explicitly portrayed as having a sexual or romantic relationship with anyone.

Even Scorsese's *Last Temptation*, which became the subject of considerable controversy, does not stray from this rule. The film concludes with a lengthy dream sequence. As Jesus is on the cross, he receives a reprieve from his tragic fate by a young girl who removes the nails and guides him off the cross and into his own marriage with Mary Magdalene. Mary becomes pregnant but dies before bearing him a child. He then marries Mary and Martha of Bethany, with whom he has several children. This indeed is the Last Temptation, but it is not sexuality so much as the lure of domesticity, being a man – a husband, father, breadwinner – like other men. While the dream sequence contains explicit images of Jesus making love, it is evident throughout that it is indeed a dream, and not "reality." At the end of the film, Jesus, like all of his cinematic counterparts, dies on the cross a virgin.

A second difficult issue is Jesus' ethnicity. The Jesus films attempt to portray him as a universal savior who remains relevant for and central to twentieth or twenty-first century western culture. This attempt seems to override any acknowledgment that Jesus was a Jew, who probably engaged in the same level of observance of Jewish law and customs as other Galilean Jews (Meier 1991).

Jesus' Jewish identity is not in doubt. His name is a short form of "Yehoshua" or "Joshua," and his home town, Nazareth, was a Jewish city in the Galilee during the period of Roman domination over Judea, Galilee, and Samaria, several decades before the first Jewish revolt against Rome (66–74). It is not just the Jesus movies, however, that are reluctant to acknowledge Jesus' Jewishness. For many, it is natural to view Jesus as something "other" than Jewish, because Christianity defines itself as "other" than Judaism (Becker and Reed 2003; Reinhartz 2005). Theologically, Jesus' Jewish identity stands in tension with belief in him as the universal Savior and Messiah who transcends any notions of religion, ethnicity, or even gender.

While Jesus' Jewishness has to a great extent been recovered in Christian theology as well as in New Testament research (Levine 2006; Fredriksen 1999; Sanders 1985), it is still difficult to discern in many of the Jesus movies made before the 1970s. Most films do portray a Jewish wedding (cf. John 2) and Jewish festivals (the Passover), because these events are described in the gospels themselves. Their portrayal, however, focuses on their christological significance and often disregards completely their Jewish context and meaning. An amusing example of this tendency can be found in D. W. Griffith's *Intolerance* (1916), in which Jesus' presence at the wedding in Cana is used to demonstrate Jesus' approval of alcohol, a point that is quite far from the meaning of the wedding story in John 2 but central to Griffith's polemic against the Temperance movement in the United States.[4]

Following the lead of theology and scholarship, recent films have been more attentive to Jesus' Jewish context and identity. Zeffirelli's *Jesus of Nazareth*, for example, lavishly portrays the Jewish rituals and celebrations, particularly in the segments dealing with the courtship of Joseph and Mary and with Jesus' own young life. *Jesus of Montreal* explicitly emphasizes Jesus' Jewish identity. The narrator of the passion play, which is performed within the contemporary frame of the film, proclaims that "Our knowledge of Jesus is so sketchy some claim he never existed. Paradoxically, Jesus wasn't Christian, but Jewish. He was circumcised and observed Jewish law. The destiny of Israel obsessed him." In Scorsese's rendition of the wedding scene, the groom recites the traditional formula, "You are sacred to me through this ring according to the laws of Moses and Israel." In *Godspell*, the clown-faced Jesus celebrates the Passover Seder while sitting on the ground surrounded by his disciples and recites the traditional Hebrew blessings over the bread and wine. In Gibson's film, Passover is also strongly evoked. At the moment of Jesus' arrest, his mother Mary wakes up with a start and says in Hebrew, "Listen ... Why is this night different from every other night? Because once we were slaves and now we are slaves no longer." This speech combines two elements from the Passover Seder:[5] the "Four Questions," usually recited by the youngest child at the Seder, and a passage from a later moment in the home-based ritual that focuses on the enslavement in Egypt from which God miraculously freed the Israelites. Mary's words recall the Passover season of Jesus' death, and its salvific importance, while also drawing attention to the fear that gripped her heart as Jesus' mother.

One major factor influencing perceptions of Jesus' Jewishness is his appearance. Most cinematic Jesus figures bear no resemblance whatsoever to the first-century Semitic male as reconstructed from the archaeological evidence.[6] The only real exceptions to this pattern are the Jesus character in the British animated/Claymation film *The Miracle Maker* (2000), who has dark skin and typically Semitic features, and the protagonist of *The Color of the Cross* (2006), who is African in appearance.[7]

In most cases, however, Jesus on the silver screen bears a strong resemblance to the Jesus of renaissance paintings and the biblical illustrations by Gustav Doré and James Tissot. He generally has a slight physique and is of medium height, with light brown hair, a short brown beard, and piercing blue eyes.[8] Perhaps the strongest influence on the visual portrayal of Jesus from the epic period to the present is Warner Sallman's 1940 painting. In the postwar period of the 1940s and 1950s, this painting was ubiquitous across all segments of American society and may have been one of the best-known art works ever created. It was reproduced in illustrated Bibles, Sunday school literature, calendars, posters, church bulletins, lamps, buttons, and even bumper stickers (Prothero 2003, 116–123; to view the image, see Henderson n.d.). The most faithful recreation of the Sallman image is that of Robert Powell, who plays Jesus in Zeffirelli's *Jesus of Nazareth*, but most other Jesus figures since the 1960s also take their cues from Sallman. This way of representing Jesus not only evokes the popular painting but also provides an obvious contrast to the Jewish enemies of Jesus as depicted in film, who inevitably have a dark coloring and stereotypical Semitic features. A clear example of this contrast can be found in *Jesus Christ Superstar*, in which the Pharisees and priests have dark curly hair and sinister voices.

It is striking that the films that are the most explicit about Jesus' Jewish identity are also those that take the greatest liberties with the gospel sources. *Monty Python's Life of Brian* (1979), while not strictly speaking a Jesus movie, emphasizes the Jewishness of its protagonist, Brian, who is an unwitting Messiah figure. The film uses, and at the same time mocks, the clichés of the Jesus film genre, including the tendency to present Jesus as a western European male. In contrast to the Jesus of popular piety, Brian is Jewish, and proud of it. When his mother tells him that his father was a Roman soldier, Brian protests, "I'm not a Roman, and I never will be!

I'm a kike, a yid, a hebie, a hook-nose, I'm kosher, Mum, I'm a Red-Sea pedestrian and proud of it!" This scene draws upon the ancient – and unhistorical – Jewish legend that Jesus was the illegitimate child of Mary and a Roman soldier.

Jesus as Savior

One of the most salient differences between canonical gospels and the Jesus movies is the role of politics. The gospels acknowledge that the events they recount took place in the context of Roman domination in Judea and Galilee. Luke's infancy narrative (Luke 1–2) sets the birth of John the Baptist and Jesus in the time of King Herod of Judea (1:1) and dates John's baptizing mission as follows: "It was the fifteenth year of the reign of Emperor Tiberius, when Pontius Pilate was governor of Judea, and Herod was ruler of Galilee, and his brother Philip ruler of the region of Ituraea and Trachonitis, and Lysanias ruler of Abilene, during the high priesthood of Annas and Caiapha" (Luke 3:1–2). Joseph and his pregnant wife Mary must travel to Bethlehem, because "In those days a decree went out from Emperor Augustus that all the world should be registered. This was the first registration and was taken while Quirinius was governor of Syria. All went to their own towns to be registered" (Luke 2:1–3). Furthermore, Roman rule is implied in the references to the denarius as the coin of the realm (Matt 18:28; 20:2; 22:15–21) and, more explicitly, in the prominent role given to Roman soldiers and the Roman governor Pilate himself in the events leading up to Jesus' execution. John 11:49–52 implies fear of Rome, as in the aftermath of Jesus' spectacular resurrection of the dead Lazarus:

> [T]he chief priests and the Pharisees called a meeting of the council, and said, "What are we to do? This man is performing many signs. If we let him go on like this, everyone will believe in him, and the Romans will come and destroy both our holy place and our nation." (11:47–48)

The Jesus movies pay much more attention to the Roman oppression of Judea and Galilee, however, than do the gospels. By emphasizing the role of Rome, the Jesus movies can bolster their claims to historicity. This emphasis is seen from the very earliest contributions to the genre. The 1923 silent film *INRI* describes Jerusalem as a city "across whose shoulders the yoke of Rome had lain heavy for almost a hundred years." Similarly, the 1935 film *Golgotha* opens with a reference to "Tiberius Caesar of Palestine," a map of Judea under Roman rule, and a declaration of Israel's strong desire to be free. In DeMille's *The King of Kings*, Judea is said to be "groaning under the iron heel of Rome." More recently, Philip Saville's 2003 film *The Gospel of John* opens with a scrolling text specifying that the Fourth Gospel, and hence the film too, is "set in a time when the Roman Empire controlled Jerusalem."

While Pilate and the members of his entourage may be cultured Romans, their soldiers are invariably presented as vicious and uncouth. In many of the epics, such as *Ben-Hur* (1959), Zeffirelli's *Jesus of Nazareth* (1979), and Young's *Jesus* (1999), Roman soldiers gallop on horseback into the villages of innocent residents, much like the villains in Westerns such as *Pale Rider* (1985) rode into frontier outposts, demanding tribute, terrorizing the townsfolk and helping themselves to food and livestock (Reinhartz 2003, 166–173; cf. Freyne 1988; 2000). Like television mafiosos, these ancient Romans often had local henchmen, such as Matthew the tax collector, who used intimidation and force when gentler persuasion failed.

One of the most disturbing scenes of Roman force is not, as some might think, the lengthy scourging of Jesus in Gibson's *The Passion of the Christ* (2004), but Pasolini's portrayal of the "Slaughter of the Innocents" (Matt 2:16) in *The Gospel According to Saint Matthew* (1964). Whereas Matthew attributes the slaughter to Herod's men, Pasolini explicitly portrays the perpetrators as Roman soldiers. The camera pans slowly across the Roman soldiers waiting on a ridge for the signal to attack the Jewish infants. Just when the suspense becomes unbearable, the leader puts two fingers in his mouth and whistles loudly, unleashing the troops on the innocents below.

Only one film acknowledges that there may have been at least some positive consequences of the Roman presence in Judea. *Monty Python's Life of Brian* (1979) portrays a meeting of one of the many protest movements in Judea that is planning a guerilla attack on Pilate's palace. To maintain the appropriate anger and sense of outrage, their leader, Reg, proclaims, "They've bled us white, the bastards. They've taken everything we had, and not just from us, from our fathers, and from our fathers' fathers." Others pipe up, "And from our fathers' fathers' fathers ... And from our fathers' fathers' fathers' fathers." Yet when Reg asks, rhetorically, "And what have they ever given us in return?!" a rather long list emerges, including the aqueduct, sanitation, the roads, irrigation, medicine, education, wine, public baths, public safety, and so on. Finally Reg, disgusted, shouts, "All right, but apart from the sanitation, the medicine, education, wine, public order, irrigation, roads, a fresh water system, and public health, what have the Romans ever done for us?" "Brought peace," says one. Reg gives up: "Oh. Peace? Shut up!"[9]

A second reason for the focus on the political context is that it allows for a greater and more explicit establishment of causality. Such films often develop a "backstory" to explain Judas Iscariot's betrayal of Jesus. They suggest that Judas was a zealot, a member of a group that strove for armed rebellion against Rome. In this backstory, Judas initially believed that Jesus would bring armed revolution; his betrayal of Jesus is in some cases a reflection of his disappointment in Jesus (Young's *Jesus*), and in others, a mistaken attempt to push Jesus toward a call to begin the revolution (*King of Kings, The Greatest Story Ever Told, Jesus of Nazareth*).

A third reason pertains specifically to films made in America and elsewhere in the decades after World War II, when society was still processing the events of the war and the necessity of liberating humankind from an oppressive, unjust, and authoritarian regime. Some of the Jesus movies explicitly evoke the postwar period by comparing the fate of the Jewish people under Rome with that under the Nazi regime. For example, *King of Kings* (1961) begins with a lengthy voiceover narration that includes the following description of Judea under Rome:

> For more than fifty years after Pompey's invasion, the history of Judea would be read by the light of burning towns. If gold was not the harvest, there was a richness of people to be gathered. The battalions of Caesar August brought in the crop. Like sheep, from their own green fields, the Jews went to the slaughter. They went from stone quarries to build Rome's triumphal arches.

This narrative explicitly recalls the postwar reflections on the Holocaust, which explicitly raised the question of whether Jews went "like sheep to the slaughter" (Reinhartz 2007, 126–129).

The movies that focus on the Roman context posit that the people of Judea and the Galilee were awaiting a messiah who would come to save the Jews from Roman oppression. This is articulated, for example, by a Roman official in *Ben-Hur*, who responds to an order to find the Jewish rebels against Rome by saying,

> Oh, you don't know. There's nothing you can put your finger on! I tell you there are strange forces at work here. For instance there's this Messiah business ... A King of Jews, who will lead them into some sort of anti-Roman paradise. [scoffs] Makes your head spin. Then there's a wild man in the desert named John who drowns people in water. The carpenter's son goes around doing magic tricks. Miracles, they call them.

In *Jesus of Nazareth*, Zeffirelli's Herod explains derisively, "The messiah is a bad dream disguised as a solution to every problem. It's a leveler of scores, a rewarder of righteousness, a scourge for the wrong-doer. It is the dream of everlasting peace."

Naturally, it is Jesus who is the long-awaited Messiah. Yet at this point in Hollywood's liberation narrative, the chain of causality breaks down. The fact is that Jesus did not liberate the Jews from Roman rule. His story pre-dates the first Jewish Revolt against Rome by approximately four decades, and, as far as we can tell, Jesus played no role either historically, ideologically or symbolically in the events that led up to the Revolt. Even more, the Jesus of the gospels rejects attempts to view him as a political revolutionary (cf. John 6:15), though the fact that he was crucified suggests that at least Rome suspected him of treason.

Conclusion

The Jesus movies allow us to "see" Jesus through the eyes of filmmakers from different eras and different perspectives. In this sense, these films also constitute interpretations of the gospels as well as of the meaning of Jesus' life and message. Yet we should not forget that the Jesus films are not historical reconstructions of Jesus' life, however loudly they may proclaim their own historicity. As we have seen, these films undermine their own claims at the same time as they state them, by the very act of attaching visual and aural elements to the canonical texts, and by adjusting the story to meet the narrative conventions of the bio-pic genre and the technological requirements of the cinema. Nor are marketing considerations to be overlooked. Like most other commercial films, the Jesus films are made with an eye to the possibility of both box office and critical success, and for those reasons they tailor their portrayals of Jesus to the market their films target. The Jesus movies reach large audiences, not only or even primarily through theater screenings but now through DVD and the internet and therefore help to shape how their viewers may perceive and understand Jesus for themselves.

Despite these considerations, including the challenges and ambiguities of the bio-pic genre itself, the cinematic Savior remains a seductive figure, the closest that most of us can hope to get to seeing and touching Jesus for ourselves.

Notes

1   The 2000 film *The Miracle Maker*, for example, reproduces a number of scenes from Zeffirelli's 1979 epic Jesus of Nazareth, and Gibson's Pilate character is similar in appearance to the Pilate of Stevens' *The Greatest Story Ever Told*.

2   On the indebtedness of this film to other genres, including Gibson's previous films, see Thistlethwaite (2004).

3   In this respect, the cinematic Jesus often resembles the superhero Spiderman, who also initially rejects romance on the grounds that it will distract him or create in him a conflict of interest with respect to his broader mission. See *Spiderman I* and *Spiderman II*.

4   On the American Temperance movement, see Young (2006).

5   The *Seder* is the traditional home-based service and celebration held on the first day of the Passover festival in Israel, or on the first two days outside of Israel.

6   See the BBC Worldwide/Reuters 2001 computer-generated reconstruction of the face of a first-century Judean male, based on the skull of a man buried in Jerusalem 2000 years ago (Walsh n.d.).

7   Culturally, the protagonist of *The Color of the Cross* seems to be African American, just as other Jesus figures seem to be American (*Last Temptation*), British (*Jesus of Nazareth*), or even Quebecois (*Jesus of Montreal*).

8   See, for example, the baptism of Jesus (Rose 1974, 168; Tissot 1899, insert in vol. 1, between pp. 62–63).

9   This transcription is taken from Screenplays for You (Raynor n.d.), which justifiably claims to provide the most complete and accurate transcription of this film available. Humorous as it is, Monty Python did not invent this scenario *ex nihilo*. The positive Roman contribution to the quality of material life in Judea is also the subject of a passage in the Babylonian Talmud, *Shabbat* 33b: "R. Judah, R. Jose, and R. Simeon were sitting, and Judah, a son of proselytes, was sitting near them. R. Judah commenced [the discussion] by observing, 'How fine are the works of these people [the Romans]! They have made streets, they have built bridges, they have erected baths.' R. Jose was silent. R. Simeon b. Yohai answered and said, 'All what they made they made for themselves; they built marketplaces, to set harlots in them; baths, to rejuvenate themselves; bridges, to levy tolls for them.' Now, Judah the son of proselytes went and related their talk, which reached the government. They decreed: 'Judas, who exalted [us], shall be exalted [by always having the privilege of speaking first in any discussion]. Jose, who was silent, shall be exiled to Sepphoris [in the Galilee]; Simeon, who censured, let him be executed'" (Epstein 1961, Seder Mo'ed 1.156).

References

Becker, Adam H., and Annette Yoshiko Reed, eds. (2003). *The Ways that Never Parted: Jews and Christians in Late Antiquity and the Early Middle Ages*. Tübingen: Mohr Siebeck.

Custen, George F. (1992). *Bio/Pics: How Hollywood Constructed Public History*. New Brunswick, NJ: Rutgers University Press.

Epstein, Isadore (1961). *The Babylonian Talmud*. English trans. London: Soncino.

Fredriksen, Paula (1999). *Jesus of Nazareth, King of the Jews: A Jewish Life and the Emergence of Christianity*. New York: Knopf.

Freyne, Sean (1988). *Galilee, Jesus, and the Gospels: Literary Approaches and Historical Investigations*. Dublin: Gill & Macmillan.

Freyne, Sean (2000). *Galilee and Gospel: Collected Essays*. Tübingen: Mohr Siebeck.

Henderson, Charles P. (n.d.). "Warner Sallman's Head of Christ: An American Icon." GodWeb. At www.godweb.org/sallman.htm (accessed April 11, 2010).

Levine, Amy-Jill (2006). *The Misunderstood Jew: The Church and the Scandal of the Jewish Jesus*. San Francisco: HarperSanFrancisco.

Meier, John P. (1991). *A Marginal Jew: Rethinking the Historical Jesus*. Anchor Bible Reference Library. New York: Doubleday.

Prothero, Stephen (2003). *American Jesus: How the Son of God Became a National Icon*. New York: Farrar, Straus & Giroux.

Raynor, Alex (n.d.). "Life of Brian, 1979, movie script." Screenplays for You. At http://sfy.ru/sfy.html?script=mp_brian (accessed June 5, 2009).

Reinhartz, Adele (2003). *Scripture on the Silver Screen*. Louisville, KY: Westminster John Knox.

Reinhartz, Adele (2005). "A Fork in the Road or a Multi-Lane Highway? New Perspectives on 'The Parting of the Ways' Between Judaism and Christianity." In Ian Henderson and Gerbern S. Oegema (eds.), *The Changing Face of Judaism, Christianity and Other Greco-Roman Religions in Antiquity* (pp. 278–293). Studien zu den Jüdischen Schriften aus Hellenistisch-Römischer Zeit. Band 2. Gütersloh: Gütersloher Verlagshaus.

Reinhartz, Adele (2007). *Jesus of Hollywood*. Oxford, New York: Oxford University Press.

Rose, Millicent, ed. (1974). *The Doré Bible Illustrations*. New York: Dover.

Sanders, E. P. (1985). *Jesus and Judaism*. Philadelphia: Fortress.

Telford, William R. (1998). "Jesus Christ Movie Star: The Depiction of Jesus in the Cinema." In C. Marsh and G. Ortiz (eds.), *Explorations in Theology and Film: Movies and Meaning* (pp. 115–140). Oxford: Blackwell.

Thistlethwaite, Susan (2004). "Mel Makes a War Movie." In *Perspectives on the Passion of the Christ* (pp. 127–145). New York: Miramax.

Tissot, James Jacques Joseph (1899). *The Life of Our Saviour Jesus Christ. Three Hundred and Sixty-Five Compositions from the Four Gospels, with Notes and Explanatory Drawings*. London: Sampson Low, Marston.

Walsh, W. John (n.d.). "Physical Appearance of Jesus." LightPlanet.com. At www.lightplanet.com/mormons/basic/christ/physical_appearance.htm (accessed May 15, 2009).

Young, Michael P. (2006). *Bearing Witness against Sin: The Evangelical Birth of the American Social Movement*. Chicago: University of Chicago Press.

Index

Note: page numbers in italics indicate illustrations. The Arabic prefix Al- is ignored in the alphabetical ordering of entries.

Abbasid Caliphate   233
'Abdu, Muhammad   246
Abe, Masao   272, 276
Abelard, Peter, and atonement   207, 209
Abgar of Edessa   501
Abhedananda, Swami   252, 256, 258, 259
Acts, Apocryphal   154–6
Acts of Andrew   154
Acts of Andrew and Matthias   154
Acts of the Apostles *see* Luke-Acts
Acts of John   3, 154–5
Acts of Paul   154–5
Acts of Peter   154–5
Acts of Peter and the Twelve Apostles   172
Acts of Pilate (Gospel of Nicodemus)   151, 153
Acts of Thomas   3, 154–6
Adam christology:
   in Christian art   497
   in Paul   2, 101–3, 104, 108
adoption, and atonement   197
adoptionism   3, 99
adoration of the Magi, in early Christian art   484–5
Aelred of Rievaulx   444–5

African Americans:
   and Great Awakening   399
   and racialization of Jesus   403, 406–7
   and women   432
African theology   315–16
   and ancestors   288–9, 387
   christologies   386–9
   and *Christus Victor*   387–8
   context   387
   and cultural analogies   7
   and Jesus as healer   389
Ahmad, Mirza Ghulam   245–6, 461–3
Ahmadiyya movement   245, 461, 463
Ahn, Byung Mu   383
Alexander of Alexandria   177, 180
Alexandrian theology   182–3, 185, 186, 381
'Ali, 'Abd Allah Yusuf   245
Allison, Dale C.   32, 312, 335 n.9
allusions:
   in classical writers   131
   in early Judaism   131
   to Old Testament   129, 132, 135–6
Alpha and Omega, in Revelation   120, 125, 128
Althaus-Reid, Marcella   437–8

Ambelain, Robert   466
Ambrose of Milan, and atonement   205
Anastasius of Sinai   188
ancestors:
    in African theology   387, 388–9
    in black American theology   403
Anderson, Hugh   285–6
Andrews, Richard and Schellenberger, Paul
        469
androcentrism   32, 34, 428, 434
Anercius, bishop of Hierapolis, epitaph   480
Anselm of Canterbury, and atonement
        203, 206–7, 208
anti-Semitism, Christian   506, 515, 521
Antiochian theology   183, 184, 186, 381
Apocalypse of Abraham   121
Apocalypse of John *see* Revelation
Apocalypse of Peter   157, 171
apocryphal literature:
    early *see* New Testament Apocrypha
    modern   7–8, 458–71
    Old Testament   65
Apocryphon of James   167, 168–9, 172
Apocryphon of John   167, 168, 500
Apollinarianism   180, 181–2
Apostles' Creed   285–6, 303
appearance of Jesus   477–8
    in early Christian art   499–502, *501*
    in film   526–7
Appiah-Kubi, Kofi   386
Al-'Aqqad, 'Abbas Mahmud, *'Abkariyyat
        al-Masih*   246
Aquinas, Thomas   3
Aquino, Maria Pilar   431–2
Arabic Infancy Gospel   149–50
Aramaic, and sayings of Jesus   310
Arcand, Denys, *Jesus of Montreal*   521,
        522, 523
Arius   177, 180
Armenian Infancy Gospel   149–50
Arnal, William   347
arrest and trial of Jesus:
    in early Christian art   490–1, *491*
    in modern fiction   514–16
art, Christian   8, 477–502
    and appearance of Jesus   499–502, *501*
    dogmatic themes   495–9

early   479–82
episodes from life of Christ   484–95
    Jesus as Good Shepherd   479–81, *480,
        500*
    Jesus as healer and wonder-worker
        482–4, *483*, 500
    Jesus as teacher of true philosophy
        481–2, 500
Arundel 404 (*Liber de Infantia Salvatoris*)
        150
Aryan Jesus   338
Asanga   277
ascension:
    in early Christian art   495
    in Gnostic texts   171–2
    in liberation theology   379
    in Luke-Acts   57–8
asceticism of Jesus   50, 258, 312, 524
Ash'ari theology   238–41
Ashoka, Edicts   271
Asia:
    christologies   380–6
    and cultural analogies   6–7
    and ecofeminism   439
    and European Jesus   380–1
    and Jesus of the poor   383–4
    Nestorianism and Monophysitism   381–2
Athanasius   176, 204, 454–5
atonement   193–209, 288
    in canonical gospels   198–200
    Christus Victor theory   203–4
    conquest theory   204
    in early church   202–7
    in Hebrews (epistle)   118, 201
    in Johannine epistles   112
    legal theories   205–7, 209
    in Luke-Acts   57, 200
    moral influence theory   207, 209,
        293–4
    noble death idea   195–6, 197
    in Old Testament   193–5
    in Pastoral Epistles   202
    in Paul   195–8, 202
    penal substitution theory   4, 208–9
    and probability of incarnation   288,
        292–3
    and purification   194, 198

atonement (*cont'd*)
  ransom theory   41, 114, 194, 200,
      202, 203, 204–5
  and Reformation   207–8
  satisfaction theory   204, 205, 206–7,
      208, 293
  substitution theory   198, 204–5
  see also sacrifice
audience, and meaning   133–5
Augustine of Hippo   176, 205–6, 386,
      455, 516
Aulén, Gustav   203–4
Aune, David   73
authors, and meaning   132–3
avatar:
  and incarnation   251–3, 255, 260
  Jesus as   5, 6, 9, 250–6, 382

Baba, Sathya Sai   258
Baigent, Michael and Leigh, Richard
      464–5, 466–7, 468
Balthasar, Hans Urs von   371
baptism:
  and creeds   176
  in John   112–13
  in Manichaeism   168
baptism of Jesus   95, 139, 309, 312
  in early Christian art   486, *487*
  in Luke   52–3
  in Mark   21, 27, 64, 329
  in Matthew   37–8
Barlaam and Josaphat tale   462–3
Barth, Karl   358, 363–4, 366, 372
Barton, Bruce, *The Man Nobody Knows*   402
Basil of Caesarea   180
Bauckham, Richard J.   109 n.12, 125, 316
Bayle, Pierre   304
Beale, G. K.   132–3
beatitudes:
  in Matthew   37–8, 275, 321
  in Q   87
Beecher, Henry Ward   400
Ben-Hur (film)   528, 529
Bentham, Jeremy   445, 450
Bernard of Clairvaux   444
betrayal of Jesus *see* Judas Iscariot
Bhagavad Gita   251, 255–6, 264

Bhavishya-Purana   463
Bingemar, Maria Clara   437
Bird, Michael   516
birth and infancy   230 n.6
  and early Christian art   484–6, *485*
  in Gnostic texts   166
  in Luke   506–7, 527
  in Matthew   506–7
  in modern fiction   506–8
  in New Testament Apocrypha   146–51
Birth of a Nation (film)   405
bisexuality   444, 449, 451, 453, 454
Al-Bistami, Abu Yazid   242–3
Black Christ   7, 404–5, 410–24
  and black nationalism   412–13, 419
  and black struggle   414–16, 417, 421
  and black theology   416–21
  in early black literature   413–14
  in film   526
  and slave Christianity   403–5, 410–12
  and womanist theology   7, 421–4
Black, Matthew   310
black theology:
  critical appraisal   420–1
  hymns   401
  see also Black Christ
Bliss, Daniel, *Jeshua*   509, 512, 516,
      517–18
blood-and-wounds theology   398
bodhisattva   463
  Jesus as   5, 9, 271, 272–3
Boff, Leonardo   379, 380
Bonino, José Miguez   380
Book of Mormon   470
Book of Thomas the Contender   168, 172
Borg, Marcus J.   303, 313–14, 334, 335
      n.9, 345
Bornkamm, Günther   307
Boswell, John   445
Brahmo Samaj   256
Bramley, William   451
branch imagery:
  in Dead Sea Scrolls   76
  in Old Testament   75
Brandon, S. G. F.   345
Brock, Rita Nakashima   209, 431, 435–6
Brown, Dan *see The Da Vinci Code*

Brown, Raymond E.   69
Buckwalter, H. Douglas   61 nn.1, 2
Buddhadâsa   276, 277, 279–80
Buddhism   267–81, 384
    anonymous   271
    and Buddhisms   267
    Jesus as bodhisattva   5, 9, 271, 272–3
    Jesus as compassionate   273–4
    Jesus as object of faith   277–8
    Jesus as savior from sin   279
    Jesus as Son of God   275–7
    Jesus as spiritual teacher   274–5
    new religious movements   269, 270
Bujo, Benezet   389
Bultmann, Rudolf   95, 306, 338, 340
Burgess, Anthony, *Man of Nazareth*   507,
        509, 512, 513–14, 515, 517–18
Burridge, Richard   97
Bush, George W.   394
Bushnell, Horace, and atonement   208–9

Cabezón, José Ignacio   276
Calvin, John, and atonement   4, 208, 209
Cameron, John, *The Messiah: In Nine Books*
        504
Campbell, John McLeod, and atonement
        208
Campbell, Lucie   401
Campbell, R. J.   209
Candasiri, Ajahn   274–5, 279, 280
Cappadocian theology   3–4, 180, 205
Caravaggio (Michelangelo Merisi), *Supper at
        Emmaus*   495
Carleton Paget, James   339
Carson, Donald A.   64
Carter, Warren   40
Cash, Johnny, *Gospel Road* (film)   403
catacombs, and early Christian art   479,
        480, 481, 495–6
catholic epistles *see* general epistles
Catholicism:
    19th-century christology   362–3, 366,
        372
    20th-century christology   367–72
    folk piety   375
    see also Roman Catholic Church
Chalcedon, Council (451):

    and Council of Ephesus   183, 184
    and Haight   370
    and Monophysitism   382
    and nature of Christ   3–4, 184–5, 190,
        264, 366, 424
    and Nestorius   185, 186, 381
    and Rahner   367–8
    and womanist theology   424, 436
Chamberlain, Houston S.   347
Channing, William Ellery   208
Chérisey, Philippe de   466–7
Cherry, Kittridge   453
Chilton, Bruce   315
China, and Nestorian Christianity   381–2
Chinese Hymn Roll   164
Christ:
    in Deutero-Pauline letters   105
    as erotic power   435–6
    of faith   306, 362, 364, 417–19
    as head of the church   106
    in Hinduism   252, 264
    in Johannine epistles   112
    and New Being   365
    in Pastoral Epistles   107
    in Paul   2, 85, 98–9, 104–5, 108
    in Q   85
    as universal   418
    see also Messiah
Christianity:
    and doctrine   270, 274, 306
    and Jesus as ultimate truth   8–9
    and Judaism   224–5
    as patriarchal   349, 429–30
    and slave Christianity   403–5, 410–12
Christmas, and Hinduism   257
christology:
    and creeds   176–91
    Dalit   383–4
    and ecclesiology   106
    of embodiment   434–9
    feminist   7, 348–9, 427–41
    from above   177, 183, 364
    from below   183, 366–7, 370, 372,
        378–9
    of Hebrews   116–18
    of John   64–75
    of liberation   431–2

christology (cont'd)
  Logos   177–8, 370
  of Luke-Acts   47, 48
  of Mark   18, 24, 25–7, 28
  of Matthew   31, 34
  modern Western   357–72
  ontological   177–8
  of Pastoral Epistles   107
  of Paul   94
  post-metaphysical   440
  of pre-Markan tradition   24–5, 26
  of Q   2, 13, 19, 20, 81–92
    christological categories   84–92
    implicit christology   83–4
  of Revelation   119–26
  and veneration of icons   188–9
  womanist   7, 421–4
  yin-yang interpretation   384
  see also adoptionism; Monophysitism;
    Nestorians
Christus Victor theories   203–4, 387–8
Churchill, Winston S.   259
citations:
  in classical writers   131
  in early Judaism   131
  of Old Testament   87–8, 95–6, 100,
    118, 128–9, 132, 135–7
    apologetic and interpretative roles
    135
    and longer traditions   138–41
civil rights movement, American   406–7
Clarke, John Henrik   413–14
Cleage, Albert   419–20, 421
Clement of Alexandria   160, 450–1, 460,
    478
Codex Tchachos   161
colonialism:
  in Asia   380, 383
  and Hinduism   259
  and Islam   234, 243–7
  in Latin America   375–7
  in North America   397–8
The Color of the Cross (film)   526, 530 n.7
Colossians (epistle), christology   105–6
Colville, John   259
Comma Johanneum   113
commercialization of Jesus   401–3, 408

communicatio idiomatum   184
compassion of Jesus   273–4
composition criticism, and Mark's Gospel
    16, 22
Cone, James   417–18, 421
Constantinople:
  First Council (381)   180–2, 190
  Second Council (553)   186–7,
    190–1
  Third Council (680)   187–8, 191
Corbu, Noël   465–6
Corley, Kathleen E.   334
Corpus Christi (play)   443, 453
cosmotheandrism   384, 385
covenant, Christ as giver   497–8
Craig, William Lane   286
Cranach, Lucas the Elder   482
creation:
  Jesus as creator in Christian art   497
  and Wisdom   67–70, 77, 103, 106,
    116, 128, 178
creeds   176–91
  of Constantinople   180–2
  and Council of Ephesus (431)   182–4
  and liturgy   176
  Nicene   3, 176, 180
  and resurrection of Jesus   286–7, 303
  and Tillich   366
Crosby, Fanny   401
"Cross Gospel"   343
Crossan, John Dominic   314–15, 320,
    334, 335 n.9, 343, 345, 348
crucifixion:
  in early Christian art   491–3, 492
  see also death of Jesus
Crusades:
  and Islam   233
  and Jews   221
Cullen, Countee   413
Cyprian of Carthage   205, 386
Cyril, bishop of Alexandria   182–4, 185,
    186

The Da Vinci Code (Brown)   7, 443, 464,
    466, 467–9, 471
Dalai Lama   271, 273–4, 276, 277, 278
Dalit theology   383–4

Daly, Mary   43, 429, 430
Daniel (book), use in New Testament
        120–1, 140, 360
Das, Shaunaka Rishi   261
Davis, Stephen T.   286, 288, 297–8
De Mesa, José M.   380
Dead Sea Scrolls:
    and branch imagery   76
    and eschatology   344
    and knowledge of Jesus   217
    and Second Temple Judaism   340–1
    use of citation and allusion   131
death of Jesus:
    as atonement see atonement
    and betrayal see Judas Iscariot
    and Buddhism   280
    in early Christian art   478
    in Gnostic texts   167, 169–71
    in Hebrews   116, 201
    and Hinduism   257–8
    in Islam   240–2, 245–7
    Jewish culpability   506, 515, 521
    in Jewish scholarship   225–6
    in John   68–9
    in Judaism   225–6
    in Luke-Acts   56–7, 137, 199–200
    in Mark   17, 27, 151, 198–9
    in modern fiction   509–10
    in Paul   96–7, 151, 196–8, 295, 303
    in Q   84–5, 89
    and Rahner   368
    in Revelation   122
    as sacrifice   3, 9
    and Schillebeeckx   369
deification:
    in Athanasius   204
    and atonement   193, 198, 203
    in Irenaeus   203
    in Paul   198
    and salvation   179–80, 184, 191
DeMille, Cecil B. see The King of Kings
descent into Hades:
    in Gnostic texts   170
    in New Testament Apocrypha   153
Deutero-Pauline epistles   105–7
Deutsch, Celia   33

dialogue:
    Christian–Buddhist   268, 273, 280
    Christian–Hindu   253, 259, 261–3
Dialogue of the Savior   166, 167
Dibelius, Martin   15
Dickson, Kwesi   388
Didache   199
disability, theology of   438
discipleship:
    in Luke   50, 59
    in Mark   19, 21, 27
    in Matthew   37, 39, 41–2
    in Q   91
Discourse of Theodosius II   155
dissimilarity criterion   309, 311, 316,
        328, 340
divinity of Jesus:
    and Barth   363–4
    and docetism   3, 113
    and ecumenical councils   177–91
    in Enlightenment thought   6, 394–5
    in feminist theology   436
    in films   521–4
    in Indian thought   382
    and Islam   237, 238–9, 247
    in Jewish thought   229
    in John   2, 521
    and Judaism   219
    in liberation theology   379
    in Luke   58
    in Mark   23, 25, 27
    in Matthew   2
    in New Testament Apocrypha   147,
        149–50
    in Pastoral Epistles   107
    in Paul   94, 104–5
    in Puritanism   394
    in Revelation   120–1, 124–6
    and sinlessness   455
Dixon, Thomas   406
docetism:
    in apocryphal literature   3, 150, 152,
        156
    and divinity of Jesus   3, 113
doctrine, and historical Jesus   270, 274,
        305, 396
Dodd, C. H.   134, 338, 343, 344

Dogen, *Shobogenzo* 272
Dogmatic Sarcophagus 495
dogmatic theology 362–3
Doré, Gustav 526
Dorsey, Thomas 401
Douglas, Kelly Brown 432
Dowling, Levi 470
Du Bois, W. E. B. 405
Du Toit, David S. 339
Duccio di Buoninsegna, *Maesta* 484
Duling, Dennis 31–2
Dunn, James D. G. 61 n.3, 103–4, 316, 343
Dürer, Albrecht, *Christ among the Doctors*
    482

early church:
    and atonement theories 202–7
    development of thought and doctrine
        3–4
Ebionites 233, 236
ecofeminism 439–40
Egerton 2 (papyrus) 151
Eiesland, Nancy 438
Eisenhower, Dwight D. 402
El Greco 484
Elizondo, Virgilio P. 376–7
Elkesaites 233, 236
embodiment, and feminist christologies
    434–9, 440
Emerson, Ralph Waldo 400
encratism 3, 449
Enlightenment 5–6
    and critical scholarship 301, 302, 304,
        337, 357–8
    and Islam 234
    and Jesus as moral exemplar 358, 394
    and miracles 6, 304, 511
1 Enoch, influence on Revelation 121–2
Ephesians (epistle), christology 105, 106–7
Ephesus, Council (431) 182–4, 185, 186,
    190, 381, 486
Epiphanius of Salamis, and Gnostics 160
Epistle of the Apostles 155, 156–7
Epistle of Barnabas 69
eschatology:
    ethical 314
    Gnostic 172–3

and historical Jesus 305–6, 323,
    344–5, 361–2, 369–70
and Islam 241–2, 245–7
of Q 83–4, 86–8, 91
realized 344
restoration 312, 342
see also kingdom of God; second coming
The Essene Letter 7, 461, 462
ethics:
    Jesus as moral exemplar 97–8, 112,
        115, 293–4, 358–9
    in Kant 358
ethnicity *see* historical Jesus
eucharist:
    and atonement theories 199, 202
    see also transubstantiation
Eusebius of Caesarea, and Gnostics 160
Eutyches 184
evangelicalism, American 394, 399–403
    and hymns 401
    and publishing industry 400, 403
    and race 405–6
Evans, Craig A. 339
exaltation of Christ:
    in Ephesians 106
    in general epistles 111
    and Haight 370
    in Hebrews 111, 116–17
    in John 133, 178, 201
    in pastoral epistles 107
    in Paul 95, 97
    in Revelation 120–1, 124
exclusivism:
    and Buddhism 272
    and Christianity 253, 273
exemplar, Jesus as 97–8, 112, 115,
    117–18, 178, 358–9, 394
existentialism, and Tillich 365
exorcist, Jesus as:
    in film 523
    in Mark 20, 21, 24, 28
    in Q 83–4
    in recent scholarship 313–14, 329–30,
        435
experience, religious:
    in feminist theology 436
    personalization 395, 399–400

expiation, and atonement   193, 200
expulsion ritual   195

Faber-Kaiser, Andreas   461
faith:
   and Buddhism   277–8
   and Christ   306, 362, 364, 417–19
   and reason   358, 372
Fanthorpe, Lionel   469
Farquhar, John N.   383
feminism:
   and androcentrism   427–8, 434
   and atonement   207, 209
   and christology   7, 348–9, 427–41
      biblical   432–4
      ecofeminist   439–40
      of embodiment   434–9, 440
      Jesus as Wisdom   32, 433
      post-Christian   429–31
   and liberation christologies   431–2
   and womanism   421–4, 430, 432
fiction, Jesus in *see* novels
Fiddes, Paul S.   209
film, Jesus in   8, 28, 504, 519–30
   and bio-pic genre   519–20, 522, 529
   and historical accuracy   520–1, 527,
      529
   and Jesus as a Jew   525–7
   and Jesus as savior   527–9
   and nature of Jesus   521–4
   and political context   527–9
   and sexuality   524–5
First Apocalypse of James   162, 167,
   168
first and last, Jesus as, in Revelation   120,
   128
Foley, John M.   138
form criticism   340, 341
   and Mark's Gospel   16, 17
Fortna, Robert   334
Fox, Richard Wightman   396, 399, 408
Fra Angelico   494, 494
free will, and sin   208, 292–3
Freud, Sigmund   445
Friedmann, Yohanan   246
From the Manger to the Cross (film)   520
fundamental theology   362–3, 366

fundamentalism:
   Christian   328
   religious   262, 264
Funk, Robert W.   286, 308, 314, 319–20,
   334

"Gabriel's Revelation"   459
Gale, Aaron M.   38
Galilee:
   in Luke   50
   in Mark   18, 19, 27
   and Q   85
Gandhi, Arun   257
Gandhi, Mohandas K. (Mahatma)   250,
   251, 257, 264, 382–3
Gardner, Laurence   469
Garvey, Marcus   413
Gautama Buddha, parallels with Jesus
   279–80
gay Jesus   7, 443–56
   in the arts   452–4
   and the gospels   444, 445–52
   in theology   454–6
Gebara, Ivone   439–40
genealogy:
   Lukan   507
   Matthean   34, 35–6, 128, 129–30, 507
general epistles, and christology   111–18,
   201
Gentiles:
   and anti-Judaism   216
   in Luke-Acts   59–60
   in Mark   19
Germanus of Constantinople   189
Al-Ghazali, Abu Hamid Muhammad   239,
   240, 247
Gibson, Mel *see The Passion of the Christ*
Girard, René   209, 371
Gnosticism   160–74
   and canonical gospels   163, 166
   and dialogues with risen Christ   156
   and eschatological role of Jesus   172–3
   and Gospel of Thomas   153
   and identity of Jesus   163–4
   and Islam   233
   and Jesus' descent to the world   165–6
   and Jesus' leaving the world   168–72

Gnosticism (*cont'd*)
  and origin of Jesus   164
  and portraits of Jesus   162–72
  and resurrection of Jesus   171, 286
  and role of Jesus   166–8
  and self-knowledge   3
  and use of portraits of Jesus   172–3
  see also Gospel of Judas; Gospel of Mary;
    Gospel of Philip; Manichaeism
God, existence   290–1
Godspell (film)   521, 526
Goel, Sita Ram   253
Gokak, V. K.   264
Golgotha (film)   527
Gompertz, Rolf, *My Jewish Brother Jesus*
    507, 509, 512, 514, 516, 517–18
González, Justo L.   376, 379
The Gospel According to Saint Matthew (film)
    520, 523, 528
Gospel of Barnabas, and Islam   237,
    244–5, 462
Gospel of the Ebionites   302
The Gospel of John (film)   520, 527
Gospel of Judas   161, 168, 458
Gospel of Mary   468
gospel music   401
Gospel of Nicodemus (Acts of Pilate)   151,
    153
Gospel of Peter   151, 319, 333, 343
Gospel of Philip   165–8, 173, 468
Gospel of Pseudo-Matthew   148–9, 151
Gospel Road: the Story of Jesus (film)   403
Gospel of Thomas   152, 167–8, 302, 309,
    505
  and historical Jesus   343–4
  and Jesus Seminar   314, 319, 321–2,
    327
  and Mary Magdalene   451
Gospel of Truth   166–7
gospels:
  and anti-Jewish attitudes   19, 215–16,
    220–1, 224–5, 227, 506, 515
  and atonement   199–201
  differences in portrayals of Jesus   302–3,
    304, 306–7, 316
  harmonization   8, 360, 486, 505, 507
  images of Jesus   1–2, 316, 342–3, 360

  and Islamic ideas of Jesus   237–8,
    239–41, 244, 246–7
  and Jewish images of Jesus   215–20, 228
  modern alternative   458
  non-canonical   444, 505, *see also* Gospel
    of Thomas
  sources   308, *see also* Q
Goss, Robert   452
grace, and salvation   205
Graham, Billy   394
Grant, Jacquelyn   422, 423, 432
Great Awakening   399
The Greatest Story Ever Told (film)   8, 520,
    521, 523, 528, 530 n.1
Green, J.   209
Greene, David   521
Gregory I (the Great), Pope   205, 206, 478
Gregory X, Pope   207
Gregory of Nazianzus:
  and atonement   205
  and christology   180, 182, 187, 455
Gregory of Nyssa   180, 205, 503 n.7
Grey, Mary   434
Griffiths, Bede   259
Griffiths, D. W., *Intolerance* (film)   525
Griffiths, Paul J.   269
Grimm, George   275
Groddeck, Franz   445
Gross, Rita M.   269–70, 272, 276
Grundmann, Walter   347
Grünewald, Matthias, Isenheim altar   453,
    494
Grünschloss, Andreas   270, 272
Gulácsi, Zsuzsanna   173
guru, and Jesus as teacher   6–7, 383
Gutiérrez, Gustavo   376, 377, 380

Hades, Jesus' descent into   153, 170
hadith   236–7, 241–2, 244, 247
Haight, Roger   370, 372
Hampson, Daphne   430, 431
Hanh, Thich Nhat   271, 273, 275, 278,
    279–80
Harnack, Adolf von   305, 361
Harrelson, Becky Jayne   453
Harris, Elizabeth J.   272
Hatch, Nathan   399

Hays, Richard   129
healer, Jesus as:
 in African theology   389
 in Christian art   *482*, 482–4, *483*, 500
 in film   523
 in Islam   235–6
 in Luke-Acts   52
 in Mark   20, 21, 24, 28
 in Matthew   33, 37–8
 in modern fiction   512
 in New Testament Apocrypha   147–8
 in Q   83
 in recent scholarship   313, 314, 330–1,
  342
Hebrew Bible *see* Old Testament
Hebrews (epistle)   116–18
 and atonement   118, 201
 and death of Jesus   117
 and exaltation of Christ   111, 116–17
 Jesus as heavenly high priest   2,
  117–18, 140
 and new covenant   118, 140
 and Old Testament   116–17, 129, 131,
  139–40
Hedrick, Charles W.   334
Hegel, G. W. F.   359, 360
Hellenism, and Islam   233
Hellenistic Christianity:
 and denial of the female   427–8
 and Jews   216
 and Mark's Gospel   20–1, 23, 25, 26–7,
  28
Hellenistic Judaism, and Paul   195, 199
Henson, John   453–4
Herbert, Edward   304
Hermas, *Shepherd*   480
Herrick, James A.   162
Heyward, Isabel Carter   435–6
Higginson, Thomas Wentworth   405–6
high priest, Jesus as   2, 117–18, 121, 140,
  364
Hill, David   31
Hinduism   250–64
 and Christian missions   253–4, 256–7,
  259–60, 262, 264, 383
 and Indian Renaissance   382–3
 Jesus as avatar   5, 6, 9, 250–6

Hippolytus, and Gnostics   160
historical criticism   6, 20–1, 31, 32, 305,
  337, 339, 360–1
historical Jesus:
 and doctrine   270, 274, 305, 396
 and Haight   370
 and homoeroticism   443–6
 and Jesus as Jew   215, 224–5, 229,
  312–13, 327, 340–1, 347, 417,
  525–7
 in Latin American theology   378–9
 and maleness   398, 400, 402, 428–9
 and Mark's Gospel   17, 19–21
 and Paul   94–8
 in recent scholarship   366, 505
  as apocalyptic figure   312–13, 316
  as non-apocalyptic figure   313–15
  see also Jesus Seminar
 and Revelation   119
 as social and political reformer   6, 223,
  315, 342, 345–6, 348, 360, 383,
  401–2, 415–16
 and universal Christ, in Buddhism   276–7
 see also quest for historical Jesus
Hodgson, Marshall G. S.   232–3
Hofius, Otfried   198
Holmén, Tom   347
Holocaust   215, 227, 347, 515, 529
Holtzmann, Heinrich Julius   305
Holy Face of Lucca   502
Holy Spirit:
 divinity   180–1, 190
 relation with Jesus Christ   180–1
 see also Wisdom
homoeroticism:
 and John's Gospel   443–50
 and Mark's Gospel   450
homoousios   3, 177, 180–1, 184–5
homosexuality   7, 443–56, 460
Honi the Circle-Drawer   313, 342, 511
Hooker, Morna D.   198
Hookham, Michael (Lama Rigzen Shikpo)
  271
Hoover, J. Edgar   402
Horrell, David   97
Horsley, Richard A.   315, 345
How, Samuel D.   410–11

Hughes, Langston, "Christ in Alabama" 413
humanity of Jesus:
  and adoptionism 3
  in American evangelicalism 396, 398
  as avatar 252–3
  and Barth 364
  and docetism 113
  and ecumenical councils 178–91
  in feminist theology 436
  in films 521–4
  in Gnostic texts 165–6
  in Islam 239–40, 242, 247
  in Jewish Christianity 3
  in Mark 1–2, 23, 239
  in Matthew 1–2
  and Nestorianism 381
  in New Testament Apocrypha 150
  and Rahner 367–8
  in Revelation 123
  and sexuality 454–5
  and sinlessness 455–6
Hunter, W. L. 405
Hurtado, Larry 101, 103, 104, 107
Husayn, Muhammad Kamil, *Qarya Zalima* 246
Hymn to Christ the Shepherd 480
hymns, evangelical 401
hypostasis:
  hypostatic union 183–4, 189–90, 252–3, 436
  and nature of Christ 177, 180, 184–5, 186–8

Ibas of Edessa 186
Ibn 'Abd al-Wahhab, Muhammad, *Kitab al-Tawhid* 244
Ibn al-'Arabi, Muhi al-Din 242–3, 244
Ibn Hazm, Abu Muhammad 'Ali 239–40
icons, veneration 8, 188–90, 191, 477, 478, 487, 495
Idealism, German 358
Ignatius of Antioch:
  and atonement 202–3
  epistles 113
Ikhwan al-Safa' theology 238–40, 242, 246

Il Messias (film) 521
images of Jesus 1–9
imitation of Christ 273
immanence, divine, in Islam 238–9, 242
incarnation:
  and Barth 364
  and Buddhism 273, 275, 384–5
  and disability 438
  and ecofeminism 439
  in feminist theology 434, 436–7, 440
  in Hinduism 251–3, 255, 260, 263
  and homosexuality 454–5
  and icons 188–90, 477
  and liberation theology 379
  probability 292–5
  and Rahner 368
  see also humanity of Jesus; kenosis
inclusivism, and Buddhism 270–2
indecent theology 437
India:
  and feminist theology 428–9
  Jesus in 258–9, 382–3
  see also Hinduism
Indian Americans, and inculturation of Jesus 397–8
Infancy Gospel of Thomas 3, 52, 146–8, 150, 151, 302
  use by novelists 505, 507
  use in films 520
infancy narratives *see* birth and infancy
influence of Jesus 1, 9
Innocent IV, Pope 205
INRI (film) 527
intercalation, in Mark 22
International Association for Krishna Consciousness (ISKCON) 251, 261
interpretation, continuity and discontinuity in 134–5
Interpretation of Knowledge 164, 168
Intolerance (film) 525
Irenaeus of Lyons:
  and atonement 203–4, 207
  and credal formulae 176
  and deification 203
  and Gnostics 160, 162, 173
  and Revelation 119
Irene, Byzantine Empress 189

Isaiah, citations   135–7, 138, 179
Iser, Wolfgang   134
ISKCON *see* International Association for
    Krishna Consciousness
Islam, images of Jesus   5, 9, 232–47
    and canonical gospels   237–8, 239–41,
        244, 246–7
    and *hadith*   236–7, 241–2, 244, 247
    historical context   232–4
    and humanity and divinity   239–40, 242
    in late scholarship   243–7
    and mysticism   242–3, 247
    and Qur'an   235–6, 240–1, 244–5, 247
    in theological schools   238–42
    and Manichaeism   233, 236
Isma'il, Shah Muhammad, *Taqwiyat al-Iman*
    244
Isra'iliyyat literature   237–8

James (epistle)   111–12
Jefferson, Thomas   394–5, 396, 400
Jeremias, Joachim   310, 311, 338
Jerusalem, Jesus' entry into, in early
    Christian art   487–8, *489*
Jesus Christ Superstar (film)   8, 396, 443,
        521, 522, 526
Jesus (film)   520, 524, 528
Jesus in India (film)   259
Jesus of Montreal (film)   521, 522, 523, 525
Jesus of Nazareth (film)   520, 521, 525,
        526, 528, 529, 530 n.1
Jesus Seminar   286, 319–34
    criticism   327–8, 346, 347–8
    and deeds of Jesus   319, 328–33
    and methodology   320–1
    and non-apocalyptic Jesus   323, 327,
        338, 344–5
    problems in understanding   323–5
    and resurrection   333
    and rules of evidence   325–6
    and sayings of Jesus   308, 314, 321–8,
        341
    voting system   320, 323–4, 327, 329
Jewish Christianity:
    and Islam   233, 236
    and Jesus as Messiah   3, 4, 20
    and Jesus as prophet   5

and Mark's Gospel   23, 25, 27
    and Revelation   120
Jewison, Norman   521
Jews:
    and blood libel   207
    and death of Jesus   506, 515, 521
    in Mark's Gospel   19
    persecution   4–5, 90, 215, 222
    see also Judaism
Johannine epistles   112–13, 201
Johannine thunderbolt   92
John the Baptist:
    and apocalypticism   344–5
    in Gnostic texts   166
    in John's Gospel   67
    in Luke's Gospel   48, 50, 52, 527
    in Mark's Gospel   19, 21, 27, 134
    in Matthew's Gospel   36–7
    see also baptism of Jesus
John of Damascus   189–90, 477
John (gospel)   64–78
    and betrayal of Jesus   513
    christology   2, 64, 508–9, 521
    date   78 n.5
    historicity   343, 450
    homoerotic readings   444, 445–50,
        453, 454
    and Jesus Seminar   321
    Jesus as Son   74–5, 76–7
    Jesus as Tabernacle   70–1
    Jesus as Temple   71–4, 76
    and miracles   483–4, 511, 512
    passion narrative   75–7
    Prologue   64–70, 76–7, 128, 454, 497
    and sacrifice   200–1
    use of Old Testament   133, 136, 139, 141
    and Wisdom and creation   67–70, 77,
        128
    and Wisdom literature   65–8
    and Wisdom and Word   65–8, 252, 433
    see also Johannine epistles
Johnson, Elizabeth   427, 433–4
Johnson, Luke Timothy   61 n.4
Jones, John William, *Christ in the Camp*   405
Josephus, Flavius   217, 301–2, 341, 505,
        520
Joshua, Rabbi   74

Judaism:
  1st-century writing about Jesus 217–18
  citations of Old Testament 131
  and denial of the female 427
  and dissimilarity criterion 309
  images of Jesus 4–5, 9, 25, 215–30
  Jesus and Jewish laity 228
  Jesus in modern scholarship 223–7
  in Middle Ages 221–3
  and ministry of Jesus 216–17
  rabbinic 69, 74, 218–20
  and re-assessment of Paul 226–7,
    229–30
  and re-evaluation of Jesus' execution
    225–6
  reclamation of Jesus 215–16, 224–5
  and two-covenant theology 227
  see also Dead Sea Scrolls
Judas Iscariot:
  in early Christian art 490, 492
  in films 520, 522, 528
  and gay Jesus 446, 453
  in Gnostic texts 459
  in gospels 513
  in Islam 241
  and Jesus Seminar 332
  in modern fiction 505, 509, 513–14, 518
  in non-canonical gospels 168, 169
Jude (epistle), christology 115
justification, and atonement 196–7
Justin Martyr:
  Dialogue with Trypho 217–18
  and Gnostics 160

Kähler, Martin 362
Kant, Immanuel:
  and atonement 208
  and Enlightenment 357, 372
Käsemann, Ernst 306–7, 309
Kaspar, Walter 373 n.3
Kazantzakis, Nikos, *The Last Temptation of
    Christ* 508, 509–10, 512, 513,
    514, 517–18, 523–4
Keck, Leander E. 84
Kennett, Jiyu (Peggy) 269
kenōsis (self-emptying) 179, 183, 384–5
Kephalaia 164, 165, 167, 169, 171–2

Kereszty, Roch 187
Kern, Iso 279
Khalidi, Tarif 243
Khema, Ayya 275
Kim, Bokin 270, 278
King, Karen 162
King, Martin Luther Jr. 406–7, 414–16,
  419
The King of Kings (film, 1927) 521, 523,
  527
King of Kings (film, 1961) 8, 520, 521, 528
kingdom of Christ, and Marcellus of Ancyra
  181
kingdom of God:
  in 19th-century scholarship 360–1
  and eschatology 305–6, 307, 312–13,
    361
  in liberation theology 379–80
  in Luke-Acts 50–1, 60–1
  in Mark 19, 20, 25
  in Matthew 36–7, 38–9, 41, 378
  in Q 83–4
  in recent scholarship 313–14, 316
Kingsbury, Jack Dean 31
Kitab Bilawhar-wa-Budhasaf 463
Klausner, Joseph 338
Kleutgen, Josef 362
Kloppenborg, John S. 343, 347
Knohl, Israel 459
Kripal, Jeffrey 451–2, 453
Ku Klux Klan, and Jesus as Klansman 406
Kümmel, Werner 18
Küster, Volker 376
Kwok Pui-Lan 439
kyrios see Lord

Lachmann, Karl 305
LaDue, William J. 379
Lakhani, Seetha 262
lamb, Jesus as 2, 121–2, 124, 125, 200,
  481
Las Casas, Bartolomé de 376
Last Judgment, in early Christian art *499,
  499*
Last Supper:
  and atonement theories 199–200
  in early Christian art 489–90, *490*

in film   520, 522
in John   446–7, 453
The Last Temptation of Christ (film)   8,
    94–5, 443, 521, 522, 523–6
Lateran Council, Fourth (1215)   207
Latin America:
    christologies   375–80
    and colonialism   375–6
    feminist christologies   431–2, 436–7
    and Jesus of history   378–9
    and Jesus as liberator of the poor   6,
        379–80
    and liberation theology   376–80
law, new, in Christian art   497–8, *498*
Law, Jewish:
    in gospels   51, 230 n.7, 313
    and homoeroticism   448, 455–6
    in James   112
    in modern fiction   509, 515
    and Temple   74
    and Wisdom   69, 74
Lee, Jung Young   384
Lee, Robert E.   405
Leo I, Pope, and Chalcedonian formula   184
Leonardo da Vinci, *Last Supper*   490
Leong, Kenneth S.   270
Lessing, Gerhard E.   304, 360
Letter of Lentulus   158
Letter of Peter to Philip   167
Levine, Amy-Jill   35, 38, 39, 40, 344
liberalism   366, 372
    and quest for the historical Jesus   305,
        338–9, 346, 358–62
liberation theology   6, 346, 376
    Asian   383
    feminist   431–2, 436–7
    hermeneutics   377–8
    and Jesus of history   378–9
    origins   376–7
    see also liberator, Jesus as
liberator, Jesus as   6, 379–80, 412,
        415–16, 417–18
Life of Issa   7, 461, 462
Lincoln, Andrew T.   107
Lincoln, Henry (Henry Soskin)   465,
        466–7, 470
Lion of Judah, Christ seen as   120, 121–2

literary criticism:
    and Mark   16
    and Matthew   32
liturgy, and creeds   176
Logos christology   177–8, 370
    and Apollinaris   182
    and Wisdom   434, 481, 497
Lord, in Old Testament usage   100
Lord, Jesus as:
    in African theology   388
    and Barth   364
    and creeds   178
    in Deutero-Pauline letters   105
    in Luke-Acts   54–5, 58
    in Mark   24, 25
    in Matthew   31, 32
    in Pastoral Epistles   107
    in Paul   26, 84–5, 100–1, 104, 108
    in Q   85–6
    in Revelation   120, 125
Love, Stuart   43 n.4
Luke-Acts   47–62
    and ascension   57–8
    and atonement   200
    and betrayal of Jesus   513
    christology   47, 48
    and Gentiles   59–60
    infancy narrative   48–50, 506–7,
        527
    Jesus as friend of the poor   2, 51, 378
    Jesus as Messiah   48–9
    and Jesus Seminar   321
    Jesus as Son of God   49–50
    Jesus' mighty deeds   52
    Jesus' public ministry   50–5
    Jesus' reign in earth   60–1
    Jesus' reign in heaven   58–60
    and Judaism   225
    message of Jesus   50–2
    passion narrative   55–7, 199
    and resurrection   57, 516
    secrecy motif   49, 53
    sources   47, *see also* Q
    titles of Jesus   52–5
    use of Old Testament   136–7
Luther, Martin, and atonement   4, 203–4,
        207–8

McCormack, Matt   292
MacGuire, George   405
Machida, Soho   269, 279
McNally, Terrence, *Corpus Christi*   443,
    453
McVann, Mark   36
Mahayana Buddhism   270, 271, 276,
    279, 384
Mahdi (Guided One)   241, 245, 247, 462
Mailer, Norman, *The Gospel According to the
    Son*   512, 514, 515, 517–18
Malcolm X (Malcolm Little)   410, 414,
    416, 418, 419–20, 424
maleness of Jesus   398, 400, 402, 428–9,
    430–1, 502
Manichaean Homilies   172
Manichaean Psalm Book   163, 164, 165,
    168, 169–70, 171
Manichaeism   161, 164
  and Augustine   206
  and Islam   233, 236
Manns, Frédéric   68–9
Manson, T. W.   338
Marcellus, bishop of Ancyra   181–2
Marjanen, Antti   162, 173
Mark, identity   15
Mark (gospel)   13–28
  apocalypse   17, 115
  and betrayal of Jesus   513
  christology   18, 24, 25–7, 28
  controversy stories   17
  as history   20–1, 27–8, 305
  and homoeroticism   450–1, 454
  and humanity of Jesus   1–2, 23, 239
  influence on other gospels   14, 28
  and Jesus Seminar   321
  and Judaism   225
  as literature   16, 21–3
  miracle stories   18
  parables   17
  passion narrative   17, 27, 151,
    199–200, 332, 378
  and pre-Markan traditions   14–15,
    16–17, 18, 19–21, 303
  priority   13, 81, 305, 343, 361
  road (*hodos*) theme   331
  secrecy motif   26–7, 305, 361

and soteriology   27, 28
  teaching about discipleship   17, 19, 21,
    27
  as theology   15, 16, 18–19, 23–7, 28
  and trial of Jesus   515
  use of Old Testament   22, 24, 129,
    133–4, 136–7, 139
Marlowe, Christopher   445
Maronites, and Islam   233
marriage and family, and the gospel   449,
    456
Marsh, Clive   339
Marshman, Joshua   256–7
Martin, Dale   452
Martyrdom of Polycarp   203
Marx, Karl   378
Mary:
  in early Christian art   484–6, *485*,
    495
  in film   521, 526
  in Qur'an   235
  as *Theotokos* (God-bearer)   182–3, 185,
    485
Mary Magdalene   219
  and crucifixion of Jesus   447, 493
  in early Christian art   493, 495
  as feminist symbol   467–9
  in film   521, 522, 523, 524–5
  possible relationship with Jesus   8, 444,
    451, 453, 464–7, 470, 524–5
  and resurrection of Jesus   57, 222, 301,
    316, 433–4, 448, 467, 495
Matera, Frank   33
Mathews, Shailer   209
Matthew (gospel)   30–42
  and betrayal of Jesus   513
  and divinity of Jesus   2
  genealogy   34, 35–6, 128, 129–30
  infancy narrative   506–8
  Jesus as rabbi   2
  and Jesus Seminar   321
  and Judaism   2, 225
  kingdom of God   36–7, 38–9, 41, 378
  passion narrative   41, 199
  priority   13
  Sermon on the Mount   38, 112, 152,
    257, 321

sources *see* Q
titles of Jesus   31–3, 41
trial of Jesus   515
use by Gnostics   163
use of Old Testament   128, 129–30,
     133, 136–7, 138, 141
and Wisdom motif   32, 34, 38
Mawdudi, Abu al- A'la, *Tafhim al-Qur'an*
     244
Maximos the Confessor   187–8
Mbiti, John S.   386, 387
meaning, role of authors and audiences
     132–5
Meier, John P.   31, 309, 312–13, 339
Melancton, Monica   428
Merriam, Dena   260
Merton, Thomas   396
Merz, Annette   308, 310–11, 313
Messiah:
   Black Messiah   412–13, 418, 419–20
   in film   529
   and historical Jesus   307, 312, 322,
        360, 508–9
   in Islam   5, 235, 245, 462
   and Jewish attitudes to Jesus   217–18,
        226, 228, 229, 515
   and Jewish Christianity   3, 4, 20
   in John   76
   in Luke-Acts   48–9, 53, 56–7, 58–9, 61
   in Matthew   31, 33, 41
   Messianic secret motif   26–7, 305, 361,
        408
   in Paul   98–9, 104
   in pre-Markan traditions   25
   in Revelation   123, 124
Metz, Johann Baptist   372 n.1
Michelangelo di Lodovici Buonarotti
     Simone, *Last Judgment*   499
Middle Ages:
   and Christian attitudes to Jews   221
   and Christian views of Jesus   4
   and Jewish views of Jesus   221–3
Miethe, Terry   286
millenarianism, 1st-century   312
minjung theology   383
The Miracle Maker (film)   521, 526,
     530 n.1

miracles:
   in early Christian art   482–4, 500
   in Enlightenment thought   6, 304, 411
   as eschatological   20, 312–13
   in film   523
   initial improbability of miracle claims
        287–8
   in Islam   235
   in John   511
   in Luke-Acts   52
   in Mark   18, 19, 20
   in modern fiction   506, 511–12
   nature miracles   332
   in rabbinic thought   219
   see also healer, Jesus as; resurrection
mission of Jesus, in fiction   508–11
mission and missionaries:
   and Hinduism   253–4, 256–7, 259–60,
        262, 264
   and Islam   233, 246
Moffett, Samuel H.   381
Moltmann-Wendel, Elisabeth   434–5
monarchianism   496
Monophysitism   233, 381–2
monothelitism   187
Montanism   156
Montefiori, Hugh   452
Monty Python's Life of Brian (film)   526–7,
     528
Moody, Dwight   401
Moore, Christopher, *Lamb*   510–11, 513,
     514, 515–16, 517–18
Moravians, and humanity of Jesus   394,
     398, 399
Morrison, Kenneth   397
Moses, Jesus as   369
   in Luke   59
   in Matthew   32, 38, 128, 130, 230 n.7
Muhammad:
   and *hadith*   236–7
   knowledge of Abrahamic faiths   233,
        236
   see also Qur'an
Müller, Max   461, 462
Murphy, Catherine   328
Muslim Brotherhood   245
Mu'tazili theology   238–41

mysticism, Islamic   242–3, 247
mystifications   458–71
    descendants of Jesus and Mary
        Magdalene   464–7
    and facts and theories   470–1
    Jesus in Kashmir   461–4
    Mary Magdalene as feminist symbol
        467–9
    and recent discoveries   459–60

Nag Hammadi texts   152, 161, 163, 164,
        171, 172
narrative criticism:
    and Mark   16, 23
    and Matthew   31, 33–5
narrative theology, and Mark   23–4
Nath, P. V.   253, 260–1
Native Americans:
    and homoeroticism   451
    and inculturation of Jesus   397–8
nature of Jesus   3–4, 359, 496, 500,
        see also divinity of Jesus; humanity
        of Jesus
Nazarene, Jesus as   75–6
Neo-Scholasticism   358, 362–3
Neo-Thomism see Neo-Scholasticism
Nestorians, Nestorianism   233, 381–2
Nestorius, bishop of Constantinople
        182–3, 185, 186
Neusner, Jacob   71, 460
New Testament:
    and anti-Judaism   19, 215–16,
        220–1
    atonement in   195–202
    Jesus in   1–2, 302
    see also John (gospel); Luke-Acts; Mark
        (gospel); Matthew (gospel); Paul;
        general epistles; Revelation
New Testament Apocrypha   3, 28,
        145–58, 302, 341, 520
    apocryphal Acts   149, 154–6
    birth and infancy narratives   52,
        146–51
    dialogues with risen Christ   156–8
    and docetism   3, 150, 152, 156
    Jesus' descent into Hades   153
    Jesus' public ministry   151–2

Neyrey, Jerome   37, 41
Nicea:
    First Council (325)   3, 177–80, 370
    Second Council (787)   188–90, 191
Nicene creed   3, 176, 180, 190, 285, 303,
        424
Nichiren   270
Niebuhr, Richard   408
Nikhilananda, Swami   261
Nirmal, A. P.   383–4
Nishida, Kitaro   276
Nishitani, Keiji   276
Niwano, Nikkyo   280
noble death idea   195–6, 197
Notovitch, Nicolas   258, 461, 462
Novakovic, Lidija   39
novels, Jesus in   8, 504–18
    betrayal of Jesus   513–14
    birth and youth   506–8
    and miracles   511–12
    mission of Jesus   508–10
    and parables   510–11, 518
    post-death appearances   516–17
    trial and death   514–16
Nyamiti, Charles   388
Nyanaponika   276

obedience of Jesus   178–9
    in early church fathers   203
    in Hebrews   116–18
    in Paul   2, 97, 102–3
    in Q   92
Old Testament:
    allusions to   129, 132, 135–6
    and atonement   193–5
    and audience   133–5
    and authorial intent   132–4
    and branch imagery   75
    citations   87–8, 95–6, 100, 118,
        128–9, 132, 135–7
    and communicative intent   132–4
    and God as Lord   100
    and intertextuality   130–1, 138
    as source for imagery   2, 25, 127–41,
        225, 360–1
    use by John   133, 136, 139, 141
    use by Luke-Acts   136–7

use by Mark   22, 24, 129, 133–4,
    136–7, 139
use by Matthew   128, 129–30, 133,
    136–7, 138, 141
use by Paul   125, 130–1, 139
use in Hebrews   116–17, 129, 131,
    139–40
use in Revelation   129
and Wisdom   65, 88
word associations   129–30
Onaiyekan, John   386, 387–8
oppression:
    and black theology   414–15, 417–20
    and feminist theology   432
    and Latin American theology   375–7,
        380
    and slave Christianity   410–11
    and womanist theology   421–4
oral tradition:
    and gospels   17, 303, 310
    and Paul   96
    reliability   316
Origen:
    and appearance of Jesus   500–1
    and Arius   177
    and atonement   204
    and Gnostics   160
    and God as eternal   178
    and idolatry   478
    and resurrection of Jesus   286
Osborn, Sarah   399
Overman, J. Andrew   38
Oxyrhynchus Papyrus 840   151

Paine, Thomas, and atonement   208
Pannenberg, Wolfhart   366–7, 372
Pannikar, Raimundo   383, 384–5
Panofsky, Erwin   469
Papias, and Mark   15
parables:
    as advertisements   402
    and Jewish views of Jesus   229
    in Manichaean texts   167
    in Mark   17, 510
    in Matthew   510
    in modern fiction   510–11, 518
Paramahansa, Sri Ramakrishnan   254

Parratt, John   390 n.3
Pasolini, Pier Paolo see The Gospel According
    to Saint Matthew
The Passion of the Christ (film)   407–8, 520,
    521, 524, 526, 528, 530 n.1
passion narratives:
    and early Christian art   490–1, 491
    and Jesus Seminar   332–3
    of John   75–7
    of Luke-Acts   55–6, 199
    of Mark   17, 27, 151, 199, 332
    of Matthew   41, 199
Pastoral Epistles:
    and atonement   202
    and christology   107
patriarchy:
    and feminist theology   345, 349, 422,
        428, 429–30, 437
    and the gospels   32, 34, 50, 449
    and womanist theology   7
Patterson, Stephen   334, 335 n.9
Paul   94–109
    Adam christology   2, 101–3, 104, 108
    appearances of Jesus to   60, 156
    and atonement   195–8, 202
    and authentic Jesus tradition   308
    and death of Jesus   96–7, 151, 196–8,
        295, 303
    disputed letters   105–7
    and divinity of Jesus   94, 104–5
    epistles   13, 94, 96
    and historical Jesus   94–8, 151, 302, 303
    Jesus as Christ   2, 85, 98–9, 104–5, 108
    Jesus as Lord   26, 85–6, 100–1, 104, 108
    Jesus as Son of God   26, 99–100, 104,
        108
    in Jewish scholarship   226–7, 229–30
    and Old Testament   125, 130–1, 135–6,
        139
    and resurrection   97, 99, 285, 333, 516
Paulinus of Nola   499
Pearson, Birger A.   160, 162
Pentecostalism, and Jesus as healer   389
Perrin, Norman   307, 309, 311
persecution:
    in early church   114, 115, 116
    of Jews   4–5, 90, 215, 222

personality cult of Jesus   400
1 Peter   113–15, 131
    use of Old Testament   136
2 Peter, christology   115–16
Philo of Alexandria, and knowledge of Jesus
        217, 505
Picknett, Lynn   467–8, 470
Picknett, Lynn and Prince, Clive   468–9
Pieris, Aloysius   381, 383
Piero della Francesca   494
Pilch, John   38–9
Plantard, Pierre   465–7, 470
Pliny the Younger   217, 302
Plockhorst, Bernhard   481
pluralism   370
    and Buddhism   267, 270–2, 385
    and Hinduism   250–1, 257, 260, 262,
        263
Pope-Levison, Priscilla and Levison, John R.
        379
postmodernism:
    and Jesus myths   458–9
    and Jesus research   348
    and miracles   511
Poussin, Nicolas   469
poverty:
    and Asian theology   381, 383–4
    and Latin American theology   375–7,
        436
    and slave Christianity   410–11
Powell, Mark Allan   33, 339
Powell, Robert   526
Prabhavananda, Swami   251, 254, 261
Prabhupadha, Srila   251
pre-existence of Jesus:
    and creeds   178–9, 180
    in Deutero-Pauline epistles   105–6
    in Gnostic texts   153–4
    in John   2, 66, 103, 147
    in Luke   48
    in New Testament Apocrypha   147
    in Paul   94, 99, 102, 103–5, 108
predestination:
    in Augustine   205–6
    in Luther   207–8
Priory of Sion   465–7, 469–70
proof-texts   138, 218

prophet, Jesus as   6, 369
    and Barth   364
    and Islam   5, 232, 236
    in John   71
    and Judaism   3, 5
    in Luke-Acts   55, 57, 134, 200, 331
    in Matthew   36–7
    in pre-Markan tradition   19–20, 24, 28
    in Q   83, 86–8
    in recent scholarship   312–13, 323,
        342, 344–5
    and Wisdom   88–9, 433
propitiation, and atonement   193, 194,
        198, 204, 205, 209
Protestantism:
    18th-century   399
    19th-century   358–62, 372, 399–401
    20th-century   363–7, 401–3
Protevangelium of James   148, 150–1
Prothero, Stephen   395–6
Proto-Orthodoxy, and humanity and
        divinity of Jesus   3, 150, 156
Psalms, citations   138–40
Pseudepigrapha   341
publishing industry, American   400, 403
Pueblo Revolt (1680)   397–8
purification, and atonement   194, 198
Puritanism, in North America   394, 399
Putnam, Bill and Wood, John Edwin   469

Q   343–4
    christology   2, 13, 19, 20, 81–92
    eschatology   83–4, 86–8, 91
    and Jesus Seminar   319, 321
    and Johannine thunderbolt   92
    as pre-dating death of Jesus   316
    and resurrection   517
    and sayings of Jesus   152, 305, 308, 314
    significance of death of Jesus   84–5, 89
    and Wisdom traditions   88–9, 92
    as written document   82
Qisas al-Anbiya' 237
quest for historical Jesus   6, 223, 301–17
    appraisal   337–49
    coherence criterion   309–10, 326
    criteria for authenticity   308–11
    difference criterion   309

double similarity criterion   311, 316, 340
embarrassment criterion   309
environmental appropriateness criterion
   310
historical plausibility criterion   310–11
language criteria   310
liberal   305, 338–9, 346, 359–62
multiple attestation criterion   309
new quest   306–7, 309, 311, 337, 340,
   343
no quest period   306, 338
old quest   303–8, 359–62, 511
reasons   302–3
sources for   301–2, 303
third quest   308–9, 316, 337–49
   critique   346–9
   distinguishing features   339–42
Questions of Bartholomew   157
Qur'an, and Islamic view of Jesus   235–6,
   240–1, 244–5, 247

rabbi, Jesus as   2, 6, 9, 24, 315, 342
Rabbula gospels   492, 493, 495
race:
   and Black Christ   410–24
   and images of Jesus   395, 403–7
   and white theology   416–17
Radford Ruether, Rosemary   427–8, 431
Radhakrishnan, S.   253, 258
Ragg, Lonsdale and Laura   462
Rahner, Karl   185, 367–8, 372
Rahula, Walpola   277–8
Rausch, Thomas   328
Ravindra, Ravi   256, 257, 261
Ray, Nicholas   520, 521
reader, interpretative role   133–6
reason, and faith   357, 372
recapitulation, in Irenaeus   203
reconciliation:
   and atonement   183, 196–7
   in Barth   364
   in black theology   419
redaction criticism, and Mark   16, 18
Redeker, Martin   359
redemption:
   in feminist theology   432, 435
   in Paul   196

Reformation, and atonement theories
   207–8
Reimarus, Herman Samuel   286, 304,
   337–8, 340, 345, 359–60
religion:
   and feeling   359
   as morality   358
Rembrandt van Rijn, "Christ Healing the
   Sick" 482, 482
Renan, Ernest   304
Rennes-le-Chateau   465–7, 469–70
repentance, in Luke-Acts   51
resurrection:
   alternative explanations   296–7
   bodily   102
   in early Christian art   493–4, 494
   in Enlightenment thought   6, 286,
      304
   evidence for   295–6
   in Gnostic texts   171, 286
   and God's purpose   288–9
   and Haight   370
   in Hinduism   258
   improbability   286–90
   in Islam   236, 240
   and Jesus Seminar   333
   and Jews   222
   in John   69
   in Luke-Acts   57, 516
   in modern fiction   516–17
   and NT Apocrypha   154, 156–7
   and Pannenberg   366–7
   in Paul   97, 99, 285, 333, 516
   in 1 Peter   114
   and Rahner   368
   and Schillebeeckx   369
   skeptical perspectives   285–99
   strong and weak senses   289–94, 298
revelation:
   and autonomy   430
   as history   366
Revelation (book)   119–26
   date   119
   and divinity of Jesus   120–1, 124–6
   and humanity of Jesus   123
   influence of Daniel   120–1
   Jesus as divine warrior   124, 136

Revelation (book) (*cont'd*)
  Jesus as lamb   2, 121–2, 124, 125
  Jesus as shepherd   122, 123
  Jesus as woman's male child   123
  and Jewish Christianity   120
  and Old Testament   129, 136
  and Son of Man   120–1, 140
revivalism, American   45, 395, 399, 400
revolutionary, Jesus as   6, *see also*
        historical Jesus, as social and
        political reformer
rhetorical criticism, and Mark's Gospel   16
Ricci, Nino, *Testament*   507, 510, 512,
        514, 516, 517–18
Rice, Anne   505, 507–8, 511, 517–18
Rida, Rashid   246
Ritschl, Albrecht   305
Roberts, James Deotis   418–19, 421
Robinson, James M.   334
Robinson, John A. T.   53
Robinson, Neal   240
Roerich, Nicholas   258
Roman Catholic Church, and liberation
        theology   377
Roman Empire, in film   527–8
Roscoe, Will   451
Rosslyn Chapel   464, 466, 469, 470
Roth, Wolfgang   28 n.5
Rousselet, Louis   260
Rowe, C. Kavin   61 n.3
Roy, Raja Rammohun   256–7, 263
Rudolph, Kurt   160

Šābuhragān (Manichaean text)   164, 172
sacrifice:
  covenant   199–200
  in early church fathers   203, 204–5
  in feminist theology   429–30
  in Hebrews   201
  and Jesus Seminar   322
  in John   200–1
  in Old Testament   193–5
  in Paul   196–8
Salafi movements   234, 243–5, 246, 247
Saldarini, Anthony   35, 38
Sallman, Warner, *Head of Christ*   396,
        402–3, 407, 526

salvation:
  in Athanasius   204
  in Augustine   205–6
  by works   202
  and ecofeminism   439
  in Gnosticism   160
  in Hebrews   117
  in Irenaeus   203
  in John   201, 521
  in liberation theology   380
  in Luke-Acts   49, 59, 200
  in Origen   204
  in Pannenberg   367
  and participation   198, 204
  in Paul   97–8
  in Rahner   368
  in Revelation   122
  in Schillebeeckx   369
  in Schleiermacher   359
  through suffering   207, 209
  and unity of Christ   182, 184, 191
  and women   427–8, 429, 430
  see also atonement; deification;
        predestination
Samartha, Stanley J.   382, 385–6
Sanatana Dharma *see* Hinduism
Sanders, E. P.   308, 311, 312, 337, 338,
        342, 343, 347
Sangharakshita, Venerable (Derek
        Lingwood)   270, 271, 273
Sanhedrin, and trial of Jesus   56, 219–20,
        226, 513–14, 516
Sankey, Ira   401
Santikaro Bhikkhu   277
Saramago, José   507–8, 510, 511, 513,
        516, 517–18
Satprakashananda, Swami   258
Saunière, Bérenger   465
Saville, Philip, *The Gospel of John*   520, 527
savior, Jesus as *see* salvation
sayings tradition:
  apocryphal   152
  and criteria of authenticity   309–10
  and Mark   19–20
  and new quest for the historical Jesus
        341
scapegoat concept   195, 196, 209, 429

Schellenberg, J. L.   298–9
Schillebeeckx, Edward   368–70, 372
Schleiermacher, F. D. E.   358–9, 372
Schmidt-Leukel, Perry   269, 272
Schnackenburg, Rudolf   66
Schneck, Richard   28 n.5
Schreiner, T.   209
Schüssler Fiorenza, Elisabeth   315, 345,
        349, 432–3
Schwager, Raymond   371–2
Schweitzer, Albert   305–6, 308, 338, 340,
        344, 345, 346, 362
Scorsese, Martin see The Last Temptation of
        Christ
Scott, Bernard Brandon   334
scripture, and tradition   358
Seal of Saints, Jesus as   243
second coming:
    in disputed Pauline epistles   105
    in feminist theology   429
    in Gnostic texts   172
    in Hinduism   255
    in James   111
    in Johannine epistles   113
    in Jude   115
    in Luke-Acts   60–1
    in Paul   100
    in 1 Peter   114
    in 2 Peter   115
    in Q   89–90
Second Great Awakening   395, 400
Second Treatise of the Great Seth   164,
        170–1
Second Vatican Council, Nostra Aetate   227
secrecy motif:
    in Gospel of Thomas   167–8
    in Luke   49, 53
    in Mark   26–7, 305, 508
Secret Gospel of Mark   444, 450–1,
        459–60, 463, 470–1
Sède, Gérard de   466
Segal, Alan F.   34
Segundo, Juan Luis   377–8
Sen, Keshub Chunder   382
Senior, Donald   41
Sermon on the Mount   38, 112, 152, 257,
        275, 321, 383

Serrano, Andres, Piss Christ (painting)   396
Setiloane, Gabriel   386
sexuality:
    in film   524–5
    and historical Jesus   443–4
Shah, Sheetal   260
Sheldon, Charles, In His Steps   401–2
Shema   101, 219
shepherd motif   8
    in early Christian art   478, 479–81,
        480, 500
    in Revelation   122, 123
Shi'ism, Nizari   246
Shroud of Turin   502
Silva, Lily de   274, 277
Simmer-Brown, Judith   271
sin:
    and atonement   205–6
    and Buddhism   270, 279
    in feminist theology   429
    and free will   208
    in Hinduism   255–6
    in Islam   240
    Jesus as sinless   455–6
Sivananda, Swami   257
Slaughter of the Innocents   280, 508,
        518, 528
slavery:
    in New Testament   114–15, 137, 196,
        294–5, 411
    in United States   396, 403–5, 410–12,
        414, 416
Smart, Ninian   268
Smith, Joseph, and Book of Mormon   470
Smith, Morton   444, 450–1, 459–60
Smith, Wilfred Cantwell   267
social gospel   209, 401–2
social scientific criticism, and Matthew's
        Gospel   35–7
Socinus (Gausto Paolo Sozzini), and
        atonement   208
Son of David:
    in 19th-century christology   360
    in Johannine epistles   112
    in Luke   49, 54, 56, 59
    in Mark   24, 25
    in Matthew   31–2, 41

Son of God:
  in African theology   387–8
  and Barth   364
  and Buddhism   275–7
  in Deutero-Pauline letters   105
  and Islam   236
  in Johannine epistles   112
  in Luke   49–50, 52–3, 56, 59
  in Manichaean texts   164, 165
  in Mark   25, 26
  in Matthew   31
  in Paul   26, 99–100, 104, 108
  in Q   91–2
Son of Man:
  and Barth   364
  and Daniel   120–1, 140, 307
  in Gnostic texts   165, 171
  and historical Jesus   322
  in Luke   54, 56–7, 60, 140
  in Mark   19, 24, 26, 27, 140
  in Matthew   31, 41, 140
  in Q   88, 89–91
  in Revelation   120–1, 140
  and suffering   90–1
Sophia see Wisdom
Sot'aesan   270
soteriology:
  and Mark   27, 28
  and Paul   101
source criticism   18
Spinoza, Baruch   304
spirituality, queer   451
Stanton, Graham N.   40, 43 n.6, 97
Starbird, Margaret   467–8, 471
Steiner, George   445–6
Stevens, George see The Greatest Story Ever
    Told
Strauss, David Friedrich   286, 302–3,
    304, 305, 338, 343, 360–1, 400
stumbling block, Jesus as   136
Subramuniyaswami, Satguru Sivaya   259
Suetonius (Gaius Suetonius Tranquillus),
    knowledge of Christianity   217,
    302
suffering:
  and American South   405–6
  and atonement   207, 209

and black slaves   411–12
and Buddhism   273, 274, 279, 280
in early Christian art   493
and evil   368–9
in feminist theology   429–30
in film   524
and kingdom of God   316
suffering servant, Jesus as   209, 306,
    524
  in Luke-Acts   137–8
  in Mark   25, 378
  in 1 Peter   114–15, 136
Sufism   242–3, 245
Sumedho, Ajahn   280
Sunim, Dae Kwang   274
supersessionism   35, 140, 226, 227
surrogacy, in womanist theology   423–4,
    430
Swarup, Ram   253
Swinburne, Richard   286, 287, 288–98

Tabernacle and Temple, Jesus as   70–4
Tacitus, Cornelius, knowledge of
    Christianity   217, 302
Tagore, Rabindranath   264
Talmud, and Jesus   219–20, 221
Tamez, Elsa   431
tawhid (divine unity), in Islam   232,
    238–9, 247
teacher, Jesus as:
  as Cynic teacher   314, 342, 345, 347
  in early Christian art   478, 481–2, 500
  in film   523
  and Jewish views of Jesus   229
  in Luke   50–1
  in Matthew   31, 33
  in pre-Markan tradition   19, 20, 24, 28
  in Q   83
  in recent scholarship   313–14, 342
Teachings of Silvanus   161–2, 164, 169
Telford, William R.   338
Temple:
  believing community as   72–4, 76–7,
    114
  Jesus as   70–4, 76
  and Torah   74
Tertullian   160, 203, 205, 386, 478

Testament of Joseph   121
Testimony of Truth   166
Theissen, Gerd   308, 310–11, 313
Theodore of Mopsuestia   183, 186
Theodoret of Cyrus   186
theology:
    blood-and-wounds   398
    Islamic, and Jesus   238–47
Theotokos (God-bearer)   182–3, 185, 485–6
Theravada Buddhism   270, 275
Thomas *see* Gospel of Thomas; Infancy
        Gospel of Thomas
Thomas, M. M.   383
Thompson, Michael B.   97
Tibetan Buddhism   273
Tillich, Paul   275, 365–6, 372, 417
Tindal, Matthew   304
Tindley, Charles Albert   401
Tissot, James   526
Titian, *Noli Me Tangere*   495
Toledot Yeshu   221–3, 225
tolerance:
    Buddhist   271, 272
    Hindu   260
tomb of Jesus   459
Torah *see* Law, Jewish
Torres, Camillo   380
Tractate Pelliot   164
traditio legis, in Christian art   497–8, *498*
tradition, and scripture   358
tradition criticism   19
transcendence, divine:
    and historical Jesus   301
    in Islam   238–9
Transcendentalism, American   400
transfiguration, in early Christian art
        486–7, *488*, 501
transubstantiation   3, 207
Treatise on Resurrection   165, 171
Tree of Life, Jesus as   164
Trinity, doctrine of   3
    and Buddhist three-body doctrine   277
    and creeds   176, 180–1
    in early Christian art   486, 495–6, *496*
    in Enlightenment thought   6
    and Islam   236, 239
Tripartite Tractate   163–4, 165, 169

truth:
    in Hinduism   250, 255, 261, 263
    Jesus as   8–9
Tuckett, Christopher M.   62 n.7
Turner, Henry McNeal   404–5, 413
two-covenant theology   227

Ueda, Shizutera   276
Umayyad Caliphate   233
uniqueness of Jesus:
    and Buddhism   270, 273, 275–7
    and Hinduism   261, 263
    and Judaism   229
    and womanist theology   424
United States:
    and chosen nation ideology   407–8
    and civil rights movement   406–7, 415
    early history   396–8
    evangelicalism   399–403, 405–6
    Great Awakening   399
    Jesus as cultural icon   7, 394–408
    and modern mystifications   470–1
    and race   395, 403–7
    Second Great Awakening   395, 400
unity of God, in Islam (*tawhid*)   232,
        238–9, 247
unity of Jesus Christ   179–91, 364, 436
universalism   271
Uphadhyaya, Brahmabandhab   383
'Uthman, Caliph   235

Vajrayana Buddhism   276
Valantasis, Richard   152
Van der Weyden, Rogier, *The Last Judgment*
        499
Velásquez, Diego, *The Coronation of the
        Virgin*   497
Vermes, Geza   310, 347
Veronica legend   502
virgin birth   8, 303, 304
    in Enlightenment thought   6
    in Gnostic texts   166
    in Islam   5
    in modern fiction   508, 512
Virgin of Guadalupe   376
Vivekananda, Swami   254, 255, 256,
        261, 263

Wahhabism   244
Walker, Alice   422, 424
Walker, David   405
Wallace-Murphy, Tim   470
Walter, Nikolaus   108 n.3
Wangerin, Walter Jr., *Jesus: A Novel*   507,
    511, 513, 516, 517–18
Weiss, Johannes   305, 361
Welch, Claude   358
Wessells, Anton   375, 387
Wilberforce, William   259
will of Jesus Christ   187–8, 191
Willett, Michael   66
Williams, Delores   423–4, 430
Williams, Michael   162
Williams, Robert   452
Willitts, Joel   32
Wilson, Charles Hackett   397–8
Winter, Dagmar   310
Wisdom:
    and creation   67–70, 77, 103, 106,
        116, 128, 178
    in Deutero-Pauline epistles   106
    in feminist theology   32, 433–4
    in Gnostic texts   169
    in John   65–70, 74–5, 433
    in Matthew   32, 34, 38
    in non-canonical literature   65–8, 70
    in Old Testament   65, 88
    and prophets   88–9, 433
    in Q   92
    and Son of Man   89–90, 322
    and Word   65–8, 124, 481
Wisdom (Book of)   65–6, 116
womanism:
    and Black Christ   7, 421–4
    and liberation theology   432
    and sacrifice   430
women:
    and Great Awakening   399
    in Luke-Acts   50

    in Matthew's Gospel   37–9, 41
    see also Mary; Mary Magdalene
Won Buddhism   270, 278
Woolston, Thomas   304
Word:
    in John   65–70, 252, 497
    and Wisdom   65–8, 124
worship:
    and christology   182, 183, 186,
        190–1
    in Revelation   125–6
    and veneration of icons   188–90,
        477–8
Wrede, Wilhelm   26, 305, 361
Wright, N. T.:
    and Jesus as Messiah   109 n.11
    and Jesus Seminar   335 n.12
    and quest for historical Jesus   303, 308,
        311, 316, 338, 339, 343
    and resurrection   516

X, Malcolm *see* Malcolm X
Xhixu, Ouyi   279

Yarbro Collins, Adela   123
Yeshe, Thubten   273, 274, 276,
    280
yin and yang   6, 384
Yogananda, Paramahansa   252, 254–5,
    258, 260, 263
Yohanan ben Zakkai, rabbi   74
Young, Robert   520, 525, 528
Young, Robert Alexander   412
Yukteswar, Sri   255–6

Zahiri theology   239–40
Zechariah (book), use in New Testament
    140–1, 200, 307
Zeffirelli, Franco *see Jesus of Nazareth*
Zen Buddhism, and Jesus   270
Zwiep, A. W.   62 nn.5, 6

Lightning Source UK Ltd.
Milton Keynes UK
UKHW031826011019
350820UK00005B/18/P